Intellectual Property Law

INTELLECTUAL PROPERTY LAW

STAVROULA KARAPAPA

Professor of Intellectual Property and
Information Law, University of Reading

LUKE MCDONAGH

Senior Lecturer in Law, City,
University of London

OXFORD
UNIVERSITY PRESS

OXFORD
UNIVERSITY PRESS

Great Clarendon Street, Oxford, OX2 6DP,
United Kingdom

Oxford University Press is a department of the University of Oxford.
It furthers the University's objective of excellence in research, scholarship,
and education by publishing worldwide. Oxford is a registered trade mark of
Oxford University Press in the UK and in certain other countries

Impression: 2

Published in the United States of America by Oxford University Press
198 Madison Avenue, New York, NY 10016, United States of America

British Library Cataloguing in Publication Data
Data available

Library of Congress Control Number: 2019937516

ISBN 978–0–19–874769–7

Printed in Great Britain by
Bell & Bain Ltd., Glasgow

Preface

We wrote this book because we find the subject of intellectual property to be a fascinating one. We hope that through this textbook students are drawn into the interconnected web of copyrights, patents, trade marks, designs, and trade secrets to discover some of the same fascination we have found. Our aim has been to explain intellectual property law through carefully-crafted practical scenarios at the start of each chapter, bringing this technical subject to life in a meaningful and engaging way for students. Within each chapter we then explain the law with reference back to this scenario, as well as offering a response to the scenario at the end of each chapter.

We are grateful to be able to draw on material from Helen Norman's *Intellectual Property Law* published by OUP. When Helen retired from writing this title, there was an opportunity to continue Helen's work whilst introducing this practical, problem-based approach. We believe the approach we have developed in this textbook achieves our aim of providing a textbook for students that is thematically rich yet centred on practical scenarios.

Stavroula Karapapa and Luke McDonagh, April 2019

Acknowledgements

The authors and publisher would like to thank the following reviewers for their invaluable contributions during the development of this title:

Dr Kimberley Barker, University of Stirling

Dr Rick Ball, University of the West of England

Professor Andrew Charlesworth, University of Bristol

Professor Ronan Deazley, Queen's University Belfast

Dr Janice Denoncourt, Nottingham Trent University

Bukola Faturoti, Robert Gordon University

Professor Tom Guthrie, University of Glasgow

Dr Barbara Henry, University of Hertfordshire

Ria Hill, University of Wolverhampton

Timothy Press, Cardiff University

Sallie Spilsbury, Manchester Metropolitan University

Wendy Steel, University of Chester

Mark Thomas, Nottingham Trent University

Dr Lingling Wei, Bournemouth University

Dr Dimitris Xenos, University of Suffolk

Dr Chen W. Zhu, University of Birmingham

Guide to the book

Intellectual Property Law is a rich learning resource, enhanced with a range of features designed to help you get the most out of the book.

Problem scenarios

Each chapter begins by setting out a 'real-life' problem related to the topic. You should have this scenario in mind as you read the rest of the chapter.

Problem question

Read this problem question carefully and keep it in mind while
through the chapter that follows. At the end of this chapter, you w
what you have learnt to the problem question and advise the rele

In early 2002 the well-known folk-pop musician Andrew Starr, who perfo
'Starr', composed a song called *All I Live For*. The melancholic lyrics to
man who falls in love with a woman who is already married to someone

Case summary boxes

Case summary boxes provide an overview of the most influential and important cases in the subject area, to help you to understand how the law has developed and why.

Slater v Wimmer [2012] EWPCC 7

In this case—heard at the Patents Count Court (now the Intellectual Prope
IPEC)—HHJ Birss concluded that in the absence of a clearly worded agree
parties, copyright in a film made by the claimant of the defendant sky-d
determined by the statutory provisions: the defendant was producer (he ha
financial arrangements) and the claimant was director (he had creative contr
each had infringed the other's rights by copying the film and communicatir

Pause for reflection boxes

These boxes help you stop, reflect on and assess the law described. They help you to consider how the law works in practice, as well as look more closely at its logic and its consistency with other principles, its policy ramifications and how it relates to other key issues.

Pause for reflection

In many instances, there is conflict between the theories outlined abo
and case law say. For example, if copyright law is justified under utilitar
period of protection now last until 70 years after the author's death, so t
are the author's successors? Here, we reach a crucial part of our prob
right is a property right that subsists for 70 *years* *after* the life of the
any property, it can be inherited. Steven's wife Sharon inherited his pr

Conclusion

Each chapter ends with a concluding section, to draw the chapter together, highlight outstanding questions, and apply the discussion back to the problem and illustrations you have considered.

1.6 **Conclusion**

This chapter has explained the history of copyright law in the UI
fluences which have shaped its content, the theoretical justificati
the extent to which they accord with the current law, and the pr
of copyright, including the crucial difference between protecting
ing the expression of that idea. We have examined some UK case
copyright's history—*Millar*, *Beckett*, *Bach*—and the key pieces of
tion from the Statute of Anne 1709 to the 1911 and 1956 Acts
statute, the CDPA 1988.

End of chapter questions

A few questions at the end of each chapter help you to think about what you have learnt, track your progress, and go back to any sections you need to spend more time on.

End-of-chapter questions

After reading the chapter carefully, try answering the following questio
visit the online resources at **www.oup.com/uk/karapapa-mcdona**

1. The assumption that the list of eight categories of protected subje
CDPA is closed is under challenge. Critically discuss.

2. How has the European standard of originality impacted on the tra
judgement' approach in the UK? Discuss by reference to relevant

3. Can invented words, short sentences or headlines attract protecti

Further reading

Suggestions for further reading give you a starting point for broadening your knowledge and taking your learning further.

Guide to the online resources

www.oup.com/uk/karapapa-mcdonagh/

Intellectual Property Law is accompanied by the following online resources which complement the book and enhance your learning experience.

Home > Law > Intellectual Property Law

Description

Resources to accompany *Intellectual Property Law*:

- General guidance on approaching problem questions
- Suggested answers to the end of chapter questions from the book
- Updates from the authors to help students keep on top of this fast-moving subject
- Web links to the major international intellectual property organisations

Download Cartridge

- General guidance on approaching problem questions
- Suggested answers to the end of chapter questions from the book
- Updates from the authors to help you keep on top of this fast-moving subject
- Web links to the major international intellectual property organizations

Contents in brief

Contents in full

European Court of Human Rights Case

Court of Justice of the European Union Cases

European Union Intellectual Property Office Cases

European Patents Organisation Cases

National Cases by Country

Australia Cases

Benelux

UK Secondary Legislation

Introduction

Introduction to copyright

Problem question

Read this problem question carefully, and keep it in mind while you are working through the chapter that follows. At the end of this chapter, you will be able to apply what you have learnt to the problem question and advise the relevant parties.

Steven Murphy was a poet who lived all his life in London, UK. He wrote at least one poem every day from the age of 21 until he died at the young age of 33. During his life, he hand-wrote the poems on paper and posted them to his friends, keeping only one hand-written copy of each poem in a drawer in his study. As stated in his letters, Steven simply wanted to share the poems with his friends—but he made clear that the poems were to be kept private. When he died his letters and writings all passed to his wife Sharon Murphy.

Earlier this year, Sharon unexpectedly saw Steven's friend Adil, an actor, speak out one of Steven's poems during a popular BBC TV programme. By coincidence Sharon had been reading the specific poem earlier that day in Steven's former study. Sharon was shocked as she is sure nobody asked Steven about this before his death, and nobody sought her permission either. She has never thought about the authorship or ownership of Steven's poems. She is unaware of how works of literature are protected under copyright. She knows nothing of the history of the law or about the requirements of protection. She has no idea what Steven's rights are in this circumstance, or even why copyright exists in the first place, nor whether she, as a surviving spouse who inherited all of Steven's property, has any rights to enforce Steven's copyright.

Advise Sharon as to the history, nature and purpose of copyright, and whether she can enforce rights over the poems, given that she inherited all of Steven's property.

1.1 Introduction

Before we can examine the key elements of the law in later chapters, we must understand what copyright is, and how it came to be. By keeping in mind the above problem question concerning the ownership of Steven's poetry, we will seek to understand what copyright is, why copyright protects works of authorship, and how this type of protection came about. As we shall see, answering the question of how and why (and for how long) a poem will be protected by copyright illustrates the simplicity of the principle at stake—that authors deserve protection for their works—as well as the complexity of the law in the area, including how questions of ownership ought to be determined once an author has passed away.

Like any legal subject, copyright law is a product of history. Here we provide a brief account of how United Kingdom copyright law has developed from the mid-16th century onward. The purpose of giving this account is to highlight two recurring themes: (i) the law's struggle to keep up with changing technology; and (ii) the effect of external influences on domestic law. We further suggest that any discussion of copyright law should not be separated from an appreciation of its theoretical justifications.

Burkitt points out (in 'Copyrighting Culture—The History and Cultural Specificity of the Western Model of Copyright' [2001] 2 *IPQ* 146) that copyright law cannot be divorced from its historical origins. However, it is wrong to assume that there is a single, unified historical account of copyright's development. Even within the so-called 'Western' model of copyright, at least four different philosophical approaches can be detected—in Britain, the USA, France, and Germany. Over time, the values inherent in these diverse legal systems have been imposed on other cultures, for example, those of Imperial China or of Aboriginal Australia, regardless of the fact that these other systems may have had no traditional notion of individually owned intellectual property rights. As we shall see, Britain was particularly influential in this regard—the 1911 Copyright Act was officially styled as an Imperial Act, and it was binding on a vast range of territories within the Empire, including Ireland (then part of the UK), Canada, South Africa, New Zealand, Australia, and India.

When was the first ever case of copyright?

It is alleged that the first ever 'case' involving copyright occurred in Ireland in the sixth century. The missionary St Columba was accused of plagiarism, having visited a particular monastery where he surreptitiously borrowed a rare book in order to copy it. Complaint was made to the High King of Meath, Diarmuid, by the owner of the original book who demanded that the copy be handed over. In giving judgment in favour of the book's owner, the King took inspiration from traditional Irish law, which was to the effect that any calf found wandering belonged to its mother, wherever the cow might be kept. His ruling was 'As to every Cow its Calf, so to every Book its Copy', a statement which is said to be the foundation of modern copyright law. (When reading this pronouncement, it should be remembered that books at that time were made of vellum, that is, cow hide.)

Bearing this in mind, along with Burkitt's argument about differing cultural traditions, we consider in this chapter the philosophical arguments advanced by United

Kingdom judges and writers as justifications for copyright protection. This is to help you, the reader, to reflect, when dealing with the material in later chapters, whether the practice of the current law lives up to its theoretical justifications.

Pause for reflection

Referring back to our problem at the beginning of this chapter, a key question might be: what is it about what Steven did, in creating his poems, that justifies giving him legal protection?

As an introduction to this reflective process, in the next part of the chapter we compare and contrast copyright law with other forms of intellectual property to demonstrate the surprising breadth of protection given to the right owner. This is despite the fact that copyright protection arises automatically—i.e. despite the widespread use of assertive symbols such as ©, copyright does not, in fact, require registration—and, in many instances, copyright arises with only a minimum expenditure of effort. You may wish to think further about the fact that such broad protection is somewhat at odds with the reasons given for protection of copyright works. Indeed, many writers argue that copyright needs to be reined in so as to accord with its justifications, but we pose the question whether it is ever possible to turn back the legal clock.

Pause for reflection

Why do you think that copyright ought not to require an application or registration process? In particular, who might benefit from this lack of registration, and who might prefer a registration system?

Generally, authors themselves are said to be the beneficiaries of the lack of a registration requirement. Since there is no application fee, or need to renew a copyright, authors are, at the outset, charged nothing for copyright protection.

Consider the case of Steven in our problem question—he never sought even to publish his poems, merely share them with friends, yet his works will be protected by copyright law in the same way the works of a famous poet such as Seamus Heaney are protected. Automatic protection is therefore advantageous to authors.

On the other hand, the lack of a register of copyright works can hinder digital uses of some works, particularly letters and photographs held by archives and libraries, since the authors of these works may no longer be known (and thus their permission cannot be sought for uses of the works). These types of works are known as 'orphan works' since we do not know who the 'parents', or authors, are. Christopher Sprigman ('Reform(aliz)ing Copyright' [2004] 57 *Stanford Law Review* 484) notes that some jurisdictions such as the US chose in the early decades of copyright protection to use a registration system, though this ceased in the 1970s. He further argues that there is a case for bringing formal registration back into use to ensure public access to copyright works. What the above divergence illustrates is that within copyright theory there is often a battle between private interests (of authors) and the wider public interest (of users and consumers).

Later in this chapter we will consider another key question—what is the difference between an idea and its expression? It is often said that copyright law does not protect ideas but the form in which they are expressed. Yet, this distinction is easy to state, but difficult to apply. Copyright case law features decisions where, on the one hand, the courts appear to have come close to protecting mere ideas; and, equally, cases where the courts appear to have failed to protect the creator's actual expression.

 Pause for reflection

On the idea/expression dichotomy, if we think back to our problem question we can observe that there is some truth to the distinction: when Steven came up with the idea of e.g. writing a poem in tribute to his wife, this would not in itself have been protectable; it was only when Steven expressed this initial idea in poetic form that copyright arose. Yet, as we will see in later cases, depending on the facts, the distinction can be hard to maintain.

1.2 History

1.2.1 The origins of copyright at the advent of the printing age

A recurring theme of copyright law is that it is a legal response—albeit belatedly—to changing technology. The advent of the Gutenberg printing press in the 15th century meant that in Europe books no longer had to be copied laboriously by hand, a skill previously practised by a few 'scriptors' in monasteries (consider the story of St Columba given above) and universities. This labour-intensive and slow method of hand-reproduction severely limited the availability of books (and, in turn, the ability of the public to read). With the printing press, the ability to reproduce text swiftly and mechanically meant that the ideas and information contained in print became readily available to the reading public for the first time.

The English reaction to this continental European invention—the Gutenberg press—involved the Tudor monarchs (specifically, Queen Mary) using the Royal Prerogative to grant a charter to the Stationers' Company in London, just as Queen Elizabeth I later granted patents to her favourite courtiers. The Stationers' Company, as a craft guild, possessed supervisory powers over its members, so that before a book could be printed a *licence* had first to be obtained. Licences were only granted to company members, who accordingly had the exclusive right to print and distribute books. The Company's powers included those to search out and dispose of any books printed contrary to law. Viewed from today's perspective, we would say that the Crown used the Company as a means of controlling printing so as to censor materials thought to be contrary to the interests of the established church or the state.

The system of licensing books was maintained throughout the English Civil War (despite the abolition of the Star Chamber) and was renewed after the Restoration by the Licensing Act 1662. In due course, however, the legislation lapsed, leaving the Company to regulate the publishing trade as best it could through its rules of membership. By now, however, the ability to copy books easily (and hence cheaply) was causing concern in the book trade. There was intensive lobbying for legislation to deal with the perceived problem of piracy, but it should be noted that most of the pressure came from the publishers themselves, that is, entrepreneurs, rather than disgruntled *authors*, the creators.

1.2.2 The Statute of Anne

The Copyright Act 1709 (the 'Statute of Anne') is said to be the first piece of copyright legislation anywhere in the world. It conferred on authors 'the sole right and liberty of printing books' for a term of 14 years from first publication, with a further period of 14 years being available if the author were still alive at the end of the first term of protection (average life expectancy being much shorter in those days). For books already printed at the date of the Act (10 April 1710) the duration of protection was 21 years. The chosen periods of protection were similar to those available for *patents* under the Statute of Monopolies 1623. Authors were able to assign their rights to others, and booksellers and printers were declared to fall within the meaning of the authors' 'assigns'.

It took many years before the scope of the Act's protections became clear. In the 18th century, as the periods of protection given under the 1709 Act began to expire, a debate ensued as to the relationship between copyright granted under the Act and the author's assumed protection under the old English common law. In other words, did the Act create a new authorial copyright or did it simply declare a right which already existed at common law? As Burkitt points out, this debate coincided with the rise of authors as autonomous professionals rather than as scribes dependent on the patronage of the ruling class.

Booksellers argued that authors had literary property in their work, justified by Lockean labour theory. This literary property, it was said, belonged to the author at common law; the author was free to assign this to a publisher, and moreover such right existed indefinitely at common law. Equally, however, there were those who argued that literature was simply a collection of ideas, too transient and fleeting to be protected as property. Finally, the courts were asked to resolve this question.

Millar v Taylor (1769) 98 ER 201 and *Donaldson v Beckett* (1774) 1 ER 837

Both of these cases concerned a book of poetry, *The Seasons*, written by one James Thompson, the copyright in which had been owned by Millar. (Given the centrality of poetry to these cases, it is worth keeping our problem, and Steven's poems, in mind.) On the expiry of the period of protection under the Statute of Anne, Taylor printed and sold 1,000 copies of the book. In *Millar v Taylor*, the Court of King's Bench upheld Millar's claim for loss of profit, holding that common law copyright had not been taken away by the Statute. Willes J, in the majority, avoided using Lockean arguments, preferring instead theories of 'natural justice' and equity. Literature should be encouraged and the author should be entitled to the fruits of his labour. Lord Mansfield, too, relied on equitable notions of fairness and the moral rights of the author. Only Yates J dissented, arguing (at p. 233) that 'nothing can be an object of property which is not capable of sole and exclusive enjoyment'. →

> Subsequently, Millar's executors sold the copyright in *The Seasons* to Beckett, who, relying on the judgment in *Millar v Taylor*, successfully obtained an injunction against Donaldson for printing and distributing further copies of Thomson's works. Donaldson appealed to the House of Lords, who referred the matter to the 12 common law judges for an opinion. By a majority, the judges in *Donaldson v Beckett* held that there was a common law copyright in published works, but by an even narrower majority they ruled that the Statute took away that right. The limited term of protection under the Statute removed the perpetual common law right upon publication.

 Pause for reflection

It is worth pausing to consider the impact of *Donaldson v Beckett* in light of recent academic research. First, as Deazley argues (in 'The Myth of Copyright at Common Law' [2003] 62 *CLJ* 106), close analysis of the case reveals that its ruling has often been misunderstood; in fact, the court denied the existence of *any* common law copyright. Nevertheless, in the aftermath Parliament appears to have assumed that the case did leave intact the author's perpetual common law copyright in unpublished works, as more than a century later this right was declared to be abolished by the Copyright Act 1911. Second, as Burkitt observes, the discussion in *Donaldson v Beckett*, in contrast to that in *Millar v Taylor*, appears to favour the economic view of copyright rather than the aesthetic. Although the judges express concerns about the dangers of creating a perpetual monopoly, the net effect of the case is the 'commodification of literature'.

1.2.3 Piecemeal legislative and judicial development of copyright doctrine

The legal developments which occurred after *Donaldson v Beckett* reflect the reactionary nature of copyright law, perpetually attempting to catch up with changes in business and technology. One of the key judicial developments concerned whether the Statute of Anne applied only to literature or also musical works.

Bach v Longman (1777) 2 Cowper 623

It was initially unclear whether the Statute of Anne—which referred expressly to books—protected works of music as expressed in sheet music. In *Bach v Longman* the case involved the composer Johann Christian Bach (son of the more famous composer Johann Sebastian Bach) suing publisher James Longman, who had published some of his compositions as sheet music without his permission. Longman claimed music was not protected by the Statute of Anne.

The court resolved this in Bach's favour by giving a broad meaning to the word 'books' in the Statute of Anne, referring to the fact that the preamble referenced the protection of 'books and other writings', so as to include sheet music. The case is a seminal one as it is the beginning of music copyright in the UK.

Apart from *Bach v Longman*, the majority of legal changes during the 18th and 19th centuries were legislative in nature and involved one or more of three possible reforms: (i) introducing new categories of work to the copyright system; (ii) adding to the scope of protection given to the right holder by entitling them to object to new forms of infringing conduct; or (iii) extending the term of protection.

Examples of the way in which new categories of work were added included the protection conferred on engravings in 1734 and 1766, on sculptures in 1798, and on paintings, drawings, and photographs in 1862. Examples of the extension of the scope of protection to include infringing conduct other than copying was the addition of the right to control performances of dramatic works in 1833 and of musical works in 1842. The duration of protection was increased to 28 years or the author's life, whichever was longer, in 1814, and to 42 years or the author's life plus seven years, whichever was longer, in 1842.

It was not until the Copyright Act 1911 (enacted in response to the international Berne Convention 1886, discussed in the next part of the chapter) that the standardized period of duration—the author's life, plus 50 years—was introduced. The same Act—which as noted earlier, applied throughout the British Empire—also put copyright in unpublished works on a statutory footing, abolishing common law copyright in the process, and repealed many of its myriad predecessors, bringing all forms of copyright work under the umbrella of a single statute.

1.2.4 External influences—international treaties on copyright

Changes to copyright law from the latter part of the 19th century onwards reflect the way in which trade became increasingly international, and eventually, global. At first, British authors received no protection in other countries, nor indeed did foreign nationals qualify for protection in the United Kingdom (*Jefferys v Boosey* (1854) 4 HLC 415). In consequence, there was nothing to stop a publisher in another country from making copies of a book written by a British author and then importing these copies into this country, often undercutting the price of the 'authorized' version of the work. Eventually, in 1886, the terms of an international system were agreed at Berne, Switzerland.

The Berne Convention 1886

The Berne Convention for the Protection of Literary and Artistic Works 1886 (signed by ten states and subsequently the subject of five major revisions) established minimum, rather than absolute, standards for the protection of copyright. Its key ingredient is the principle of *national treatment*. An author of one Contracting State is entitled to the same protection in another Contracting State as the authors of the latter receive. Another fundamental principle is that Contracting States may not impose any formality such as registration as a precondition of protection.

As long as the Berne minimum standards are in place there can be differences in detail between the laws of Contracting States as to the types of work protected, the scope of protection, and the duration of protection. Thus, 'national treatment' does not guarantee that an

→

→

author from France will receive the same treatment under UK law as he or she is entitled to in France; rather it means that the French author will receive the same treatment as a British author can expect in the UK.

Thinking back to our problem question, this would mean that Steven, as a citizen of the UK and an author of poems, could expect comparable national treatment in other Contracting States (most countries in the world). Luckily for Steven, a poem is well established as a valid work of copyright in all Contracting States, so his works would be protected; however, as we shall see later on, the duration of his copyright could vary from state to state, as some states, such as the US and UK (via the EU) have legislated to extend duration beyond the Berne minimum term to life, plus 70 years.

Although one of the founding signatories of the Berne Convention, the UK did not incorporate the Convention into domestic law until the Copyright Act 1911, the impetus for change coming from the 1908 version of the Convention. Later revisions to the Berne Convention (in 1928, 1948, 1967, and 1971) prompted further legislative reforms, specifically the Copyright Act 1956 ('the 1956 Act') and the Copyright, Designs and Patents Act 1988 ('CDPA').

Although it is the paramount treaty, the Berne Convention is not the only international agreement which has affected the content of domestic copyright law. The Rome Convention on the Protection of Performers, Producers of Phonograms and Broadcasting Organisations 1961 (the so-called 'neighbouring rights' convention) has also had a major effect at ensuring protection for performers, sound recordings, and broadcast rights (although it must be noted that UK law protected sound recordings and broadcasts before the advent of the Convention). Thus, its main effect in the UK has been with regard to the rights of performers to control the recording of their performances. The UK initially fulfilled this obligation by means of the criminal law, set out in the Performers' Protection Acts 1958–1972; but as a result of case law intervention during the 1980s, civil redress for 'bootleg' recordings was created by Part II of the CDPA (in 1988), which remains the major piece of UK copyright legislation. Further protection for performers has been added to Part II of the CDPA as a result of EU Directives. However, the most recent expansion (the creation of moral rights for performers) has come not from the EU but from WIPO—the World Intellectual Property Organization—based in Geneva. The WIPO Performers and Phonograms Treaty 1996 ('WPPT') and the WIPO Copyright Treaty 1996 ('WCT') enhanced the protection afforded to performers and copyright owners.

 Pause for reflection

In our problem question above, Steven's actor friend Adil read out one of Steven's poems on a BBC TV programme. This would be considered to be a performance for the purposes of performers' rights protection under UK copyright law, and Adil would have rights over this performance independent of Steven's rights over the poem itself. For example, Adil must give permission for his performance to be broadcast. We will consider performers' rights in more detail in later chapters.

Why is it so important to authors that copyright be protected not just in their home jurisdiction, but internationally? We have already discussed the fact that at the time of the Statute of Anne, publishers and booksellers were all-powerful, and authors had little influence on legislation. Uma Suthersanen ('Bleak House or Great Expectations?' in H. Porsdam (ed.), Copyright & Other Fairy Tales (Edward Elgar, 2006), 40) argues that during the 19th century, the literary author emerged as a stakeholder in international copyright politics. The most popular authors of the Victorian era, notably Victor Hugo and Charles Dickens, had become aware of the sheer amount of pirate editions of their works available elsewhere, especially in the US. Both authors were strong advocates for international copyright.

 Pause for reflection

Reading the problem at the beginning of the chapter, it is worth considering the following: what would the consequences be if Steven's poem had been read out in a US PBS TV programme rather than a UK BBC one?

Due to the existence of international copyright, Steven's works would be protected under copyright in the US, and the same rights issues would arise (issues that in our problem are of great concern to his wife Sharon).

1.2.5 European Union legislation

As noted above, the three major legislative reforms to United Kingdom copyright law in the 20th century (the Acts of 1911, 1956, and 1988) can each be attributed to obligations under the Berne Convention (of which there are now well over 160 country signatories). In the last three decades, however, the driving force for the reform of domestic copyright law has been the EU, with no fewer than 11 Directives requiring alteration to UK copyright legislation. Although the UK is currently on a path to exit the EU—'Brexit'—the UK plans to maintain EU-derived legislation within domestic law for the immediate post-Brexit period. As a result, EU law is still of great importance to intellectual property and will remain so for some time.

For convenience, the EU Directives can be grouped together as follows. First, there are those which deal with the impact of digital technology, namely: the Semiconductor Directive (Council Directive 87/54/EEC of 16 December 1986 on the legal protection of topographies of semiconductor products [1987] OJ L 24/36); the Computer Programs Directive (Council Directive 91/250/EEC of 14 May 1991 on the legal protection of computer programs [1991] OJ L 122/42 now codified as Directive 2009/24/EC of the European Parliament and of the Council of 23 April 2009 [2009] OJ L 111/16); the Database Directive (Directive 96/9/EC of 11 March 1996 on the legal protection of databases [1996] OJ L 77/20); and the Information Society Directive (Directive 2001/29/EC of the European Parliament and of the Council of 22 May 2001 on the harmonisation of certain aspects of copyright and related rights in the information society [2001] OJ L 167/10). It is the fourth of these which has had the most wide-ranging effect on the general principles of copyright law (particularly with regard to the issues of *originality*, *infringement*, and *defences* to infringement) and on *neighbouring rights* such as those of performers. We will discuss the Information Society Directive further in the following chapters on copyright.

The second batch of EU directives deal with the relationship between copyright and broadcasting, namely: the 'Television without Frontiers' Directive (Council Directive 89/552/EEC of 3 October 1989 on the co-ordination of certain provisions concerning the pursuit of television broadcasting activities [1989] OJ L 298/23); and the Copyright Broadcasting Directive (Council Directive 93/83/EEC of 27 September 1993 on the co-ordination of certain rules concerning copyright and neighbouring rights applicable to satellite broadcasting and cable re-transmission [1993] OJ L 246/15).

A third category of directive deals specifically with the rights of artists when an original work of art is resold, the Droit de Suite Directive (Directive 2001/84/EC of the European Parliament and of the Council of 27 September 2001 on the resale right for the benefit of the author of an original work of art of [2001] OJ L 272/32).

Finally, a number of directives impact upon the law of copyright generally, namely: the Rental Rights Directive (Council Directive 92/100/EEC of 19 November 1992 on rental right and lending right and on certain rights related to copyright in the field of intellectual property [1992] OJ L 346/61, now codified as Directive 2006/115/EC of the European Parliament and of the Council of 12 December 2006 [2006] OJ L 376/28); the Copyright Term Directive (Council Directive 93/98/EC of 29 October 1993 harmonising the term of copyright protection [1993] OJ L 290/9, now codified as Directive 2006/116/EC of the European Parliament and of the Council of 12 December 2006 [2006] OJ L 372/12, amended in relation to sound recordings and performances by Directive 2011/77/EU of the European Parliament and of the Council of 27 September 2011 [2011] OJ L 265/1); the Enforcement Directive (Directive 2004/48/EC of the European Parliament and of the Council of 29 April 2004 on the enforcement of intellectual property rights [2004] OJ L 157/45); and Directive 2012/28/EU of the European Parliament and of the Council of 25 October 2012 on certain permitted uses of orphan works [2012] OJ L 299/5. It is expected that a new EU Copyright Directive will be passed during 2019—Article 11 will require companies that use media publishing content to pay when it is 'linked' in commercial circumstances; Article 13 will require platforms such as Twitter to filter content uploaded by users in case it is protected by copyright. Depending on the Brexit timetable, it is not clear at time of writing whether the UK would adopt the Directive or mirror its rules, post-Brexit.

One result of international treaty obligations (Berne, Rome) and EU legislation (directives) is that the framers of UK copyright legislation no longer have much freedom of choice with regard to the types of right which are recognized, the scope and duration of protection, and the defences available to an infringer. At the same time, the UK is a net exporter of copyright materials, due to its successful literary, musical, and film industries, so it is in the UK's interest that copyright be protected internationally.

 Pause for reflection

We do not know yet what the outcome of Brexit will be. UK copyright law will not immediately change once Brexit occurs, as the government has stated that EU legislation will be, where

→

→ possible, incorporated into domestic law. Thereafter the UK may—depending on the terms of any eventual trade deal with the EU—decide to make changes to domestic copyright law that are not in line with current EU principles, on subjects such as originality, infringement, and defences to infringement. This brings up the potential to reform copyright in line with the UK economy's needs and the needs of users, especially the areas related to mass digitisation, 'fintech' (i.e. financial technology), and the fourth industrial revolution (i.e. the digital revolution). Reform is not a new idea: the Hargreaves Review of Intellectual Property and Growth (hereafter 'Hargreaves'), published in May 2011, made ten recommendations, including changes to copyright defences/exceptions, designs, and enforcement. Changes to copyright exceptions post-Hargreaves were effected by statutory instrument, whilst the revisions to design law were made by the Intellectual Property Act 2014. These are relatively minor revisions which comply with EU law. Crucially, as noted earlier, in the aftermath of Brexit it may be possible to enact more radical changes to copyright. Once you have read through this book's copyright chapters, ask yourself the following question: what would be your priority, if you were tasked with reforming UK copyright post-Brexit?

1.3 The justifications for copyright protection

Here we return to a fundamental question: why should an author have copyright in the work the author creates? How can we justify this? As we shall see, there are several competing theories, including utilitarianism, labour-based theory, and a philosophical personality-based justification.

 Pause for reflection

The utilitarian justification states that authors like Steven should be given a limited monopoly either as an incentive to create or as a reward for having created something which enriches society. The labour (or natural law) theory put forward by the English thinker John Locke argues that the product of the intellect of a person like Steven belongs to them, in the same manner as any tangible artefact they have laboured to create out of 'the commons'. The continental European philosophical theory associated with the German philosophers Immanuel Kant and Georg Hegel states that intellectual creations are an extension of the author's personality—in our case, Steven's—and should therefore be accorded property rights.

Most scholars accept that authors like Steven do something in creating e.g. poetry that is useful, or aesthetically pleasing, and that consequently deserves some protection, either in and of itself as an intellectual and pleasurable activity, or as an incentive or reward for the effort expounded. The debate—and the devil, as they say—is in the detail: how much protection; how long should it last; who benefits?

These philosophical arguments were considered in the context of UK copyright law by Sir Hugh Laddie (in 'Copyright: Over-strength, Over-regulated, Over-rated' [1996] 18 *EIPR* 253). Laddie referred to 'three sacred principles' which underpin copyright law: that one should not steal what belongs to another (which assumes that ideas are property, a point considered further later); that a person should be entitled to own the product of the intellect just as much as he or she might own a piece of furniture he or she has carved from a tree (the Lockean labour theory); and that it is in society's interests to reward those who are inventive, or to encourage creativity, as this will in the long term improve everyone's standard of living. However, Laddie further argued that these sacred principles do not justify the current breadth of copyright legislation. In particular, he highlighted the unwarranted expansion of copyright to provide three-dimensional protection for two-dimensional artistic works; the availability of additional damages; the 'overlong' term of protection; the low test of originality coupled with the ease of creation; the availability of criminal sanctions; and the narrow nature of the UK's fair dealing defence when compared with the fair use defence in the US. We shall cover these debates in the chapters that follow this one.

In the US, the economic justification of copyright holds sway. Landes and Posner (in 'An Economic Analysis of Copyright Law' [1989] 18 *Journal of Legal Studies* 325) consider in detail the economics of copyright as an incentive to create. They argue that the need for copyright protection has increased over time as modern technology has reduced the time needed to make copies as well as enabling more perfect copies to be made. Further, various rules of copyright can be regarded as attempts to promote economic efficiency by balancing the consequences of enhanced protection against the need to encourage greater creativity. By contrast, Breyer (in 'The Uneasy Case for Copyright: A Study of Copyright in Books, Photocopies and Computer Programs' (1970) 84 *Harv LR* 281) argues that extensions to copyright protection are both unnecessary and harmful. Having reviewed both the moral rights and incentive theories, he questions whether it is necessary to attribute property rights to creativity. Further, he states that the non-economic goals served by copyright law are not an adequate justification for the copyright system, as other arrangements could be made to protect an author's dignitary rights. It must be stressed that both of these seminal pieces were written before the advent of the digital age, which has reduced to almost zero the cost of making perfect copies of a work. Rahmatian (in 'Copyright and Commodification' [2005] 26(2) *EIPR* 371) argues that to merely suppose that the world would be a better place if copyright were not treated as a property right and if creativity were not treated as a commodity ignores the real issue. The problem, he says, is that lawmakers, under pressure from the international entertainment industry, forget that there is a need for restrictions on the power which flows from the proprietary nature of copyright.

 Pause for reflection

In many instances, there is conflict between the theories outlined above and what statutes and case law say. For example, if copyright law is justified under utilitarianism, why does the period of protection now last until 70 years after the author's death, so that those who benefit are the author's successors? Here, we reach a crucial part of our problem question—copyright is a property right that subsists for 70 years *after* the life of the author. Moreover, like any property, it can be inherited. Steven's wife Sharon inherited his property upon his death,

➡

→

including his poems as copyright works. She now is the owner of these works, and it is from her any permissions to use the work should be sought. The oft-stated justification for this is that it allows the families of authors who die young to continue to receive royalties for the exploitation and publication of the author's works for a long time after death. While this is laudable, the jury is out on whether 70 years is nonetheless too long a period to allow this, given that it means that Sharon's heirs will also likely inherit Steven's works for a period of time upon her death (unless she lives to be over 100 years old).

Another salient question is as follows: if copyright law is justified under Locke's labour theory, why is the threshold for originality, required for copyright protection, set so low that items like professional directories (*Waterlow v Rose* [1995] FSR 207) and lists of television programmes (*Independent Television Publications v Time Out* [1984] FSR 64) are protected? We will explore this question of originality further in the next chapter, but for now we can accept that Steven's poems are sufficiently original to be protected.

Finally, if Hegelian personality theory is the justification, why does United Kingdom law treat copyright as an economic right which can be bought and sold like any other commodity, with freedom of contract the guiding principle, rather than treating it as a dignitary right unique to its author? Here it is worth pointing out that during his lifetime Steven could have sold the rights to his poems to e.g. a publisher, but instead he decided only to circulate the poems privately. Copyright ownership now belongs to Sharon, who, in the absence of any express term from Steven's will (and we have no evidence such a term exists), could decide to sell the rights to the poems to a publisher. Such a decision, by a late owner, might be questioned under the Hegelian theory, as it goes against the will of the creator. (At this stage, we can also note that under copyright there are principles called 'moral rights' that are concerned with the will and reputation of the author, and we will examine these in a later chapter.)

1.4 Comparing copyright with other intellectual property rights

It is worth pointing out at this stage that there are a number of aspects of copyright that do not apply to other intellectual property rights like patents and trade marks. Understanding these differences will help you to distinguish between the different types of intellectual property right as you read through this book.

1.4.1 Ease of creation

As we saw earlier, the existence of copyright protection does not depend on registration, something that marks copyright out from patents and registered trade marks. Indeed, under Article 5(2) of the Berne Convention, Contracting States must not impose any formal requirements (e.g. registration) for the 'enjoyment and exercise of these rights'.

Copyright in a work therefore arises automatically and instantaneously, upon the act of creation, provided certain simple conditions are satisfied. The key criteria are: the work must be original; it must be recorded in a material form; and the author or the work must qualify for United Kingdom protection by being 'connected' in some way to a Contracting State of the Berne Convention, the Universal Copyright Convention ('UCC') or the World Trade Organization ('WTO').

 Pause for reflection

With regard to our problem, we have already accepted that Steven is a UK citizen whose works are original (though we'll explore originality in greater depth in the next chapter). Finally, we know that they were fixed—recorded—in the form of the paper he wrote them onto. Thus, there is no reason to doubt that Steven's poems are works of copyright.

1.4.2 Scope of protection

It might be assumed that if an intellectual property right can easily be created, the protection conferred on its owner must be relatively limited. The contrary is the case. On the one hand, copyright is not a true *monopoly* right in the same sense as a *patent* or a *registered design*, so proof of independent creation is always a defence to an infringement action—indeed, it is the corollary of the requirement of originality. However, the breadth of copyright can be judged from the fact that it protects the rightholder in a wide range of scenarios: (i) the copying of the work by another; (ii) issuing tangible copies of the work (by sale or rental); (iii) performing the work in public; (iv) communicating the work to the public by intangible means (by broadcasting it or uploading it onto a website); and (v) adapting the work. These five forms of conduct are known in the CDPA as 'restricted acts' and are categorized as acts of primary infringement.

 Pause for reflection

Copyright is not a single right, but a bundle. In our problem, Steven was the author and holder of these rights until his death, at which point they passed to Sharon, who is the current owner of the bundle.

We will consider *infringement* in detail in the chapters that follow. For present purposes, we can simply note that it is not necessary for the whole of the work to be copied, as liability arises should a 'substantial part' be taken, 'substantial' being assessed qualitatively not quantitatively (*Hawkes & Son v Paramount Film Services* [1934] Ch 593 & *Infopaq International A/S v Danske Dagblades Forening* Case C-5/08 [2009] ECR I-6569). Further, copying can be indirect as well as direct and the copier does not even have to copy the source work consciously (*Francis Day & Hunter v Bron* [1963] Ch 587). Innocence is therefore not a defence to the acts of primary infringement, although it may affect the award of *damages* (CDPA s. 97). Not only is the primary infringer liable for taking the work, but liability can be imposed for secondary infringement, so that anyone who subsequently deals knowingly in infringing copies in the course of trade may be sued.

Pause for reflection

In our problem, Adil has undertaken (iii) above—a public performance of the work without Steven's (or Sharon's) permission. Indeed, we can see from the details of our problem scenario that Steven expressly forbade public sharing of his work. This is an act of primary infringement. The BBC meanwhile have committed (iv) by broadcasting the performance of the work, which was also without permission. Both of these appear to be clear infringements of Steven's copyright, which may be enforced by Sharon as the copyright owner. (In later chapters we will discuss defences to allegations of infringement, but they are not necessary to discuss at this point.)

One other aspect of the breadth of the copyright infringement action should be mentioned, which is that someone who authorizes the commission of an infringing act is just as much an infringer as someone who copies or who sells infringing copies. The word 'authorizes' has been held to encompass not just conduct whereby the defendant 'sanctions, countenances or approves' the behaviour of another, but also where the defendant exhibits 'indifference from which authorisation may be inferred': *Moorhouse v University of New South Wales* [1976] RPC 151. The significance of authorization has increased in the era of the internet, as it has been held that the act of authorization need not be committed in the UK as long as the act of primary infringement occurs here (*ABKCO Music v Music Collection International* [1995] RPC 657). As we shall see in the later chapter on copyright infringement the implications of the *ABKCO* decision for websites which enable UK visitors to download music and films should be considered in the context of cases involving s. 97A CDPA web-blocking orders—orders requiring internet service providers to block access to websites that allow unlicensed download of copyright works (*Twentieth Century Fox & others v British Telecommunications Plc* [2011] EWHC 1981 (Ch)).

 Pause for reflection

Have you ever downloaded an unlicensed film or song from the internet (i.e. without paying for it)? If so, you may well have committed copyright infringement. For many years, the music industry took a hard line against such acts of infringement, but in recent years both the music and film/TV industries have moved away from the 'punitive' approach to enforcing copyright and instead have focused on new business models involving cheap, easy-to-use online services such as Spotify, YouTube and Netflix. This chimes with the Hargreaves Review in 2011, which grappled with copyright in the digital age and recommended that legal access to copyright materials be made easier for consumers. By contrast, as noted earlier, the upcoming EU Copyright Directive in 2019 takes a firmer approach by requiring platforms to filter content uploaded by consumers in case it breaches copyright (Article 13).

A further difference exists between copyright and registered forms of intellectual property protection. Patents, trade marks, and designs can be declared invalid for failing to comply with the relevant statutory requirements, and trade marks may also be revoked for mismanagement, e.g. non-use. In contrast, copyright, once established, cannot be declared invalid, although a court may hold that the work in question is incapable of enforcement on grounds of public policy, e.g. immorality (promotion of adultery and 'free love'): *Glyn v Western Feature Film Co* [1916] 1 Ch 261 (though it must be emphasized that such cases are extremely rare and public morality has changed significantly since 1916).

1.4.3 Involvement of the criminal law

A challenge which faces both copyright and trade mark owners is how to combat commercial piracy. Both the CDPA and the Trade Marks Act 1994 ('TMA') (in, respectively, ss. 107 and 92) impose criminal sanctions where an act of infringement is committed by way of trade. Such liability is not confined to counterfeiters, but applies equally to the copyright owner's business competitors (*Thames & Hudson v Design & Artists Copyright Society* [1995] FSR 153). The maximum penalties, police search and seizure powers, and the ability of the court to order forfeiture of seized items were rationalized by the Copyright, etc and Trade Marks (Offences and Enforcement) Act 2002 and the penalties were increased by the Digital Economy Act 2010. The 2002 Act did not, however, make any changes to the type of behaviour prohibited by the 1988 and 1994 Acts. Enforcement of s. 107 CDPA and s. 92 TMA is delegated to Local Authority Trading Standards Departments, with confiscation orders available to the magistrates' court under the Criminal Justice Act 1988 (Confiscation Orders) Order 1995. Trading Standards Departments have increased powers as a result of s. 107A of the CDPA having been brought into force on 6 April 2007 by the Criminal Justice and Public Order Act 1994 (Commencement No. 14) Order 2007.

A more universal concern is the impact of counterfeiting. Counterfeiting is no longer confined to luxury brands but to medicines, car parts, and foodstuffs, with the obvious implications for consumer safety. EU law accordingly enables the intellectual property owner to call on the assistance of the customs authorities in the fight against counterfeiting by means of Regulation (EU) 608/2013 of the European Parliament and of the Council of 12 June 2013 concerning customs enforcement of intellectual property rights [2013] OJ L 181/15. The intellectual property owner can notify customs authorities who have power to prevent the importation of suspect goods at the point of entry. The goods in question are liable to forfeiture and destruction.

 Pause for reflection

With respect to our problem scenario, there is no element of criminal law at play in what Adil or the BBC have done—it is a question of copyright infringement and will potentially result in civil penalties, not criminal ones.

1.4.4 No liability for use

Traditionally, there has always been one significant limitation on the scope of copyright protection. The purchaser of a legitimate copy of a work is free to use it in whatever way he or she chooses. Thus, someone who buys a book, besides being at liberty to read it, can use it to light a fire, tear out the pages, prop up the leg of a table with it, or do any other sort of conduct, provided that what has been done is not within the list of 'restricted acts' which are the prerogative of the copyright owner.

 Pause for reflection

In line with the above, Adil and other friends of Steven could have destroyed their copies of the letters/poems, which had been freely sent to them by Steven, because the physical letters had become their property (although the underlying poems remained the property of Steven under copyright).

To some extent the advent of digital technology means that the purchaser's freedom to use a copyright article needs re-evaluating. To give one simple example, in order to use computer software, the program must be copied into the computer's memory. Whilst a licence to do so may readily be implied in the case of someone who buys a legitimate copy of software, the purchasers of a pirated copy will not be so protected and so will infringe each time they use the software, even if such use is for a legitimate purpose such as word-processing a letter or an essay. Further, whilst s. 28A CDPA provides the defence of making a temporary copy of any work as part of a technological process for a lawful purpose, such defence does not apply to computer software.

1.4.5 The fragmentary nature of copyright

As noted earlier, unlike patents and trade marks, copyright is not a unitary right, but a bundle or collection of different rights. It therefore has a fragmentary nature. This can be demonstrated with two examples.

First, each type of copyright work can, as a result of the list of 'restricted acts' found in s. 16 CDPA, be reproduced in a multiplicity of ways. If this is combined with the way in which copyright protection arises automatically in every Contracting State of the Berne Convention, Universal Copyright Convention, and WTO, the owner of a copyright work will have (quite literally) thousands of rights which exist worldwide.

Example 1 —*The Lord of the Rings* by JRR Tolkien

The trilogy *The Lord of the Rings* was written by J.R.R. Tolkein, who died in 1973. His literary executor (his son Christopher) has, by virtue of s. 16 CDPA, the right to control the following until the end of 2043:

- the 'reproduction' of the trilogy (indeed, each part of the trilogy) 'in any material form';
- the first sale of each copy of the books, together with the rental of any copies;
- any public performance of the books, such as a reading or recitation;
- their communication by intangible means, whether by broadcast or by the internet;

➙

→

- their adaptation, for example if they are turned into plays, or converted into pictorial form, or translated.

Consequently, there are hardback rights, paperback rights, serialization rights, talking book rights, dramatisation rights, film rights, radio and television broadcast rights, and the right to control the translation of the books into any language (consider how many languages there are worldwide). These rights exist not just in the UK, but in each state which is a signatory to the Berne Convention, the Universal Copyright Convention, or the WTO (well over 160 countries worldwide). Each one of these rights can be assigned or licensed to third parties, either collectively or individually.

As noted earlier, copyright's fragmentary nature, combined with the lack of registration and the lengthy duration of protection, makes the task of identifying who owns which right very complicated, particularly if the first author of the works has passed away, meaning that potential users need to contact the author's estate for permission (consider also the 'orphan works' mentioned earlier).

In our problem scenario Sharon, as the inheritor of Steven's copyright, has the right to exercise the above rights against anyone who attempts to use Steven's works without permission.

The second illustration of the fragmentary nature of copyright highlights the way in which one individual tangible product, for example a film DVD, may consist of a large number of individual copyrights. Some of these rights will flow from the copyright in another 'source' work, others will be independent of it, but the owners of each of these rights will need to give their permission before the film itself can be made, exhibited in public, communicated to the public, or copies of it sold or hired to the public.

Example 2 —*Death in Venice* by Thomas Mann

Consider the novel *Death in Venice*, written by Thomas Mann (1875–1955), which was first published in 1912. The novel was originally in German, but was translated into English by, amongst others, H.T. Lowe-Porter and Stanley Appelbaum. Visconti's 1971 film *Death in Venice* is based on the novel and has music by Gustav Mahler as its soundtrack. A film will have a screenplay (the story) and dialogue, as well as music, costumes, and sets. All of these—the novel, the translation, the film, the music, the script, the sets/costumes—could be copyright works in their own right, but equally they might be derived from earlier works. Thus, the screenplay and dialogue of *Death in Venice* might be derived directly or indirectly from the original novel, or from an English translation of that novel (or indeed a translation of the novel in another language).

Try to identify everyone who might have owned prior copyrights and who therefore would have had to give their consent to the making and subsequent exhibition of the film *Death in Venice*.

1.4.6 Duration

For most categories of work listed in s. 1 of the CDPA, the simple rule of thumb is that protection lasts for a period of the author's life plus 70 years (this rule is applicable throughout the whole of the EU, but Berne only requires life plus 50 years, and some countries such as New Zealand maintain this shorter term). Notably, despite the ease of creation, copyright in a work lasts far longer than either patent or design protection, and as previously explained, is not liable to revocation or invalidity proceedings.

However, there is a further complication awaiting the copyright lawyer in practice. The provisions of the CDPA apply only to works created after its operative date (1 August 1989). Regarding works created before that date, the principle found in Sch. 1 to the Act is that copyright will continue to subsist in an 'existing' work *after* commencement only if it subsisted therein *before* commencement (the so-called 'gateway' provision). In practice, therefore, it will be necessary to refer to the old law in respect of works created before 1989. The wording of previous copyright legislation will be relevant in deciding whether the work was of a type which was capable of protection, whether the author of the work qualified for protection (indeed, what the relevant definition of 'author' was at the time the work was created), and what the duration of the work originally was.

Pause for reflection

Consider a novel written in 1910 where, because the author died in 1950, copyright will remain in force until 2020. The novel will have to meet the criteria for protection set out, not in the 1956 Act, nor even in the 1911 Act, but in the Copyright Act 1842, because of the general principle that whether a work attracts United Kingdom copyright depends on the law in force when the work was made. Therefore, even though such a novel should continue to be protected under the CDPA, it will have to meet the criteria in legislation well over 150 years old!

It is worth recalling that Sharon (and potentially her heirs, or anyone she assigns—sells—the copyright to) will be able to control the use of the works for 70 years after Steven's death. In what year will the duration of Steven's works end?

Once the copyright in a work has expired, then that work passes into what is called the 'public domain' and is therefore free for everyone to use. However, this simple statement requires qualification. Many successful copyright works are often the subject of continuous revision or updating by their owners. Each time a new version of the work emerges, provided enough original creative effort has gone into the revision, a fresh copyright will arise. A good example of this is the Mickey Mouse cartoon character, whose appearance over the decades has been subtly altered.

Sawkins v Hyperion Records [2005] 1 WLR 3281

In this case, a very old piece of music by the French composer Lalande, which was in the public domain, became the subject of a copyright dispute. Dr Lionel Sawkins, a musicologist, conducted extensive research and revised fragments of Lalande's works so as to make them playable by a modern orchestra. As the creator of the modern 'performing edition' of the music, and having expounded sufficient creative original effort, the court held that Dr Sawkins was entitled to copyright in that version.

A final example can be observed where a work long out of copyright (if indeed it ever had protection) is incorporated into another copyright work. If e.g. a new edition of Shakespeare's plays is printed, although the plays themselves have never been protected by copyright, the publisher may have copyright in the typographical arrangement of the words on the printed page under s. 8 CDPA. The publisher can therefore object to the copying of that layout even though the content of the book itself is not protected. However, if a rival publisher brings out its own edition of Shakespeare's plays, following its own new layout/arrangement, this would not be a violation of copyright law.

1.5 The idea/expression dichotomy

One of the fundamental tenets of copyright law is that copyright does not exist to protect ideas, but rather the form in which they are expressed: *Donoghue v Allied Newspapers* [1938] Ch 106 at p. 109. This deceptively simple statement conceals what is perhaps the greatest challenge facing the student of copyright: how to draw the dividing line between an idea and its expression.

1.5.1 Idea versus expression: legislation

As Spence and Endicott point out ('Vagueness in the Scope of Copyright' [2005] 121 *LQR* 657) the CDPA itself gives little indication of this challenge. Section 1(1) merely declares that 'copyright is a *property* right which subsists . . . in the following descriptions of *work*' whilst s. 2(1) states that the owner of the copyright in '*a work of any description*' has the '*exclusive right*' to do the acts . . . *restricted by the copyright*' in a work of that description. Article 9(2) of the Agreement on Trade-Related Aspects of Intellectual Property Rights ('TRIPs Agreement'), however, makes the clear distinction between ideas and expression. It should be remembered (as Gervais points out) that the TRIPs Agreement itself, in Article 9(1), expressly incorporates both the provisions of the Berne Convention and the background discussions which are used to interpret its key provisions.

1.5.2 Idea versus expression: case law

Green v Broadcasting Corp of New Zealand **[1989] 2 All ER 1056 and** *Norowzian v Arks Ltd (No 2)* **[2000] FSR 363**

Earlier we discussed our problem scenario and noted that Steven's mere idea of writing a love poem would not be protectable, though the text of his poem itself, provided it is original, would be protected. However, there are many examples where the distinction is much less clear. Several cases can be used to illustrate this. In *Green v Broadcasting Corp of New Zealand* [1989] 2 All ER 1056 the Judicial Committee of the Privy Council held that there was no copyright infringement where the defendant copied the format for a television talent show: all that had been taken was the mere idea. Nevertheless, close reading of the case reveals that the claimant could quite easily have identified key elements in each programme, such as the

→

→

running order, catchphrases and other stage business which might (with careful pleading) have been claimed as a dramatic work. Similarly, in *Norowzian v Arks Ltd (No 2)* [2000] FSR 363 the defendant advertising agency, in creating a television advert called Anticipation for GUINNESS, had borrowed the claimant's idea of editing a film by a technique known as 'jump cutting' so that the actor appeared to make movements which were physically impossible. It was held that there had been no copying of the claimant's dramatic work, nor of his original film (called Joy). Although decided on the narrow point that there had been no taking of the claimant's work, it could be argued that what had been taken was the idea of how to edit the film in a particular way, not any particular copyright work. Nevertheless, it could be argued that the claimant's 'creativity' lay in the editing technique as much as in his film. Copyright law does not offer protection.

Despite these two illustrations, there are many other examples in the cases of where the courts appear to be conferring protection on ideas themselves.

Elanco v Mandops [1980] RPC 213

In order to sell a specific type of weed-killer, the defendant had to produce an appropriate instruction leaflet. Having changed the first version of its leaflet on the claimant's insistence so as to try to avoid copyright infringement, the defendant was nonetheless successfully sued for having reproduced the wording in its second leaflet (even though this had been carefully redrafted in order to avoid taking the wording of the claimant's instructions). The second leaflet consisted principally of factual information (usually regarded as falling below the threshold for copyright protection) yet its publication was still found to be an infringement of the claimant's leaflet. It is tempting to conclude here that the Court of Appeal (in contrast to the Privy Council in *Green*) was protecting the underlying idea, not its expression.

1.54.3 Idea versus expression: can the line be clearly drawn?

The most recent illustration of the difference between taking the ideas in another's work and taking the expression is the fascinating case of *Baigent and Lee v Random House Group Ltd* [2007] FSR 579, which involved the bestselling novel *The Da Vinci Code*.

Baigent and Lee v Random House Group Ltd [2007] FSR 579

The authors of a book, *The Holy Blood* and *The Holy Grail*, sued the publishers of Dan Brown's bestselling novel, *The Da Vinci Code*, alleging copyright infringement by copying the 'central theme' of their work. Upholding the decision of Peter Smith J at the High Court, the Court of Appeal held that although there had been copying (evidenced by points of similarity between the two works), what had been taken fell on the wrong side of the dividing line between ideas and their expression. The claimants' alleged 'central theme' (that descendants of Christ had married into the French royal family in the fifth century) was not the 'structure or architecture'

→

→ of their book (which would have been capable of protection). Instead, the 'central theme' amounted to no more than a series of generalized propositions, at too high a level of abstraction to qualify for copyright protection. It was not the product of originality by the claimants. Lloyd LJ (with whom Mummery LJ expressly agreed) declared (at [5]) that copyright does not subsist in ideas. It protects the expression of ideas, not the ideas themselves. Unhelpfully, perhaps, he then added that no clear principle 'is or could be laid down . . . to tell whether what is sought to be protected is on the ideas side of the dividing line, or on the expression side'. Unfortunately, outside of the specific literary facts of the case, the net result of the case confirms the idea/expression divide but offers minimal guidance as to how it should be applied.

 Pause for reflection

Throughout copyright law (particularly in infringement cases) you will find references to 'the idea/expression dichotomy'. Do you agree with Lloyd LJ in *Baigent* that it is not possible to state the distinction in such a way that it can be applied consistently in all cases? Are there any doubts about the line between idea and expression in our problem scenario?

1.6 Conclusion

This chapter has explained the history of copyright law in the UK and the external influences which have shaped its content, the theoretical justifications for copyright and the extent to which they accord with the current law, and the principal characteristics of copyright, including the crucial difference between protecting an idea and protecting the expression of that idea. We have examined some UK cases which are central to copyright's history—*Millar, Beckett, Bach*—and the key pieces of UK copyright legislation from the Statute of Anne 1709 to the 1911 and 1956 Acts and the key present statute, the CDPA 1988.

Turning to our problem scenario, we can state with confidence that during his lifetime Steven Murphy was an author and owner of copyright in his poems as literary works—which appear to be original and were fixed in hand-written form. When he died, the copyright in his works would have all passed, along with his other property, to his heirs—in this case his widow, Sharon Murphy. Under current UK copyright, the duration of protection is 70 years from the author's death, so Sharon, as owner, is in a position to enforce copyright in Steven's works. We can advise her that this is justified under copyright theory—copyright law has been designed to give protection not just to authors during their lifetime, but also to their heirs, a factor particularly significant when an author dies young and leaves family members behind.

By performing Steven's copyright work without permission, Adil has likely committed copyright infringement—a subject we will focus on in more detail in the chapters that follow this one. By recording and broadcasting Adil's performance of Steven's poem, the BBC have also likely infringed the copyright work now owned by Sharon. We will see in the later chapters 21 and 22 that in such circumstances a licence agreement could be reached with the parties—and failing that there are several remedies Sharon could claim, including an injunction to prevent future performances and damages to compensate for the use of the work without permission. As a first step, Sharon could consider asking Adil to refrain from future performances of Steven's poem, and ask the BBC for compensation for the use of the work without permission. If these requests are not met with a satisfactory answer, she can consider filing a copyright claim at the Intellectual Property Enterprise Court (IPEC).

End-of-chapter questions

After reading the chapter carefully, try answering the following questions. For answer guidance visit the online resources at **www.oup.com/uk/karapapa-mcdonagh/**

1. Has copyright protection expanded so far that protection can no longer be justified? If so, would it not be better to abolish copyright altogether?

2. Can a new adaptation of a public domain work be protected by copyright?

3. Is the idea/expression dichotomy a useful one, or is it simply misleading?

Further reading

For understanding the history, nature, and purpose of copyright, the following readings are highly recommended:

Breyer, S. 'The Uneasy Case for Copyright: A Study of Copyright in Books, Photocopies and Computer Programs' [1970] 84 *Harv LR* 281
Takes a sceptical view of 'copyright expansionism' from a US perspective, arguing that extending the duration of copyright is not justified to encourage the creation and distribution of new works.

Burkitt, D. 'Copyrighting Culture—The History and Cultural Specificity of the Western Model of Copyright' [2001] 2 *IPQ* 146
Examines copyright in historical perspective, including key early cases.

Deazley, R. 'The Myth of Copyright at Common Law' [2003] 62 *CLJ* 106
Argues that the House of Lords in Donaldson v Beckett *explicitly denied the existence of any common law copyright and that the legislative basis for copyright must take into account societal goals as well as the interests of authors and publishers.*

Gervais, D. 'The Compatibility of the Skill and Labour Originality Standard with the Berne Convention and the TRIPs Agreement' [2004] 26(2) *EIPR* 75
Explores whether the TRIPS Agreement requires a higher standard of originality than that present in several common law countries such as the UK.

Laddie, H. 'Copyright: Over-strength, Over-regulated, Over-rated' [1996] 18 *EIPR* 253
Considers whether the exclusive rights protected by copyright have gone too far and may be causing negative societal and economic impacts.

Landes, W. and Posner, R. 'An Economic Analysis of Copyright Law' [1989] 18 *Journal of Legal Studies* 325

Takes a 'law and economics' approach to copyright, justifying it on the basis of economic efficiency.

Rahmatian, A. 'Copyright and Commodification' [2005] 26(2) *EIPR* 371

Examines the justifications for copyright and questions whether they are satisfactory or necessary.

Spence, M. and Endicott, T. 'Vagueness in the Scope of Copyright' [2005] 121 *LQR* 657

Considers the inherent vagueness of the doctrines of 'substantial part' and 'idea–expression dichotomy' in the context of copyright case law.

Sprigman, C. 'Reform(aliz)ing Copyright' [2004] 57 *Stanford Law Review* 484

Argues that in the US the lifting of the requirements of copyright formalities (e.g. registration) during the 1970s may have actually harmed public access to works, and that formalities should be restored.

Suthersanen, U. 'Bleak House or Great Expectations?' in H. Porsdam (ed.), *Copyright & Other Fairy Tales* (Edward Elgar, 2006), 40

Takes a historical view of the role that well-known writers such as Charles Dickens played in turning 'authors' into 'stakeholders' in 19th-century political negotiations over copyright.

Vaver, D. 'Rejuvenating Copyright' (1996) 75 *Can BR* 69

Argues that as copyright law has expanded it has become overly complex, noting that it requires a firmer and more simplified moral centre in order to resonate with the public.

Copyright

Subsistence of copyright

Problem question

Read this problem question carefully and keep it in mind while you are working through the chapter that follows. At the end of this chapter, you will be able to apply what you have learnt to the problem question and advise the relevant parties.

Adam is a freelance photographer, photographing, in particular, baby clothes for an online retailer, Baby Home Ltd. He customarily takes pictures of the clothes as such from various angles to be used as references in online sales via the Baby Home website. He also takes portrait pictures of babies wearing them. As part of Baby Home's new marketing campaign, he wanted to create a single, iconic image to feature in the promotional materials of the company. Having taken numerous shots, he chose a photograph of a baby boy wearing an outfit in Baby Home's most distinctive fabric and driving a plastic car, resembling Baby Home's logo. Once the photograph was taken, he manipulated it on his computer using a well-known piece of software called Photoshop. He had the idea of making the baby on the toy car stand against a blurred background by enhancing the colour contrast. Soon after his pictures went online, he was informed that one of Baby Home's competitors started using an image featuring a baby seated on a differently shaped toy car with a similarly enhanced visual effect. He also found out that simple, representative images of Baby Home's clothes taken by other photographers feature on websites of other online retailers selling Baby Home merchandise.

Advise Adam on the subsistence of copyright protection in his photographs.

2.1 Introduction

Our problem scenario concerns subsistence of copyright. Subsistence is a central requirement for copyright protection—unless it is established that copyright subsists in your work, you cannot make a viable claim that someone else has used your work without permission.

Section 1 of the Copyright, Designs and Patents Act 1988 ('CDPA') declares that copyright is a property right which subsists in an exhaustive, or closed, list of eight different categories of 'work'. It reads:

> *Copyright is a property right which subsists . . . in the following descriptions of work*
>
>   *(a) original literary, dramatic, musical or artistic works*
>
>   *(b) sound recordings, films or broadcasts*
>
>   *(c) the typographical arrangement of published editions*

All categories of subject matter included in s. 1 CDPA are called 'works' and can in principle be protected by copyright. Literary, dramatic, musical, and artistic works are regarded as being the intellectual product of a human author who has expended originality—defined as 'skill, labour and judgement' (in accordance with the traditional UK test for originality) or 'intellectual creation' (in line with the more recent EU-derived test). This group of works has traditionally been referred to in the UK under the category of 'authorial' works; meanwhile, protection is also offered to what are known as 'entrepreneurial' works—sound recordings, films, broadcasts, and the typographical arrangement of published editions (copyright works that result from the investment of capital by an enterprise, although this is not to deny that there will be human creativity involved). As we shall see, the UK's exhaustive list and the division between authorial and entrepreneurial works have been challenged by recent EU rulings.

 Pause for reflection

With respect to our problem scenario, we can note that photographs are protected under s. 4(2) CDPA. This part of the legislation should be referred to when discussing copyright in Adam's photographs. We will explore this category of photographs in more detail below.

The concept of work as protected subject matter has *not* been harmonized legislatively through the European Copyright Directives. As a result not all EU Member States take the same approach to defining the 'work' (*Nova v Mazooma* [2007] EWCA Civ. 219; [2007] RPC 25). In some EU Member States, for example, entrepreneurial works are not protected by copyright but by a system of 'neighbouring rights' (a narrower scope of protection). This is in line with the Berne Convention (Art. 2(1)), which merely indicates that protection should be offered to 'literary and artistic works' but offers no stipulation about how this is to be achieved.

The principal difference in the approaches followed by different EU countries is the 'open' list versus the 'exhaustive' (closed) list of protected subject matter. For example,

France follows an 'open list' approach of protected subject matter, whereas in the UK, protection is afforded to the exhaustive, or closed, list we considered earlier (i.e. to the eight categories of work *only*). Therefore, in the UK in order to attract copyright protection a creation must fall within the definition of one or more of these categories; if not, protection is precluded. The exhaustive nature of the closed list incorporated in s. 1 CDPA is supplemented by statutory definitions that elaborate on the concept of the categories of protected work (e.g. ss. 3 and 4 CDPA).

However, recent cases of the Court of Justice of the EU ('CJEU') adopt a broad definition of what protectable subject matter is—and in this regard these decisions challenge the UK's exhaustive list approach (The CJEU is currently constituted of two courts: The Court of Justice, informally referred to as the 'ECJ', and the General Court. In this work 'CJEU' will be used to refer collectively to the jurisprudence of both courts). Moreover, these cases shed light on the concept of 'work' by establishing that protection is available to subject matter that is the intellectual creation of its author. It all started in the case of *Infopaq*.

Infopaq International A/S v Danske Dagblades Forening Case C-5/08 [2009] ECR I-6569

In *Infopaq*, the Court held that 'copyright . . . is liable to apply only in relation to a subject-matter which is original in the sense that it is its author's own intellectual creation' (at [37]). The case involved the storing and subsequent printing out of 11-word extracts from daily newspapers. This criterion of 'author's own intellectual creation' is crucial.

The approach developed in *Infopaq* was later elaborated in *Bezpečnostní softwarová asociace—Svaz softwarové ochrany v Ministerstvo kultury,* Case C-393/09, [2010] ECR I-13971 (BSA), a case involving the question of whether graphic user interfaces could be protected by copyright. The Court of Justice found that an interface can be protected in its own right (and not as a computer program) as an original 'work' if it is its 'author's own intellectual creation' (at [40–42], [44–46]). This suggests that under EU law, binding on the UK at least until the post-Brexit period, the term 'work' has a broad definition—potentially broader than that envisaged by the UK's closed list.

 Pause for reflection

It is possible that the closed list of protected subject matter under s. 1 CDPA may not be compatible with European copyright law in light of this recent expansion of the concept of 'work' at European level. Some commentators (E. Rosati, 'Closed Subject-Matter Systems are no Longer Compatible with EU Copyright' [2014] 12 *GRUR Int* 1112) argue that the UK's approach may have to be adjusted in light of CJEU jurisprudence which avoids such classification and instead accords protection to any and every 'intellectual creation': Case C-5/08 *Infopaq International A/S v Danske Dagblades Forening* [2009] ECR I-6569 at [33–37] (*Infopaq*); Case C-393/09 *Bezpečnostní softwarová asociace—Svaz softwarové ochrany v Ministerstvo kultury* [2010] ECR I-13971 at [45–46].

In *SAS Institute Inc v World Programming Ltd* [2013] EWHC 69 (Ch), Arnold J expressed a clear view on the matter and, in discussing whether a programming language of a computer

→

➡
program qualifies as a work, he held that:

> In the light of a number of recent judgments of the CJEU, it may be arguable that it
> is not a fatal objection to a claim that copyright subsists in a particular work that the
> work is not one of the kinds of work listed in section 1(1)(a) of the Copyright, Designs
> and Patents 1988 and defined elsewhere in that Act. Nevertheless, it remains clear
> that the putative copyright work must be a literary or artistic work within the meaning
> of Article 2(1) of the Berne Convention (at [27]).

Until the implications of the CJEU case law are made clear, the eight categories of protected
subject matter under s. 1 CDPA remain the starting points in considerations over claims to
copyright protection, but we must be open to new ways of accommodating unusual copyright
works. At the same time there are some limits—in the recent case C-310/17 *Levola Hengelo
BV v Smilde Foods* BV ECLI:EU:C:2018:899 (13 Nov 2018) the CJEU ruled that the taste of
food was not protected as it did not fall under the category of 'work'.

The remainder of this chapter will set out the detailed requirements which must be
met before copyright protection will arise in the UK. The requirements can be summarized in a four-question approach:

- does the alleged 'work' fall within one of the recognized categories listed in s. 1
  CDPA (also taking into account recent CJEU case law on the broad approach to
  'work')?
- if so, does it possess originality (defined as 'intellectual creation' in recent CJEU
  case law)?
- if so, is it recorded in a permanent form (fixed)?
- if so, is its author qualified for protection by being 'connected' to the UK?

All of the above questions must be answered in the positive for copyright protection
to arise.

2.2 Categories of copyright work

2.2.1 Literary, dramatic, and musical works

Although, as we have seen above, the UK system of 'closed' categories of work is under
pressure from the influence of EU rulings, it is nonetheless worth examining the various types of work in detail, as there is a rich body of case law that remains relevant to
understanding copyright law in the UK.

2.2.1.1 Literary works

Section 3(1) CDPA provides that a literary work is any work, other than a dramatic or
musical work, which is *written, spoken or sung*. Although the words 'other than' suggest
there is no overlap between literary work on the one side, and dramatic or musical work
on the other, the distinction between these categories of work is not always self-evident.

While it is relatively easy to distinguish words from music, it may be more difficult to draw the line between a literary work and a dramatic work. In the case of an opera, for example, the script could be classed as a dramatic work but the words of the songs as literary works. This distinction ought not to cause a problem, as UK courts consider that it is possible for a work to fall into more than one category, depending on the context; e.g. a film can be classed as a dramatic work if it is performed in public (*Norowzian v Arks Ltd* [2000] FSR 363).

'Writing' is defined in s. 178 CDPA (the general definition section for Part I) to mean 'any form of notation or code, whether by hand or otherwise and regardless of the method by which, or medium in or on which, it is recorded'. The section contemplates copyright in the spoken word. As Phillips illustrates (in 'Copyright in Spoken Words—Some Potential Problems' [1989] *EIPR* 231), the combined effect of s. 3(2) and 3(3) means that words when spoken are inchoate copyright. Once fixed, they become literary works. Fixation (i.e. putting the words in permanent form) could be simultaneous, for example, via sound recording; or belated, for example by someone writing the words down from memory some time after the event. Returning to the statutory definition, s. 3(1) adds that the term 'literary work' includes a table or compilation, other than a database; a computer program; preparatory design material for a computer program; and a database.

Section 3 does not offer further indication on what counts as a literary work. In order to understand the scope of protection available we must examine the case law. The starting point is the classic case of *University of London Press v University Tutorial Press* [1916] 2 Ch 601 in which Peterson J accorded protection to university examination papers. Peterson J explained that 'literary work' did not require that the item possessed any sort of intellectual merit; rather, the phrase was analogous to the term 'printed matter' so that anything committed to paper was protected. The net effect is that a wide range of everyday items fall within the scope of copyright, for example, a five-letter code for sending messages (*Anderson & Co v Lieber Code Co* [1917] 2 KB 469), football pools coupons (*Ladbroke v William Hill* [1964] 1 WLR 273), greyhound race forecast cards (*Bookmakers Afternoon Greyhound Services v Wilf Gilbert* [1994] FSR 723), and lists of TV programmes (*Independent Television Publications v Time Out* [1984] FSR 64).

2.2.1.1.1 Words, titles, headlines

Literary works can attract protection under copyright law irrespective of their literary or scientific merit. The length of a work is irrelevant, and even short expressions such as a title or a headline can attract protection as long as they are sufficiently original. Nonetheless, although there is no *de minimis* principle many cases have excluded certain works from protection with reference to their length, because it is less likely that a very short work will be sufficiently original. There have been cases where song titles were found not to be protected (*Francis Day v Twentieth Century Fox*); and the argument that an invented word—Exxon—should be treated as a literary work was rejected by the Court of Appeal in *Exxon Corporation v Exxon Insurance Consultants* [1982] RPC 69 because it did not provide 'information, instruction or pleasure of a literary kind', i.e. it lacked sufficient original literary character (*per* Stephenson LJ at p. 88). Similarly, factual information at the front of a diary was denied protection in *Cramp v Smythson* [1944] AC 329 because it was commonplace; and in *Navitaire Inc v EasyJet Airline Co* [2005] ECDR

160, which relied on the reasoning in the *Exxon* case, individual command names in a computer program were held incapable of copyright protection as literary works.

More recently, however, CJEU jurisprudence has affirmed that, with the caveat that a single word would not be protected, there is no quantitative limit on the length of a copyright work. A headline or a short sentence, e.g. 11 words, could be protected by copyright if considered to be sufficiently original in the sense the expression is the author's own intellectual creation (*Infopaq*).

 Pause for reflection

Infopaq has increased the likelihood that short expressions will be classed as literary works under UK copyright law. The Court of Appeal applied *Infopaq* in *Newspaper Licensing Agency v Meltwater Holding BV* [2012] RPC 1 (reversed on a different point by the Supreme Court in *Public Relations Consultants Association Ltd v Newspaper Licensing Agency Ltd* [2013] RPC 469). Here, a text extract of not more than 256 characters—comprising the headline from an article, the first few words after the headline and the context of the keyword—was held to qualify for copyright protection.

2.2.1.1.2 Computer programs

Due to the fact that they comprise 'code', computer programs are protected as literary works. At an international level, this is stipulated in Art. 4 of the WIPO Copyright Treaty 1996 and Art. 10(1) of the TRIPS Agreement 1996. At a European level, Art. 1(1) of the Computer Programs Directive (Directive 91/250/EEC on the legal protection of computer programs (OJ L122 17 May 1991)) clarifies that Member States must protect computer programs as literary works within the meaning of the Berne Convention (Art. 2(1)). Art. 1(2) also indicates that protection is available 'to the expression in any form of a computer program' but not to the ideas and principles underlying any element of a computer program. No exhaustive definition of a computer program is offered in the Directive.

In the UK the definition of what amounts to a computer program has been developed by the courts. In *Navitaire v Easyjet Airline Co* [2006] RPC 3, at [80], Pumfrey J found that individual command names used in a system of airline bookings could not be considered as literary works. Citing *Exxon* as authority, Pumfrey J held that 'single words in isolation are not to be considered as literary works' (at [81]). Protection could also not be afforded to a series of commands (a computer language). On the basis of recital 14 of the EU Computer Programs Directive, protection is not available to programming languages to the extent that they comprise ideas and principles.

SAS Institute Inc v World Programming Ltd C-406/10 (CJEU Grand Chamber) [2012] 3 CMLR 4

The CJEU affirmed this position in *SAS Institute Inc v World Programming*. The claimant had developed a sophisticated software system that enabled its users to carry out a wide range of

➞

→

data processing tasks, especially statistical analysis. In order to be able to run application programs developed in SAS language and to develop new ones, customers had to carry on licensing the use of the SAS system, otherwise they would have to rewrite all their application programs. The defendant, World Programming, developed its own software (WPS) that emulated the functionality of the SAS software components. They did not have access to the source code of the SAS system and did not copy the structural design of the source code of the SAS components. The allegation was that they had indirectly copied, by using the SAS manuals, the computer programs that comprised the SAS components. Arnold J referred the case to the CJEU, seeking clarification, inter alia, as to whether the functionalities of a computer program are protected by copyright pursuant to Art. 1(2) of the Computer Programs Directive. The Grand Chamber of the CJEU found that:

> Article 1(2) of Directive 91/250 must be interpreted as meaning that neither the functionality of a computer program nor the programming language and the format of data files used in a computer program in order to exploit certain of its functions constitute a form of expression of that program and, as such, are not protected by copyright in computer programs for the purposes of that directive (at [46])

 Pause for reflection

A major reason for the exclusion of data formats and files from the scope of copyright is the reference to 'intellectual creation' as the benchmark of what qualifies as protectable subject matter. As Gervais and Derclaye observe ('The scope of computer program protection after SAS: are we closer to answers?' [2012] 8 *EIPR* 34) the Court's statements at [39] and [45] are hard to reconcile. On the one hand, the CJEU clearly states that '[n]either the functionality of a *computer program nor the programming language and the format of data files* used in a computer program in order to exploit certain of its functions constitute a form of expression of that program for the purposes of Art. 1(2) of Directive' and further that 'to accept that the functionality of a computer program can be protected by copyright would amount to making it possible to monopolise ideas, to the detriment of technological progress and industrial development'. On the other hand, it states that 'the SAS language and the format of SAS's data files *might be protected, as works,* by copyright under Directive 2001/29 if they are their author's own intellectual creation'. How can the court say that functionality, e.g. language and format of data files, is not a form of expression and then say that data formats or a language can be protected as a work if they are their author's own intellectual creation? Ideas, even 'original' ones, are not protectable by copyright. This is why the above-named scholars suggest that data formats and languages should not be protected by copyright. Do you agree with their suggestion?

2.2.1.1.3 Compilations and databases

A compilation or collection of other works can be protected, of itself, as a copyright work. This has long been known, as stated in the House of Lords decision in *Ladbroke v William Hill* in 1964, a point further emphasized in *Ravenscroft v Herbert* [1980] RPC 193. A significant thing to note, however, is that where the collection/compilation is of existing copyright works, it will infringe unless licences from the owners of the previous works have first been obtained.

Importantly, the UK's domestic law on compilations and collections has been altered by EU legislation—namely, Council Directive 96/9 on the legal protection of databases [1996] OJ L 77/20, as implemented by The Copyright and Rights in Databases Regulations 1997 (SI 1997/3032). The Directive creates a two-tier system of protection for databases, dependent on whether or not intellectual activity was involved in their creation. A collection of information may therefore under UK law now attract via two possible means of protection:

- as a copyright work, provided that it satisfies the test of originality and qualifies for protection as a database or compilation under Arts 1 and 3 of the Directive and s. 3(1)(d) of the CDPA. 'Database' is defined in Art. 1 of the Directive as 'a collection of independent works, data or other materials arranged in a systematic or methodical way and individually accessible by electronic or other means'. In the CDPA s. 3(1)(d)—as required by Art. 3 of the Directive—provides that databases and compilations may be viewed as literary works.

- as a database (as defined in Art. 1 of the Directive) in which the *sui generis* database right exists—not because of originality—but by virtue of Art. 7 of the Directive because it has arisen as a result of 'substantial investment'.

The most important recent case decided with respect to protecting databases under copyright is the CJEU decision in *Football Dataco v Yahoo! UK Ltd and others* (C-604/10) [2012] 2 CMLR 24. We will look at this case in detail in the discussion of originality given later on 2.7.1. of this chapter. The most significant case on the *sui generis* database right is C-203/02 *British Horseracing Board v William Hill Organisation Ltd* [2004] ECR I-10415, which we will also discuss later on.

2.2.1.2 Dramatic works

Section 3 CDPA gives no guidance for what a dramatic work is other than stating that it includes a work of dance or mime, which means that this type of work does not have to have words to be protected (though many dramatic works—such as film and theatre scripts—do feature words). From s. 3(2) and 3(3) we know that a dramatic work need not be written down as long as it is recorded in some medium, such as film, even if the recording is unauthorized.

Turning to case law, a dramatic work must be 'a work of action, with or without words or music, which is capable of being performed before an audience' (*Norowzian v Arks Ltd* [2000] FSR 363). This idea—that a dramatic work is necessarily *performative*—is clearly central to the concept of a dramatic work, but it begs the question: what counts as a performance?

Norowzian v Arks Ltd [2000] FSR 3634

In *Norowzian v Arks Ltd*, the claimant—a film-maker—had shown a film to an advertising agency in the hope they would make use of it in an ad campaign. The advertising agency

→

→

rejected the film. Nonetheless, that same agency later released a TV advertisement for Guinness that appeared to use ideas, techniques, and styles very similar to those displayed in the film, including 'jump-cuts' that made a single dancing man seem as if he was in multiple places in the room simultaneously. Since no use of the claimant's actual original film had been made by the advertising agency—merely use of the 'jump-cut' techniques and the dancing man—the claimant was forced to argue that his film itself was a dramatic work, and that the advertisement agency had infringed upon it by making their own film of a dancing man using jump-cut techniques. This led to the following interesting question: can the broadcast of a film be a 'performance' such that the film should be protected as a dramatic work? The Court of Appeal held that a film could indeed be a dramatic work in itself because it is a work of action that is capable of being performed before an audience:

> Where a film is both a recording of a dramatic work and a dramatic work in itself they do not exclude an overlap. In other cases there will be no overlap. Sometimes a film will simply be a recording of something which is not a dramatic work. At other times, it will not be a recording of a dramatic work but a dramatic work in itself.

Presumably, the performance of a dramatic work must be by a human being, as it has been held that a video game cannot be categorized as a dramatic work: *Nova Productions Ltd v Mazooma Games Ltd* [2007] RPC 589. Meanwhile, television game show formats, despite their enormous commercial value, are probably not protected by copyright in the UK. In the Privy Council case of *Green v Broadcasting Corp of New Zealand* [1989] RPC 700—which concerned copyright law in New Zealand—the bundle of elements that made up the TV format for the talent show *Opportunity Knocks* was held to not be protected. The court noted that the content of the show would vary with each edition and thus it lacked the 'scripted' character required for a dramatic work to subsist.

In the UK case of *Miles v ITV Network Ltd* [2003] WL 23192242, the claimant alleged that he had, in 1998, given promotional material for a cartoon format to ITV and that ITV had subsequently copied his cartoon format in their programme *Dream Street*. However, there was evidence that ITV had made plans for *Dream Street* in 1997, a point which fatally undermined the claimant's argument. The dismissal of the case at the summary level was affirmed by the High Court as the case was seen as too weak to proceed to full trial (see also *Michael Mitchell v BBC* [2011] EWPCC 42).

Interestingly, in practice the television and media industry tends to operate on the basis that TV formats *are* protectable. For instance, in 2005 the makers of *Pop Idol* and *X-Factor* came to an out-of-court settlement over similarities between their formats; and more recently, the producers of the popular BBC show *Great British Bake Off* claimed they had a right to the format of training amateurs to be experts in a particular field. Nonetheless, in the UK the case law suggests TV formats are not in themselves protectable.

2.2.1.3 Musical works

The CDPA s. 3 defines a musical work as 'a work consisting of music, exclusive of any words or action intended to be sung, spoken, or performed with the music'. From the wording of s. 3(1) it is clear that in the case of a song, the words (literary work) and music (musical work) are separate copyright works and so may be owned by different people. However, as explained later on in this chapter, where the song is produced in collaboration between the lyricist and composer, it is treated as a work of co-authorship for the sole purpose of determining the duration of protection.

The fixation requirement applies before protection takes effect, as required by s. 3(2) and s. 3(3), but the courts have held that the musical work can exist before it is formally written down or recorded (*Hadley v Kemp* [1999] EMLR 589).

For musical works, the definition of what can be considered a musical work is broad. In *Lawson v Dundas* 12 June 1985, unreported, the four-note tune used as the ident of Channel 4 was held to be a copyright work. In *Bamgboye v Reed* [2004] EMLR 61, the addition of a drum accompaniment to a piece of music was sufficient to confer protection on the claimant. By contrast, in *Coffey v Warner/Chappell Music Ltd* [2005] FSR 747, the singer's vocal expression, pitch contour, and syncopation were held not capable of being regarded as a copyright work, because they were not sufficiently separable from the remainder of the work to constitute a musical work in their own right. The leading case on defining the musical work is *Sawkins v Hyperion Records* [2005] 1 WLR 3281.

Sawkins v Hyperion Records [2005] 1 WLR 3281

The judgment of Mummery LJ in *Sawkins v Hyperion Records* [2005] 1 WLR 3281 at [53–56] is the key statement of what a musical work can consist of. Mummery LJ remarked that according to 'ordinary usage' the essence of music is combining sounds for listening to. Music, he related, is not the same as 'mere' noise. Yet, although many people think of music as an organized performance played from a musical score, Mummery LJ confirmed that the existence of a written score (sheet music) is not essential for the existence of a musical work protected by copyright—any form of fixation is sufficient. Furthermore, the musical work itself must be distinguished from its fixation because the fixation, whether in a written score or on a record, is not in itself the music in which copyright subsists.

Taking a broad view, Mummery LJ also suggested that there is no reason why a recording of spontaneous singing, whistling, or humming, or even improvisations of sounds, with or without musical instruments, should not be regarded as 'music' for copyright purposes. Mummery LJ further remarked that musical notes are not necessarily the only thing protected by copyright—and that it would be wrong to deny copyright to the other elements that make some contribution to the sound of the music when performed, such as directions for tempo, volume, and other 'performance indicators'. Mummery LJ therefore took into account that the way a performance occurs may be an integral part of a musical work. This also implies that atonal, avant-garde music could be protected.

Overall, the broad definition of musical work envisaged by Mummery LJ is to be preferred to that of the more 'traditional' view of Park J in *Hadley v Kemp*, where it was assumed that the creation of music had to involve the writing down (or at least the recording) of the notes divorced from any input from the performers.

Moreover, it is clear from *Sawkins v Hyperion* and from *Fisher v Brooker* [2009] 4 All ER 789 that while a newly created musical work is certainly protected by copyright—provided it is original—*adaptations* and *arrangements* of that work can also be protected with separate copyrights (though if the work a musician is arranging is in copyright he or she would require a licence from the original composer in order for his or her version to be published, or else the later version would infringe the initial copyright).

The consequence of this is that musicians who thrive on improvised performances of established standard compositions—such as jazz and folk musicians—can claim copyright in their arrangements. These copyrights are authorial and are separate from any performers rights the musicians might hold, which we will discuss in a later chapter.

2.2.2 Artistic works

Section 4(1) CDPA provides the meaning of the phrase 'artistic work' and is divided into three paragraphs. It covers, first, graphic works, photographs, sculptures, or collages, irrespective of their artistic quality; second, works of architecture; and finally, works of artistic craftsmanship. Further elaboration is provided in s. 4(2), which explains that a 'graphic work' includes (a) any painting, drawing, diagram, map, chart, or plan; and (b) any engraving, etching, lithograph, woodcut, or similar work.

This indiscriminate list of items covers both two-dimensional and three-dimensional art forms, the latter comprising works of architecture (which according to s. 4(2) CDPA can be either buildings or models for buildings); sculptures (the term of which includes any cast or model made for the purposes of sculpture); and works of artistic craftsmanship. It is arguable that s. 4 is conservative in its definition of an artistic work. Some of the 'installation' art found today in e.g. the Tate Modern would not easily fall within the statutory definition. The statement in para (a) that the types of art listed do not have to possess artistic quality means that, in theory, the judiciary do not have to decide whether something deserves protection on the basis that it is 'art'. Despite this, the sparse definition of 'artistic work' in the legislation means that some cases appear to have been decided on the basis of assumptions which may not accord with the expectations of the creator of the work in question.

As with s. 3, we have to look to case law for elaboration, taking the key words and phrases in s. 4 in turn.

2.2.2.1 Graphic works

Section 4(2) 'defines' graphic work by giving a list of various two-dimensional art forms. The first of these is a 'painting'. It has been suggested (in *Merchandising Corporation of America v Harpbond* [1983] FSR 32) that this involves 'representation or depiction by colours on a surface' which immediately begs two questions: i) could a blank canvas be a 'painting'; and ii) what is a 'surface'? We do not have case law on the first point. However, the *Harpbond* case answered the second question with the decision that a person's face could not be a 'surface'—on the facts, stage make-up for the singer Adam Ant was not protected by copyright for this reason (the court further suggesting that the lack of permanence of the make-up was also fatal to copyright protection being granted).

Of the remaining items in the list in s. 4(2), the most important is probably the word 'drawing'. However, the commercial significance of this category of artistic works is minimal because of the defence in s. 51 CDPA which means that the intellectual property owner is unable to rely on copyright to prevent another person from making articles to that design, but instead must rely on unregistered design right.

The case law on what is a 'drawing' reveals that even mundane articles can receive protection. In *Hutchison Personal Communications v Hook Advertising* [1995] FSR 365, a logo for a mobile phone network consisting of an inverted 'R' (which looked like a rabbit's head) was held to be a work. In *Bernstein v Sidney Murray* [1981] RPC 303 rough fashion sketches were protected. Technical drawings are also included, so that drawings for machine parts (*British Northrop v Texteam Blackburn* [1974] RPC 57); circuit diagrams (*Anacon v Environmental Research Technology* [1994] FSR 659); and an architect's plans (*Jones v London Borough of Tower Hamlets* [2001] RPC 407) have all been held to attract copyright (an architect's plans fall within para (a) of s. 4(1), whereas buildings fall within para (b)). Lastly, cartoons (such as *Popeye*) are artistic works within the CDPA: *King Features Syndicate Inc v O & M Kleeman Ltd* [1941] AC 417.

A two-page document containing written instructions for setting up a loom to create a woollen plaid fabric was found to be both a literary work and an artistic work in *Abraham Moon & Sons Ltd v Thornber*, [2012] EWPCC 37; [2013] FSR 17. That copyright was infringed by the manufacture and sale of another woollen plaid fabric copied from the mill's design. According to Birss HHJ:

> Artistic copyright must relate to the content of the work of the artist and not the medium in which it is recorded. It is or should be a 'content' copyright and not a 'signal' copyright. The visual image of Skye Sage if it was fixed in a material form as a drawing would be protected by artistic copyright. It seems to me that to deny artistic copyright in this case – despite the fact that the visual image is indeed fixed in a material form – is to confuse the medium with the message (at [106]).

It might be thought that the terms 'engraving' and 'etching' are concerned with types of pictorial representation only, but two cases have given them wide meanings so that three-dimensional objects fall within their scope. First in the New Zealand case of *Wham-O Manufacturing Co v Lincoln* [1985] RPC 127 it was held that plastic frisbees made by extrusion mouldings were engravings and the wooden models for the moulds were sculptures. Then in *Hi-Tech Autoparts Ltd v Towergate Two Ltd* [2002] FSR 254 it was held that rubber car mats with grooves cut in them to help drainage were etchings. These two cases should be contrasted with the decisions on sculptures (discussed later).

2.2.2.2 Photographs

Section 4(2) CDPA explains that the word 'photograph' means 'a recording of light or other radiation on any medium on which an image is produced or from which an image may by any means be produced and which is not part of a film'. This definition, which draws a distinction between still and cinematic photography, is wide enough to cover all types of photographic activity, ranging from celluloid to X-ray to digital imagery.

Nevertheless, the extent to which photographs *should* be protected by copyright has proved somewhat controversial. In *Graves' Case* (1869) LR 4 QB 715 it was held that a photograph of an engraving was itself an artistic work. The case has been criticized on the ground that there was no originality, but also justified on the basis that the technology of the time required a greater effort on the part of the photographer than do today's digital cameras, so that there must have been skill, labour, and judgement expended.

> ### *Antiquesportfolio.com Ltd v Rodney Fitch & Co Ltd* [2001] FSR 345
>
> In *Antiquesportfolio.com Ltd v Rodney Fitch & Co Ltd* [2001] FSR 345 the principle that there is copyright in photographs, no matter how simple, was upheld. Skill, labour, and judgement, Neuberger J remarked, may be found in three ways, either in the photographer's choice of subject matter, or in things like camera angle, lighting, and so on, or by the photographer being in the right place at the right time. The one exception might be when a 'slavish imitation' is taken of a two-dimensional copyright work, for example by photocopying a drawing, although Neuberger J did not decide the point.
>
> Applying this case to our problem scenario, we should consider the following question: would all of Adam's photographs be protected by copyright under the *Antiques Portfolio* test?

The thinking in *Antiques Portfolio* was applied by HHJ Birss QC in *Temple Island Collections Ltd v New English Teas Ltd* [2012] FSR 321 when he decided that an otherwise monochrome photograph of a red bus crossing Westminster Bridge—with the distinctive red colour standing out in contrast to the remaining monochrome image of Parliament—was protected by copyright. His reasoning is in line with the CJEU's rulings in *Infopaq* and Case C-145/10 *Eva-Maria Painer v Standard Verlags GmbH* (2011), where it was held that a photograph can be protected by copyright provided it is the 'author's own intellectual creation'.

> **Pause for reflection**
>
> What about the scope of protection afforded to photographic copyright? It should be noted that in relation to copyright in photographs the basic rule is that independent creation is always a defence to infringement. As Lupton explains (in 'Photographs and the Concept of Originality in Copyright Law' [1988] 10 *EIPR* 257) the outcome may be different if the first photograph to be taken has involved creative effort in the choice of scene, lighting, camera angle, exposure and so on. Were this to be the case, then its owner may be able to stop another person taking a similar photograph, at least where there is evidence that he or she had seen the first photograph and so had the opportunity to copy its composition. This argument was accepted in the *New English Teas* case.
>
> With Adam's photos and our problem scenario in mind, it is worth asking the following question: what is the distinction between the idea and expression in the creation of a photograph? Is this an area where the distinction is not useful?
>
> Could someone who owns copyright in a simple holiday snapshot of a famous building (for example, the Louvre Museum in Paris) prevent someone else from taking a similar picture? Would this not be too overreaching? There is no judicial guidance in the UK as to whether pointing a camera and pressing the button demonstrates sufficient 'labour, skill, and judgement' to qualify for protection. Simple portraits can be protected on the basis of sufficient creative freedom in light of the *Painer* case (at [87]–[93]).
>
> Think again of the problem question at the start of this chapter. There are three different sets of pictures: the simple shots of the clothes as products to be sold online, portrait photographs
>
> →

→ of children, and the photoshopped image featuring the company's logo. You will need to examine each type of photo in turn to determine whether some or all of the photos are protected by copyright. The discussion of originality below will be central to your advice to Adam.

A much misunderstood (and often inaccurately reported) case is *Bauman v Fussell* (1953) [1978] RPC 485. It concerned a photograph of a cockfight. The copyright owner subsequently attempted to sue for infringement in respect of a painting of the same scene. The decision of the Court of Appeal was *not* that there was no copyright in the photograph, but that there had been no substantial taking from it. Although the scene had been copied, the alleged infringer had not taken the key features of the picture. Usually, therefore, an action for the infringement of photographic copyright will have to be based on an exact reproduction, as happened in *Gabrin v Universal Music Operations Ltd*, [2004] ECDR 18, where a photograph of Elvis Costello had been taken for publicity purposes, and was subsequently turned into a poster publicising his concerts. Many years later, the poster was used to create the cover of a CD. Patten J held that in principle there had been indirect copying of the original photograph, a point strictly speaking *obiter*, as the action was defeated on the ground that the claimant had no title to sue.

Pause for reflection

Considering the problem question at the beginning of the chapter, what are your initial thoughts about advising Adam? What you will learn in 2.6 below in originality will also prove crucial to the advice you will give Adam, but even at this early stage you can give him some indication of what the crucial factors will be.

2.2.2.3 Sculptures

The term 'sculpture' is stated by s. 4(2) CDPA to include any cast or model made for the purposes of sculpture. Cases have discussed whether *any* three-dimensional object could be a sculpture or whether the word imports some sort of artistic requirement. In *J & S Davis v Wright* [1988] RPC 403 Whitford J held that dental impression trays were not sculptures (in part because they were not permanent). In *Metix (UK) Ltd v G.H. Maughan (Plastics) Ltd* [1997] FSR 718 Laddie J decided that cartridges used to mix chemicals were not sculptures. In so holding, he accepted counsel's definition of a sculpture as 'a three-dimensional work made by an artist's hand'. This implies that functional three-dimensional articles should not be treated as artistic works but are best left to design right protection.

The policy of denying that functional three-dimensional articles are sculptures was made explicit by Mann J at first instance in *Lucasfilm Ltd v Ainsworth* [2012] 1 AC 208, a case concerned with alleged copyright in the Stormtrooper helmets in the film *Star Wars*. Having reviewed the previous case law on 'sculptures', he discussed ([2009] FSR 103 at [118]) the proper meaning of the word. Considering the 'normal' sense of the word, he stated that not every three-dimensional object can be regarded as a sculpture. According to Mann J, a sculpture should have, as part of its purpose, a visual appeal in the sense that it might be enjoyed for that purpose alone, whether or not it might have another purpose. The purpose was that of the creator, the 'artist's hand' referred to by Laddie J in *Metix*. An artist (in the realm of the visual arts) created something because it had visual appeal which was to be enjoyed as such. It had to have the intrinsic quality of being intended to be enjoyed as a visual thing. For that reason, items such as model soldiers had correctly been treated as sculptures, but the frisbee in *Wham-O* should not have been, nor should the moulds for the toasted sandwich maker in *Breville Europe plc v Thorn EMI Domestic Appliances Ltd* [1995] FSR 77. What mattered was whether the maker intended the object to have a visual appeal for its own sake (see further J. Pila, 'An Intentional View of the Copyright Work' [2008] 71 *MLR* 535). So, for example, a pile of bricks in an art gallery would amount to a sculpture, but a pile of bricks left outside a house by a builder would not. Mann J's decision that the helmets were not sculptures and his approach to the meaning of the word was endorsed by both the Court of Appeal and the Supreme Court.

2.2.2.4 Collages

The case of *Creation Records v News Group Newspapers* [1997] EMLR 444 provides a useful link between the concept of a sculpture and that of a collage. It concerned a collection of random items in a swimming pool to be photographed for the cover of the Oasis album *Be Here Now*. The collection was held not to be a sculpture (again, the conservative assumptions made by copyright law are apparent) and although the assembly might be considered as a collage, it did not obtain copyright because it was not permanent. The requirement of permanence is considered later on.

2.2.2.5 Buildings

The word 'buildings' is stated by s. 4(2) CDPA to include any fixed structure and a part of a building or fixed structure. It should not be assumed that copyright in works of architecture is confined to grandiose public buildings such as art galleries or cathedrals. In *Meikle v Maufe* [1941] 3 All ER 144, copyright was held to exist in showrooms on Tottenham Court Road, London, the infringement being by the building of an extension which matched the original facade and interior. In *Hay v Sloan* (1957) 12 DLR 2d 397 (a case concerned with suburban housing) the judge speculates as to how low the threshold for works of architecture might be, contemplating that even a crenellated pigsty might be a copyright work.

2.2.2.6 Works of artistic craftsmanship

The phrase 'artistic craftsmanship' is not defined in the CDPA, but as a composite concept it involves two elements, artistry and craftsmanship, both of which must be satisfied. As regards what is 'artistic', the consensus seems to be that it equates to 'eye appeal'—something which appears to have an aesthetic quality.

Hensher Ltd v Restawile Upholstery (Lancs) Ltd [1976] AC 64

As to who should decide whether an object meets that criterion, the House of Lords offered five different suggestions in *Hensher Ltd v Restawile Upholstery (Lancs) Ltd* [1976] AC 64, a case involving the design for a three-piece suite, admittedly at the lower end of the market.

→

→

Although all of their Lordships agreed that the object in question was not artistic, their justifications differed substantially. Lord Reid said that the test to decide whether a work was artistic was whether 'any substantial section of the public genuinely admires and values a thing for its appearance [78G]'. To Lord Morris, the question would ultimately need to be addressed by courts on the basis of evidence. Taking a different approach, Lord Simon of Glaisdale said that 'the statutory phrase is not "artistic work of craftsmanship" but "work of artistic craftsmanship" and that this distinction accords with the social situation in which Parliament was providing a remedy. It is therefore misleading to ask, first, is this a work produced by a craftsman, and secondly, is it a work of art? It is more pertinent to ask is this the work of one who was in this respect an artistic-craftsman. It follows that the artistic merit of the work is irrelevant . . . it follows, again, that whether the subject matter is or is not a work of artistic craftsmanship is a matter of evidence; and the most cogent evidence is likely to be from those who are either themselves acknowledged artists-craftsmen or concerned with the training of artists-craftsmen — in other words, expert evidence [94–95]'.

These varying comments should be seen as *obiter* for two reasons, namely the concession by counsel that the prototype for the furniture was a work of craftsmanship, and the finding that there was no copyright because the original prototype had been destroyed once production commenced. The lack of permanence is yet again the excuse for denying protection to a functional object.

Discussing inter alia *Hensher Ltd v Restawile Upholstery (Lancs) Ltd*, Masiyakurima offers an interesting insight by reference to works of artistic craftsmanship in the light of the *Infopaq* decision, arguing that UK courts should replace 'artistic quality' tests with an analysis of the work as an expression of the author's 'intellectual creation' (P. Masiyakurima, 'Copyright in works of artistic craftsmanship: an analysis' [2016] 36(3) *OJLS* 505).

The issue of who decides whether a particular work of craftsmanship is artistic was resolved in *Merlet v Mothercare plc* [1986] RPC 115 where the Court of Appeal confirmed that it is the intention of the creator which is paramount. Here, therefore, a baby cape was not a work of artistic craftsmanship because its designer intended it primarily to be a means of protecting the infant from the weather.

Further clarification of what is a work of artistic craftsmanship can be found in the case of *Vermaat v Boncrest Ltd* [2001] FSR 43. The court said that it had to be possible to say that the author was both a craftsman and an artist. A craftsman was a person who made something in a skilful way and who took justified pride in his workmanship. An artist was a person with creative ability who produced something with aesthetic appeal. Further, it was not necessary for the same person to conceive and execute the work, so that if two or more people combined to design and make an article, there was no reason why it should not be regarded as a work of artistic craftsmanship. Again, however, the finding in the case was that the work was not protected in copyright: although the articles (bedspreads) were a product of craftsmanship, they lacked artistry. An additional factor emerges at first instance in the decision in *Guild v Eskandar Ltd* [2001] FSR 38 (overturned on appeal on different grounds: [2003] FSR 23). Rimer J thought that where the original article (here, knitwear) had been made by machine it could not be a work of craftsmanship, so that protection (if any) was by means of design right under Part

III CDPA. Whether an article has been made by hand or machine is therefore crucial. *Hensher* and *Boncrest* (together with Australian case law) were relied on by Mann J at first instance in *Lucasfilm* in deciding that the Stormtrooper helmets were not works of artistic craftsmanship, a conclusion confirmed on appeal.

A rare case in which a claim that a work was one of artistic craftsmanship succeeded was *Shelley Films v Rex Features* [1994] EMLR 134 which concerned the film costumes, sets, and masks for *Frankenstein*.

2.3 Films

The definition of 'film' is to be found in s. 5B CDPA, as amended. A film means a recording on any medium from which a moving image may by any means be produced. A film soundtrack receives dual protection, being treated both as part of the film and as a sound recording in its own right. The CDPA 1988 Sch. 1 states that copyright in such films will expire at the end of 50 years from the end of the calendar year in which that Act came into force.

2.4 Sound recordings

Under the CDPA, 'sound recording' means a recording of sounds, from which sounds may be reproduced, or a recording of the whole or part of a literary, dramatic, or musical work, from which sounds reproducing the work or part may be produced, regardless of the medium on which the recording is made or the method by which the sounds are reproduced or produced (s. 5A, as amended). Sound recordings are not limited to recordings of music but of any sound, and the definition is wide enough to cope with changing technology.

 Pause for reflection

Think back to the problem at the start of the chapter. Can you see an analogy between the act of pressing the 'record' button to create a sound recording and pressing the 'click' button to take a photograph? Should simply pressing the record button be enough for copyright protection to arise, or should some element of creative choice be required for sound recordings (as it is for photographs)?

2.5 Broadcasts

The CDPA operates in the global telecommunications market. The Act has to be read in conjunction with the Broadcasting Acts 1990 and 1996 and the relevant EU legislation—Council Directive 89/552/EEC of 3 October 1989 on the co-ordination of certain provisions concerning the pursuit of television broadcasting activities [1989] OJ L 298/23 (the 'Television without Frontiers Directive'), Council Directive 93/83/EEC of 27 September 1993 on the co-ordination of certain rules concerning copyright and neighbouring rights applicable to satellite broadcasting and cable re-transmission (the 'Copyright Broadcasting Directive') [1993] OJ L 246/15 and the Information Society Directive (Directive 2001/29/EC of the European Parliament and of the Council of 22 May 2001 on the harmonisation of certain aspects of copyright and related rights in the information society [2001] OJ L 167/10, known as 'Infosoc').

Under s. 6 of the Infosoc Directive, the term 'broadcast' means 'an electronic transmission of visual images, sounds or other information'. It must be either transmitted for simultaneous reception by members of the public being capable of being lawfully received by them, or else be transmitted at a time determined solely by the person making the transmission for presentation to members of the public. The definition therefore covers cable and wireless broadcasts, terrestrial and satellite, analogue and digital, as well as information such as teletext. It does not include any internet transmission unless this takes place simultaneously on the internet and by other means, or is a concurrent transmission of a live event, or is a transmission of recorded moving images or sounds forming part of a programme service offered by the person responsible for making the transmission, being a service in which programmes are transmitted at scheduled times determined by that person. This definition draws a clear distinction between a broadcast and the making of information, images, and sounds available on the internet.

2.6 Typographical arrangements

The one uniquely British category of copyright work (which is not found in any of the International Conventions) is set out in s. 8 CDPA, namely protection for the published editions of literary, dramatic, or musical works which do not reproduce the typographical arrangement of a previous edition. Given changes in technology, it is arguable that this category of work is an anachronism. Copyright under s. 8 is separate from that (if any) in the work itself and is conferred on *publishers* in respect of the layout *only* of printed editions of books, periodicals, plays, and music (i.e. only works falling within s. 3). A typeface (as opposed to the layout of the printed page) is protected as an artistic work.

Section 8 was scrutinized by the House of Lords in *Newspaper Licensing Agency Ltd v Marks & Spencer plc* [2003] AC 551. Relying on Australian authority, their Lordships held that in respect of newspapers, it is the whole edition, not individual articles, which is protected by s. 8. Therefore, in photocopying press cuttings on 'lifestyle' issues for internal distribution the defendant had not infringed the s. 8 right as it had not reproduced the whole published edition.

2.7 The requirement of originality

Originality is the paramount criterion of copyright protection. For this reason, as we shall see there are a great many cases that consider how to define the level of originality required for a piece of literature, drama, music, or art to be protected.

2.7.1 The meaning of originality in relation to literary, dramatic, musical, and artistic works

Section 1(1)(a) CDPA declares that copyright subsists in every *original* literary, dramatic, musical, or artistic work. As Gervais puts it, originality is at the very core of copyright (D. Gervais, 'The Compatibility of the Skill and Labour Originality Standard with the Berne Convention and the TRIPs Agreement' [2004] 26 *EIPR* 75). The Act does not define originality but its notion has been shaped through case law.

As early as in 1916, in *University of London Press v University Tutorial Press*, Peterson J (at p. 608) stated that originality means 'source' and not inventiveness, in that the work should *originate* with the author. In the UK the requirement developed to mean that author must expend the necessary skill, labour, and judgement in the creation of the work. As Lord Pearce put it in *Ladbroke v William Hill* at p. 291 'the word "original" does not demand original or inventive thought, but only that the work should not be copied but should originate from the author'. It is important however to consider *what kind* of skill, labour, and judgement has been involved. In *Interlego v Tyco* [1989] AC 217 the Privy Council held that minor adjustments to the engineering drawings for LEGO bricks were too minimal to result in fresh copyright protection being given: 'Skill, labour or judgement merely in the process of copying cannot confer originality . . . A well-executed tracing is the result of much labour and skills but remains what it is, a tracing' (at [262]).

This minimalist definition of 'originality' conflicts, according to Gervais, with the intention of the makers of the Berne Convention who regarded the term as meaning 'creativity'. The thinking in the *University of London Press* (endorsed by the House of Lords in *Ladbroke v William Hill*) is attributable, Gervais argues, to the fact that at the time there was no recognition of the tort of misappropriation. Had Peterson J been able to make use of a case such as *International News Service v Associated Press* (1918) 248 US 215, where the US Supreme Court protected the business investment in a news telegraphy service through the action for unfair competition, instead of defining originality in terms of the right to protect investment, he might have given it the true meaning of the author's intellectual endeavour.

Originality is not defined as a general copyright principle under EU legislation. It is only by reference to databases, computer programs, and photographs that the relevant Directives indicate that, to be protected, these works ought to be their 'author's own intellectual creation' (Directive 2009/24/EC (computer programs), Art. 1(3); Directive 96/9/EC (databases), Art. 3(1); Directive 2006/11/EC (term), Art. 6 (photographs)). This European standard of originality has been extended to cover all copyright works in a line of recent rulings of the Court of Justice of the EU—meaning that originality is now a harmonized concept across the EU.

In *Infopaq* the CJEU held that 11-word extracts from daily newspapers can attract copyright protection: 'it is only through the choice, sequence and combination of those words that the author may express his creativity in an original manner and achieve a result that is an intellectual creation' (at [45]). With this ruling, *Infopaq* delineated the European qualifying standard according to which such protection ought to apply, namely the 'author's own intellectual creation'. This was accepted in the UK copyright cases of *Meltwater* and *SAS* as the standard of originality, though the extent to which it differs, if at all, from the prior standard of 'skill, labour, and judgement' is an open question.

C-145/10 *Eva-Maria Painer v Standard VerlagsGmbH and Others* (Third Chamber) [2011] ECR I-12533

With a view to understanding originality in the context of our problem scenario, it is worth considering in detail the most significant CJEU case on photographs and the 'author's own intellectual creation'—*Painer* (2011). In *Painer*, the Court was called to examine whether a realistic portrait photograph of a child at nursery school can attract copyright protection. Relying on *Infopaq*, the Court found that 'a portrait photograph can . . . be protected by copyright . . . such photograph is an intellectual creation of the author reflecting his personality and expressing his free and creative choices in the production of that photograph' (at [94]). The case is significant if one considers that portrait photographs in such a context often allow only a very minor degree of creative freedom. However, as the court affirmed, by making free and creative choices, the author of a portrait photograph can stamp the work created with his 'personal touch' (at [92]) and qualify for copyright protection.

Keeping this ruling on originality in mind should help you to advise Adam about copyright in his photographs.

Another important CJEU case involved fixture lists of football leagues in England and Scotland. In *Football Dataco Ltd and others v Yahoo! UK Ltd and others*, Case C-604/10, the Court was called to assess whether the notion of the 'author's own intellectual creation' within the meaning of Art. 3 of the Database Directive requires more than significant labour and skill from the author, and if so, what that additional requirement is. The creation of annual fixture lists involved some skill and labour and was not purely mechanistic and on that basis the Court found that fixture lists could attract copyright protection if, by virtue of the selection and arrangement of the content, they constitute the author's own intellectual creation (at [28]–[29]). Relying on its previous rulings, the Court held that this 'criterion of originality is satisfied when, through the selection or arrangement of the data which it contains, its author expresses his creative ability in an original manner by making free and creative choices . . . and thus stamps his "personal touch"' (at [38]).

  Pause for reflection

Will the CJEU decisions in *Infopaq*, *Football Dataco*, and *Painer* require a rethink of the UK originality requirement? Rahmatian ('Originality in UK Copyright Law: The Old 'Skill and Labour' Doctrine Under Pressure' [2013] 44(4) *IIC* 4) argues that these changes will not actually have a major impact on the British standard of originality. Indeed, UK cases decided in the aftermath of the CJEU decisions, such as *Meltwater* and *SAS*, indicate that UK courts have made a smooth transition from 'skill, labour, and judgement' to the new threshold of the 'author's own intellectual creation'. In fact, in many cases there may be little real distinction between the two tests due to considerable overlap between 'skill and labour' and 'intellectual creation'.

The transposition of the European standard of originality in the UK can be observed through examining two major decisions—*Meltwater* and *Temple Island Collections*—in detail. In *Newspaper Licensing Agency Ltd and others v Meltwater Holding BV and others* [2010] EWHC 3099 (Ch), Proudman J found that 'headlines involve considerable skill in devising and they are specifically designed to entice by informing the reader of the content of the article in an entertaining manner' (at [70]), referring to the *Infopaq* originality standard. The Court of Appeal ([2011] EWCA 890 Civ) affirmed this position.

In *Temple Island Collections v New English Teas* [2012] EWPCC 1, HHJ Birss relied, inter alia, on the *Infopaq* test in deciding whether the photoshopped image of a red bus (on a monochrome background) crossing the Westminster Bridge could be classified as an original photograph. He held that:

> The composition of an image will certainly derive from the 'angle of shot' . . . but also from the field of view, from elements which the photographer may have created and from elements arising from being at the right place at the right time. The resulting composition is capable of being the aggregate result of all these factors which will differ by degrees in different cases. Ultimately however the composition of the image can be the product of the skill and labour (or intellectual creation) of a photographer and it seems to me that skill and labour/intellectual creation directed to that end can give rise to copyright (at [27]) . . . These elements above derive from and are the expression of the skill and labour exercised by [the photographer], or in *Infopaq* terms, they are his intellectual creation (at [53]).

 Pause for reflection

Consider the problem question at the start of this chapter. Now that you have considered originality in further detail, decide how the *Painer* standard of originality would apply to Adam's three categories of photographs: the simple shots of the clothes as products to be sold online, portrait photographs of children, and the photoshopped image featuring the company's logo. In particular, following *Temple Island*, is Adam's photoshopped image sufficiently original to attract copyright protection?

In light of your conclusion on this point, what rights might copyright in a photoshopped or digitally manipulated image give to the copyright holder, i.e. Adam?

When we study infringement in a later chapter we will discuss the consequences of this in detail—for now you should consider the following question: would it mean that another photographer's similarly digitally manipulated image of e.g. the baby and car, with colour contrasting, would infringe Adam's 'original' one? This is important as in our problem one of Baby Home's competitors has done just this.

2.7.2 The meaning of originality in relation to films, sound recordings, broadcasts, and published editions

In s .1(1)(b) and (c) and in the wording of ss. 5, 6, and 8 (which define sound recordings, films, broadcasts, and published editions) the word 'original' does not appear. Instead each provision declares that the particular category of work does not attract copyright 'to the extent that it is a copy of' a previous sound recording, film, broadcast, or published edition. This raises the question of whether these particular categories of works must be original. Whilst it could be argued that the omission of the word 'original' might be significant, the requirement that the work be 'not copied' is entirely consistent with the *University of London Press* case.

Further, it should be noted that films fall within the scope of the Berne Convention and are therefore subject to the requirement of originality.

2.7.3 Specific issues concerning originality

Peterson J's definition of 'originality' in the *University of London Press* case has been addressed in other cases too that have further refined the scope of the legal requirement of originality.

2.7.3.1 Revisions by or with the consent of the author

The first aspect of originality which requires further discussion is where the author of a work (assuming that he or she is also the owner, or else has the owner's permission) revises the work. Does the updated version of the work attract fresh copyright? Cases indicate that it is a question of degree as to whether enough originality has been expended on the revision. The fact that it is a question of degree means, in effect, that it lies in the court's discretion whether to accord fresh copyright to the amended work.

In *Interlego v Tyco* [1989] AC 217, the Privy Council held that minor adjustments to the engineering drawings for LEGO bricks were too minimal to result in fresh copyright protection being given. Yet, in *Cala Homes v Alfred McAlpine Homes East Ltd* [1995] FSR 818, Laddie J held that revisions made to an architect's plans for houses had been done with enough skill, labour, and judgement to attract fresh copyright. It did not matter that the alterations had been done by the claimant's employees at the direction of the initial architect. It is worth noting, however, that the judge's conclusion that there was a new copyright in the revised drawings may have been influenced by the fact that the defendant had flagrantly copied the plans.

 Pause for reflection

What is the differentiating factor in *Cala Homes* and *Interlego*? In finding that a work is original, what matters is not the *amount* of originality that was invested, but the finding that the labour/creativity involved is of the *right kind*.

2.7.3.2 Arrangements and adaptations (derivative works)

Where someone other than the original author uses the source work in a transformative way, e.g. via alterations or modifications, a new copyright may arise in the later work, which is typically classed as an arrangement or adaptation (or in the US, as a derivative work). Whether copyright arises in the new expression depends on how much originality is invested by the second author. Minor changes will not lead to the creation of a new work—original, authorial changes are required (*Brighton & Dubbeljoint Co Ltd v Jones* [2005] FSR 288).

Where the source work is no longer subject to copyright, because the term of protection has expired (or indeed if it never had copyright protection in the first place) then the second author's efforts may result in there being copyright in the revised or edited work. A finding of originality will depend on the level of creativity (skill, labour, judgement) invested in the later work.

A prime example of this is *Sawkins v Hyperion Records* where the claimant was held to be the owner of copyright in a new 'performing' edition of ancient music. In this case, Dr Sawkins, a musicological scholar and a world authority on Lalande, a 17th-century French composer, had completed modern performing editions of three of Lalande's *grands motets*. Mummery J held that 'the effort, skill and time which . . . Dr Sawkins spent in making the 3 performing editions were sufficient to satisfy the requirement that they should be "original" works in the copyright sense. This is so even though (a) Dr Sawkins worked on the scores of existing musical works composed by another person (Lalande); (b) Lalande's works are out of copyright; and (c) Dr Sawkins had no intention of adding any new notes of music of his own' (at [36]).

 Pause for reflection

A classic issue arising by reference to derivative works is whether the second work can attract protection in its own right or whether it amounts to an infringement of the pre-existing work. The issue has not been subject to harmonization at EU level and the practice in Member States varies, with some states requiring the altered material to be a personal intellectual creation, and others requiring some additional authorial input. The possibility of protecting arrangements and adaptations has long been recognized in the UK, insofar as the arrangement/adaptation demonstrates 'some quality or character which the raw material did not possess, and which differentiates the product from the raw material' (*Macmillan v Cooper* (1924) 40 TRL 186, 188).

What is less certain is whether protection can extend to appropriation art, namely the use of pre-existing works with little or no transformation applied to them with the view to recontextualize, rather than alter, those works (R. H. Chused, 'The Legal Culture of Appropriation Art: The Future of Copyright in the Remix Age' 17 Tul. J. Tech. & Intell. Prop. 163 (2014)).

2.7.3.3 Compilations and databases

Whether a collection or compilation itself meets the requirement of originality depends on the amount of effort expended on its assembly. As ever, the threshold in UK law is low. Copyright protection has been conferred on items such as professional directories even where these are assembled using factual information stored on a card-index: *Waterlow v Reed* [1992] FSR 409. Then, in *Waterlow v Rose* [1995] FSR 207, the Court of Appeal held that the owner of copyright was entitled to stop the defendant from *using* the directory in order to write to those listed in it asking them to complete a questionnaire so that it could collect its own data.

The correctness of conferring copyright on factual compilations has been debated in other jurisdictions, with varying outcomes. In the US, a higher threshold of creativity than the traditional UK standard was imposed by the US Supreme Court in *Feist Publications v Rural Telephone Service Co* (1991) 111 Sup Ct 1282. The opposite conclusion was reached in Australia in *Desktop Marketing Systems Pty Ltd v Telstra Corporation Ltd* (2002) 192 ALR 433, a case which, like *Feist*, involved a telephone directory. The court held that in assessing whether a factual compilation is an original work, the labour and expense of collecting the information can be taken into account. Consequently, what the court called a 'whole of the universe' compilation was capable of attracting copyright. The Supreme Court of Canada took a different view in *CCH Canadian Ltd v Law Society of Upper Canada* SC [2004] 1 SCR 339 where it declared that to be 'original', the work must originate from an author, not be copied from another work, and must be the product of an author's exercise of skill and judgement. The exercise of skill and judgment required to produce the work must not be so trivial that it could be characterised as a purely mechanical exercise.

With respect to databases, Art. 3 of the Directive was considered by the CJEU in Case C-604/10 *Football Dataco Ltd v Yahoo! UK Ltd, Stan James (Abingdon) Ltd and others*, 1 March 2012 where it was said that copyright protection depends on whether the selection or arrangement of the data which it contains amounts to an original expression of the creative freedom of its author. Art. 7 of the Directive was, in part, given a narrow interpretation by the CJEU in Case C-203/02 *British Horseracing Board v William Hill Organisation Ltd* [2004] ECR I-10415. The Court ruled that the 'substantial investment' which is required as a condition of protection must relate to obtaining and verifying data. The copyright holder must have committed its resources to seeking out existing independent materials or to monitoring their accuracy. Just collecting facts and figures is not enough. Equally, with regard to how the *sui generis* database right is infringed, a 'substantial part evaluated qualitatively and quantitatively' (the test for infringement in the Directive) means that the volume of data taken by the defendant must be compared with both the total volume of the contents and the claimant's investment in obtaining, verifying, or presenting those contents. However, the Court took a broader view of the restricted acts of 'extraction' and 'utilization', so that the database owner could object to any unauthorized act of appropriation even if the contents had been made accessible to the public.

The views expressed in the *British Horseracing Board* case have been reiterated by the CJEU in Case C-304/07 *Directmedia GmbH v Albert-Ludwigs-Universität Freiburg* [2008] ECR I-7565 and Case C-545/07 *Apis-Hristovich EOOD v Lakorda AD* [2009] ECR I-1627. In the former case, concerning a database of poetry, the Court stated that whilst the database right does not prevent consultation of a database (which the owner may or may not restrict to those who have paid), transfer of material from the protected database to another database following an on-screen consultation can still amount to an 'extraction'. It was immaterial whether the extraction depended on a technical means such as downloading or photocopying, or whether there was manual recopying. Neither did it matter that the alleged infringer had omitted some of the items from the protected database whilst adding others, nor whether the extraction was to create another database, whether in competition with the original or not. In the second case, which concerned databases of Bulgarian legislation and case law, the CJEU pointed out that under the Directive, 'extraction' covered both permanent and temporary transfer (the difference between which depended simply on the duration of storage in another medium). It repeated that it did not matter whether the extraction led to the creation of a new database, even if organizationally different from the protected database (so the alleged infringer's motives were immaterial) and that the fact that the two databases shared physical and technical characteristics could be evidence of extraction. Further, it did not matter if the contents of the protected database were publicly accessible or consisted of official materials: the database right protects the investment in obtaining and verifying such data.

2.7.3.4 Reports of the spoken word

Section 3(1) CDPA contemplates that the spoken word can attract copyright protection once it is recorded, even if the recording is done by another person. This in turn raises the question of whether someone who makes a report of a speech can acquire copyright *in the report* as a separate work. If, for example, a celebrity is interviewed by a reporter, the interview is recorded using, say, an MP3 device, and the reporter then subsequently produces a written report of the interview containing not just extracts of the words spoken by the celebrity but his or her own comments and observations on the interview, a number of different copyrights can be identified. These are:

- the literary work consisting of words spoken by the celebrity, assuming these pass the minimum threshold for copyright protection, the celebrity owning the copyright as author unless it can be argued that the interview, being an interactive process, leads to joint authorship between the celebrity and journalist. Copyright will arise in the words spoken once the speech is recorded (s. 3(2)) even if the recording is done by someone else (s. 3(3) CDPA);

- the sound recording of the interview. Whilst the recording operates under s. 3(2) to 'fix' the copyright in the spoken word, it will of itself be protected under s. 5A CDPA; and

- the reporter's story of the interview, assuming that this last mentioned possesses sufficient originality through the expenditure of skill, labour, and judgement to attract fresh copyright or else, under *Infopaq*, involves enough intellectual creativity.

The use of the recording of the interview for the purposes of reporting current events would be governed by the defence in s. 58 CDPA. Interestingly, the written report based on the recording would not be within the defence as it is not a 'direct' record, and theoretically infringes the spoken word copyright as an indirect copy (assuming substantial taking) although doubtless in most cases the celebrity is only too glad to receive the oxygen of publicity.

One of the oldest and most famous UK copyright cases—*Walter v Lane*—is worth considering in light of this analysis of the combination of s. 3(3) and the current requirement of originality.

Walter v Lane [1900] AC 539

In *Walter v Lane* [1900] AC 539 a leading politician, Lord Rosebery, made a series of speeches during an election campaign, those speeches being written down in shorthand by a reporter from *The Times* where the speeches were subsequently published. The House of Lords held by a majority of 4:1 that the defendant had infringed the copyright in the reports by publishing a book containing the speeches.

Browne Wilkinson J in *Express Newspapers v News (UK)* [1990] 3 All ER 376 (a case where the key facts occurred after the operative date of the CDPA) suggested that *Walter v Lane* is still good law. In the *Express Newspapers* case, involving a 'tit-for-tat' copying of so-called 'exclusive' interviews by rival tabloid newspapers, the defendant paper had interviewed Marina Ogilvy (a member of the Royal family), the interview (which had lasted some eight-and-a-half hours) being edited subsequently by its reporter. Browne Wilkinson J held that in reproducing the text of the interview, the claimant had infringed the defendant's copyright. There was both copyright in the words spoken by Ms Ogilvy and in the reporter's edited version of the interview. However, a matter left open for debate was the extent to which there can be copyright in the news itself, as opposed to a report of the news.

A strange case on copyright in spoken word is *Cummins v Bond* [1927] 1 Ch 167, where a spiritual medium claimed copyright over séance writings she produced whilst in a trance state. Eve J found that the writings 'could not have reached us in this form without the active co-operation of some agent competent to translate them from the language in which they were communicated [Aramaic] to [Cummins] into something more intelligible to persons of the present day [archaic English]'. It was hence held that 'the authorship rests with this lady, to whose gift of extremely rapid writing coupled with a peculiar ability to reproduce in archaic English matter communicated to her in some unknown tongue we owe the production of these documents' (at [173]).

 Pause for reflection

MacQueen (in '"My tongue is mine ain": Copyright, the Spoken Word and Privacy' (2005) 68 *MLR* 349) points out that there are a number of difficulties in according copyright to the spoken word. Although the spoken word (even in informal contexts) can in principle be original and attract copyright protection, according to MacQueen, 'copyright is not necessarily the protection which is required in the particular case, with perhaps the now extended action for breach of confidence being the most significant alternative legal avenue to protection of speech from the unsought intrusions of others. But with regard to the protection of the spoken word in its own right, copyright appears to strike an apt balance between the interests of those uttering the words and those who, for a wide variety of reasons, would disseminate them to a wider world.'

2.8 How copyright protection arises

2.8.1 Absence of formalities

Although copyright was initially a registered right, it has become an unregistered right since the beginning of the 20th century. This means that protection arises automatically and there is no need to satisfy any formalities, such as registration, deposit, or renewal. The abolition of formalities is expressly stated in Art. 5(2) of the Berne Convention: 'The enjoyment and exercise of these rights shall not be subject to any formality'. Although the absence of formalities has benefits, including the ease and low cost of acquiring and maintaining copyright protection, when it comes to the enforcement of copyright through infringement proceedings owners may have to prove that they are entitled to copyright protection. This is when they will have to show that the subsistence requirements are met.

The non-lawyer often confuses the question of whether copyright exists with *proof* that it exists. It must be stressed that copyright comes into being the moment the work is made. Proof as to the identity of its creator and the date of its creation can be effected through digital recordings/email, or by the old-fashioned method of posting a copy of the work (by recorded delivery) to a trusted person or organization (for example a solicitor or bank). Needless to say, there are businesses who advertise that they can help aspiring authors or composers to 'register' their copyright (naturally, for a fee) by being the recipients of copies of the work.

 Pause for reflection

Despite some obvious benefits coming with the automatic subsistence of copyright, the elimination of formalities has resulted to a lack of sufficient or adequate identifying information on works. To some commentators, this is one of the reasons behind the increased number of 'orphan' works, namely works whose copyright holder cannot be identified or located after diligent search by users who wish to engage in acts that require permission. Orphan works represent a challenge in copyright to the extent that they form a large body of our cultural heritage that may remain unused due to the impossibility of clearing permission. Although there are only estimates as to the numbers of orphan works, the British Library has stated that over 40% of *all* existing in-copyright works have potentially orphaned (British Library, 'Intellectual Property: A Balance—The British Library Manifesto', September 2006, point 5). Via the EU Orphan Works Directive, it is now possible for organizations such as museums and libraries to make use of orphan works, and to keep any resulting royalties in trust for any authors/owners who may come out of the woodwork in the future (Directive 2012/28/EU of the European Parliament and of the Council of 25 October 2012 on certain permitted uses of orphan works (Text with EEA relevance)).

Thinking back to our problem scenario, it is worth recalling that many of the orphan works held by e.g. the British Library and the National Archives are photographs of historical interest. The consequence of the low originality threshold, combined with the lack or registration, means that there are hundreds of thousands of 'orphan photos'.

2.8.2 Fixation

The requirement that a work must be recorded owes its origins to the Berne Convention—Art. 2(2) permits its Contracting States to stipulate that works shall not be protected 'unless they have been fixed in some material form'.

Section 3(2) of the CDPA provides that copyright does not exist in a literary, dramatic, or musical work unless the work is recorded 'in writing or otherwise'. Defining 'writing', s. 178 declares that it '*includes* any form of notation or code, whether by hand or otherwise, and regardless of the method by which, or medium in or on which it is recorded'.

The requirement of fixation does not expressly cover artistic works (s. 3(2)). Although in cases such as *Metix (UK) Ltd v G.H. Maughan (Plastics) Ltd* at p. 721, Laddie J remarked *obiter* that a sculpture in ice would be a copyright work, other cases indicate that courts have denied protection to alleged artistic works on the ground that they were not permanent (as examples, consider the outcomes in *Hensher Ltd v Restawile Upholstery (Lancs) Ltd*, *Creation Records v News Group Newspapers*, *J & S Davis v Wright*, and *Merchandising Corporation of America v Harpbond*).

 Pause for reflection

Can certain works of modern art, such as contemporary art installations, qualify for protection? Are they 'fixed'? Can the requirement of permanence as developed in case law be seen a means of filtering out-of-copyright works which the judges consider do not deserve protection?

With regard to our problem, remember that fixation is unproblematic for photos in and of themselves as the very existence of the photo is itself a proof of fixation!

2.8.3 Qualification for copyright protection

Copyright does not subsist in a work unless the qualification requirements are satisfied as regards:

(a)   the author (s. 154);

(b)   the country in which the work was first published (s. 155);

(c)   in the case of a broadcast, the country from which the broadcast was made (s. 156).

The simple rule is that the author or the work must in some way be connected with the UK or a country to which the CDPA extends or to a country to which the Act applies. A work will qualify for protection if the author was, at the material time, a qualifying person. 'Qualifying person' means, under s. 154, that the author was a citizen of or was domiciled in or was resident in the UK or a country to which the Act extends or a country to which the Act applies at the relevant date.

If for some reason the author was not a qualifying person (for example, our author might be a national of North Korea who has never left that country), the final way the work can obtain UK copyright (under ss. 155 and 159) is by reference to the place it was first published. In effect, what needs to be shown is that the work was first published either in the UK or in an 'extension' country or in a Convention country. It should be noted that the Act refers to countries to which it 'extends' (broadly speaking, colonies and dependent territories) and to countries to which it is deemed to 'apply'. This latter category, for the sake of convenience, are referred to as 'Convention countries', that is, Contracting States of the Berne Convention (for literary, dramatic, musical, and artistic works, and films), the Rome Convention (for sound recordings and broadcasts), or any member of the World Trade Organization (WTO).

For literary, dramatic, musical, or artistic works, the material time is: for published works, the time of first publication, and for unpublished works the time when the work was made (s. 154(4)). For sound recordings, films, and broadcasts, material time is when the work was made, and for typographical arrangements of published editions it is the time when the edition was first published (s. 154(5)).

2.9 **Conclusion**

In this chapter we have looked at the requirements for subsistence of copyright protection.

First, an alleged 'work' needs to fall within one of the recognized categories listed in s. 1 CDPA. We have seen that in the UK there is a closed list of protectable subject matter but this exhaustive approach may need to be rethought in light of the jurisprudence of the Court of Justice. Second, a work needs to be original to be protected. We have seen that this is likely the case when the author has invested the right kind of skill, labour, and judgement in the creation of the work. We have also seen that an author who creates a derivative work can also attract copyright if there was additional skill and effort involved. Third, some categories of protected subject matter, namely literary, dramatic, and musical works, ought to be recorded in a permanent form to be protected. Finally, authors need to qualify for protection by being 'connected' to the UK.

Turning to our problem scenario, we can advise Adam that in general terms, he would be considered the author and owner of the copyright in his photographs. In light of EU case law such as *Infopaq* and *Painer*, as followed in UK cases such as *Meltwater* and *SAS*, we can observe that the creative choices Adam makes in arranging the subjects of his photographs are sufficient for those photographs to be considered works of 'intellectual creation' bearing the personal 'stamp of the author'. This would also be the case under the more traditional UK standard of 'skill, labour, and judgement' (*Ladbroke*). Moreover, the efforts Adam makes with photoshop are comparable with those of the photographer/author in *Temple Island* bolstering his authorship claim further. Thus, on subsistence, the copyright issues are clear.

However, there are several other issues of interest in this set of facts that will only become clear as we proceed through the chapters. For now, we can flag up the following issues and keep them in mind in the upcoming chapters: (i) ownership; (ii) infringement; (iii) licensing.

For instance, it is clear Adam has been engaged/commissioned to take these photographs for an online retailer—Baby Home Ltd. But who owns the works? We must ask what legal agreement is in place between Adam and Baby Home. As we will consider in more detail in chapter 3, in the absence of an agreement between the parties that says otherwise, for such commissioned works Adam would be considered the author/owner of the copyright. If there is an agreement, does the agreement provide that Adam must assign copyright in the photographs to Baby Home, or does he grant a mere licence to Baby Home for specific uses? In terms of the use of Baby Home images on online retail websites, the agreement between the parties should specify whether Baby Home has the right to allow its retailers to do this. (The later chapter 21 covers issues of licensing and assignment in more detail.) The fact that a competitor has used a very similar photo means that, as in *Temple Island*, there may have been infringement of copyright in the photo, since key elements appear to have been taken without permission. This is something we will deal with in the later chapter on copyright infringement. Resolving the question of who owns the rights to the photographs will enable us to advise Adam on whether he can take legal action or whether Baby Home, as owner or licensee, should take the action (or whether both should be claimants in the case).

End-of-chapter questions

After reading the chapter carefully, try answering the following questions. For answer guidance visit the online resources at **www.oup.com/uk/karapapa-mcdonagh/**

1. The assumption that the list of eight categories of protected subject matter under s. 1 CDPA is closed is under challenge. Critically discuss.

2. How has the European standard of originality impacted on the traditional 'skill, labour and judgement' approach in the UK? Discuss by reference to relevant cases.

3. Can invented words, short sentences or headlines attract protection under UK copyright and, if so, under which conditions?

4. Is the helmet of the Stormtrooper character featuring in Star Wars eligible for copyright protection?

5. A student keeps notes during a lecture of intellectual property law. Another student records the lecture with a dictaphone. Does copyright subsist in the notes and/or the recording?

6. An atmospheric art installation features neon lights hanging from the gallery's ceiling. A critic referred to it as 'shafts of glimmering light striking their way from the ceiling to the floor'. Can it be protected by copyright?

7. Can the portrait photograph of a child at nursery school that was taken by a freelance photographer be protected by copyright?

8. Can an 11-word extract from a newspaper article attract copyright protection?

9. A musicologist works on the unfinished music scores of a 17th-century composer and produces performing editions of music that can be thereinafter orchestrated. Does copyright subsist in modern performing editions of the out-of-copyright music?

Further reading

Arnold, R. 'Joy: A Reply' [2001] 1 *IPQ* 10
   Considers copyright in dramatic works and films.

Brennan, D.J. and Christie, A. 'Spoken Words and Copyright Subsistence in Anglo-American Law' [2000] 4 *IPQ* 309
   Examines spoken words, originality, and fixation of copyright works.

Cullabine, J. 'Copyright in Short Phrases and Single Words' [1992] 14 *EIPR* 205
   Ask the question of whether a very short work, including a single word, can be accepted as a copyright work—includes analysis of Exxon.

Derclaye, E. '*Infopaq International A/S v Danske Dagblades Forening* (C-5/08): Wonderful or Worrisome? The Impact of the ECJ Ruling in *Infopaq* on UK Copyright Law' [2010] 32 *EIPR* 247
   Considers the impact of Infopaq *on the UK originality standard.*

Gervais, D.J. 'The Compatibility of the Skill and Labour Originality Standard with the Berne Convention and the TRIPs Agreement' [2004] 26 *EIPR* 75

Takes an interesting comparative view of the skill and labour originality standard in light of international copyright treaties.

Gervais, D.J. and Derclaye, E. 'The scope of computer program protection after SAS: are we closer to answers?' [2012] 34 *EIPR* 565

Analyses SAS and its implications for computer programs.

Griffiths, J. '*Infopaq, BSA* and the "Europeanisation of United Kingdom Copyright Law' [2011] 16 *MALR* 59

A forensics exploration of the impact of recent CJEU decisions on the UK standards of copyright protection.

Lupton, K. 'Photographs and the Concept of Originality in Copyright Law' [1988] 10 *EIPR* 257

A classic article on photographic copyright in the UK.

MacQueen, H. '"My tongue is mine ain": Copyright, the Spoken Word and Privacy' [2005] 68 *MLR* 349

Argues that protection for the spoken word can be justified by the privacy and personality interests of speakers.

McDonagh, L. 'Plays, Performances and Power Struggles—Examining Copyright's "Integrity" in the Field of Theatre' [2014] 77 *MLR* 533

Considers the dramatic work and its peformative qualities, which differentiate it from the literary work.

Pila, J. 'An Intentional View of the Copyright Work' [2008] 71 *MLR* 535

An examination of the authorial perspective of copyright.

Phillips, J. 'Copyright in Spoken Words—Some Potential Problems' [1989] 11 *EIPR* 231

Considers originality and fixation in the context of spoken words.

Rahmatian, A. 'Originality in UK Copyright Law: The Old "Skill and Labour" Doctrine Under Pressure' [2013] 44(4) *IIC* 4

Explores whether the UK standard of originality has actually been altered by the impact of the CJEU case of Infopaq.

Rahmatian, A. 'Music and Creativity as Perceived by Copyright Law' [2005] 3 *IPQ* 267

Uses musicological literature to examine copyright's notion of the musical work.

Rosati, E. 'Closed Subject-Matter Systems are no Longer Compatible with EU Copyright' [2014] 12 *GRUR Int* 1112

Argues that the UK's closed list system is no longer compatible with CJEU rulings.

3 Authorship and ownership

Problem question

Read this problem question carefully and keep it in mind while you are working through the chapter that follows. At the end of this chapter, you will be able to apply what you have learnt to the problem question and advise the relevant parties.

In early 2002 the well-known folk-pop musician Andrew Starr, who performs under the name 'Starr', composed a song called *All I Live For*. The melancholic lyrics to the song describe a man who falls in love with a woman who is already married to someone else, and as a result the man's love goes unrequited. The lyrics, chord progression and melody of the song *All I Live For* were written by Starr for voice and solo guitar, but after playing the song privately to his friends and getting their feedback, he decided that the final recorded version would benefit from some mandolin accompaniment to give it a more earthy, folk music sound.

Sarah Wilson is an acoustic mandolin player who works primarily as an orchestral performer with the High Holborn Mandolin Orchestra. In May 2002, having seen Sarah's orchestra perform at the Royal Albert Hall, Starr went backstage and asked Sarah if she would be willing to perform on the recording of *All I Live For*. She accepted his offer. During the rehearsal and recording process, Sarah added several musical motifs to *All I Live For*, as well as an extended mandolin solo. Both the motifs and the solo were improvised by Sarah over the guitar chords to *All I Live For*. Starr was very happy with Sarah's additions and in the final recorded version of the song her mandolin motifs and solo are heard prominently.

The agreement between Starr and Sarah Wilson was that she would play the mandolin on his track for a one-off performer's fee of £340. Starr paid her this fee in cash immediately after the recording. No agreement was made between them regarding the consequences of any musical additions or authorial contributions made to the song by Sarah Wilson.

When first released in 2003 the song was not a hit, but from 2014 onwards the song grew in prominence and popularity due to its use as the theme song for a hit Netflix sitcom. Since early 2014 the song has generated more than £200,000 per year in copyright royalties. All royalties currently go to Andrew Starr.

→

> →
>
> After the recording session, Sarah Wilson went back to her regular orchestral career. She did not think again about the song until she heard her mandolin playing while scrolling through Netflix in June 2016. Angry, she called Starr and asked him to share some of the royalties. He refused.
>
> Sarah wishes to know whether her contributions to the track give her any authorial interest in it. Advise Sarah on the rules of authorship and joint authorship under copyright.

3.1 Authorship and ownership

It is very important to understand the way the law evaluates authorship of copyright works—including what happens when two or more authors collaborate on a joint work. Moreover, it is crucial to distinguish between authorship and ownership of copyright works, as the two do not necessarily coincide. The reason for this, as explored in detail below, is that an author may decide to license or assign (transfer) the ownership of the work to a third party, such as a publisher, in exchange for money, i.e. royalties. In such a case the author would still be classed as the author of the work, but would no longer own the economic rights to control the 'restricted acts'.

3.1.1 What is an author?

The author is typically the first owner of the work. Thus, identifying the 'author' of a copyright work is the first step in identifying its ownership, as even if the ownership has been transferred, there will always be some legal link back to the author through e.g. a contract of assignment. But how can we determine who is the author? Section 9 CDPA gives the answer, but maintains a distinction between authorial and entrepreneurial copyrights.

In the case of literary, dramatic, musical, and artistic works, s. 9 CDPA simply declares that the person who creates the work is the author. However, in relation to disputed claims, such as in the case of joint authorship, deciding as a matter of fact what amounts to creative input is not always easy.

 Pause for reflection

In our problem scenario we will need to evaluate the creative actions of each party to assess questions of authorship and joint authorship to do with the popular song *All I Live For*. Who could plausibly make authorship/ownership claims in this scenario?

Furthermore, where a literary, dramatic, musical, and artistic work is computer-generated, the author is said to be person making the arrangements 'necessary for the creation of the work'. As yet, there is no guidance from case law as to where to draw the line between where a computer is merely a tool in the hands of a creative person and where it is the computer which generates the work, nor is there any guidance as to the meaning of 'arrangements necessary for the creation of the work'. This question is sure to become more important in future as the process of automation continues, and machine-led creation via artificial intelligence becomes more normal a.k.a. the 'fourth industrial revolution' (A. Ramalho, 'Will Robots Rule the (Artistic) World? A Proposed Model for the Legal Status of Creations by Artificial Intelligence Systems' 21 *Journal of Internet Law* [2017], 12–25).

In the case of entrepreneurial copyrights, there are significant differences in detail. In the case of a sound recording, the author is the producer (in contrast to the position under the 1956 Act); for films, the authors are deemed to be the principal director and the producer; whilst for broadcasts it is the person who makes the broadcast. For published editions, it is the publisher who is the author. Section 178 CDPA defines the producer of a sound recording or a film as the person who makes the necessary arrangements for its creation. Again, it must be stressed that the CDPA merely provides a starting point, and that in many instances contractual arrangements will be used to determine the matter.

Slater v Wimmer [2012] EWPCC 7

In this case—heard at the Patents Count Court (now the Intellectual Property Enterprise Court or IPEC)—HHJ Birss concluded that in the absence of a clearly worded agreement between the two parties, copyright in a film made by the claimant of the defendant sky-diving over Everest was determined by the statutory provisions: the defendant was producer (he had made the necessary financial arrangements) and the claimant was director (he had creative control), and as joint authors each had infringed the other's rights by copying the film and communicating it to the public.

Consider our problem scenario, which involves authorship/joint authorship of a musical work: is there a clearly worded agreement between the two parties about authorship/ownership? If not, we will have to pay close attention to statutory guidance in determining these issues.

3.1.2 Ownership of copyright

Section 11(1) CDPA provides that initial ownership of copyright vests in the 'author' of the work. This deceptively simple rule is merely a starting point in the process of identifying the owner. In UK law (in contrast to other jurisdictions) copyright is freely assignable. In many sectors of the economy (for example in the media and entertainment industries) it is standard practice for there to be extensive (not to say complex) contractual arrangements dealing with copyright ownership.

3.1.2.1. Distinguishing between the intangible work and its material embodiment

Because copyright is an intangible right, it is necessary to distinguish between the ownership of the medium in which a work is embodied from the ownership of the copyright itself. This point was made in *Re Dickens* [1935] Ch 267 where it was held that the beneficiary under a will of unpublished manuscripts was not entitled to the copyright in them (though s. 93 CDPA now provides for copyright in unpublished manuscripts to pass with a bequest of such papers).

Pause for reflection

The distinction between the work and the material form in which the work is embodied was neatly illustrated by a row over the estate of Stieg Larsson, author of *The Girl with the Dragon Tattoo*. Eva Gabrielsson was Larsson's long-term partner until he died suddenly in 2004, but because they were unmarried and he died without a will, his copyrights passed upon his death to his living relatives—his brother and father. For several years, it was thought that Larsson had written a final novel, the only copy of which was saved on a laptop initially owned by Larsson's magazine, but that ended up in the possession of Gabrielsson after Larsson's death. In this case, Gabrielsson possessed the material form in which the copyright work existed (the laptop and word processor) but the copyright in that work was owned by Larsson's estate. In the end, it transpired that the final novel was not in a publishable form, and the row petered out—but it shows that ownership of a physical copy of a work does not equate to a copyright interest in that work.

3.1.2.2 Works made in the course of employment

The only statutory exception to the basic rule that authors are the first owners of copyright is in s. 11(2) which provides that literary, dramatic, musical, and artistic works and films created in the course of employment belong to the author's employer, subject to any contractual arrangement to the contrary. There is no equivalent provision for the other types of work—the entrepreneurial works—yet one could imagine (say) a journalist making an electronic recording of an interview. Would the journalist be regarded as the 'author' i.e. producer of the sound recording because, in the words of s. 178, he or she has made the arrangements necessary for the making of the sound recording, or would that work belong to the employer?

The wording of s. 11(2) should be compared with that of s. 39 Patents Act. 'In the course of employment' in the former provision is arguably a more flexible concept (and hence subject to a degree of judicial discretion) than the notion of 'normal duties . . . such that an invention might be expected' found in the latter. It is beyond the scope of this work to go into the vast number of employment law cases on whether a person is an employee so we shall confine ourselves to those decisions where ownership of copyright was at stake.

In *Stevenson, Jordan & Harrison v MacDonald & Evans* (1952) 69 RPC 10 the Court of Appeal held that the copyright in a book written by an accountant belonged to his estate, not his employer, with the exception of one chapter which was based on a project which his firm, who were management consultants, had undertaken. He was not employed to deliver lectures or write books. This can be contrasted with *Beloff v Pressdram Ltd* [1973] RPC 765.

Beloff v Pressdram **[1973] RPC 765**

In a copyright case, a memorandum written by the claimant—Nora Beloff—while she worked as a journalist at *The Observer*, was the subject of dispute. Crucially, Beloff was unable to maintain her claim because she did not own the work in question. The memorandum was considered a work made in the course of her employment, which thus belonged to *The Observer* (as employer) rather than to Beloff (employee).

One useful test as to whether a work is written in the course of employment is whether the employee could have been ordered to produce the work. In *Noah v Shuba* [1991] FSR 14, Mummery J held that a consultant epidemiologist who had, in his spare time, written a paper on good hygiene practices for tattoo parlours, was the owner of the copyright. Even though his secretary had typed the manuscript, he could not have been ordered to write the paper by his employers.

One common misconception concerns works that have been commissioned. By 'commission' we mean that A asks B to write a book or a play or a piece of music or create an artistic work and agrees *unconditionally* to pay for the work in any event. In other words, it must be possible for A to sue B for breach of contract if he does not complete the work and for B to sue A for non-payment (*Gabrin v Universal Music Operations Ltd* [2003] EWHC 1335 (Ch)). There is *no* rule in UK law that the person who commissions a work is the owner of copyright in it. The normal rule applies, i.e. that the author is the first owner.

Pause for reflection

With respect to commissioning of works, when considering our problem one important thing becomes clear—even if we accept that Andrew Starr 'commissioned' a musical performance from Sarah Wilson, it does not mean that Andrew necessarily owns the copyright in what results. As we shall see later in the chapter, however, it is more accurate to analyse the dispute between Andrew and Sarah as one concerning joint authorship, than that of a commissioned work.

There are two ways in which a person who commissions a work can become the copyright owner. The first is to enter into an agreement complying with s. 91 CDPA. This provides for the assignment of future copyright and requires a written agreement signed by the putative author of the work to hand over the work to another. If the conditions of the section are met, the copyright vests automatically in the **assignee** once the work is created. Second, a commission may give rise to a claim in equity, either for an **exclusive licence**, or for equitable title to the work. A court has the power to imply a suitable term to this effect into the contract to give effect to the parties' intentions but will only imply the absolute minimum necessary to make the contract work: *R Griggs Group Ltd and others v Evans and others* [2005] FSR 706.

Pause for reflection

In light of the above, we can see that in our problem scenario, the lack of a written agreement between Andrew and Sarah may prove to be important. What terms could potentially be implied in this case? Who might have granted an implied licence, and to whom?

Under the Copyright Act 1956 s. 4 there was a rule that the commissioner of certain types of artistic works (photographs and portraits) was the copyright owner. This rule was abolished by the CDPA, but will continue to apply to such works created before its operative date. Section 104 CDPA assists the claimant in any copyright infringement action by creating a number of presumptions as to existence and ownership of copyright. The net effect is that the onus is on the defendant to disprove.

3.1.3 Why is the distinction between authorship and ownership important?

Having identified who is the author of a work, it is necessary to keep separate the authorship and ownership issues in copyright law. As noted earlier, the author of a work may not be the owner of copyright in that work. This is critical, because it is the *owner* who can sue for infringement of copyright and who has the ability to assign or license the right, in whole or in part (see CDPA s. 96 and ss. 90–93 respectively). Even in the absence of ownership, the issue of authorship remains relevant to: (a) whether the work attracts UK protection; (b) the calculation of the length of the term/duration of copyright protection; and (c) the determination of whether moral rights have arisen (something we will cover in a later chapter).

Under s. 11(2) CDPA, works created under employment contracts and in the normal course of employment are typically owned by the employer. Thus, a work such as an instruction manual for a piece of equipment written in the course of employment will be owned by the employer (who may well be a company whose assets are subsequently transferred as part of a corporate acquisition); however, the life of the human author (employee) will determine the duration of copyright protection for the work. As we shall see in the next sub-section, authorship and ownership of copyright works is even more complicated in the case of works that are authored and owned jointly.

3.2 Joint authorship

Section 10 CDPA provides that copyright protects works of joint authorship. The definition of a work of joint authorship is very precise—it must *not* be possible to identify each author's respective contribution (it must truly be a joint endeavour). So, for example, a book written by two people in which one writes chapters 1, 3, 5, and 7 and the other writes chapters 2, 4, 6, and 8 will *not* be a work of joint authorship as each person's contributions can be identified and distinguished. The rights of joint owners are set out in s. 173(2) CDPA.

Further, case law has made clear that each alleged co-author 'must share responsibility for the form of expression' and make 'a significant and original contribution to the creation of the work', phrases which have become a judicial mantra when deciding a claim for joint authorship. However, deciding what amounts to creative input is not always easy.

Unsuccessful claims for a share of royalties arising from alleged joint authorship include *Lawson v Dundas* (*The Times*, 13 June 1985) where Whitford J held that the claimant had contributed nothing towards the orchestral arrangement of the Channel 4 musical ident; *Fylde Microsystems v Key Radio Systems Ltd* [1998] FSR 449, where simply correcting 'bugs' in software was insufficient to confer joint authorship; *Ray v Classic FM plc* [1998] FSR 622, where it was held that the claimant was the sole author of a database of classical music, although the court granted the defendant radio station an exclusive licence to use the database as an implied term of the contract; and *Hadley v Kemp* [1999] EMLR 589, where Park J held that Gary Kemp was the sole author of the songs performed by the group Spandau Ballet as the compositions were complete before rehearsals began (despite the fact that a prominent saxophone solo lasting 16 bars was added by band-member Steve Norman during the rehearsal and recording of the song).

Post-*Hadley v Kemp*, musicians have been more successful at claiming joint authorship of pop songs. In *Beckingham v Hodgens* [2003] EMLR 376 the Court of Appeal held that there was a work of joint authorship—the released version of the song *Young at Heart*—after the addition of a violin riff by the claimant during the recording session. A similar outcome occurred in *Bamgboye v Reed* [2004] EMLR 61, where the claimant's contribution was the addition of drum accompaniment to a tune called *Bouncing Flow*. The most recent, leading case on joint authorship of musical works is *Fisher v Brooker*.

Fisher v Brooker [2009] 1 WLR 1764

This saga concerned the 1967 hit *A Whiter Shade of Pale*, initially composed, in demo form, by Gary Brooker. Brooker then went into the recording studio with a group of musicians who became known as Procol Harum. During the recording, Matthew Fisher added an organ line inspired by Bach's *Air on a G String*. The final recorded arrangement was released in 1967 and became a huge hit. Brooker was credited as the author of the work and received 100% of all royalties. In 2005, a High Court claim was brought by Fisher asserting a share in the joint authorship in the final recorded arrangement of *A Whiter Shade of Pale*.

The High Court decided that Fisher's contribution easily met the test of joint authorship— it was a sufficiently original contribution to the overall work, i.e. the arrangement ([2007] EMLR 256), amounting to a 40% share. However, the Court of Appeal decided that although Fisher was a joint author of the recorded arrangement of the song, he had waited too long to take his claim, and thus should not be awarded joint ownership ([2008] EWCA Civ 287).

In 2009, the House of Lords reversed the Court of Appeal and restored the original judgment of the High Court that the claimant was entitled to 40% of the ownership. However, they stated that since Fisher had not taken legal action until 2005, he could be said to have given Brooker an implied licence to make use of his interest in the work up to that point. Thus, Fisher was only entitled to royalties from 2005 onwards.

Music cases bring up a number of interesting dilemmas for copyright lawyers. For instance, in both *Beckingham v Hodgens* and *Fisher v Brooker* it was possible to identify, respectively, the violin line and the organ line in each piece of music. Could it really be said that the contribution of each author—initial composer, later performing musician—was not distinct, as required by s. 10? It could be, of course, that it was easier to make a finding of joint authorship despite the express wording of s. 10, in view of the complexity of working out the parties' separate contributions had this not been the case. On the other hand, the courts could be interpreting s. 10 to mean that a released version of a pop song is a unitary work, and even if separate parts can be identified (as will always be the case in music cases) the contributions should be seen as fulfilling the requirements of s. 10. Furthermore, a key element of analysing joint authorship claims in music cases is identifying the specific work in dispute. In *Fisher v Brooker*, what was in dispute was in fact the recorded arrangement of the original composition written by Brooker. Under copyright, both are copyright works, with the arrangement being an adaptation of the initial work. The recorded arrangement featured Fisher's famous organ solo—whereas the original composition by Brooker featured no organ part at all—and it was this recorded arrangement that was of commercial value (it became a hit). Fisher was a joint author of the recorded arrangement of the song, and thus entitled to a share of it. In *Hadley v Kemp*, by contrast, the judge struggled with the distinction between the original composition of Kemp, and the later musical additions added by Steve Norman and other band-members in the studio. If the judge had made the distinction between the composition (copyright work) and the arrangement (a later adaptation of that work, which is a copyright work in itself) the judge may have found it easier to find that Norman was a joint author of the final arrangement.

 Pause for reflection

Having analysed disputes over the authorship of music such as *Fisher*, we should return to our problem scenario. A number of things become clear: first, the hit version of *All I Live For* can be seen as an arrangement of the original composition written by Andrew; second, it is clear that what Sarah added is significant and original and therefore this hit arrangement can be viewed as a work of joint authorship between Andrew and Sarah (since they collaborated on it in the same way Brooker and Fisher collaborated on *A Whiter Shade of Pale*); third, there is no written agreement between Andrew and Sarah that specifies what should happen to any copyright interest Sarah acquired through her creative contribution—in the absence of such an agreement a court would likely award Sarah a joint share in the musical work (the proportion may be determined by the court e.g. 60/40); fourth, in terms of sharing of royalties, cases such as *Fisher* show that if a joint author takes no action for several years to assert her interest in the work, the court may be unwilling to award 'back royalties' for that period that has passed—instead the court will only require sharing of royalties from the point at which the claim was made (which in Sarah's case is 2016).

One of the key elements in maintaining a joint authorship claim is showing proof, or evidence, of joint authorship. In musical cases, such as our problem scenario, the evidence will often be obvious, as the saxophone or organ part (or mandolin part in Sarah's case) will be audible in the recording of the song. But what about other types of creative works, such as dramatic works, where contributions made by e.g. a director or actor may not be clearly reflected in the final work?

Brighton & Dubbeljoint Co Ltd v Jones [2004] EWHC 1157 (Ch)

It is not only music that can lead to interesting disputes concerning authorship. *Brighton* involved a dispute over a dramatic work—the popular play *Stones in His Pockets*. The director

➡

→

of the original 1996 production of the play, Pamela Brighton, and the original theatre company that put on the production, Dubblejoint, took a case against Marie Jones, the playwright, after a subsequent production of the play became successful in the West End and on Broadway.

Brighton's main claim was that she ought to be awarded joint authorship of the play because she had suggested several changes to the play, including lines of dialogue and character directions, during rehearsals. However, the evidence for this claim was sketchy—there was no recording of the rehearsals, and no written proof of contributions. The court ultimately held that in light of the poor quality of the evidence, whatever Brighton's contribution was it was not sufficient for joint authorship: the changes suggested by Brighton to the script were of the usual sort to be suggested by a director, and the playwright had the final say as to whether these changes were accepted.

However, Brighton's second claim—infringement—largely succeeded due to a different authorship question. Brighton testified that early on, to encourage Jones to start work on the play, she had faxed her an opening scene she had written (effectively, a dramatic work). Brighton presented the original fax sent to Jones in court. The court found that elements of this opening scenario remained in the final play, written by Jones, and that elements of the later play (Jones' work) were thus derived from this opening scene (Brighton's work). However, the court also found that Jones had been impliedly authorized to use the draft opening script in writing the play in 1996, and this implied licence had not been revoked when the play was re-written in 1999. For future exploitation of the play, however, a licence from Brighton would be required based on the use of her initial dramatic work. Not for the first time, implied licences were found by the court as a practical way of resolving the complexities in the case.

3.2.1 Lyrics and music

The Copyright and Duration of Rights in Performances Regulations 2013 (SI 2013/1782), implementing Directive 2011/77/EU of the European Parliament and of the Council of 27 September 2011 [2011] OJ L 265/1, have amended s. 10 CDPA by providing for there to be works of co-authorship. Such works arise where there is collaboration between the author of a musical work and the author of a literary work where the two are created in order to be used together, i.e. a song. The sole purpose of the amendment is to provide for a change in the calculation of the term of protection, explained later on in this chapter.

3.3 Duration of copyright

Once it has been established who the author(s) and owner(s) are, it is important to consider whether the work is still protected by copyright—and thus requires a licence for use—or whether the term has expired, and the work is in the public domain. The term of protection for copyright is one area where EU law has had a significant impact on the CDPA. In common with similar legislation in other jurisdictions, such as Australia and the US, the Copyright Term Directive has lengthened the duration of most categories of copyright work to 70 years, beyond the minimum requirements of the

Berne Convention (50 years). In so doing, it sought to limit the benefit of the extended period of protection to works the authors of which are nationals of the European Economic Area (EEA) or the country of origin of which is the EEA. Section 15A CDPA gives a detailed definition of the term 'country of origin', determined primarily by the place of first publication, but if the work is unpublished, then by the nationality of the author.

3.3.1 Duration for literary, dramatic, musical, and artistic works

The Copyright Term Directive was implemented by The Duration of Copyright and Rights in Performances Regulations (SI 1995/3297). Section 12 CDPA, as amended, now provides that the term of protection for literary, dramatic, musical, and artistic works shall be the author's life, plus 70 years, calculated from the end of the calendar year when the author died. In the case of works of joint authorship and co-authorship, the calculation is based on the death of the last author to die. The overriding condition, however, is that the author must be an EEA national or the work's country of origin must be in the EEA. If this is not the case, then the term of protection is to be that laid down by the law of the country of origin.

The duration of protection applies regardless of the type of work found within ss. 3 and 4, regardless of how much effort went into its creation, and regardless of whether the work is published or unpublished. There are, however, a number of exceptions. Thus, in the case of works of unknown authorship, the term is 70 years from creation, or 70 years from making available to the public, provided that the making available happened within 70 years of creation; in the case of computer-generated works the period is 50 years from creation.

 Pause for reflection

If copyright law is meant to reflect the underlying policy of encouraging or rewarding creativity, is it right that the term of protection for literary, dramatic, musical, and artistic works is the same regardless of the merits of the work? Why should a mobile phone ringtone get the same length of protection as a symphony?

3.3.2 Duration for films

Section 13B CDPA, as amended, provides for film copyright to expire at the end of 70 years from the death of the survivor of the principal director, the author of the screenplay, the author of the dialogue, or the composer of music specially created for and used in the film. As ever, there is the condition that one of the authors of the film must be an EEA national or the country of origin of the film must be an EEA Contracting State. If this is not the case, the film is accorded the same term of copyright as in its country of origin. Following the EU Copyright Term Directive, the UK implemented the Copyright and Related Rights Regulations 1996 (SI 1996/2967) accorded the producer the status of co-author of the film (by amending s. 9 CDPA).

3.3.3 Duration for sound recordings

The term of protection for sound recordings has been amended on a number of occasions, in order to implement the original version of the Copyright Term Directive, the Information Society Directive, and the latest amendment to the Copyright Term Directive (Directive 2011/77/EU of the European Parliament and of the Council of 27 September 2011 [2011] OJ L 265/1). Section 13A CDPA provides that copyright expires at the end of 50 years from the end of the calendar year in which the recording was made, or if during that period it is published, 70 years from publication, or if during that period the recording is not published but is made available to the public by being played in public or communicated to the public, 70 years from being made available. Again, the requirement is that the author of the sound recording (the definition of which is provided by s. 9 CDPA, explained earlier) must be an EEA national. If that is not the case, the duration of protection is to be that accorded in the author's own country.

3.3.4 Duration for broadcasts

The most straightforward period of protection is for broadcasts. Section 14 CDPA, as amended, states that the term is 50 years from the end of the calendar year of first broadcast, provided that the author of the broadcast is an EEA national. If this is not the case then the length of protection is that provided in the author's own country.

3.3.5 Duration for published editions

The period of protection for published editions is unaffected by the Copyright Term Directive and therefore remains at 25 years from the end of the calendar year of first publication.

3.4 Conclusion

This chapter has explained: how to determine whether someone is an author of a work; how to establish who owns a copyright work; how to distinguish between a copyright work and the material form in which the work is embodied; how to evaluate a joint authorship claim for a work; and how the duration of protection is determined.

Turning to our problem question, explain the concept of joint authorship under s. 10 of the CDPA. Outline its central requirements: that each joint author make a sufficiently original contribution; towards a joint enterprise; and that the contributions to the work are not separable (a compilation is not a joint work but a collection of separate works).

Discuss those UK cases which are central to the concept of joint authorship, such as *Fylde Microsystems* and *Brighton v Jones*, but with a particular emphasis on music cases since the problem is a music-related one: *Hadley v Kemp, Beckingham v Hodgens, Bamgboye v Reed, Fisher v Brooker*.

Explain to Sarah that the cases that followed *Hadley v Kemp*—and especially the seminal case of *Fisher v Brooker*—demonstrate that it is possible for her to make a successful claim in the circumstances. Here she has made a significant and original contribution to the eventual recorded arrangement of the song—initially written by Andrew Starr—and that the released arrangement is a musical work under the CDPA for which she should claim a joint share. Following cases such as *Beckingham* and *Fisher*, Sarah is on solid legal standing to be named as a joint author of this work. The proportion of authorship awarded to her is likely to be like the share awarded to Matthew Fisher in *Fisher v Brooker*, where he was given a 40% share of the work for contributing the organ solo. However, as in *Fisher v Brooker*, the court is likely to say that because Sarah did not assert her rights at the time, she effectively gave an implied licence to Andrew Starr to use their joint work as he saw fit, and that this implied licence was only revoked once Sarah began her copyright claim in 2016. This means Sarah will not be entitled to claim back royalties from 2003, but that she will be entitled to claim royalties from 2016 onward.

End-of-chapter questions

After reading the chapter carefully, try answering the following questions. For answer guidance visit the online resources at **www.oup.com/uk/karapapa-mcdonagh/**

1. Consider the problem question at the start of this chapter. How would you advise Andrew about any future dealings he might have with 'session musicians'?

2. Is it a good idea that authors can assign—transfer—their economic rights in a copyright work to another party, e.g. a publisher or record company? Why might the negotiation over this be unbalanced (i.e. in the favour of the publisher or company)?

3. Is the duration of copyright in literary, artistic, dramatic, and musical works at the appropriate length? What about for sound recordings?

4. Consider the following examples:

   • A producer and director make a film together without a formal agreement on copyright—who owns the copyright in the film?

   • During the final recording session of a new pop song, a musician contributes a dramatic organ solo to the song, which was initially composed by another musician. The song goes on to be a hit. How can the authorship of the song and ownership of the copyright work be determined?

   • A popular novelist completes his final novel just before dying. His (unmarried) lifelong partner owns the laptop featuring the completed novel, but due to the rules of inheritance, the copyright in the work passes automatically to the estate of the author, i.e. his closest living relatives—his father and brother. Should the laptop owner (his life partner) be compelled to hand over the intangible work contained within the tangible laptop to the copyright owners (the estate)?

   • The duration of copyright in James Joyce's works expired in 2012. Does this mean that the works are in the public domain? What does this mean for new creators who wish to adapt Joyce's works?

Further reading

For understanding the authorship, joint authorship, ownership, and duration of copyright works, the following readings are highly recommended:

Chander, A. and Sunder, M. 'The Romance of the Public Domain' [2004] 92 *Cal. L. Rev.* 1334
Critical analysis of the public domain concept, focusing on resources and availability of public domain materials.

Cooper, E. 'Joint authorship and copyright in comparative perspective: the emergence of divergence in the UK and USA' [2015] 62 *Journal of the Copyright Society of the USA* 245
Looks at differences between the US and UK approaches to joint authorship.

Ginsburg, J. 'The Concept of Authorship in Comparative Copyright Law' [2002–2003] 52 *DePaul L. Rev.* 1063
Takes a comparative approach to the concept of authorship and ownership of copyright works.

Jaszi, P. 'Toward a Theory of Copyright: The Metamorphoses of "Authorship"' *Duke Law Journal* 455
A theoretical analysis of authorship, taking into account several different philosophical approaches.

McDonagh, L. 'Rearranging the Roles of the Performer and the Composer in the Music Industry— the Potential Significance of Fisher v Brooker' [2012] 1 *IPQ* 64–76
Considers the impact of the Fisher case on musical authorship and performance.

Ramalho, A., 'Will Robots Rule the (Artistic) World? A Proposed Model for the Legal Status of Creations by Artificial Intelligence Systems' [2017] 21 *Journal of Internet Law* 12–25
A cutting-edge analysis of the recent debate about AI creativity and copyright.

Infringement of copyright

4

Problem question

Read this problem question carefully and keep it in mind while you are working through the chapter that follows. At the end of this chapter, you will be able to apply what you have learnt to the problem question and advise the relevant parties.

Robert Williams is a visual artist. He has recently created a blog, where he keeps a diary of his work, including images of his drawings and paintings, and notes on his thoughts on art. Because the blog is meant to enhance visibility of Robert's work, there is no access control protocol.

Robert has recently found out that images of his artwork have been published in various websites and social media platforms, without his consent.

User Charlotte98 has published a folder on a publicly-accessible social media website, entitled 'Art I heart: R. Williams', where she includes a copy of practically every drawing and painting that Robert has ever posted on his blog. Charlotte98 also offers to print any of these images and to sell them on canvas for a suggested price on an e-commerce website.

A major search engine features thumbnails, i.e. small-sized copies, of Robert's work in its Images service.

Another artist and blogger, John Collins, casually places on his blog hyperlinked headings to other art websites, including Robert's posts. Recently, John took place in a collective art show where he exhibited a collage, which—among others—included a small piece of one of Roberts paintings, entitled 'Tree of life'; the piece used depicted one of the most characteristic elements of the painting, namely the colourful leaves of a tree painted in Robert's distinctive technique.

Robert comes to you for legal advice.

4.1 **Introduction**

In this chapter, we look at what the copyright holder can do to prevent others exploiting the work. In discussing the scope of protection accorded to the copyright owner, we reconsider the justifications for copyright and the idea/expression divide in relation to the statutory requirement that the defendant must have taken a substantial part of the claimant's work.

Because copyright protection does not depend on registration, there is no equivalent in copyright law of the counterclaim (usually raised in relation to registrable forms of intellectual property) to remove the right from the register. Instead, the existence of one or more of the key elements which must be satisfied before copyright arises may well be disputed by the defendant, so all the issues concerned with the subsistence of copyright must be kept in mind.

There are two types of copyright infringement within the Copyright, Designs and Patents Act 1988 ('CDPA'): primary infringement and secondary infringement. Primary infringement (s. 16) takes place when an individual carries out any of the following activities without the consent of the copyright holder:

- Copying the work
- Issuing copies of the works to the public
- Renting or lending the work to the public
- Performing, showing, or playing the work in public
- Communicating the work to the public
- Making an adaptation of the work or doing any of the above in relation to an adaptation

Sections 22–26 CDPA 1988 offer the legislative framework for secondary liability. Examples of this form of liability include:

- Importing infringing copies
- Possessing of or dealing with infringing copies
- Providing the opportunity for making infringing copies

It is usually retailers or publishers that may be found liable for secondary infringement.

In primary infringement, the defendants are directly involved in copying, performing, issuing to the public, etc. the copyright work, whereas secondary infringement involves people who deal with infringing copies, or facilitate such copying or other activities that are restricted by copyright. Besides this difference that has to do with the scope of rights, there is also difference on the mental element. Unlike primary infringement that does not require knowledge or intention to infringe on the part of the alleged infringer and is hence subject to strict liability, secondary infringement occurs where the defendant—during the commercial exploitation of copies or articles adapted to making copies—knew or had reason to believe that activities in question are wrongful. This is assessed on the basis of an objective test: what matters is what a reasonable person would have thought in the relevant circumstances.

Before discussing the specific aspects of primary and secondary infringement, and seeing how the relevant legal provisions could apply by reference to our scenario question, it is important to understand some important elements on the nature of copyright infringement.

4.2 Primary infringement

4.2.1 The difference between use and infringement

Copyright law draws a distinction between the right of property in a tangible object in which a copyright work is embodied, and the intangible right of property in the work itself (*Re Dickens* [1935] Ch 267). Copyright infringement entails taking the work without the consent of its owner, rather than any dealing with the physical object. The consequence is that the lawful owner of the physical item (whether acquired by gift or purchase) is free to deal with it as they wish, as long as a restricted act is not committed. Thus the recipient of a letter from a celebrity, being the owner by way of gift of the piece of paper on which the letter is written, may sell that letter at auction, but the purchaser will not be able to publish extracts of the letter in a newspaper without the consent of the copyright owner. The purchaser of a book of modern poetry can study the poems, but cannot read them aloud at a poetry evening held at a local village hall. A computer user can view material from the internet on screen but may not print or save it to disc. This is because the acts of publishing the letter (i.e. reproducing it in the newspaper and then selling copies of the paper), performing the poetry in public, or saving a file to disc are all restricted acts which the copyright owner alone is entitled to enjoy or license.

 Pause for reflection

Can you think how the activities referred to in the scenario question affect Robert's copyright and in particular the acts restricted by copyright as listed in s. 16?

The distinction between using the object embodying a work and taking the work itself has been eroded with the advent of digital technology. To give one example, with digital technology, every use of the work requires making copies, which is one of the restricted acts. For this reason, special exceptions to rights, otherwise called activities permitted by copyright, have been introduced in order to address the digital challenge, such as the exception available for temporary and transient copying. The means whereby a computer stores internet material in a temporary cache to enable it to be viewed falls within the defence of making temporary copies in s. 28A CDPA: *Public Relations Consultants Association Ltd v Newspaper Licensing Agency Ltd* [2013] RPC 469 at [31].

4.2.2 Copyright infringement as an interference with property

As a statutory tort, the commission of one or more of the primary acts of copyright infringement will give rise to strict liability. Copyright infringement is an interference with the right of property conferred on the copyright owner by s. 1 CDPA, and so the state of mind of the infringer is irrelevant. The claimant does not have to prove that the defendant knew that copyright existed in the source work, nor that what was done amounted to infringement. Conversely, where the defendant simply takes the underlying idea of the claimant's work rather than the work itself, the fact that he knew that he was doing so makes no difference and the claimant's action will still fail (*Baigent & Lee v Random House Group Ltd* [2007] FSR 579).

The principle that the infringer's state of mind is irrelevant is, however, qualified in three ways. Knowledge is crucial for liability for secondary infringement, and in relation to primary infringement, the innocence of the defendant that copyright existed (determined objectively) means that damages may not be awarded (s. 97(1) CDPA), although this does not affect the award of any other remedy. For certain acts of communication to the public, such as hyperlinking, knowledge of the infringement is also required (see Case C-160/15 *GS Media BV v Sanoma Media*, [48], [51]).

4.2.3 Copyright infringement need not be for profit

In contrast to patents, designs, and trade marks, copyright is the one form of intellectual property where there can be liability for infringement committed in the home, at least under current United Kingdom law. Contrary to popular belief, copyright infringement does not have to be committed in the course of trade (indeed, copyright infringement which is committed commercially attracts both civil and criminal liability). Private and domestic use is not a *general* defence to copyright infringement (though many argue that it should be), but some defences in the CDPA (for example, the so-called 'time-shift' defence in s. 70) do protect the copyist as long as certain conditions are met. The common reaction to the fact that copying a protected work in the home gives rise to liability is that such a law is unenforceable. Nevertheless, right owners (or industry associations representing their interests) are growing increasingly aggressive in their pursuit of home infringers (as an example, see *Polydor Ltd v Brown* [2005] EWHC 3191 (Ch)).

4.2.4 Arguments raised in a copyright infringement action

As with any action to enforce an intellectual property right, it is important to identify what the claimant's case can be.

The claimant will need to establish four things: first, that they are the owner or exclusive licensee of one or more rights in a 'work' entitled to copyright protection under United Kingdom law. The fragmentary nature of copyright should be remembered. Thus a 'complex' work such as a film or broadcast may contain a number of other works, each one of which will in turn consist of a collection of rights. Each of these rights can be dealt with separately, and indeed may have been the subject of a series of transactions (that is, assignment or licensing) in the past (as an example see *Governors of the Hospital for Sick Children v Walt Disney* [1966] 2 All ER 321). Presumptions set out in ss. 104 and 105 CDPA assist the claimant in establishing the right to sue, the net effect being to put the onus of proof on the defendant to show that the claimant is not entitled. By s. 101 CDPA, an exclusive licensee has the right to sue for infringement as if it were the owner of copyright.

The second item to be proved is that the defendant has committed one or more of the restricted acts of primary infringement listed in s. 16 CDPA, or else has authorized another to commit such an act.

Third, the claimant should show that the defendant's work has derived from the copyright work and there is a causal connection between the claimant's and defendant's works.

Finally, the claimant must demonstrate that the restricted act relates to the whole of the copyright work or a substantial part of it, although it does not matter whether the defendant took directly or indirectly from the claimant's work.

We examine these elements in detail below.

4.3 Acts restricted by copyright

The framework provision for primary infringement is s. 16 CDPA. According to this section, the copyright owner has the exclusive rights to:

- copy the work ('reproduction right')
- issue copies of the work to the public ('distribution right')
- rent or lend the work to the public
- perform, show, or play the work in public ('public performance right')
- communicate the work to the public ('communication right')
- make an adaptation of the work or do any of the above in relation to an adaptation ('adaptation right').

These exclusive economic rights allow the copyright owner to exploit the work in various ways. Their scope determines the activities that—if carried out without the consent of the copyright owner—amount to infringement of copyright. This means that anyone who carries out these activities, or who authorizes another to carry them out, is liable for primary infringement of copyright, unless they have received the permission of the copyright owner or can show that the activity is covered by one of the available defences.

 Pause for reflection

Keeping in mind the exclusive rights afforded to authors by virtue of the CDPA, go back to the scenario question and think of ways in which the various activities of Charlotte98, the search engine, and John Collins may have affected Robert's exclusive rights.

Since 1710, when the Statute of Anne offered authors protection only against copying, there has been steady expansion of the types of activity that fall within the control of the copyright holders. To a large extent this was the result of external pressures, such as the evolution of technology. For instance, the communication right was introduced to cover electronic transmission (such as radio or TV broadcasting) and later it was expanded to cover the making available of works on the internet. The bundle of rights granted to an owner has also grown in the light of the implementation of European Directives. The Information Society Directive harmonizes the right of reproduction, communication to the public, and distribution, and the scope of rights has been interpreted through the case law of the Court of Justice of the European Union ('CJEU'). Notably, however, two rights have not been harmonized at European level: the public performance right and the adaptation right.

The traditional understanding is that the acts restricted by copyright listed in ss. 16–20 are subject to the rules of strict liability. It is immaterial whether the defendant knew or had reason to believe that the work was protected by copyright. What matters is that the defendant carried out one of the acts restricted to copyright on the claimant's work. The practical implication of this is that the state of the mind of the defendant does not matter in determining liability for acts of so-called primary infringement. However, CJEU case law has had an impact on this traditional understanding, in particular with respect to the right of communication to the public. Certain acts of communication on the internet, such as linking to a work made available on another website, amount to infringement only if the defendant had knowledge of the infringement. As we will see later in this chapter, certain acts of communication to the public on the internet imply an assessment of the state of the mind of the defendant (see Case C-160/15 *GS Media BV v Sanoma Media*).

Each of the exclusive economic rights—otherwise referred to as acts restricted by copyright—receives individual treatment in the sections that follow.

4.3.1 Copying: s. 17

4.3.1.1 The meaning of 'copying'

This exclusive right, often referred to as the reproduction right, covers every description of copyright work, and includes the making of temporary copies or copies which are incidental to some other use of the work (subject to the defence in s. 28A). The right to copy is also called reproduction right because copying results in the creation of new copies of the work.

Section 17 deals with each category of work in turn. In relation to literary, dramatic, musical, and artistic works, 'copying' is defined in s. 17(2) to *mean* reproducing the work in any material form, including storing the work in any medium by electronic means. An additional form of copying in relation to artistic works only is provided by s. 17(3), which declares that copying *includes* the making of a three-dimensional version of a two-dimensional work and vice versa. So, for example, making a toy based on a cartoon drawing or taking a photograph of a sculpture or of a work of architecture would fall within the provision. Section 17(4) declares that copying in relation to a film or broadcast *includes* making a photograph of the whole or part of an image forming part of the film or broadcast (thereby confirming the earlier Court of Appeal decision in *Spelling Goldberg v BPC Publications Ltd*). Finally, s. 17(5) explains that copying a typographical arrangement *means* making a facsimile copy; in other words, the category of work covered by s. 8 CDPA will only be infringed by activities such as photocopying or scanning. There must be a facsimile copy of the whole published edition and nothing less will suffice: *per* Lord Hoffmann in *Newspaper Licensing Agency Ltd v Marks & Spencer plc* [2003] 1 AC 551 at [20].

What amounts to copying a work will be coloured by the statutory definition of the work itself. Whilst copyright in a literary, dramatic, musical, and artistic work will be infringed by its being reproduced in *any* material form, the definition of a sound recording (see s. 5A) as 'a recording of sounds from which sounds may be reproduced' means that, in order to infringe, the copy must itself reproduce sounds: in other words a sound recording would not be infringed by someone writing down the sounds on paper. Similarly, a film, being 'a recording from which a moving image may be reproduced' will only be infringed by something which reproduces the recording of the moving image. Copyright in a recipe is not infringed by making a cake (*J & S Davis v Wright* [1988] RPC 403).

Pause for reflection

Copying by reference to films and sound recordings appears to be subject to a narrower definition than the one used with regard to literary, dramatic, musical, and, artistic works. Writing extrajudicially, Arnold J has made a distinction between 'signal' and 'content' copyright (Arnold, R. 'Content Copyrights and Signal Copyrights: the Case for a Rational Scheme of Protection' [2011] 1 *QMJIP* 272). Films, sound recordings, and broadcasts are subject to 'signal' copyright: what is protected with regards to these kinds of work is not the content as such—e.g. the words, storyline, music—but the signal, namely the recording of images or sounds. Keep this distinction between content and signal copyright in mind as it will be useful in understanding copyright infringement in photographs, which we will be discussing in more detail later.

Copying can occur in several ways. The defendant may make an exact copy of the claimant's work, or may take only part of the work adding something of his or her own (in which case they will be both an infringer of what has been taken and the creator of the added matter), or may create a work which appears to be similar. However, one guiding principle is that the simpler the source work, the greater degree of copying is required. In *Kenrick v Lawrence* (1890) 25 QBD 99, a drawing of a hand explaining to voters how to vote was so simple that it could only be infringed by an exact copy. Likewise in *Guild v Eskandar Ltd* [2003] FSR 23, knitwear designs were held to be so basic that the defendant could escape liability by adding extra detail.

It is often stated that the right to copy is the core of copyright (see e.g. the Commission's Green Paper, 'Copyright and Related Rights in the Information Society', (1995) COM(95) 382 final, p. 49). It is considered to be the core because most of the infringing acts require copying. This assumption is challenged on the internet, however, to the extent that every act in relation to a copyright work involves the creation of copies, even mere cached copies in the computer's temporary memory.

On the internet, some copies of works are made for primarily functional purposes. An example concerns thumbnails, namely reduced-sized images that feature as results in search engines, museum websites, or other archives of artistic and photographic works. Although there have been no cases on thumbnails in the UK, Courts in Europe have found that copying such images and making them available online may amount to copyright infringement. However, there is a growing body of EU case law that exempts such activities from infringement on the basis of legal principles, such as the doctrine of implied consent. Indicatively, the German Supreme Court (Bundesgerichtshof) (*Vorschaubilder I*, 29 April 2010, I ZR 69/08, 14–15) ruled that a website owner who had not activated technological protection to block the automated indexing and displaying of online content by search engines had implicitly consented to the use of her works in an image search service. The US approach is more liberal in that thumbnails have been found permissible under the so-called fair use doctrine on the basis of the new function that they may appoint to the original artistic work and of the public interest objectives they may embody (indicatively: *Perfect 10 v Amazon.com*, 508 F 3d 1146, 15474; *Kelly v Arriba Soft Corporation*, 336 F 3d 811 (CA9 2003)).

Pause for reflection

The CDPA follows a technologically neutral approach on the construction of the concept of copying. With regards to literary, dramatic, artistic, and musical works, copying means 'reproducing the work in any material form' (s. 17(2)). Very similar is the stipulation of the Information Law Directive which covers copying by 'any means and in any form'. It is not clear however whether copying can also include instances where the work is transformed in some way and, if so, to what extent can a work be changed. English courts have been reluctant to accept that such transformative uses qualify as copying and have hence developed the criterion that the derived work has to be 'objectively similar' to the copyright work for the activity in question to amount to an act of copying (*Francis Day Hunter v Bron* [1963] Ch 587, 623). In order to infringe, the derived form has to be a representation of the original work in whole or in part. Otherwise the right of adaptation would cover such transformative uses. It is worth noting that the adaptation right has not been harmonized at the European level, with the exception of databases and computer programs.

Going back to the scenario, how many acts of copying with regards to Robert's work took place? How many acts of copying has Charlotte98 carried out? What about the thumbnail images? Can they qualify as reduced-size copies of Robert's works? What about the hyperlinked text? Does the link on its own qualify as copying? Why not?

4.3.1.2 Indirect copying

Section 16 CDPA provides for liability to be imposed whether the defendant takes from the claimant's work directly or indirectly. Examples of indirect copying include *Bernstein v Sydney Murray* [1981] RPC 303, where it was held that making garments which copied those sold by the claimant infringed the copyright in the claimant's drawings for those garments; and *Plix Products v Winstone* [1986] FSR 608 where the New Zealand Court of Appeal held that where the defendant had made containers in which Kiwi fruits could be transported by following the specifications and verbal instructions given by the New Zealand Kiwifruit Association, which in turn had based its standards on packaging designed by the claimant, the defendant had infringed the claimant's copyright drawings. In *Gabrin v Universal Music Operations Ltd* [2004] ECDR 18, Patten J held that the defendant recording company had infringed the claimant photographer's copyright when it had produced a CD cover based on a print which in turn had been based on the original photograph of Elvis Costello taken some 20 years earlier. In each

DIAGRAM 4.1 *Indirect copying*

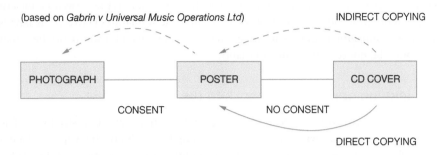

of these cases, the defendant copied the claimant's work *indirectly*, namely through intermediate instances, such as a copy or an illustration of the claimant's work.

Because of the importance of understanding the concept of indirect copying, we set out an illustration in Diagram 4.1 below. Whilst the illustration shows indirect copying only one step away from the original (as in the *Gabrin* case), there is no reason in principle (subject to the requirement of substantial taking) how many steps removed from the original work the indirect copy may be. An example could include the creation of drawings of a three-dimensional object, which was the result of someone else's drawings. There could be a case of indirect copying even where the person making the drawings had not seen the original drawings.

4.3.1.3 Subconscious copying

As liability for copyright infringement does not depend on the defendant's state of mind (*Baigent & Lee v Random House Group Ltd*), it is possible for a defendant to commit copyright infringement even though they are unaware that they are copying the claimant's work. Subconscious copying is an argument usually found in cases concerned with musical copyright, where the claimant will contend that the defendant must have heard the tune in question so that they became familiar with it and then unwittingly reproduced it later on. The allegation of subconscious copying failed in *Francis Day & Hunter v Bron*, where the court accepted that there was similarity but insufficient evidence of derivation. In *EMI Music Publishing v Papathanasiou* [1993] EMLR 306, Whitford J rejected the claim that the defendant (professionally known as Vangelis) had based his tune 'Chariots of Fire' on an earlier piece. The only similarity between the two tunes was one particular phrase, which was commonplace, and viewed overall the pieces were not alike.

Subconscious copying may also be invoked in cases involving copyright protected designs. In *John Kaldor Fabricmaker v Lee Ann Fashions* [2014] EWHC 3779 (IPEC), the claimant was a fabric designer who brought an action against a fashion company for copyright and design infringement. The defendant had received a brief from Marks & Spencer ('M&S') to pitch fabrics for use in M&S's Per Una clothing collection. The defendant approached the claimant, requesting it to produce some sample fabrics, one of which was the 'JK Fabric' design. The defendant chose not to use any of the claimant's designs and it instructed one of its own designers to design a fabric. In February 2013, the claimant became aware of a dress sold by M&S in its Per Una range made from a fabric, which had been supplied by the defendant. The defendant claimed that instead of specific instructions, she was given a general design brief. This claim was accepted by the High Court as there was no sufficient reason to rebut this evidence. The Court did not find the similarities between the fabrics sufficiently compelling to draw a strong inference of copying and it was hence held that the designer did not copy the claimant's fabric.

4.3.2 Issuing copies of the work to the public: s. 18

Section 18 CDPA covers two aspects of the copyright owner's right of distribution. The principal provision deals with the right to issue tangible copies of the work by placing them in circulation within the EEA, namely, in addition to the UK and the other 27 EU Member States, also Norway, Iceland, and Liechtenstein. Section 18A deals with the right to control the rental or lending of the work to the public. Whilst the former applies to all categories of work, the latter applies only to literary, dramatic, musical, and artistic works (other than works of architecture and a work of applied art), films, and sound recordings.

The principal provision, s. 18, has been amended twice since its original enactment. Both in its original and amended form, it creates a new type of restricted act, as explained by Sterling (in 'Copyright, Designs and Patents Act 1988: the New Issuing Right' [1989] 11(8) *EIPR* 283) and by Phillips & Bently (in 'Copyright Issues: the Mysteries of Section 18' [1999] *EIPR* 133). Previously there was liability for publishing a *work*. As explained by the House of Lords in *Infabrics v Jaytex Ltd* [1981] 1 All ER 1057, 'publishing' is a one-off occurrence—either a work is published or it is not. The consequence under the old law was that if a copyright owner wanted to object to dealings in further copies of the work which had not been approved, they had to establish liability for secondary infringement. The current situation is that there is liability for issuing *copies* of the work. Hence the copyright owner is given the ability to control the first sale of *each and every copy made*, a point confirmed by Laddie J in *Nelson v Rye & Cocteau Records* [1996] 2 All ER 186 at p. 208.

Consider as an example an author who licenses a publisher to print 2,000 copies of a book but states that only 1,000 copies are to be distributed. The first 1,000 copies are quickly sold out. The publisher then sells the remaining 1,000 without seeking the author's permission. Under the old law, the work would have been regarded as 'published' so that the author had no right to object to the distribution of additional copies. Under s. 18, this is infringement.

Reference to the origin of the wording in the Rental Rights Directive (now codified as Directive 2006/115/EC of the European Parliament and of the Council of 12 December 2006 [2006] OJ L 376/28) reveals that the section is meant to incorporate the doctrine of intra-EU exhaustion of rights, so that whilst the copyright owner cannot object to the issuing of copies which have previously been put in circulation within the EEA, they can object to the issuing of copies which have previously been put in circulation outside the EEA. It has been confirmed by the CJEU in Case C-479/04 *Laserdisken ApS v Kulturministeriet* [2006] ECR I-8089 that Member States no longer have a discretion to maintain any doctrine of international exhaustion of rights in relation to copyright. Further, the separate rental right in copyright (s. 18A) is a deliberate exception to the doctrine of exhaustion: Case C-61/97 *Egmont Films v Laserdisken* [1998] ECR I-5171.

The traditional justification for the exhaustion principle within the EU was one based on property law: copyright exhaustion marked the distinction between two distinct, yet colliding, forms of property: the intellectual property rights on the work and the right of ownership over the embodiment thereof, i.e. the tangible medium (copy, product). The common law doctrine on the alienation of property offers a normative justification for copyright exhaustion. In *Dickens v Hawksley* [1935] Ch 267, 274 CA it was explained that:

> The common law, therefore, had this conception with regard to rights of property in a literary work written, marked or impressed or otherwise recorded upon some material thing namely, that the material thing might, as a subject of property, be separated from the literary work recorded on it and that the literary work might be regarded as an incorporeal subject of property and be owned separately from the material thing upon which it was recorded.

Arguably a key aspect of the property justification for copyright exhaustion is the 'tangibility' of the medium in which the intellectual creation has been incorporated, which can be distributed in hand-to-hand transactions and qualify as an object of property (*see* Karapapa, S. 'Reconstructing copyright exhaustion in the online world' [2014] (4) *IPQ,* 304). The relevance of tangibility to exhaustion was discussed in Case C-419/13 *Art & Allposters International BV v Stichting Pictoright* (22 January 2015). Allposters used to market reproductions of famous paintings—inter alia—in the form of canvases. These canvas transfers were made by transferring an image from a paper poster of the work to a canvas through a chemical process. In this case, the CJEU held that exhaustion of the distribution right covers the tangible object incorporating a work. The practical consequence is that exhaustion of the distribution right does not apply in cases where a reproduction of a protected work that was marketed in the EEA with the copyright holder's consent has undergone an alteration of its medium and is placed on the market in the new form.

 Pause for reflection

It is not clear at the moment how the withdrawal of the United Kingdom from the European Union will impact on the exhaustion of the distribution right. European exhaustion is an expression of the fundamental freedom of movement of goods as protected by the Treaty on the Functioning of the European Union ('TFEU'). The exit of the United Kingdom from the European Union could have repercussions on rights that are effective in the whole Union, including copyright, but also EU trademarks, community designs, and European unitary patents. The operation of European exhaustion means that parallel importation is permitted within the EU single market, essentially allowing the resale of goods at lower prices.

If the United Kingdom leaves the European Union without negotiating its entry into the EEA, European exhaustion and the relevant provisions will stop applying in the United Kingdom. The practical implication will be that products that are already placed on the market in the EEA will no longer be freely imported in the United Kingdom, and the other way around, unless the rightholder authorizes this parallel importation.

In order to understand the meaning of 'issue to the public', subsection 18(3) CDPA 1988 indicates that when a copy is in circulation subsequent acts of 'distribution, sale, hiring or loan of copies' and/or importation do not infringe. Distribution does not include 'rental' or 'lending', which receive separate protection. *Peek & Cloppenburg v Cassina* [2008] ECR I-2731 clarified the broad scope of the concept of distribution, which according to Art. 4(1) of the Information Society Directive covers 'any form of distribution to the public by sale or otherwise', such as e.g. donation, endowment, or exchange. A German court asked the CJEU whether distribution 'by sale or otherwise' could cover display of copyright works in a warehouse and their use on the spot by customers. According to the CJEU, such a use was not found to qualify as an act of distribution as it did not entail transfer of ownership. The phrase 'or otherwise' only covers instances where ownership of the goods is transferred. Note however that in Case C-5/11 *Donner* (21 June 2012), the CJEU adopted a slightly broader definition of 'distribution', finding that this concept can include various acts such as agreement to sell, sale, entrance delivery (at [26]–[30]). Any of these activities can result in distribution.

The meaning of 'issue to the public' can be further exemplified by considering as an example the normal chain of distribution of a book (from author to publisher to wholesaler to retailer to purchasing public) illustrated by Diagram 4.2 below. Is (as Philips & Bently discuss) the issuing right concerned with the *disposition* of the copies (i.e. once copies of a book have been supplied to a wholesaler the right is exhausted), or is issuing concerned with the *destination* of the copies (i.e. the right is only exhausted once copies are purchased by *the public*)? The answer to the question makes a crucial difference to the position of the retailer and should be compared with the law as it stood under the 1956 Act decision of *Infabrics v Jaytex*. If the issuing right is spent once a copy of

DIAGRAM 4.2 *Section 18 CDPA*

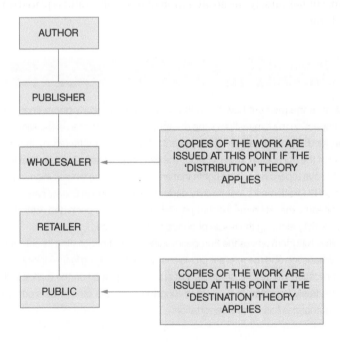

the work has been *disposed* of to the first person in the chain of distribution, then any person further down the chain can deal with that copy without restriction. However, if the issuing right is only spent once it reaches its destination (i.e. the public), then a retailer will be liable for infringing the issuing right. As yet there is no guidance on this point, but reference to the exhaustion of rights case law concerning trade marks suggests that the key fact is whether the first person acquiring the goods has the power of disposal of them: that is, they have legal title (Case C-16/03 *Peak Holding AB v Axolin-Elinor AB* [2004] ECR I-11313). By analogy, this points to the disposition theory. In view of the legislative origins of s. 18, the matter awaits resolution by the CJEU.

Pause for reflection

In our problem scenario, does Charlotte98 issue copies of Robert's work to the public by making copies on canvas? To what extent if at all does the exhaustion principle apply?

Pause for reflection

An interesting aspect of s. 18 is that it changes the relationship between primary and secondary infringement. In contrast to what was said on the old law in *Infabrics v Jaytex*, it is now possible for a retailer to be made liable for primary infringement. Thus, if an author has not given permission for particular copies of the work to be distributed, or if the copies in question were first marketed outside the EEA, then the person who supplies them in the United Kingdom has committed a restricted act. This point is controversial and there is a conflict between s. 18 and the definition of infringing copy for the purposes of secondary infringement in s. 27 (see later).

Do you think the distribution theory or the destination theory is the most appropriate interpretation of s. 18 CDPA? How is the concept of exhaustion of the distribution right likely to change in light of the withdrawal of the United Kingdom from the European Union?

4.3.3 Performing, showing, or playing the work in public: s. 19

Under s. 19, the performance of a literary, dramatic, or musical work in public is a restricted act, as is the playing or showing in public of a film, sound recording or broadcast. The performance right therefore does not apply to artistic works, a point which may surprise some of today's exponents of modern art, but which is entirely in keeping with the assumptions underlying the CDPA about the nature of creativity.

The public performance right has not been subject to European harmonization. An important aspect of the British public performance right is that it overlaps to a certain extent with the right of communicating works to the public as envisaged under the Information Society Directive 2001/29/EC. In particular, s. 19 CDPA 1988 contains a definition of 'performance', which includes the delivery of speeches and sermons, and 'any mode of acoustic and visual presentation'. An example of the overlap between the British public performance right and the EU right of communicating works to the public arose in *Football Association Premier League v QC Leisure*, Joined Cases C-403/08 and C-429/08 [2011] ECR I-9083. In this case, the CJEU held that showing the broadcast of a football match on a TV screen in a pub was an act of communicating works to the public. This activity however would very comfortably fall under the public performance right as described in the CDPA 1988. The CJEU also implicitly found in Case C-162/10 *Phonographic Performance (Ireland) Ltd v Ireland* [2012] 2 CMLR (29) 859, that the playing of sound recordings is an act of communication to the public. In Case C-283/10 *Circul Globus Circul Globus Bucureşti v UCMR—ADA* [2011] ECR I-12031, the CJEU clarified that playing live music before a circus audience was an act of public performance, instead of an act of communication to the public, and that because public performance has not been subject to harmonisation this was not a matter regulated under European law. The boundary between an act of public performance and an act of communication to the public remains unclear. We will examine below how the CJEU has elaborated on the concept of the public in the context of the right of communicating works to the public.

To understand the meaning of the term 'public' under domestic jurisprudence by reference to the right to perform, show, or play the work in public we need to refer to case law. The early decision in *Duck v Bates* (1884) 13 QBD 843 provided a relatively narrow interpretation of the phrase, so that a performance of a play by hospital staff for patients was held to be in private. Modern case law makes clear that what matters is the relationship between the spectator of the performance and the copyright holder, not the relationship between the spectator and the person providing the performance: *PRS v Harlequin Record Shops* [1979] 2 All ER 828. Anything outside the domestic sphere is 'in public'. As Greene LJ stated in *Jennings v Stephens* (at 485):

> [T]he expression 'in public' must be considered in relation to the owner of the copy-right. If the audience considered in relation to the owner of the copyright may properly be described as the owner's 'public' or part of his 'public', then in performing the work before that audience he would in my opinion be exercising the statutory right conferred upon him.

Hence, the staging of a play in a Women's Institute (*Jennings v Stephens* [1936] Ch 469), a concert in a private club (*PRS v Rangers Club* [1975] RPC 626), and the provision of background music in factories (*Ernest Turner v PRS* [1943] Ch 167) and shops (*South African Music Rights Organisation v Trust Butchers* [1978] 1 SA 1052) have all been held to be 'in public'. It does not matter whether the performance is live or by means of a recording or through a radio. Relevant factors include the relationship of the party initiating the performance to the audience and whether the audience was paying for the use.

4.3.3.1 The role of collective management organizations

Management of the performing right in music provides a useful illustration of the role of copyright collecting societies, although such organizations are found across the spectrum of copyright. We take as our example the Performing Right Society ('PRS'), founded in 1914 as a non-profit-making company limited by guarantee and part of a worldwide network of sister organizations, which collects royalties on behalf of its members, primarily composers, whenever their music is performed in public or communicated to the public. PRS is now part of an alliance with the Mechanical Copyright Protection Society ('MCPS') whose task is to grant licences for the recording and distribution of copyright music. The two organizations between them deal with all aspects of the recording, distribution, performing, and communication of copyright music in the United Kingdom.

The starting point is that a composer, songwriter, or music publisher, on becoming a member of PRS, assigns the performing and communication rights set out in ss. 19 and 20 CDPA to the Society (by contrast, MCPS does not take an assignment but acts as agent to collect royalties for the recording and distribution of recordings of copyright music under ss. 17 and 18 CDPA). In the case of copyright music which is performed in public (whether live or via a recording or by means of a radio or television broadcast), PRS grants a blanket licence to the controller of the premises where the performance occurs. In the case of the communication of copyright music, it grants a specific licence to the organization which is going to use the music in a radio or TV broadcast. In the blanket licence scheme, there are over 40 different tariffs depending on the nature of the business activity in which the music is used, ranging from cinemas to pubs to hairdressing salons to aircraft to ringtones for mobile phones. Premises are checked by inspectors to ensure that they have the appropriate licence. Failure to obtain a licence will result in PRS commencing proceedings against the owner of the premises for copyright infringement. Where music (whether live or recorded) is used in a broadcast, there is likewise a range of tariffs depending on how the music is going to be used, such as in radio and television advertisements, as background music for a play or documentary, as an ident for a particular radio station, or in hospital or student radio broadcasts. Resulting royalties are divided between the members, who number about 50,000. Disputes about licensing schemes are dealt with by the Copyright Tribunal under s. 149 and Sch. 6 CDPA.

Other copyright management societies include the Copyright Licensing Agency ('CLA') (which deals with the photocopying of literary, dramatic, and musical works), the Newspaper Licensing Agency ('NLA') (managing the rights of newspapers and periodicals over both tangible and intangible media), the Design and Artists Copyright Society ('DACS') (controlling the use of artistic works), and Phonographic Performance Ltd ('PPL') (which licenses the public performance of sound recordings). A business, such as a hairdresser, which uses CDs to play background music to its customers, will need both a PRS and PPL licence.

4.3.4 Communicating the work to the public: s. 20

Section 20 CDPA, amended as a result of Art. 3 of the Information Society Directive 2001/29/EC, provides for the copyright owner's right of communicating works to the public. The Directive in turn was influenced by the Copyright Treaty 1996 of the World Intellectual Property Organization ('WIPO'), which introduced right of communicating works to the public in international copyright.

In contrast to s. 18 which deals with distribution of the work by tangible means (i.e. physical copies), s. 20 is concerned with electronic, intangible means of distribution and therefore covers both broadcasting and the internet. Accordingly the right of communication to the public covers two distinct acts of electronic transmission, namely broadcasting the work (s. 20(2)(a)) and making the work available to the public in such a way that members of the public may access it from a place and at a time individually chosen by them (s. 20(2)(b)). Therefore, the right of communication to the public includes in fact two distinct rights: the broadcasting right and the 'making available' right. It applies to all categories of copyright works with the exception of typographical arrangements of published editions.

4.3.4.1 The meaning of communication to the public according to the CJEU and the concept of the 'new public'

The scope of the communication right has been clarified owing to a number of references that reached the CJEU. The scope of the right is understood to be fairly broad. In Case C-306/05 *Sociedad General de Autores y Editores España v Rafael Hoteles SA* [2006] ECR I-11519, the CJEU observed that, even though the Directive did not define 'communication to the public', the phrase should be given a wide interpretation so as to give broad protection to authors. Whilst installing television sets in hotel rooms was not an act of 'communication', using the sets to provide TV programmes to customers was. With regard to the meaning of 'the public', the CJEU said (at [40]) that what matters is that the transmission is to a public different from that targeted by the original act of communication, i.e. a new public. Similarly, in Cases C-403/08 and C-429/08 *Football Association Premier League Ltd and others* [2011] ECR I-9083, the CJEU said that 'communication to the public' requires the work to be transmitted to a new public, i.e. one not contemplated by the copyright owner at the time of the initial transmission. It did however make plain that the right of communicating works to the public is separate from the reproduction right, so that the defendant had infringed the communication right by screening football matches in her pub using a satellite decoder purchased in another EU State without the copyright owner's permission. However, the reproduction right had not been infringed because the copies of the broadcast stored in the decoder's cache were within the temporary copying defence, explained later.

The Court's emphasis on there being a new public means that s. 20 covers not just those who indulge in unlicensed file sharing activities (*Polydor Ltd v Brown* [2005] EWHC 3191, *Dramatico Entertainment Ltd v BSB Ltd* [2012] RPC 665) but also those whose service enables viewers to catch up on free-to-air programmes they may have missed (Case C-607/11 *ITV Broadcasting Ltd v TV Catchup Ltd*, 7 March 2013).

Perhaps the most controversial aspect of the right of communicating works to the public is hyperlinking, which was addressed in more than one instances by the Court of Justice. In Case C-466/12 *Nils Svensson and Others v Retriever Sverige AB*, the CJEU addressed the question whether hyperlinks constitute an act of communication to the public. According to the CJEU, there were two cumulative conditions that need to be met: first, there should be an act of communication; secondly, this communication should be addressed to a 'public' (at [16]). It is only two paragraphs, [19] and [20] in this case, addressing whether hyperlinks amount to an act of communication. Applying by analogy *Sociedad General de Autores y Editores España v Rafael Hoteles*, communication was defined to mean making works available 'to a public in such a way that the persons forming that public may access it, irrespective of whether they avail themselves of that opportunity' (at [19]). Without entering into a detailed analysis of the nature of the relevant rights, the CJEU assumed that hyperlinks amount to an act of communication and held that the retransmission of works should be addressed to a 'new public' to be infringing (at [24]). In *Svensson*:

> the public targeted by the initial communication consisted of all potential visitors to the site concerned, since, given that access to the works on that site was not subject to any restrictive measures, all internet users could therefore have free access to them (at [26]).

The practical consequence is that rightholders that do not block access to their websites through access restriction protocols are assumed to have offered free access of their content to a public comprised by 'all internet users'. It has been argued that this introduces an implied licence reasoning in the context of the right of communicating works to the public (Karapapa, S. 'The Requirement for a "New Public" in EU Copyright Law' [2017] *EL Rev* 63).

Pause for reflection

Much of the controversy surrounding *Svensson* has to do with the way in which the Court applied the 'new public' requirement. This has been said to introduce a 'waiver *erga omnes* (or at least, as to all members of the intended public)' that has: 'the unfounded and illegitimate effect of exhaustion of the communication to the public right or, rather, the scope of that right is *reduced* by the court from the outset' ((ALAI) Opinion on the criterion 'New Public', developed by the Court of Justice of the European Union (CJEU), put in the context of making available and communication to the public, adopted on 17 September 2014, 15–16). We have examined the legal principle of exhaustion by reference to the distribution right. The Information Society Directive 2001/29/EC clearly states in Art. 3(3) that exhaustion does not apply to electronic communications. In the online context exhaustion only applies to software by virtue of Case C-128/11 *Usedsoft GmbH v Oracle International Corp,* which is meant to introduce a *lex specialis*, applicable only to software. What is more, in the *FAPL* case (Joined Cases C-403/08 and C-429/08, 4 October 2011, ECLI:EU:C:2011:631), where a UK based pub owner had imported decoders from Greece, the Court of Justice did not uphold the AG's opinion according to which there was no difference between the sale of goods and the provision of services because restrictions on fundamental freedoms must, as a general rule, be justified by reference to the same principles (AG Opinion, ECLI:EU:C:2011:43, [183]).

Although bearing a similar effect, *Svensson* does not introduce exhaustion (see Karapapa, S. 'The Requirement for a "New Public" in EU Copyright Law' [2017] *EL Rev* 63) but it embraces an implied licence rationale similar to that upheld in German jurisprudence. According to the German doctrine of implied licence rightholders who fail to take positive steps to ensure that an activity remains prohibited are assumed to have given their implicit consent. The construal of the concept of the new public in *Svensson* follows a very similar reasoning.

Going back to the problem scenario, do the hyperlinks that John Collins posts on his blog qualify as an infringement of the communication right? What does *Svensson* instruct? Would your answer be different should Robert had introduced an access control mechanism in his blog?

Pause for reflection

It has been argued that hyperlinks do *not* amount to an act of communication, because they are meant to signpost an electronic address (European Copyright Society, Opinion on the Reference to the CJEU in Case C-466/12, *Svensson*, 15 February 2013 at [40]). Indeed, hyper-

→

→

links serve as location tools and in this regard they do not involve the transmission of content, which is an important element of the communication right according to the 2003 WIPO Guide. The concept of electronic transmission is also central in the way in which s. 20 CDPA 1988 is drafted.

As the European Parliament has acknowledged, 'the ability to freely link from one resource to another is one of the fundamental building blocks of the Internet' (European Parliament, Committee on Legal Affairs, Draft Report on the Implementation of Directive 2001/29/EC of the European Parliament and of the Council of 22 May 2001 on the harmonisation of certain aspects of copyright and related rights in the Information Society, 15 January 2015, 2014/2256(INI), point 15).

Should hyperlinks be subject to copyright protection, what do you think the impact will be on internet freedom? How are internet users likely to be affected?

4.3.5 Adaptation: s. 21

The restricted act of adaptation applies to literary, dramatic, and musical works only, and so is the one type of infringement which is not of general application. Further, the definition of 'adaptation' is much narrower than might be expected and will apply in very limited circumstances.

'Adaptation' is stated by s. 21(3) to mean, in relation to a literary or dramatic work, its translation, turning a play into a book and vice versa, or turning the work into a pictorial format suitable for newspapers and magazines (but *not* turning a story or play into pictures to be published as a *book*). In relation to musical works it means arranging or transcribing the work. There are separate provisions dealing with the adaptation and translation of computer programs and databases. The section further provides that an adaptation is made when it is recorded in writing or otherwise. Once so recorded, it is also infringement to copy the adaptation, issue copies, perform it, and communicate it to the public (s. 21(2) CDPA).

Section 21 concludes by declaring that no inference is to be drawn as to what does or does not amount to copying a work. The dividing line between copying and adaptation is therefore left unclear, but in view of the narrow scope of s. 21 and the breadth of s. 17, a claimant is more likely to allege that the defendant has committed altered copying rather than adaptation.

In our problem scenario, does John Collins carry out an unauthorized adaptation of Robert's work by including part of it in his collage?

4.3.6 Authorization: s. 16(2)

Copyright holders are also given the right to authorize others to carry out any of the re-stricted activities. Indeed, copyright infringement has a broader reach than other forms of intellectual property rights, in that it imposes liability for the conduct of others. Naturally, as a statutory tort, the normal rules of vicarious liability for an employee's conduct will apply (*PRS v Mitchell & Booker* [1924] 1 KB 762) and the opportunities for employees to commit infringing conduct (for example by photocopying literary works or by downloading material from the internet) are numerous. For that reason, any responsible business should have a clearly stated policy warning employees of the implications of such conduct.

The most significant aspect of being liable for the conduct of others is to be found in s. 16 CDPA. The section imposes liability should someone 'authorize' the commission of a restricted act, and according to *ABKCO Music v Music Collection International* [1995] RPC 657, there can be liability where the act of authorization is committed outside the United Kingdom as long as the restricted act (copying, issuing, performing, etc) occurs within the jurisdiction.

The limits of 'authorization' need to be understood. The term 'authorize' has been given its dictionary meaning of 'sanction, countenance or approve' in *Falcon v Famous Players Film Co* [1926] 2 KB 474, 491 (Bankes LJ). In the same case, Atkin LJ offered an alternative definition of 'authorize' as 'to grant or purport to grant a third person the right to do the act complained of, whether the intention is that the grantee shall do the act on his own account or only on account of the grantor' (at 499). In *Moorhouse v University of New South Wales* [1976] RPC 151 the High Court of Australia defined 'authorize' to mean 'sanction, countenance and approve' but added that authorization also occurred where there were acts of indifference from which permission to infringe could be inferred. The University was therefore held to have authorized its students to commit infringement by photocopying because of the absence of suitable warning notices in the library. The significant facts of the decision should be noted. It involved the provision of copyright materials as well as the equipment necessary to make the copies. In other cases, claimants have failed to establish liability for authorization because one or other of these key ingredients was absent. Thus in *CBS v Ames* [1981] 2 All ER 812, a record shop was held not to have authorized the copying of sound recordings when it had sold blank tapes and allowed its customers to hire the records. It had supplied the recording medium but not the recording equipment. In *Amstrad Consumer Electronics plc v British Phonographic Industry Ltd* [1986] FSR 159, the Court of Appeal held that to supply a double-headed cassette deck on its own was not enough to 'authorize', because the element of control over the users of such machines was lacking. Also, the manufacturer of the deck (which had sought a declaration that its advertisements for the machine were lawful) could not be said to have incited copyright infringement because the incitement was not directed to identifiable individuals, but to the public at large. However, the court added that the manufacturer's conduct might amount to 'inciting' the commission of a crime under what is now s. 107 CDPA.

This last remark led one of the record companies who belonged to BPI to attempt to obtain an injunction against Amstrad for persistent breaches of the criminal law in *CBS Songs Ltd v Amstrad Consumer Electronics plc* [1988] AC 1013. Amstrad used to manufacture and market double-deck cassette recorders which could be used for infringing purposes—copying cassettes without permission from the copyright holders. The House of Lords distinguished between 'facilitating' infringement and 'authorizing' it, adding that even if Amstrad had incited the commission of criminal conduct (which it had not because the advertisements were not directed at particular individuals), such criminal liability did not entitle record companies to obtain an injunction to restrain infringement under civil law. Lord Templeman (at p. 1060) thought the position was 'lamentable' because the record companies and their artists were powerless to stop the home taping of music. By selling the recorder, the defendants may have facilitated copying in breach of copyright without purporting to authorize it.

> ### Twentieth Century Fox Corp v Newzbin [2010] EWCH 608 (Ch)
>
> An important case on authorization for infringement is *Twentieth Century Fox Film Corp v Newzbin* [2010] EWHC 608 (Ch). A Usenet website, Newzbin, was found liable for infringement of copyright by authorizing copying of the claimants' films. The defendant owned and operated a website on Usenet that allowed users to upload and view messages on electronic bulletin boards. Third parties had uploaded films on Usenet without a licence from the relevant copyright holders. Newzbin employed a team of editors to ensure that all messages relating to a copy of a film (or other work) had been identified and put in an index. By so doing, Newzbin engaged in a deliberate course of conduct knowing that the vast majority of material was infringing and that its users carried out copyright infringement by making unauthorized downloads. Referring to *CBS Songs Ltd v Amstrad,* Kitchin J held that 'authorize' means the grant or purported grant of the right to do the act complained of, which could be express or implied from the relevant circumstances but it does not extend to mere enablement, assistance, or even encouragement.

One minor form of secondary liability for the conduct of another is to be found in s. 25(1) CDPA which deals with where a defendant permits a place of public entertainment to be used for a public performance. This should be understood in the context of the primary restricted act of performing a copyright work in public, and of the role of copyright collecting societies in licensing premises for the public performance of music and sound recordings, discussed later.

> **Pause for reflection**
>
> Do you agree with the House of Lords in *CBS v Amstrad* that the law of copyright is deficient if it does not assist the copyright owner to prevent the supply of equipment which facilitates copying? Is imposing a levy on such equipment the answer?

4.4 Objective similarity and derivation

The key feature of copyright infringement which distinguishes it from patents, trade marks, and registered designs is that the claimant must show that there is a causal link between the copyright work and the alleged infringement. Therefore, independent creation will always be a defence to copyright infringement (*Kleeneze Ltd v DRG Ltd* [1984] FSR 399). This particular feature of copyright protection enables the defendant to put forward a number of different explanations as to how the alleged infringement came to resemble the claimant's work. The fact that the two works are similar may be a matter of coincidence, or it may be that the defendant's work was first in point of time so that the claimant might be the copyist. Equally, both works might be derived from a common source (*Roberton v Lewis* (1960) [1976] RPC 169; *Warwick Films v Eisinger* [1969] 1 Ch 508). Lastly, the defendant may simply try to convince the court that their work was independently created, with no 'borrowing' from the claimant's work. However, where the defendant had the opportunity to copy the source work or is assumed by the court to have known of the claimant's creation, a court may well be reluctant to accept such an argument.

The requirement that the claimant's work must be the source of the alleged infringement was summed up by Diplock LJ (as he then was) in *Francis Day & Hunter v Bron* [1963] Ch 587, where he stated that in order for a claim of copyright infringement to succeed, there must be objective similarity and derivation.

4.4.1 Objective similarity

The requirement of objective similarity requires the court to compare the source work with the alleged infringement. The purpose of such a comparison is to enable the court to decide whether the similarities are more likely to be the result of 'copying rather than coincidence', taking into account whether the similarities are 'close, numerous and extensive' and disregarding similarities which consist of commonplace or unoriginal information, or general ideas (see Lord Millett in *Designers Guild Ltd v Russell Williams (Textiles) Ltd* [2000] 1 WLR 2416 at [39]). Such a comparison is carried out objectively and is of the work as a whole. Judges frequently warn against the dangers of making too detailed a comparison of minor elements, or of fragmenting the work into its constituent parts (*Baigent & Lee v Random House Group Ltd*, relying on *Ladbroke v William Hill* [1964] 1 WLR 273). Thus in *Francis Day & Hunter v Bron*, the Court of Appeal, when required to compare two popular songs, avoided a note-by-note analysis of the music but instead considered the overall impression the two works would have on the listener, in particular the first eight bars of each song. As a general point, strong similarities raise a strong inference of copying (*Forensic Telecommunications Services Ltd v Chief Constable of West Yorkshire* [2011] EWHC 2892 (Ch)).

The comparison may not only be of the expression used by the author of the source work, but also of that work's structure or 'architecture'. Hence, in *Corelli v Gray* (1913) 30 TLR 116, it was held that even though the language used by the claimant had not been copied, the taking of incidents and plots from the claimant's novel and turning them into a play amounted to infringement. Sargant J, at first instance ((1913) 29 TLR 570), emphasized that, whilst copyright is not a true monopoly because proof of independent creation is always a valid defence, it does prevent the misappropriation of the first author's skill, labour, and judgement. If the creator's efforts have been taken, it is no argument to say 'but I only took the concept'. However, protecting the structure or 'architecture' of a work in the name of preventing misappropriation of effort can at times come very close to protecting the underlying idea (*Baigent & Lee v Random House Group Ltd*).

4.4.2 Derivation: 'causal link'

Derivation means that there must be a causal link between the claimant's and defendant's works. The claimant's work must be the *source* of the infringement. The length of the causal chain does not matter, because s. 16 CDPA expressly protects against indirect taking, so that a copy of a copy of a copy of a copy of the source work will infringe.

Solar Thomson v Barton [1977] RPC 537

A good example of derivation is the Court of Appeal's decision in *Solar Thomson v Barton* [1977] RPC 537. The claimant was the patentee for a system of conveyor belts which included pulleys with special rubber linings. When the linings wore out, the defendant, who helped to maintain machinery of one of the claimant's customers, made his own replacement linings, and when threatened with copyright infringement (the claimant asserting copyright in the drawings for the machinery) sent a pulley to a third-party designer and asked them to design a replacement lining. The Court of Appeal held that because the instructions left the third-party designer little choice, the replacement created by the third party was an infringement of the claimant's copyright drawings. Although the case today would be decided under unregistered design law rather than the law of copyright, it is a useful illustration both of how long the causal chain of derivation can be, and of liability for indirect copying.

An example of direct rather than indirect derivation can be found in *LB (Plastics) v Swish Products* [1979] RPC 551. The claimant had designed a drawer system for self-assembly furniture. The House of Lords agreed with Whitford J that there had been infringement because the defendant had seen the claimant's drawings for the furniture. Tellingly, Lord Wilberforce remarked (at p. 619) that where, as here, there are 'striking similarities' between the two works together with an 'opportunity to copy', then a finding of copyright infringement is a logical conclusion.

In contrast, in *Purefoy Engineering v Sykes Boxall* (1955) 72 RPC 89, there was no derivation where rival manufacturers each produced a catalogue of their own range of machine tools. Neither had copied from the other and the similarity of the two catalogues was coincidence. In *Warwick Films v Eisinger*, a film script was held not to have been copied from the claimant's book about the trials of Oscar Wilde, as the defendant film company had relied on the original court transcripts as the source for the screenplay.

Michael Mitchell v British Broadcasting Corp [2011] EWPCC 42

In *Michael Mitchell v British Broadcasting Corp* [2011] EWPCC 42, Birss J held that '[t]he defendant's work must be causally connected to the work of the original author. If it is an independent work, then, though identical in every way, there is no infringement' (at [33]). This case concerned a group of cartoon characters, called 'Bounce Bunch', that Mr Mitchell created for use in animated television programmes for children. He submitted a proposal to the BBC including drawings of the characters, a synopsis, and a summary of the pilot episode but his proposal was not successful. About a year later, the BBC started broadcasting a children's programme, 'Kerwhizz', and according to Mr Mitchell, there was striking similarity between the human characters in Kerwhizz and those of the Bounce Bunch. As Birss J explained, in an action for infringement of artistic copyright, the court has to carry out a visual comparison

→

> →
>
> between the claimant's and the defendant's designs to assess whether the similarities are sufficiently close, numerous, and extensive to establish that they were the result of copying and not of a mere coincidence. As Birss J observed at [23], if the plaintiff demonstrates sufficient similarity, not in the works as a whole but in the features which he alleges have been copied, and establishes that the defendant had prior access to the copyright work, the burden passes to the defendant to satisfy the judge that, despite the similarities, they did not result from copying.

4.4.3 Derivation: the test

Of the two elements identified by Diplock LJ, it must always be remembered that copyright is essentially concerned with derivation rather than with overall similarity (*per* Lord Millett in *Designers Guild Ltd v Russell Williams (Textiles) Ltd* at [39–41]). One should avoid laying too much emphasis on overall similarity, otherwise there is the danger of treating copyright infringement as if it were passing off.

> *Designers Guild Ltd v Russell Williams (Textiles) Ltd* [2000] 1 WLR 2416
>
> Lord Millett explained the three-stage test for infringement, especially where there has been what is called 'altered copying'. The first step is the identification of those features of the defendant's work which the claimant alleges have been copied. The correct approach requires an overall comparison to be made. Next, if the claimant demonstrates similarities and shows that the defendant had the opportunity to copy, the burden of proof passes to the defendant to show that despite the similarities, these did not result from copying. Last, once it is established that the defendant's work incorporates features of the source work, it must be decided whether these features are a substantial part, assessed by reference to their importance to the source work, *not* their importance to the alleged infringement. Although Lord Millett was speaking in the context of artistic copyright (a design for curtain fabric), the test applies to any other category of copyright work where only part of the work is taken: *Baigent & Lee v Random House Group Ltd.*

4.5 The requirement of substantial taking

Section 16 CDPA, the 'umbrella' provision on primary infringement, states that the infringement may relate to the whole of the protected work or a substantial part of it. There are many cases which declare that what is 'substantial' is a matter of quality not quantity, so that the percentage of the claimant's work taken does not matter, the principal authority being *Ladbroke (Football) Ltd v William Hill (Football) Ltd.*

Substantiality depends on its importance in relation to the copyright work, and not the defendant's work (*Designers Guild Ltd v Russell Williams (Textiles) Ltd* [2001] FSR 11). The protection of skill and labour was declared by their Lordships in *Designers Guild* to be the overall purpose of copyright law.

> ### *Hyperion Records v Warner Music* (17 May 1991) (unreported)
>
> *Hyperion Records v Warner Music* (17 May 1991) (unreported) also stresses this point, namely that substantiality has to be assessed in relation to the copyright work. Hyperion Records, who owned copyright in a sound recording of the medieval chant, *O Euchari*, applied for a summary judgment, alleging that their copyright had been infringed when a band, The Beloved, copied eight notes from their sound recording and incorporated them into their music track, called *Happiness*. Although it was clear that *O Euchari* was a copyright work, Hyperion Records argued that those first eight notes were also a distinct work in their own right. Judge Laddie QC remarked that 'if the copyright owner is entitled to redefine his copyright work so as to match the size of the alleged infringement, there would never be a requirement for substantiality' (at 8). This case is important as it stresses that the part that has been taken is assessed in terms of its importance to the plaintiff's work, not the defendant's work. It is immaterial whether the part taken forms an unimportant part of the defendant's work, and it is also irrelevant whether the defendant expended independent skill, labour, and judgement. At the same times, it does not matter whether the defendant has repeatedly used part of the copyright-protected work, as is often the case in samples and remixes.

The test is ultimately a qualitative one, assessing the originality—and hence the protectability—of the portion taken in light of the so-called idea/expression dichotomy. In *Ravenscroft v Herbert* [1980] RPC 193, the plaintiff, who had written a non-fiction book entitled *The Spear of Destiny*, claimed infringement of his copyright by the defendant in his book of fiction called *The Spear*. The allegation was that the story spun by the defendant had depended heavily on the plaintiff's work. The defendant admitted using the plaintiff's book as a source of inspiration for his novel and the Court hence found for the plaintiff on the basis that the defendant had written the prologues using the same characters, incidents, and interpretation of events.

In *Baigent v Random House* [2006] EWHC 719, the High Court was called to determine a claim from authors of a work of 'historical conjecture' entitled *The Holy Blood* and *The Holy Grail*, that alleged that the central theme of their work was copied in Dan Brown's *Da Vinci Code*. Dismissing the claim, the High Court found that copyright did not protect ideas at such a high level of abstraction and that in any case the relevant themes were not a substantial part of the plaintiffs' work.

> ### *Temple island Collections Ltd v New English Teas Ltd & Nicholas John Houghton* [2012] EWPCC 1
>
> A recent important case concerns the photograph of a red Routemaster bus: *Temple Island Collections Ltd v New English Teas Ltd & Nicholas John Houghton* [2012] EWPCC 1. The claimant had taken the picture of a red bus travelling across Westminster Bridge with the Houses of Parliament; he then used Photoshop to enhance the visual contrast so that image
>
> →

would be in grey scale whereas the red colour of the bus would be depicted as bright as possible. The defendants did not copy the plaintiff's image but created a visually similar image through a collage of various pictures. Referring to a long line of authority, Birss J held that determining what a substantial part is involves a qualitative rather than a quantitative examination and has to take into account the elements of the work that have a visual significance. In artistic works in particular, what matters is the final output of the creative process and less so the skill and labour that has been invested in their creation. In the present case, despite the differences in the creative process, the visual similarity between the works was substantial and hence infringement was established.

Pause for reflection

Some commentators have criticized this decision. Andreas Rahmatian for instance ('Temple Island Collections v New English Teas: an Incorrect Decision based on the Right Law?' [2012] 34(11) *EIPR* 796) has argued that the decision has extended the copyright protection for photographs and their digital manipulation unsatisfactorily widely. In *Temple Island Collections*, Birss J stressed that the claimant's work should not be seen as a mere photograph, but as a 'photographic work' with some artistic element (at [66]).

Could the distinction between signal copyright and content copyright be relevant here? What do you think?

In order to determine whether a substantial part of a work was taken, it is first important to determine what is the work: to define its parameters; establish the death of protection; and distinguish the protected from the non-protected parts.

Pause for reflection

Going back to our problem scenario, is the part of Robert's painting that features in John Collins' collage a substantial part of that work? How is this to be assessed? To what extent is the *Temple Islands Collections* case relevant in this context?

4.5.1 Substantial taking: the test

How substantial taking is to be determined has been summarized as follows.

Baigent & Lee v Random House Group Ltd [2007] FSR 579

Mummery LJ in *Baigent & Lee v Random House Group Ltd* at [124] sets out the nature of the inquiry undertaken by the court in a copyright infringement action, an inquiry which, he says,

> →
> should be carried out chronologically. First, there should be an analysis of the similarities between the alleged infringement and the original copyright work, because unless similarities exist, there is no arguable case of copying. Second, it should be asked what access, direct or indirect, did the author of the alleged infringing work have to the source work, because unless there is evidence from which access can be proved or inferred, the crucial causal connection between the two cannot be established. Third, did the author of the alleged infringement make some use of material derived by him, directly or indirectly, from the original work? Fourth, if the defendant contends that no such use is made, what is his explanation for the existence of similarities between the two works? Fifth, if use was made of the source work, did this amount to a 'substantial part' of it? Finally, what factors support the conclusion that what has been taken is a 'substantial part' of the original?

Cases illustrating the 'traditional' United Kingdom view that substantial taking looks to quality rather than quantity include *Hawkes & Son v Paramount Film Services* [1934] Ch 593, where a 30-second extract from the Colonel Bogey march included in a news film of a public ceremony was held to infringe the music copyright; and *Spelling Goldberg v BPC Publications Ltd* [1981] RPC 280, where the use of one frame from one episode of the *Starsky & Hutch* television series to make a poster amounted to substantial taking. In both of these decisions, what was taken was the creator's expression, in contrast to *Norowzian v Arks Ltd* [2000] FSR 363, where arguably what was taken was not the copyright work (a film) but the technique (jump cutting) used to create the expression.

The general rule is that in order to distinguish between the protected parts from the non-protected part of a work the idea/expression dichotomy plays a central role. Non-original and/or public domain parts are not protected, and the same applies to the underpinning ideas as such. Non-literal elements however do receive protection. In *Designers Guild Ltd v Russell Williams (Textiles) Ltd*, Lord Hoffmann held that copyright subsists in the literary, artistic, or other authorial aspects of a work, to the extent that these meet the protection requirements. This means that the ideas underpinning a work, e.g. the characters or plot of a novel, are parts of what confers originality to the work and part of what is protected against infringement.

For certain categories of works such as computer programs and databases, however, it is important to draw the line between ideas and expressions, particularly because alternative forms of protection for the non-authorial aspects of such works are available (including, for example, patent protection for technical aspects of computer programs and the sui generis database right for non-original databases).

In *SAS Institute Inc v World Programming Ltd* [2013] RPC 421, Arnold J, in applying the ruling of the CJEU (Case C-406/10, [2012] RPC 933), assumed that *Infopaq* (which we extensively discussed in chapter 2 on subsistence) was the right test, so that in order to infringe, the defendant must reproduce something which amounts to the intellectual expression of the author. Consequently, copying the language in which a computer program was written did not infringe (subsequently confirmed [2013] EWCA Civ 1482).

Pause for reflection

As Spence and Endicott remark (in 'Vagueness in the Scope of Copyright' (2005) 121 *LQR* 657) even the House of Lords in *Designers Guild Ltd v Russell Williams (Textiles) Ltd* barely addresses the issue of substantiality, although Lords Hoffmann and Scott do state that what has to be considered, when deciding whether a substantial part of the claimant's work has been copied, is whether the infringer has taken the 'skill and labour' of the original author.

Spence and Endicott further argue that by not defining 'substantial' with greater precision, and by running together the issue of whether there has been copying with whether that copy is a substantial part of the original work, the House of Lords in *Designers Guild* comes close to saying that 'what is worth copying is worth protecting'. The thinking in *Designers Guild* also makes it harder to identify the dividing line between an idea and its expression, a fundamental issue of copyright set out in Art. 9(2) of the TRIPs Agreement. Lastly, the impact of the CJEU's ruling in Case C-5/08 *Infopaq International A/S v Danske Dagblades Forening* [2009] ECR I-6569 on the meaning of 'originality' may require a re-evaluation of 'substantial taking'.

In relation to the requirement of substantial taking, would it be desirable or possible to have clear judicial guidance on what is the 'substance' of a work? Would greater reliance on the justifications for copyright protection assist? What do you think?

4.6 Secondary infringement of copyright

4.6.1 Acts of secondary infringement

Liability for secondary infringement of copyright occurs when the defendant undertakes commercial dealings in infringing copies. The relevant conduct is set out in ss. 22 and 23 CDPA. It comprises, in summary, importing (except for private and domestic use), possessing, selling, letting or hiring, offering for sale or hire, exhibiting in public, and distributing. 'Commercial dealings' is not limited to those who trade in goods, so that in *Pensher Security Door Co Ltd v Sunderland City Council* [2000] RPC 249 a local authority was held liable for the installation of security doors in a council-owned block of flats when the doors infringed the claimant's design. The sections are therefore concerned with tangible copies only.

Sections 22 and 23 are subject to two preconditions which must be satisfied before the defendant can be held to have infringed. These are the requirement of knowledge, and the fact that the defendant must have been dealing in infringing copies.

4.6.2 The requirement of knowledge

Both of the previously mentioned provisions are qualified by the phrase 'which he knows or has reason to believe'. This imposes an objective standard, so that the defendant is to be judged by a reasonable person in that line of business: *LA Gear v Hi-Tec Sports plc* [1992] FSR 121; *Vermaat v Boncrest Ltd (No. 2)* [2002] FSR 331. To ensure that a retailer is fixed with notice that they are dealing in suspect goods, the copyright owner can write, and the retailer is deemed to have the requisite knowledge 21 days after the date of the letter, as 21 days is a sufficient period of time for the defendant to make the necessary inquiries and to obtain legal advice: *Monsoon Ltd v India Imports of Rhode Island* [1993] FSR 486. To continue trading in the counterfeit goods after that will risk the award of additional damages for flagrant infringement under s. 97 CDPA.

4.6.3 The definition of 'infringing copy'

The second requirement is that the defendant must have been dealing with infringing copies of the claimant's work. This may seem self-evident. However, the definition of 'infringing copy', set out in s. 27 CDPA, is problematic in a number of ways:

- it fails to take into account the impact of s. 18 which creates the distribution right;
- it is in conflict with the case law of the CJEU with regard to international exhaustion of rights; and
- the actual wording of the section gives rise to practical uncertainties.

 Pause for reflection

Do the copies of Robert's work that Charlotte98 sells on printed canvases qualify as infringing copies?

4.6.3.1 The wording of s. 27

Section 27(2) declares that an article is an infringing copy if its making constituted an infringement. This means that where a work is copied by a counterfeiter (whether in the United Kingdom or any other country adhering to the Berne Convention or the World Trade Organization ('WTO')) the articles in question (for example, CDs or DVDs) will be infringing copies. Any person who subsequently deals in such copies, provided they have the requisite knowledge, will commit secondary infringement.

The real difficulty lies in the wording of s. 27(3) which reproduces (though with alterations) similar provisions in the 1956 Act. It states that an article is also an infringing copy if it has been or is proposed to be imported into the United Kingdom and its making in the United Kingdom would have constituted an infringement of the copyright or a breach of an exclusive licence. This wording contains an artificial assumption, namely that had the imported article (made elsewhere) been made in the United Kingdom, its manufacture 'would have constituted an infringement'. Section 27(5) contains an exception to s. 27(3) for those instances where the CJEU's case law on intra-EU exhaustion of rights applies.

4.6.3.2 The interpretation of the section

So how has the assumption (or hypothesis) in s. 27(3) been interpreted? There are two interpretative approaches. First, the court could assume that the articles were made in the United Kingdom by the person who *actually* made them in the country of export, which requires only one hypothesis, namely as to the place of the manufacture of the goods. Second, the court could assume that the articles were made in the United Kingdom by the person who imported them into the United Kingdom. This requires the making of two hypothetical assumptions, one as regards the identity of the maker and the other as regards the place of manufacture.

CBS Ltd v Charmdale [1980] 2 All ER 807

The first interpretation was that adopted by Browne-Wilkinson J (as he then was) in *CBS Ltd v Charmdale* [1980] 2 All ER 807. Here the defendant had imported copies of sound recordings into the United Kingdom and was sued for secondary infringement by the subsidiary company (who was an exclusive licensee) of the copyright owner, CBS Inc. The records had been made in the USA by the parent company. Browne-Wilkinson J decided that the wording of the 1956 Act required the court to make but one hypothesis. Here the goods had been made by the copyright owner. Had that person made them in the United Kingdom rather than in the USA, they would not have been infringing copies. The defendant was not liable.

The second interpretation was applied by the New Zealand High Court in *Barson v Gilbert* [1985] FSR 489, the relevant New Zealand legislation being identical in substance to the 1956 Act. The justification for making a double hypothesis was that to hold otherwise would undermine the position of the exclusive licensee in New Zealand, who would be exposed to price competition from parallel imports.

The net effect of the two alternatives is that the *Charmdale* interpretation creates a doctrine of international exhaustion of rights (which renders s. 27(5) redundant) because it is assumed that the actual maker of the goods made them in the United Kingdom. Articles obtained indirectly from the copyright owner can never amount to infringing copies. The *Barson v Gilbert* solution enables the copyright owner to keep parallel imports out of the United Kingdom unless the articles have originated in the European Economic Area ('EEA'), in which case s. 27(5) will apply to provide the importer with the defence of intra-EU exhaustion of rights.

 Pause for reflection

The inclusion of s. 27(3) as an alternative definition of 'infringing copy' to that found in s. 27(2) is erroneous (it must be emphasized that s. 27(2) is entirely acceptable). Why did Parliament see fit to base the provision on sections found in the 1956 Act even though s. 18 CDPA created the distribution right, which as we explained earlier, has built into it the EU policy that there should be no international exhaustion of rights? Further, Parliament added an alternative within s. 27(3) itself, so that the imported article can either infringe copyright or breach an exclusive licence. This means that there may or may not be international exhaustion of rights, depending on whether the copyright owner has appointed an exclusive licensee for the United Kingdom. Unlike patents and trade marks, there is no means for a third party to find out whether an exclusive licensee has been appointed, as there is no register to consult. Is it logical to have the

→

> *Charmdale* rule applying where there is no licensee and *Barson v Gilbert* applying where there is? In any event, as the CJEU has stated in Case C-479/04 *Laserdisken ApS v Kulturminis-teriet*, Member States no longer have any discretion to maintain a policy of international exhaustion of rights in copyright. The presence or absence of an exclusive licensee is therefore irrelevant to the ability of the copyright owner to prevent non-EEA parallel imports.

 Pause for reflection

Is Charlotte98 committing secondary infringement by reference to Robert's work?

4.7 Conclusion

In this chapter, we have discussed the statutory provisions which deal with primary and secondary infringement. We have seen what the differences between these two kinds of infringement are and what kinds of activities fall under their scope. We have also examined the scope that is afforded to the exclusive rights under copyright and the nature of copyright infringement as a statutory tort. We have also explained the test for determining copyright infringement, namely the conditions that courts consider when assessing whether a particular activity amounts to infringement or not. This assessment involves defining the parameters of the work, distinguishing protected from non-protected elements, and identifying whether the part that has been taken is a substantial part thereof.

Going back to our problem scenario, Robert should be advised on each of the activities in turn. There is a strong inference of copyright infringement with regards to the activities of Charlotte98. Her account on a publicly-accessible social media website contains verbatim copies of every artistic piece that Robert has posted on his blog and this amounts to an act of reproduction (s. 17) and a substantial taking of Robert's work (*Baigent v Random House Group; Designers Guild Ltd v Russell Williams Ltd; ITV v TV Catchup Ltd; Ladbroke (Football) v William Hill; Ravenscroft v Herbert*). She is also offering the artwork for sale through an e-commerce website, this amounting to unauthorized commercial dealing with infringing copies (s. 23) and hence an act of secondary infringement (Charlotte98 may also be liable for primary infringement if she prints the artwork on canvas herself). There is a knowledge requirement for secondary infringement, which means that Charlotte98 should know or have reason to know that she is dealing with infringing copies and this is subject to an objective standard, namely that of a reasonable person in that line of business (*LA Gear v Hi-Tec Sports plc*). Robert should be advised to write to Charlotte98 and ask her to stop selling his work, as it will be deemed that she will have requisite knowledge 21 days after the date of the letter (*Monsoon Ltd v India Imports of Rhode Island*). To continue trading in the counterfeit goods after that will risk the award of additional damages for flagrant infringement under s. 97 CDPA.

With regard to the thumbnails, Robert should be advised that prima facie this activity amounts to an infringement of the reproduction right. Although there have not been any relevant cases discussed in the UK, Robert should be advised that there is a growing body of EU case law that exempts thumbnails from infringement on the basis of the implicit licence principle (e.g. German Supreme Court, *Vorschaubilder I*) and that he can apply technological protection on his website to block search engines from indexing and displaying his pictures.

As regards the hyperlinks that John Collins places on his blog, Robert should be advised that according to the case law of the CJEU hyperlinks are said to amount to an act of communication to the public (s. 20, *Nils Svensson and Others v Retriever Sverige AB*). According to the same case law, it is when such a communication is addressed to a 'new public' (also see e.g. *ITV Broadcasting Ltd v TV Catchup Ltd*) that there is infringement of the right of communication to the public and because Robert did not have an access control protocol to his blog this requirement would not be met. *Svensson* instructs that rightholders that do not block access to their websites through such protocols are assumed to have offered free access of their content to a public comprised by 'all Internet users'.

As for the use of Robert's painting in John's collage, it is important to assess this taking under the spectrum of the test for copyright infringement. John's collage at least in part derives from Robert's artwork and this part will likely be considered substantial. It should be explained that substantiality depends much more on the quality than on the quantity of what has been taken (*Ladbroke v William Hill*) and that it is assessed on the basis of its importance to the copyright work, i.e. Robert's work (*Designers Guild v Russell Williams*). The part taken is the most characteristic and visually significant part of Robert's work (see also *Temple Island Collections Ltd v New English Teas*) and there is hence a strong case of copyright infringement.

End-of-chapter questions

After reading the chapter carefully, try answering the following questions. For answer guidance visit the online resources at **www.oup.com/uk/karapapa-mcdonagh/**

1. Which new restricted acts have been introduced to address the internet challenge?

2. What is the test for copyright infringement? In which way does the idea/expression dichotomy play an important role in understanding whether infringement took place?

3. What is the meaning of the concept of the new public in the context of the right of communicating works to the public? Which are the key cases of the Court of Justice of the European Union that have developed this concept, which defines the scope of the right? What is the likely impact of this new test on the scope of copyright protection?

4. The exhaustion principle is the legal basis upon which protected works can lawfully be resold. To what extent, if at all, can this principle cover the electronic dissemination of digital copies?

Further reading

For understanding the scope of acts restricted by copyright and therefore this scope of copyright infringement, the following readings are recommended:

Arnold, R. 'Content Copyrights and Signal Copyrights: the Case for a Rational Scheme of Protection' [2011] 1 *QMJIP* 272

Develops insights on the distinction between content copyright and signal copyright. You can read this article keeping in mind the Temple Island Collections *case.*

Chacksfield, M. 'The Hedgehog and the Fox, a Substantial Part of the Law of Copyright?' [2001] 23(5) *EIPR* 259

Offers a discussion on the test for determining copyright infringement in the UK.

Ginsburg, J. 'The (new?) Right of Making Available to the Public', in D. Vaver and L. Bently (eds) *Intellectual Property in the New Millennium* (Cambridge University Press, 2004)

Considers the legislative history of the right of communication of works to the public in the context of its international dimension.

Karapapa, S. 'Reconstructing copyright exhaustion in the online world' [2014] (4) *IPQ*, 304

Discusses the normative impediments towards 'digital' exhaustion.

Karapapa, S. 'The Requirement for a "New Public" in EU Copyright Law' [2017] 1 *EL Rev* 63

Offers an overview of the doctrinal development of the requirement of the 'new public' by reference to the right of communication to the public.

Rahmatian, A. 'Temple Island Collections v New English Teas: an Incorrect Decision based on the Right Law?' [2012] 34(11) *EIPR* 796

Offers a critical account on the 'Red Bus' case and reflects more broadly on the test for copyright infringement.

Spence, M. and Endicott, T. 'Vagueness in the Scope of Copyright' (2005) 121 *LQR* 657

Examines the seminal case of Designers Guild v Russell Williams Textiles *and considers whether it is desirable that key issues, such as substantial taking, should be left vague.*

Sterling, J.A.L. 'Copyright, Designs and Patents Act 1988: the New Issuing Right' [1989] 11(8) *EIPR* 283

Explains the differences between the former restricted act of 'publishing' a work and the issuing right in s. 18 CDPA.

Stokes, S. 'Copyright and the Reproduction of Artistic Works' [2003] 25 *EIPR* 486

Offers a critical account on the Theberge v Galerie d'Art du Petit Champlain Inc *case.*

Defences

5

Problem question

Read this problem question carefully and keep it in mind while you are working through the chapter that follows. At the end of this chapter, you will be able to apply what you have learnt to the problem question and advise the relevant parties.

Philip Stamos is a junior journalist, who recently got a job at a monthly magazine, *Cinema*. His first job is to report on the story of a famous actress, Brigitte James, who died in a car crash 15 years ago. In his story, he quotes an extensive passage from the book of Alex Gordon, the author of Brigitte's biography. As a big fan of Brigitte, Philip is quite critical on that passage which comments on the dubious acting talent of Brigitte. In the article, he also includes images of Brigitte taken by various photographers, and in all instances he cites their names or the name of the photo agency on the photographs.

Matthew Owen, a university professor of film studies, asks Philip to teach a pro bono class on the life and contribution of Brigitte James to cinema. Philip prepares his slides using the photographs he has used for his newspaper article, without citing the names of the photographers, as they could not fit well in the slides. He has also added a short video of about eight seconds featuring one of Brigitte's famous cinema scenes and he plays the video during his class before Matthew's students.

While doing his research in order to write the article, Philip makes a copy of a TV-broadcasted documentary on actresses from the 60s to watch when he finds some time off of work.

Georgina Nicholson, Philip's girlfriend, recently took a 'mooc' class on intellectual property and has alerted Philip that he may face legal liability in case he uses copyright material without seeking authorization from copyright holders. Philip seeks your legal advice on whether the use of copyright materials in his article and slides is legally permitted or whether he should clear licences from the various rightholders. He is also unsure on whether he is breaking the law by having made a copy of the TV documentary. Advise Philip.

5.1 **Introduction**

Defences against copyright infringement usually take the form of the so-called exceptions and limitations to copyright, which are meant to enhance and maintain a balance of interests between copyright holders and users. Exceptions allow individuals to carry out an exclusive act in relation to a copyright work, without asking authorization from the copyright holder and without having to pay remuneration. Limitations on the other hand allow individuals to carry out an exclusive act in relation to a copyright work in return for paying remuneration to the copyright holder.

Copyright exceptions and limitations are available for a number of reasons. These may reflect the need to protect fundamental human rights, such as the freedom of speech or freedom of press. Examples of such permitted uses include, for instance, parody and news reporting. There are also exceptions available for public policy reasons, such as those available for educational establishments, libraries, and archives.

We will go through the relevant statutory and non-statutory defences to infringement, keeping in mind the scenario question and the way in which Philip's activities may be permitted by copyright or not.

5.2 **Overview**

Discussion of the defences to copyright infringement immediately presents three challenges. First, the defences are numerous: there are now well over 50 to be found in the Copyright, Designs and Patents Act 1988 ('CDPA'), in addition to those available at common law, the list having been added to as a result of the Hargreaves Report. Second, the statutory defences are all fact-specific: by this we mean that they are only available to a defendant if the infringing conduct has occurred in a particular factual scenario. If the defendant's conduct does not fall within the parameters set out in the relevant section, the defence is not available. So, for example, prior to the Hargreaves' amendments, there was the defence of dealing with a work for the purposes of criticism or review in s. 30(1) CDPA (now replaced with the defence of quotation). Although the words 'criticism' and 'review' were not to be interpreted too narrowly (*Pro Sieben Media AG v Carlton UK Television Ltd* [1999] 1 WLR 605), they did not cover taking the claimant's work for the purposes of a comparative advertisement which alleged that the defendant's magazine was better than the claimant's as this was not 'criticism or review' of the work (*IPC Media Ltd v News Group Newspapers Ltd* [2005] FSR 752). Finally, each of the statutory defences is hedged about with restrictions and conditions. Some defences apply to all categories of copyright work, but many apply only to some. Some defences require due acknowledgement to be made, others do not. Attention to detail becomes paramount.

At the international level, the protection of exceptions and limitations takes the form of a general test that legislators should apply each and every time they are about to introduce permitted uses under national law. Both the Berne Convention Art. 9(2) and the WIPO Copyright Treaty 1996 Art. 10(1) provide for what is commonly referred to as the 'three-step test', namely that any limitations or exceptions to the rights of authors (1) should be confined to certain special cases which (2) do not conflict with a normal exploitation of the work and which (3) do not unreasonably prejudice the legitimate interests of the author.

At the EU level, Art. 5 of the Information Society Directive (2001/29/EC) contains a long list of available exceptions and limitations, which have not been mandatory for Member States to implement and hence harmonization in this area of copyright law has remained minimal. The scope of the available exceptions and limitations is significantly narrow, covering only few, specifically defined activities. What is more, exceptions and limitations should be subject to strict interpretation according to EU copyright (Case C-435/12, *ACI Adam and Others* (2014), [23]; Case C-5/08, *Infopaq* [2009] ECR I-06569, [56]), although more recently the Court of Justice seems to have departed from the doctrine of strict interpretation of exceptions and limitations where fundamental rights such as freedom of expression are involved (see Case C-201/13 *Johan Deckmyn and Another v Helena Vandersteen and Others*, ECLI:EU:C:2014:2132, [22]; for a comment see Geiger, C. et al., 'Limitations and exceptions as key elements of the legal framework for copyright in the European Union, Opinion of the European Copyright Society on The Judgment of the CJEU in Case C- 201/13 Deckmyn' (2015) 46(1) *IIC* 93–101). This has an impact on user freedom as the permitted uses are very specific and their scope is narrowly framed.

The United Kingdom has revised its list of available exceptions and limitations twice after the enactment of the Information Society Directive 2001/29/EC: in 2003 in light of the implementation of the Directive and in 2014 following the so-called Hargreaves Review of intellectual property and growth. The framework of copyright exceptions and limitations in the UK is particular as it includes a sui generis form of copyright defence alongside the various exceptions and limitations: fair dealing. Fair dealing allows certain uses to be carried out for the purposes of non-commercial research or study, criticism, or review, or for the reporting of current events. In the 2014 copyright reform, the UK introduced new exceptions for parody and data analysis and enlarged the scope of fair dealing, educational exceptions, and library privileges. What is more, as a result of the 2014 copyright reform certain exceptions cannot be overriden by contractual terms and conditions.

Laddie J in *Pro Sieben* stated that 'Chapter III of the Act consists of a collection of provisions which define with extraordinary precision and rigidity the ambit of various exceptions to copyright protection. Although it is apparent that these provisions are designed to address situations where there are thought to be public policy grounds for restricting the copyright owner's rights, it is the legislature which has specified where and the extent to which the public policy overrides the copyright' ([1997] EMLR 509, 516). The specificity of UK legislation should be contrasted with the approaches of other jurisdictions, such as the 'fair use' defence in §107 of the US Copyright Act. Fair use is a test for judicial application comprising four non-exclusive statutory factors, i.e. (1) the purpose and character of the use, including whether such use is of a commercial nature or is for nonprofit educational purposes; (2) the nature of the copyright-protected work; (3) the amount and substantiality of the portion used in relation to the copyright-protected work as a whole; and (4) the effect of the use upon the potential market for or value of the copyright-protected work.

 Pause for reflection

Various scholars have positively commented on the flexibility that such a judicial test allows judges, as opposed to the very detailed provisions available under UK and EU copyright law

➡

→

(see e.g. Hugenholtz P.B. and Sentfleben M., 'Fair Use in Europe: In Search of Flexibilities', November 2011, available at http://www.ivir.nl/publicaties/download/912). Indeed, even though there is a long list of available exceptions enumerated in the respective provisions of EU and UK copyright, their respective scope is significantly narrow, covering only a few, specifically defined instances. Because of the lack of a flexible framework, like the US fair use test, legal uncertainty remains as to the lawfulness and legality of many activities emerging as a result of technological advancement. This is particularly so in light of digitization and the internet which have altered the ways in which copyright works are used. For instance, distance-learning methods may require transmission of copyright works in ways that traditional copyright exceptions are too limited to cover. Similarly, libraries and archives can make copies for preservation purposes, but this privilege cannot safely cover displaying these copies in their dedicated electronic premises. Many online services, such as media monitoring and meta-search engines, operate on the basis of routine extraction and copying of material that may be copyright protected.

The way in which defences to copyright infringement are drafted has an impact on the balance of rights of copyright holders and end-users. Indeed, exceptions and limitations represent a balancing act between copyright and other entitlements or objectives, such as fundamental freedoms or public policy concerns, including freedom of speech or the protection against unfair competition.

Exceptions and limitations serve as defences against allegations for copyright infringement and not as user rights. In this light, users are not entitled to turn against rightholders in case their benefit to permitted uses is limited, e.g. by way of technological protection measures that disable copying a copyright work in digital form. As Burrell points out (in 'Reining in Copyright Law: Is Fair Use the Answer' [2001] *IPQ* 361) it is too easy to blame Parliament for this state of affairs where the balance of copyright law seems tilted in favour of the right owner at the expense of the user. There is ample evidence, he suggests, that judges are more likely to favour the claimant rather than the defendant even where statute appears to confer on the court a measure of discretion.

As we will see, however, effort has been made in the recent reform of UK copyright law so that some copyright exceptions and limitations will be enforceable against possible contractual limitation.

5.3 Arguments raised in a copyright infringement action

As with any action to enforce an intellectual property right, it is important to identify what the defendant's case can be.

The arguments open to the defendant are as follows:

a. to deny that the claimant is the owner or licensee of the copyright work, in other words, they are not entitled to sue. An example of this argument succeeding can be found in *Beloff v Pressdram Ltd* [1973] RPC 765 where the copyright work in question (an internal office memorandum) was held to belong not to the claimant but to her employer, as it had been written in the course of employment;

b. to deny that the work in question is entitled to United Kingdom copyright protection. This denial raises a number of separate points. First, that what has been taken is not a work but a mere idea (*Baigent & Lee v Random House Group Ltd* [2007] FSR 579) or is everyday factual information (*Cramp v Smythson* [1944] AC 329) or else falls below the threshold of copyright protection (*Francis Day v Twentieth Century Fox* [1940] AC 112); second, that even if it is a work, it is not original (*Interlego v Tyco* [1989] AC 217); next, even if it is an original work, it has not been recorded in permanent form (*Creation Records v News Group Newspapers* [1997] EMLR 444); next, that the author of the work did not qualify for protection under United Kingdom law; or, lastly, that even if all the other elements for the subsistence of copyright were satisfied, the term of protection has expired. The defendant may raise one or more of these arguments in the alternative;

c. in relation to primary infringement, to deny that any infringing conduct has been committed. One particular aspect of such denial is to plead that the defendant's work was independently created and therefore was not derived from that of the claimant. Alternatively, if infringing conduct is admitted, the defendant may deny that what was taken amounted to a substantial part of the work, or argue that what was taken was not the expression but the idea;

d. in relation to secondary infringement, to deny that the infringing conduct has been committed, or if this is admitted, to deny that the defendant had the requisite knowledge and/or that the articles dealt with by the defendant were infringing copies;

e. to claim that their allegedly infringing conduct falls within any of the acts permitted by copyright;

f. last, if entitlement to sue, subsistence of copyright, and infringing conduct are all admitted, or are found by the court to be established, the defendant may seek to rely on one or more of the myriad statutory defences to copyright infringement set out in the CDPA, or else to plead one or more of the more general, non-statutory defences.

We have already explored in chapter 4 instances that could be classified as denials of the elements of infringement (a–d). In this chapter we will examine the so-called acts permitted by copyright and statutory defences to copyright infringement (e–f).

5.4 General statutory defences: fair dealing

The comments made earlier about how copyright defences are fact-specific and subject to different preconditions can be illustrated by the following chart, Table 5.1. This sets out the principal general defences (which we shall deal with under the umbrella term of 'fair dealing'), and indicates which categories of work are covered by which defence and the requirements attached to each. For the sake of ease of understanding we have omitted some of the detail concerned with computer programs and databases.

TABLE 5.1   *Copyright defences: categories of work(s) and requirements*

Section	Factual situation	Category of work(s)	Condition(s)
28A	Making temporary copies.	All except computer programs, databases, and broadcasts.	1. Must be transient or incidental; and 2. Must be an essential part of a technological process; and 3. Must not have any independent economic significance; and 4. Must be to enable the transmission of the work in a network or to enable a lawful use of the work.
29(1)	Non-commercial research.	All categories.	Must be accompanied by a sufficient acknowledgement unless this is impossible for reasons of practicality.
29(1C)	Private study.	All categories.	1. Must be done by the researcher or student personally; 2. Must be a single copy.
29A	Data analysis for non-commercial research.	All categories.	Must be accompanied by a sufficient acknowledgement unless this is impossible for reasons of practicality.
30(1)	Quotation for purposes such as criticism or review.	Any work.	1. Must be accompanied by a sufficient acknowledgment; 2. Must have been lawfully made available to the public.
30(2)	Reporting current events.	Any work other than photographs.	Must be accompanied by a sufficient acknowledgement unless the reporting was by sound recording, film, or broadcast where this would be impossible for reasons of practicality.
30A	Caricature, parody, or pastiche.	All categories.	-
31	Incidental inclusion in an artistic work, sound recording, film, or broadcast, including issuing copies, performing or communicating the work containing the source material.	Any work, but a musical work, words spoken or sung with music, or a sound recording or broadcast containing such music or words is not to be regarded as incidentally included where the inclusion is deliberate.	-

Pause for reflection

Are the general defences set out in ss. 28–31 CDPA logical in the way they apply to different categories of copyright work and in the conditions which must be fulfilled before they can be used?
   Which of the fair dealing defences above can be used in Philip's case? To what extent can these
apply?

5.4.1 Applying the fair dealing provisions

The leading case on the application of the provisions is *Pro Sieben Media AG v Carlton UK
Television Ltd*. The Court of Appeal explained that two steps must be taken sequentially,
namely a determination of whether the appropriate factual scenario (for example reporting current events or quotation) has been made out, and then, if it has, whether the
defendant's dealing was fair. Both of these are to be determined objectively (through
the eyes of the reasonable person) without regard to the defendant's opinions or intentions: *Pro Sieben; Hyde Park Residence Ltd v Yelland* [2000] 3 WLR 215.

Pause for reflection

Despite the clarity of *Pro Sieben*, one issue omitted from all the cases is a discussion of the
policy underlying the application of the defences. Such policy, argues Griffiths (in 'Preserving
Judicial Freedom of Movement—Interpreting Fair Dealing in Copyright Law' [2000] *IPQ* 164)
could be that derogations from rights of property should be strictly construed or equally that
freedom of expression should prevail. Instead, he says, what can be discerned from the cases
is the pragmatic need to preserve judicial discretion. In contrast to Burrell (in 'Reining in Copyright Law: Is Fair Use the Answer?' [2001] *IPQ* 361), Griffiths suggests that the majority of cases
display a considerable degree of flexibility.
   This is an area where the last decade has witnessed a marked increase in the volume of case
law. It may be too soon to say which of these two views is correct but in the light of recent case law
from the CJEU which affirmed the principle of strict interpretation of copyright exceptions and limitations (see e.g. Case C 5/08, *Infopaq International*, [56]) it can be argued that there is not much
room for flexibility.

5.4.1.1 Non-commercial research and private study

According to s. 29 CDPA, the exception for research and private study applies to all types
of copyright work, and to recordings of performances of works. Fair dealing for research
and private study is allowed only if the purpose of the use is non-commercial research
and/or private study, the use of the materials is fair, it is carried out by researchers or
students for their own use only, and there is sufficient acknowledgement of the source.

   Research and private study refer to different activities, with research covering work that is
carried out by an individual either for the benefit of an organization or for the promotion
of knowledge, whereas private study is made for the individual's own benefit, often as part
of the pursuit of a formal qualification. Drawing a distinction between research and private

study is important to the extent that fair dealing for non-commercial research also requires that the source of the materials is sufficiently acknowledged. Note that fair dealing covers only non-commercial research, which is meant to exclude profit-making activities, either directly or indirectly. This is to be understood as research that is not made for profit either directly or indirectly and, hence, commercial researchers are not covered by the exception.

An important aspect of the exception of s. 29 is that it is personal and that it can be invoked as a defence against allegations for infringement only by researchers and students, or by people making copies on their behalf. For instance, although librarians can make copies for researchers and students to the extent that they are satisfied that the person requesting the copy requires it for research or private study, and insofar as that person is not provided with more than one article from the same journal or with more than a reasonable proportion of any other published work, lecturers cannot benefit from this exception and supply copies of the same journal article to all the students in their class. As affirmed in *Universities UK Ltd v Copyright Licensing Agency Ltd* ([2002] EMLR 35 [35]), 'If a lecturer were to instruct every member of his class to make copies of the same material, we consider that this too would not be fair dealing. But the mere distribution of a reading list, without any instructions to copy, is not in our view an infringement of copyright at all.'

5.4.1.2 Text and data analysis

Section 29A and Sch. 2(2)1D of the Copyright Designs and Patents Act 1988 provide an exception that enables researchers to make copies of works 'for text and data analysis', namely computational analysis of anything recorded in the work. The exception, that was introduced in UK copyright in 2014 following the Hargreaves Review, is very important in the online context. Electronic analysis of large amounts of copyright works allows researchers to discover patterns and trends that usual 'human' reading may not have the capacity to detect. This process, known as 'text and data mining', may reveal information that is available in the works being mined but has not yet been expressly stipulated. For example, the processing of data included in scientific papers in a particular medical field could indicate an association between a drug and a side effect, even though those papers do not expressly state that such a connection exists.

The exception applies only where the computational analysis is for the purpose of non-commercial research and the source is sufficiently acknowledged (unless this is practically impossible). Although text and data analysis mainly regards literary works, the exception covers all categories of copyright works, and there is also a parallel exception covering recordings of performances. It is also indicated that copyright is infringed if the copy made is transferred to another person, or when it is used for other purposes than those covered by the exception.

5.4.1.3 Quotation, criticism, review

Before the copyright reform of October 2014, UK copyright allowed for the use of a work for the purpose of criticism and review, but quotations for more general purposes were not permitted. The current s. 30(1), however, makes allowance for two activities: there is an exception for criticism and review and a more general exception covering quotations. Even though both exceptions cover all categories of copyright work, they are subject to a number of conditions, namely that (a) the purpose of the use is quotation, criticism, or review; (b) the material used is already available to the public; (c) the use is fair; (d) and the source is sufficiently acknowledged. An additional proportionality requirement is set by reference to the quotation exception, in that the use of the quoted matter should extend no further than what is required in order to achieve the stated purpose.

The impetus towards a more broadly framed quotation exception at the EU level has been repeated in the recently adopted Copyright Directive in the Digital Single Market. Recital 21(b) acknowledges that:

> Despite some overlap with existing exceptions or limitations, such as the ones for quotation and parody, not all content that is uploaded or made available by a user that reasonably includes extracts of protected works or other subject-matter is covered by Article 5 of Directive 2001/29/EC. A situation of this type creates legal uncertainty for both users and rightholders. It is therefore necessary to provide a new specific exception to permit the legitimate uses of extracts of pre-existing protected works or other subject-matter in content that is uploaded or made available by users. Where content generated or made available by a user involves the short and proportionate use of a quotation or of an extract of a protected work or other subject-matter for a legitimate purpose, such use should be protected by the exception provided for in this Directive.

It is specified that such an exception should be applicable only under the conditions of the so-called three-step test, according to which the exception should only be applied (1) in certain special cases (2) which do not conflict with normal exploitation of the work or other subject matter concerned, and (3) do not unreasonably prejudice the legitimate interests of the rightholders.

A quotation of a work for the purpose of criticism or review, can include not only a review of the merit of the work at issue but also its philosophy or broader context. The quotation could also be used in order to criticize another work. In *Time Warner v Channel 4 Television* [1994] EMLR 1, the Court of Appeal accepted that a television programme criticizing the copyright owner's decision to prohibit the exhibition and distribution of the film *A Clockwork Orange* could not be separated from criticism of the content of the film itself. In *Pro Sieben*, the same court held that the use of an extract from the claimant's television interview with Mandy Allwood, who was expecting octuplets, was an integral part of the defendant's criticism of the evils of 'cheque book journalism'.

There is no definition of fairness in the context of the exception and this determination is subject to the court's assessment of the particular facts of a case. In *Hubbard v Vosper* [1972] 2 QB 84, Lord Denning observed:

> You must consider first the number of quotations and extracts. Are they altogether too long to be fair? Then you must consider the use made of them. If they are used as a basis for comment, criticism or review, that may be fair dealing. If they are used to convey the same information as the author, for a rival purpose, that may be unfair. Next you must consider the proportions. To take long extracts and attach short comments may be unfair. However, short extracts and long comments may be fair. Other considerations may come to mind also.

 Pause for reflection

Applying this test to Philip's use of the quote in his article, can he benefit from the quotation defence, should Alex Gordon bring a case against him? To what extent is Philip covered by s. 30(1)? What about the critical comments he makes?

5.4.1.4 Reporting of current events

Journalists and reporters often need to use copyright materials, e.g. short textual extracts, in order to report on current events. Section 30(2) allows this use when (a) the material used is not a photograph; (b) the use of the material is fair; and (c) accompanied by sufficient acknowledgement.

It has been stated that the term 'current events' should be given a wide meaning. 'Current events' includes not only political news but sport: *BBC v BSB* [1992] Ch 141. Whether the term extends to events which occurred more than one year ago is less clear, but it can cover commenting on media coverage generated by allegations made about past events: *Hyde Park Residence Ltd v Yelland*.

A contemporaneous sporting event, such as a cricket match, has been found to be a current event for the sake of the defence (*England And Wales Cricket Board Ltd & Anor v Tixdaq Ltd & Anor* [2016] EWHC 575 (Ch)). Arnold J held in [112] that:

> the exception must be given a 'living' interpretation, at least in the sense that it must be interpreted in manner that takes into account recent developments in technology and the media. In these circumstances . . . these provisions should now be interpreted more broadly than they may have been in the past.

Pause for reflection

Could the eight-minute video that Philip embeds in his slides for the University class fall under the definition of a current event? Why not?

5.4.1.5 Parody, caricature, pastiche

One of the most welcome revisions to copyright defences must be the introduction of fair dealing by way of parody. As Spence explains (in 'Intellectual Property and the Problem of Parody' (1998) 114 *LQR* 594), there are numerous meanings of the term 'parody', not least because it can be used in countless ways, for example in political debate, in commerce, in advertising, and to entertain. He suggests that in the context of intellectual property, it can be taken to mean, broadly speaking, 'the imitation of a text for the purpose of commenting, usually humorously, upon either that text or something else'. 'Target' parodies, he says, seek to comment on the text or its creator; 'weapon' parodies involve the use of that text to comment on something else. Spence puts forward two reasons why parody should receive special treatment namely 'transformative activity' and free speech. We considered 'transformative activity' in the context of originality, where it was noted that a person who takes another's work and adds to it using their own creative endeavour will have copyright in the addition even though they have infringed the source work (*ZYX Music v King* [1995] 3 All ER 1). However, while other jurisdictions such as the USA and Germany recognize transformative use as part of the fair use defence, under UK law such use does not receive special treatment. Free speech as a justification for parody is recognized in some countries (see Rütz, 'Parody: A Missed Opportunity' [2004] *IPQ* 284), particularly those with written constitutions.

Up to now, UK law treated parody no differently from other types of transformative use. It was suggested by Younger J in *Glyn v Western Feature Film Co* ([1916] 1 Ch 261 at

p. 268) that a parody should not infringe if the parody itself amounted to an original work, but this appears to be the only decision where a parody was given special treatment and further, the principal argument in that case was whether the source work was debarred from copyright protection on grounds of public policy. Cases since have held that whether or not a parody infringes depends solely on the issue of substantial taking. Thus, in *Joy Music v Sunday Pictorial* [1960] 2 QB 60 (an example of weapon parody) there was no infringement of the copyright in song lyrics where the defendant's newspaper article proposed a new set of words commenting satirically on a speech by Prince Philip. The new words could be sung to the music of the original song, but the music itself was not reproduced: it was left to the reader's imagination to add the new words to the music. In *Schweppes v Wellingtons* [1984] FSR 210 (an example of target parody), Falconer J held that there had been substantial taking of the claimant's labels for tonic water bottles. The fact that the defendant was attempting to parody the style of the label in selling 'joke' products was neither here nor there. Likewise, in *Williamson v Pearson* [1987] FSR 97 the use of a well-known song in a television advert, albeit with altered lyrics, was held to be substantial taking of the musical work.

At the European level, the permissible scope of the parody exception was examined in Case C-201/13 *Deckmyn*. In this case, the Court of Justice confirmed that the concept of parody must be regarded as an autonomous concept of EU law, having two essential characteristics: (i) it must evoke existing work whilst being noticeably different from it; and (ii) it must constitute an expression of humour or mockery. This case will have an impact in the national interpretations on the appropriate scope of the parody defence. Griffiths explains in detail the possible impact of *Deckmyn* on the scope of the United Kingdom's new parody exception in 'Fair Dealing after Deckmyn—The United Kingdom's Defence for Caricature, Parody or Pastiche' in M. Richardson and S. Ricketson, *Research Handbook on Intellectual Property in Media and Entertainment* (Edward Elgar, 2017).

 Pause for reflection

Even though there is now a parody defence to copyright infringement, this will have no effect if at the same time the defendant commits trade mark infringement. In *Ate My Heart Inc v Mind Candy Music* [2011] EWHC 2741 interim relief was granted to restrain the release on YouTube of a song performed by a cartoon character 'Lady Goo Goo' which infringed the registered mark LADY GA GA by means of dilution. Humour, it seems, has no part to play in trade mark law.

5.4.1.6 Are the circumstances of the defence established?

Despite the statement in *Pro Sieben* that whether the relevant circumstances have been met is an objective test, it has been constantly stated that key words such as 'current events' should be given a wide meaning. 'Any attempt to plot their precise boundaries is doomed to failure' *per* Robert Walker LJ in *Pro Sieben* at p. 614.

Therefore 'current events' includes not only political news but sport: *BBC v BSB* [1992] Ch 141. Whether the term extends to events which occurred more than one year ago is less clear, but it can cover commenting on media coverage generated by allegations made about past events: *Hyde Park Residence Ltd v Yelland*.

It is unclear whether the 'quotation' defence (which replaces 'criticism or review') will operate in the same way. The old defence included not just the work taken but another work or a performance of the work, as well as the work's underlying ideas or its moral or social implications.

Fraser-Woodward Ltd v British Broadcasting Corporation & Brighter Pictures Ltd [2005] FSR 762

Mann J upheld the 'criticism or review' defence where a documentary series *Tabloid Tales*, made by the second defendant and broadcast by the BBC, had included images of newspaper articles containing the claimant's photographs. The images had been broadcast to support the programme's criticism of the 'cult of celebrity', seeking to show that some celebrities, such as Victoria Beckham, were adroit at manipulating the popular press.

5.4.2 Assessing 'fairness'

'Fair dealing' is a legal term used by reference to the assessment of the lawfulness of a use of copyright work that would otherwise amount to infringement. Once it is established that the defendant's conduct falls within the specific factual requirements of a particular defence, the court must then determine, objectively, whether the taking was fair. There is no legal definition of what is fair or unfair in this context, but as Lord Denning once remarked (in *Hubbard v Vosper* [1972] 2 QB 84 at p. 94), what is 'fair' is a question of degree, adding that ultimately it is a matter of impression. Nevertheless, from the Court of Appeal's decision in *Pro Sieben* it is possible to identify a number of factors to be considered. None is conclusive, but all form part of the assessment of fairness. Depending on the circumstances of the case, some factors may weigh more heavily than others. In *Ashdown v Telegraph Group Ltd* ([2001] EWCA Civ 1142; [2002] RPC 5; [2002] ECDR 32), the three most important factors have been identified to be:

(1) The degree to which the alleged infringing use competes with exploitation of the copyright work by the owner;

(2) Whether the work has been published or not;

(3) The extent of the use and the importance of what has been taken.

Considering these in more detail, the amount taken is not conclusive one way or the other. In *Hubbard v Vosper*, Megaw LJ suggested that taking the whole of a short work might be fair in certain cases of criticism or review. In the *Time Warner* case, it was held that incorporating 12-and-a-half minutes of the film in a 30-minute television programme was acceptable.

Whether the defendant's use competes with the claimant's exploitation of the work is a key factor. In *Sillitoe v McGraw Hill* [1983] FSR 545, the court concluded that the use made by the defendant of extracts of contemporary novels as part of its study guides was driven by the commercial imperative of making money. The defendant's motives equally can have a bearing: in *Associated Newspapers v News Group Newspapers* [1986] RPC 515, the only motive in publishing private correspondence of the Duke and Duchess of Windsor was to boost newspaper sales, whereas in *Pro Sieben* the court accepted that the defendant's motives had been to expose the evils of cheque book journalism.

However, even if the defendant is driven by a desire to expose an untruth, that will count for nothing if the information could have been communicated to the public by other means. In *Hyde Park v Yelland*, although the defendant newspaper editor was concerned to show the truth about the visit of Princess Diana to the Villa Windsor in Paris, it was not necessary to infringe the copyright in the CCTV security video by printing stills in *The Sun*: the information could have been conveyed by other means. The fact that the video had been unlawfully obtained (through a disgruntled former employee of the claimant) meant conclusively that the dealing was not fair.

 Pause for reflection

Does the way in which 'fairness' is assessed in the 'fair dealing' defences produce certainty for those who wish to make lawful use of another's copyright work?

Going back to the scenario question, how could fairness be construed by reference to Philip's activities that could benefit from fair dealing (e.g. criticism and review)? How do the *Ashdown* factors apply in Philip's critical review on Alex Gordon's quote?

Prior to the introduction of the Human Rights Act 1998 in October 2000, there was some debate that the Act would require courts in copyright infringement actions to have greater regard to Article 10 of the European Convention on Human Rights ('ECHR') (freedom of expression).

Ashdown v Telegraph Group Ltd [2001] 4 All ER 666

An early opportunity to test this hypothesis occurred in *Ashdown v Telegraph Group Ltd* [2001] 4 All ER 666, a case which conveniently combined the defences of fair dealing, in the public interest, and freedom of expression. The defendant newspaper group had obtained a copy of a confidential minute taken by the claimant in a previous meeting with the then Prime Minister which it published as part of a major article about the extent of the collaboration between the Liberal Democrat and Labour parties. This resulted in an action for breach of confidence and copyright infringement. The Court of Appeal accepted that when interpreting the CDPA, a court had to apply the Act in a manner which accommodates the right to freedom of expression. However, it then decided that the facts of the case did not give rise to 'one of those rare cases' where Art. 10 ECHR 'trumped' copyright, and proceeded to apply the fair dealing defences in favour of the claimant. The reasons given for dismissing the defendant's reliance on s. 30(2) were that the defendant's use competed commercially with the claimant's intended autobiography, it had been motivated by profit, the minute was previously unpublished, and the amount taken from the source work was disproportionate.

Pause for reflection

Griffiths argues (in 'Copyright Law after Ashdown—Time to Deal Fairly with the Public' [2002] 3 *IPQ* 240) that the judgment is less than satisfactory in that it demonstrates an unwillingness to engage substantively with the requirements of Art. 10. The factors to be taken into account when determining fairness were, he says, applied in a formulaic and inflexible manner.

Do you agree with this view? Do you think that the Court of Appeal in Ashdown genuinely took the right to freedom of expression fully into account when applying the fair dealing defence to a newspaper?

Which ones of the aforementioned fair dealing defences cover Philip's activities? To what extent are they applicable and how would fairness be assessed should that case had to reach the court?

5.5 General statutory defences: temporary copying

Section 28A CDPA states that:

> Copyright in a literary work, other than a computer program or a database, or in a dramatic, musical or artistic work, the typographical arrangement of a published edition, a sound recording or a film, is not infringed by the making of a temporary copy which is transient or incidental, which is an integral and essential part of a technological process and the sole purpose of which is to enable—(a) a transmission of the work in a network between third parties by an intermediary; or (b) a lawful use of the work; and which has no independent economic significance.

The exception covering temporary copies was the only mandatory exception included in Art. 5(1) of the Information Society Directive 2001/29/EC. The permitted use allows for the creation of temporary copies on the internet, such as caches, and the policy objective behind the introduction of the exception at the EU level was to enhance the efficiency of electronic networks.

The concept of temporary copying and its appropriate scope have been discussed by the Court of Justice in cases *Infopaq International A/S v Danske Dagblades Forening* (C-5/08) [2010] FSR 495 (*Infopaq I*); *Infopaq International A/S v Danske Dagblades Forening* (*Infopaq II*) (C-302/10), 17 January 2012; *Football Association Premier League Ltd v QC Leisure* (C-403/08) and *Karen Murphy v Media Protection* (C-429/08) [2011] ECR I-9083, [2012] 1 CMLR 29; and *Public Relations Consultants Association Ltd v Newspaper Licensing Agency Ltd and Others,* Case C-360/13, 5 June 2014. The Court of Justice affirmed that the concept transient or incidental copying within the meaning of Art. 5(1) of the Information Society Directive does not involve the creation of material records that can only be destroyed by means of discretionary human intervention (*Infopaq I* and *Infopaq II*).

Temporary copying in light of yet another media monitoring service similar to that at issue in *Infopaq I* and *II* was discussed in the *Meltwater* case, which originated in UK proceedings. Meltwater News Service was making available to its subscribers the relevant data on its website, without having cleared a license with the Newspaper Licensing Agency Ltd, which represents over 1,300 newspaper publishers. Overturning the decisions of the High Court of Justice and the Court of Appeal of England and Wales, the UK Supreme

Court held that the creation of transient copies of result data in the memory and on the screen of the subscribers' computers in the context of media monitoring merely enabled the works to be viewed and this is not an act restricted by copyright. According to Lord Sumption, '[i]t is not enough that forensic ingenuity can devise a method of extending to some extent the life of copies which are by their nature temporary' (*Public Relations Consultants Association Ltd v Newspaper Licensing Agency Ltd* [2013] UKSC 18; [2013] 2 All ER 852 [32]). The CJEU agreed with the Supreme Court's decision and reasoning.

5.6 Statutory defences: miscellaneous

The remaining defences in the CDPA can be subdivided according to whether they deal with the defendant's particular situation (for example the visually impaired, education, libraries, archives, public administration) or with particular works (for example computer programs, databases, designs, typefaces, works in electronic form). We select four of the latter category for further discussion.

5.6.1 Use of notes or recordings of spoken words

The defence found in s. 58 CDPA should be seen as the obverse of the fact that copyright subsists in the spoken word. The section provides that where a record of spoken words is made, in writing or otherwise, for the purpose of reporting current events or broadcasting the whole or part of the work, it is not an infringement of any copyright in the words as a literary work to use the record or material taken from it for that purpose, provided the record is a direct record of the spoken word and the making of the record was not prohibited by the speaker, the use made of the record was not of a kind prohibited by the speaker before the record was made, and the use is by or with the authority of a person who is lawfully in possession of the record. This means, for example, that where a reporter electronically records a conversation with a celebrity or a politician, although the latter will own the copyright in the words spoken, the reporter will be at liberty to use the recording either for the purpose of reporting current events or to include in a broadcast. If, however, what is used is not a direct record (so if the notes or recording are copied the *copy* cannot be used) or if the recording is stolen, then the defence will not apply. It is, on the wording of the section, open to the interviewee to prohibit the making of the record. If (say) a reporter, despite the prohibition, persists in taking notes or making a recording, this would operate to 'fix' the copyright in the spoken word but the recording would be of no real value because it could not be exploited without infringing copyright.

5.6.2 Time shifting

It is in relation to broadcasts that we find another example of where private and domestic use can be a defence to copyright infringement. Yet again s. 70 CDPA (as amended) is subject to a number of restrictions. It provides that the making of a recording of a broadcast *solely* for the purpose of enabling it to be viewed or listened to at a more convenient time does not infringe copyright in the broadcast nor any material comprised in it. The recording must be made on domestic premises (and hence not in a café or other commercial establishment—*Sony Music Entertainment (UK) Ltd v Easyinternetcafe Ltd* [2003] FSR 882) and there can only be one reason for the making of the recording. Hence someone who systematically records broadcasts of films so as to build up their own collection would not be within the defence. Further, s. 70(2) provides that where a lawfully made recording is then sold or hired or offered for sale or hire or communicated to the public it then becomes an infringing copy. So again, if the home taper then makes the recording available on a file-sharing website (which would amount to 'communicating to the public'), they would no longer have the benefit of s. 70.

Pause for reflection

It should be noted that the Information Society Directive 2001/29/EC includes a copyright exception that allows private use to the extent that this is not directed towards any commercial purposes, either directly or indirectly, and on condition that the rightholders receive fair compensation, the concept of which has been elaborated in a number of cases that were brought before the Court of Justice of the European Union ('CJEU') (see indicatively: Cases C-462/09 *Thuiskopie*; C-435/12 *ACI Adam*; C-463/12 *Copydan*, C-572/13 *Hewlett-Packard*; and C-470/14 *Egeda*). This exceeds the scope of mere time shifting and allows users to go ahead with a broader set of activities. There is a wealth of case law from the Court of Justice on this exception (and mostly on the requirement of fair compensation).

A limited private copying exception that would correspond to consumer habits and expectations was introduced in UK copyright in the 2014 copyright reform (former s. 28B and Schedule 2 (1B) of the Copyright, Designs and Patents Act 1988). However, it was soon quashed in a judicial review brought by the British Academy of Songwriters, Composers and Authors (BASCA), the Musicians' Union (MU) and UK Music (see *BASCA v Secretary of State for Business and Innovation* [2015] EWHC 1723, and follow-up judgment [2015] EWHC 2041). These three bodies challenged the Government's decision to introduce a private copying exception into UK copyright law, arguing that it was unlawful as it failed to provide fair compensation to rightholders in line with European law. This means that copying for private and non-commercial purposes, that goes beyond mere time shifting, is no longer permitted in the United Kingdom.

Going back to our problem scenario, could Philip benefit from s. 70 regarding the copy of the documentary for time shifting purposes? Which are the particular conditions of this exception and to what extent can Philip's copy of the documentary be covered?

5.6.3 Educational defences

The use of copyright protected works is a necessary component of the learning process and copyright includes a number of exceptions that permit the use of such materials for educational purposes. These exceptions are found in ss. 32–36 CDPA.

Perhaps the most important exception for educational purposes is the one allowing the use of any type of works 'for the sole purpose of illustration for instruction'. Teachers or students are allowed to copy a work to the extent that this is done for the purpose of offering or receiving instruction (or in the context of preparing to do so) and copying takes place with a view to illustrate a point about the taught subject matter. The concept of 'giving and receiving instruction' is as broad as to cover copying in the context of setting exam questions, making them available to students, and responding to exam questions. It is accepted that minor uses, such as displaying a small portion of a work on a whiteboard, will be permitted, but those uses that would have an impact on the sales of teaching materials should be subject to a licence. In order for the exception to apply, (a) the use should be fair; (b) its purpose should be non-commercial; and (c) there should be sufficient acknowledgement.

Educational establishments are also allowed to make copies of extracts of certain types of work (with broadcasts and artistic works excluded).

Several other exceptions allow copyright works to be used for educational purposes, such as: the compilation of anthologies for educational use that include published literary or dramatic works; performing, playing, or showing copyright literary, dramatic, or musical works in the course of activities of an educational establishment; recording of a broadcast for use in an educational establishment. There is also an exception allowing an educational establishment to make copies of extracts of certain types of work for the purpose of instruction.

 Pause for reflection

Which of the aforementioned exceptions for educational purposes cover the use of copyright materials that Philip has added in his slides? To what extent? Is it permissible not to cite other authors' work in his slides (i.e. photographers' names) and to include a short video which is subject to overlapping copyrights?

5.6.4 Incidental inclusion

The defence of 'incidental inclusion' was considered in *Football Association Premier League v Panini (UK) Ltd* [2004] 1 WLR 1147, CA.

Football Association Premier League v Panini (UK) Ltd [2004] 1 WLR 1147, CA

At first instance it was suggested that 'incidental' should mean casual, inessential, subordinate, or merely background. Consequently the defence was not available to the defendant who had produced collectible stickers with pictures of football players which showed the claimant's logo as well as their club's badge. The appearance of the logo was an integral part of the photograph and so was not incidental. In upholding the appeal, the Court of Appeal said that 'incidental' and 'integral' were not necessarily opposites, and thought it more appropriate to ask why the work had been included in the infringement on both commercial and aesthetic grounds. Here it was important to the defendant's business that the pictures showed players wearing their club's shirt, so the use of the logo was not incidental. In any event, the defendant's product (albums to put the stickers in) was a literary not artistic work and so the defence did not apply (yet another example of the idiosyncrasies of the general defences in the CDPA). In contrast, in the *Fraser-Woodward* case it was held that in respect of the one photograph not covered by the criticism or review defence, the television programme had focused on the headline within which the photograph had been inserted by the newspaper. As the photograph had been there in the original newspaper page, its use in the programme was incidental.

5.7 Statutory defences: in the public interest

In common with the law of breach of confidence that we will be examining later in this book a defence that copyright infringement was justified 'in the public interest' may be pleaded. Indeed, most of the cases in which the defence has been raised involved both causes of action. There is a subtle difference between arguing that disclosure is 'in the public interest' and 'of public interest'. The need to know gossip and trivia do not justify an infringement of copyright.

The defence was first recognized (although it was rejected on the facts) in *Beloff v Pressdram*, where Ungoed-Thomas J (at p. 56) stated that the disclosure must be of 'matters, carried out or contemplated, in breach of the country's security, or in breach of law, including statutory duty, fraud, or otherwise destructive of the country or its people, including matters medically dangerous to the public; and doubtless other misdeed of similar gravity'. Since then, the law has moved on from this strict approach so that there is no longer a requirement that there must be a 'misdeed'. The best illustration of the defence in a copyright infringement action is to be found in *Lion Laboratories v Evans* [1984] 2 All ER 417 where the Court of Appeal accepted that the defendant ought to be able to reproduce the claimant's internal papers which revealed that its breathalyser was faulty. Had the defendant not been able to do so, there was a serious chance that large numbers of motorists would be wrongly convicted of drink-driving.

When the CDPA was enacted, the Government belatedly introduced a statutory provision codifying the public interest defence. Section 171(3) provides that 'nothing in this part affects any rule of law preventing or restricting the enforcement of copyright on grounds of public interest or otherwise'. As Burrell suggests (in 'Reining in Copyright Law: Is Fair Use the Answer' [2001] *IPQ* 361), at first glance this appears to amount to an express statutory recognition of the public interest defence.

However, in *Hyde Park Residence Ltd v Yelland*, the Court of Appeal adopted a different view, the majority holding that there was no defence of in the public interest and that all the section did was to restate the point that equitable remedies are discretionary. Burrell points out that in so doing, they ignored the legislative history of the provision as well as earlier case law and academic writing. A differently constituted Court of Appeal in *Ashdown v Telegraph Group Ltd* at [58] held that copyright could restrict freedom of expression so that a defence in the public interest should be available, although it did not apply in the case. However, the public interest defence received a far narrower treatment in *Ashdown* than it did in *Lion Laboratories*, the court suggesting that it would apply only in 'very rare' circumstances. As Burrell says, the combined effect of *Yelland* and *Ashdown* has been to restrict a defence that Parliament intended to be much broader despite the coming into force of the Human Rights Act. Subsequent decisions, such as that in *HRH Prince of Wales v Associated Newspapers Ltd* [2007] 3 WLR 222, indicate that this approach is unlikely to change in the near future.

5.8 Contractual override and copyright exceptions

An issue that came to prominence with digitisation and online uses of copyright works was the possibility that rightholders could contractually forbid users from carrying out activities that would otherwise be covered by a permitted use. This issue has attracted intense scholarly discussion, with most commentators arguing in favour of mandatory exceptions that cannot be waived through contractual terms. This was particularly so with regards to exceptions that find their justificatory basis on fundamental human rights, such as freedom of speech or freedom of press (e.g. parody and news reporting). Other exceptions, however, such as those that are available for the fulfilment of public policy objectives, would be rendered meaningless in case that rightholders could re-write the limits of the property rights bestowed upon them.

The issue of contractually overridden exceptions is not regulated at the EU level but it was at the heart of the 2014 reform of UK copyright law in the aftermath of the Hargreaves Review. The Government's aim was to offer legal certainty and to ensure that licensing does not restrict acts that are beneficial to society as a whole.

The newly introduced exceptions (namely quotation, parody, text and data mining) and some of the amended exceptions (i.e. research and private study, illustration for instruction, interlibrary loans, and recoding of broadcasts for archival purposes) include a provision, according to which 'to the extent that a term of a contract purports to prevent or restrict the doing of any act which, by virtue of this section, would not infringe copyright, that term is unenforceable'. The above mentioned exceptions cannot generally be set aside by contract and where contractual terms restrict users from taking advantage of an exception they are unenforceable. However, some of the exceptions that were amended in 2014 do not include a provision to regulate their relationship with possible contractual override and there are also some exceptions that are subject to a complex regime in their relationship with contract law (e.g. the exception of s. 35(4) CDPA allowing the recording of broadcasts by educational establishments applies 'if, or to the extent that, licences are available authorizing the acts in question and the educational establishment responsible for those acts knew or ought to have been aware of').

5.9 Non-statutory defences

5.9.1 Acquiescence

The general equitable defence of acquiescence may be raised in a copyright infringement action. However, its meaning is quite precise. In *Film Investors Overseas Services SA v Home Video Channel Ltd* Times, 2 December 1996, the court stressed that the claimant's conduct must amount to a misrepresentation, so that there is an intimation to the defendant, on which the defendant relies, that copyright will not be enforced. Consequently, mere delay in commencing proceedings is not acquiescence: *Farmers Build Ltd v Carier Bulk Handling Materials Ltd* [1999] RPC 461 CA.

Fisher v Brooker [2009] 1 WLR 1764

The defence was considered by the House of Lords in *Fisher v Brooker* [2009] 1 WLR 1764 where Lord Neuberger (at [62]–[63]) remarked that he did not think that acquiescence added anything to two other equitable defences, namely laches and estoppel. Whichever of the three defences was deployed, the basic question was whether it would be unconscionable for the

→

> → claimant to go back on his word. In the present case, this would only be met if the defendants could show that they had reasonably relied on the claimant not wanting to claim a share in the royalties of *A Whiter Shade of Pale*, that they had acted on this reliance, and that it would be unfairly to their detriment if the claimant was now permitted to enforce his rights. The three criteria had not been established. In any event, such equitable arguments were more appropriate to the question of equitable relief rather than a claim to a property right granted by statute.

5.9.2 Public policy

A defendant may choose to argue that the claimant's copyright should be unenforceable on the general principle (found throughout intellectual property) that it is contrary to public policy. Although there is no statutory basis for this defence, it was recognized as long ago as *Glyn v Western Feature Film Co*, where the court accepted the defendant's argument that the source of its film, the claimant's novel, did not deserve protection because it encouraged adultery.

When applying the public policy defence, it is important to distinguish between where the claimant's conduct is not deserving of protection from where the copyright work itself is disentitled to protection. This difference was endorsed by the House of Lords in *AG v Guardian Newspapers (No. 2)* [1990] 1 AC 109 ('*Spycatcher*'). The point is neatly illustrated by *ZYX Music v King* where although the claimant was an infringer (by virtue of having reproduced an earlier pop hit) this did not prevent it from enforcing its own copyright in its arrangement against the defendant.

The principles which guide the court in applying the public policy defence were restated by the Court of Appeal in *Hyde Park Residence Ltd v Yelland and others*, relying on Lord Goff's opinion in *Spycatcher*. It said that the court will not enforce copyright if the work is immoral, scandalous, contrary to family life, contrary to public health or safety, or the administration of justice, or where it incites others to commit such harm. In keeping with the underlying policy that restrictions on a property right should be narrowly construed, these are strict criteria.

5.9.3 Implied licence

As consent is always a defence to any intellectual property infringement action, a defendant may attempt to argue that they had permission. However, the argument of implied licence rarely succeeds, as the court will only imply permission to commit a restricted act if this is necessary to make an *existing* agreement between the parties effective. The principles on which the court will act were set out in *R Griggs Group Ltd and others v Evans and others* [2005] FSR 706. As regards the implied licence defence, in *Banier v News Group Newspapers* [1997] FSR 812, the court declined to imply a licence to publish photographs which had already appeared in another newspaper, as the parties were not in a contractual relationship. Even where a licence has previously been granted, the court may be reluctant to make a finding of an implied licence if there has been a lengthy period of time since the earlier grant: *Gabrin v Universal Music Operations Ltd* [2003] EWHC 1335 (Ch)).

Pause for reflection

The implied licence defence has become more and more relevant in the online context. Recently, the CJEU has upheld a principle that echoes an implied licence rationale by reference to hyperlinks. In *Svensson* (*Nils Svensson and Others v Retriever Sverige AB*, Case C-466/12, 13 February 2014), the Court held that 'the public targeted by the initial communication consisted of all potential visitors to the site concerned, since, given that access to the works on that site was not subject to any restrictive measures, all internet users could therefore have free access to them'.[*footnote omitted*] (at [26]). This meant that the copyright holders—by not applying access restriction protocols—were assumed to have offered free access of the content to 'all internet users'. The failure of copyright holders to actively restrict access to their protected works can be assumed to imply that the work was intended to be made accessible to the public.

5.9.4 Exhaustion of rights

The application of the exhaustion of rights defence (implicit in s. 18 and s. 27 CDPA) is far from straightforward. Normal principles will apply to the first sale within the European Economic Area ('EEA') of tangible goods containing copyright material, and Member States do not have any power to continue to apply international exhaustion to non-EEA goods (Case C-479/04 *Laserdisken ApS v Kulturministeriet*). Where, however, copyright products are licensed, the rental right in such goods can never be exhausted (Case C-61/97 *Egmont Films v Laserdisken*); equally, other rights, such as the performance right, may not be exhaustible (Case 158/86 *Warner Bros v Christiansen* [1988] ECR 2605). What is more, in *Allposters* (Case C-419/13), the Court of Justice confirmed that exhaustion does not cover works that have been subject to modifications and in this light the copyright holder can oppose the distribution of the modified work, even if he had agreed to the distribution of the original work.

An important aspect of the exhaustion doctrine is that it applies to the distribution right but it is not equally available to the right of communicating works to the public. This means that the communication of works on the internet is not equally 'exhausted' and remains within authorial control. The only exception to this rule is software. In Case C-128/11 *UsedSoft GmbH v Oracle International Corp*, 3 July 2012, the CJEU ruled that exhaustion applies not only where the software is supplied on a physical medium, but where it is distributed by means of downloads from a website. It is an open question whether exhaustion should also apply online and the CJEU has been called to give its response in a pending referral from the Rechtbank Den Haag (Court of The Hague) in a case concerning a second-hand e-book trader: *Tom Kabinet*.

 Pause for reflection

The operation of European exhaustion legitimates parallel imports within the EU single market, hence enabling private importers to profit from the resale of goods at lower prices than those charged by the official retailer. Exhaustion enables the creation of legitimate second hand mar-

→

> →
> kets. It is not clear at the moment what the impact of Brexit on the exhaustion principle shall
> be. If the United Kingdom leaves the European Union without negotiating entry into the EEA,
> the exhaustion principle would cease to apply in the United Kingdom.

5.10 Proposals for an EU-wide flexible standard in dealing with exceptions and limitations

More flexibility in copyright law could arguably overcome the uncertainty concerning new uses of copyright works. The so-called Wittem Group has proposed a half-open structure of copyright limitations that follows the wording of the three-step test but is adjusted in a way that makes the test suitable for judicial examination (Wittem Group, European Copyright Code, 2010, available at http://www.jipitec.eu/issues/jipitec-1-2-2010/2622/wittem-group-european-copyright-code.pdf). This can be seen as a proposal that combines the advantages of legal security and predictability associated with the 'closed list' of exceptions and limitations under the UK and EU legal tradition with the flexibility and adaptability to technological change that the US fair use doctrine offers.

The European Parliament urged for an evaluation of the Information Society Directive in the area of exceptions and limitations, proposing the introduction of a flexible tool such as the fair use test in EU copyright (European Parliament, Committee on Legal Affairs, Draft Report on the Implementation of Directive 2001/29/EC of the European Parliament and of the Council of 22 May 2001 on the harmonization of certain aspects of copyright and related rights in the Information Society, 15 January 2015, 2014/2256(INI)). The EU Parliament vote on September 2018, however, does not incorporate such a proposal (see Copyright in the Digital Single Market ***I, Amendments adopted by the European Parliament on 12 September 2018 on the proposal for a directive of the European Parliament and of the Council on copyright in the Digital Single Market (COM(2016)0593—C8-0383/2016–2016/0280(COD), P8_TA-PROV(2018)0337).

Pause for reflection

What do you think? Would a general test for judicial application be a preferable system in determining the appropriate scope of exceptions and limitations?

5.11 Conclusion

In this chapter we have examined the statutory and case law defences against copyright infringement. We have seen that there are a number of instances where certain activities are exempt from infringement and the purpose of a particular activity is important in assessing its fairness and permissibility thereafter. Courts have elaborated on the appropriate scope of permissible uses, which has been enlarged in the aftermath of the

2014 copyright reform. We have also seen that there are discussions at the European Parliament towards the introduction of a general rule in assessing whether a particular use is permitted or not.

In terms of Philip's activities in the problem question, it is important to identify the particular exceptions and limitations that could cover each one of these activities. Philip should be advised that the quotation from Alex Gordon's book and the critical comments are very likely to be covered by s. 30(1) CDPA, insofar as he pays attention to the length of the quote and makes sure that Alex's book is appropriately referenced. It should be explained that all the conditions of the exception of s. 30(1) should apply and that this section makes allowance for uses (a) the purpose of which is quotation, criticism, or review; (b) the material used is already available to the public; (c) the use is fair; (d) and the source is sufficiently acknowledged. The words 'criticism' and 'review' are not to be interpreted too narrowly (*Pro Sieben Media AG v Carlton UK Television Ltd*), and this leaves room for a broader understanding of the terms: a quotation of a work for such purposes can include not only a review of the merit of the work at issue but also its philosophy or broader context. Philip should be advised that there is no definition of fairness and that this would be a matter of fact and degree. Case law indicates however that there are certain conditions that are often considered in relevant examinations, including—but not limited to—the number of quotations and extracts; their length; the use that is made of them (*Hubbard v Vosper*). For his use to be fair and permitted, he should pay attention to the length of the quotes (*England And Wales Cricket Board Ltd & Anor v Tixdaq Ltd & Anor*), which at the moment is excessive.

With regards to the use of photographs in the article, Philip should be advised that fair dealing for the reporting of current events (s. 30(2)) cannot apply, primarily because this exception does not cover photographs. Fair dealing for the purposes of quotation, criticism, or review (s. 30(1)) is allowed for any type of copyright work and it could be available. Philip attributes the photograph to the relevant rightholders but he needs to make sure that these photographs are already available to the public. It will also be important for him to be able to show that he makes use of these photographs for the purposes of substantiating his article and to put those pictures into context, i.e. to explain their relevance to his article, as the law sets a requirement for the use to be genuinely for the purposes of quotation, criticism, or review. For the use of the photographs to be fair, the length of the copied material matters but copying the whole work could in principle be justified depending on the context. A critical question would be whether the use of those photographs comes in conflict with the normal exploitation of the photographs from their rightholders, i.e. whether the said use competes commercially with the rightholders.

The same ought to apply by reference to the use of the photographs in the slides for the lecture. With regard to the sufficient acknowledgement requirement that is set by law, this requirement is not strict in cases where it is practically impossible to cite the source. So, Philip should be advised to make a reference to the relevant rightholders in each and every instance where this is feasible.

The short video that he has embedded in his slides could be covered by the quotation exception subject to the conditions of s. 30(1). The additional proportionality requirement available for the quotation exception would have to be met in that the use of the quotation must extend no further than is required to achieve its purpose. This particular use could also benefit from the educational exceptions, and in particular the one available in s. 32 CDPA, which allows for illustrations for instruction. Such a use according to the statute does not infringe copyright in the work insofar as the dealing is (a) for a non-commercial purpose, (b) by a person giving or receiving instruction (or preparing for giving or receiving instruction), and (c) accompanied by a sufficient acknowledgement (unless this would be impossible for reasons of practicality or otherwise). According to the guidance of the Intellectual Property Office, 'minor uses, such as displaying a few lines of poetry on an interactive whiteboard, will be permitted, but uses which would undermine sales of teaching materials will still need a licence'. Philip's use of the video could be covered by the educational exception, as he is giving instruction and the class is given pro bono. He should be advised to give reference details on the video.

Finally, regarding the copy of the TV-broadcasted documentary, Philip should be advised that the time shifting exception of s. 70 CDPA could apply. Section 70 allows for the making of a recording of a broadcast for the purpose of enabling it to be viewed or listened to at a more convenient time. It is a requirement that the recording must be made on domestic premises and not in a commercial establishment (*Sony Music Entertainment (UK) Ltd v Easyinternetcafe Ltd*).

End-of-chapter questions

After reading the chapter carefully, try answering the following questions. For answer guidance visit the online resources at **www.oup.com/uk/karapapa-mcdonagh/**

1. Which are the main arguments that a defendant can bring forward against allegations for copyright infringement?

2. Which are the statutory and non-statutory defences against copyright infringement?

3. Which are the key elements of fair dealing defences? How is fairness to be determined under established case law?

4. The case law intrepreting the CDPA provisions on infringement of copyright and the defences thereto fails to strike a reasonable balance between the rightholder and those who wish to make use of the work. Discuss.

5. Is the closed list of available defences an efficient mechanism in the online context or an open ended test for judicial interpretation would be a preferable solution?

Further reading

For understanding the scope of acts restricted by copyright and therefore this scope of copyright infringement, the following readings are recommended:

Angelopoulos, C. 'Freedom of Expression and Copyright: the Double Balancing Act' [2008] 3 *IPQ* 328

Considers the interplay between copyright protection and freedom of expression and offers insights on how a possible conflict between these legal orders should be approached.

Bradshaw, D. 'Copyright, Fair Dealing and the Mandy Allwood Case; The Court of Appeal gets the Max out of a Multiple Pregnancy Opportunity' [1999] 10(5) *Ent LR* 125

Offers critical insights on the Pro Sieben *case and its impact.*

Burrell, R. 'Reining in Copyright Law: Is Fair Use the Answer' [2001] 4 *IPQ* 361

Argues that although it might be desirable in the interests of flexibility to adopt a more general 'fair use' defence, judicial practice has failed to take adequate account of the interests of the users of copyright material, so that without a change of attitude, relaxing legislative requirements would not have any effect.

Geiger, C. et al., 'Limitations and exceptions as key elements of the legal framework for copyright in the European Union, Opinion of the European Copyright Society on The Judgment of the CJEU in Case C- 201/13 Deckmyn' (2015) 46(1) *IIC* 93–101

Offers a critical exposé of the Deckmyn case and takes a particular focus on the doctrine of strict interpretation of exceptions and limitations and its appropriate application.

Griffiths, J. *'Copyright Law after Ashdown*—Time to Deal Fairly with the Public' [2002] 3 *IPQ* 240

Considers the Court of Appeal's judgment in Ashdown v Telegraph Group *and considers that despite the court's apparent acceptance of the Human Rights Act, its treatment of the fair dealing defences is weighted in favour of the copyright owner at the expense of the public interest.*

Griffiths, J. 'Preserving Judicial Freedom of Movement—Interpreting Fair Dealing in Copyright Law' [2000] 2 *IPQ* 164

Considers which principles ought to colour the interpretation of the fair dealing defences in the CDPA, but concludes that most cases have been characterized by judicial flexibility.

Griffiths, J. 'Fair Dealing after Deckmyn—The United Kingdom's Defence for Caricature, Parody or Pastiche' in M. Richardson and S. Ricketson, *Research Handbook on Intellectual Property in Media and Entertainment* (Edward Elgar, 2017)

Offers insights on how the UK fair dealing defence on parody will be impacted in light of the Deckmyn *case.*

Hugenholtz P.B. and Sentfleben M., 'Fair Use in Europe: In Search of Flexibilities', November 2011, available at http://www.ivir.nl/publicaties/download/912

Addresses the lack of flexibility in the context of copyright exceptions and limitations under the EU copyright framework.

Karapapa, S. *Private copying: The Scope of User Freedom in EU Digital Copyright*, Routledge Research in Intellectual Property (Routledge, 2012)

Offers an overview of the private copying exception available in the Information Society Directive and the way in which it was implemented in the various EU Member States and offers normative insights on the application of this copyright exception at the EU level.

McDonagh, L. 'Headlines and Hyperlinks: UK Copyright Law Post-Infopaq—Newspaper Licensing Agency Ltd and Others v Meltwater Holding BV and Other Companies' (2011) 1 *Queen Mary Journal of Intellectual Property Law* 2, 184

Considers the protection available to hyperlinks in the light of recent cases of the CJEU.

Rütz, C. 'Parody: A Missed Opportunity?' [2004] 3 *IPQ* 284

Comments on how the United Kingdom's implementation of the Information Society Directive failed to take the opportunity to make parody a defence to copyright infringement.

Sims, A. 'The Public Interest Defence in Copyright Law: Myth or Reality?' [2006] 6 *EIPR* 335
Offers an overview of the public interest defence.

Spence, M. 'Intellectual Property and the Problem of Parody' (1998) 114 *LQR* 594
Considers the various ways in which parody ought to receive special treatment in UK copyright law.

Wittem Group, European Copyright Code, 2010, available at http://www.jipitec.eu/issues/
jipitec-1-2-2010/2622/wittem-group-european-copyright-code.pdf
Offers a proposal for a single pan-European legal instrument on copyright.

Moral rights

6

6.1 Introduction

From a human rights perspective, the distinction between economic and moral rights can be traced back to Art. 27(2) of the Universal Declaration of Human Rights. This article reads: '[e]veryone has the right to the protection of the moral and material interests resulting from any scientific, literary or artistic production of which he is the author' (Universal Declaration of Human Rights, U.N. Doc. A/RES/217(III) (Dec. 10, 1948)). The protection of the moral interests of the authors finds justification not only in the context of human rights but also under a special set of copyright rules that offer protection to non-pecuniary interests of the authors.

The Copyright, Designs and Patents Act 1988 ('CDPA') recognizes four main moral rights: the right to be identified as the author or director of a work (this is the so-called paternity right); the right to object to derogatory treatment of a work (the so-called integrity right); the right to object to a false attribution of authorship in the case of a literary, dramatic, musical, and artistic work or a film; and the right of privacy in commissioned photographs and films.

In this chapter, we look at these non-pecuniary interests of the authors, keeping in mind the scenario question with a view to understanding the ways in which moral rights are protected and may be infringed under UK copyright law.

6.2 The concept of moral rights and their justification

As Ginsburg observes (in 'Moral Rights in a Common Law System' [1990] 4 *Ent LR* 121) the term 'moral rights', translated from the French *droit moral*, is not concerned with morality but with non-pecuniary interests, just as the French term *dommage moral* denotes non-economic loss in the law of tort. The notion of rights personal to the creator was identified by Lord Mansfield in *Millar v Taylor* (1769) 98 ER 201, who remarked that without protection, an author would not be the master of the use of his own name and would have no control over the correctness of his own work. Ginsburg argues that protection of moral rights is justified because the rights improve the climate in which authors and artists create their works. Knowing that they will receive credit for what they have created and that their work will survive in its intended form may be more important than pecuniary gain. The protection of moral rights, she says, sends a message that society cares about creation and about authorship. It also provides the public with information about who created a work and helps avoid deception by preventing wrongful attribution of authorship.

As Ricketson describes (in 'Moral Rights and the Droit de Suite: International Conditions and Australian Obligations' [1990] *Ent LR* 78), the recognition of moral rights can be traced back to France in the early 19th century. Subsequently Germany and other civil law members of the Berne Convention began to provide similar protection for authors, principally the rights of integrity, paternity, and disclosure. To a very large extent, the protection of certain inalienable moral rights in some jurisdictions, such as France and Germany, was founded on Hegel's personality theory (Georg Wilhelm Friedrich

Hegel, *Hegel's Philosophy of Right* 45 (trans. T.M. Knox (Oxford University Press, 1952) (1821)). Common law members of the Berne Convention tended not to grant moral rights, although piecemeal protection for authors was available through other means, such as the actions for defamation, passing off and breach of contract (for an example of breach of contract being used to prevent the derogatory treatment of a dramatic work, see *Frisby v BBC* [1967] Ch 932). Moral rights were first introduced into the Berne Convention by the Rome revision of 1928, although the text reflected a diplomatic compromise between those countries keen to enhance authorial rights and those who wanted the freedom to choose other means of protection outside copyright law.

The current provision on an author's moral rights is Art. *6bis* of the 1971 version of the Convention. It declares that independently of the author's economic rights, and even after the transfer of the same, the author shall have the right to claim authorship of the work and to object to any distortion, mutilation, or other modification of, or other derogatory action in relation to the said work, which would be prejudicial to his honour or reputation. It also requires Contracting States to ensure that these rights are to last at least until the expiry of the author's economic rights. As Ricketson observes, the obligation to keep moral rights independent of economic rights does not mean that the former should be treated as inalienable, i.e. incapable of assignment, although many countries choose to do so. Equally, there is nothing in Art. *6bis* to prevent Contracting States from allowing authors to assign or waive their moral rights just as they can assign or waive copyright.

 Pause for reflection

Are moral rights human rights? As Willem Grosheide observes ('Moral rights' in Derclaye, E. (ed.) *Research Handbook on the Future of EU Copyright* (Edward Elgar, 2009, 242, 247), two schools of thought have developed on the relationship between moral rights and human rights: the first school holds that human rights and intellectual property rights are in conflict and, in case of conflict, human rights prevail. The second school of thought maintains that, human rights and intellectual property rights are compatible and pursue the same objectives, however, a balance needs to be stuck between private property rights and public access to works. According to this second approach, moral rights could be seen as human rights.

Note that, even though moral rights protection is offered at the international level, notably the Berne Convention, moral rights have not been subject to European harmonization.

6.2.1 The treatment of moral rights in other jurisdictions

It might be assumed that there are two models for treating moral rights, namely the civil law and common law systems. Not so. Dworkin (in 'The Moral Rights of the Author: Moral Rights and the Common Law Countries' (1994–1995) 19 *Colum-VLA Journal of Law & the Arts* 229) explains how the United Kingdom, United States, Australia, and Canada have each, over the years, adopted different strategies in relation to authorial rights, with

Canada being closest to the civil law model. Further, as Dietz explains (in 'The Moral Right of the Author: Moral Rights and the Civil Law Countries' (1994–1995) 19 *Colum-VLA Journal of Law & the Arts* 199) the approach of civil law countries is far from standardized.

Philosophically, some countries (such as Germany) view moral rights as an integral part of copyright (the so-called monist view) whilst others (typically, France) treat moral rights and copyright as two separate entities, each with its own characteristics, particularly with regard to duration and alienability (the dualist view). There are further variations with regard to categories of moral rights, their duration, and whether they are capable of waiver. Types of moral rights which are recognized include not just the 'core' rights of paternity and integrity, but the divulgation (disclosure) right and the right to repent or withdraw the work. Duration of moral rights can be perpetual (as in France and Spain) or dictated by the length of the copyright term (as in Germany). Similarly, there is divergence as to whether moral rights can be waived, whether such waiver (if permitted) is subject to any test of reasonableness, and whether moral rights can be denied to particular categories of work, such as computer programs. It is not surprising that Dietz declares Art. 6*bis* to be 'minimalist'.

6.2.2 Moral rights in the United Kingdom

The CDPA 1988, in Part I, Chapter IV, formally introduced the moral rights of the author into United Kingdom law in fulfillment of Art. 6*bis*. Two moral rights—the right of paternity and right of integrity—arise in respect of those categories of work covered by the Berne Convention (i.e., literary, dramatic, and musical works; artistic works; and films).

The other two Chapter IV rights are not the result of the Berne Convention. The right to object to a false attribution of authorship in the case of a literary, dramatic, musical, and artistic work or a film was present in the Copyright Act 1956. The right of privacy in commissioned photographs and films was inserted belatedly into the CDPA and was a necessary consequence of the change to rules on ownership of copyright in commissioned photographs. Whilst previously the person who commissioned a family photograph would own the copyright in it and thus be able to control its publication, s. 9 CDPA now provides for the author of the work (i.e. the photographer) to be the first owner. Commissioning a work no longer gives rise to a right of ownership, although a term as to equitable ownership of copyright or an exclusive licence to exploit it may be implied by the court into the contract of commission in order to give effect to the parties' expectations (*R Griggs Group Ltd and others v Evans and others* [2005] FSR 706).

A further right has now been added. It is debatable whether this is an economic right or a moral right, although Ricketson argues that it is economic in nature. This is the artist's resale right. Found initially in Art. 14*ter* of the Berne Convention, it was introduced into EU law by the *Droit de Suite Directive* (Directive 2001/84/EC of the European Parliament and of the Council of 27 September 2001 on the resale right for the benefit of the author of an original work of art of [2001] OJ L 272/32, (throughout this chapter, the 2001 Directive)). This was implemented into United Kingdom law by The Artist's Resale Rights Regulations 2006 (SI 2006/346) (the 'Regulations').

We shall examine each of these rights individually, and then consider the provisions which are common to them all (in part because of its unclear status, the artist's resale right will be considered seprately in chapter 7).

6.3 The right of paternity or attribution

Under CDPA s. 77, the author of a literary, dramatic, musical, or artistic work or film has the right to be identified as its author. The right arises in circumstances which may be described as 'commercial dealings' with the work, although as ever with the CDPA, there are significant differences in detail between the different categories of work.

In the case of literary and dramatic works (other than words intended to be spoken or sung with music) and adaptations of such works, the author has the right to be identified whenever the work is published commercially, performed in public, communicated to the public (i.e. by being broadcast or placed on the internet), or when copies of a film or sound recording including the work are issued to the public (s. 77(2)). In the case of a musical work (which includes for these purposes the words which are to be sung or spoken with music, and any adaptation of the work) the identification right arises whenever the work is published commercially, or when copies of a sound recording including the work are issued to the public, or when a film where the soundtrack includes the work is shown in public (s. 77(3)). There are similar rights for artists (when a work is published commercially, exhibited, or communicated to the public), for architects and for film directors (when the film is shown in public, communicated to the public, or copies are issued to the public) (ss. 77(4)–(6)).

'Identification' means that the author's name must appear on each copy of the work issued to the public, but if that is not appropriate, then it must be given in some other manner likely to bring his or her identity to the notice of the person acquiring a copy. In the case of a building, the architect should be identified 'by appropriate means visible to persons entering or approaching the building', and where a work is being performed or exhibited, identification must be in a manner likely to bring the author's identity to the attention of the audience. In each case, the identification must be clear and reasonably prominent.

There are some interesting anomalies in s. 77, as Dworkin observes. In contrast to literary and dramatic works, there is no right to be identified as the composer of music when the musical work is performed or communicated to the public. Thus there is no obligation to identify the composer where music is provided in public premises, such as shopping malls, pubs, and discothèques, regardless of whether the performance of the music is live or by means of a sound recording. Thus in the example at the start of the chapter, the composer of the songs has no right to be identified at the rock concert. Nor is there any requirement for broadcasting organizations to identify the creators of musical works. It was said during the Parliamentary debates that it would be far too inconvenient for broadcasters if they had to acknowledge the composer of every tune played on the radio or used as the theme tune of a television programme or included in a broadcast advertisement. By contrast, although an artist does not have the right to control the 'performance' of the artistic work under s. 19 CDPA, he or she does have the right to be named should the owner of the tangible copy decide to display the work in public.

However, before the right of paternity can arise, it has to be asserted. According to s. 78(2), assertion can either be general or in relation to specific (restricted) acts. It *has* to be made in writing, either when the copyright is assigned to a third party, or by any other written instrument. No guidance is given in the Act as to what sort of wording suffices.

In the case of the public exhibition of an artistic work, s. 78(3) provides for two methods of assertion. First, the assertion can be made when the artist parts with possession of the original by ensuring that their name appears on the work or its frame (the CDPA has a somewhat narrow view of what constitutes an artistic work). Second, the right can be asserted when the right to reproduce the work is licensed.

Section 78(4) provides that an assertion which is made under s. 78(2) upon the assignment of copyright binds the assignee of copyright and anyone claiming through them, even if they did *not* have notice of the assertion, whereas a general assertion binds *only* those to whom notice of the assertion is brought. In relation to the public exhibition of artistic works, any third party acquiring the work is bound by an assertion made by the artist when parting with possession of the work, but where the reproduction right is licensed, the right binds the licensee and anyone receiving a copy of the work. The separate treatment accorded to artistic works in comparison with other categories of work together with the differing effects of assertions on third parties (exacerbated by the lack of any registration system) are typical of the complexities found in the CDPA.

 Pause for reflection

The requirement to assert the right of paternity has been the subject of considerable criticism. First, as Ginsburg points out, the drafters of the CDPA appear to have misunderstood Art. 6*bis* which simply states that 'the author shall have the right to claim authorship of the work'. Parliament has twisted a straightforward personal right into a complex commercial transaction. Further, such obligation to assert an author's basic right may well breach the requirement in Art. 5*bis* that Contracting States may not impose any formality as a precondition for protection under the Convention.

To make matters worse, s. 79 CDPA provides for a number of instances of when the right to be identified as author does not arise. Under s. 79(2), certain categories of work, namely computer programs, typefaces and computer-generated works, are excepted. Under s. 79(3), works created in the course of employment do not receive protection if the employer consents to the relevant infringing act, and likewise, any work made for the purpose of reporting current events does not attract the right (s. 79(5)) nor does the right apply where a literary, dramatic, musical, or artistic work is published with the author's consent in a newspaper, magazine or other periodical or in a reference work (s. 79(6)). Certain categories of author, therefore, particularly employees and journalists, receive harsh treatment. There are also exceptions for works which are Crown or Parliamentary copyright, or where the copyright was originally vested in an international organization. Finally, under s. 79(4), the right is excluded where a number of defences to copyright infringement apply, in particular those of fair dealing and incidental inclusion. Since these exceptions appear in the Berne Convention in relation to copyright rather than moral rights, one may only assume that Parliament was more concerned with the interests of those who exploit copyrights than with those of copyright creators.

Has the United Kingdom really fulfilled its obligations under the Berne Convention to give effect to the right of paternity? What do you think?

Pause for reflection

Going back to our problem scenario, does the journalist commit an infringement of the paternity right by not naming an author? As we will see, moral rights are non-transferable and inalienable by virtue of s. 87.

6.4 The right of integrity

The author of a literary, dramatic, musical, or artistic work or film has the right to object to its derogatory treatment (s. 80). In contrast to the right of paternity, the right of integrity does not have to be asserted, but it seems that the scope of available protection under the CDPA is narrower than that accorded under the Berne Convention.

The problem lies in s. 80(2) which defines both 'treatment' and 'derogatory'. 'Treatment' means any addition to, deletion from, alteration to, or adaptation of the work. However, it does not include the translation of a literary or dramatic work, nor the arrangement or transcription of a musical work if this involves no more than a change of key. It was said in the Parliamentary debates that translation and transposition preserve the basic integrity of a work, yet as Cornish observes (in 'Moral Rights under the 1988 Act' [1989] 12 *EIPR* 449), of all the ways of misrepresenting an author's true worth, poor translation must be the most frequent occurrence. He also questions whether the exclusion in respect of the transposition of musical works can really be justified.

These criticisms apart, s. 80(2) is narrower than Berne in two regards: the words 'distortion, modification or mutilation' in Art. *6bis* are arguably wider than 'addition', 'deletion' and 'alteration' in s. 80(2); and second, the latter omits the key phrase in Art. *6bis* 'other derogatory action *in relation to* the said work' (emphasis supplied). As Dworkin argues, this means that an artist could object if a portrait is defaced (such as by adding a moustache to the subject), but could not object if the portrait is placed in an unfavourable location in a gallery or included in a book of pornography or if it was destroyed or allowed to fall into disrepair.

According to s. 80(2), 'derogatory' means that the treatment amounts to a distortion or mutilation of the work, or is otherwise prejudicial to the honour or reputation of the author or director.

The grammatical structure of s. 80(2) should be compared with that of Art. *6bis*. The section appears to impose a double condition, first that there should be 'treatment' (or rather, mistreatment) of the work, and then that this treatment must be prejudicial to the author's honour or reputation.

A further difficulty is whether the requirement of prejudice should be decided subjectively or objectively. As Sprawson comments (in 'Moral Rights in the 21st Century: A Case for Bankruptcy' [2006] *Ent LR* 58), moral rights are personal in nature and a reflection of the personality of the creator. How could an objective assessment of what is derogatory be compatible with the nature of a personal right? Nevertheless, in what little United Kingdom case law there has been so far on the right of integrity, the courts have adopted an objective approach to the question of what is derogatory (rather like the test for what is defamatory) so that the author's hurt feelings are not taken into account.

Pause for reflection

Art. 6*bis* of the Berne Convention lays down the minimum standard of protection and it is up to contracting states to decide whether to stick to this minimal requirement by applying an objective test to determine prejudice to authors' honour and reputation (e.g. the United Kingdom) or not. In countries where a higher standard of moral rights prediction is available, alterations that come in conflict with ethical, political, or even artistic beliefs of the author could be seen as an infringement of the integrity right. Even in those countries however a role of reason is incorporated into their national statutes. In Germany, for instance, the author's interest in the work that is allegedly subject to prejudice should be legitimate (see German Copyright Act, § 14).

Whereas the minimalist approach offers greater legal certainty, the maximalist view offers a stronger form of protection to authors. Which system is more efficient in your view?

It is not clear whether the concept of derogatory treatment requires a distortion or mutilation of the work and/or a prejudice to the honour or reputation of the author or director. A number of cases have addressed the issue.

In *Tidy v Trustees of the Natural History Museum*, 29 March 1995, unreported, a cartoonist unsuccessfully objected to his posters of dinosaurs being turned into postcards: even though he gave the gallery of the Natural History Museum the right to show some of the cartoons he had drawn, he claimed that his integrity was violated when the gallery reduce the size of the cartoons and added coloured backgrounds to black and white drawings when putting the cartoons in a book. Rattee J decided the question of prejudice through the eyes of a reasonable person, although he did not explain whether this was the reasonable artist or the reasonable member of the public.

In *Pasterfield v Denham* [1999] FSR 168, revisions to a tourist information leaflet were held not to be derogatory. For a treatment to be derogatory 'what the plaintiff must establish is that the treatment accorded to his work is either a distortion or a mutilation that prejudices his honour or reputation as an artist. It is not sufficient that the author is himself aggrieved by what has occurred' (at [182]).

Similarly, in *Confetti Records v Warner Music UK Ltd* [2003] EMLR 790, Lewison J concluded that the addition of rap words to a song was not derogatory, but the court may have been hampered by the facts that the witnesses could not agree on the meaning of the words and the author did not object to what had been done. Importantly, the court rejected the claimant's argument as there was no sufficient evidence of a prejudice to the claimant's honour or reputation and in lack of such evidence the court was not prepared to infer prejudice.

Even though the aforementioned cases have addressed prejudice to the author's honour or reputation it is not entirely clear whether this assessment should be subject to a subjective or objective standard. Taking the objective standpoint of a reasonable person however seems to be more appropriate, especially if it is accepted that the meaning of reputation is the same as in defamation law.

There are two cases where a claim for derogatory treatment has succeeded, namely *Delves-Broughton v House of Harlot Ltd* [2012] EWPCC 29 where the discussion of the issues was minimal, and *Morrison Leahy Music Ltd v Lightbond Ltd* [1993] EMLR 144.

Delves-Broughton v House of Harlot Ltd [2012] EWPCC 29

In *Delves-Broughton v House of Harlot Ltd,* a photographer sought damages from a clothing designer for copyright infringement and forward derogatory treatment of her work by displaying one of her photographs on their website that had been cropped and had its background removed. On the question of derogatory treatment, the court observed that the composition of the original photograph was the result of considerable amount of time and effort, and that it was artistically meaningful for the claimant to retain the background in the picture. Whereas the modifications at issue were not prejudicial to the claimant's honour or reputation, and they did not amount to mutilation, there was distortion and hence a derogatory treatment of the work.

Morrison Leahy Music Ltd v Lightbond Ltd [1993] EMLR 144

In *Morrison Leahy Music Ltd v Lightbond Ltd*, in awarding interim relief, Morritt J held that there was an arguable breach of s. 80(2) CDPA. The creation of a medley of songs (in a sound recording to be called *Bad Boys Mega Mix*), the songs having been written by the second claimant, George Michael, took both the words and music out of their original context and so was prejudicial to the author's honour or reputation.

These cases can be read in conjunction with the Canadian case of *Snow v The Eaton Centre Ltd* 70 CPR 2d 105 where the temporary festooning of Christmas decorations on sculptures of Canada geese hanging in a shopping mall amounted to a breach of the artist's right of integrity.

 Pause for reflection

Indeed, an addition to or mutilation of a work may constitute a derogatory treatment of the author's production. What happens, however, in cases where someone legitimately acquires an original artistic work and destroys the material object that has been bought? Could destruction of the single manifestation of a work, e.g. a sculpture, qualify as a derogatory treatment? Scholarship is divided on this issue, with some commentators arguing that destruction amounts to mutilation and others claiming that the author's reputation can no longer be harmed once the work disappears from sight. Art. 6*bis* of the Berne Convention remains silent, leaving contracting states the liberty to introduce their national provisions. In the United Kingdom there is no case law on the matter and hence the issue remains unclear. French courts have offered remedies in cases of destruction of artwork, even though there is no consistent approach to be assumed. For instance, in *Bezombes* (1981) 108 RIDA 162, protestors dismantled a sculpture displayed in a church because they thought it was blasphemous; they were found liable for violating the artist's moral rights. In *Rousel v Grenoble* (1977) 91 RIDA 116, however, there was no infringement found in a case where a municipality destroyed a sculpture placed in the Grenoble Municipal Park to avoid safety risks because their conduct was dictated by necessities of public safety.

Pause for reflection

Going back to our problem scenario, how would you advise Mary? Did Ninna London Ltd violate her integrity right and, if so, how is derogatory treatment to be established? What about the out of context use of Mary's photograph by Bella magazine? Could this also qualify as derogatory treatment of her picture?

The circumstances when the right of integrity is infringed are listed in s. 80(3)–(6) CDPA, and as with the right of paternity, essentially involve commercial exploitation of the affected work. In the case of a literary, dramatic, and musical work, under s. 80(3) the infringing conduct must involve commercial publication, performance, or communication of the work, or issuing copies to the public of a sound recording or film which includes a derogatory treatment of the work. In the case of artistic works, s. 80(4) provides that infringement occurs when the work is published commercially, exhibited, or communicated to the public, although for certain three-dimensional works (namely models for buildings, sculptures, and works of artistic craftsmanship) there is liability when a graphic work or photograph containing the derogatory treatment is issued to the public. Such protection does not apply to works of architecture in the form of the building itself, although the architect may demand that where there is derogatory treatment his or her identification is removed from the building (s. 80(5)). This means that the derogatory treatment of the building is not of itself actionable, and further, if the architect has not been identified under s. 77, he or she has no redress. One may speculate why graphic representations of three-dimensional works do not receive protection against communication to the public, unlike two-dimensional works such as the photograph in dispute in *Delves-Broughton*. One can easily envisage a situation where a photograph of an artistic work which has been the subject of derogatory treatment (such as the sculptures of the geese in *Snow v The Eaton Centre*) is posted on a website, yet unlike literary, dramatic, and musical works there is no redress for communicating intangible two-dimensional copies of the work, only issuing tangible copies. In the case of films, under s. 80(6) the director can object where the film is shown in public, communicated to the public, or copies of it are issued to the public.

In contrast to the right of paternity, there is also liability for secondary infringement under s. 83. This provision is worded in an almost identical fashion to s. 23 CDPA. The author, artist, or director can therefore object where there are commercial dealings in infringing copies of the work which has been the subject of derogatory treatment. By 'commercial dealings' is meant conduct such as possession in the course of a business, selling, hiring, public exhibition, and distribution. Just as with secondary infringement of copyright, it must be proved that the defendant knew or had reason to believe that he was dealing in an infringing copy. The assessment of the defendant's knowledge will, as under s. 23, be done through the eyes of the reasonable trader in his position: *LA Gear v Hi-Tec Sports plc* [1992] FSR 121; *Vermaat v Boncrest Ltd (No 2)* [2002] FSR 331.

As with the right of paternity, there are numerous exceptions and qualifications to the right, found respectively in ss. 81 and 82. Just as with s. 79, there is no protection for computer programs, computer-generated works, any work made for the purposes of reporting current events, and works created for publication in newspapers, magazines, periodicals, and reference works (CDPA s. 81(1)–(4)), so journalists are denied protection. There is a further exception where the treatment of the work has been done in order to avoid the commission of an offence or by the BBC in order to prevent the work offending against 'good taste or decency' (s. 81(6)). This last exception is subject to the requirement that where the author or director has been identified, then there must be a 'sufficient disclaimer'. Again, where the right of paternity has not been asserted under s. 77, the requirement of the disclaimer will not apply.

Under s. 82, the right of integrity is curtailed in certain cases. These are where ownership of the copyright in the work was vested in the author's or director's employer under s. 11; or else was Crown or Parliamentary copyright; or else was vested in an international organization; and the treatment of the work was done with the consent of the copyright owner, unless the author or director was identified at the time of the relevant act or had previously been identified in or on published copies of the work. As with s. 81(6), a sufficient disclaimer removes liability. The effect of these provisions means that (just as with the right of paternity) employee-creators are vulnerable to the loss of the right of integrity. They are bound by their employer's consent (seemingly having no redress if they do not agree with what the employer has done), and have no protection at all where the right of paternity has not been asserted. As we have seen, inequality of bargaining power may mean that the author was not aware of the implications for the integrity right if the paternity right is not asserted.

 Pause for reflection

To what extent does the language of s. 80(2) CDPA offer effective protection to creators who wish to object to the derogatory treatment of their works? Has the United Kingdom truly fulfilled its obligations under the Berne Convention to give effect to the right of integrity?

6.5 False attribution of authorship

Under s. 84, a person can object to the false attribution of authorship of a literary, dramatic, musical, or artistic work or the false attribution of being the director of a film. The right also applies to any adaptation of the source work. An interesting aspect of this right is that it is conferred on authors and non-authors alike, and it is also closely related to entitlements arising from other areas of law such as libel, defamation, and passing off.

The right is infringed when copies of the work containing the false attribution are issued to the public, or in the case of an artistic work, where it is exhibited in public. There is also infringement where a literary, dramatic, and musical work which has wrongly attributed authorship is performed in public or communicated to the public (i.e. it is broadcast or placed on a website) or, in the case of a film, it is shown in public or communicated to the public. Like the integrity right, there is liability for secondary infringement, that is, dealing in infringing copies in the course of a business with the appropriate knowledge.

> ### Clark v Associated Newspapers [1998] 1 All ER 959
>
> An example of s. 84 in operation is *Clark v Associated Newspapers* [1998] 1 All ER 959, where the claimant (a politician and successful author) successfully alleged that a satirical column in the *London Evening Standard* entitled 'Alan Clark's Secret Election Diary' and, later, 'Alan Clark's Secret Political Diaries' would be assumed by readers to be his work. The defendant's indication that the column had been written by another, although in capital letters, would not be noticed by the average reader, who was, assumed the judge, a commuter 'skim reading' the newspaper during the journey home after work.

Another important case concerning of false attribution of authorship is *Noah v Shuba* [1991] FSR 14. We have already discussed this case on employer's ownership (at **3.1.2.2.**). A consultant epidemiologist wrote a guide to hygienic skin piercing. A magazine falsely attributed to him two sentences he had not written: *'Follow clinic procedure for aftercare. If proper procedures are followed, no risk of viral infections can occur.'* Misquotations can also result in infringement of s. 84.

 Pause for reflection

Could the mistaken attribution of the photograph to Mary by Bella magazine qualify as infringement of s. 84? Under which conditions?

6.6 Privacy in photographs and films

As mentioned earlier, s. 85 was added to the CDPA in the latter stages of its progress through Parliament. It creates a right of privacy in photographs and films which have been commissioned for private and domestic purposes. The commissioner of the photograph or film has the right to object to copies of the work being issued to the public, or the work being exhibited in public, or the work being communicated to the public (that is, by broadcast or via the internet). Liability is imposed not just on the person who commits such conduct, but on someone who authorizes such conduct.

There are, however, a number of exceptions to the right of privacy, as a result of the application of a number of defences to copyright infringement. Of particular note are the defences of incidental inclusion and Parliamentary and judicial proceedings.

6.7 Moral rights where there are joint authors

Section 88 deals with the rights of paternity, integrity, objection to false attribution, and privacy where there are joint authors. The right of paternity means the right of *each* author to be identified, but each author must assert the right for themselves. Similarly, each joint author has the right to object to derogatory treatment. In the case of false attribution, an author can object to any false statement as to the authorship of the work of joint authorship and to the false attribution of joint authorship where it is a work of sole authorship. Likewise, the rights under s. 85 belong to joint commissioners of the photograph or film. In each case, waiver by one joint author binds that person only and does not affect the rights of others.

6.8 Duration and property rights

The duration of moral rights is catered for by s. 86. With the exception of the right found in s. 84, the duration of moral rights is coterminous with the duration of copyright. The right to object to false attribution lasts for the lifetime of the person wrongly attributed as author and for 20 years after their death.

 Pause for reflection

As Stamatoudi observes (in 'Moral Rights of Authors in England: the Missing Emphasis on the Role of Creators' [1997] 4 *IPQ* 478) the logic in providing a shorter period of protection to the right which is the converse of the paternity right is questionable, especially if regard is had to the justifications for moral rights.
Do you agree with this view?

Moral rights remain personal to the author and cannot be assigned, CDPA s. 94. Upon the death of the author, in respect of the rights of paternity, integrity, and privacy, s. 95 creates a series of precise rules as to who inherits the rights. They are to pass primarily to the person to whom the rights in question were bequeathed by the author's will, but if none, then to the person to whom the copyright in the work was bequeathed, and should neither of these apply (i.e. there was no specific bequest in the will or the author died intestate), then the rights pass to the author's personal representatives. In all cases, however, the person inheriting the right is bound by any consent or waiver given by the author in their lifetime.

However, any damages recovered for infringement of any of these moral rights after the author's death will not necessarily pass to the person who owns the rights. Section 95(6) declares that the damages devolve as part of the author's estate as if the right of action had subsisted immediately before his death. What this means is that even though an author might have bequeathed their moral rights to one person, or even where there is no bequest of moral rights, but a bequest of copyright which carries with it the author's moral rights by implication under s. 95(1)(a) or (b), the named beneficiary will not get the damages. Instead, these will go, in all probability, to the author's residuary beneficiary. Permitting an author to bequeath their moral rights to a named individual but then not allowing that person to receive compensation should the rights be infringed defies logic.

 Pause for reflection

In our problem scenario, can Mary claim infringement of the paternity right with regards to her grandfather's photograph? Why not?

The right to object to false attribution receives separate treatment from the other three moral rights. After the author's death it is actionable only by the author's personal representatives and so cannot be the subject matter of a specific bequest in a will, whether of moral rights or of copyright.

6.9 Remedies for the infringement of moral rights

Infringement of the rights of paternity, integrity, objection to false attribution, and privacy is declared by s. 103 CDPA to be actionable as a breach of statutory duty owed to the person entitled to the right. Such infringement is actionable by the author of the work, not any subsequent owner to whom the copyright might have been assigned: *Confetti Records v Warner Music UK Ltd.*

The usual remedy for breach of statutory duty will be damages, but as yet there is no guidance on how the calculation will be made. The author will have suffered no pecuniary loss, so one can envisage the defendant arguing for nominal damages to be awarded. How would it be possible to quantify hurt feelings? Further, the ability to award additional damages, set out in s. 97 CDPA, is in that part of Chapter VI which is entitled 'Rights and Remedies of the Copyright Owner'. Given that s. 103 has a separate heading 'Remedies for Infringement of Moral Rights', it is arguable that no power exists to award additional damages for flagrant infringement of moral rights.

Section 103(2) contains a further provision likely to diminish the author's rights. It provides that in the case of derogatory treatment, the court may, if they think it is an adequate remedy, grant an injunction prohibiting the doing of any act unless a disclaimer is made. The court is to approve the terms and the manner of the disclaimer, the purpose of which is to disassociate the author from the treatment of the work. This means that the infringing work can still be exploited commercially so that the defendant is in effect given a licence to commit derogatory treatment. What is unclear is how the disclaimer is to be brought to the attention of the public. As Stamatoudi comments, placing a disclaimer on the label of a sound recording will not inform those who hear the recording in a nightclub that the works contained in the recording have been the subject of derogatory treatment. It is also unclear whether injunctive relief under s. 103(2) is in addition to or in substitution for damages.

 Pause for reflection

Which are the remedies you would advise Mary to pursue?

6.10 Transitional arrangements

As befits the introduction of new rights in the CDPA, there are transitional provisions to be found in Sch. 1 to the Act.

There is to be no liability for anything done before the commencement date of the Act (1 August 1989). The rights of paternity and integrity are not to apply to any films made before that date, nor to any literary, dramatic, musical, or artistic work of any author who died before that date. In other words, the Act applies retrospectively to works in copyright when it came into force, provided the author was alive at that date. The limitation with regard to films means that the United Kingdom courts will not have to deal with the thorny issue of whether the colourisation of old black and white films infringes the author's right of integrity.

6.11 Waiver and consent

Despite the fact that moral rights cannot be assigned during the author's lifetime, as both Dworkin and Cornish observe, the moral rights régime is emasculated by the fact that the author may either consent to conduct which would otherwise infringe, or may waive, their rights.

Both consent and waiver are dealt with by s. 87 CDPA. The section declares that any of the Chapter IV rights may be waived, provided that this is in writing and signed by the person giving up the right. Such waiver may be in relation to a specific work or groups of work or to works generally, whether existing or future. If made in favour of the copyright owner, the waiver extends to that person's licensees and successors in title unless there is a statement to the contrary. However, s. 87(4) compounds the problem considerably by declaring that the section is not to be taken as excluding the operation of the general law of contract or estoppel in relation to an informal waiver. Therefore, despite the earlier statement that a waiver must be in writing, an author may find that due to conduct amounting to estoppel, his or her moral rights have been lost. We have already noted how in many instances, the right of integrity only survives if the right of paternity has been asserted. The combination of the conditions in ss. 81 and 82 with s. 87(4) presents yet further traps for the vulnerable author. It is a matter of speculation whether the case law on inequality of bargaining power could be extended to lack of assertion, consent, or waiver in the case of moral rights.

6.12 Exceptions

Moral rights are subject to a number of limitations under the 1988 Act.

Section 79(3) lays down an exception to the attribution right, according to which the right does not apply where the employer or copyright owner authorized the reproduction, etc, of the work. The attribution right will also not be infringed where the activity at issue amounts to fair dealing for the purpose of reporting current events by means of a sound recording, film, broadcast, or cable programme (s. 79(4)(a)). These provisions correspond to s. 30(2)–(3) CDPA, which lays down the requirement of sufficient acknowledgement. Section 79 also lists a number of limitations to the attribution right, including incidental inclusion of the work, its use for the purposes of examination, parliamentary or judicial proceedings, and government inquiries.

Pause for reflection

As we have seen in chapter 5, the exception for caricature, parody, or pastiche is not subject to the requirement of sufficient acknowledgement. Even though a parodist could benefit from the exception without indicating the source of the original work, the paternity right is still applicable. What does this mean for the scope of the parody exception? Will parodists commit an infringement of the paternity right each and every time they decide to make a parody of the work?

With regards to the integrity right, an exceptions listed in s. 82 CDPA 1988 dictates that the integrity right does not apply to anything done in relation to a work created by an employee by or with the authority of the copyright owner unless the author or director is identified at the time of the relevant act, or has previously been identified in or on published copies of the work. Even in such cases, the integrity right is infringed where a sufficient disclaimer exists, namely a clear indication that the work has been subject to treatment that the author or director has not authorized. Section 81(6) further indicates that the integrity right is not infringed by anything done for the purpose of avoiding the commission of an offence, complying with a duty imposed by or under an enactment, or in the case of the BBC, avoiding the inclusion in a programme broadcast by them of anything which offends against good taste or decency or which is likely to encourage or incite to crime or to lead to disorder or to be offensive to public feeling, provided, where the author or director is identified at the time of the relevant act or has previously been identified in or on published copies of the work, that there is a sufficient disclaimer.

 Pause for reflection

Ginsburg argues that the CDPA is a poor model for common law countries to adopt when protecting moral rights. It leaves creators in a worse position then they were before. In particular, she says, s. 78 which requires the right of paternity to be asserted, derives from a 'perverse' interpretation of Art. 6bis and may be in breach of the Berne Convention obligation that no formality may be imposed. Further, the number of exceptions both to the right of paternity and the right of integrity, and the fact that moral rights can be waived lead one to conclude that the provisions are half-hearted, perhaps because their drafters seem to have lacked real conviction as to the desirability of moral rights. A plausible explanation may be that Parliament was primarily concerned to preserve the interests of those who exploit copyright works rather than protect the interests of creators.

6.13 Conclusion

In this chapter, we have explored the relationship between copyright, moral rights, and human rights and we have examined the way in which an author's moral rights have been introduced into United Kingdom law by the CDPA. We have also addressed the various moral rights available under the CDPA and their respective scope.

In our problem scenario, Mary Alexander should be advised that she has a strong case against Ninna London Ltd for infringement of her integrity right (s. 80) and that she can claim damages. In *Delves-Broughton v House of Harlot Ltd,* a case with very similar facts, the court found that even though the relevant modifications were not prejudicial to the claimant's honour or reputation, and they did not amount to mutilation, there was distortion and hence a derogatory treatment of the work.

Mary can also claim infringement of her moral rights against Bella magazine, and in particular she can claim infringement of her integrity (use of image out of context) and false attribution rights (mistaken attribution of photograph). Regarding the infringement of her integrity right (s. 80) she should be advised that not many cases have succeeded on the ground of mere out-of-context use of works as it has been difficult to meet the derogatory treatment requirement (*Tidy v Trustees of the Natural History Museum; Pasterfield v Denham*). As for the mistaken attribution of someone else's photograph to Mary, Mary can object to it on the basis of s. 84, which gives authors and non-authors alike the right not to have a literary, dramatic, musical, or artistic work falsely attributed to them as author (*Clark v Associated Newspapers; Noah v Shuba*). Mary should be advised that according to s. 103 CDPA an infringement of her moral rights is actionable as a breach of statutory duty.

With regard to the journalist's lack of attribution of the picture taken by Mary's grandfather, Mary should be advised that, unlike economic rights, moral rights are non-transferable and inalienable (ss. 94–95) (even though they last for the life of the author plus 70 years after the author's death, s. 86).

End-of-chapter questions

After reading the chapter carefully, try answering the following questions. For answer guidance visit the online resources at **www.oup.com/uk/karapapa-mcdonagh/**

1. Which are the main criticisms against the assertion requirement of the paternity right?

2. How is the concept of derogatory treatment understood under UK copyright law? Which are the leading cases that have determined its scope? How does the UK test for assessing whether integrity of the work has been violated differ from other jurisdictions?

Further reading

For understanding the protection available to moral rights, the following readings are recommended:

Cornish, W. 'Moral Rights under the 1988 Act' [1989] 12 *EIPR* 449
   An overview of the introduction of moral rights by the CDPA.

Dietz, A. 'The Moral Right of the Author: Moral Rights and the Civil Law Countries' (1994–1995) 19
   Colum-VLA Journal of Law & the Arts 199
   A survey of the protection of moral rights in various civil law countries.

Dworkin, G. 'The Moral Rights of the Author: Moral Rights and the Common Law Countries' (1994–1995) 19 *Colum-VLA Journal of Law & the Arts* 229

An overview of the common law treatment of moral rights, with particular emphasis on the CDPA.

Ginsburg, J. 'Moral Rights in a Common Law System' [1990] 4 *Ent LR* 121

A powerful critique of the half-hearted adoption of moral rights by the USA and United Kingdom.

Ricketson, S. 'Moral Rights and the Droit de Suite: International Conditions and Australian Obligations' [1990] 3 *Ent LR* 78

An account of the obligations imposed by the Berne Convention and how common law countries like Australia have struggled to accommodate these.

Sprawson, R. 'Moral Rights in the 21st Century: A Case for Bankruptcy' [2006] *Ent LR* 58

A concise critique of the introduction of moral rights for performers.

Stamatoudi, I. 'Moral Rights of Authors in England: the Missing Emphasis on the Role of Creators' [1997] 4 *IPQ* 478

A comparison of the treatment of moral rights in France, Germany, and the United Kingdom.

Waisman, A. 'Rethinking the Moral Right to Integrity' [2008] 3 *IPQ* 268

Argues that the right of integrity would be better understood by clarifying the distinction between modifying the work and modifying its support (i.e. the physical medium).

Related rights

Problem question

Read this problem question carefully and keep it in mind while you are working through the chapter that follows. At the end of this chapter, you will be able to apply what you have learnt to the problem question and advise the relevant parties.

Andrea Ferrano is a singer who aspires to become a world famous rock star. He has just published an album, as an independent production, funded by his family, in order to use it as a demo with music production companies. To increase visibility of his work, he uploads a music track on a video-sharing website. This soon becomes a success and he is invited to give a concert in a music hall in London, accompanied by an orchestra and a troupe of six dancers. At the end of the concert, a music producer approaches Andrea and offers to sign a music publishing contract with him for his first solo album. A few days later, he finds a video on a video-sharing website featuring his performance in London. He was never asked to give his permission. The same video-sharing website user, with the username 'xris1088', has also uploaded a copy of Andrea's music track and has embedded ads on it, gaining revenue from advertising.

Because Andrea is new to the music industry, he has questions on how to better protect his work. He knows that he has intellectual property rights over his performances but he is not sure whether both videos that xris1088 has posted on a video-sharing website qualify as an infringement of his rights. He also wants to know what other rights subsist in the performance he made during the concert in London. Another issue that interests him is whether he can apply digital locks on his work once his solo album is out, to what extent he can protect his work against unauthorized copying, and whether legal protection is also available for the particular way in which the various music tracks will be compiled in the album and included in a playlist on an online music channel.

7.1 **Introduction**

This chapter completes the copyright picture by dealing with related rights. These are related to, but fall outside, the protection afforded by copyright law. They include: performer's rights; the *sui generis* database right; rights relating to technological protection measures and rights management information; and the artist's resale right. We will be discussing these rights, alongside the scenario question at the start of this chapter. Subject to discussion shall also be the press publisher's right, which has been seen as a way to resolve the newspaper crisis that the press faced in the aftermath of online news websites and aggregators.

7.2 **Rights in performances**

7.2.1 **The nature of performers' rights**

It used to be said that there could be no copyright in a performance (as opposed to the work performed) because a performance was too fleeting and lacked the requisite permanence to be a work (see Lord Denning in *Ex parte Island Records* [1978] Ch 122). The underlying assumption was that a performance could only occur before a live audience in a theatre or concert hall, and that once delivered, all that remained was the recollection of the audience. This narrow view, separating the work from its presentation, should be contrasted with the opinion of Mummery LJ in *Sawkins v Hyperion Records* [2005] 1 WLR 3281 that a performance may be an integral part of a musical work. In any event, developing technology over the last century (initially analogue, but latterly digital) has led to performances being captured with increasing ease in a variety of media, such as sound recordings, films, and broadcasts. In turn, such media themselves are capable of digital manipulation and transmission worldwide. As an example, consider the millions of videos captured on mobile phones and posted on YouTube.

 Pause for reflection

What about the video of Andrea's performance that xris1088 posts on a video-sharing website? Could this be protectable under the related right that is available to performers?

7.2.2 **The Rome and WPPT Conventions**

Article 7 of the Rome Convention obliges Contracting States to protect performers by giving them the right to prevent any unauthorized broadcast or communication to the public of the performance, any unauthorized fixation of the performance, and the reproduction of any fixation of the performance. A 'performer' is defined by Art. 3 to mean an actor, singer, musician, dancer, or other person who acts, sings, delivers, declaims, plays in, or otherwise performs literary or artistic works. Article 19 declares, however, that once a performer has consented to the incorporation of their performance in a visual or audio-visual fixation, Art. 7 is to have no further application. The Convention therefore assumes that the performer's principal concern is with the unauthorized broadcast or sound recording of the performance. It should be remembered that the wording of the Convention will have been influenced by the technology of its day. It has not been revised since.

However, the Rome Convention has been supplemented by the WIPO Performances and Phonograms Treaty ('WPPT'). Article 2 contains a slightly broader definition of 'performer' in that it adds the activity of interpretation to the conduct expected of a performer and includes 'expressions of folklore' within the list of works to be performed. It then expands the protection conferred on performers by granting them, in Arts 5 to 9, moral and economic rights. The latter entitles the performer to control the broadcasting and fixation of unfixed performances, and the reproduction, distribution, and rental of copies of sound recordings of their performances. In addition, under Art. 15, performers are to enjoy the right to equitable remuneration for the direct or indirect use of sound recordings published for commercial purposes or for any communication to the public, Art. 15(4) making clear that 'communication to the public' includes posting on the internet.

7.2.3 Pre-1988 United Kingdom law

Prior to the Copyright, Designs and Patents Act 1988 ('CDPA'), the Rome Convention was implemented by the Performers Protection Acts 1958–1972 ('PPA'). The PPA imposed criminal liability for making a film or recording of a performance without the performer's written consent; selling, hiring, distributing by way of trade any such films or records; using such a film or recording for the purposes of public performance; and making an unauthorized broadcast of the performance. Interestingly, the PPA gave performers protection against unauthorized filming, in contrast to the Rome Convention. The PPA required proof of knowledge on the part of the defendant, both as to the commission of the act itself and as to the lack of written consent from the performer. Liability was subject to the defence that the recording was for private and domestic use. The defence failed in *Helliwell v Piggott-Sims* [1980] FSR 582 where the defendant had made a number of recordings of rock concerts for the specific purpose of exchanging them with other enthusiasts.

The *Helliwell* case provides a nice illustration of the phenomenon which led to pressure for change. This was the problem of 'bootleg' recordings of concerts and other live performances. As explained by Lord Denning in *Ex parte Island Records*, modern technology enables a member of the audience at a concert to make an unauthorized recording of the performance, and then manufacture and distribute multiple copies of that recording. The making of the recording amounts, of course, to copyright infringement under s. 17 CDPA, being a reproduction in any material form of the words and music performed at the concert, so that the copyright owner (and indeed any copyright management society responsible for collecting royalties for the reproduction right) has redress against the bootlegger and anyone dealing in infringing copies: *Carlin Music Corporation v Collins* [1979] FSR 548. However, the economic interests of the performers and those of any recording company with whom they might have had an exclusive recording contract are also being undermined by the activities of bootleggers.

The issue which therefore confronted the court in *Ex parte Island Records* and later cases was whether breach of legislation which imposed criminal penalties for bootleg recordings could give rise to protection in civil law for the performers and their recording companies. Under the principles of general law established in *Gouriet v Union of Post Office Workers* [1978] AC 435 and *CBS v Amstrad* [1988] AC 1013, breach of a criminal statute will not give rise to a claim by the 'victim' in civil law unless either the claimant was a member of a class whom the Act in question was intended to protect (so that there would be a claim at common law for breach of statutory duty) or the claimant suffered injury to a private right or incurred special damage (both giving rise to a claim in equity). Could the performers and their recording companies bring themselves within either of these categories?

Whether a performer could bring a claim at common law for breach of statutory duty depended on their being able to show that the legislation in question was passed to protect a particular class of persons, that they were a member of that class, and that the penalty found in the Act was imposed for failure to perform a defined duty (*Cutler v Wandsworth Stadium* [1948] KB 291). Despite the view of the majority of the Court of Appeal in *Ex parte Island Records* and of Harman J in *Shelley v Cunane* [1983] FSR 391 (a case concerning bootleg recordings of Pink Floyd) that the PPA was the wrong sort of Act to give rise to an action for breach of statutory duty, following the *obiter* comments of Lord Diplock in *Lonrho v Shell Petroleum* [1982] AC 173, it began to be accepted that such a claim was allowable against bootleggers. So in the first instance cases of *Ekland v Skripglow Ltd* [1982] FSR 431 and *Silly Wizard Ltd v Shaughnessy* [1984] FSR 163 the performers in each case were allowed to claim against the bootlegger. However, in the former case the claimant and defendant were in a contractual relationship, the terms of which had been breached by the defendant, and in the latter case the performer was also the owner of the copyright in the music being performed, so that there were special factors favouring the performer.

Rickless v United Artists [1988] QB 40

The definitive Court of Appeal decision came in *Rickless v United Artists* [1988] QB 40 where it was held, upholding Hobhouse J at first instance, that Peter Sellers' estate could object to the making of another *Pink Panther* film from discarded 'out-takes'. In confirming the award of $1 million damages, Browne-Wilkinson VC observed that uncertainties about the action remained, particularly whether protection survived the death of the performer and how long the right was to last.

As to whether recording companies could claim in equity because of damage to their economic interests in the exclusive recording contract with performers, the case law went in the opposite direction. Initially, in *Ex parte Island Records*, the Court of Appeal thought there should be a remedy. This, however, was doubted in *Lonrho v Shell Petroleum* and *Shelley v Cunane* and ultimately rejected by the Court of Appeal in *RCA v Pollard* [1983] Ch 135, a case concerned with bootleg recordings of Elvis Presley to which Presley's estate had not been joined as party. The court concluded that the bootleg recordings didn't destroy the exclusive recording contract with the performer, they merely made the contract less valuable. There was therefore no special damage.

7.2.4 **The CDPA Part II: overview**

Part II CDPA can in one sense be viewed as a culmination of the case law discussed in the preceding paragraphs. It gave effect to the thinking of the Court of Appeal in *Rickless v United Artists* by conferring civil law protection on performers; and overturned the decision in *RCA v Pollard* by giving rights to those recording companies which have exclusive recording contracts with performers.

However, Part II has since been amended four times in order to take account of obligations imposed on the United Kingdom as an EU Member State. These obligations flow from:

a. the Rental Rights Directive (Council Directive 92/100/EEC of 19 November 1992 on rental right and lending right and on certain rights related to copyright in the field of intellectual property [1992] OJ L 346/61, now codified as Directive 2006/115/EC of the European Parliament and of the Council of 12 December 2006 [2006] OJ L 376/28);

b. the Information Society Directive (Directive 2001/29/EC of the European Parliament and of the Council of 22 May 2001 on the harmonisation of certain aspects of copyright and related rights in the information society [2001] OJ L 167/10);

c. Directive 2011/77/EU of the European Parliament and of the Council of 27 September 2011 [2011] OJ L 265/1, which amends the consolidated version of the Copyright Term Directive (Directive 2006/116/EC of the European Parliament and of the Council of 12 December 2006 [2006] OJ L 372/12); and

d. the WPPT. In the case of the WPPT, the EU is a signatory to the Convention.

Although there is no Directive on moral rights for performers, Recital 19 to the Information Society Directive makes clear that it regards Member States as bound by all the obligations of the WPPT. As a result, the United Kingdom Government took the view that the WPPT was in effect an EU Treaty, so that moral rights for performers could be introduced by secondary legislation under the European Communities Act 1972.

 Pause for reflection

As Simon-Fhima observes (in 'The Introduction of Performers' Moral Rights' [2006] *EIPR* 552, 600) the resulting Performances (Moral Rights etc) Regulations 2006 (SI 2006/18) were produced very speedily at the expense of Parliamentary scrutiny. Simon-Fhima suggests that the use of secondary legislation was prompted by a desire for Parliamentary expediency together with fear of action by the EU for non-implementation of the WPPT.

When passing The Performances (Moral Rights etc) Regulations 2006, the United Kingdom Government took the opportunity to restructure Part II of the CDPA into Chapters dealing with economic rights of performers (this category being divided into non-property and property rights) and their moral rights. For the sake of convenience, however, we deal with these rights in the historical order in which they were created, namely non-property rights (the original rights created by Part II CDPA), property rights (derived from the Rental Rights Directive), rights in respect of the internet (flowing from the Information Society Directive), and moral rights (the result of obligations under the WPPT).

7.2.5 The CDPA Part II: general matters

Before looking at these four aspects of performers' protection in turn, we must consider Chapter 1 of Part II. It consists of just two sections, ss. 180 and 181 which contain, respectively, some (but not all) key definitions and the requirements for qualification for protection. Section 180(1) has been described as a 'chatty introduction' to what follows (*Experience Hendrix LLC v Purple Haze Records Ltd* [2007] FSR 769 at [24] *per* Jacob LJ). The section declares that economic rights and moral rights are to be conferred on performers. Rights are also to be conferred on persons who have exclusive recording contracts with performers when illicit recordings of performances are made without the performers' consent. We may note the change of terminology, with the term 'illicit recording' being substituted for Lord Denning's more colourful 'bootleg recording'. The term 'illicit recording' is itself defined by s. 197 CDPA as meaning the recording of the whole or any substantial of a performance which is made otherwise than for private purposes without the consent of the performer. It is irrelevant where the recording is made. 'Exclusive recording contract' is defined by s. 185 to mean a contract between a performer and another person under which that person is entitled to the exclusion of all others (including the performer) to make recordings of the performance with a view to commercial exploitation.

Section 180(2) provides the definitions of 'performance' and 'recording'. The former means a dramatic performance, a musical performance, a reading or recitation of a literary work, or a performance of a variety act or similar presentation. Section 211 provides that 'literary work' is to have the same meaning as in Part I CDPA. That being so, does this mean that the literary work must be 'fixed', in which case Part II cannot apply to improvised performances? The wording of both the Rome Convention and the WPPT imply that the work being performed must be susceptible of copyright protection, although it is unclear whether they apply to works in the public domain, such as a Shakespeare play or Beethoven symphony. As Simon-Fhima explains, academic opinion is divided as to whether there must be some pre-existing script for Part II protection to arise.

A further difficulty is that the subsection adds that the performance must be 'a live performance given by one or more individuals'. 'Live' is not defined in the CDPA but it might be assumed that it requires the performance to be before an audience rather than in a film or recording studio. If this were so, *Rickless v United Artists* would have a different outcome today (leaving on one side the breach of contract aspect of the case), as Peter Sellers' performances were in a film studio rather than in a theatre. Nevertheless, Vinelott J in *Bassey v Icon Entertainment plc* [1995] EMLR 596 held that a studio performance fell within Part II CDPA so that the singer had redress when copies of a recording which she had vetoed were issued without her consent.

Section 180(2) defines 'recording' as a film or sound recording of the performance, whether this is made directly from the performance itself, made from a broadcast of the performance, or made directly or indirectly from another recording of the performance. We may note that like the PPA, Part II CDPA is broader than the Rome Convention in protecting the performer against the filming of the performance as well as by an unauthorized sound recording.

Section 181 sets out the precondition that in order to attract protection, the performance must be a qualifying performance, i.e. it must be given by a qualifying individual or take place in a qualifying country. Further detail is provided by s. 206, which operates in a similar fashion to s. 153 CDPA with regard to qualification for protection for copyright works. A 'qualifying individual' is someone who is a national of or resident in the United Kingdom, a Member State of the European Union, or a country designated by Order in Council as giving reciprocal protection. As with Part I CDPA, the Copyright and Performances (Application to Other Countries) Order 2013 (SI 2013/536) lists the relevant countries, which are basically signatories to the Rome Convention. If the performer is not a qualifying individual, then protection may be claimed where the performance occurred in a qualifying country, that is, the United Kingdom, a Member State of the European Union, or a signatory to the Rome Convention. In order for the company with an exclusive recording contract to receive protection, it too must be a qualifying person, i.e. it must be incorporated in the United Kingdom or another qualifying country, and it must have a substantial business activity in such territory (CDPA ss. 185(2) and 206(1)).

 Pause for reflection

Is Andrea's performance eligible for protection? Which are the relevant requirements?

7.2.6 Performers' non-property rights

The non-property rights of the performer are set out in ss. 182, 183, and 184 CDPA. The first of these sections gives a performer the right to object to the making of an illicit recording of a performance, the broadcasting of a performance, or the making of an illicit recording from a broadcast of the performance (such as where someone makes a recording of a live broadcast with the intention of selling copies of the recording). Under s. 183, the performer's rights are infringed if the illicit recording is shown or played in public or communicated to the public (that is, posted on the internet), and under s. 184, the performer's rights are also infringed by importation or other commercial dealings, such as sale or hire of copies of the illicit recording.

In parallel to the performer's rights with regard to illicit recordings, ss. 186, 187, and 188 create rights for those recording companies which have exclusive recording contracts with the performer. Thus the recording company can object to the making of an illicit recording of the performance (s. 186), to the showing or playing in public of that recording or the communication to the public of that recording (s. 187), and the importation of or other commercial dealings in copies of the illicit recording (s. 188). However, the rights of the recording company are not independent, because where the performer consents to the making of the recording, that consent binds the recording company (ss. 186(1), 187(1), 188(1), and 193(2)). The performer's consent may be given in relation to a specific performance, a specific description of performances (for example, all those given on a particular concert tour or given in a particular country), or performances generally, in all cases whether past or future (CDPA s. 193(1)) and will also bind anyone who inherits the performer's non-property right (s. 193(3)).

The right to object to illicit recordings of performances is retrospective, i.e. it applies to performances occurring before 1 August 1989: s. 180(3) CDPA. Furthermore, it does not matter that the performance took place in a country which at the time was not a qualifying country if that country subsequently joins the EU or the Rome Convention.

Experience Hendrix LLC v Purple Haze Records Ltd [2005] EMLR 417

In *Experience Hendrix LLC v Purple Haze Records Ltd* [2005] EMLR 417, Hart J held that the fact an illicit recording had been made of a Jimmy Hendrix concert in Sweden at a time when Sweden was not an EU Member State was irrelevant. If performances in the United Kingdom were given retrospective treatment by s. 180(3), it would be illogical not to give protection to performances taking place elsewhere.

In a separate case involving the same parties, the Court of Appeal held that it was also irrelevant that the performer had died before the CDPA came into force. The right of a performer's successors to object to illicit recordings was recognized in *Rickless v United Artists* and Parliament had originally provided that the rights should last for 50 years after the date of the performance, the rights surviving for the benefit of the performer's estate: *Experience Hendrix LLC v Purple Haze Records Ltd* [2007] FSR 769, CA.

Section 189 provides for a number defences ('permitted acts') which can be raised where there has been a breach of the performer's economic rights (both non-property and property). The list of the 25 separate defences is set out in Sch. 2 CDPA. They mirror many of the defences to copyright infringement found in Part I Chapter III CDPA. As might be expected, the defences are set out in detailed fashion and are subject to numerous qualifications and conditions.

The duration of rights in performances is dealt with by s. 191, amended by the Copyright and Duration of Rights in Performances Regulations 2013 (SI 2013/1782) ('the 2013 Regulations') so as to implement Directive 2011/77/EU of the European Parliament and of the Council of 27 September 2011 [2011] OJ L 265/1. The Directive was the EU's response to numerous calls from the pop stars of the 1950s and 1960s for the term of protection for sound recordings and performances to be extended. Section 191 accordingly provides for the right to expire 50 years from the performance or if, during that period, a recording of the performance (other than a sound recording) is released ('release' here meaning 'published, played or shown in public, or communicated to the public'), 50 years from release, or if a sound recording is released, 70 years from that release. No account is to be taken of any unauthorized release. If the performer is not a European Economic Area ('EEA') national, the right is to have the same duration as in the performer's own country.

The new provisions concerning the duration of performers' rights are retrospective. The 2013 Regulations accordingly contain complex transitional provisions which are beyond the scope of this work.

Section 192A CDPA declares that the performer's non-property rights cannot be assigned, in other words, like moral rights, they remain personal to the performer. They can, however, pass on death, either to the person to whom such rights were bequeathed, or, if there is no such bequest, to the performer's personal representatives. As with moral rights, s. 192A(5) provides that any damages recovered by the personal representatives for an infringement of the rights after the performer's death devolve as part of his or her estate, that is, they go to the residuary beneficiary and not to the person to whom the right was bequeathed. Section 192B likewise provides that the recording company's rights to object to illicit recordings are not assignable or transmissible.

 Pause for reflection

The CDPA provides in s. 194 that breach of the performer's non-property right is actionable as a breach of statutory duty. Because the same remedy is provided for infringement of moral rights, it can be argued that the provisions on a performer's non-property rights betray a similar approach to the provisions on an author's moral rights.

This should be contrasted with the remedies provided for infringement of the performer's property rights, explained later. One might speculate as to how damages under s. 194 might be calculated, although it should be remembered that the sum awarded ($1 million) in *Rickless v United Artists* was considerable. There are, however, the additional remedies of delivery up and seizure of illicit recordings set out in ss. 195 and 196, whilst ss. 198 to 204 deal with criminal penalties to be imposed on those who make, deal with, or use illicit recordings.

 Pause for reflection

To what extent can Andrea object to the making of xris1088's video of his performance, and the making of that video available to the public on a video-sharing website? Which are the relevant legal provisions that he can rely on?

7.2.7 Performers' property rights

Part II CDPA was amended in 1996 in order to give effect to the Rental Rights Directive. The Directive anticipated the effect of the WPPT by conferring copyright-type rights on performers to control the exploitation of *legitimate* copies of their performances.

Section 182A begins by creating the performer's reproduction right, that is, the right to control the making of copies of a qualifying performance. Like s. 17 CDPA, it provides that the copy can be direct or indirect and can be of the whole or a substantial part of the performance. It includes the making of transient (i.e. temporary) copies or those which are incidental to some other use of the recording.

Sections 182B and 182C provide for rights analogous to those found in ss. 18 and 18A CDPA, namely the distribution right and the rental and lending right. As with copyright, the distribution right is the right to control the issuing of copies to the public of the recording and the section contains the principle of exhaustion of rights, so that the distribution right is 'spent' where copies are put on the market within the EEA but not where they are first put in circulation outside the EEA. Just as with s. 18, there is no guidance yet about the point at which copies are issued *to the public*. It is, however, clear, that 'issuing' requires the transfer of ownership or possession: Case C-456/06 *Peek & Cloppenburg KG v Cassina SpA* [2008] ECR I-2731. The rental right in s. 182C is similarly concerned with the supply of tangible copies of the performance. 'Rental' means that copies are made available for use on terms that the copies will or may be returned for a direct or indirect economic advantage, whereas 'lending', which must be by an establishment which is accessible to the public (i.e. a library), does not involve a commercial advantage to that establishment. Rental and lending do not involve making the copies available for performance, playing in public, communication to the public, for reference use, or interlibrary transactions. The separate rental right in copyright (s. 18A) is a deliberate exception to the doctrine of exhaustion (Case C-61/97 *Egmont Films v Laserdisken* [1998] ECR I-5171) and one must assume that the same applies to the rental right in a performance.

Last, s. 182D gives the performer the right to demand equitable remuneration when a commercially published sound recording of a qualifying performance is played or communicated to the public (whether by being broadcast or posted on the internet). The right to remuneration cannot be assigned except to a copyright collecting society but on the death of the performer is treated as his or her personal property. Likewise, the right cannot be restricted by contractual provisions. In the case of dispute about the amount of equitable remuneration, the matter is to be decided by the Copyright Tribunal.

The reproduction, issuing, and rental rights are declared by s. 191A to be property rights. In consequence, they receive the same treatment as copyright, so that they can be assigned and licensed (s. 191B), with exclusive licensees being granted the same procedural rights as exclusive licensees of copyright (s. 191D). Also like copyright, there can be an assignment of future rights (s. 191C). The performer's property right passes on death in the usual way, and in parallel to copyright law (CDPA s. 93), where a will bequeaths an unpublished sound recording, the performer's right passes under that bequest. In the case of an assignment of the rental right in a sound recording or film to the producer thereof, the performer retains the right to equitable remuneration, which can only be assigned to a copyright collecting society. According to *Bourne v Davis* [2006] EWHC 1567, where there is more than one performer, each performer has individual rights which they can control, so that one member of a group cannot assign the property rights of the others. The 2013 Regulations add, in s. 191HA, that the performer has the right to terminate an assignment of the reproduction, distribution, and communication rights or the performer's property rights in a sound recording of a performance where the producer of that recording has, at the end of 50 years, failed to issue sufficient quantities of the recording or failed to make it available to the public by electronic transmission. The 50-year period is calculated from the first publication or making available to the public of the sound recording. Termination of the assignment has the effect of triggering the expiry of the copyright in the sound recording, thus leaving the producer, as owner of the copyright in the sound recording, without an enforceable right.

In the case of the infringement of the performer's property right, ss. 191I and J confer remedies which are identical to those given to a copyright owner by ss. 96 and 97 CDPA, that is, damages, injunctions, an account of profits, and additional damages. The generosity of this provision should be contrasted with s. 194 which treats infringement of the performer's non-property right as a breach of statutory duty. One can only assume that additional damages will not be available against a bootlegger.

 Pause for reflection

Is the different treatment accorded to the performer's non-property and property rights with regard to ownership and infringement justified?

7.2.8 Performers' rights in respect of the internet

As part of the range of property rights accorded to a performer, the 2003 amendments to the CDPA (implementing the Information Society Directive) introduced the right found in s. 182CA, namely the right to control the making available to the public of recordings of a qualifying performance. The section makes clear that the right refers specifically to communication via the internet ('by electronic transmission in such a way that members of the public may access the recording from a place and at a time individually chosen by them'). For this reason, there are specific provisions in s. 191JA enabling the award of injunctions against internet service providers who have actual knowledge that another person is using the service to infringe a performer's property right.

The communication right is treated in exactly the same manner as the other property rights of the performer explained in the previous section with regard to ownership and infringement.

 Pause for reflection

Going back to our scenario question, can Andrea claim infringement of his reproduction right against xris1088's copy of his music track on a video-sharing website? Can he demand equitable remuneration for xris1088's communication of his music track to the public?

7.2.9 Performers' moral rights

Under the WPPT, the protection for a performer's moral rights is limited to live aural performances. This means that visual performances are not protected, although the word 'aural' suggests that the right is not limited to music and so would apply to the aural part of a dramatic performance. Be that as it may, the CDPA is not so constrained. Because of the wording of Chapter 1 of Part II, the definition of 'performance' in s. 180(2) must apply to all sections dealing with a performer's rights, so the CDPA is wider than the WPPT.

Section 205C creates the paternity right for a performer. There is the right to be identified whenever anyone produces or puts on a qualifying performance in public, broadcasts a live qualifying performance, communicates to the public a sound recording of a
qualifying performance, or issues copies of such a recording to the public. The manner
of identification depends on the circumstances of the performance, i.e. whether it is a
performance in public, a broadcast of the same, a sound recording which is communicated to the public, or copies of a sound recording which are issued. However, in the
case of a performance by a group, it is sufficient if the group is identified. 'Group' means
two or more performers who have a particular name by which they may be collectively
identified.

Like the author's moral right of paternity, the performer's right must also be asserted.
Section 205D is worded in almost identical fashion to s. 78, except of course that it does
not replicate the special provisions about artistic works. The effect of assertion on third
parties is the same.

There are eight exceptions to the paternity right set out in s. 205E. The right does
not apply where it is not reasonably practicable to identify the performer (would this
apply to a large symphony orchestra?), nor does it apply to any performance given for
the purpose of reporting current events or advertising goods or services. Certain of the
defences in Sch. 2 which apply to a performer's property rights apply also to the right of
paternity, namely news reporting, incidental inclusion, examinations, judicial proceedings, and Royal Commissions.

The right to object to derogatory treatment (the integrity right) is set out in s. 205F.
Whilst this does not have to be asserted, the manner in which it can be infringed is
narrower than the paternity right. The performer may only object if the performance is
broadcast live or is played in public or communicated to the public by means of a sound
recording 'with any distortion, mutilation or other modification that is prejudicial to
the reputation of the performer'. It will be appreciated that this wording is even narrower than the equivalent for the author's right of integrity in s. 80. Given the case law
on s. 80, it is likely that an objective test will be applied. Section 205F, in contrast to s.
205C, does not contain any special treatment for groups. As with the author's right of
integrity, there is secondary liability for dealing in sound recordings which infringe the
integrity right (s. 205H).

The exceptions to the integrity right are narrower than those to the paternity right.
They include performances given for the purpose of reporting current events, and alterations to a performance which are part of 'normal editorial practice', a phrase likely
to produce litigation. Where the alteration is to avoid the commission of an offence or
made by the BBC to avoid the inclusion of offensive material in a broadcast, and the
performer has been identified, there is no infringement of the right only where there
is an adequate disclaimer. The conclusion must be that if the right of paternity has not
been asserted, then there is no need for the disclaimer.

The duration of the moral rights is coterminous with the performer's economic
rights, so that the governing factor is the date of the performance. Just as with an
author's moral rights, a performer's moral rights can be waived or be the subject of
consent, s. 205J being worded in an identical manner to s. 87. The performer's moral
rights are personal to the performer and cannot be assigned (s. 205L), but they can be
transmitted on death. Section 205M mirrors the wording of s. 95, so that the performer

may bequeath their moral rights to a named individual, but failing that the moral rights pass to the person who has been bequeathed the performer's property rights, and failing that they pass to the performer's personal representatives. Section 205M(5) contains an identical provision to s. 95(5), explained earlier, so that where there is an action for infringement of the performer's moral rights after their death, the damages are dealt with as part of the performer's general estate.

The remedies for infringement of moral rights are set out in s. 205N. Infringement is actionable as a breach of statutory duty. In the case of infringement by derogatory treatment, the court is able to grant an injunction on terms which permit the infringer to continue with their conduct provided there is an appropriate disclaimer. As mentioned in the discussion of s. 103(2) earlier, this means that the infringing work can still be exploited commercially so that the defendant is in effect given a licence to commit derogatory treatment. Equally, it is not clear how the disclaimer is to be made known to the audience of the broadcast or those who hear the sound recording being played.

Unlike the performer's non-property rights, the performer's moral rights are not retrospective. The provisions in the CDPA apply only to performances occurring after 1 February 2006.

7.3 The *sui generis* database right

Europe has a dual regime for the protection of databases, which was launched via the Database Directive (Directive 96/9/EC of the European Parliament and of the Council of 11 March 1996 on the legal protection of databases, OJ L 077, 27 March 1996): copyright protection and the database right. Databases that are their author's own intellectual creation, i.e. 'original' databases, receive copyright protection and databases which do not meet the originality requirement but their making involves a substantial investment ('non-original' databases) are protected by a database right of lesser duration than copyright. The database right, which is referred to as a *sui generis* right, is a novel form of intellectual property and no Member State had a comparable legal instrument in place before its enactment. For this reason, the interpretation of its precise scope has proven difficult by the Member States and the European Free Trade Association ('EFTA') countries, which implemented the Directive into their legislation. It is a distinct form of protection afforded to commercially valuable databases that would otherwise fail to be protected under copyright law. Because it has some similarities to copyright but still be a distinct right with its own conditions of application it can be referred to as 'quasi-copyright'.

At the time of the adoption of the Directive, the differences in the originality standard as a prerequisite for copyright protection of databases was considered an impediment to the free movement of 'database products' within the EU. Whereas common law Member States, notably the United Kingdom and Ireland, had adopted a 'sweat of the brow' approach, requiring considerable skill, labour, or judgement in gathering together a compilation, *droit d'auteur* Member States required a higher standard of protection, namely they were affording protection to 'intellectual creations'. To avoid distortions in trade, the Directive adopted a two-tiers approach as an attempt to harmonize the threshold of 'originality'.

In this light, databases are protected by copyright if—and only if—by reason of the selection or arrangement of their contents, the database constitutes the author's own intellectual creation. Databases which are not eligible for copyright protection but are commercially valuable, being the result of substantial investment, receive protection under the *sui generis* right that is meant to reward the maker of the database for the investment in deploying financial resources and/or the spending of time, effort, and energy.

The database right applies irrespective of the eligibility of that database for protection by copyright or by other rights. In this light, many databases that receive copyright protection may also benefit from the database right (Art. 7(4) of the Database Directive). The overlap matters because infringement and exceptions to infringement are not identical for both rights. For example, the repeated and systematic extraction of *insubstantial* parts of the database may infringe the database right in circumstances where copyright infringement cannot be established.

 Pause for reflection

There is a substantial overlap between the copyright and the *sui generis* protection for databases. This is mostly due to the fact that both types of protection cover the same subject matter. As a result, the person who has put his intellect in the creation of the database and, additionally, invested substantially in the obtaining and the verification of the database's contents qualifies both for copyright and *sui generis* protection. Nonetheless, the two types of protection differ in terms of subsistence requirements, exclusive rights afforded, and applicable exceptions and limitations. Consequently, even though the two regimes present some similarities, they are not totally on a par with each other.

7.3.1 Meaning of database

Section 3A(1) of the CDPA defines a database to mean 'a collection of independent works, data or other materials which—(a) are arranged in a systematic or methodical way, and (b) are individually accessible by electronic or other means.' It is generally understood that a 'database' is more than a mere collection of data and it can include works of authorship or other subject matter. Websites, multimedia works (i.e. collections of many different types of works in structured and unified format, such as CD-ROMs or a web resources), and collections of works available online, such as bulletin board services, may qualify for database copyright, if they meet the originality requirement, or they may receive protection by the database right if their creation is the result of substantial investment.

However, compilation of music on a CD is excluded both from copyright and *sui generis* protection. Recital 19 of the Database Directive indicates that 'as a rule, the compilation of several recordings of musical performances on a CD does not come within the scope of this Directive, both because, as a compilation, it does not meet the conditions for copyright protection and because it does not represent a substantial enough investment to be eligible under the sui generis right[.]' This implies that cost and labour in producing and compiling the phonographic recordings collected on a music CD are not taken into account as 'investment' for the purposes of the database right.

Pause for reflection

Can Andrea's compilation of music tracks in the album qualify as a database and be eligible for either copyright protection or protection from the database right, or both? Why not? What about the playlist?

The broad definition of 'database' has been stressed by the Court of Justice of the European Union ('CJEU') in *Fixtures Marketing Ltd v 'OPAP'* (Case C-444/02, [2004] ECR I-10549, at [20], [25] and [32]). The case involved the unauthorized extraction of a substantial number of pairings of football teams playing against each other and their transfer to four of OPAP's websites. The CJEU held that the term 'database' had a broad scope, covering 'any collection of works, data or other materials, separable from one another without the value of their contents being affected, including a method or system of some sort for the retrieval of its constituent materials' (at [32]). Fixture lists fell under this definition as—even though the interest of a football league mainly rests in the overall result of the various matches in that league—data concerning the date, the time, and the identity of the teams in a particular match have independent value because they provide interested third parties with information (at [34]).

7.3.2 The *sui generis* database right

According to section 13(1) of the Copyright and Rights in Databases Regulations 1997, 'a property right ("database right") subsists . . . in a database if there has been a substantial investment in obtaining, verifying or presenting the contents of the database.' 'Obtaining' refers to the collection the materials comprising the database, 'verification' to the checking, correcting, and updating of the contents of the database and 'presentation' to the form in which the compiled data are communicated.

The maker of the database is the person who takes the initiative in obtaining, verifying, or presenting the contents of a database and assumes the risk of investing in that obtaining, verification, or presentation (s. 14(1)). With regards to employee inventions, the employer is regarded as the maker of the database, subject to any agreement to the contrary (s. 14(2)). A database is made jointly if two or more persons acting together in collaboration take the initiative in obtaining, verifying, or presenting the contents of the database and assume the risk of investing in that obtaining, verification, or presentation (s. 14(5)). There is a presumption that the maker of the database is the owner of the database right in it (s. 15).

Database protection is conferred to the investment in the obtaining, verification, and presentation of the contents of a database. The investment as a requirement for protection may be in respect of financial, human, or technical resources and/or the expenditure of time, effort, and energy. The database right is not meant to protect the investment deployed in the creation of the materials that form the contents of a database. This important distinction has been highlighted in a number of cases that have been brought before the CJEU.

In *Fixtures Marketing Ltd v Oy Veikkaus Ab* (Case C-46/02, [2004] ECR I-10365), the CJEU held that the investment in the creation of a database may consist in the deployment of human, financial, or technical resources. To be protected by the database right, investment has to be substantial both qualitatively and quantitatively, meaning that it is both quantifiable resources and efforts that cannot be measured, such as intellectual effort or energy, that are taken into account. As a result, where the person creating the database also creates the materials contained in the database is not excluded from protection. However, protection is available so long as the maker of the database establishes that the obtaining, verification, and presentation of the contents of that database required substantial investment that was *independent* from the investment in the creation of the materials that form the contents of the database. The CJEU also held that the expression 'investment in . . . the obtaining . . . of the contents' under Art. 7(1) of the Database Directive should be understood to refer to the resources used to seek out existing independent materials and collect them in the database rather than to the resources used for the *creation* of materials as such. The mere creation of data does not fall within the ambit of substantial investment in the obtaining of the contents of the database and does not qualify for *sui generis* database protection.

British Horseracing Board Ltd and Others v William Hill Organisation Ltd (Case C-203/02, [2004] ECR I-10415)

In *British Horseracing Board Ltd and Others v William Hill Organisation Ltd* (Case C-203/02, [2004] ECR I-10415), a referral from the UK Court of Appeal, the CJEU held that the resources used to draw up a list of horses in a race and to carry out checks in that connection do not constitute investment in the obtaining and verification of the contents of the database in which that list appears. As a result, the Court drew a distinction between the resources used in the *creation* of materials contained in a database and the *obtaining* of such materials. The *sui generis* database right is afforded only to the latter activity. Thus, bodies like the British Horseracing Board that *create* the data in order to assemble the contents of a database and do not *obtain* these data from others, do not receive database protection and, consequently, cannot license their own data to third parties.

Fixtures Marketing Ltd v AB Svenska Spel (Case C-338/02, [2004] ECR I-10497)

The CJEU followed the same distinction in *Fixtures Marketing Ltd v AB Svenska Spel* (Case C-338/02, [2004] ECR I-10497), where it held that the notion of 'investment . . . in the obtaining of the contents' referred to the resources used to seek out existing independent materials and to collect them in the database. It did not cover the resources used for the *creation* of materials making up the database's contents. 'Sole-source' databases, namely databases where the status of the maker of the database and the proprietor of the underlying information coincide in the same person or entity are protected as long as additional 'substantial investment' in the obtaining of the data can be demonstrated.

The beneficiary of the *sui generis* right is entitled to prevent extraction or re-utilization of the whole or of a substantial part of the contents of the database (s. 16). 'Extraction', in relation to any contents of a database, means the permanent or temporary transfer of those contents to another medium by any means or in any form. 'Re-utilization', in relation to any contents of a database, means making those contents available to the public by distribution of copies, by renting, by online or other forms of transmission. The acts of repeated and systematic extraction or re-utilization of insubstantial parts of the contents of the database are prohibited where those acts conflict with a normal exploitation of the database or prejudice unreasonably the legitimate interests of the maker of the database. A decisive factor is the harm caused to the investment.

The database right, as a property right subsisting in the database may be transferred, assigned, or granted under a licence. The term of protection of the database right is set out in s. 10 of the Regulations and it expires at the end of the period of 15 years from the end of the calendar year in which the making of the database was completed. However, if the database is made available to the public before the end of that period, the right continues to endure for 15 years from the date on which the database was first made available to the public. In case that the database is substantially updated or modified as a result of an accumulation of successive additions, deletions, or alterations, to the extent of being considered as a substantial new investment, a fresh 15-year term of protection is provided.

7.3.3 Permitted acts in relation to a database

Section 19 indicates that a *lawful user* of a database which has been made available to the public in any manner shall be entitled to extract or re-utilize insubstantial parts of the contents of the database for any purpose. A lawful user in relation to a database is any person who has been given the right to access and use the database by a licence or other authorization from the beneficiary of the *sui generis* right. Where under an agreement a person has a right to use a database, or part of a database, which has been made available to the public in any manner, any term or condition in the agreement shall be void in so far as it purports to prevent that person from extracting or re-utilizing insubstantial parts of the contents of the database, or of that part of the database, for any purpose.

Section 20 of the Copyright and Rights in Databases Regulations 1997 states that the database right in a database which has been made available to the public in any manner is not infringed by *fair dealing* with a substantial part of its contents if (a) that part is extracted from the database by a person who is apart from this paragraph a lawful user of the database, (b) it is extracted for the purpose of illustration for teaching or research and not for any commercial purpose, and (c) the source is indicated. This exception to the database right flows from Art. 8 of the Database Directive which lays down a mandatory provision. Substantiality in this context is evaluated in terms of quality and/or quantity and/or a combination of both. A lawful user of a database which is made available to the public may not perform acts which conflict with the normal exploitation of the database and unreasonably prejudice the legitimate interests of its maker or the interests of holders of copyright or related rights in respect of the contents of the database (Art. 8(2) and (3)).

Public lending is to a certain extent allowed. Section 12(2) of the Copyright and Rights in Databases Regulations 1997 specifies that the making of a copy of a database available for use, on terms that it will or may be returned, otherwise than for direct or indirect economic or commercial advantage, through an establishment which is accessible to the public shall not be taken for the purposes of this Part to constitute extraction or re-utilization of the contents of the database.

In implementation of Art. 15 of the Database Directive, s. 296B specifies that where under an agreement a person has a right to use a database or part of a database, any term or condition in the agreement shall be void in so far as it purports to prohibit or restrict the performance of any act which would but for s. 50D infringe the copyright in the database. This is an important provision as it clarifies the relationship between contract and limitations to the database right in that contractual restrictions to the rights and obligations of lawful users are void.

 Pause for reflection

An interesting aspect of the contractual restriction of lawful uses arose in *Ryanair v PR Aviation* (Case C-30/14, EU:C:2015:10). In this case, the CJEU held that Art. 15 of the Database Directive, which declares null and void contracts excluding permitted uses under Arts 6(1) and 8 of the Directive, does not apply to databases that—albeit falling under the definition of a database—cannot be protected by copyright or the database right. According to Art. 6(1), a lawful user can perform acts that are necessary to access the contents and to carry out a normal use of the contents of the database, and according to Art. 8 the lawful user has a fully fledged 'right' to extract and/or re-utilize insubstantial parts of a database that has been made available to the public. In *Ryanair*, the CJEU had to determine whether PR Aviation had a defence for the extraction and re-utilization of Ryanair's database of flight data in order to carry out price comparisons and to book flights subject to the payment of a commission. The use was in breach of the terms and conditions included in Ryanair's website, which prohibited unauthorized screen scraping and price comparisons. The case reaches a paradoxical conclusion: databases that cannot be protected under either copyright or the database right can benefit from stronger contractual protection than protected databases. Even though the Directive expressly states that contracts restricting permitted activities from lawful users shall be null and void, the CJEU interpreted the provision as available not to subject matter that qualifies as a database under the Directive but to databases that *qualify for protection* under the Directive. This has the odd effect that makers of non-protected databases enjoy full freedom of contract, unlike the makers of databases that happen to qualify for copyright or the database right (see M. Borghi and S. Karapapa, 'Contractual Restrictions on Lawful Use of Information: Sole-source Databases Protected by the Back Door?' [2015] 37(8) *EIPR* 505).

7.4 Technological protection measures and rights management information

Rightholders can use 'self-help' mechanisms, in the form of technological protection measures, in order to exploit their works that are made available to the public in digital form. In the digital environment, one of the greatest risks that rightholders face is the ease of copying and subsequently making the work available. Technological protection measures include encryption and access control mechanisms, and they can have an important role in enabling rightholders to enhance offer of content to consumers and protect themselves against unauthorized copying. The application of technological protection measures is reinforced by laws prohibiting the circumvention of such measures through civil and criminal actions. These legal provisions apply by reference to copyright but also by reference to performer's rights and the *sui generis* database right.

 Pause for reflection

Going back to the scenario question, Andrea should be made aware of the following legal framework that is available with regards to the legal protection against the circumvention of technological protection measures.

The protection on technological protection measures was first introduced at the international level in 1996 through the WIPO Copyright Treaty ('WCT') and the WPPT. These Treaties require the introduction of adequate legal protection and effective legal remedies against the circumvention of technological measures applied to copyright protected works and phonograms (WCT Art. 11; WPPT Art. 18).

The implementation of this international obligation in Europe took place via the Information Society Directive (Art. 6), which requires Member States to provide adequate legal protection against the circumvention of any effective technological measures, which the person concerned carries out in the knowledge, or with reasonable grounds to know, that he is pursuing that objective. The anti-circumvention protection is also applicable with respect to technological measures applied voluntarily by rightholders. As a result, bypassing technological measures, such as DVD region-code restrictions, is illegal.

Member States are also obliged to provide adequate legal protection against: the manufacture, import, distribution, sale, rental, advertisement for sale or rental, or possession for commercial purposes of devices, products, or the provision of services, which are promoted, advertised, or marketed for the purpose of circumvention; have only a limited commercially significant purpose or use other than circumvention; are primarily designed, produced, adapted, or performed for the purpose of enabling or facilitating circumvention. The purpose of the legal protection on technological measures is to ensure a secure environment for the provision of interactive 'on-demand' services, so that members of the public may access protected works from a place and at a time individually chosen by them.

There are three categories of provision in the CDPA addressing situations where a person facilitates access to works that they are not entitled to use or receive. First, ss. 296ZA–ZF offer protection in cases involving the circumvention of effective technological measures that have been applied to a copyright work other than a computer program, and a person who does anything which circumvents those measures knowing, or with reasonable grounds to know, that he is pursuing that objective. Second, s. 296 covers specifically computer programs on which a technical devise has been applied and a person knowing or having reason to believe that it will be used to make infringing copies: (i) manufactures for sale or hire, imports, distributes, sells or lets for hire, offers or exposes for sale or hire, advertises for sale or hire, or has in his possession for commercial purposes any means the sole intended purpose of which is to facilitate the unauthorized removal or circumvention of the technical device; or (ii) publishes information intended to enable or assist persons to remove or circumvent the technical device. Finally, ss. 297–299 covers the reception of transmissions, in implementation of the Conditional Access Directive 98/84/EC.

An interesting aspect on the legal protection afforded to technological protection measures was highlighted in Case C-355/12, *Nintendo Co. Ltd and Others v PC Box Srl and 9Net Srl* (ECLI:EU:C:2014:25). In this case, the CJEU held that in order to qualify for legal protection under Art. 6 of the Information Society Directive, technological protection measures embedded into videogame consoles must respect the principle of proportionality, in the sense they should not prohibit devices or activities which have a commercially significant purpose or use other than to circumvent the technical protection (at [30]). This would require looking into whether technological measures directed at the games themselves—instead of the console—would offer adequate copyright protection. When assessing the purpose of the defendant's device, the assessment of the national court would have to focus on whether it was used to facilitate unauthorized copies of Nintendo games or alternatives to those games ([31]–[38]). In this light, it can be said that where rightholders apply measures that disproportionately exclude a big number of lawful activities, such measures will not receive protection because an equally big number of circumvention tools will be used towards lawful activities.

The Information Society Directive also offers protection to 'rights-management information' which is defined as any information that identifies the work, the author, or any other rightholder, or information setting the terms and conditions of use of the work (Art. 7(2)). Member States are obliged under Art. 7(1) to provide for adequate legal protection against any person who knowingly performs any of the following acts: the removal or alteration of any electronic rights management information; the distribution, importation for distribution, broadcasting, communication, or making available to the public of works from which electronic rights management information has been removed or altered without authority.

Section 296ZG CDPA offers protection against the circumvention of electronic rights management information, covering instances where a person, knowingly and without authority, removes or alters electronic rights management information which (a) is associated with a copy of a copyright work, or (b) appears in connection with the communication to the public of a copyright work, and where that person knows, or has reason to believe, that by so doing he is inducing, enabling, facilitating, or concealing an infringement of copyright. It also applies where a person, knowingly and without authority, distributes, imports for distribution, or communicates to the public copies of a copyright work from which electronic rights management information (a) associated with the copies, or (b) appearing in connection with the communication to the public of the work, has been removed or altered without authority and where that person knows, or has reason to believe, that by so doing he is inducing, enabling, facilitating, or concealing an infringement of copyright. Knowledge is a requirement in both instances, meaning that accidental removal of data is permitted, and so is the deliberate removal of metadata in cases where the person has no reason to think that infringement is likely to occur.

Pause for reflection

The application of technological protection measures could potentially prevent activities that are permitted by copyright exceptions. Dusollier, Poullet, and Buydens acknowledge that technological measures are 'blind' in that they cannot comprehend the subtleties of the law (S. Dusollier, Y. Poullet, and M. Buydens, 'Copyright and Access to Information in the Digital Environment' (2000) XXXIV(4) *Copyright Bulletin* 4, 22–23). This was highlighted in *Scarlet Extended SA v Société belge des auteurs, compositeurs et éditeurs SCRL (SABAM)* (C-70/10, [52]), where the CJEU stated that a filtering system of online user behaviour could undermine freedom of information by not distinguishing between lawful and unlawful content.

The intersection between technological protection measures and copyright exceptions was addressed at the international level through the WIPO Treaties. Article 11 of the WIPO Copyright Treaty and Art. 18 of the WIPO Performances and Phonograms Treaty state that contracting parties should provide adequate legal protection and effective legal remedies against the circumvention of technological protection measures used by the rightholders in connection to the exercise of their rights and capable of restricting activities, in respect of their works, which are not authorized by the rightholders concerned *nor permitted by the law*. This means that the protection to technological measures should not apply in respect of permitted activities, such as copyright exceptions and limitations.

According to Art. 6(3) of the Information Society Directive, the definition of technological protection measures does not address their relationship to exceptions, inferring that the intersection of technological protection measures and exceptions is not settled. Art. 6(3) reads that 'the expression "technological protection measures" means any technology, device or component that, in the normal course of its operation, is designed to prevent or restrict acts, in respect of works or other subject-matter, which are not authorized by the rightholder of any copyright or any right related to copyright.'

Under UK law, if the owner of a technological protection measure does not allow a person with a legitimate right to access the protected content to bypass the technological protection may receive a 'notice of complaint' to the Secretary of State (s. 296ZE CDPA). The Secretary of State may give to that rightholder such directions as appear to the Secretary of State to be requisite or expedient for the purpose of (a) establishing whether any voluntary measure or agreement relevant to the copyright work the subject of the complaint subsists, or (b) (where it is established there is no subsisting voluntary measure or agreement) ensuring that the relevant rightholders of that copyright work make available to the complainant the means of carrying out the permitted act the subject of the complaint to the extent necessary to so benefit from that permitted act.

7.5 The artist's resale right

Some jurisdictions (notably France) have for some time conferred on artists a special right that enables them to receive a royalty on any subsequent sale of their original works of art. This right, which is known as the resale right or *droit de suite*, aims to encourage the production of unique art forms which, by nature, cannot be distributed *en masse.* The rationale underlying the resale right is that whereas works of contemporary artists do not sell on a reasonable price at the time of their creation, they may later be resold for continually increasing sums.

Found initially in Art. 14*ter* of the Berne Convention, the artist's resale right was introduced into EU law by the *Droit de Suite Directive* (Directive 2001/84/EC of the European Parliament and of the Council of 27 September 2001 on the resale right for the benefit of the author of an original work of art of [2001] OJ L 272/32, throughout this chapter, the '2001 Directive'). This was implemented into UK law by The Artist's Resale Rights Regulations 2006 (SI 2006/346) (the 'Regulations').

Recital 3 of the 2001 Directive (which the United Kingdom opposed) states that the purpose of the *droit de suite* is to ensure that artists share in the economic success of their original works of art, Recital 4 adding that the resale right is an integral part of copyright and is an essential prerogative for authors. The recitals continue with the declaration that the majority of Member States recognize the resale right and that harmonization of laws is required in the interests of the internal market. One of the United Kingdom's concerns was that the Directive would have an adverse effect on the London art market, with the risk that business would be diverted to other countries, such as Switzerland or the USA (with the exception of the state of California which has a resale royalty act protectable under Civil Code s. 986), which do not have a resale right.

The Directive offers a broad and non-exhaustive definition of the 'dealers of works of art', covering in essence sales performed by any professional intermediary, including auction houses, private galleries, and online auction sites insofar as there is a connecting factor between the sale and the EU resale right legislation. Article 3 of the Directive obliges Member States to set a minimum sale price from which the subsequent sales of the work shall be subject to the resale right and Art. 4 contains an extensive and detailed list of rates for the calculation of the royalties. By virtue of Art. 8 of the Directive, the resale right lasts for life of the author plus 70 years after his death.

The Regulations which implement the Directive into United Kingdom law provide that the author of a work of art in which copyright subsists is to be paid a royalty on any sale of the work (provided the sale occurred after the date of the Regulations) which is a resale subsequent to the first transfer of ownership by the author. In other words, the resale right is triggered by any transaction subsequent to the first sale by the artist, whereby ownership of the tangible medium of the work of art is transferred to another. It is therefore irrelevant who owns the copyright, rather what matters is ownership of the physical object. The work must, however, be the subject of copyright protection. 'Work' means any work of graphic or plastic art such as a picture, collage, painting, drawing, engraving, print, lithograph, sculpture, tapestry, a ceramic, an item of glassware, or a photograph. This should be compared with the somewhat narrower list of 'artistic works' in s. 4 CDPA. The Regulations add that the right also applies to limited copies of the work provided these have been made by or with the authority of the author, although no definition is given of what is a 'limited copy'. Unlike the Berne Convention which extends the resale right to manuscripts, the 2001 Directive and the Regulations are limited to works of art.

In contrast to the moral rights set out in Part IV CDPA, any waiver of the right is to be of no effect. The Regulations further provide that the resale right cannot be assigned, whether during the artist's lifetime or by the artist's successors. The right can, however, be bequeathed under the artist's will or pass on their intestacy. Once inherited, the artist's heirs may also pass on the entitlement on their death. However, where the right has been bequeathed to a charity, it may be transferred to another charity, a provision obviously designed to assist museums and art galleries. The resale right is to last as long as copyright. However, when implementing the Directive, the United Kingdom took advantage of the option set out in Art. 8(2) of the 2001 Directive, so that the right is not available to the heirs of any artists who died before 1 January 2010. The United Kingdom notified the EU Commission on 18 December 2008 that it intended taking advantage of a further option set out in Art. 8(3) by extending the period by which the resale right does not accrue to the artist's heirs for a further two years. This meant that until 1 January 2012 the right was only available to living artists.

A number of transactions are exempted from the right. It does not apply to the first transfer of ownership by the artist themselves, whether this is by sale, gift, or on death. Similarly, it does not apply to any resale within three years of the first transfer where the price was less than €10,000, nor does it apply to private sales, i.e. those where the seller, buyer, or their agents are not art-market professionals. Lastly, the right does not apply to commercial sales (either by auction or private treaty) where the price was less than €1,000.

 Pause for reflection

The resale right does not cover the first transfer of ownership by the artists themselves but the first transfer is covered by the distribution right. Unlike other categories of works, however, where the authorial control over every subsequent transfer of the work is exhausted after the first act of putting the works in circulation within the EEA, the resale right gives authors of artistic works some control over subsequent acts of distribution in that they receive royalties over subsequent sales of their works.

The right is available to artists who are 'qualifying individuals', that is, EEA nationals or nationals of those countries listed in Sch. 2 of the Regulations. An artist's heirs (once they are entitled to the right after 2012) need not be qualifying individuals in order to enjoy the right, but if they are not qualifying, they are not able to transmit the right in turn when they die. In contrast to copyright, qualification for protection is based solely on nationality, so that the country of domicile or residence is irrelevant.

The calculation of the royalty to be paid on resale is set out in detail in Sch. 1 of the Regulations. Payment of the royalty is the responsibility of the seller, who is jointly and severally liable with the seller's agent (if any) or failing that, the agent of the buyer, or, if there is no such agent, the buyer. The United Kingdom has decided that royalties should be managed for artists by collecting societies, the two currently involved being the Design and Artists Copyright Society and the Artists' Collecting Society.

> **Pause for reflection**
>
> It is often argued that, given that the resale right is personal to the artist, and cannot be waived or assigned, it should be regarded as a moral right. This approach focuses principally on the personality rights of authors and is premised on the view that artists and their works are in a continuing relationship, even after the works are sold. It is under this natural law justification of intellectual property rights, which is available mostly in civil law traditions, notably in continental Europe, that the resale right is seen as a moral right. The legal nature of the resale right, however, remains debatable, and some scholars, e.g. Ricketson, argue that it is economic in nature.

7.6 Press publisher right

Following a public consultation on the Role of Publishers in the Copyright Value Chain and on the 'Panorama Exception' (23 March 2016), the Commission published on 14 September 2016 a proposal for a Directive on Copyright in the Digital Single Market, which suggests granting press publishers the exclusive rights of reproduction and making their press publications available for digital use.

This related right to press publications publications, which is included in notorious Article 11 of the proposed Copyright Directive, is meant to address concerns on the so-called 'newspaper crisis', which has been marked with the shift from print to digital press. Indeed, even though the audience of press publications has grown considerably, the exploitation and enforcement of the rights in publications has become increasingly difficult. Moreover, revenues in the press-publishing sector have declined and newspaper advertising sales in Europe have dropped.

The proposed right will have the effect that news aggregators will not be able to copy hyperlinked headlines or snippets, i.e. short extracts, of news items without clearing permission from press publishers.

The issue has been addressed already in numerous Member States but the approaches they followed vary considerably. In Belgium, France, and Italy, for instance, Google and national press publishers have concluded special agreements on the use of newspaper articles in Google News. In other Member States the issue was addressed with the introduction of new legislation. This was in particular the case of Germany and Spain that have regulated the online exploitation of news content through the so-called 'Google tax' laws. These initiatives have been welcomed with skepticism from scholars and there is a referral before the CJEU regarding the lawfulness of the German ancillary right (*VG Media Gesellschaft zur Verwertung der Urheber- und Leistungsschutzrechte von Medienunternehmen mbH v Google Inc*, C-299/17, OJ C 309, 21–22, 18 September 2017).

The proposed right to press publications has also become source of a heated debate, having received intense opposition from various parliamentary Committees and national delegations, for the reason that the proposed right lacked sufficient justification and was not adequate in meeting its stated objectives. Scholarly criticism too has focused on the argument that the proposed right is unnecessary, undesirable, fundamentally misconceived, and unlikely to achieve anything apart from adding to the complexity and cost of operating in the copyright environment (see e.g. L. Bently et al, 'Response to Article 11 of the Proposal for a Directive on Copyright in the Digital Single Market, entitled 'Protection of Press Publications concerning Digital Uses' on behalf of 37 Professors and Leading Scholars of Intellectual Property, Information Law and Digital Economy' (5 December 2016)).

Indeed, there is no hard evidence that the right can achieve its stated objectives, notably to facilitate rights clearance and enforcement in the press publishing industry, and its scope and duration are excessive. The right is also broadly designed to cover a number of digital activities beyond mere hyperlinking, such as scanning, indexing, posting snippets, certain forms of text mining, and headlines embedding links, meaning that the right could have the undesirable effect of granting protection to information rather than original subject matter. Such an effect could possibly involve a monopolization of information that is in contrast with basic principles of copyright protection and also the very rationale of Art. 11, namely to enhance public access to information.

 Pause for reflection

What will the impact of Art. 11 be for news aggregators?

7.7 Conclusion

This chapter outlined the legal protection that is available to the so-called related rights. Each one of the rights we discussed (with the exception of the legal protection that is available to technological protection measures) is specific in terms of rightholders (performers, artists, press publishers) or the subject matter concerned (non-original databases). The chapter explained the relationship between copyright and rights in performances, and the incremental protection which has been accorded to performers following a series of amendments to the CDPA. It also discussed the *sui generis* database right and the specific conditions under which the makers of a database can be rewarded for the investment they put in obtaining, verifying, or presenting the contents of the database. Subject to discussion has also been the legal protection afforded against the circumvention of technological protection measures. Finally, a related right for press publishers that is included in the proposed Copyright Directive has also been subject to discussion.

With regards to our problem question, Andrea should know that performers have both economic rights and moral rights. In terms of non-property rights, Andrea has a claim against xris1088 for the unauthorized copying of the performance in London under s. 182, which gives performers the right to object to the making of an illicit recording of a performance, the broadcasting of a performance, or the making of an illicit recording from a broadcast of the performance (such as where someone makes a recording of a live broadcast with the intention of selling copies of the recording). What is more, he has a claim of infringement against xris1088 according to s. 183, because the illicit recording is shown or played in public or communicated to the public by being posted on the internet. Andrea also has a claim against xris1088 for copying the music track and posting it on the video-sharing website under 182A, outlining the performer's reproduction right. He can also claim equitable remuneration from xris1088 under ss. 182CA and 182D for having posted on the internet a commercially published sound recording of a qualifying performance.

With regards to Andrea's question on the various rights which might exist, these are:

- the words and music of each song may have separate copyright, with the lyricist and composer being the authors and first owners of each respectively. Such copyrights will probably have been assigned to a music publishing or management company. Even if they have not, the right to control the public performance of the music will have been assigned to the Performing Right Society who will collect and administer the royalties for any public performance of the song;

- the person who made the orchestral arrangement of the music will have copyright in the arrangement. Again, such copyright will probably have been assigned to another;

- the person who created the choreography for the dancers will have copyright in this as a dramatic work;

- regardless of the ownership of the copyright in the various works in the previous list, their creators will each have the moral rights of paternity and integrity in the works they have created. Whilst such moral rights cannot be assigned during each author's lifetime, it is possible that these rights might have been lost through waiver when the copyrights mentioned earlier were assigned;

- the rock star, orchestra, and dancers will each have rights in their respective performances. These rights consist of the non-property right to object to the making of any illicit recording of a performance, a property right to control the reproduction and distribution of permitted recordings of the performance, and a right to control the dissemination of the performance by electronic means. As with moral rights, the non-property right remains personal to the performer during their lifetime, but the property right can be assigned to another; and

- lastly, the rock star, orchestra, and dancers will have the performers' moral rights of paternity and integrity. Again such rights cannot be assigned during the lifetime of each performer, but may be lost through waiver.

On the matter of technological protection measures, Andrea should be advised that such 'self-help' mechanisms are available to rightholders and there are legal provisions reinforcing their application. Sections 296ZA–ZF offer protection against the circumvention of effective technological measures that have been applied to a copyright work other than a computer program; section 296ZA applies where a person does anything which circumvents those measures knowing, or with reasonable grounds to know, that they are pursuing that objective.

With regards to the question on whether rights subsist on the compilation of the music tracks on the album, such a compilation is excluded both from copyright and *sui generis* protection. This flows from Recital 19 of the Database Directive that excludes the compilation of several recordings of musical performances on a CD from protection. The playlist, however, is likely to qualify for protection as a database, either by copyright or the database right (depending on the standard of originality or investment), if it meets the conditions of s. 3A(1) CDPA (also *Fixtures Marketing Ltd v 'OPAP'* (Case C-444/02, [2004] ECR I-10549)). It does not matter that his works may also be included in the database; what would matter is that there has been substantial investment in the obtaining, verification, and presentation of the contents of the database required that was *independent* from the investment in the creation of the materials which form the contents of the database (*Fixtures Marketing Ltd v Oy Veikkaus Ab,* Case C-46/02, [2004] ECR I-10365).

End-of-chapter questions

After reading the chapter carefully, try answering the following questions. For answer guidance visit the online resources at **www.oup.com/uk/karapapa-mcdonagh/**

1. Do the provisions of the CDPA with regard to performers' moral rights adequately fulfil the United Kingdom's obligations under the WPPT?

2. What is the meaning of substantial investment as a requirement for the subsistence of the database right? Which are the key cases that have discussed its meaning?

3. What is your opinion about the press publisher right? For which reasons has it been criticized by scholarly literature?

Further reading

For understanding the protection available to related rights, the following readings are recommended:

Bently, L. et al, 'Response to Article 11 of the Proposal for a Directive on Copyright in the Digital Single Market, entitled 'Protection of Press Publications concerning Digital Uses' on behalf of 37 Professors and Leading Scholars of Intellectual Property, Information Law and Digital Economy' (5 December 2016). Available at https://www.cipil.law.cam.ac.uk/sites/www.law.cam.ac.uk/files/images/www.cipil.law.cam.ac.uk/documents/ipomodernisingipprofresponsepresspublishers.pdf
A critical approach to the (proposed) press publishers' right.

Banternghansa, C. and Graddy, K. 'The impact of the Droit de Suite in the UK: an Empirical Analysis' (2011) 35(2) *Journal of Cultural Economics* 81
An empirical analysis of actual changes in the UK auction market for art that is subject to the Droit de Suite.

Borghi, M. and Karapapa, S. 'Contractual restrictions on lawful use of information: sole-source databases protected by the back door?' [2015] 37(8) *EIPR* 505
Discusses the issue of sole-source databases in the light of Ryanair v PR Aviation.

Derclaye, E. 'The European Court of Justice Interprets the Database Sui Generis Right for the First Time' [2005] 30 *EL Rev* 420
Considers the impact of four European Court of Justice rulings, including British Horseracing Board Ltd v William Hill Organisation Ltd, which examined the scope of the sui generis database right under the Database Directive.

Dusollier, S., Poullet, Y., and Buydens, M. 'Copyright and Access to Information in the Digital Environment' (2000) XXXIV(4) *Copyright Bulletin* 4

Offers insights on the database right, copyright exceptions and limitations, and the use of contracts and technology in the protection of copyright.

Ricketson, S. 'Proposed International Treaty on Droit de Suite/Resale Royalty Right for Visual Artists' SG15-0565, June 2015

A study reviewing the arguments in favour of introducing a new treaty on resale royalty rights for visual artists and outlining the principal features of such an agreement.

Simon-Fhima, I. 'The Introduction of Performers' Moral Rights' [2006] *EIPR* 552

A very detailed analysis of the introduction of moral rights for performers as a result of the United Kingdom's implementation of the WIPO Performances and Phonograms Treaty 1996, arguing that the method of implementation and the slavish following of the authors' moral rights régime has led to stunted rights for performers.

Stokes, S. 'Droit de Suite: an Artistic Stroke of Genius? A Critical Exploration of the European Directive and its Resultant Effects' [2012] 34(5) *EIPR* 305

A critical overview of the Resale Rights Directive.

Passing Off

Passing off

Problem question

Read this problem question carefully and keep it in mind while you are working through the chapter that follows. At the end of this chapter, you will be able to apply what you have learnt to the problem question and advise the relevant parties.

Natalia Danova has owned a dance school in central Winchester for just over ten years. Through her practice, she has developed a new method for delivering ballet classes, which combines elements of the English and the Russian Schools of Ballet. She believes that the 'Danova Method' can increase consciousness of the body because the upper body, legs, and feet are involved in every movement. On her website, www.danova.co.uk, and in the flyers she has printed to promote her practice, she explains how this innovative method of teaching ballet helps dancers in elementary levels to progress fast. She has been repeatedly praised in the local press and the *Winchester Times* has published an article including her interview and explaining how the 'Danova Method' works.

She has recently found out that a dance school in Hackney has made a tremendous success using the 'Danova Method' for their ballet teaching, without having sought her consent. They even use the method as a selling point on their website, www.stardancing.co.uk, where they use quotes from Natalia's interview in the *Winchester Times*: 'the method has the unparalleled ability to help children gain consciousness of their body'. They also state on their website that more than 150 children registered in their junior class during the course of last year.

Natalia is frustrated and comes to you for legal advice. What is the available course of action for her and what are her chances of success?

8.1 Introduction

In the United Kingdom, there is no obligation to register a trade mark. Protection has always been available at common law for marks in use, by means of the action for passing off. In consequence, a trade mark owner has the freedom to choose whether to register their mark, or whether to rely on common law protection. Indeed s. 2 of the Trade Marks Act 1994 ('TMA') declares that nothing in the Act affects the law of passing off.

In this chapter, we will discuss the tort of passing off which protects the goodwill of a trader from misrepresentation; in parallel to the examination of the elements that are essential in a passing off action we will keep in mind the scenario question and the legal advice to Natalia Danova.

8.2 Preliminary matters

8.2.1 The relationship between passing off and the law of registered trade marks

It may seem odd to discuss the law of passing off before the law of registered trade marks is considered in detail. Nevertheless, we believe that there are good reasons to examine passing off at this stage. These reasons are as follows.

8.2.1.1 Passing off and trade mark function

We have seen how a number of different commercial functions are affected by trade marks. They tell the consumer about where the goods come from, they enable the consumer to choose between competing brands, they guarantee the consistency of quality of the goods, and they act as the means to create goodwill. All of these functions are reflected, in various ways, in the case law on passing off. However, as a result of the key ingredients of the tort, the origin function has come to dominate. This may prove to be something of a straightjacket should it be thought appropriate to develop passing off in the future; alternatively, it could be seen as a way to ensure that the power of the brand owner is kept within reasonable bounds.

8.2.1.2 Passing off and trade mark registrability

Prior to the TMA, passing off was the means to protect unregistrable marks. It acted to 'fill the gaps' in the registration system. Colour schemes, shapes, and the appearance of products ('get-up') were not capable of registration before 1994 but could, in appropriate circumstances, be protectable as common law trade marks. The TMA enables a far greater range of subject matter to be capable of registration, so it might be thought that passing off is now of less value. Nevertheless, some of the concepts used in passing off have been transposed into the law of registration. For example, proving acquired distinctiveness for the purposes of the proviso to TMA s. 3(1) has many characteristics of proving reputation as part of passing off, establishing a likelihood of confusion in opposition proceedings under the relative grounds for refusal is similar to the element of misrepresentation in passing off, and the protection of marks with a reputation, again in opposition proceedings, has much in common with the way that passing off has protected strong common law marks against dilution.

8.2.1.3 Passing off and trade mark infringement

In the same way, many passing off notions have been transferred into the law of trade mark infringement. Establishing likelihood of confusion for the purposes of TMA s. 10(2) has much in common with passing off; and again, the infringement action to protect marks with a reputation shares features with passing off. Passing off, however, has a further role. It is usually pleaded in the alternative when a claimant brings an action for trade mark infringement. Should there be a successful counterclaim that the trade mark is invalid or should be revoked for mismanagement, then at least the claimant has something to fall back on (see *United Biscuits (UK) Ltd v Asda Stores Ltd* [1997] RPC 513 for an example of where the passing off claim became crucial once the registered marks had been revoked for non-use).

8.2.1.4 Passing off in the future

It may be asked, if the law of registered trade marks has become more flexible and has appeared to adopt many of the attributes of passing off, does the passing off action have a future? We will discuss this issue in greater detail at the end of this chapter, but for the moment, the following comments can be made:

- the greater flexibility in the law of registered trade marks owes more to the driving force of the CJEU in offering guidance as to the meaning of key words and phrases in the Trade Marks Directive (Council Directive 89/104/EEC of 21 December 1988 on the approximation of the laws of Member States relating to trade marks [1989] OJ L 40/1, now codified as Directive 2008/95/EC of the European Parliament and of the Council of 22 October 2008 [2008] OJ L 299/25) rather than any express incorporation of the values of passing off;

- passing off will always have a role to play for the trader who chooses not to register their mark (or who cannot register it, for whatever reason);

- the policy question which has to be answered is whether it is appropriate for passing off to expand. If it is concluded that passing off should develop further, then the elements which at present have to be proved to succeed in a passing off action will need to be reconsidered.

8.2.2 The nature of passing off

In *Erven Warnink BV v Townend & Sons* [1979] AC 731 at p. 730 Lord Diplock remarked that passing off was a 'protean tort'. By this he meant that passing off was a flexible form of action, one that could and should respond to changing business practices. Indeed, Lord Diplock argued forcefully in the case that passing off must develop into the action for unfair competition. Other judges have not been so liberal in their approach, most notably Lord Scarman in *Cadbury-Schweppes v Pub Squash Co* [1981] RPC 429.

The term 'protean' to describe passing off is appropriate in another sense. It suggests that the tort is difficult to pin down. The elusive nature of the tort is attributable to two things. First, it is entirely a product of case law. In consequence, it is always possible to find decisions which appear not to fit in with first principle or which contradict other cases. For this reason, constructing a logical justification for the tort is extremely difficult. Whilst most cases appear to treat passing off as a means of consumer protection, there are others which have granted a business protection against conduct which amounts to misappropriation, the theft of something of value which is nevertheless intangible. In other words, passing off in these cases is protecting the trader's investment rather than the consumer.

Second, in passing off it is for the claimant to prove each of the three ingredients of the tort. These elements are interdependent, so that strength in one area can offset a weaker case in another. However, what really matters is the quality of the evidence which the claimant adduces. The reason why so many cases fail is down to the claimant's inability to prove a key ingredient of the action. From the point of view of evidence, passing off is much more onerous than a claim for trade mark infringement. This may help to answer the question 'why register'?

 Pause for reflection

On the basis of these preliminary considerations, it is clear that Natalia cannot benefit from trade mark protection in that there is no indication that she has registered a mark by reference to the 'Danova Method'. Can she, however, claim protection under passing off? We examine the elements of a passing off action below.

8.3 The elements of passing off

8.3.1 The definition of passing off

Most cases today rely on one leading definition (or perhaps, description) of passing off. This was developed in *Reckitt & Colman v Borden (JIF LEMON)* [1990] 1 WLR 491.

Reckitt & Colman v Borden (Jif Lemon) [1990] 1 WLR 491

In this case, Lord Oliver set out what has come to be called 'the classic trinity'. He stated that first, a trader must establish that he has goodwill or a reputation (the difference between these two terms is explained in section 8.3.2.2) attached to the goods or services which he or she supplies; second, the trader must demonstrate that the defendant has made a misrepresentation (whether intentional or not) leading or likely to lead the public to believe that the goods or services offered by the defendant are the goods or services of the claimant; and last, the trader must demonstrate that he or she has suffered or is likely to suffer damage by reason of the erroneous belief caused by the defendant's misrepresentation. The three elements are interdependent, and each element is a question of fact. It is up to the claimant to convince the court as to the existence of each one.

8.3.2 Reputation

8.3.2.1 What is reputation?

In one sense, reputation can be considered the equivalent of factual distinctiveness in the law of registered trade marks. Whether the claimant has reputation (or goodwill) is a question of fact, and hence entirely dependent on evidence showing that consumers recognize the sign as indicating origin. This is sometimes referred to in the cases as acquiring 'secondary meaning'. By 'sign' we mean a name, colour, shape, or anything else which sends the consumer a message about the commercial origin of the goods. Almost any sign (but not every sign) is capable of protection through passing off.

 Pause for reflection

A sign may not qualify for registration as a trade mark but it could receive protection under passing off. It might be unregistrable because as a word it describes the quality of the goods (like the phrase 'camel hair belting' in *Reddaway v Banham* [1896] AC 199) or it is a word indicating geographical origin (like the name 'Stone Ale' in *Montgomery v Thompson* [1891] AC 217 or 'Yorkshire Relish' in *Powell v Birmingham Vinegar Brewery Co* (1896) 13 RPC 235) or because as a container it indicates the nature of the product inside (as in *JIF Lemon* itself). As long as there is proof of factual distinctiveness, the sign will be capable of protection in passing off. However, where the sign has *not* been used to indicate commercial origin, but instead has designated a particular type or model of product, then this does not suffice. An example of this is *Burberrys v Cording* (1909) 26 RPC 693 where the claimant had used the name 'Slip On' for a particular type of raincoat. Also, the court may not be convinced that the sign can be described separately from the goods in which the claimant trades, and so is not regarded as a trade mark at common law. In *Cadbury v Ulmer* [1988] FSR 385 protection was denied for the shape of the Flake chocolate bar simply because it was the product itself which the claimant was trying to protect. Alternatively, the sign might not be visible to the consumer when the goods are purchased, like the Blu Tack pads in *Bostick v Sellotape* [1994] RPC 556.

8.3.2.2 Reputation and goodwill

Reputation cannot exist in isolation. It must be attached to a particular business. Reputation depends on the claimant being a trader (and not just a private individual), so that the claimant must have a business interest to protect (*Oxford Blue Trade Mark*, Registry, 23 March 2004). This business interest is usually called goodwill. 'Goodwill', as a type of intangible property, is not easy to define, even though it can be transferred and is capable of being valued for the purpose of a company's balance sheet. It has been described (in a tax case) as 'the attractive force which brings in custom' and 'that which distinguishes an old business from a new' (*per* Lord Macnaghten in *IRC v Muller & Co's Margarine Ltd* [1901] AC 217). The relevant date for determining whether a claimant has established the necessary reputation or goodwill is the date of the commencement of the conduct complained of (see e.g. *Cadbury-Schweppes Pty Ltd v The Pub Squash Co Ltd* [1981] RPC 429; *Roger Maier, Assos of Switzerland SA v ASOS Plc, ASOS.com Ltd* [2015] EWCA Civ 220 [2015] ETMR 26).

As Lord Diplock explained in *Star Industrial Co v Yap Kwee Kor* [1976] FSR 217 at p. 269, a passing off action is a remedy for the invasion of a right of property, not in the mark, name, or get-up improperly used, but in the business or goodwill in which it has been used. Goodwill, as the subject of proprietary rights, is incapable of subsisting by itself. It has no independent existence apart from the business to which it is attached.

In *Bhayani Law Limited v Taylor Bracewell LLP* [2016] EWHC 3360 (IPEC), HHJ Hacon held that reputation by itself does not found an action in passing off and that '[g]oodwill cannot in law subsist as a thing alone—it is indivisible from the business with which it is associated' (at [26]–[27]). The learned Judge moved on to remark that '[t]his is to be distinguished from reputation which exists by itself. A solicitor celebrated for his or her expertise may enjoy the highest possible reputation and this will be personal, attaching only to that individual. But reputation alone cannot form the basis of an action for passing off, no matter how high the wattage of celebrity' (at [28]).

This is in line with the Supreme Court's ruling in *Starbucks (HK) Ltd v British Sky Broadcasting Group Plc* [2015] UKSC 31; [2015] ETMR 31. In this case, the Court found that in a passing off claim the defendant had to establish that it had actual goodwill in the relevant jurisdiction and that the notion of goodwill involved the presence of clients or customers in the jurisdiction with regards to the products or services at issue. As the Court stressed with regards to what amounts to a sufficient business to amount to goodwill, 'it seems clear that mere reputation is not enough' (at [52]), as a long line of authorities establish.

 Pause for reflection

Having discussed the meaning of reputation and goodwill, has Natalia attracted reputation and/or goodwill by reference to her dancing method?

8.3.2.3 Limitations on goodwill

Goodwill is limited, both in time and geographically. It is also divisible, so that if business is carried on in several countries, a separate goodwill attaches to it in each. As regards its geographical scope, for our purposes this will normally be within the United Kingdom (or part of it). The existence of goodwill in the United Kingdom depends on there being customers in this country who are not members of a special class, in other words, they must be members of the general public (*per* the Court of Appeal in *Anheuser-Busch Inc v Budejovicky Budvar NP* [1984] FSR 413). This was also affirmed by the Supreme Court in *Starbucks (HK) Ltd v British Sky Broadcasting Group Plc* [2015] UKSC 31; [2015] ETMR 31, where the Court relied on a number of passing off cases from various jurisdictions (e.g. Ireland, Canada, New Zealand, Australia, South Africa, Hong Kong, and Singapore etc), to hold that 'such goodwill involves the presence of clients or customers in the jurisdiction for the products or services in question. And, where the claimant's business is abroad, people who are in the jurisdiction, but who are not customers of the claimant in the jurisdiction, will not do, even if they are customers of the claimant when they go abroad' (at [47]).

As regards the duration of goodwill, it may survive after a business ceases to trade, but only for a limited period. How long goodwill can survive after a business closes is a question of fact (*Ad-Lib Club v Granville* [1971] FSR 1). If the claimant has no intention of re-opening the business, then that points to the conclusion that goodwill has entirely disappeared (*Star Industrial Co v Yap Kwee Kor; Foster v Brooks* [2013] EWPCC 18). Another trader is then free to adopt the same or similar sign to the one used by the defunct business. By contrast, in *Jules Rimet Cup Ltd v The Football Association Ltd* [2008] FSR 254 the court accepted that the FA had never given up the intention to use the cartoon character 'World Cup Willie' (used to promote the 1966 World Cup), so that the symbol's goodwill survived 40 years.

8.3.2.4 Length of use to establish goodwill

It should not be assumed the claimant has to demonstrate many years' use of the sign in order to prove the existence of goodwill, provided that the remaining ingredients of passing off are present. In *Stannard v Reay* [1967] RPC 589, three weeks' use of the name 'Mr Chippy' for a mobile fish'n'chip van sufficed. Despite such a short period of use, the claimant obtained an injunction to prevent the defendant from operating a rival van under the identical name. However, the claimant was helped by the fact that his business had operated in a clearly defined location (the Isle of Wight) and there was evidence of damage to that business, as there had been a marked loss of sales as soon as the defendant began trading.

Pause for reflection

What about the more than ten years that Natalia is in business? Would this be considered sufficient time in establishing goodwill?

In *Jadebay Ltd v Clarke-Coles Ltd (t/a Feel Good UK)* [2017] EWHC 1400 (IPEC); [2017] ETMR 34, the IPEC considered whether passing off could arise by reference to a device mark that was used on Amazon listings. The claimants were selling their products (flagpoles) on Amazon as being 'by DesignElements'. Although set up by one seller, an Amazon listing can be used by multiple sellers that sell the same product and Amazon selects one, usually the one selling at the lowest price, as the default seller that is promoted in the listing. The defendant had used the claimants' listings on Amazon to sell its own product, although from a different Chinese manufacturer. By undercutting the price of the claimants' flagpoles, they were set as the default sellers, thereby capturing the majority of sales from the listings within a given period. Following *Stannard v Reay*, the IPEC held that goodwill might be established after trading for a very short time but the claimant had to show goodwill that was more than trivial. In the present case, the IPEC was satisfied that goodwill associated with the sign had accrued to the claimants ([96]–[98]).

Pause for reflection

The *Jadebay* case seems to affirm the emergence of a new form of infringement online, that may become more common in the future. Other online platforms, such as eBay, have features similar to Amazon's, such as the 'Sell one like this' service that could be used to copy information from one listing to another.

8.3.2.5 Exclusive reputation

The basic rule is that the reputation has to be exclusive to the claimant. However, in a number of cases, there may be two or more undertakings sharing that reputation. This may come about, first, where two companies independently of each other start using the same sign at more or less the same time. Where this coincidence happens, each will acquire a separate reputation and neither can stop the other from using the name in question. An example of this is *Anheuser-Busch Inc v Budejovicky Budvar NP* [2000] RPC 906, where Budweiser was the trade mark of two rival companies, one American and one Czech. The net outcome was that the two companies were forced to coexist, neither having a right of priority over the other. Second, it is possible for two businesses to acquire their reputation from a common source. A case within this unusual category is *Sir Robert McAlpine Ltd v Alfred McAlpine plc* [2004] RPC 711 where the two companies were originally part of the same family business which had been divided along geographical lines. In such cases, each undertaking, it was held, had to ensure that they did not cause customers to mistake one firm for the other. Each co-owner was under a duty not to 'erode the exclusivity of the other's name'.

8.3.2.6 Shared reputation

The most frequent example of shared reputation has occurred in a family of cases, each one of which concerns the protection of a product which has special qualities. The product will originate from a specific geographical area which because of its climate or terrain imparts the particular quality to the product, or else the product is made to a unique recipe. Any of the businesses which make the product share the reputation, and can, therefore, sue a third party for passing off.

The cases on shared reputation have so far mostly concerned drinks or foodstuffs. Thus it has been held that champagne can only come from the Champagne district of France and has to be made by a unique method. There is no such thing as 'Spanish Champagne' (*Bollinger v Costa Brava Wine Co* [1961] RPC 116) and to call a drink made from pear juice 'Champagne perry' is a misrepresentation (*Bulmer v Bollinger* [1978] RPC 79). Further, calling a sparkling elderflower drink 'Elderflower Champagne' will dilute the unique quality of the Champagne name, even if customers are not confused: *Taittinger v Allbev* [1993] 2 CMLR 741. Similarly, the name 'sherry' is reserved for a fortified wine produced in the Jerez region of Spain, so that there cannot be a product called 'British sherry' (*Vine Products v MacKenzie* [1969] RPC 1). Scotch whisky is similarly protected, and must originate from Scotland (*Walker v Ost* [1970] RPC 489).

The protection afforded to advocaat in *Erven Warnink v Townend & Sons Ltd* was somewhat different, as here what mattered was not the place of production, but the precise recipe and particular ingredients. In *Diageo North America Inc v Intercontinental Brands (ICB) Ltd* [2010] EWCA Civ 920, it was held that this category of passing off was not limited to products perceived as being of a superior quality: to hold otherwise would deny protection to the claimant's goodwill. Here, selling an alcoholic drink under the name 'Vodkat' without clear labelling to indicate that it was not vodka misled the public, particularly as the get-up of the claimant's leading brand of vodka (Smirnoff) had been copied. And in *Fage UK Ltd v Chobani UK Ltd* [2014] EWCA Civ 5, protection was given to Greek yoghurt, so that similar products created by the use of thickening agents rather than by straining could not be labelled with the protected name.

> ### Chocosuisse Union des Fabricants Suisses de Chocolat v Cadbury Ltd [1999] RPC 826
>
> The case which can be considered the most extreme of the shared reputation cases (and one relied on in the *Diageo* case) is *Chocosuisse Union des Fabricants Suisses de Chocolat v Cadbury Ltd* [1999] RPC 826. Its outcome was dependent on the specific finding of fact that the use of the name 'Swiss chocolate' had led UK customers to expect a particular quality. The Court of Appeal found that the defendant had committed passing off by selling its product under the name 'Swiss Chalet'.
>
> However, Chadwick LJ highlighted some of the difficulties presented by this category of passing off. For example, how extensive must the trade of the claimant be in order for them to share in the goodwill? Here, it was held that the first claimant, a trade association, could not sue as it did not have any UK goodwill to protect, although the second and third claimants, as manufacturers within the class, could. How should an individual trader prove that they are a member of the class? How long do they have to be in the class before they can sue? Where (as here) the product is not subject to any regulatory control, how is the class to be defined and how exact does the recipe have to be (many of the other passing off cases involving unique products are subject to detailed national and/or EU rules which set out where and how the product can be made). Last, in the case of an unregulated product, can the members of the class change the recipe? It will be clear from this discussion that much of the detail remains to be worked out with regard to this type of passing off.

Other passing off cases concern instances of false associations to a trade association or to a trade mark proprietor. An interesting passing off case was heard at the IPEC, concerning use of the term 'The National Guild of Removers and Storers' in web advertisements, where that use would convey the false impression that a removals and storage business was member of a trade association (*National Guild of Removers and Storers Ltd v Bee Moved Ltd* [2016] EWHC 3192 (IPEC)). Trade associations can bring an action for passing off and in order to determine whether there was a likelihood of deception, a substantial number of the claimant's customers or potential customers would have to be deceived and any misrepresentation would have to be more than transitory.

On another occasion, the IPEC found that a garage repairing and maintaining cars conveyed the message that the use of the claimant's signs did no more than render the average consumer unable to determine whether there was an economic link between the two parties, as opposed to causing the average consumer to take the view that there was such a link and, on that evidence, the Court would have concluded that there had been no passing off (*BMW AG v Technosport London Ltd/George Agyeton* [2016] EWHC 797 (IPEC); [2016] ETMR 31).

 Pause for reflection

Can goodwill subsist in the 'Danova Method'? If so, under which conditions?

8.3.3 **Misrepresentation**

8.3.3.1 The meaning of misrepresentation

The second of Lord Oliver's 'classic trinity' is misrepresentation. As Lord Parker in *Spalding v Gamage* (1915) 32 RPC 273 at p. 284 explained, a false statement is the basis of the action. That false statement can be made expressly, though express misrepresentation is rare. More usually, the misrepresentation is implied, by the imitation of the claimant's sign. From this, we can see that the false statement can be by words or conduct.

Further detail on the requirement of misrepresentation is given by Lord Diplock in *Erven Warnink BV v Townend & Sons*. He stated that the misrepresentation must be made by a trader in the course of trade, to the defendant's prospective customers or ultimate consumers. It must be calculated to injure the business of another, and it must cause actual damage to the claimant's goodwill or be likely to do so. By 'calculated', Lord Diplock added, the misrepresentation must be likely to cause confusion (that is, 'on the balance of probabilities'). However, somewhat unhelpfully, Lord Diplock added that just because all the elements listed by him were satisfied did not mean that passing off had been established.

8.3.3.2 The effect of the misrepresentation

The crucial issue, however, is what effect the false statement has on the minds of the claimant's customers. According to the cases, the misrepresentation must lead customers to make an association with the claimant. It must make them think that this was 'something for which the [claimant] was responsible' (see the remarks of Goff and Buckley LJJ in *Bulmer v Bollinger*). So, for example, in *Associated Newspapers v Insert Media* [1991] FSR 380, the Court of Appeal held that where the defendant inserted advertising leaflets without permission inside magazines published by the claimant, the public would assume that the material had been approved or authorized by the claimant. In *United Biscuits (UK) Ltd v Asda Stores Ltd*, Robert Walker J held, when confronted by the defendant's lookalike 'Puffin' biscuits (the wrappers of which had been deliberately designed to evoke those for the Penguin biscuits made by the claimants), customers would think that the supermarket had asked the claimant to make the biscuits for it, when it had not.

The effect of the misrepresentation on the mind of the consumer must, therefore, produce confusion as to the trade origin of the defendant's product (if passing off is to develop, the requirement of origin confusion would prove to be a major restriction on expansion). Quite simply, if the consumer is not confused about the source of the defendant's product, there can be no liability for passing off. Two major cases make this point.

Hodgkinson & Corby v Wards Mobility Service **[1995] FSR 169**

In Hodgkinson & Corby v Wards Mobility Service [1995] FSR 169, the claimant alleged that by reproducing the shape of its cushions (used by healthcare professionals when nursing the chronically ill), the defendant had committed passing off. It was held that upon seeing the cushion, the relevant consumer would not have been confused into thinking that the cushions were made by the claimant. In the absence of origin confusion there could be no passing off.

Harrods v Harrodian School [1996] RPC 697

In *Harrods v Harrodian School* [1996] RPC 697, the defendant had set up a preparatory school on the site of a sports club previously owned by the famous department store. The majority of the Court of Appeal held that although customers might 'call to mind' the name of the claimant when confronted by the name of the school, they would not be misled into thinking that the store had endorsed or approved the school. We may note the powerful dissenting judgment of Sir Michael Kerr. He remarked that although the basic ingredients of passing off were well established, their application to individual cases 'remained elusive'. He thought that the public, on seeing the defendant's name, would assume that the claimant was in some way 'mixed up' with the school. Further, the extensive reputation of the claimant had to be taken into account when deciding confusion. The deliberate choice of name by the defendant amounted to mis-appropriation. The damage inflicted in this case was the blurring or erosion of the distinctiveness of the name in question.

 Pause for reflection

In the light of Lord Diplock's comments in the *Advocaat* case about the role of passing off, which do you find more convincing in the *Harrods* case, the majority or minority view?

In *Comic Enterprises Ltd v Twentieth Century Fox Film Corp* [2016] EWCA Civ 41 [2016] ETMR 22, the Court of Appeal of England and Wales held that there is a distinction between misrepresentation and confusion (at [157]). The case concerned an appeal from Twentieth Century Fox against a finding that its well-known *Glee* TV series infringed a registered series of device marks incorporating the word 'Glee', owned by a comedy club business. Even though the evidence on confusion was admissible, confusion in this case did not establish that Fox had been guilty of any misrepresentation actionable in passing off. It was noted that the scope of protection conferred by the law of passing off is not the same as that afforded by a registered trade mark. In considering a claim for infringement, the court need not restrict its consideration to the particular way the mark has been used and the goodwill that has been generated in connection with it, and may take into account a notional and fair use of the mark in relation to all of the goods and services for which it is registered, on condition that all of the other conditions for protection are also satisfied (at [159]).

8.3.3.3 Proof of confusion

A further problem is how does the claimant satisfy the court that there is a likelihood of confusion? Unlike their German counterparts, UK courts are sceptical about the worth of survey evidence (see *Dalgety Spiller Foods v Food Brokers* [1994] FSR 505). They would rather have witnesses who will come to court to give evidence in person. An example is *Neutrogena v Golden Ltd t/a Laboratoires Garnier* [1996] RPC 473, where the claimant's solicitor emailed her staff to see how many had been confused by the defendant's television advert for shower gel, those replying then being asked to explain to the court how they had been misled by the defendant. Such evidence clearly had an impact on the result of the case.

 Pause for reflection

How could Natalia establish confusion? Could she use a similar method to that used in *Neutrogena v Garnier*?

8.3.3.4 The recipient of the misrepresentation

The defendant's false statement must, according to Lord Diplock, be made to the customer. But who is this person and what is their level of intelligence? One misconception is that the test is that of the 'moron in a hurry'. Reference to the origin of the phrase (in *Morning Star Co-operative Society Ltd v Express Newspapers Ltd* [1979] FSR 113) reveals that the judge remarked that '*even* the moron in a hurry' would not confuse the defendant's newspaper *The Daily Star* with *The Morning Star* published by the claimant, which implies that the average consumer is somewhat smarter than suggested. In the law of registered trade marks the notional consumer is deemed to be reasonably well informed, reasonably observant, and circumspect (Case C-342/97 *Lloyd Schuhfabrik Meyer & Co GmbH v Klijsen Handel BV* [1999] ECR I-3819). There is no reason why a similar standard should not be appropriate in passing off.

8.3.3.5 Misrepresentation and keyword advertising/'targeting'

Cases on passing off in the context of keyword advertising are very rare. Search engines enable users to search online for relevant content and to present users with a list of 'clickable' links to certain websites in response to key queries. Search engines track the volume of searches on the basis of keywords and the amount of traffic that these searches generate. Advertisers pay on the basis of clicks but not on the basis of 'impressions' ('pay per click'). Most of the cases on keyword advertising have to do with allegations on trade mark infringement (e.g. *Google France Sarl v Louis Vuitton Malletier SA* (C-236/08); *Google France Sarl v Centre National de Recherche en Relations Humaines (CNRRH) Sarl* (C-238/08); *Google France Sarl v Viaticum SA* (C-237/08) EU:C:2010:159; [2010] ETMR 30).

Victoria Plum Limited v Victorian Plumbing Limited **[2016] EWHC 2911 (Ch); [2017] ETMR 8**

Victoria Plum Limited v Victorian Plumbing Limited [2016] EWHC 2911 (Ch); [2017] ETMR 8, is the first case where keyword advertising was held to be passing off. Mr Justice Henry Carr held that there was a propensity for confusion and there was nothing in the relevant advertisements to indicate the absence of a connection between the parties. A substantial proportion of the relevant public were hence likely to have been misled into believing that the claimant was—or was connected with—the first defendant, this amounting to misrepresentation. In these circumstances, the Judge found that there is a likelihood of damage (at [161]).

In *Argos Ltd v Argos Systems Inc* [2017] EWHC 231 (Ch); [2017] ETMR 19, the High Court of England and Wales had to consider a case of an alleged infringement arising because of the use of the Argos mark in the domain name of a US company. Many internet users based in the United Kingdom had visited the defendant's website as a result of their mistake in assuming that the claimant operated the '.com' domain name. The defendant had registered the '.com' domain name lawfully and properly before the claimant had thought of registering it themselves: it was not done with the view to attracting website traffic from internet users based in the United Kingdom. The claimant's allegation on 'targeting' could only be sustained taking into consideration the content featuring on the defendant's homepage, including the relevant advertisements. In terms of the perception of the average consumer, neither the whole nor any sufficient part of the defendant's website was targeted at the United Kingdom and, hence, the use of the Argos sign was not considered to be made within the United Kingdom. On the basis of this finding, the Court found in the defendant's favour. Although the claimant had goodwill, the passing off claim had to fail as material misrepresentation to the public could not be established, nor could damage, nor that the defendant's domain name was an instrument of fraud ([202], [219], [223]–[224], [361]).

 Pause for reflection

Going back to our scenario question, can misrepresentation be established by reference to the use that the Hackney dance school made of the 'Danova Method'? How can this be established?

8.3.3.6. Misrepresentation and character merchandising

Character merchandising refers to the practice whereby famous personalities may use their image or name to endorse and associate themselves with products or services. The same form of protection covers fictional characters, that may be applied to merchandise.

Under certain conditions, celebrities (and the owners of fictional characters) may be able to control the use of their image through passing off. This offers an important stream of protection, as UK law does not currently recognize image rights or a right to personality. As Kitchin LJ noted in *Fenty v Arcadia* [2013] EWHC 2310 (Ch), a case involving the use of a picture of Rihanna on t-shirts sold by Topshop without her permission, '[t]here is in English law no "image right" or "character right" which allows a celebrity to control the use of his or her name or image.' This means that '[a] celebrity seeking to control the use of his or her image must therefore rely upon some other cause of action such as breach of contract, breach of confidence, infringement of copyright or, as in this case, passing off.'

Passing off claims in the context of personality merchandising were also invoked in *Irvine and another v Talksport Ltd* [2002] EWHC 367 (Ch). A picture of Eddie Irvine, a well-known former Formula One driver, holding a mobile phone was used on a flyer promoting the rebranding of a station from Talk Radio to Talksport. Irvine claimed that the flyer falsely implied that he was endorsing Talksport. Laddie J upheld the claim, holding that Irvine had 'a property right in his goodwill' and that he could 'protect from unlicensed appropriation consisting of a false claim or suggestion of endorsement of a third party's goods or services'.

Protection through the action of passing off may also be available to fictional characters. In *Mirage Studios v Counter Feat Clothing Co Ltd* [1991] FSR 145 (the *Ninja Turtles* case), Sir Nicholas Browne-Wilkinson upheld that the public expected goods bearing the image of well-known cartoon characters to be subject to a licence.

8.3.4 **Damage**

In the third element of the 'classic trinity', the claimant must establish that there has been or will be damage. Such damage must harm the goodwill of the claimant's business. It must be more than minimal, but need not be actual. A threat of damage will suffice provided all the other elements of passing off are established, but proof of damage will make passing off easier to establish.

8.3.4.1 Harm to goodwill: loss of custom

As Carty explains (in 'Heads of Damage in Passing Off' [1996] *EIPR* 487) damage on its own is not enough, otherwise passing off becomes a tort of unfair competition. The damage must be *to* the claimant's goodwill. Because passing off exists to prevent origin confusion, diversion of custom as a result of the defendant's misrepresentation will cause a loss of sales revenue for the claimant. This is the normal form of harm and is illustrated by the facts of *Stannard v Reay*.

Customer confusion may also have other unexpected consequences. In *Neutrogena v Golden Ltd t/a Laboratoires Garnier* [1996] RPC 473, the defendant's Neutralia shower gel had been advertised on television in a way that some viewers found distasteful. A number of complainants, however, confused the defendant's products with the claimant's Neutrogena skin-care range. The court found that harm had been caused to the claimant's goodwill. Even in *Erven Warnink BV v Townend & Sons*, where the misrepresentation consisted of product misdescription rather than the creation of origin confusion, the damage consisted of lost sales of the genuine Advocaat.

 Pause for reflection

To what extent can Natalia claim loss of custom? Bear in mind that her dance school is based in a different location from that of the Hackney dance school.

8.3.4.2 Other forms of harm

It is in this area of damage that the passing off cases appear most inconsistent. Forms of harm have been recognized which do not accord with the concept of origin confusion. The cases may be individually explicable because of the way in which evidence of harm was presented, but that does not make them any easier to reconcile with first principles. It is perhaps a case of the tail wagging the dog.

One particular category of harm identified by Carty is devaluation of reputation. This occurred in *Spalding v Gamage* where the defendant had sold footballs that had been made by the claimant, but described them in advertisements as being of first-class quality when in fact they had been disposed of as faulty stock. There was thus no origin confusion (the balls were, after all, made by the claimant) but the harm done to goodwill was apparent. Another example of devaluation can be found in *Annabel's (Berkeley Square) v Schock* [1972] RPC 838, where a high-class London nightclub, Annabel's, successfully restrained the defendant from carrying on the business of an escort agency under the name Annabel's Escort Agency. The public's perception that escort agencies were in some way 'not nice' meant that, as Carty puts it, the claimant might be 'tarred with the same brush', should the public confuse the two. A more extreme case is *Rolls-Royce Motors v Dodd* [1981] FSR 519, where Megarry J accepted that the claimant had suffered damage to the image of its product (luxury cars) by the defendant's having affixed the Rolls-Royce badge to his home-built racing car powered by an aeroplane engine. The problem with this particular case is that it ignores the fact that the defendant wasn't actually trading in cars, and so didn't meet Lord Diplock's criteria for misrepresentation in passing off.

Another form of harm, which has been recognized, according to Carty, is loss of control. The argument here is that the defendant's conduct will reduce the claimant's ability to expand their business into new areas at some date in the future, or else will deter potential licensees from coming forward. The former aspect was recognized in *Lego System AB v Lego M Lemelstrich* [1983] FSR 155 where the claimant toy manufacturer successfully sued a company which made plastic irrigation equipment. Falconer J accepted the argument that one day Lego might wish to expand into other types of plastic product.

Irvine v Talksport Radio [2002] 2 All ER 414

The effect of the defendant's conduct on future licensees was a key ingredient in Laddie J's decision in *Irvine v Talksport Radio* [2002] 2 All ER 414. Here, the defendant had 'doctored' a digital image of the claimant so that he appeared to be listening to one of their radio broadcasts rather than using his mobile phone. The claimant had proved that he had an established goodwill in merchandising his image, so the conclusion had to be that if the defendant's conduct was not restrained, others would try to 'cash in' on the claimant's image without paying royalties.

 Pause for reflection

The form of harm which Carty argues is hardest to reconcile with origin confusion is dilution. The ability of the owner of a strong trade mark to use passing off to prevent others selling dissimilar goods was recognized in *Eastman Photographic Materials Co v John Griffiths Cycle Co* (1898) 15 RPC 105, where the use of Kodak, already well known for cameras, was enjoined in respect of bicycles. In *Taittinger v Allbev*, the Court of Appeal recognised that the value of the name 'Champagne' would be weakened were it to be used in relation to a fruit-flavoured drink, even though there was little evidence of consumer confusion. Peter Gibson LJ remarked that

→

> 'blurring or erosion of the uniqueness that now attaches to the word champagne' was the harm being done and Mann LJ accepted that the claimant's case rested on the premise 'that the word champagne has an exclusiveness which is impaired if it is used in relation to a product . . . which is neither champagne nor associated with or connected to the businesses which produce champagne'. Carty argues that *Taittinger* involved no misrepresentation and no harm to goodwill. The decision, she says, 'refashions passing off by the back door'. Further difficulties are presented by *Harrods v Harrodian School*. Although the majority found that there was no actionable misrepresentation, Sir Michael Kerr adopted in full the thinking in *Taittinger*. Millett and Beldam LJJ do not deal adequately with all the arguments in *Taittinger*, and so, according to Carty, dilution remains as a form of harm protected by passing off.

 Pause for reflection

In our scenario question, can damage be established and, if so, how can it be substantiated?

8.4 Defences to passing off

8.4.1 General defences

The normal way in which a defendant will resist a passing off action is to challenge whether the claimant has actually established each of the three ingredients of the tort. The claimant cannot succeed if one or more of the 'classic trinity' is missing. In each instance, however, as mentioned earlier, much may depend on the quality of evidence produced by the claimant to prove the 'classic trinity'.

So, for example, the claimant may not have convinced the court that the particular sign has acquired a secondary meaning, as in *Cadbury v Ulmer* where the court was not satisfied that the shape of its chocolate bar had come to indicate trade origin. Alternatively, the claimant may have failed to show that there has been a material misrepresentation, as was the case in *Harrods v Harrodian School*. Even if there was a material misrepresentation, there might be insufficient evidence of customer confusion. This was the reason why the Court of Appeal in *Bulmer v Bollinger* did not find in favour of the Champagne houses who sought to show that customers might be misled if Babycham was sold as 'the genuine Champagne perry'. Incidentally, the case provides a neat illustration of judicial prejudices. The assumptions made by the Court as to who was the typical consumer of champagne and who drank Babycham would no doubt today be regarded as politically incorrect. Finally, there may be failure to prove damage to goodwill. A key issue in *Cadbury-Schweppes v Pub Squash Co* was the inability of the claimant to show that there had been a loss of sales following the launch of the defendant's lemonade. It should be remembered, though, that the Privy Council in this case adopted a very orthodox view of passing off and refused to accept other forms of harm, such as the misappropriation of the imagery used in the claimant's television adverts.

8.4.2 No common field of activity

The defence of 'no common field of activity' is one which is sometimes pleaded. It means that the claimant and defendant are not in the same line of business. The requirement that claimant and defendant be competitors does not appear in Lord Oliver's 'definition' in *JIF Lemon*, so does the defence actually exist? Certainly, in the past, there have been a number of cases which recognized the defence. All of these involved the practice of character merchandising. The high point of the defence is the decision in *McCulloch v May* (1947) 65 RPC 58, where it was held that a children's radio presenter could not stop a cereal manufacturer from using his name to sell the product. With one notable exception (*Mirage Studios v Counter-Feat Clothing* [1991] FSR 145) UK courts have been unreceptive to the notion of protecting fame through passing off. This unwillingness to accord protection is perhaps one reason why the defence is only to be found in the merchandising cases.

The best explanation of the 'defence' is to be found in *Annabel's (Berkeley Square) v Schock*, where the Court pointed out that it is more difficult for a claimant to establish a likelihood of confusion if the parties are not in direct competition. In other words, 'no common field of activity' is not a defence as such, but rather is one aspect of whether the misrepresentation by the defendant is likely to deceive the public into thinking the celebrity has endorsed the product.

More recently, the Court of Appeal in *Harrods v Harrodian School* saw fit to say that the requirement of a common field of activity did not form part of the formula for passing off. Equally, Laddie J in *Irvine v Talksport Radio* was dismissive of the need to show that the parties were in competition, preferring instead to focus on the harm to the claimant's goodwill. We have already noted how the loss of potential licensees was a key factor in proving harm to goodwill.

 Pause for reflection

Can the Hackney-based dance school invoke a defence against an allegation of passing off in terms of their unauthorized use of the 'Danova Method'?

8.5 Varieties of the tort

Passing off can be committed in an infinite variety of ways. We set out here examples of these, grouped together for convenience under two main headings. The headings derive from a point made by Lord Diplock in *Erven Warnink BV v Townend & Sons* where he described passing off as being subdivided into two categories. He called these 'orthodox' and 'extended' passing off. The latter category includes those cases which concern product misdescription, or else harm to goodwill other than through origin confusion. The context in which Lord Diplock made those remarks was, of course, his policy statement that passing off ought to expand to deal with any sort of unfair trading practices. Some have since doubted whether this subdivision actually exists, but we use it here as a means of organizing the case law.

The illustrations of the tort should be considered always in light of Lord Oliver's 'classic trinity', the three interdependent factors which go to make up passing off. In essence, we are here concerned with the different ways in which the defendant can misrepresent to a customer that 'this is something for which the claimant was responsible'.

8.5.1 Orthodox passing off

The following may be considered as examples of 'orthodox' passing off:

8.5.1.1 Names

A well-established illustration of passing off is where the claimant's name is used as the name of the defendant's business. The name taken by the defendant can be that of an individual (*Biba Group Ltd v Biba Boutique* [1980] RPC 413); that of a company (*Harrods Ltd v R Harrod Ltd* (1924) 41 RPC 74); or the claimant's trading name (*Brestian v Try* [1958] RPC 161). Where the claimant has traded under a descriptive name, then the scope of protection will be quite narrow, and the defendant can avoid liability by choosing a slightly different name: *Office Cleaning Services Ltd v Westminster Window & General Cleaners Ltd* (1946) 63 RPC 39.

The protection of trading names appears to have been extended by analogy to telephone numbers in *Law Society v Griffiths* [1995] RPC 16. Here the defendant was held to have committed passing off by choosing a telephone number for his accident helpline which was only one digit different from that of the claimant's helpline. The misrepresentation occurred as a result of the defendant's silence in not correcting customers' assumptions that they had contacted the claimant for legal advice.

One question which is often asked is whether passing off can actually prevent a trader using their own name. The answer would seem to be 'yes'. If claimant and defendant have the same name, then the onus is on the defendant to *ensure* that customers are not misled: *Boswell-Wilkie Circus v Brian Boswell Circus* [1986] FSR 479.

I N Newman Ltd v Adlem [2005] EWCA Civ 741

An illustration of this harsh rule can be seen in *I N Newman Ltd v Adlem* [2005] EWCA Civ 741. Here, the defendant had sold his business as a funeral director to the claimant's predecessor in business, but then set up a new business using his own name, which he also registered as a trade mark. Overturning the first instance decision, a majority of the Court of Appeal held that the goodwill of the original business had been transferred to the claimant. Accordingly, by trading in his own name the defendant had failed to do enough to ensure that customers would not be misled. Passing off was therefore established, and the defendant's trade mark registration was invalid under s. 47(2) TMA.

The net effect is that the 'own name' defence in passing off is far narrower than the equivalent defence in trade mark infringement, despite the fact that, as we will see in chapter 14, the new position of the EU Trade Mark package of 2015 limits the 'own name' defence only to natural persons. There also appears to be no decided case in passing off where the defence has succeeded: *Reed Executive plc v Reed Business Information Ltd* [2004] RPC 767.

Pause for reflection

Although the 'own name' defence has a narrow scope of application, it was partly upheld in *Property Renaissance Ltd (t/a Titanic Spa) v Stanley Dock Hotel Ltd (t/a Titanic Hotel)* [2016] EWHC 3103 (Ch); [2017] ETMR 12. In this case, the proprietor of the UK trade mark 'Titanic Spa' succeeded in its passing off claim against the owners of the Titanic Hotel Liverpool. The defendant could not rely on the 'own name' defence with regards to past acts of infringement; however, provided that it undertook to place a prominent notice on its website making clear that it is not connected to the claimant, the own name defence could succeed in respect of the future ([128]–[137]).

8.5.1.2 Trade marks

The traditional use of passing off has always been to protect the claimant's unregistered trade mark. Whether the trade mark was descriptive or geographical was irrelevant, provided factual distinctiveness was established. If that factual distinctiveness was exceptionally powerful, then it was possible to prevent the use of the name on dissimilar goods: see *Eastman Photographic Materials Co v John Griffiths Cycle Co* and *Lego System AB v Lego M Lemelstrich*.

8.5.1.3 Get-up of the product

However, perhaps the most significant group of cases in 'orthodox' passing off (before the 1994 reforms) shows how the claimant could protect the get-up of their goods. By 'get-up' we mean the shape of packaging and of containers, the use of colour schemes, the layout of and typeface used on labels, indeed *any* aspect of the goods' *appearance* which helps the consumer to identify trade origin. This is sometimes referred to as 'trade dress'.

Examples of cases falling within this group include *William Edge & Sons v Niccolls* [1911] AC 693, where the House of Lords conferred common law protection on the packaging of 'dolly blue' whitening for laundry which had been sold in little muslin bags with a stick attached, so that it had the appearance of a doll. In *Combe International v Scholl (UK) Ltd* [1980] RPC 1 the appearance of the product was the special packaging used on 'odour-eater' insoles. In *United Biscuits (UK) Ltd v Asda Stores Ltd*, as we have already seen, what was protected was the style of the wrappers on PENGUIN chocolate biscuits, even though the brand name used by the defendant on its biscuits (PUFFIN) was held not to be confusingly similar. The case is a rare example of passing off being successfully used to deal with a problem debated (somewhat inconclusively) and then ignored by Parliament when implementing the Directive and recently raised as an issue for possible reform by the 2006 *Gowers Review of Intellectual Property* at para 5.82, namely how to provide brand owners with protection against supermarket 'own-brand lookalikes' (a matter likely to be resolved by the recast EU Trade Marks Directive).

Containers for liquids are another typical instance of passing off being used to protect get-up. Cases include *John Haig v Forth Blending* (1953) 70 RPC 259 where the shape of the dimple whisky bottle was held to have acquired secondary meaning, and, of course, *JIF Lemon* itself, where the appearance of a plastic lemon for lemon juice (described by Lord Oliver as resembling a hand grenade) was held to have acquired '100% factual distinctiveness'. The fact that the claimants obtained their evidence of distinctiveness on Shrove Tuesday (when customers who don't normally buy fresh lemons were buying the claimant's product to put on their pancakes) might have had something to do with the successful outcome!

In *George East Housewares Ltd v Fackelmann Gmbh & Co KG & Anor* [2016] EWHC 2476, the IPEC dismissed a passing off claim brought by the company that makes and distributes retro-style conical kitchen measuring cups under the brand name TALA in the United Kingdom. The claimant claimed goodwill in many variations of cup and the judge found that '[i]t is clear that the interior of that cup was copied from the Claimant's cups, down to some stray inverted commas that are printed in one of the columns' (at [21]). However, the judge also stressed that, because of some 'conspicuous differences', particularly between the exteriors of the cups, any confusion by members of the trade or consumers would be too low and hence 'an average end consumer would not be led to assume from the get-up of the Defendants' cups that any of them are Tala cups, or that they come from the same manufacturer or are otherwise linked in trade to the Claimant' (at [79]).

In *London Taxi Corp Ltd (t/a London Taxi Co) v Fraser-Nash Research Ltd* [2016] EWHC 52 (Ch); [2016] ETMR 18, Sir Arnold dismissed a passing off claim regarding models of London black taxi-cabs because the claimant was unable to establish misrepresentation. As the learned Judge held in [296], 'there [was] no evidence that the shape of the new Metrocab [was] likely to lead consumers of taxi services to believe that it [came] from the same source as LTC's taxis, as opposed to being a licensed London taxi'.

 Pause for reflection

Indeed, consumers do not usually see colours and shapes as trade marks. In consequence, they need to be 'educated' that the sign does indicate origin, so far more factual distinctiveness needs to be proved. Relevant to this is the nature of the sign itself. So, as regards colours, the 'garish' scheme of purple and green pharmaceutical capsules was protected in *Hoffmann-La Roche v DDSA* [1972] RPC 1 but the 'very ordinary' pale blue colour of tablets in *Roche Products v Berk Pharmaceuticals* [1973] RPC 473 was not. The descriptive nature of the sign (green and yellow for cans of lemonade) may help to explain the result of *Cadbury-Schweppes v Pub Squash Co* where, it will be remembered, the Privy Council thought it significant that there was no evidence of confusion, which in turn was attributable to the lack of distinctiveness. This again highlights the interdependence of the ingredients in Lord Oliver's 'classic trinity'.

8.5.1.4 Effect of the TMA

Since 1994, the law of registered trade marks has changed dramatically and such revolution is bound to have an impact on passing off, as follows:

- the test for registrability is considerably broader than before. The key word in the definition of trade mark in TMA s. 1 is 'sign'. The CJEU has interpreted this to mean anything which sends a message to any of the senses, so that in principle colours, sounds, and smells can all be registered as trade marks. The shape of products and their packaging are specifically mentioned as types of registered marks. The implication must be that those passing off cases giving protection to trade dress will decline in importance;

- some of the 'get-up' cases will need to be reconsidered in light of the CJEU's comments about trade mark function in Case C-206/01 *Arsenal Football Club v Matthew Reed* [2002] ECR I-10273. The dismissal of the claim for passing off in *Cadbury v Ulmer* on the ground that the appearance of the Flake bar did not have 'trade mark significance' is at odds with the comments of AG Colomer about the role of trade marks in the modern consumer era. The rejection of the claim in *Bostick v Sellotape* because the product was not visible at point of sale likewise contradicts what the CJEU said: that the perception of the mark by the end user is as important as the views of the actual purchaser;

- the scope of protection accorded to the owner of a registered trade mark has been extended. Under previous law, protection was limited to the goods of the registration. Today, the owner can sue for infringement where the registered mark is used on identical, similar, or dissimilar goods. Consequently, cases like *Eastman Photographic Materials Co v John Griffiths Cycle Co* and *Lego System AB v Lego M Lemelstrich* appear to be redundant. The TMA ss. 5(3) and 10(3) introduce protection against dilution. If passing off is restricted by its definition to origin confusion, what does it add (if anything) to the law of registered trade marks?

8.5.2 Extended passing off

'Extended' passing off involves a misrepresentation which does not cause origin confusion, but results in some other form of harm to the claimant's goodwill. The cases can be grouped together as follows:

8.5.2.1 False suggestion of superior quality

This particular form of 'extended' passing off has long been recognized. In *Spalding v Gamage*, the defendant advertised the claimant's goods as being first class when in fact they were defective and had been disposed of as scrap. The House of Lords held that although the defendant had sold genuine goods, the false statement as to their quality caused harm to the claimant. Such harm was not caused by origin confusion, but by customers ceasing to buy the claimant's goods because they believed they had declined in quality. Another example of this type of passing off is *Wilts United Dairies v Thomas Robinson* [1958] RPC 94, where the tins of the claimant's condensed milk sold by the defendant were past their 'sell by' date. Similarly, in *Sodastream Ltd v Thorn Cascade Ltd* [1982] RPC 457 there was held to have been passing off when the defendant supplied refilled gas canisters for the claimant's fizzy drinks machines.

8.5.2.2 Geographical origin

We have considered how the names of unique products had been protected, products such as champagne, sherry, advocaat, Swiss chocolate, and Greek yoghurt. Whilst this category of passing off, which deals with product misdescription rather than origin confusion, is well established, the uncertainties surrounding the precise limits of the case law were discussed in *Chocosuisse Union des Fabricants Suisses de Chocolat v Cadbury Ltd*.

A further difficulty is that there is an overlap between this category of passing off and two other forms of intellectual property protection. First, TMA ss. 49 and 50 provide, respectively, for the registration of collective and certification trade marks. The function of a collective mark is to indicate who is entitled to use the mark (normally, members of a trade association which owns the mark) whereas the function of a certification mark is to indicate that goods or services comply with certain objective standards (concerning, for example, material, safety, or quality) which are laid down by regulation. An example of a certification mark is the 'wool mark' used on garment fabric, or the British Standards 'Kite Mark'. Second, there is EC Regulation 2081/92 [1992] OJ L 208/1, repealed and replaced by Council Regulation (EC) No 510/2006 of 20 March 2006 [2006] OJ L 93/12, on the protection of geographical indications and designations of origin for agricultural products and foodstuffs. This enables producers of regional products to register the name of the place where the product originates with the EU Commission in Brussels. Such protection is not, however, as powerful as might first be assumed. Much depends on the wording of the regulations in the country of origin. So, for example, in Case C-108/01 *Consorzio del Prosciutto di Parma v Asda Stores Ltd* [2003] ECR I-5121, the CJEU accepted that although the name 'Parma ham' was protected under EU law, the Italian regulations governing its use were not capable of having direct effect throughout the EU. In consequence, the trade association which oversaw the application of the name was unable to stop the defendant from selling pre-sliced, prepackaged Parma ham in the United Kingdom, even though Italian law required otherwise.

8.5.2.3 Advertising campaigns

A possible use of 'extended' passing off is to prevent the defendant from taking the idea underlying the claimant's advertising campaign. What is being taken is not any copyright material, such as words or music, but the misappropriation of the *concept* of the advert. It will be remembered that the Privy Council did not accept such an argument in *Cadbury-Schweppes v Pub Squash Co* despite clear evidence that the defendant had set out deliberately to copy the sporting theme of the claimant's advert for lemonade. However, other cases have tentatively suggested that passing off might be used in this way, at least where the defendant deliberately sought to take advantage of another's successful campaign. The suggestions can be found in *RHM Foods v Bovril Ltd* [1983] RPC 275 and *Elida Gibbs v Colgate-Palmolive* [1983] FSR 95, although both involved applications for interim relief. The cases do not, of course, fit in with the decision in *Pub Squash*.

8.5.2.4 Comparative advertising

Can comparative advertising amount to passing off? Normally, the answer is 'no', because if the defendant compares two products side-by-side there cannot be origin confusion: *Bulmer v Bollinger*. If the comparison is not explicit, but rather, implied (i.e. the defendant refers to the claimant's product in an indirect way), this may amount to passing off. In *McDonald's Hamburgers Ltd v Burgerking (UK) Ltd* [1986] FSR 45 the defendant launched an advertising campaign on the London underground which used the phrase 'It's Not Just Big, Mac'. Whitford J held that by so referring to the claimant's 'flagship' product the defendant had committed passing off.

> ### Kimberly-Clark v Fort Sterling [1997] FSR 877
>
> In *Kimberly-Clark v Fort Sterling* [1997] FSR 877, the defendant launched a new range of toilet tissue, Nouvelle, with a special promotional offer which declared that if customers were not satisfied, they could exchange it for Andrex, which was made by the claimant. Laddie J held that on seeing the defendant's packaging, consumers would assume that the claimant had approved the offer or that Nouvelle was actually made by the claimant. The average shopper would not stop to read a disclaimer in very small print which acknowledged that Andrex was the claimant's trade mark.

8.5.2.5 Reverse passing off

As might be supposed, 'reverse' or inverse passing off involves a false statement which is the exact opposite of that which is usually found in passing off. In 'orthodox' passing off, the defendant misleads customers by stating that his or her goods are those of the claimant. In 'reverse' passing off, the defendant misleads by saying that the claimant's product is made by the defendant. An example of such conduct occurred in *Bristol Conservatories v Conservatories Custom Built* [1989] RPC 455, where customers were shown a catalogue of the claimant's products but were led to believe that the goods had been made by the defendant.

 Pause for reflection

To what extent would it be possible to fit both 'orthodox' and 'extended' passing off into Lord Oliver's formula in *JIF Lemon*?

8.6 The foreign claimant and the protection of well-known marks under the Paris Convention

8.6.1 The foreign claimant rule

The first part of Lord Oliver's 'classic trinity' requires the claimant to have a reputation or goodwill in the United Kingdom. How does this apply to an overseas company which does business in the United Kingdom? What has to be proved before it can bring a passing off action?

The starting point is to identify what sort of activity is being conducted in the United Kingdom. This could range from having business premises within the United Kingdom (such as a factory or an office), to having a facility to process orders for goods or bookings for services, to having customers within the jurisdiction who might have bought one of the claimant's products when on holiday or on a business trip overseas. Finally, the firm might have a reputation in the United Kingdom, but otherwise no other business presence. Which of these satisfies the requirement of goodwill? What is certain is that the need to show goodwill is satisfied if there are business premises. The presence of a manufacturing facility or similar will therefore suffice. An extreme example is *Sheraton Corporation v Sheraton Motels* [1964] RPC 202, a decision which has been doubted by some. The decision was to the effect that the ability to receive hotel bookings amounted to United Kingdom goodwill, even though the claimants did not at the time have any hotels in the United Kingdom. Similarly, in *Hotel Cipriani Srl v Cipriani (Grosvenor Street) Ltd* [2010] RPC 485, the Court of Appeal confirmed that the claimant hotel group had United Kingdom goodwill because customers either made direct bookings with the group or instructed travel agents to do the same.

However, we live in a shrinking world. Surely the presence of customers alone should suffice? A resounding rejection of this proposition occurred in *Alain Bernadin v Pavilion Properties Ltd* [1967] RPC 581, where it was said that a foreign claimant must have both business presence *and* customers in the United Kingdom before being able to sue for passing off. The narrow approach is remarkable, given the old case of *Panhard Levassor SA v Panhard-Levassor Motor Co Ltd* [1901] 2 Ch 513, where the court restrained the use of the name of a French car company by the defendant, even though the claimant's only business 'presence' was the existence of several English customers who had in the past purchased the claimant's cars.

Two decisions have since set the record straight as regards what will suffice for local goodwill. The Court of Appeal in *Anheuser-Busch Inc v Budejovicky Budvar NP* (1984) declared that the minimum necessary to enable an overseas undertaking to sue for passing off is the presence of customers in the United Kingdom who can be misled by the defendant's misrepresentations. The court did say, however, that those customers had to be members of the public, not visiting foreign nationals such as members of the American armed forces. As a result, the claim for passing off failed because at the time, the claimant's trade mark *BUDWEISER* for beer was not known to the general public, having been supplied only to US forces personnel stationed temporarily within the United Kingdom. It has since been held that the two companies involved in this case, one American and one Czech, have concurrent rights to the *BUDWEISER* mark: *Anheuser-Busch Inc v Budejovicky Budvar NP* (2000). A more liberal approach still can be discerned in the judgment of Browne-Wilkinson VC in *Peter Waterman Ltd v CBS (The Hit Factory)* [1993] EMLR 27. He rejected the claimant's attempt to sue for passing off, holding that it had failed to demonstrate that the nickname accorded to its business had acquired distinctiveness. However, he went on to observe that any misrepresentation made to customers in England is an interference with that goodwill wherever it was situated. Although the defendant was based in New York, its recording studio was known to those in the entertainment industry in London and it therefore had sufficient use of the name in the United Kingdom to acquire goodwill.

These *obiter* comments by Browne-Wilkinson VC echo the conclusions of Graham J in *Maxim's Ltd v Dye* [1977] 1 WLR 1155. In a far-thinking judgment, he held that the owners of Maxim's restaurant in Paris could obtain an injunction simply because the name was 'known' to the public as a result of 'spill over' advertising in films, television, or magazines. In other words, he took a 'global' approach to the existence of goodwill. This accords with how the matter is dealt with in other common law jurisdictions. In Australia, for example, it has been held that reputation alone is sufficient to enable a foreign litigant to sue for passing off: *Conagra Inc v McCain Foods (Aust) Pty Ltd* (1992) 106 ALR 465.

8.6.2 **The impact of TMA s. 56**

The presence of TMA s. 56 necessitates a review of the previously discussed case law on what amounts to protectable goodwill in the case of a foreign claimant. The section implements the United Kingdom's obligations under Art. 6*bis* of the Paris Convention for the Protection of Industrial Property 1883. It provides that the proprietor of a well-known mark is entitled to obtain an injunction to prevent the use or registration of a trade mark which is identical or similar to his mark, in relation to identical or similar goods or services, where the use of the same is likely to cause confusion. The section, however, does not enable the award of damages: *Hotel Cipriani Srl v Cipriani (Grosvenor Street) Ltd*. The purpose of s. 56 is to enable overseas trade mark owners, who have neither registration nor use of their mark in the United Kingdom, to prevent others misappropriating it providing that they can establish that their mark is well known. Individuals or organizations domiciled in the United Kingdom cannot rely on this provision, again because of the wording of the Paris Convention: *Jules Rimet Cup Ltd v The Football Association Ltd* at [73]. The section implies that sufficient 'knowledge' of the mark is enough, a more relaxed test than proving that the claimant has protectable goodwill.

8.6.3 The meaning of 'well-known mark' under the Paris Convention

The question prompted by TMA s. 56 is 'what is a well-known mark'? An answer can be found in *LE MANS Trade Mark Application*, Appointed Person, 8 November 2004. Here, the organizers of the 24-hour motor race opposed an application by a garage proprietor to register the name 'Le Mans' for his garage business. Richard Arnold QC referred to the *Joint Recommendation Concerning Provisions on the Protection of Well Known Marks* adopted by WIPO in September 1999. This document listed the factors which ought to be taken into account by a court or registry when deciding whether a mark is well known for the purposes of Art. *6bis* of the Paris Convention. The criteria include: the degree of recognition of the mark; how much and for how long it has been used; the amount of advertising and publicity accorded to the mark, and for how long such advertisements have been running; the geographical 'reach' of the mark; whether it possesses inherent or acquired distinctiveness; the degree of exclusivity enjoyed by the mark and the extent of use of the same or similar marks by third parties; the nature of the goods or services provided under the mark, and how those goods and services reach the public; whether the reputation of the mark symbolises quality goods; and the extent of the commercial value attributed to the mark. In the instant case the opponents clearly met these criteria.

The question which therefore remains, in the light of the remarks of Browne-Wilkinson VC in *Peter Waterman Ltd v CBS (The Hit Factory)* and Graham J in *Maxim's Ltd v Dye*, is whether s. 56 requires Lord Oliver's classic trinity to be completely rewritten.

8.7 The future of passing off

Since the introduction of a system of registering trade marks in 1875, passing off has often been regarded as the means of 'filling in the gaps' in trade mark law. The 1994 reforms have considerably broadened the law of registered trade marks. This increase in scope applies to both registrability and infringement. Further, the judicial recognition of the functions which trade marks perform has been liberalized by the CJEU's decision in *Arsenal v Reed*. If registered trade marks are no longer restricted by origin function, where does that leave passing off, with its insistence that the defendant's misrepresentation must produce a likelihood of confusion on the part of the consumer?

Our discussion of passing off has shown how the case law has a pendulum effect. There are times when the courts are adventurous and want to expand passing off so that it becomes a tort of unfair competition. As illustrations of this, the judgments in *Vine Products v MacKenzie* and *Erven Warnink BV v Townend & Sons* specifically mention the need for passing off to be flexible and respond to changes in business practices. Both of these cases involve passing off by product misdescription, and both argue for the need for protection against unfair competition. Equally, the Court of Appeal in *Taittinger v Allbev* saw no need for there to be customer confusion, instead conferring protection against dilution. This suggests that passing off doesn't just protect goodwill, but the unique selling power of the brand name itself. Indeed, it has been suggested that passing off *ought* to be regarded as unfair competition by Aldous LJ in two cases, *BT plc v One in a Million* [1999] FSR 1 at p. 18 and *Arsenal Football Club v Matthew Reed* [2003] RPC 696 at [70]. For some commentators such as Carty, however, this is stretching passing off too far, so that it is in danger of losing sight of its rationale.

In contrast, there are just as many instances of when the courts are restrictive in their thinking. One prime example is *Cadbury-Schweppes v Pub Squash Co* where the Privy Council expressly refused to countenance any expansion of the tort beyond the traditional confines of origin confusion, despite there being clear evidence that the defendant had deliberately sought to 'free-ride' on the claimant's success. The certainty from having precise rules was preferable to flexibility. Similarly, the majority of the Court of Appeal in *Harrods v Harrodian School* held that in the absence of proven confusion there could be no liability. Another case reaching the same conclusion is *Hodgkinson & Corby v Wards Mobility Service*, where Jacob J remarked that there 'is no tort of copying. There is no tort of taking another man's market or customers. Neither the market nor the customers are the plaintiff's to own.'

Jacob LJ (as he had become) later observed in *L'Oréal SA v Bellure NV* [2008] RPC 196 at [141] that:

> the basic economic rule is that competition is not only lawful but a mainspring of the economy. The legislator has recognised that there should be exceptions. It has laid down the rules for these: the laws of patents, trade marks, copyrights, and designs have all been fashioned for the purpose. Each of them have rules for their existence and (save for trade marks) set time periods for existence. Each has their own justification. It is not for the judges to step in and legislate into existence new categories of intellectual property rights. And if they were to do so they would be entering wholly uncertain territory.

 Pause for reflection

In an era of emerging new technologies, is it preferable to have specific intellectual property rights which are clearly defined, or should the law be flexible enough to respond to changing business practices?

If we had a crystal ball, what might it tell us about the future of passing off? In simple terms, the question is one of policy. *Should* passing off develop into a form of protection against unfair competition, or should it remain as a strictly defined, alternative means of protection to registered trade marks? During the last decade and a half, the Government has resisted three separate attempts to introduce a law of unfair competition by means of legislation, although the *Gowers Review* has identified the need to protect brand owners against supermarket imitations. It seems unlikely that the judiciary will provide the means for change (especially in view of the expansion of registered trade marks). Academic opinion is divided.

8.7.1 **In favour of unfair competition**

The principal argument in favour of passing off being developed into a general tort of unfair competition is that the United Kingdom has an obligation under the Paris Convention to provide such a form of redress. Such a cause of action would, in an era when copying is all too easy, provide protection for an individual's creative endeavours, and would add flexibility. The relevant arguments can be found in A. Horton and A. Robertson, 'Does the UK or the EC Need an Unfair Competition Law?' [1995] *EIPR* 568.

8.7.2 **Against unfair competition**

The arguments against having a general tort of unfair competition are perhaps stronger. Spence argues (see 'Passing Off and the Misappropriation of Valuable Intangibles' (1996) 112 *LQR* 472) that there is no theoretical justification for unfair competition. He further contends that the action would be too general to provide any guidance for judges. As Parliament has already legislated to provide specific forms of protection, it would be wrong to go outside those boundaries (see *Victoria Park Racing v Taylor* (1937) 58 CLR 479 at p. 509 (*per* Dixon J) (Australian HC) and *Moorgate Tobacco v Philip Morris* [1985] RPC 291 at pp. 236–40 (*per* Deane J) (Australian HC)). If additional protection is required, then there should be *sui generis* legislation to deal with particular problems. Carty argues (in 'Dilution and Passing Off: Cause for Concern' (1996) 112 *LQR* 632) that the introduction of an action for unfair competition would lead to unnecessary judicial interference in the marketplace. There is also the perennial argument about opening the litigation floodgates.

8.8 **Conclusion**

This chapter has explained the elements which go to make up the tort of passing off: the 'protean' nature of the tort, both with regard to its potential to develop into a broader means of redress against unfair competition, and the numerous inconsistencies and contradictions which are to be found in the cases; and the likely impact of the Trade Marks Act 1994 on the tort and how it might change in the future.

With regards to our problem question, Natalia should be advised that a passing off claim against the Hackney-based dance school has good prospects of success. It is important that all three conditions of the *JIF Lemon* test (namely goodwill, misrepresentation, and damage) apply cumulatively. On goodwill, what is subject to protection is the specific method of teaching ballet, as a service, along with the name that has been given to this method. These have received public recognition over the past ten years, not only through Natalia's practice, but also from the appearances of the 'Davona Method' in local press (*IRC v Muller*). The Hackney dance school enters into a misrepresentation as a false statement of fact (*Spalding v Gamage*) that is demonstrated both by the presentation of the 'Danova Method' on their website and through their practice of it. It is an operative misrepresentation that takes place through a statement that explicitly links the Hackney school to Natalia's school, implying that their services and those of Natalia are related. Damage can be established in light of the loss of a licensing opportunity, that could perhaps emerge through franchising (*Mirage Studios*).

End-of-chapter questions

After reading the chapter carefully, try answering the following questions. For answer guidance visit the online resources at **www.oup.com/uk/karapapa-mcdonagh/**

1. The tort of passing off has no effective role to play in the modern intellectual property régime. Discuss.
2. What is the difference between confusion and misrepresentation in passing off actions?

Further reading

For understanding the passing off action, the following readings are recommended:

Carty, H. 'Dilution and Passing Off: Cause for Concern' (1996) 112 *LQR* 632
Argues that a tort of unfair competition would be bad for business.

Carty, H. 'Heads of Damage in Passing Off' [1996] 18 *EIPR* 487
Argues that Taittinger v Allbev *is wrong to recognize dilution as a form of harm to goodwill in passing off.*

Carty, H. 'Passing Off: Frameworks of Liability Debated' [2012] 2 *IPQ* 106
Argues that passing off should remain firmly based in Lord Oliver's 'classic trinity'.

Davis, J. 'Why the United Kingdom Should Have a Law against Misappropriation' [2012] 69 *CLJ* 561
Argues that trends in passing off show that remedies for misappropriation are necessary to protect investment in the attractiveness of brands.

Gowers Review of Intellectual Property, December 2006, available on the Treasury website at: hm-treasury.gov.uk
Offers an overview of the extent to which passing off protection applies.

Griffiths, J. 'Star Industrial Co Ltd v Yap Kwee Kor: The End of Goodwill in the Tort of Passing Off' in Douglas, S., Hickey, R., and Waring, E. (eds.) *Landmark Cases in Property Law* (Hart Publishing, 2015) 277
Outlines the continuing significance of Star Industrial Co Ltd v Yap Kwee Kor.

Horton, A. and Robertson, A. 'Does the UK or the EC Need an Unfair Competition Law?' [1995] 12 *EIPR* 568
Argues for the introduction of a general tort of unfair competition.

Spence, M. 'Passing Off and the Misappropriation of Valuable Intangibles' (1996) 112 *LQR* 472
Argues that general torts, such as misappropriation or unfair competition, are not justified theoretically and would not assist judges to decide cases.

Wadlow, C. 'Hotel Cipriani Srl v. Cipriani (Grosvenor Street) Ltd [2010] EWCA Civ 110: the Court of Appeal draws the line on whether a foreign business has an English goodwill or not' [2011] 33(1) *EIPR* 54
A critical account on the Cipriani *case.*

Trade Marks

PART 4

Trade marks

Problem question

Read this problem question carefully and keep it in mind while you are working through the chapter that follows. At the end of this chapter, you will be able to apply what you have learnt to the problem question and advise the relevant parties.

George Giannopoulos is a chemist and a wine connoisseur. He has recently started running his own winery in Southampton, using grapes that have been cultivated under specific climate conditions in his village, called Kefalovriso, in Peloponnese, Greece. He produces a sweet wine, commonly known in Greece as Mavrodaphne, and he sells it via wine retailers in South West England as 'Kefalovriso wine' or 'Mavrodaphne of Kefalovriso'. Because the wine has become very popular and the increase of his sales is incrementally high, George wants to start selling in supermarkets too and he is thinking of registering the name of the wine as a trade mark. He has gained some goodwill under the names 'Kefalovriso wine' and 'Mavrodaphne of Kefalovriso' but he is also considering the option of registering a new name for the wine, 'Giannopoulos Estate'.

In his spare time he has developed a perfume using undertones of the wine he is producing. Incidentally, his wife, Sophia, tells him that the fragrance smells tremendously like the fragrance 'Muse' by famous designer Joan Kipling that sells for over £100 per 50ml. George was thinking of naming the perfume after his wife, 'Sophia', which happens to mean 'wisdom' in Greek. Given the strong similarity of the two scents, he considers the possibility of selling his fragrance at a lower price than Joan Kipling as a 'Muse' smell-alike product, calling his fragrance 'Muse' but indicating in the packaging that this fragrance just smells like Joan Kipling's perfume. He thinks this may save him time in advertising the product and gaining a share in the fine fragrances market, while at the same time making it clear to consumers that this is just a cheaper alternative to the expensive perfume.

George comes to you for legal advice. Advise George whether the names that he has in mind for his products can function as trade marks.

Keep in mind that there may be other issues worth considering, e.g. grounds for refusing the registration of the trade mark and infringement, but we will be addressing these in the following chapters.

9.1 **Introduction**

The purpose of this chapter is to deal with themes which recur throughout the chapters which follow, dealing with trade mark registrability, infringement, and exhaustion of rights. We consider the historical uses of trade marks, showing how, in some ways, little has changed with respect to how trade marks form a bridge between the manufacturer and consumer of goods. The development of trade mark law is set out, with the objective of emphasizing the cultural change which has occurred since 1994 in United Kingdom trade mark law as a result of EU reforms.

Next, we compare and contrast trade marks with other forms of intellectual property. This comparison will show that trade marks do not always fit in with the assumptions which underlie intellectual property protection. They do not reward creativity nor provide an incentive to innovate. Instead, their justification lies in the economics of the consumer society. Many (e.g. Naomi Klein) would argue that the rise of consumerism has led to an overvaluation of trade marks, with the rights of the trade mark owner prevailing over the interests of the consumer and of society itself.

We also examine the commercial functions fulfilled by trade marks in the age of the consumer, with the objective of showing the dilemma inherent in trade mark law, keeping in mind the issues raised in the scenario question. If the function of trade marks is simply to tell the consumer about the commercial origin of the goods, this has a restrictive effect on the ability to register trade marks, and to protect them through the action for infringement. If, however, trade mark protection is enhanced to reflect the selling power of brands as image carriers, then they become barriers to entry and impede competition.

9.2 **The history of trade marks**

9.2.1 **Ancient use of trade marks**

The use of trade marks developed long before their legal protection. It is not possible to pinpoint accurately when the concept of ownership first evolved, nor when mankind first began to trade by bartering or selling goods, but it is reasonable to assume that the use of a symbol or sign to designate either ownership or commercial origin must have developed contemporaneously with these events. Ancient cave paintings in France show how trade marks were first used to claim ownership of cattle by the practice of burning (or branding) the hides of the animals with a symbol, the term 'brand name' today being a relic of this ancient custom. The use of a trade mark to designate the trade origin of goods goes back furthest in ancient China, where marks are thought to have been placed on pottery as long ago as 3000 BC. A good deal of information is available about ancient pottery, because it lasts almost indefinitely. Excavations from ancient Egypt, Asia Minor, India, and Crete have all revealed potters' marks, and indeed marks used by other crafts, notably goldsmiths, ironsmiths, and brickmakers.

Nevertheless, it is Greek and Roman antiquities which are most revealing of the historical background of trade marks. In Greece, vases, jars, and pottery objects were marked in various ways; for example, amphorae used to export wine were marked with the name of the maker, the place of origin, and an official mark, the latter presumably signifying fitness to drink. Thousands of Roman trade marks have been catalogued, particularly those used on clay lamps. Roman goods were exported throughout the Roman Empire and their remains have been found in numerous countries across Europe and beyond. Even bread found in the ruins of Pompeii was found to bear the maker's stamp.

9.2.2 Medieval use of trade marks

Use of trade marks in the Middle Ages falls again into these two broad categories, namely marks to show ownership and merchants' marks. Schechter (in his seminal work, *Historical Foundations of Trade Mark Law* (Columbia University Press, 1925)) describes these as proprietary and production marks.

9.2.2.1 Proprietary marks

The use of the proprietary mark on goods (i.e. branding them as a means of showing ownership) can be considered similar to the adoption of heraldic devices. The practical significance of such branding becomes clear when it is remembered the frequency with which goods might be affected by piracy or shipwreck. Where goods had been lost in transit, the seller or original owner could reclaim them, if they were later recovered, by proving that they bore his mark. Throughout the trading cities of Northern Europe, laws were passed enabling merchants to get back lost or stolen goods upon proof of entitlement to their mark. In England, Stat. 27 Ed III Chap 13 (1353) facilitated the recovery of goods in this manner, the statute being invoked as late as *Hamilton v Davis* (1771) 5 Burr 2732. Here, Lord Mansfield held that the claimant was entitled to recover certain hogsheads of tallow, lost en route from Ireland to Liverpool, from the defendant, even though it could not be established how the defendant had acquired the goods.

9.2.2.2 Production marks

When considering the use of production marks, two things need to be remembered, first the overwhelming power of the Craft Guilds, and the fact that the public bought goods direct from the maker. Not only in England, but throughout continental Europe, virtually all industry up until the fifteenth century was organized in towns and cities by the Guilds, who, in return for the grant of a monopoly over a particular product, saw it as their function to preserve high standards of quality. Goods were marked so that poor workmanship could be identified and punished. Consequently, as a form of consumer protection, there were numerous national, local, and Guild regulations providing for the compulsory marking of goods, and setting out criminal penalties for breach. Examples include breadmakers, brewers, weavers and, of course, gold and silversmiths.

9.2.3 The rise of the age of the consumer

How then did the trade mark evolve from the production mark, designed to create collective goodwill for the Guild, to the asset mark of today, creating individual goodwill for the trader in question? Again, the answer lies in trading conditions. So long as goods were bought by the consumer dealing directly and face to face with the craftsman there was no need for a trade mark as an indication of origin (although one was needed as a guarantee of quality). Trading in the Middle Ages was by and large very localized, with consumers and craftsmen living in the same community, although as Schechter explains, cloth and cutlery were two trades which from a relatively early date were located in only a handful of towns, so that the resulting goods had, of necessity, to be transported over long distances to reach consumers. Moreover, with the craftsman usually having his place of business in the same vicinity as others of the same type and being closely controlled by his Guild, it was difficult for him to acquire any individual goodwill or indulge in any real form of competition, whether fair or unfair. It is only when goods of a durable nature are transported that the trade mark as a mark of origin acquires any significance.

The decisive event, therefore, which changes trade marks from what Schechter calls liability marks to asset marks, is the Industrial Revolution. Once technology enables goods to be mass-produced in a mill or factory, and then transported to cities many miles away, the producer and consumer are separated. The maker's mark therefore has a different role to fulfil. It is needed to identify the source from which satisfactory goods have come. Nevertheless, the explosion in the use and exploitation of trade marks does not really happen until the latter part of the 20th century. What matters is the way in which retailing habits change, from selling goods in small, personalized outlets (the local shop), to selling in sophisticated, multi-national hypermarkets offering thousands of competing brands of prepackaged, 'designer' goods from around the world. The advent of internet shopping is likely to have a further impact on the role of the trade mark.

 Pause for reflection

How does the use of trade marks today compare with their use in previous times?

9.3 The development of United Kingdom trade mark law

9.3.1 Trade mark law before 1875

Aldous LJ in *Marks & Spencer plc and others v One in a Million Ltd* [1998] 4 All ER 476 tells us that the first ever reported trade mark case is *Southern v How* (1618) Popham 143. Close examination of the case (which has five different reports) shows that it has nothing whatsoever to do with the law of trade marks, being an agency dispute. As Schechter tells us, the only link with trade marks lies in an irrelevant remark by the judge, Doderidge J, in which he recalls a case heard many years earlier about the counterfeiting of a trader's mark. Reported trade mark cases do not actually appear until the 19th century, and then, as one would expect of that time, they fall into two groups, those decided at common law and those decided in equity.

9.3.1.1 Common law cases

At common law, the protection of trade marks evolved from the action on the case for deceit. It took a few attempts before the principle was clearly established. So, for example, in *Sykes v Sykes* (1824) 3 B & C 543, the court held that it was important that the defendant placed his imitation of the claimant's mark on goods which were of inferior quality, whilst in *Blofeld v Payne* (1833) 4 B & Ad 409 the court said that what mattered was the defendant's fraudulent intent rather than the quality of the goods. Similarly, in *Crawshay v Thompson* (1842) 4 Man & G 358 the court stressed that if the defendant had acted innocently, there could be no liability even if the mark he had placed on his goods was confusingly similar to that of the claimant. What mattered, therefore, was not the quality of the goods, nor the effect of the statement on the consumer, but whether the defendant *intended* fraudulently to supplant the claimant.

9.3.1.2 Cases in equity

It took a little while for the Court of Chancery to catch up with the courts of common law. In *Blanchard v Hill* (1742) 2 Atk 484, Lord Hardwicke refused to grant an injunction to restrain the defendant from placing the claimant's trade mark on playing cards for the simple reason that to give protection would create an unfair monopoly. Freedom to trade was likewise used as the reason for denying equitable relief by Lord Eldon in *Cruttwell v Lye* (1810) 17 Ves 335. However, it was eventually recognized that the 'get-up' of a business could be protected in *Knott v Morgan* (1836) 2 Keen 213, where Lord Langdale MR restrained the defendant from using the same words, colour scheme, and lettering on his omnibuses as were already used by the claimant in his rival enterprise.

A significant shift in thinking occurred in *Millington v Fox* (1838) 3 My & Cr 338, where Lord Cottenham granted an injunction on the ground simply that a trade mark was 'property', treating it as conferring the same rights on its owner as entitlement to a piece of land. Use of the mark by another amounted to trespass. The defendant's state of mind was irrelevant. It was sufficient that the claimant's mark had been reproduced on the defendant's steel bars.

Thereafter, Chancery cases fall into two groups. There are those where it was held that likelihood of deception was a precondition to equitable relief and there are those which treated trade marks as property. An example of where the Court of Chancery followed the common law and insisted on deception is *Perry v Truitt* (1842) 6 Beav 66. However, this case and others like it (such as *Croft v Day* (1843) 7 Beav 84 and *Burgess v Burgess* (1853) 3 De G, M & G 896) tell us that equity differed from the common law in its approach to deception, concentrating not on the defendant's state of mind but on the *effect* of the false statement on the consumer. An example of the property approach is *Hall v Barrows* (1863) 4 De G, J & S 150, where the Lord Chancellor, Lord Westbury, treated trade marks as analogous to patents and copyright for the purposes of infringement.

9.3.2 Trade mark law after 1875

After 1875, the developments are legislative rather than judicial. There were two key events in that year.

First, the Judicature Acts 1873–5 reorganized the court structure, creating a single High Court of Judicature. Within that, the Chancery Division was to have responsibility, inter alia, for patents, copyright, and trade marks. The Acts also declared that where there was a conflict between the rules of common law and equity, equity was to prevail. In the case of protection of trade marks, the House of Lords, in *Reddaway v Banham* [1896] AC 199 and *Spalding v Gamage* (1915) 32 RPC 273, based its statements of principle for the tort of passing off firmly on the thinking in *Perry v Trufitt*, stressing the importance of the effect of the defendant's false statement on the mind of the purchaser. Both cases deny that trade marks, at common law, are a species of property in their own right. Instead, the right of property which is protected is the goodwill of the claimant's business.

Second, there was the Trade Marks Registration Act 1875. As its name indicates, this introduced (after much lobbying by business) the first system of registration of trade marks. Thereafter, the scheme of protection for trade marks in the United Kingdom is divided into two, namely the registration system, and the tort of passing off for unregistered (or 'common law') trade marks. The 1875 Act can be regarded as primarily procedural in its effect (that is, it provided a system of registration but did not change the underlying case law concept of a trade mark) and was followed by a string of subsequent Acts (10 in total). The most important of these were the Trade Marks Act 1905 (which provided a statutory definition of a trade mark for the first time) and the Trade Marks Act 1938 (which provided for marks to be capable of assignment separately from the goodwill of the business and for marks to be licensed).

9.3.3 Reform of the 1938 Act

Reform of the Trade Marks Act 1938 was considered in detail by the Mathys Committee in 1974 (*British Trade Mark Law and Practice* Cmnd 5601), but the only change recommended by that Committee which was implemented was the introduction of the registration of service marks as a result of the combined effect of Trade Marks (Amendment) Act 1984 and the Patents, Designs and Marks Act 1986. Even this reform was horrendously complicated, with two separate versions of the 1938 Act existing side-by-side, one dealing with marks for goods and one dealing with marks for services.

The Government White Paper *Reform of Trade Marks Law* (Cm 1203) in September 1990 identified a number of reasons why the trade mark system was in urgent need of reform:

- the 1938 Act was horribly out of date and having two parallel versions made it unwieldy, in addition to which it was written in language which judges had frequently criticised for being obscure. The fact that the 1938 Act was stated to be a consolidating measure meant recourse to earlier legislation or even pre-1875 case law, surely not appropriate at the end of the 20th century;

- the United Kingdom had to fulfil its obligations to WIPO by ratifying the latest (1967) version of the Paris Convention for the Protection of Industrial Property 1883 and by joining the Protocol Relating to the Madrid Agreement Concerning the International Registration of Marks 1989;

- most important, however, were the United Kingdom's EU obligations which required it to implement the First Trade Marks Directive (Council Directive

89/104/EEC of 21 December 1988 on the approximation of the laws of Member States relating to trade marks [1989] OJ L 40/1) ('the Directive') (now codified as Directive 2008/95/EC of the European Parliament and of the Council of 22 October 2008 [2008] OJ L 299/25) and to provide for formal links between the United Kingdom Trade Mark Registry and the European Union Intellectual Property Office ('EUIPO'), the body responsible for running the EU trade mark system under Regulation (EU) 2015/2424 of the European Parliament and the Council amending the Community trade mark regulation (the Amending Regulation), and the Community Trademark Regulation (Council Regulation (EC) 40/94 of 20 December 1993 [1994] OJ L 11/1, now codified as Council Regulation (EC) No 207/2009 of 26 February 2009 on the Community trade mark [2009] OJ L 78/1) ('the Regulation').

The net result of the White Paper was the Trade Marks Act 1994 ('TMA'). Given the pressures for reform, one might assume that the Act would revolutionize the law of trade marks. Unsurprisingly, UK judges have, in many instances, continued to cling to principles developed under previous Acts. If anything, the driving force for change has been provided by European institutions.

9.3.4 Conclusion: the historical legacy

The preceding historical account shows several things. First, the way in which trade marks are *used* has, in some ways, changed little, even though trading conditions today are far removed from those of previous times. Although medieval use was primarily to guarantee quality, use since the Industrial Revolution has been to tell the consumer about the origin of the goods. Trade marks have always been messengers. They are the communications link between the manufacturer and ultimate consumer (not necessarily the purchaser) of the goods.

The legal history of trade marks shows that the principles articulated in the early cases continue to influence today's law. There is the perennial concern that trade marks create unfair monopolies. Further, the perception of early cases that the key to the protection of trade marks was the effect of the defendant's false statement on the consumer rather than the right of property in the mark remains today. It is bound up in the judicial concern not to create monopolies. In turn, it raises one of the underlying debates in the law of trade marks, namely whether trade mark law exists to protect consumers or the trade mark owner. If the answer is that the law protects the owner of the mark, how then is the balance to be struck between protecting brands and ensuring free competition?

 Pause for reflection

Given the pressures for reform, and the importance of brands to the consumer economy, is it surprising that the 1994 Act was the first major piece of trade mark legislation for over 50 years?

9.4 **The nature of trade marks**

9.4.1 **Key characteristics**

9.4.1.1 Exclusivity

Like other forms of intellectual property, the TMA declares (in s. 9) that registration of a trade mark confers exclusive rights on its owner. Thus as with patents and copyright, trade marks confer negative rights to stop others (*Inter Lotto (UK) Ltd v Camelot Group plc* [2003] 3 All ER 191).

9.4.1.2 Proprietary nature

The TMA further states in ss. 2 and 27 (in contrast to the historical debate) that registered trade marks and indeed, pending applications for trade marks, are property rights. The conclusion has to be, therefore, that unregistered marks do not possess the characteristics of property, but all registered marks do. For unregistered 'common law' marks protected by passing off, the property right resides in the goodwill of the business in which the mark has been used.

But are trade marks really proprietary in nature? Certainly, registered marks *look* like any other form of intangible, personal property. They can be bought and sold, permission can be granted to others to use them, they can be mortgaged, and a value can be placed on them (indeed, successful brand owners declare the value of trade marks in a company's balance sheet, sometimes as a means of deterring a takeover bid).

However, the entry of a trade mark on the register does not mean that its existence is guaranteed. As with any other form of registrable right, the Registry does not guarantee the validity of a trade mark (TMA s. 70) and it is possible to apply to have a trade mark declared invalid under s. 47 because at the time of registration it did not comply with the Act. Further, and more significantly, a trade mark can be revoked for mismanagement under s. 46. 'Mismanagement' basically comprises three things: that the proprietor has failed to use the mark for a given period of time (if you don't use it you lose it) or the proprietor has allowed the mark to become generic or the proprietor's conduct has caused the mark to become deceptive. As English property law does not have any concept of abandonment, the ability to revoke a trade mark suggests that as a property right it does not quite fit the standard model.

9.4.1.3 Monopolistic nature

Starting with *Blanchard v Hill*, there are numerous cases where judges have denied a trade mark protection on the ground that to do so would create an 'unfair monopoly'. Modern examples include the House of Lords in *Re Coca-Cola Trade Marks* [1986] RPC 421, where Lord Templeman asserted, without reasoning, that a bottle could not be a trade mark because of the anti-competitive effect of granting registration to a shape. Another example is the judgment of Jacob J in *British Sugar plc v James Robertson & Sons Ltd* [1996] RPC 281. Although his thoughts were no doubt coloured by the fact that the claimant's mark 'Treat' was highly descriptive of their product (a sweet topping) and therefore invalid, his remarks about powerful businesses seeking to close off large parts of the English language by registering undeserving trade marks are indicative of a negative attitude.

The term 'monopoly' is used by economists to indicate that an undertaking is the only source of supply for a commodity. This is not the case with trade marks. Just because 'Nike' is registered for footwear does not mean that other companies cannot make and sell trainers. They can do so as long as they adopt a different brand name for their product. If the name 'Crocodile' is registered for shoes, that does not prevent a television company from making a documentary about crocodiles. Perhaps it is the ease with which a trade mark can be created together with its potential duration which produces this adverse reaction.

9.4.2 Comparison with other forms of intellectual property

9.4.2.1 Overlap

Trade marks do overlap with other forms of intellectual property protection, particularly copyright and designs. For example, it is now possible to register the shape of a product as a trade mark. That shape might be a sculpture for the purposes of copyright law, or it might be a design, whether registered or unregistered. A trade mark which consists of a picture might also be a copyright work. In *R Griggs Group Ltd and others v Evans and others* [2005] FSR 706 it was held that artwork which combined the two previous logos for Doc Martens boots was a copyright work, but because it had been created so as to enable the new trade mark to be registered, there was an implied term in the contract to the effect that the artist would assign ownership of the copyright to the trade mark owner. Further, it is now possible to register a musical tune as a trade mark: Case C-283/01 *Shield Mark BV v Joost Kist* [2003] ECR I-14313. Unless the musical work is out of copyright (as it was in *Shield Mark*, where the tune was *Für Elise* by Beethoven) then there will have to be an assignment ensuring that title to the copyright is vested in the trade mark owner.

However, such dual protection is not always available. Even though time and effort have been spent in creating a trade mark, this does not equate to 'skill, labour, and judgement' for the purposes of copyright law, so that an invented word trade mark will not qualify as a literary work under s. 3 of the Copyright, Designs and Patents Act 1988 ('CDPA').

> *Exxon Corporation v Exxon Insurance Consultants International*
> **[1981] 3 All ER 241**
>
> In *Exxon Corporation v Exxon Insurance Consultants International* [1981] 3 All ER 241, the Court of Appeal held that the invented word 'Exxon', adopted by the claimant as its new corporate name and trade mark, did not qualify for copyright protection, even though several million dollars had been spent researching the new brand. The company was therefore unable to stop an unrelated organization from adopting the same name. The case, were it to be decided today, might have a different outcome because of the broader scope of protection given to registered marks under ss. 5 and 10 TMA.

9.4.2.2 Differences

9.4.2.2.1 Ease of creation

The popular perception of copyright is that it requires the expenditure of creative effort by the author or artist (a perception which does not necessarily accord with the law). Most patents today result from huge investment in research. By contrast, almost anyone can think up a trade mark. The courts have accepted that the level of creativity can be very low (Case C-329/02 P *SAT.1 SatellitenFernsehen GmbH v OHIM (SAT.2)* [2004] ECR I-8317). Even a colour can be a trade mark. That being so, perhaps it is justifiable to some extent to refer to trade marks as unfair monopolies.

9.4.2.2.2 Limited protection

However, unlike patents and designs (which can be seen as absolute monopolies) but like copyright, the scope of protection for the trade mark owner is limited. Once a trade mark is registered, its proprietor can object to the use of the identical or similar sign in relation to identical, similar, or dissimilar goods or services. Protection is absolute in the case of an identical sign used in relation to identical goods. However, where there is only similarity, the owner must prove that there is a likelihood of confusion on the part of consumers. Where there is no likelihood of confusion, or where the goods are dissimilar, then the owner has to show that the mark has a reputation and that the conduct of the defendant is an attempt to take unfair advantage of or cause detriment to the distinctive character or repute of the mark. Moreover, for each category of protection, it is necessary to show not only that the trade mark has been used in the course of trade, but also that it has been used 'in relation' to goods and services, and that such use affects the interests of the trade mark owner: Case C-206/01 *Arsenal Football Club v Matthew Reed* [2002] ECR I-10273. The requirement of 'trade mark use' therefore acts as a limit on the trade mark owner's monopoly.

9.4.2.2.3 Justification

It is in relation to why we recognize intellectual property that the biggest difference between trade marks on the one hand, and patents, designs, and copyright on the other, is apparent. Patents, designs, and copyright are susceptible to a number of different justifications. The trouble is that whether one believes in John Locke's labour theory, in Benthamite utilitarianism, in rewards and incentives, or the personality of the author, none works for trade marks.

Instead, arguments in support of trade marks lie in economic theories about the importance of consumer choice. As Landes & Posner explain (in 'Trademark Law: An Economic Perspective' (1987) 30 *Journal of Law & Economics* 265), trade marks are best justified by the hypothesis that the law is trying to promote economic efficiency. Trade marks reduce consumer search costs (imagine, they say, having to ask for a jar of instant coffee without having a brand name available). Further, the protection accorded to trade marks encourages manufacturers to maintain quality, so that satisfied customers will return time and time again to buy their favourite product. Trade marks therefore promote competition.

However, although trade marks have the beneficial effect of helping consumers choose what to buy, there is a negative aspect to this. Trade marks create barriers to entry. Imagine a company wishes to launch a new brand of instant coffee. The advertising expenditure in bringing this product to the attention of customers already loyal to Kenco or Nescafé would run into millions (in 1991 the then United Kingdom Monopolies and Mergers Commission estimated that it would cost £5 million to launch a new brand of coffee). Powerful brands therefore can be a disincentive to competitors.

9.4.2.2.4 Duration

Ironically, despite the ease of creation, and different theoretical basis, trade marks, unlike patents, designs, and copyright, do not have a finite duration. Provided the owner pays the renewal fees promptly every ten years, and provided there is no risk of a third party bringing a revocation action under TMA s. 46, a trade mark could potentially last forever. Trade Mark No. 1 (the first ever to be registered under the 1875 Act) is the Bass Red Triangle mark for beer. It is still in force today.

9.5 Trade mark functions

In 1927, Frank Schechter, in his article 'The Rational Basis of Trade Mark Protection' (1927) 40 *Harv LR* 813, argued forcefully that the true function of a trade mark was 'to create and retain custom'. He further suggested that to require a claimant to show likelihood of confusion amongst consumers was too narrow a form of protection, and that the rationale of trade mark law demanded that they be protected against dilution, what he referred to as the gradual 'whittling away' of the mark's distinctive character.

In this section, we consider the commercial functions performed by trade marks, with the objective of deciding whether there has been legal recognition of those functions and whether Schechter's hypothesis has actually been achieved. Five possible functions can be identified: trade marks function as indications of origin, product differentiators, guarantors of consistent quality, advertising, or investment tools.

 Pause for reflection

Do the differences between trade marks and other categories of intellectual property rights mean that we should be less ready to brand them as 'unfair monopolies'?

The Court of Justice of the European Union ('CJEU') developed the so-called 'functions argument' in Case C-487/07 *L'Oréal v Bellure* [2009] I-05185, whereby in cases involving the use of an identical sign in relation to identical products or services, the functions of a mark 'include not only the essential function of the trade mark, which is to guarantee to consumers the origin of the goods or services, but also its other functions, in particular that of guaranteeing the quality of the goods or services in question and those of communication, investment or advertising' (at [58]). It is worth noting that *L'Oréal* involved the use of the names of famous perfumes for cheaper, smell-alike products. Deviating from the Court's position in *Adam Opel/Autec* (Case C-48/05 [2007] ECR I-01017) this newly elaborated doctrine has been received enthusiastically by some commentators and with skepticism from others. In *Adam Opel/Autec*, the Court had found that the essential function of a trade mark is not affected by referential use (namely, the use of the Opel trade mark as a sign for toy models) and that protection could be in principle sought under Art. 5(2) of the Trade Marks Directive which offers extended protection to marks with a reputation. In *L'Oréal*, however, the Court took a different stance by introducing a broader scope of protection to trade mark owners in cases where referential use of their trade marks is made, without including false or inaccurate statements on the attributes of the original mark. To be precise, indications in comparison lists mentioning particular famous brands by reference to smell-alike perfumes were found to affect the functions of trade marks, even though there was no confusion or false statement with regards to the origin of the expensive products. The functions discussion has not only raised scholarly debate, but it also manifests discrepancies at institutional EU level.

Most importantly, however, it raises a question of principles: What is the appropriate approach towards function analysis in double identity cases from the perspective of the principles of EU trade mark law? In particular, how should such an analysis be construed in a way that reflects broader legal principles developed in the area of EU trade mark law?

 Pause for reflection

What would your advice to George be with regards to the marketing of his perfume in light of *L'Oréal*?

9.5.1 **Origin function**

From the early 19th century, UK judges have assumed that the only function which a trade mark fulfils is to indicate to the consumer the commercial origin of the goods. But does it matter if the consumer does not know the precise identity of the business which launched the goods in the first place? According to Lindley LJ in *Powell v Birmingham Vinegar Brewery Co. Ltd* (1896) 13 RPC 235 at p. 250, a customer can be misled and can mistake one trader's goods for another even though they do not know the identity of either. The trader whose mark is imitated is 'just as much injured in his trade as if his name was known as well as his mark'. Similarly, Warrington LJ in *McDowell's Application* (1926) 43 RPC 313 at p. 337 declared that if it was shown that consumers had been misled by the defendant's mark, it did not matter whether they did or did not know the precise source of the goods.

The Trade Marks Act 1938, in s. 68, defined a trade mark as 'a mark used or proposed to be used in relation to goods for the purpose of indicating . . . a connection in the course of trade between the goods and . . . [the] proprietor'. The definition permeated all aspects of that Act, and was shown in due course to have two particularly restrictive effects.

First, it meant that celebrities (or rather, the successors of deceased celebrities) could not register the name of that person, because the name did not indicate the origin of the goods. In *Elvis Presley Trade Marks* [1999] RPC 567, the Court of Appeal upheld an opposition to the application to register the names 'Elvis' and 'Elvis Presley' on the grounds that a consumer, on seeing a bar of 'Elvis' soap, would not think that it was a particular brand of soap, coming from a particular manufacturer, but that it commemorated the singer. The court did not seem concerned that to deny registrability would allow others to make free use of the Elvis name, nor did it take into account the public perception of merchandising. It did, however, decide that the late singer's signature could be registered as a trade mark. Unfortunately, the *Elvis Presley* case, decided under the 1938 Act, appears to have been carried over into the present legislation. In both *Diana, Princess of Wales Trade Mark* [2001] ETMR 254 and *Jane Austen Trade Mark* [2000] RPC 879, the names of the two deceased individuals were held not capable of registration because they did not indicate origin, and were accordingly devoid of distinctive character under TMA s. 3(1)(b). The matter has not yet been referred to the CJEU, and there must be some doubt as to whether the *Elvis Presley* decision's attitude to celebrities' names accords with the Directive's policy on registrability.

Second, the origin function, strictly applied, had significant implications for the protection accorded to the trade mark owner against infringers. In *Arsenal Football Club v Matthew Reed* [2001] RPC 922, Laddie J held that the defendant, who had sold unauthorized football merchandise from his stall, had not committed trade mark infringement. Fans, on seeing the famous Gunners' logo would not think that the scarves and T-shirts originated with the Club. Instead, they were simply badges of allegiance. Laddie J did, however, refer the case to the CJEU, who approached the matter in an entirely different manner. In Case C-206/01 *Arsenal Football Club v Matthew Reed* [2002] ECR I-10273, the Court declared that 'the essential function of a trade mark was to guarantee the identity of origin of the marked goods or services to the consumer or end user by enabling him, without any possibility of confusion, to distinguish the goods or services from others which have another origin'. It added that the trade mark must offer a guarantee that all the goods or services bearing it have been manufactured or supplied under the control of a single undertaking responsible for their quality. Clearly, here, the defendant's clothing had not been approved by the Club, and so the guarantee offered by the trade mark was false. There had therefore been infringement. The CJEU made clear that the trade mark owner had to be protected against those who wished to take unfair advantage of the trade mark. Hence, the trade mark owner's rights, set out in the Directive and the TMA, were there to enable the owner to protect his specific interests. On the return from Luxembourg, Laddie J ([2003] 1 CMLR 382) refused to apply the CJEU's ruling, however, the Court of Appeal ([2003] RPC 696) accepted it.

To put the matter another way, under *Arsenal*, the protection accorded to the mark reflects its functions, which in turn reflect the interests of the owner. The issue of trade mark infringement is approached from the viewpoint of the owner of the mark, not the consumer of the goods. Consequently, 'origin function' has a wider meaning under the TMA than it did under the 1938 Act, being concerned with the interests of the consumer in the quality of the goods and the interests of the proprietor in protecting the investment in the trade mark against free-riding. However, the CJEU appears to have retreated somewhat from its pro-trade mark owner views in *Arsenal*.

 Pause for reflection

With regards to George's wine, can the names 'Kefalovriso wine' or 'Mavrodaphne of Kefalovriso' be regarded as indicating the company from which the wine originates or just the geographical origin of the grapes/wine? What would your advice to George be? What about the use of the word mark 'Giannopoulos Estate'?

9.5.2 Product differentiation function

TMA s. 1(1), based on Art. 2 of the Directive, expresses the function of trade marks in a different way. It states that a trade mark means 'any sign . . . which is capable of distinguishing the goods or services of one undertaking from those of other undertakings'. It might be thought that this is simply a modern reformulation of the origin function, but the CJEU appears to be saying otherwise. In Case C-299/99 *Philips Electronics BV v Remington Consumer Products* [2002] ECR I-5475, at [47–50] it asked whether the mark enabled the consumer to choose one product from another, confident that the goods had originated from one particular business which was responsible for their quality. In other words, this function reflects the economic role of trade marks (advocated by Landes and Posner) in promoting consumer choice and lowering consumer search costs.

That the product differentiation function is not the same as the origin function is supported by the way in which the CJEU has developed the notion of the average consumer as the arbiter of a range of matters under the Directive. Just as the notional skilled addressee is used to impart objectivity in the law of patents, so the average consumer is deployed to decide a number of issues in trade mark law. These include whether a sign has the potential to be a trade mark under Art. 2, whether it falls foul of any of the Absolute Grounds for Refusal in Art. 3, and whether it conflicts with another mark, in the context either of the Relative Grounds for Refusal or in the context of infringement proceedings. The consumer is also used to decide issues of revocation, in particular whether the trade mark has been allowed to become deceptive or generic. The notional consumer therefore holds a pivotal role.

9.5.3 Guarantee function

When we speak of a trade mark acting as a guarantee, the word 'guarantee' is not used necessarily in the contractual sense. Instead, we mean that the mark tells the consumer that the goods they are about to buy have the same quality as previously purchased items. 'Guarantee' therefore indicates consistency.

Spalding v Gamage (1915) 32 RPC 273

The House of Lords in *Spalding v Gamage* (1915) 32 RPC 273, a passing off case, recognized the guarantee function of trade marks. Here the defendant had purchased a consignment of the claimant's footballs but advertised them as being of first-class quality when in fact they were seconds. It was held that this misrepresentation harmed the goodwill of the claimant's business. Consumers, used to buying high-quality products, would be put off from purchasing any more because of their bad experience.

Another example of the guarantee function being recognized in a passing off case is *United Biscuits (UK) Ltd v Asda Stores Ltd* [1997] RPC 513. Robert Walker J held that by deliberately copying the appearance of the wrappers in which the claimant's PENGUIN biscuits were sold, the defendant supermarket made its customers believe that its own PUFFIN biscuits had been made by the claimant and would therefore be of similar quality.

The CJEU has recognized the importance of a trade mark guaranteeing the consistency of a product in several cases dealing with the parallel importation of goods.

> ### Case C-10/89 *SA CNL-Sucal NV v Hag GF AG* [1990] ECR I-3711
>
> Consumer expectations played a major part in its decision in Case C-10/89 *SA CNL-Sucal NV v Hag GF AG* [1990] ECR I-3711 (*'Hag II'*). As a result of government intervention after World War II, there were two versions of Café Hag decaffeinated coffee available to European consumers, one made by the original trade mark owner in Germany, the other by a company which had acquired the trade mark registration in Belgium. The CJEU thought it relevant that purchasers would be confused by the different quality and taste of the rival products. As a result, the original German owner of the mark could sue its Belgian rival owner for infringement. The fact that historically the two trade mark registrations in Belgium and Germany had been owned by the same enterprise was irrelevant.

Case C-143/00 *Boehringer Ingelheim v Swingward Ltd and Dowelhurst* [2002] ECR I-3759 shows how consumer preferences can play a part when medicines imported from another EU Member State are then reboxed or relabelled so that their instructions are available in the local language. The CJEU stated that consumers rely on the trade mark as a means of ensuring that (legitimate) goods have not been interfered with by the importer. The trade mark therefore guarantees the *safety* of the goods.

In Case C-59/08 *Copad SA v Christian Dior Couture SA* [2009] ECR I-3421 the Court considered that the sale of luxury goods by a licensee to third parties which were not part of a selective distribution network might affect *the quality of the goods themselves*, thereby entitling the trade mark owner to sue the licensee for trade mark infringement under Art. 8 of the Directive and negating consent to first marketing for the purpose of the doctrine of exhaustion of rights. In Schechter's words, the trade mark helps to retain business.

The ruling of the CJEU in *Arsenal v Reed* also mentions the role of the trade mark in guaranteeing consistency. This guarantee, according to the Court, is an aspect of the product differentiation function found in Art. 2 of the Directive.

A parallel can be drawn here between the modern role of trade marks and how they were used in medieval times. In the era of the Craft Guilds, trade marks told purchasers that goods were of a certain standard. The same is true today. There is therefore a consumer protection aspect to trade marks just as there was previously.

9.5.4 Advertising function

The core of Schechter's hypothesis is that the advertising function of a trade mark must be protected. He declares that 'the mark sells the goods'. Therefore, its selling power must be protected against those who wish to take unfair advantage of its reputation. In the case of successful brands, there will be many who wish to 'free-ride' on the strength of the mark.

Close examination of the CJEU's ruling in *Arsenal v Reed* indicates that the Court agrees. The CJEU stated that 'for that guarantee of origin, which constitutes the essential function of a trade mark, to be ensured, the proprietor must be protected against competitors wishing to take unfair advantage of the status and reputation of the trade mark by selling products illegally bearing it'. Although the statement is integrated into the Court's declaration that trade marks guarantee the consistency and origin of the goods, its use of the phrase 'unfair advantage' is significant.

Further, Schechter's hypothesis is part of UK law in another respect. The TMA, implementing two optional provisions in the Directive, contains in ss. 5(3) and 10(3) a specific form of protection for trade marks which have a reputation. They confer on a trade mark's owner the ability either to oppose the registration of or to prevent the use in trade of an identical or similar mark which seeks to take unfair advantage of or cause detriment to the distinctive character or repute of the earlier mark. Arguably (though some would disagree) the two subsections introduce the doctrine of dilution into UK law. Dilution (as a form of harm to a trade mark with a reputation) has long been recognized in US and Benelux trade mark law. The doctrine states that a mark with a reputation can be harmed in a number of ways. First, the mark can be 'watered down' by use on non-competing goods. Over a period of time it will lose its distinctive quality. To paraphrase Schechter, if the use of Rolls-Royce on lipsticks, hamburgers, or steam shovels is not prevented, then the Rolls-Royce trade mark for cars will be undermined. Another form of harm is that a mark with a reputation can be tarnished if it is used on non-competing goods which have an unsavoury or unwholesome connotation.

CLAERYN/KLAREIN (1976) 7 IIC 420

The best known example of tarnishing as a form of dilution is the leading Benelux Court of Justice decision of *Claeryn/Klarein* (1976) 7 IIC 420. Here, the owner of the Claeryn trade mark for Dutch gin was able to prevent Colgate using Klarein for a toilet cleaning liquid. Both marks were pronounced in an identical manner in Dutch. The court thought that consumers would not wish to be reminded of bleach when drinking a glass of high-quality gin.

Last, a competitor may 'free-ride' on a mark with a reputation by using an identical or similar mark as a means of gaining quick access to the market.

At first, UK courts failed to understand the elements of TMA ss. 5(3) and 10(3). In *Baywatch Production Co Inc v The Home Video Channel* [1997] FSR 2, it was held that proof of likelihood of confusion was required and that viewers of the *Baywatch* television series would not be misled by a soft-porn programme, *Babewatch*, shown on cable television. The meaning of the two subsections was explained by the CJEU in Case C-251/95 *Sabel BV v Puma AG* [1997] ECR I-6191. It stated that likelihood of confusion is not required, as the provisions pursue a different objective, namely that of protecting marks with a reputation.

Case C-487/07 *L'Oréal SA v Bellure NV* [2009] ECR I-5185

The Court confirmed its ruling in *Sabel v Puma* in the later decision of Case C-487/07 *L'Oréal SA v Bellure NV* [2009] ECR I-5185. It clarified that the owner of such a mark is protected (provided all the other elements of the provision are satisfied) against the three types of harm mentioned earlier, namely the 'whittling away' or 'blurring' of the mark's distinctive character, 'tarnishment' or 'degradation' where the mark is used by the third party in a way which reduces its power of attraction, and 'parasitism' or 'free-riding' where the third party seeks to exploit, without paying any financial compensation, the marketing effort expended by the proprietor in order to create and maintain the mark's image.

 Pause for reflection

What would your advice to George be with regards to the marketing of his perfume vis-à-vis the advertising function of trade marks?

Sections 5(3) and 10(3) of the TMA (and the parent provisions in the Directive) leave the origin function far behind. It does not matter that the consumer is not confused. Instead, any case under these provisions will consider the investment made by the owner in the mark. The trade mark is treated as a valuable asset in its own right. It is to be protected against those who wish to misappropriate its selling power. Schechter calls this 'the commercial magnetism' of the mark. Such language also appears in the Opinion of AG Colomer in *Arsenal v Reed*. He states that the trade mark acquires a life of its own, making a statement about quality, reputation and even, in certain cases, a way of seeing life. Further, the messages it sends out are autonomous. A distinctive sign can indicate at the same time trade origin, the reputation of its proprietor, and the quality of the goods it represents. As Loughlan remarks (in 'Trade Marks: Arguments in a Continuing Contest' [2005] *IPQ* 294), trade marks carry values, associations and relations from one sphere to another. Trade marks link the economy and culture by investing consumer products with social and symbolic values. The irony is, of course, that in some instances, trade marks no longer make a statement about the origin of the goods but about the aspirations of the purchaser. However, if the commercial magnetism of the trade mark is protected, there are implications not only for free competition but for freedom of speech. There is a danger that cultural icons, which should be free for all to use, become private property.

9.5.5 Investment function

The CJEU intimated that a trade mark may have yet further functions which can be protected by the infringement action in its ruling in *L'Oréal SA v Bellure NV*. At [58] it stated that besides the 'essential' origin function, there were others including guaranteeing the quality of the goods or services and those of communication, investment, or advertising.

Whilst the Court did not elaborate further in its ruling in *L'Oréal SA v Bellure NV* on the communication and investment functions, it did discuss the investment function in Case C-323/09 *Interflora Inc v Marks & Spencer plc* [2011] ECR I-8625 at [60–62], where the claimant ultimately succeeded in preventing the defendant retailer from using the claimant's name as an internet adword on Google for its own flower delivery service (see *Interflora Inc v Marks & Spencer plc* [2013] EWHC 1291). Noting that trade marks are often 'instruments of commercial strategy . . . used to develop consumer loyalty', the CJEU explained that even though this 'investment function' overlapped with the advertising function, it was none the less distinct. When the use by a competitor of an identical sign for identical goods substantially interfered with the proprietor's use of its trade mark to acquire or preserve a reputation capable of attracting consumers and retaining their loyalty, the third party's use must be regarded as adversely affecting the trade mark's investment function.

Pause for reflection

Which of the commercial functions performed by trade marks is the most appropriate in the current age of the consumer? Are there any dangers in protecting the 'commercial magnetism' of trade marks?

9.6 The impact of EU law

9.6.1 The need for harmonization

One of the fundamental principles of the Treaty on the Functioning of the European Union ('TFEU') (formerly the Treaty of Rome) is the establishment of the internal market, in which all the Member States are treated as a single territory for the purposes of the free movement of goods, services, persons, and capital. Fairly early in the development of the common market (as it was originally called) it was realized that the territorial nature of intellectual property rights was an obstacle to achieving the goals of the EU. Not only do such rights enable their owners to prevent the importation of goods from one Member State to another, but different Member States have different standards of protection. What is regarded as a trade mark in one state might be incapable of registration in another.

From the early 1980s, the EU Commission adopted a 'twin-track' policy towards accommodating intellectual property rights into the internal market. Although Art. 345 TFEU (formerly Art. 295 EC) declares that national rules on property ownership are not to be affected by the Treaty (so that the grant of intellectual property rights is a matter left to Member States) the objective of achieving a 'level playing field' enabled the Commission to legislate for the standardization of national rights and for the creation of pan-European unitary rights. The legal vehicles for these two solutions were, respectively, a Directive and a Regulation.

9.6.2 The Trade Marks Directive

The Directive is declared to be a partial harmonization measure only. It seeks to standardize the 'core' of trade mark law, by setting out what can be a trade mark, what objections can be made to it when an application to register it is made, how the mark is to be compared with prior rights, and the protection conferred on its owner to stop third parties infringing it. The Directive also deals with revocation of trade marks, with the requirement to use a mark, and with the ability of the owner to license the mark.

In many ways, the most important part of the Directive is its Recitals. These set out the reasons behind the Directive and are often utilized by the CJEU in dealing with questions referred to it by national courts under Art. 267 TFEU (formerly Art. 234 EC). Of particular significance, using the numbering in the consolidated (2008) version of the Directive, are Recital 10, which declares that trade marks are to receive the same level of protection in all Member States, although states are free to confer greater protection if they so wish; and Recital 11, which includes a statement as to the function of trade marks and the criteria to be taken into account when deciding whether there is a likelihood of confusion.

To those used to UK legislation, with its proliferation of detail, the language of the Directive may seem stark. It is, of course, a product of the civil law tradition, where legislation is couched in broad statements of principle, with the detail being supplied in court rulings. For this reason, the case law of the CJEU on its interpretation is extremely important for all substantive aspects of trade mark law. Not only does the Directive itself introduce new statutory principles into UK trade mark law, but case law has extended those principles even further. The revolution in trade mark law expected when the TMA was passed has come not from within the UK legal system, but from outside.

 Pause for reflection

Have UK courts recognized fully the impact of EU legislation on UK trade mark law? What impact will the exit of the United Kingdom from the European Union have on UK Trade Mark law?

9.6.3 The EU Trade Mark Regulation

Trade mark applicants now have a choice when it comes to obtaining protection. They can either obtain national protection in the United Kingdom (and indeed in other individual Member States) by the filing of separate national applications or they can obtain an EU trade mark registration from EUIPO. The EU trade mark is a unitary right, that is, it is effective throughout the whole of the European Union. The unitary concept creates an 'all or nothing' system. If the trade mark is invalid (for example because it is descriptive or deceptive in one Member State or conflicts with a prior right in one Member State) it is invalid for the whole European Union (though there are provisions allowing it to be converted into national registrations).

The substantive provisions of the Regulation (dealing with what can be a trade mark, what objections can be made to it in application proceedings, how it is to be compared with prior rights, and the scope of protection accorded to the owner) are substantially identical to the equivalent Articles in the Directive. Decisions from EUIPO (which also deals with EU designs) can be appealed to the General Court and thence (on a point of law only) to the CJEU. Therefore, in the context of trade mark law, the CJEU has parallel jurisdiction, namely to act as the ultimate appellate body to decisions of EUIPO, and to provide preliminary rulings on the interpretation of the Directive to national courts. The resultant case law, dealing as it does with two substantially identical EU measures, is therefore entirely interchangeable.

 Pause for reflection

What is the likely impact of the exit of the United Kingdom from the European Union on the ability of UK based individuals and legal entities to benefit from EU trade mark registrations?

9.6.4 Interpretation of the TMA

When asked to interpret a Directive, the CJEU, in keeping with the civil law tradition, will adopt the teleological style of interpretation, that is, it will consider the legislation in the light of its objectives, making use of working papers and discussions which preceded its enactment. Because of the influence of the Directive on the content of the TMA (in essence it lowers the test for registrability and broadens the scope of protection conferred on the owner), the meaning of the TMA can no longer be determined by the Chancery Division, the Court of Appeal, or the Supreme Court. The CJEU is the only body which can give a conclusive ruling on its meaning. At national level, the Directive must be used as an aid to interpreting the TMA. Words and phrases which have their counterparts in earlier law must bear the meaning allocated to them by the CJEU, rather than that which developed in UK case law during the previous 100 years.

9.6.5 Recent developments

On 23 March 2016, Regulation (EU) 2015/2424 of the European Parliament and the Council amending the Community trade mark regulation (the Amending Regulation) entered into force. The Amending Regulation, which applies as and from 1 October 2017, brought about changes to the name of the Office to the European Union Intellectual Property Office, which is now called European Intellectual Property Office ('EUIPO') instead of Office for Harmonisation of the Internal Market ('OHIM'); the name of the trade mark administered by the Office from Community Trade Mark ('CTM') to European Union Trade Mark; and the fee system for trade marks. Some changes also applied to examination proceedings, absolute grounds, opposition and cancellation, relative grounds, and appeals. We will be referring to these changes where appropriate in the following chapters.

9.7 Conclusion

This chapter has explained the use of trade marks over the centuries; the origins of United Kingdom trade mark law; the commercial functions which trade marks fulfil and how such functions are regarded by the courts; and the way in which EU reforms have impacted on domestic trade mark law.

George should be advised that the answer to disputed questions of trade mark law is normally provided by considering the purpose of a trade mark which, broadly speaking, is to function as a guarantee of origin to those who purchase or use the product. This guarantee is meant to ensure that the consumer or ultimate user of the products or services will be able without any possibility of confusion to distinguish that product or service from products which have another origin (*La Roche & Co AG v Centrafarm; Arsenal Football Club v Reed; Zino Davidoff SA v A&G Imports Ltd*). By reference to the word marks that George is currently using by reference to his wine, namely 'Kefalovriso wine' and 'Mavrodaphne of Kefalovriso', he should be made aware that passing off protection may be available (see chapter 8). In terms of the suitability of these names as trade marks, however, George should be advised that these names may not be able to function as trade marks, the reason being that they are descriptive of essential qualities of the goods themselves, either by denoting the geographical origin of the products or by referring to geographical origin and the specific type of wine. On that basis it is not likely that they can perform the origin or product differentiation function that trade marks ought to serve. (*Philips Electronics BV v Remington Consumer Products*). The word mark 'Giannopoulos Estate' is more likely to operate as a badge of origin for the products at issue.

With regards to the perfume, George should be advised that in the aftermath of *L'Oréal v Bellure* using the smell-alike connotation in conjunction with the word 'Muse' is not a good idea. In cases involving the use of an identical sign in relation to identical products or services, as is the case here, the functions of a mark do not only include the essential function of the trade mark, i.e. to act as badges of origin, but also its other functions, namely to guarantee the quality of the goods or services and also other aspects, such as the communication, investment, or advertising. *L'Oréal* has the effect that, even though a trader does not mislead the public with false or inaccurate statements on the attributes of products or services, the functions of trade marks are affected (and thereinafter infringement can take place). The wiser policy would be for George to enter the market with the 'Sophia' word mark as a product differentiator and guarantor of origin of the perfume he produces.

End-of-chapter questions

After reading the chapter carefully, try answering the following questions. For answer guidance visit the online resources at **www.oup.com/uk/karapapa-mcdonagh/**

1. If we abandon the origin function as the proper rationale for trade mark protection, then the modern trade mark will become a powerful means to suppress fair competition. Discuss.

2. Can a trade mark function as a guarantee of consistent quality? Discuss.

Further reading

For understanding the protection available to trade marks, the following readings are recommended:

Davis, J. 'Locating the Average Consumer: His Judicial Origins, Intellectual Influences and Current Role in European Trade Mark Law' [2005] 2 *IPQ* 183

Examines the way in which the CJEU has developed the average consumer as the arbiter of key issues under the Directive and Regulation.

Gangjee, D.S. 'Property in Brands' LSE Law, Society and Economy Working Papers 8/2013 (available from www.lse.ac.uk/collections/law/wps/wps.htm)

Traces the emergence of a new res within European trade mark law due to the CJEU's recognition of functions other than the origin function.

Klein, N. *No Logo* (Harper Collins, 2000)

A critique of the power of brands.

Kur, A. 'Trade marks function, don't they? CJEU jurisprudence and unfair competition practices,' (2014) 45(4) *IIC*, 434

Considers the functions of trade marks in the light of the CJEU case law.

Landes, W. and Posner, R. 'Trademark Law: An Economic Perspective' (1987) 30 *Journal of Law & Economics* 265

Explores the economic justification for trade mark protection.

McDonagh, L. 'From Brand Performance to Consumer Performativity: Assessing European Trade Mark Law after the Rise of Anthropological Marketing' (2015) 42(4) *Journal of Law and Society* 611

An alternative view to the position that brand image is protected even where there is no harm to the underlying mark.

Schechter, F.I. 'The Rational Basis of Trade Mark Protection' (1927) 40 *Harv LR* 813

Argues for the protection of the selling power of brands through the doctrine of dilution.

Schechter, F.I. *Historical Foundations of Trade Mark Law* (New York: Columbia University Press, 1925)

A comprehensive account of the use of trade marks throughout Europe up to the 19th century.

Tarawneh, J. 'A new classification for trade mark functions' [2016] 4 *IPQ* 352

Argues for a new classification for trade mark functions as indicators, incentives, and stimulators.

Registration of a 'sign' 10

Problem question

Read this problem question carefully and keep it in mind while you are working through the chapter that follows. At the end of this chapter, you will be able to apply what you have learnt to the problem question and advise the relevant parties.

Becky Jones has recently taken over a family business that sells party poppers, hats, and balloons. The products have been sold for the past 25 years under the name 'Caramel Bubble'. Her company has a registered UK trade mark over the word sign 'Caramel Bubble' for goods in Class 28 of the Nice Classification ('novelty toys for playing jokes and for parties, for example, carnival masks, paper party hats, confetti, party poppers and Christmas crackers'). Becky believes that if she adopts a more efficient marketing strategy her sales will increase. She commissions Faye Dean, an independent marketing expert, to look into market trends and offer marketing advice. Faye is a strong proponent of unusual marketing techniques and suggests that Becky uses the smell of caramel on the packaging of the balloons in order to create a memorable impression to consumers. There is nobody else in the market of party supplies that does this and a caramel smelling packaging is likely to give Becky a competitive edge. Faye also suggests using a distinctive colour combination on the packaging of the goods using blue, white, and red, which are thought to be very appealing colours to those purchasing party supplies according to her marketing study. Faye also thinks that a consistent music theme would work well in the advertisements of the company. She suggests using a seven-note extract from Vivaldi's *Summer* followed by the sound of a popping balloon.

Before going ahead with the implementation of this marketing strategy, Becky comes to you for legal advice. She wishes to retain some form of exclusivity over the new marketing tools of representing her work and requests information on whether the three-colour combination, the smell of caramel attached to her party supply products, and the music theme that Faye suggested can in principle attract protection as UK trade marks. She also wants to know what are the procedural steps for registering UK trade marks and around how much time it will take for the marks to receive protection.

10.1 Introduction

Unlike passing off protection that is not subject to formalities, trade marks ought to be registered in order to receive legal protection. Whether a trade mark can be registered appears at first glance to be deceptively simple. There are certain conditions that need to be met. In particular, the sign in question must satisfy the definition of 'trade mark', and it must not be prohibited by any of the absolute or relative grounds of refusal (examined in chapters 11 and 12 respectively), all of these issues being judged through the eyes of the average consumer. Nevertheless, there is a huge body of case law to be digested. Furthermore, such case law reveals that there are tensions between the pre-1994 attitude of UK courts towards trade marks and the more liberal views of EU tribunals.

The United Kingdom transposed the provisions of Directive 2015/2436 into national law through the Trade Marks Regulations 2018. The Regulations came into force on 14 January 2019. With effect from 15 January 2019, Directive 2008/95/EC has been repealed. However, references to the Directive will be made in cases where the CJEU has offered interpretative guidance on trade mark law that still remain valid and relevant. The Regulation (EU) 2017/1001 of the European Parliament and of the Council of 14 June 2017 on the European Union trade mark ('EUTMR'), entered into force on 1 October 2017. It contains a number of provisions that had to be developed by secondary legislation, consisting of the Implementing Regulation (EU) 2017/1431 ('EUTMIR') outlining the rules for implementing certain provisions of Council Regulation (EC) No 207/2009 on the European Union trade mark and the Delegated Regulation (EU) 2017/1430 ('EUTMDR') supplementing Council Regulation (EC) No. 207/2009 on the European Union trade mark and repealing Commission Regulations (EC) No 2868/95 and (EC) No 216/96.

10.2 Overview of the issues

Whether a trade mark is capable of registration depends on three requirements. First, whether the subject matter of the application satisfies the definition of 'trade mark' in s. 1 of the Trade Marks Act 1994 ('TMA'), second whether there are any objections to the application under the absolute grounds for refusal in s. 3 (see chapter 11), and last, whether there are any prior rights which could prevent registration under the relative grounds for refusal in s. 5 (chapter 12). These three aspects of registrability will be considered in sequence.

This chapter takes a particular focus on the registration of trade marks in the United Kingdom and outlines the meaning of a 'sign' as the protectable subject matter.

10.2.1 The incoming tide of European law

The registrability of trade marks is a subject where the First Trade Marks Directive (Council Directive 89/104/EEC of 21 December 1988 on the approximation of the laws of Member States relating to trade marks [1989] OJ L 40/1, now codified as Directive (EU) 2015/2436 of the European Parliament and of the Council of 16 December 2015 to approximate the laws of the Member States relating to trade marks [2015] OJ L 336 ('the new Directive')) ('the Directive') and the consequent interpretation of the Directive by the European Court of Justice (Court of Justice of the European Union and General Court) has had a radical impact on UK domestic trade mark law. The torrent of references by national courts under Art. 267 of the Treaty on the Functioning of the European Union ('TFEU') (reviewed by Peter Turner-Kerr in 'EU Intellectual Property Law: Recent Case Developments' [2004] *IPQ* 448) has produced definitive guidance on the meaning of almost every aspect of the definition of a trade mark and its suitability for registration. It is not clear what the relevance of Art. 267 will be in light of the exit of the United Kingdom from the European Union. In case the United Kingdom remains in the European Economic Area, even though courts will lose their ability to query the interpretation of EU law, they will still have to apply EU legislation.

Another, complementary, body of case law (where the Court of Justice ('ECJ') acts as the appellate body for decisions of the General Court in reviewing decisions of the Boards of Appeal of OHIM (Office for Harmonization in the Internal Market; now the EU Intellectual Property Office ('EUIPO')) has also emerged under the European Union Trademark Regulation (now Regulation (EU) 2017/1001 of the European Parliament and of the Council of 14 June 2017 on the European Union Trade Mark ('EUTMR')). Because the wording of the substantive Articles in the Directive and Regulation is virtually identical, the two bodies of case law are interchangeable.

Examination of United Kingdom cases shows that the judiciary has taken time to appreciate the impact of the 'Europeanization' of trade mark law. At times, they have appeared reluctant to abandon the legacy of the Trade Marks Act 1938. Many decisions in the early days of the TMA made use of reasoning derived from pre-1994 cases (as examples, see the discussion of the phrase 'capable of distinguishing' by the Court of Appeal in *Philips Electronics NV v Remington Consumer Products* [1999] RPC 809 and in *Bach Flower Remedies Ltd v Healing Herbs* [2000] RPC 513, and the assessment of 'likelihood of confusion' in *British Sugar plc v James Robertson & Sons Ltd* [1996] RPC 281). Adaptation to the brave new world of the Directive has undoubtedly been helped by the way in which the United Kingdom Trade Marks Registry ('the Registry') has frequently revised the *Trade Marks Registry Works Manual* (available online from the UK Intellectual Property Office ('UKIPO') website at www.ipo.gov.uk) in the light of CJEU rulings, although it is likely that in light of the exit of the UK from the EU those decisions may retain a continuous relevance. Lord Denning in *Bulmer v Bollinger* [1974] Ch 401 had observed that 'when we come to matters with a European element, the treaty is like an incoming tide. It flows into the estuaries and up the rivers. It cannot be held back. Parliament has decreed that the treaty is henceforward to be part of our law. It is equal in force to any statute.' His lordship's remarks about the incoming tide have never seemed so apposite.

10.2.2 Theoretical issues

We have previously examined the functions performed by trade marks. We noted how the origin function dominated United Kingdom trade mark law under the 1938 Act, and proved to be a straightjacket when deciding issues of registrability and infringement. The product differentiation function (enabling the consumer to choose between competing brands), the guarantee function, and the advertising and investment function have all been recognized in case law. As a result of the decision of the CJEU in Case C-206/01 *Arsenal Football Club v Matthew Reed* [2002] ECR I-10273 and also C-487/07 *L'Oreal & Ors v Bellure & Ors*, ECLI:EU:C:2009:378, trade mark function has the potential to go far beyond that of simply indicating origin. This theoretical debate underpins much of the case law on registrability (see indicatively A. Kur, 'Trade marks function, don't they? CJEU jurisprudence and unfair competition practices,' [2014] 45(4) *IIC* 434).

10.2.3 The importance of the average consumer

Trade mark law depends heavily on the perception of the average consumer, in the same way that patent law relies on the person skilled in the art in order to assess key issues (see chapters 15–18). The average consumer lays down the foundation for discussions that will follow in later chapters. Indeed, consumer perception is central for both formally recognizing when a sign qualifies as a trade mark and in the context of infringement provisions, that we will be looking into later (chapter 13) (see on the concept of the average consumer G. B. Dinwoodie and D. S. Gangjee, 'The Image of the Consumer in European Trade Mark Law' in D. Leczykiewicz and S. Weatherill (eds), *The Image(s) of the Consumer in EU Law* (Hart Publishing, 2015). Article 2 of the Directive (also Art. 3 of Directive 2015/2436) states that a trade mark must be capable of distinguishing the goods or services of one undertaking from those of another. In plain English, trade marks help consumers to choose and therefore act as messengers between the manufacturer of a product and the end user. The average consumer (a hypothetical being) is the arbiter of registrability.

10.2.3.1 The characteristics of the average consumer

The CJEU first gave guidance as to the characteristics of the average consumer in Case C-342/97 *Lloyd Schuhfabrik Meyer & Co KG v Klijsen Handel BV* [1999] ECR I-3819 at [26]. It said that the average consumer is deemed to be reasonably well informed and reasonably observant and circumspect. However, their level of attention will vary depending on what sort of product is being purchased. Thus, someone spending £300 on a food mixer will pay greater attention and be less likely to be confused between competing brands than (say) someone pushing a trolley round a supermarket (*Whirlpool Corporation v Kenwood Ltd* [2010] RPC 51). Equally, someone buying a car (Case C-361/04 P *Ruiz-Picasso v OHIM* [2006] ECR I-643) or a mobile phone (Case C-16/06P *Les Editions Albert Réné Sarl v OHIM* [2008] ECR 10053) pays greater attention to detail.

The concept of the average consumer was further elaborated in *The London Taxi Corporation Limited trading as the London Taxi Company v (1) Frazer-Nash Research Limited and (2) Ecotive Limited* [2016] EWHC 52 (Ch), where the average consumers of taxis, notably the iconic London cabs, were not considered to be the users of the taxi services but the taxi drivers themselves. Arnold J explained that taxis are expensive and specialized vehicles, and the average consumers for the purposes of assessing validity and infringement would be the knowledgeable and careful purchasers, namely the taxi drivers. As users of the service instead of users of the good as such, members of the public could not qualify as average consumers in that their level of attention was deemed fairly low (at [159]–[163]).

 Pause for reflection

In our scenario question, who is the average consumer of party supply products? Should those attending parties be excluded from the concept of the average consumer, applying by analogy the *London Taxi* case?   →

→
Does the choice of the average consumer as the person to decide issues of registrability of trade marks really guarantee consistency and objectivity?

10.3 An outline of the registration procedure

10.3.1 The procedure at the United Kingdom Trade Marks Registry

By way of background information, we will first outline the registration procedure; further detail is available from the UKIPO website. In essence, the procedure can be broken down into six steps, as illustrated in Diagram 10.1.

DIAGRAM 10.1 United Kingdom Trade Mark Application procedure

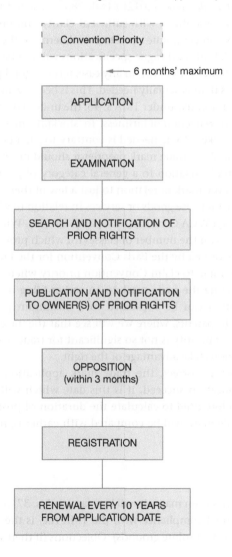

10.3.2 **Filing**

The starting point is for the applicant to complete Form TM3, available from the Registry website. Before doing so, the prudent applicant would undertake a search of the register to identify whether there are any prior rights which might conflict with the intended mark.

Besides the choice of the mark itself, the principal decision will be which list of goods and services the mark is to be registered to, as trade marks are registered in respect of specific items (s. 32(2)(c)). There are 34 classes of goods and 11 classes of services listed in the World Intellectual Property Organisation's (WIPO's) Nice Agreement for the International Classification of Goods and Services 1957 (incorporated into United Kingdom law by means of Sch. 4 of the Trade Marks (Amendment) Rules 2001). The classes group related products together; for example Class 3 contains cleaning substances and Class 5 medical preparations. It is possible to make multi-class applications. However, many of the classes are very wide. The CJEU in Case C-307/10 *Chartered Institute of Patent Attorneys v Registrar of Trade Marks* [2012] ETMR 783 has stated that the list of goods and/or services must be 'identified with sufficient clarity and precision to enable the competent authorities and economic operators to determine the extent of protection conferred by the mark'. Wide and vague specifications will not be allowed (see UKIPO's Practice Amendment Notice PAN 3/13). In any case, it is not good practice to apply for a wider range of products than is actually needed. This is because any person can apply to revoke a trade mark for non-use under TMA s. 46, the underlying policy being that the Register should be a true reflection of business. To 'stockpile' marks or to register marks for goods which are unlikely to be needed is contrary to such policy: *Imperial Group v Philip Morris* [1982] FSR 72. A trade mark proprietor should not be able to monopolize the use of a trade mark in relation to a general category of goods or services merely because they had used the mark in relation to just a few of them and the mark should remain registered only for those goods or services in relation to which it has been used (*Maier v ASOS Plc* [2015] EWCA Civ 220, [2016] 2 All ER 738). What is more, the cost of the application depends on the number of classes for which protection is sought.

As with any right governed by the Paris Convention for the Protection of Industrial Property 1883, it is possible to claim Convention priority when filing a trade mark (s. 36 TMA), thus backdating the trade mark to an earlier filing in another Convention country. The application can be backdated to a maximum period of six months. However, in contrast to patents, where we will see that the 'race to the patent office' door is crucial, claiming priority is not so significant for trade marks and only a small percentage of applications take advantage of the right.

If all the paperwork is correct, the trade mark application is accorded a filing date. Should the application succeed, it is this date which will become the date of registration and therefore used to calculate the duration of protection. It is also the date at which the trade mark will be compared with earlier rights under the relative grounds provision.

10.3.3 **Examination**

Once the application has been made, it will be examined (s. 37). Examination basically covers two things: formal compliance with the TMA (i.e. is the paperwork in order), and compliance with s. 3 (absolute grounds). Objections (if there are any) are normally dealt with by correspondence. The TMA does not expressly give the applicant a right to a hearing, but such right can be inferred from a number of provisions, e.g. s. 37(3). Appeals from the Examiner's decision are normally dealt with by a judicial officer, the Appointed Person, under s. 76, or by the Patents Court.

10.3.4 Search and examination report

One impact of the 2007 changes is that there is no longer any examination of the application under the relative grounds for refusal. Instead, the Registry conducts a search of earlier registered rights and notifies the results to the applicant, but will do no more than this. It is up to the applicant to decide whether to amend the statement of goods so as to avoid conflict, to withdraw the application, or to continue with it. The applicant has two months within which to respond to the examination report. If nothing is heard, the Registry assumes that the applicant wishes to continue.

10.3.5 Publication and notification

If there are no objections, or they are overcome, the mark is accepted. It is then advertised in the *Trade Marks Journal*, a weekly publication now available online (https://www.ipo.gov.uk/t-tmj.htm). When publication occurs, the Registry informs the owners of any UK registered marks identified in the examination report. It also notifies the owners of any relevant community or internationally registered trade marks but only if they have 'opted in' to the notification procedure. The applicant has no right to a hearing about the Registry's intention to notify, nor can such a decision be appealed.

10.3.6 Opposition

Third parties have a fixed period from the date of publication within which to file an opposition to the application. The initial period is two months, but this can be extended on request by one further month. The request for the extension can only be made online. Thereafter, no further extension of time is possible.

The grounds of opposition fall into the same categories as objections by the Registrar, namely that the subject matter of the application does not meet the definition of 'trade mark' or that it is prohibited by the absolute grounds. Any third party can raise such objections and it does not matter whether or not the same matters were considered during examination of the application. However, there is one further objection which can only be raised by the owner of an earlier right, namely that the application should be rejected under the relative grounds for refusal because it conflicts with this earlier right.

As with the Registrar's objections, opposition can be dealt with by paperwork or by means of a hearing, with appeal to the Appointed Person or the court.

An alternative to filing an opposition is for a third party to make written observations to the Registrar under s. 38(3). Although the person making the observations does not become a party to any proceedings, the Registry can re-open the case. Further, the observations will be entered on the file and will thus be available to any third party who subsequently tries to challenge the mark for lack of validity.

Should the opponent lose the opposition, the applicant should not assume that this is the end of the matter, as the owner of the earlier right has five years within which to bring invalidity proceedings under TMA s. 47(2).

10.3.7 Registration

If no opposition is filed, or if any opposition is overcome, the mark is registered for an initial period of ten years. The period of registration is calculated from the filing date. Registration is only prima facie evidence that the mark is valid (s. 72). It can always be challenged for lack of validity by any third party under s. 47(1) (absolute grounds) and by the owner of the earlier right under s. 47(2) (relative grounds) within five years. The effect of s. 72 is to place the burden of proving invalidity on the third party. Should the mark be removed from the Register as a result of invalidity proceedings, the disgruntled owner has no redress, as s. 70 declares that the Registrar does not warrant the validity of the registration of any mark.

The registration process of a UK trade mark can be synopsized in Diagram 10.2 below.

DIAGRAM 10.2 UK trade mark registration process

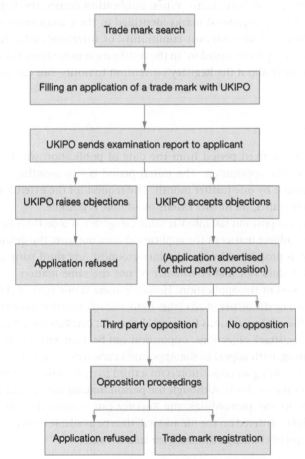

A trade mark registration can be renewed every ten years and is therefore capable of indefinite duration, subject to any challenge for revocation or invalidity.

 Pause for reflection

On the basis of the aforementioned discussion, what would your advice to Becky be regarding the process of registering trade marks in the United Kingdom?

10.3.8 The registration procedure at the EU and international level

Those interested in securing trade mark protection in countries other than the United Kingdom can apply to the trade mark office in each country. However, European and international application systems are also available and these routes of registration have numerous potential benefits, including an easier application process, lower cost, and less paperwork.

10.3.8.1 European trade mark protection

Those interested in securing trade mark protection in countries which are members of the European Union can apply for a European Union Trade Mark ('EUTM') through the European Union Intellectual Property Office ('EUIPO'). Details of the registration process of EU trade marks are available at the EUIPO website, at www.euipo.europa.eu. Applicants must use one of the 23 official languages used in the European Union and indicate a different second language from the five official languages that are in use at the EUIPO.

10.3.8.2 International trade mark protection

To apply for an international trade mark in countries which have signed up to the Madrid Protocol, applicants must already have an existing application or registration of a trade mark in the United Kingdom. The Madrid Protocol is an international instrument governed by WIPO, which lists in its website the various member countries that can be covered by an international application. An applicant filling an application through the UK office can submit an international application only for a sign identical to the UK trade mark application or registration. This can take place either at the same time the UK application is filed or later. The application is examined by WIPO, which forwards the application to the national IP (intellectual property) offices of the designated countries once the application is in order. It is up to the national offices to determine whether the trade mark application is acceptable for registration. Information on opposition proceedings is available at the WIPO website, www.wiop.int.

10.4 The meaning of 'mark'

10.4.1 The statutory framework until January 2019

The definition of 'trade mark' is set out in TMA s. 1, derived from Art. 2 of the Directive. Note that this provision was amended on January 2019 in implementation of the trade mark reform provisions incorporated in the new Directive and the Regulation ('EUTMR').

Current s. 1(1) TMA reads that '"trade mark" means any sign which is capable

(a) of being represented in the register in a manner which enables the registrar and other competent authorities and the public to determine the clear and precise subject matter of the protection afforded to the proprietor, and

(b) of distinguishing goods or services of one undertaking from those of other undertakings.

A trade mark may, in particular, consist of words (including personal names), designs, letters, numerals, colours, sounds or the shape of goods or their packaging.' This provision implements the new Directive and Regulation and departs from the formerly applicable graphical representation standard. In the context of this section, the wording 'may consist of' is a phrase which indicates potential. Whether the thing applied for actually *is* a trade mark is determined under s. 3. Section 1, however flawed its wording, should be seen as a very low threshold.

The provisions list (non-exhaustively) the things which can be a trade mark. The inclusion of shapes (i.e. three-dimensional marks as opposed to 'designs' which are two-dimensional pictures) has the effect of reversing the House of Lords' decision in *Re COCA-COLA Trade Marks* [1986] RPC 421. Here it was decided that a bottle could not be a trade mark 'because it would create an unfair monopoly', even though it is possible to protect the shapes of goods through the action in passing off. More recently, in Case T-411/14 *Coca-Cola v OHIM* EU:T:2016:94; [2016] ETMR 25, the General Court rejected the registration of the Coca-Cola bottle as an EU trade mark because it was not sufficiently distinctive and it had also not acquired distinctiveness through use.

Three particular decisions of the CJEU give insight as to the purpose of Art. 2 of the Directive (now Art. 3 of the 2015/2436 Directive) and are an aid to interpreting s. 1. The Court has said that this Article simply sets out the minimum requirements for registrability (Case C-404/02 *Nichols plc v Registrar of Trade Marks* [2004] ECR I-8499, *per* AG Colomer at [32]) and that the list of subject matter is not exhaustive (Case C-283/01 *Shield Mark BV v Joost Kist* [2003] ECR I-14313, *per* AG Colomer at [22]). Most importantly (and, in contrast to the test under s. 3, the absolute grounds), the policy of the Directive is simply to define the *types* of sign of which a trade mark may consist without regard to the list of goods or services for which the applicant seeks protection (Case C-363/99 *Koninklijke KPN Nederland NV v Benelux-Merkenbureau (POSTKANTOOR)* [2004] ECR I-1619). In other words, the test under s. 1 is to be carried out in the abstract. The views of the CJEU as to the scope of the definition of a trade mark under the Directive are, of course, conclusive: because of this, the differences in wording between s. 1 and Art. 2 (now Art. 3) in the end do not matter.

10.4.2 The definition of trade mark in the new reform package

Following the 2015 reform of trade mark law, trade marks will no longer have to be graphically represented. According to Art. 3 of the new Directive:

A trade mark may consist of any signs, in particular words, including personal names, or designs, letters, numerals, colours, the shape of goods or of the packaging of goods, or sounds, provided that such signs are capable of:

(a) distinguishing the goods or services of one undertaking from those of other undertakings; and

(b) being represented on the register in a manner which enables the competent authorities and the public to determine the clear and precise subject matter of the protection afforded to its proprietor.

This mirrors the provision incorporated in Art. 4 of the Regulation ('EUTMR'). Article 3 of the EU Trade Mark Implementing Regulation ('EUTMIR') outlines the specific rules and requirements for the representation of some of the most popular types of trade mark. It specifies in its first paragraph that

[t]he trade mark shall be represented in any appropriate form using generally available technology, as long as it can be reproduced on the register in a clear, precise, self-contained, easily accessible, intelligible, durable and objective manner so as to enable the competent authorities and the public to determine with clarity and precision the subject-matter of the protection afforded to its proprietor.

Pause for reflection

The new provision implements the principle of 'what you see is what you get'. This enables the representation requirement to better serve its purpose, i.e. to enhance legal certainty, by allowing competent authorities and the public to determine the subject matter of protection clearly and precisely. It is also expected that—because searches will be clearer and easier—the objection rate for unconventional trademarks, such as sounds and colours, will be reduced.

Do you think that it will be now easier to register marks that it has not been possible to register until recently, such as smells or tastes? Graphic representation has been a key impediment in registering scents as trade marks for reasons that we will be exploring in more detail in the sections that follow. As we will see, although it may not be possible for scents to meet the new representation requirement, taking a significant part of brand identity outside the scope of trade mark protection, it will be considerably easier for other signs to be registered, such as sounds or colours, including single colours or colour combinations.

Section 1 consists of three ingredients: the requirement of 'a sign', the need to represent such a sign clearly and precisely, and for the sign to be 'capable of distinguishing' goods or services.

10.4.3 Sign

The choice of the word 'sign' is deliberately broad. According to Jacob J in *Philips Electronics NV v Remington Consumer Products* [1998] RPC 283 at p. 298 a 'sign' is 'anything which conveys information'. Most people think of a trade mark as being a word (a brand name such as KLEENEX), and indeed the same judge remarked in *British Sugar plc v James Robertson & Sons Ltd* [1996] RPC 281 at p. 305 a word is 'plainly included within the meaning of sign'. The CJEU has gone much further, stressing the policy of the Directive in encouraging registration. In Case C-273/00 *Sieckmann v Deutsches Patent- und Markenamt* [2002] ECR I-11737, AG Colomer (at [20]–[21]) commented that human beings receive messages with the help of all their senses, so that a message which can be understood by any of the five senses could be a trade mark. Further, in

Case C-283/01 *Shield Mark BV v Joost Kist* [2003] ECR I-14313, AG Colomer (at [30]) repeated the point that trade marks do not have to be visual messages. However, in Case C-321/03 *Dyson Ltd v Registrar of Trade Marks* [2007] ECR I-687 the Court ruled that a transparent dust collecting bin for a vacuum cleaner was a concept, not a sign.

Such an adventurous attitude is in contrast to UK law under the Trade Marks Act 1938. For many years there was a debate as to whether a product could be a trade mark of itself, or whether the trade mark had to be able to be described separately from the goods (see the narrow views of the Court of Appeal in *Re James's Trade Mark* (1886) 33 Ch D 392). In *Interlego AG's Trade Mark Applications* [1998] RPC 69 (a case decided under the pre-1994 law) it was held that the appearance of the LEGO brick could not be a trade mark for LEGO bricks, because the mark could not be described separately from the goods. However, a trade mark could cover the whole surface of the goods. In *Smith, Kline & French Laboratories Ltd v Sterling Winthrop Group Ltd* [1976] RPC 511, the House of Lords held that the two-tone colour scheme of pharmaceutical capsules was registrable. However, the product was the cold-cure contents of the capsule, and the trade mark was applied to (and therefore separate from) the goods.

A further debate in pre-1994 law was whether the trade mark had to be visible at point of sale. In *Unilever's Application* [1980] FSR 286 the court rejected an application to register the red and white stripes in the applicant's toothpaste because the mark could not be seen by the purchaser when buying the goods. This decision should be re-evaluated in light of the CJEU ruling in *Arsenal Football Club v Matthew Reed*, where the Court stated that the perception of the end user of the goods should be considered as well as that of the initial buyer. By way of postscript, two further attempts to obtain protection for the red and white stripes of SIGNAL toothpaste also failed. In *Re Unilever plc's Application* [1984] RPC 155 the application consisted of a picture of the tube with a 'slug' of striped toothpaste being squeezed onto the brush. This, said the court, was simply a picture of the product itself and could not be registered. In *Unilever Ltd's Trade Mark (Striped Toothpaste No 2)* [1987] RPC 13, Hoffmann J (as he then was) rejected another application for two reasons; first, the stripes were functional not decorative (they indicated the two components, dentifrice and mouth freshener, and so described the goods) and second, other traders might want to use the colour scheme.

 Pause for reflection

Going back to our scenario question, do the musical theme, colour combination, and smell that Becky considers registering by reference to her party supply products qualify as 'signs' eligible for protection as UK trade marks?

10.4.4 **Capacity of representation**

10.4.4.1 Capacity of graphic representation (until January 2019)

Before January 2019, the requirement of representation of trade marks was one of graphic representation. Form TM3 contained an 8cm by 8cm space within which the applicant had to enter the proposed mark. Where this was a word or a two-dimensional picture, the requirement was non-problematic. Reference to the broad meaning accorded to the word 'sign' reminds us, however, that anything which conveys a message to any of the senses is potentially registrable. Case law has shown that anything other than a word or picture (for example, shapes, colours, and all sensory marks) faced difficulty with the requirement of graphic representation.

Case C-273/00 *Sieckmann v Deutsches Patent- und Markenamt* [2002] ECR I-11737

The purpose of graphic representation was explained by the CJEU in Case C-273/00 *Sieckmann v Deutsches Patent- und Markenamt* [2002] ECR I-11737. The Court said that 'graphic representation' required the mark to be shown visually to enable it to be identified precisely. The sound operation of the registration system demanded this, first so that the scope of protection was clear, and second to make the Register accessible for all the key players, that is, the state (as manager of the Register) and other traders. Consequently, the representation had to be 'clear, precise, self-contained, easily accessible, intelligible, durable and objective'. These are often called the '*Sieckmann* 7' requirements. In principle, a smell could be registered as a trade mark (because it sent a message to the consumer); however, the CJEU declared that the three methods proposed by the German trade mark registry for graphically representing the smell of cinnamon, namely a chemical formula (which in fact would only have revealed the substance not its smell), a written description, or a sample, did not meet the above-mentioned criteria. The Court was constrained by the form of the Art. 267 TFEU reference which had asked a series of closed questions rather than seeking general advice as to how a smell might be represented.

Pause for reflection

In the light of *Sieckmann*, the earlier decision by the Board of Appeal of OHIM in *Vennootschap Onder Firma Senta Aromatic Marketing's Application* (Case R 156/1998–2) [1999] ETMR 429 that the smell of freshly cut grass for tennis balls was registrable must now be regarded as totally unsafe. Although the registrability of smells as trade marks is not entirely foreclosed, the clarity and specificity of the *Sieckmann* criteria appears to elude many applicants (see in this regard S. Karapapa, 'Registering Scents as Community Trademarks' [2010], *The Trademark Reporter*, 100 (6), 1335–1359).

In Case T-305/04 *Eden SARL v OHIM* [2005] ECR II-4705 the application was for a trade mark described as 'the smell of ripe strawberries' in respect of cleaning preparations, stationery, leather goods, and clothing. The application form merely showed a picture of a strawberry, accompanied by the words 'the smell of ripe strawberries'. The General Court upheld the decision of OHIM that this was not a valid graphic representation of the trade mark.

Was the CJEU in *Sieckmann* correct to say that a smell could in principle be a trade mark and then reject the proposed methods of graphic representation? How could a smell be shown on the Register in such a way as to meet the *Sieckmann* criteria? Do you agree with the position of the EU legislature that included the '*Sieckmann* 7' requirements in Art. 3 of the Implementing Regulation (EUTMIR)?

10.4.4.2 Further CJEU cases

The CJEU itself has relied on the *Sieckmann* criteria on three further occasions. Sound marks were the subject of *Shield Mark* where the Court said that tunes were capable of graphic representation (through the use of musical notation) but other sound marks not so, as a description in words, a spectrogram, or a sound recording, were not sufficient. Because of the way the case was referred by the Benelux authorities, the CJEU did not have to consider whether sound marks were objectionable under the absolute grounds, nor how they might be dealt with in an infringement action. Colour marks were considered in Case C-104/01 *Libertel Groep BV v Benelux-Merkenbureau* [2003] ECR I-3793. Here the CJEU declared that in principle, single colours could potentially be trade marks and were to be represented graphically by the use of an internationally recognized method of identification, such as the Pantone system. In Case C-49/02 *Heidelberger Bauchemie GmbH v Deutsches Patent- und Markenamt* [2004] ECR I-6129, the CJEU said that where the mark consists of more than one colour, the representation must also include a systematic arrangement associating the colours in a predetermined and uniform way.

It was visually represented by a photograph, and while photographs were appropriate for three-dimensional marks claiming a particular form of packaging, they were less appropriate for colour marks that might not be confined to any specific shape of goods. The description was unambiguous with regard to the Pantone shades, but it was not so clear in relation to the respective proportions and the arrangement of dark and light purple.

In order to determine precisely an EU trade mark consisting of a combination of colours, those colours have to be represented in accordance with a specific arrangement or layout, featuring the colours in a predetermined and uniform way, so as to prevent numerous other combinations of those colours which would not enable consumer recollection of a particular combination (*Red Bull GmbH v EUIPO* (T-101/15) EU:T:2017:852; [2018] ETMR 11 at [55]).

10.4.4.3 United Kingdom cases

United Kingdom decisions display a similar attitude towards the graphic representation of non-standard marks: precision is the key. With regard to smell marks, in *John Lewis of Hungerford Ltd's Trade Mark Application* [2001] RPC 575 it was held not enough merely to use words to describe a smell (again, cinnamon). The depiction of colours as trade marks was the subject matter in *Ty Nant Spring Water Ltd's Trade Mark Application* [2000] RPC 55, where it was held that to identify a colour (cobalt blue used on mineral water bottles) by its refractive index was not sufficiently ascertainable. And in *Swizzels Matlow Ltd's Trade Mark Application* [1998] RPC 244, the attempt to register a shape trade mark by writing on Form TM3 'a chewy sweet on a stick' failed. It remains a mystery why the applicant thought that these words explained clearly what the shape was and why it didn't put a drawing or photograph of the product in the space provided. A more complex reason for refusing the application occurred in *Société des Produits Nestlé SA v Cadbury UK Ltd* [2013] EWCA Civ 1174: although the applicant had identified the colour purple for its chocolate products by the appropriate Pantone reference, the application form stated that the mark would be the 'predominant' colour on the packaging which the Court of Appeal thought introduced an element of uncertainty. In *Glaxo Wellcome UK Ltd (t/a Allen & Hanburys) v Sandoz Ltd* [2016] EWHC 1537 (Ch), HHJ Hacon held that the visual representation of a sign including the photograph of an inhaler and a verbal description specifying two Pantone codes for the colour purple as applied to the inhaler was neither sufficiently precise nor uniform and was hence not appropriate for a colour mark which might not be confined to any specific shape of goods. In *J W Spear & Sons Ltd and Mattel Inc v Zynga Inc* [2013] EWCA Civ 1175, an attempt to register 'an infinite number of permutations' of the size, lettering, numbering, and colour of SCRABBLE tiles was held invalid: what was depicted was neither a sign nor did it comply with *Sieckmann* with regard to graphic representation.

10.4.4.4 Capable of clear and precise representation (from January 2019)

Up until recently, the *graphic* representation requirement of a mark was a *sine qua non* of the existence of the trade mark. Visual delineation of the mark was a simple yet essential condition ensuring that the mark would serve its basic function, namely to differentiate the origin of goods and services. With the multiplication of trade mark registrations over the years, finding available marks, such as words, figurative signs, or colours, became increasingly difficult and resulted in exploration of alternative signs, such as smells or sounds, to function as indications of origin. Following these market trends, the law evolved by eliminating the graphical representation requirement which was to a large extent an impediment to registrability, whilst endorsing the CJEU jurisprudence, most notably *Sieckmann*.

The new requirement will allow for a wider range of representations even though filing of specimens or samples seems to be excluded. Various different formats will now be allowed, including JPEG, MP3, MP4, OBJ, STL, and X3D depending on the type of mark. Some forms of unconventional marks, such as sound marks, motion marks, multimedia marks, and holograms marks, will now be easier to register. This includes colour marks, including single colour or colour combination marks, which, however, will have to include both the representation and in addition a reference to a generally recognized colour code, such as Pantone, Hex, RAL, RGB, or CMYK. Because to date there is generally available technology allowing for the reproduction of smells or tastes, registration of such marks does not still seem possible although it is not to be excluded should such a technology emerge.

One of the first cases that addressed the new representation requirement is Case R 200/2017-2 *Giro Travel Company v Andreas Stihl AG & Co KG*, where Andreas Stihl attempted to register the colours grey and orange, specified under the RAL system, for chainsaws (Class 7). There was also the following verbal description: 'The colour orange is applied to the top of the housing of the chainsaw and the colour grey is applied to the bottom of the housing of the chainsaw.' Settled case law of the CJEU indicates that the colours should be systematically arranged in a predetermined and uniform way (C-49/92 *Heidelberger Bauchemie GmbH*, ECLI:EU:C:2004:384) and that the representation of the sign and its description should be evaluated together. In the present case, references and explanations that were provided by the applicant when filling the application cannot be considered as part of the representation of the sign as they cannot be seen in the publication of the mark on the register and they are only available to third parties when studying the entire file. If these elements were seen to form a part of the representation, of the mark then such a representation would not meet the '*Sieckmann* 7' requirements, i.e. that the mark's representation must be clear, precise, self-contained, easily accessible, intelligible, durable, and objective.

Pause for reflection

In our scenario question, Becky seeks advice on the registration of a number of signs as UK trade marks, namely a multi-colour combination, a smell mark, and a music theme for advertisements. To what extent can these satisfy the clear and precise representation requirement? Will it be possible to register all relevant signs under the system of clear and graphic representation? Why is it still difficult to justify registering smells as trade marks?

10.4.5 Capable of distinguishing

In contrast to the UK courts (whose grappling with 'capable of distinguishing' is discussed later in the context of absolute grounds) the CJEU has adopted straightforward thinking about the meaning of the phrase.

Case C-299/99 *Philips Electronics BV v Remington Consumer Products* [2002] ECR I-5475

In Case C-299/99 *Philips Electronics BV v Remington Consumer Products* [2002] ECR I-5475, at [47–50] the CJEU pointed out that Art. 2 (now Art. 3) was concerned with the function of a trade mark. Did the mark enable the consumer to choose one product from another, confident that the goods had originated from one particular business which was responsible for their quality? Further, said the Court, Art. 2 treats all categories of trade mark the same. Particular types of mark (for example, shapes, as in the *Philips* case itself) were to be subjected to the same test, namely, did the sign guarantee the origin of the product?

The presence of the word 'capable' in Art. 2, together with the CJEU use of the word 'enable' in its ruling in *Philips v Remington* is significant. When combined with the Court's pronouncements on how Art. 2 should be applied in *Nichols* and *POSTKANTOOR*, it becomes clear that the only question is whether the particular category of sign (for example, a colour, a shape, a smell, or a sound) has the potential to act as a trade mark. In other words, *could* this sign help a consumer to choose between competing products (whether *in fact* it actually does so is a matter for determination under the absolute grounds)? So, in *Shield Mark*, AG Colomer (at [20]) said that sounds can *in principle* be trade marks (emphasis supplied). The same approach has been used by OHIM and the General Court. In Case T-316/00 *Viking Umwelttechnik GmbH v OHIM* [2002] ECR II-3715 at [23–24], the General Court emphasized that there was a distinction between whether signs of a particular category (here, colours) could in principle be trade marks and whether they actually were so.

By reference to shape marks, the CJEU held in *Jaguar Land Rover Ltd v Office for Harmonisation in the Internal Market (Trade Marks and Designs) (OHIM)* (T-629/14) EU:T:2015:878; [2016] ETMR 12, that only a mark which departed significantly from the norm or customs of the sector had a distinctive character, the reason for this being that such a mark can fulfill its essential function of indicating origin.

Pause for reflection

In our scenario question, what is your advice to Becky? Are the signs she wishes to register capable of distinguishing her goods from those of other undertakings? What are the key elements to consider in offering legal advice to her?

10.5 Conclusion

In this chapter, we have discussed the procedure in order to register a UK trade mark and we have also elaborated on the meaning of the concept of a trade mark. We have seen that the definition of 'trade mark' in s. 1 of the TMA consists of three elements: there is need for a sign, and this sign should be capable of graphic representation, and capable of distinguishing. We have seen that the graphic representation requirement has been an impediment towards the registration of certain non-conventional marks, such as colours, shapes, and sensory marks. With the 2015 trademark reform, however, the graphic representation requirement was eliminated and replaced by the requirement that the mark is capable of clear and precise representation. This applies to registrations of European Union trade marks since 1 October 2017, when the Regulation ('EUTMR') entered into force. The requirement for clear and precise representation was introduced into United Kingdom trade mark law on January 2019. The law of the CJEU explaining that the Directive was intended to encourage registration remains valid, in that the three elements comprising the definition of the trade mark are to be assessed in the abstract, that is, without reference to the goods or services of the application. The key question is whether what has been applied for has the potential to send a message to consumers to help them choose between competing brands. It will be at the stage of examination to assess whether any absolute grounds for refusing the registration of the trade mark exist (to be examined in chapter 11).

With regards to our scenario question, Becky should be advised about the six-step Registry procedure (filing of the application, examination, search, publication and notification, opposition, and registration). If no one objects, the registration process takes about four months. All three signs that Becky wishes to register are in principle protectable subject matter and can be registered on condition that they meet the definition of trade mark (and there are no absolute or relative grounds for refusing the application, as we will see later). The definition of a trade mark according to s. 1 of TMA 1994 requires three elements: (i) a sign, (ii) that is capable of clear and precise representation, (iii) 'which is capable of distinguishing goods or services of one undertaking from those of other undertakings'. The colour combination, music theme, and smell of caramel qualify as signs. Even though they do not feature in the list of signs included in s. 1, the list is meant to be non-exhaustive. With regards to the representation requirement, such a representation has to be 'clear, precise, self-contained, easily accessible, intelligible, durable and objective' according to Case C-273/00 *Sieckmann v Deutsches Patent- und Markenamt* [2002] ECR I-11737. The requirement will be more easily met by reference to the colour combination and the music theme (an extract from Vivaldi's *Summer* followed by the sound of a popping balloon), especially in light of the forthcoming abolition of the graphic representation requirement at national level (since January 2019) and its replacement by a system of clear and precise representations which can be supported by submission of electronic files containing the mark, such as JPEG files containing the colour combination and an audio file with the music theme. The registration of the smell of caramel however will remain equally difficult as it was under the system of graphic representation, with the smell of fresh cut grass for tennis balls being one of the very few successful applications; following *Sieckmann*, it is extremely onerous for smells to meet the '*Sieckmann 7*' criteria, which remain part of the new representation system.

End-of-chapter questions

After reading the chapter carefully, try answering the following questions. For answer guidance visit the online resources at **www.oup.com/uk/karapapa-mcdonagh/**

1. What is the process of registering UK trade marks?
2. The choice of the average consumer as the arbiter of registrability is uncertain and consequently unhelpful. Discuss.
3. What are the objectives and anticipated benefits of the abolition of the graphic representation requirement?
4. Will the 2015 EU reform of the trade mark system have an impact on the registrability of certain marks, mostly unconventional trade marks?

Further reading

For understanding the protection available to trade marks, the following readings are recommended:

Davis, J. 'Locating the Average Consumer: His Judicial Origins, Intellectual Influences and Current Role in European Trade Mark Law' [2005] 2 *IPQ* 183

Examines the way in which the CJEU has developed the average consumer as the arbiter of key issues under the Directive and Regulation.

Dinwoodie, G. B. and Gangjee, D. S. 'The Image of the Consumer in European Trade Mark Law' in D. Leczykiewicz and S. Weatherill (eds), *The Image(s) of the Consumer in EU Law* (Hart Publishing, 2015)

Insights on the concept of the average consumer under EU trade mark law.

Firth, A., Gredley, E., and Maniatis, S. 'Shapes as Trade Marks: Public Policy, Functional Considerations and Consumer Perception' [2001] 23 *EIPR* 86

Explains the underlying policy issues regarding the registration of shape trade marks and the role of the consumer in deciding registrability.

Fields, D. and Muller, A. 'Going Against Tradition: the Effect of Eliminating the Requirement of Representing a Trade Mark Graphically on Applications for Non-Traditional Trademarks' [2017] 39(4) *EIPR* 238

Considers the impact of the elimination of the graphic representation requirement on the registrability of non-traditional trade marks.

Friedmann, D. 'EU Opens Door for Sound Marks: Will Scent Marks Follow?' [2015] 10(12) *JIPLP* 931

Argues that the abolition of the graphic representation requirement will open the door for the initial registration of non-traditional trade marks in the EU.

Gangjee, D. S. 'Paying the Price for Admission: Non-Traditional Marks Across Registration and Enforcement' in Irene Calboli and Martin Senftleben (eds), *The Protection of non-traditional Marks: Critical Perspectives* (Oxford University Press, 2018)

Considers the registrability of non-conventional trade marks in the light of the tensions generated by their admission.

Karapapa, S. 'Registering Scents as Community Trademarks' [2010] *The Trademark Reporter* 1335

An overview of the protection available to scent trade marks in the light of the graphic representation requirement.

Kur, A. 'Trade Marks Function, Don't They? CJEU Jurisprudence and Unfair Competition Practices,' [2014] 45(4) *IIC* 434

Considers the functions of trade marks in the light of the CJEU case law.

Turner-Kerr, P. 'EU Intellectual Property Law: Recent Case Developments' [2004] 4 *IPQ* 448

Surveys many of the key cases on registrability under the absolute and relative grounds.

11 Absolute grounds for refusal of registration

Problem question

Read this problem question carefully and keep it in mind while you are working through the chapter that follows. At the end of this chapter, you will be able to apply what you have learnt to the problem question and advise the relevant parties.

JollyBrush Ltd has recently entered the market of hair products. They are selling their products in hair salons in the United Kingdom but they plan making them available for sale in various outlets, including supermarkets and online retailers.

JollyBrush's star product is a super nourishing hair mask that restores dry damaged hair and treats split ends just 15 minutes after applying it. JollyBrush has put it on the market under the name 'CareHair'. They also state on the packaging that this is a 'super intensive treatment mask with healing minerals from Bath, Somerset'. The product becomes such an immediate success that many users have started saying they will 'carehair' (used as a verb) their hair instead of applying a nourishing mask.

JollyBrush has also developed a new detangling brush for professional use that can detangle hair very efficiently, while it's rinsed. They call it the 'CareTangle'. It comes in a very unusual half-moon shape, featuring a set of elastic bristles on one side that enables the brush to detangle hair with extreme ease. JollyBrush is concerned that competitors will be copying this shape as they have not yet taken steps in ensuring that it will be protected.

JollyBrush has not applied to register any trade marks for their two key products yet and they come to you for legal advice. They query whether it is feasible to register various signs as UK trade marks, in particular the words 'CareTangle' and 'CareHair'; the colours fuchsia and gold, or fuchsia on its own, that they use in packaging of their products; the shape of the 'CareTangle'; and the geographical indication 'Bath, Somerset' for both products. Finally, they want to know whether they can also get trade mark protection for the words 'super intensive treatment' as they plan to put other hair treating products in the market and want to be commercially known as those offering the super intensive protection.

Advise JollyBrush.

11.1 Introduction

What brings together Toblerone and Kit-Kat chocolates, Clipper cylindrical lighters, the Rubik's Cube, Louboutin shoes, the three stripes of Adidas, and London Taxi Company cabs? All these products, along with more other products, have been part of the trend involving the desire to register non-conventional marks as trade marks. It is not always feasible to register such signs as trade marks as they may be refused registration on the basis of the so-called absolute grounds for refusal of trade marks from registrability. The absolute grounds for refusal are found in the Trade Marks Act 1994 ('TMA') s. 3 (based on Art. 3 of the Directive and also featuring in Art. 4 of the recast Directive). The section lists objections to registrability based on the mark's own characteristics. To be refused registration, the mark should possess some innate quality which prevents registration. For instance, the mark applied for may be descriptive, generic, or it may lack distinctiveness. Marks that go against public policy or marks that are immoral will also be refused protection. The TMA contains a number of negative objections in contrast to its predecessor (which required an applicant to show that the mark applied for was positively entitled to registration).

In this chapter, we will be looking into all the objections that impede registration of trade marks at the examination stage and we will also be looking into the proviso of s. 3, according to which such objections may be overcome and marks that are initially barred from protection can be protected if they have acquired distinctiveness through use.

11.2 Overview

Provided the 'sign' has passed the very nominal test in s. 1 (discussed in chapter 10), it is assumed registrable unless the Registry (or an opponent) can show that it falls within one or more of the absolute grounds in s. 3.

Overall examination of s. 3 shows that there is one general subsection (s. 3(1)) which applies to all types of trade marks, no matter what they are. Section 3(1) is subject to a proviso, concerned with acquired (or factual) distinctiveness which does not apply to the remaining subsections. Subsections 3(2) to 3(6) apply to specific cases only. So, only Three-dimensional shape marks fall within s. 3(2). Section 3(3)(a) and (b) deal respectively with marks which are contrary to public policy or are deceptive, and s. 3(4) and (5) deal respectively with marks which are contrary to any provision of United Kingdom or EU law, or which consist of or contain any specially protected emblems, such as coats of arms, state flag, or the Olympic symbol. Finally, s. 3(6) deals with applications made in bad faith. Each of the later subsections is more specific than the earlier ones. Section 3 could therefore be regarded as an upside-down pyramid. A further point is that each of the absolute grounds is separate. An applicant might succeed in arguing that one of the grounds does not apply, but still be caught out by another.

The onus of proof is on the Registrar, not the applicant. The list in s. 3 is finite.

Two of the key elements that are important and that we will be examining by reference to each absolute ground for refusing applications are the underlying policy and the test that has to be applied.

11.2.1 Policy

In providing guidance for national courts on the meaning of Art. 3, the Court of Justice of the European Union ('CJEU') has gone out of its way to state the underlying policy for each of the absolute grounds. Whilst UK courts have tended to declare a blanket rule that particular signs must be left free for other traders, the CJEU has been more specific and has provided a justification for each of the objections. We will be examining these underlying policy justifications in the following sections.

11.2.2 The test to be applied

The common factor throughout CJEU case law on absolute grounds is the 'concrete test'. This means that the mark applied for is examined with reference to the goods and services of the application through the eyes of the relevant consumer (*POST-KANTOOR*). This is in contrast to Art. 2 (now Art. 3 of the recast Directive), where the mark is considered in the abstract, on its own, and *without* reference to the goods. The effect of the concrete test is to concentrate on the consumer's perception of the mark and the messages it sends.

11.3 Absolute grounds: the general provision

Section 3(1) consists of four separate paragraphs. However, para (a) is distinct from the other three, for two reasons. First, it contains the word 'sign' whilst the others use the phrase 'trade mark'. Second, the proviso to subsection (1) applies to paras (b), (c), and (d), but not to para (a).

Case C-265/00 *Campina Melkunie BV v Benelux-Merkenbureau (BIOMILD)* [2004] ECR I-1699

With regard to paras (b), (c), and (d), the CJEU has said (in Case C-265/00 *Campina Melkunie BV v Benelux-Merkenbureau (BIOMILD)* [2004] ECR I-1699) that each is independent of the others, although they overlap. A mark could fall within one but not the other two, or it could fall within all three. Whichever is the case, this does not matter, as the mark will be denied registration if it is caught by one of the objections alone. Each paragraph must be interpreted in the light of its underlying policy. Further, each paragraph has a different policy (Case C-329/02 P *SAT.1 SatellitenFernsehen GmbH v OHIM (SAT.2)* [2004] ECR I-8317).

11.3.1 Section 3(1)(a): signs not satisfying s. 1

Section 3(1)(a) declares that signs not satisfying s. 1 shall not be registered; in other words, if something is either not a 'sign' or incapable of clear and precise representation or incapable of distinguishing it will fall within para (a).

> ## Case C-383/99 P *Procter & Gamble Company v OHIM (BABY DRY)* [2001] ECR I-6251
>
> The status of s. 3(1)(a) was considered by AG Jacobs in Case C-383/99 P *Procter & Gamble Company v OHIM (BABY DRY)* [2001] ECR I-6251, where he declared (at [63–70]) that Art. 7(1)(a) of the Regulation (the equivalent of Art. 3(1)(a) of the Directive and Art. 4(1)(a) of the recast Directive) was tautologous, a repetition of the definition of 'trade mark'.

The Court of Appeal has since accepted the view that s. 3(1)(a) is not a separate ground of refusal if there is no objection under s. 1 or the remainder of s. 3: *West (t/a Eastenders) v Fuller Smith & Turner plc* [2003] FSR 816. The previous Court of Appeal pronouncement in *Bach Flower Remedies Ltd v Healing Herbs* should therefore be treated as unsafe. Case law decided by OHIM under the Regulation reveals that Art. 7(1)(a) is never referred to as a ground of objection. Further, in *Philips v Remington*, the CJEU confirmed that if a mark is factually distinctive, there is not a separate objection that it is incapable of distinguishing.

11.3.2 Section 3(1)(b): marks devoid of distinctive character

Section 3(1)(b) prohibits the registration of trade marks that are devoid of any distinctive character. According to Jacob J in *British Sugar* (at p. 306), the phrase 'requires consideration of the mark on its own, assuming no use. Is it the sort of word (or other sign) which cannot do the job of distinguishing without first educating the public that it is a trade mark?' In other words, is the mark inherently distinctive? Does it say to the consumer (who has no prior experience of the product) 'I am a trade mark'? The General Court in Case T-305/02 *Nestlé Waters France v OHIM* [2003] ECR II-5207 explained it another way. Does the trade mark help the consumer make a repeat purchase if they liked the goods, or avoid them if they had a bad experience?

> ### Pause for reflection
>
> A point that many have found puzzling is the relationship between s. 1 and s. 3 and in particular how to fit together the phrase 'capable of distinguishing' in s. 1 with 'devoid of distinctive character' in s. 3(1)(b). It now seems settled that the relationship between s. 1 and s. 3 is the difference between the *potential* of the sign to distinguish, considered in the abstract, and whether it *actually* does so, either inherently or factually (see *Philips Electronics NV v Remington Consumer Products per* Jacob J at p. 289). This approach has been endorsed by the General Court and ECJ. The latter has said that even though the 'sign', considered in the abstract, has the potential to function as a trade mark under s. 1, it must still be assessed concretely under s. 3 to see whether it actually does so, or whether there is an objection to it (*POSTKANTOOR*).

11.3.2.1 The policy underlying s. 3(1)(b)

The policy of s. 3(1)(b) was first set out in *Libertel*, where the Benelux court asked about the registrability of the colour orange for telephone equipment and services. The CJEU said that the public interest was aimed at the need not to restrict unduly the availability of *colours* for other traders in the same field of business (the Court did not refer to 'trade marks' generally). However, in *Nichols* and *SAT.2* the CJEU modified its thinking. It said that para (b) does not have the policy of requiring certain signs to be left free for other traders (which should be compared with the policy underlying s. 3(1)(c)). Instead, the public interest cannot be separated from the essential function of a trade mark. The policy underlying para (b) is solely concerned with whether the sign in question acts as a trade mark. In *SAT.2*, the CJEU further observed that para (b) does not require much creativity or imagination by the creator of the mark. It is enough that the trade mark enables consumers to identify the origin of the product. In respect of word marks and picture marks, therefore, the test would seem fairly easy to satisfy. This is not necessarily so in the case of colours, shapes, and sensory marks (non-standard marks), even though the Court has said that the section draws no distinction between different categories of trade mark (Cases C-53/01, 54/01 & 55/01 *Linde AG, Winward Industries Inc & Rado Uhren AG v Deutsches Patent- und Markenamt* [2003] ECR-I 3161). This is because consumers perceive non-standard marks as part of the product itself.

11.3.2.2 The test to be applied

The test to be applied under para (b) is the concrete test, confirmed by the CJEU in *Philips v Remington* at [63]. The mark is considered in relation to the list of goods and services on Form TM3 through the eyes of the reasonably attentive consumer. Does such a person regard the sign as a trade mark, taking into account all the relevant circumstances, remembering that the average consumer will make an overall assessment of the mark? The concrete test, dependent as it is upon consumer perception, helps to explain why, even though s. 3(1)(b) is to be applied in an identical manner to all types of mark, certain signs (shapes, colours, sounds, and smells) are more likely to be found lacking in inherent distinctiveness. For example, in *Viking v OHIM*, it was held that a grey-green colour scheme on garden tools would be viewed by customers as relating to the finish of the product rather than indicating origin.

11.3.2.2.1 *Examples of the test being applied*

There is now an extensive body of case law from the CJEU demonstrating the application of the concrete test to decide whether a mark lacks distinctive character.

Case C-404/02 *Nichols plc v Registrar of Trade Marks* [2004] ECR I-8499

In Case C-404/02 *Nichols plc v Registrar of Trade Marks* [2004] ECR I-8499, the CJEU was asked by the United Kingdom Patents Court how surnames should be treated. Former practice in the United Kingdom had been to check in the phone book to see how often the name occurred, and if there was more than a certain number of entries, to deny registrability because

→

→ other traders might want to use the mark. The CJEU simply said that it depended on consumer perception: did the average purchaser regard the name as a trade mark for the particular goods (in this instance, vending machines)?

Shape marks have fared less well under s. 3(1)(b), simply because the average consumer does not normally think that the shape of goods indicates origin. Thus, a cigar shape for chocolate bars was not registrable (Cases T-324/01 and T-110/02 *Axion SA & Christian Belce v OHIM* [2003] ECR II-1897). Similarly, the Coca-Cola bottle was held to be a mere variant of the shape of a bottle that did not enable consumers to distinguish Coca-Cola's goods from those of other undertakings and it was hence devoid of distinctive character (*Coca-Cola Co v Office for Harmonisation in the Internal Market (Trade Marks and Designs)* (OHIM) (T-411/14) EU:T:2016:94; [2016] ETMR 25). The shape of the Clipper cylindrical lighter was also declared invalid as the shape consisted exclusively of the shape of the product, which was necessary to obtain a technical result and was hence devoid of distinctive character (*Flamagas SA v EUIPO* (T-580/15) EU:T:2017:433; [2017] ETMR 33).

The same principle applies to colours (*Libertel* and *Viking*) and surface decoration applied to the goods (Case T-36/01 *Glaverbel v OHIM* [2002] ECR II-3887).

 Pause for reflection

What about the colour and shape marks that JollyBrush wishes to register as UK trade marks? Could they been seen as devoid of distinctive character? Why not?

Trade marks, however, may be composite creations. They may consist of a combination of words and numerals, shapes and colours, words and pictures. The individual elements taken separately may each lack distinctive character. However, the court will not break the mark down into its component parts (sometimes called 'salami slicing'), but will instead make an overall assessment, because that is what the consumer would do. The combination itself may therefore be distinctive (*SAT.2*). There have been a considerable number of cases before the CJEU on appeal from OHIM concerning the appearance of detergent tablets. In each case the Court has consistently applied the concrete test and asked how the average consumer would see the mark. Unless the applicant seeks to rely on the proviso to show evidence of factual distinctiveness, the consumer does not see the combined colour and shape as indicating the origin of goods: Cases C-468/01 P to C-472/01 P and C-473 and 474/01 P *Procter & Gamble Co v OHIM* [2004] ECR I-5141.

For some time now, there has been a trend of trying to register slogans as trade marks. These slogans (sometimes called 'strap lines') are used in conjunction with the main brand name. The approach of UK courts used to be that a slogan was an invitation to try the product and therefore could not be a trade mark (*HAVE A BREAK Trade Mark* [1993] RPC 217). The only pre-1994 example of a registrable slogan was *I CAN'T BELIEVE IT'S YOGURT Trade Mark* [1992] RPC 533, where it was accepted that the slogan had been used as the only brand name on the goods. By contrast, the CJEU has applied the concrete test to slogan marks. It has said that there is no need for a slogan to be particularly creative, but that normally the consumer would not regard a strap line as indicating origin (Case C-64/02 P *OHIM v Erpo Möbelwerk GmbH* ('*The Principle of Comfort*') [2004] ECR I-10031).

A mark consisting of an advertising slogan is likely to be distinctive if, apart from its promotional function, the relevant public immediately perceives it to be a badge of commercial origin (*Qualität hat Zukunft* (T–22/12), EU:T:2012:663; *Interroll v OHIM (Inspired by efficiency)* (T-126/12), EU:T:2013:303). Distinctiveness will not be affirmed where the semantic content of a word mark is primarily perceived as indicating a characteristic of the product relating to its market value which, whilst not specific, comes from promotional or advertising information (*Puma SE v EUIPO* (Case T-104/16) ECLI:EU:T:2017:153; [2017] ETMR 23).

It is up to the applicant to show factual distinctiveness under the proviso. In Case C-353/03 *Société des Produits Nestlé SA v Mars UK Ltd* [2005] ECR I-6135, and in contrast to the views of the Court of Appeal, the CJEU ruled that it did not matter that the slogan had been used in conjunction with another trade mark, because even a secondary mark could, in appropriate circumstances, acquire factual distinctiveness in its own right.

A final point is that where the trade mark has been applied for in respect of multiple classes of goods, the Registry is required to consider the application of s. 3(1)(b) (and indeed the rest of s. 3(1)) to each item listed: *POSTKANTOOR*; and Case C-239/05 *BVBA Management Training en Consultancy v Benelux-Merkenbureau* [2007] ECR I-1455. The net result is that the mark may be inherently distinctive of some goods or services but not of others. In Case T-173/00 *KWS Saat v OHIM* [2002] ECR II-3843, the colour orange was held inherently distinctive of consultancy services but not so for seeds nor the equipment used to sow them.

 Pause for reflection

Has the CJEU been too kind to trade mark applicants in its interpretation of 'devoid of distinctive character'?

11.3.3 Section 3(1)(c): descriptive signs

In essence, s. 3(1)(c) prohibits the registration of trade marks consisting exclusively of descriptive signs. The presence of the word 'exclusively' suggests that a narrow interpretation of the provision could be adopted, but the case law of the CJEU has shown otherwise.

11.3.3.1 What is a descriptive sign?

Section 3(1)(c) prohibits the registration of 'signs or indications' which 'designate the kind, quality, quantity, intended purpose, value . . . or other characteristics of goods or services'. It therefore covers not just words which describe the goods, but other types of signs (for example colours, like the red and white stripes in *Unilever's Application* indicating ingredients). Similarly, the section prohibits the registration of words which describe 'other characteristics' of the goods. In Case C-498/01 P *OHIM v Zapf Creation AG (NEW BORN BABY)* [2004] ECR I-11349 the term 'new born baby' described the characteristics of dolls. Where a word has several possible meanings, it suffices if one of those describes the characteristics of the goods: Case C-191/01 P *OHIM v Wm Wrigley Junior Co (DOUBLEMINT)* [2003] ECR I-12447.

 Pause for reflection

On the basis of the exclusion of descriptive words from registration as trade marks, what would your advice to JollyBrush be by reference to their willingness to register the words 'super intensive treatment'?

11.3.3.2 New words

But what if the trade mark consists of a new, made-up word, the component parts of which are descriptive (what the CJEU calls a 'neologism')? The Court has said (in *BIOMILD* and *POSTKANTOOR*) that the mark must be looked at as a whole to see if it conveys a descriptive meaning. It will be denied registration 'unless the mark as a whole creates, both aurally and visually, an impression far removed from that produced by a simple combination'. An example of an unsuccessful neologism is *FROOT LOOPS Trade Mark* [1998] RPC 240, where the mark was rejected because when spoken it directly described the goods (breakfast cereals). It sounded like 'fruit loops'. Similarly, the word mark 'iGrill' was refused registration due to being descriptive: it was a neologism connoting an interactive grill or a grill which employed information technology (*Weber-Stephen Products LLC v EUIPO* (T-35/17), EU:T:2018:46). The same applied to the mark IWATCH, where the 'I' prefix and the WATCH suffix were descriptive, as was the combination of the two (*Apple Inc v Arcadia Trading Ltd* [2017] EWHC 440 (Ch); [2017] ETMR 28).

Conversely, 'UltraPlus' was registrable because it was an unusual combination of words. Even though taken individually the component parts were descriptive, the overall mark was not the normal way that consumers would refer to microwave ovenware: Case T-360/00 *Dart Industries Inc v OHIM* [2002] ECR II-3867.

 Pause for reflection

What about the words 'CareTangle' and 'CareHair'? Can these neologisms be in principle protected as UK trade marks?

11.3.3.3 Geographical names

Section 3(1)(c) also bars the registration of geographical names. The meaning of 'geographical name' was explained by the CJEU in Cases C-108/97 and 109/97 *Windsurfing Chiemsee Produktions und Vertriebs GmbH v Boots und Segelzubehor Walter Huber* [1999] ECR I-2779 at [31–35]. It means that consumers currently associate the name with the place where the goods come from. The place can be the source of the goods either now or in the future. Consequently, a 'fanciful' geographical name (such as 'North Pole' for bananas) can always be registered because consumers are unlikely to believe that those goods originate from that location. Equally registrable are names of places which consumers do not (and are unlikely to) associate with the goods. In Case T-379/03 *Peek & Cloppenburg KG v OHIM* [2005] ECR II-4633, the General Court, on appeal from OHIM, held that although there was a town called 'Cloppenburg', German consumers did not associate the name with the production of goods and/or services. It was therefore not a 'geographical name'. Similarly, registration of the mark 'The Berkshire Eye Clinic' was refused registration as a trade mark on the basis that it was purely descriptive of a geographical origin within TMA s. 3(1)(c) and it had not acquired a distinctive character as a result of use (*Berkshire and Hartley LLP's Trade Mark Application*, No.3107552).

In short, the trade mark should be an indication of trade origin, not geographical origin.

Pause for reflection

Is the geographical name 'Bath, Somerset' excluded as descriptive by virtue of s. 3(1)(c)? Is your answer the same by reference to both the hairbrush and the nourishing mask?

It should be noted, however, that certain geographical names (e.g. Champagne) may receive protection as collective/certification marks or as *sui generis* geographical indications ('GI'), namely as signs used on products that have a specific geographical origin and possess qualities or reputation owing to that origin. Unlike a trade mark, which is used to distinguish the goods and services of one undertaking from those of other undertakings, offering its proprietor the right to exclude others from using the trade mark, a geographical indication manifests that a product is produced in a certain location and has characteristics owing to that location. Agricultural products are typically influenced by specific local factors, e.g. climate and soil. Examples include 'Darjeeling Tea' which originates in Darjeeling in India, or 'Roquefort' for cheese produced in France. At the EU level there are three forms of protecting geographical indications and traditional products: protected designations of origin ('PDO'), protected geographical indications ('PGI'), and traditional specialities guaranteed ('TSG'). The legal basis of these forms of protection is EU Regulation No. 1151/2012 of the European Parliament and of the Council of 21 November 2012 on quality schemes for agricultural products and foodstuffs.

11.3.3.4 Foreign descriptive words

Case C-421/04 *Matratzen Concord AG v Hukla Germany SA* [2006] ECR I-2303

An illustration of the concrete test in relation to foreign descriptive words is Case C-421/04 *Matratzen Concord AG v Hukla Germany SA* [2006] ECR I-2303. A Spanish court had sought guidance as to whether a word which was descriptive of the goods (mattresses) in German

→

> → was registrable in Spain. The evidence was that most Spanish people did not know the meaning of the word 'matratzen' ('mattress' in German) and so would not view it as descriptive of the goods. The CJEU ruled that where a word which is descriptive of the characteristics of the goods in the language of Member State B (Germany) is sought to be registered in Member State A (Spain), it should not be refused registration unless consumers in Member State A are capable of identifying the meaning of the (foreign) word. In other words, the Court adopted the mantle of the average Spanish consumer to decide what information was conveyed about the product by the mark.

11.3.3.5 The underlying policy

The public interest underlying s. 3(1)(c) has been stated in a restrictive fashion by the CJEU, in *DOUBLEMINT* (at [29–32]) and *POSTKANTOOR* (at [54–55]). The CJEU declared that the Directive pursues an aim that descriptive signs can be freely used by all. Because of the phrase 'may serve' in the Directive, descriptive signs must be left free for other traders, whether they want to use them today, or whether they *might* want to use them in the future. This is, however, not an absolute rule because of the presence of the proviso as to acquired distinctiveness (*Windsurfing Chiemsee*).

Note the difference in the underlying policy of s. 3(1)(b) and s. 3(1)(c).

11.3.3.6 The test

Even though the underlying policy is stricter, s. 3(1)(c) is applied in the same manner as s. 3(1)(b). The concrete test is used to decide what information about the goods or services is conveyed to the average consumer by the proposed trade mark—in other words, how would the consumer refer to such goods? Where the mark consists of a number of elements, it is to be considered as a whole.

> **Case C-383/99 P *Procter & Gamble Company v OHIM (BABY DRY)* [2001] ECR I-6251**
>
> A controversial decision is Case C-383/99 P *Procter & Gamble Company v OHIM (BABY DRY)* [2001] ECR I-6251. On appeal from OHIM, the CJEU held that the mark (a combination of two known words) was 'syntactically unusual' because the normal way in English of referring to the characteristics of babies' nappies would have been to refer to a 'dry baby'. The case should now be treated with caution for two reasons. First, the CJEU did not mention the policy of preventing the registration of descriptive marks, in contrast to its earlier ruling in *Windsurfing Chiemsee* and its later statements in *DOUBLEMINT* and *POSTKANTOOR*. Second, in *DOUBLEMINT* itself, the Court made plain (at [32]) that an application will be refused under s. 3(1)(c) if at least one of the possible meanings of the mark describes the goods.

Pause for reflection

Can the decision of the CJEU in *BABY DRY* be reconciled with what was said in *DOUBLEMINT*?

11.3.4 Section 3(1)(d): generic marks

There are two separate limbs to s. 3(1)(d). A mark will be refused registration if it has become customary, either in the current language, or in the *bona fide* and established practices of the trade. The wording of the provision is not concerned with whether the word (or whatever) is common, but whether it is customary *in the trade*, that is, whether it is being used by other traders in the relevant product, or indeed, whether it is used by customers to refer to that product. In *Wm Wrigley Jr Co's Application (LIGHT GREEN)* [1999] ETMR 214, an application to register the colour light green for confectionery was refused as the mark was already widely used by other sweet manufacturers. The United Kingdom Trade Marks Registry has offered further examples of marks which can be considered customary (i.e. generic), such as star devices for brandy or 'Red Lion' for public house services.

11.3.4.1 Underlying policy

The public interest of para (d) is, according to the CJEU, the same as under para (c), that is, it protects the interests of other traders (Case C-517/99 *Merz & Krell GmbH & Co v Deutsches Patent- und Markenamt*, (*BRAVO*) [2001] ECR I-6959). However, the CJEU, in clarifying the overlap between the two paragraphs, stated that the use of the mark does not have to be descriptive of the goods. Section 3(1)(d) does differ from s. 3(1)(c) in that it deals with signs which are actually in use in trade, rather than signs which other traders *might* want to use.

11.3.4.2 The test

As with all aspects of s. 3, the test is the same, namely the concrete test. The sign is considered in relation to the products listed on Form TM3 through the eyes of the notional consumer: Case C-371/02 *Björnekulla Fruktindustrier AB v Procordia Food AB* [2004] ECR I-5791 (a case on the parallel ground of revocation found in s. 46(1)(c)). As the Appointed Person explained in *STASH Trade Mark*, 3 September 2004, there must be clear evidence that by the application date the mark is used by third parties to such an extent that it has become customary (that is, 'usual') in the trade for the relevant goods or services. In *STASH* itself, evidence of two uses of the mark by third parties before the application date did not amount to customary use. Much will depend on the nature of the market. The amount of use required will be far less where the products are specialised than where they are bought by members of the public.

Pause for reflection

Does the fact that a portion of JollyBrush customers use the word 'CareHair' customarily in order to refer to the way in which they treat their hair mean that the sign has become customary in trade and will hence be refused registration under s. 3(1)(d)?

11.3.5 The proviso to s. 3(1): distinctiveness acquired through use

The proviso to s. 3(1) makes clear that marks which are caught by paras (b), (c), and (d) can still be registered where the applicant can show acquired distinctiveness. This is a major exception to these three objections: *Windsurfing Chiemsee*. The proviso is nicely explained by the Appointed Person in *AD2000 Trade Mark* [1997] RPC 168 as the difference between nature and nurture. A mark which began life by being inherently non-distinctive, descriptive, or generic can still be registered if after use the relevant customers come to regard it as indicating origin. Such use must be before the application date.

> **Cases C-108/97 and 109/97 *Windsurfing Chiemsee Produktions und Vertriebs GmbH v Boots und Segelzubehor Walter Huber* [1999] ECR I-2779**
>
> The factors to be taken into account when deciding whether a 'significant proportion' of relevant consumers recognize the mark were listed by the CJEU in Cases C-108/97 and 109/97 *Windsurfing Chiemsee Produktions und Vertriebs GmbH v Boots und Segelzubehor Walter Huber* [1999] ECR I-2779 at [45–51]. The Court explained that there should be an overall assessment of the evidence, taking into account the nature of the sign in question. A 'weak' trade mark, such as a shape, colour, or highly descriptive name will require far greater evidence of use, although there is no objection to the fact that the mark may have been used alongside another brand name or as part of the get-up of the product: *Société des Produits Nestlé SA v Mars UK Ltd*. The other factors are the market share held by the mark, how intensive, widespread, and long-standing the use of it has been, the amount invested in advertising, and what proportion of consumers recognize the mark (although the CJEU stressed that there was no fixed percentage—it all depends on the facts). Other evidence can come from those in the same line of business, as the Court said that supporting statements from chambers of commerce and other trade associations were relevant to determining acquired distinctiveness. Evidence concerning a mark's global turnover but not capable of proving that the mark had acquired distinctive character throughout the European Union is not sufficient (*Ecolab USA, Inc. v EUIPO* (Case T-150/16) ECLI:EU:T:2017:490; [2017] ETMR 40). Even though it is not necessary to provide the same types of evidence for each Member State (*Green/Yellow* (T-137/08), EU:T:2009:417), proof shall be deemed insufficient if it is not provided for certain Member States (*FOUR-BAR SHAPE* (T-112/13), EU:T:2016:735).

The challenge of complying with the *Windsurfing* criteria is shown by Case T-16/02 *Audi AG v OHIM* [2003] ECR II-5167. It was held that the applicant had failed to satisfy the test simply by filing evidence of how many cars it had sold or exported under the name TDI, because the volume of sales by itself did not prove that consumers viewed it as a trade mark.

In *Societe des Produits Nestlé SA v Cadbury UK Ltd* [2017] EWCA Civ 358; [2017] ETMR 31, it was held that an inherently non-distinctive mark can only acquire distinctive character if it is used in such a way that it can guarantee origin and in case where such a mark is used as part of, or in conjunction with, a registered trade mark, it is necessary that a significant proportion of the relevant public perceives the goods as originating from a given undertaking. By reference to the shape of the iconic London cab, the Court of Appeal held that it did not have inherent distinctive character and it had also not acquired distinctive character through use as it was not an indication of origin according to public perception (*London Taxi Corp Ltd (t/a London Taxi Co) v Frazer-Nash Research Ltd* [2017] EWCA Civ 1729; [2018] ETMR 7).

Similarly, Adidas' three parallel stripes in respect of clothing, footwear, and headgear in Class 25 were not found to have acquired distinctiveness through use on the grounds that the evidence produced, although impressive in terms of the advertising expenditure, was not linked to the mark as registered, or to relevant goods; the same applied by reference to the results of surveys which did not serve to establish that the mark had become distinctive through use (*Adidas AG v Shoe Branding Europe BVBA*, R 1515/2016-2 [2017] ETMR 22).

Use to support a claim of acquired distinctiveness under the TMA must be within the United Kingdom. This poses interesting questions when the mark is used on a website which is not targeted at UK customers (see *800-FLOWERS Trade Mark* [2002] FSR 191). In view of the discussion about trade mark function in *Arsenal Football Club v Matthew Reed*, such use might include promotional use.

Pause for reflection

Does the proviso to s. 3(1) not mean that the interests of other traders can be overridden? By reference to the scenario question, to what extent will the proviso to s. 3(1) be relevant?

11.4 Absolute grounds: specific provisions

The remaining subsections of s. 3 are specific in their application. However, because of the independent nature of the absolute grounds, even if an applicant manages to convince the Registry that the mark is unobjectionable under these other provisions, it is still possible for the application to fail under s. 3(1).

11.4.1 Shape marks

Shapes (that is, three-dimensional objects) are specifically mentioned in s. 1 as examples of trade marks. There is a separate set of absolute grounds which apply *only* to shape marks in s. 3(2) although shape marks themselves are subject to the full list of objections in s. 3. The CJEU has held, in *Linde*, that s. 3(2) is an independent ground of objection and should be applied first, *before* s. 3(1). In consequence, if an application is rejected under s. 3(2), evidence of acquired distinctiveness will be of no assistance (*Philips v Remington*). Even if the shape, or any other characteristic (as per the implementation of the recast Directive) does not fall within any of the specific prohibitions in s. 3(2), it still needs to be considered under s. 3(1) to see if it is distinctive, descriptive, or common to the trade.

The most usual objection under s. 3(1) to shape marks is that they are devoid of distinctive character. Thus in Case C-238/06P *Develey Holding GmbH v OHIM* [2007]

ECR I-9375, protection was denied to the rather ordinary appearance of a squeezable sauce bottle. Very unusual shapes may, exceptionally, be inherently distinctive; examples include Case T-128/01 *DaimlerChrysler Corporation v OHIM* [2003] ECR II-701 (a car radiator grille) and Case T-460/05 *Bang & Olufsen A/S v OHIM* [2007] ECR II-4207 (the shape of a loudspeaker). Overcoming the objections under s. 3(1) by proof of acquired distinctiveness will not be easy. Sufficient evidence of use (complying with the *Windsurfing Chiemsee* criteria) must be produced to show that consumers recognize the shape as indicating origin. Consumers do not do this readily: *Bongrain's Application* [2005] RPC 306.

 Section 3(2), it must be repeated, applies only to three-dimensional marks, not two-dimensional picture marks: *Re August Storck KG's Trade Mark Application*, Appointed Person, 9 October 2007.

11.4.1.1 The origin of s. 3(2)

The three paragraphs of s. 3(2) can be summed up as comprising natural shapes, technical shapes, and aesthetic shapes. It is generally agreed that the wording is derived from the Benelux Uniform Trade Mark Act 1971. Strowel (in 'Benelux: A Guide to the Validity of Three-dimensional Trade Marks in Europe' [1995] *EIPR* 154) gives decided examples under that legislation of the three types of prohibited shapes. For natural shapes, he suggests an egg box, an umbrella, or a carrier bag, and gives the LEGO brick as an example of a technical shape. With regard to aesthetic shapes, there have been Benelux cases involving a set of miniature china houses or a children's bath in the shape of a scallop shell. However, Strowel argues that this exclusion does not bar the registration of shapes added to foodstuffs such as chocolate, ice cream, crisps, or drink bottles. It is, he says, necessary to ask *why* the consumer bought the goods. The shape is not the prime reason for the purchase. Even if the goods cost more because of the trade mark, this is not the 'substantial' value required by the wording of the Directive. Strowel also argues that s. 3(2) is a derogation from the very broad definition of 'trade mark' in s. 1 and so should be interpreted narrowly. In implementation of the recast Directive, the TMA makes references not only to shapes but also to 'another characteristic' of goods that may either result from the nature of the goods themselves, be necessary to achieve a technical result, or give substantial value to the goods.

11.4.1.2 The policy underlying s. 3(2)

The public interest underlying s. 3(2) has been set out by the CJEU. In *Philips v Remington*, relying on its earlier statement in *Windsurfing Chiemsee* about the policy of s. 3(1)(c), the Court said that shapes falling within the wording of the provision had to be left free for all other traders to use. It would seem, therefore, that the policy of s. 3(2) is not about avoiding overlap with patents and designs, but ensuring competitors' freedom of choice.

 Pause for reflection

Going back to our scenario, can the shape of the detangling brush qualify for trade mark protection or is this a functional shape giving substantial value to the product and hence a shape that has to remain free for all other traders to use? Why does trade mark law avoid offering protection to such kinds of shapes?

11.4.1.3 The scope of the shape exclusions

Shape objections have been considered by the CJEU in a number of cases. In *Philips v Remington*, contrary to the arguments advanced by Strowel, the Court gave a relatively broad interpretation of the technical shapes exclusion, rejecting the argument that it was irrelevant that the same result could be achieved by other means. The word 'necessary' in s. 3(2)(b) was interpreted to mean 'attributable'. It added to this in Case C-48/09 P *Lego Juris A/S v OHIM* [2010] ECR I-8403 where guidance was given as to how the essential characteristics of a shape are to be determined. The Court of Justice held that 'the presence of one or more minor arbitrary elements in a three-dimensional sign, all of whose essential characteristics are dictated by the technical solution to which that sign gives effect, does not alter the conclusion that the sign consists *exclusively* of the shape of goods which is necessary to obtain a technical result' (at [52]).

The CJEU has also stated that, for the purpose of examining the functionality of the essential characteristics of a sign, the basis for consideration should be the graphical shape alone without taking into account non-visible functional elements; by reference to Rubik's cube, for instance, such elements included the rotating capability of the cube (Case C-30/15P *Simba Toys GmbH & Co KG v EUIPO*, EU:C:2016:849; [2017] ETMR 6).

In Case T-508/08 *Bang & Olufsen v OHIM* [2011] ECR II-6975, the General Court considered the aesthetic shapes exclusion. Building on existing jurisprudence, it said that the policy of s. 3(2)(c) is the same as that of s. 3(2)(b) and that the views of the consumer are not conclusive. Further, if a particular shape became a unique selling point of the product (here, the sculpture-like shape of a loudspeaker), then it was caught by the prohibition.

An interesting recent case on the third exclusion on shape trade marks (Art. 3(1)(e)(iii)) arose by reference to the distinctive red colour attached to Christian Louboutin shoes (Case C-163/16 *Christian Louboutin* et al *v Van Haren Schoenen BV*). The Advocate General issued two opinions with regards to that case (ECLI:EU:C:2017:495, ECLI:EU:C:2018:64) expressing doubts that the colour red as such could perform the essential function of a trade mark, namely to act as a badge of origin, when used out of context and not attached on the shape of the sole. In the opinion of the Advocate General, the colour mark had to be equated with a sign that consists of the shape of the goods and that '[t]he concept of a shape which "gives substantial value" to the goods . . . relates only to the intrinsic value of the shape, and does not permit the reputation of the mark or its proprietor to be taken into account'. The Court of Justice did not share the same view, however, and held that Art. 3(1)(e)(iii) had to be interpreted as meaning that a sign consisting of a colour applied to the sole of a high-heeled shoe, does not consist exclusively of a 'shape', within the meaning of that provision (ECLI:EU:C:2018:423).

No case has yet been referred to the CJEU on natural shapes.

 Pause for reflection

Is the conclusion of the CJEU in *Philips v Remington* about the meaning of s. 3(2)(b) consistent with the argument that s. 3(2) is a derogation from the policy of s. 1 and should be construed narrowly?

Note that the recast Directive has expanded the exclusions to registrability beyond shapes. Art. 4(1)(e) states that registration will be refused by reference to signs which consist exclusively of the shape, *or another characteristic*, which results from the nature of the goods themselves; the shape, *or another characteristic*, of goods which is necessary to obtain a technical result; the shape, *or another characteristic*, which gives substantial value to the goods. There have not yet been any cases shedding light on particular aspects of such characteristics but there is a pending referral before the CJEU that may offer interpretative guidance (Case C-21/18 *Textilis Ltd, Ozgur Keskin v Svenskt Tenn Aktiebolag*, OJ C 94, 12 March 2018, p. 13–14).

11.4.2 Marks contrary to public policy

Section 3(3)(a) prohibits the registration of marks contrary to public policy or morality. There are similar prohibitions against granting protection to offensive subject matter in patent and design law.

Re Ghazilian's Trade Mark Application [2001] RPC 654

The leading decision is *Re Ghazilian's Trade Mark Application* [2001] RPC 654. The case explains that what matters is not whether a section of the public considers the trade mark distasteful, but whether it would cause outrage, and so be likely significantly to undermine current religious, family, or social values. Again, we may note the role of the consumer, as the censure must be amongst an identifiable section of the public. Each case must be decided on its own facts, so a higher degree of outrage amongst a small section of the community may well suffice.

Ghazilian has been applied on several occasions, including '*standupifyouhatemanu. com*', Trade Marks Registry, 20 November 2002, where the attempt to register the name of a website as a trade mark was refused as being likely to incite football hooliganism. In *Basic Trade Mark SA's Trade Mark Application (JESUS)* [2005] RPC 611 the choice of the name JESUS was held likely to cause offence to a significant section of the public. By contrast, in *Woodman v French Connection UK Ltd*, Registry, 20 December 2005, an attempt to have the mark FCUK declared invalid as being contrary to s. 3(3)(a) failed. Although there had been complaints to the Advertising Standards Authority that the mark was too close to a particular expletive, there was no evidence to suggest that FCUK-branded goods had themselves caused outrage. Any offence that had been caused had not been as a result of the use of the mark itself, but rather by the context in which an individual trader had chosen to use the letters in promotional material.

 Pause for reflection

An interesting development of recent years has been the discussion on plain packaging for tobacco products and its relationship with public policy from a health perspective. The Standardised Packaging of Tobacco Products Regulations 2015 No. 829, which came into force on May 2016, lay down the legal framework governing tobacco products and the introduction of

→

→

rules towards their standardizing their packaging. This has the effect that the tobacco industry will no longer be in a position to rely on distinctive features or trade mark protected elements in order to distinguish their goods from those of other undertakings.

In *R (on the application of British American Tobacco (UK) Ltd) and Others v Secretary of State for Health* [2016] EWHC 1169 (Admin); [2016] ETMR 38, tobacco companies claimed that the Regulations were in breach of their fundamental right to respect for property, including their trade marks and goodwill and this resulted in unlawful expropriation of their property rights without fair compensation. Green J rejected these claims holding that the limitation of such property rights is done for entirely proper and legitimate reasons, in an attempt to reach a fair balance between the property right and public health.

Note that s. 13 of the Regulations states that nothing in these Regulations forms an obstacle to the registration of a trade mark under the TMA or gives rise to a ground for the declaration of invalidity of a registered trade mark under s. 47(1) of that Act (grounds for invalidity of registration).

11.4.3 Deceptive marks

Section 3(3)(b) prohibits the registration of trade marks which are deceptive to the public, for example as to the nature of the goods. Here, the legislation places the applicant in a dilemma. The easiest route will be to choose a known word as a means of selling goods. However, there is a fine line between descriptiveness and deceptiveness. As explained in *ORLWOOLA Trade Mark* (1909) 26 RPC 683, 850, (and it is important to remember how the mark would have been spoken) if the goods are as described by the known word (here the goods were textiles) the mark is unregistrable because it is totally descriptive. If the goods do not possess those properties, the mark is deceptive. The assessment of deceptiveness under s. 3(3)(b) is effected through the eyes of the reasonably well-informed, observant yet circumspect consumer who is used to 'hype' (*Kraft Jacobs Suchard Ltd's Application (KENCO THE REAL COFFEE EXPERTS)* [2001] ETMR 585).

Case C-259/04 *Emanuel v Continental Shelf 128 Ltd* [2006] ECR I-3089

The CJEU has provided guidance on deceptive marks. In Case C-259/04 *Emanuel v Continental Shelf 128 Ltd* [2006] ECR I-3089, the applicant for revocation was a famous fashion designer whose reputation increased dramatically when she created the wedding dress for the Princess of Wales in 1981. A trade mark consisting of her name and a logo was registered in 1994. As a result of financial difficulties, she had assigned her business to a company in 1996, becoming an employee of the business. Thereafter, there were successive transfers of the business which ultimately was owned by the defendant. In the meantime, the applicant had resigned. The defendant's predecessor had applied to register further marks consisting of the applicant's name. She opposed these applications under s. 3(3)(b) and sought revocation of the earlier mark under s. 46(1)(d) on the ground that it had become deceptive as to the origin of the goods. The CJEU ruled that the word 'deceive' in Art. 3 of the Directive referred to the intrinsic

→

→

characteristics of the trade mark. The sign must objectively deceive the public by virtue of its qualities. Where the trade mark was a person's name and had been assigned as part of the business, it did not deceive the public even if it created the mistaken impression that that person took part in the creation of the goods for which the mark was used.

 Pause for reflection

Going back to our scenario question, could the descriptive statement 'super intensive treatment' be also seen as deceptive? Why, or why not?

11.4.4 Marks contrary to law and specially protected emblems

Section 3(4) and s. 3(5) can be considered together. Respectively, they prohibit the registration of trade marks which are contrary to United Kingdom or EU law and trade marks consisting of or containing specially protected emblems. Section 3(4) includes trade marks which breach UK legislation, such as the Trade Descriptions Act 1968, the Plant Varieties Act 1997, the Hallmarking Act 1973, or the London Olympic Games and Paralympic Games Act 2006. EU secondary legislation includes EC Regulation 510/2006 on the protection of geographical indications and designations of origin for agricultural products and foodstuffs ([2006] OJ L 93/12). This enables geographical names to be registered where the area produces food or drink with unique properties (for example 'Stilton' for cheese).

Section 3(5) is amplified by s. 4, which deals in detail with such matters as the Royal Coats of Arms, words indicating royal patronage, national flags, and the flags and emblems of international organizations. An illustration is *COMBINED ARMED FORCES FEDERATION Trade Mark*, Registry, 24 July 2009, where it was held that a combination of the Union Flag, the words of the applicant organization, and a crown would lead the average consumer to think that the user of the mark had royal patronage or mislead them into believing that it was an organ of the state.

11.4.5 Marks obtained in bad faith

Lastly, s. 3(6) prohibits the registration of a trade mark to the extent that the application was made in bad faith. 'Bad faith' was considered by the Court of Appeal in *Harrison v Teton Valley Trading Co (CHINA WHITE)* [2004] 1 WLR 2577. It said that the objection is only available in limited circumstances, where the applicant's conduct amounts to dishonesty or where the applicant's conduct falls short of the standards of acceptable commercial behaviour observed by reasonable and experienced men in the area in question. The test involves a mixture of the subjective and objective: there must be a realization by the applicant that what he was doing would be regarded by honest people as in bad faith. According to the Court of Appeal, this requires an inquiry into what the applicant knew, and whether a reasonable person would think the conduct was wrong. However, it is not necessary to show that the applicant thought that what he was doing was dishonest: *AJIT WEEKLY Trade Mark* [2006] RPC 633, Appointed Person.

'Bad faith' has been considered by the CJEU in Case C-529/07 *Chocoladefabriken Lindt & Sprüngli AG v Franz Hauswirth GmbH* [2009] ECR I-4893. Although the Advocate General provided a comprehensive review of the meaning of the phrase, the Court's ruling gives little clear guidance. The Court simply lists the factors to be taken into account and leaves the matter to be determined by the national court. These are only indicative and account can be taken of other factors, such as the origin of the contested sign and its use since its creation (*PayPal, Inc v EUIPO/Hub Culture Ltd* (Case T-132/16) [2017] ETMR 30).

An example of bad faith is attempting to register a mark knowing that it belongs to someone else (*MICKEY DEES (NIGHTCLUB) Trade Mark* [1998] RPC 359) or with a view to foreclosing the use of the mark by other traders (*Imperial Group plc v Philip Morris Ltd* [1982] FSR 72). However, there is no bad faith where there is a degree of uncertainty as to entitlement: *Gromax Plasticulture Ltd v Don & Low Nonwovens Ltd* [1999] RPC 367. Applying for a two-dimensional mark when it will be used in a three-dimensional form is not, without more, evidence of bad faith: *Robert McBride Ltd's Application* [2005] ETMR 990.

 Pause for reflection

Are the policy grounds underlying the various parts of s. 3 consistent? If not, does it matter?

11.4.6 New absolute grounds

The recast Directive lists yet three more absolute grounds for the refusal or invalidity of trade marks. These are listed in Art. 4(1)(j)–(l) and have been introduced in UK law as ss. 4A-4D. They include trade marks which are excluded from registration pursuant to Union legislation or international agreements to which the Union is party, providing for protection of traditional terms for wine; trade marks which are excluded from registration pursuant to Union legislation or international agreements to which the Union is party, providing for protection of traditional specialities guaranteed; trade marks which consist of, or reproduce in their essential elements, an earlier plant variety denomination registered in accordance with Union legislation or the national law of the Member State concerned, or international agreements to which the Union or the Member State concerned is party, providing protection for plant variety rights, and which are in respect of plant varieties of the same or closely related species.

11.5 Conclusion

In this chapter, we discussed the absolute grounds for refusing trade mark applications. We have seen that in implementation of the Directive, s. 3 TMA contains a list of situations where the intellectual property office may refuse to register the trademark (or it may later invalidate the trade mark). A mark, for example, may lose its status as a trade mark if is not recognized as distinctive by the relevant section of the market or if it has become the generic term of particular goods or services. We have seen that absolute grounds for refusal are that: the mark does not meet the requirements for the definition of a trade mark; it is devoid of distinctive character; it is made of signs or symbols that describe qualities or features of the relevant goods or services; it has become customary in current language; it consists purely of the shape of goods or their packaging; and/ or it is contrary to public policy or morality. Applicants can overcome the absolute ground(s) of refusal of lack of distinctiveness if they can demonstrate that the mark has acquired distinctiveness through use, as per the proviso of s. 3(3).

By reference to the scenario question, JollyBrush should be advised about their chances in registering and retaining registration of each one of the marks in question. Regarding the neologisms, 'CareTangle' and 'CareHair', the CJEU has said in *BIOMILD* and *POSTKANTOOR* that the mark, looked at as a whole, will not be registered 'unless the mark as a whole creates, both aurally and visually, an impression far removed from that produced by a simple combination'. The word 'CareTangle' is an unusual word combination and it is very likely that it can attract protection as a trade mark by reference to the goods at issue, namely goods falling under Class 21 of the Nice Classification. 'CareHair' is also an invented word (a combination of two known words) that can be seen as 'syntactically unusual' under the test developed in Case C-383/99 P *Procter & Gamble Company v OHIM (BABY DRY)* [2001] ECR I-6251 and can be registered for goods in Class 3. However, it may be subject to absolute grounds on the basis that the invented word tends to become customary in current language; should this be the case, the mark will become generic, even if registration is initially successful, and may be invalidated.

Regarding the registration of colours, the test requires considering the mark in relation to the list of goods and services through the eyes of the reasonably attentive consumer: does such a person regard the sign as a trade mark, taking into account all the relevant circumstances, keeping in mind that the average consumer will make an overall assessment of the mark? As regards the registration of a single colour, e.g. in the present case the colour fuchsia, the CJEU has clarified in *Libertel*, that the public interest was aimed at the need not to restrict unduly the availability of *colours* for other traders in the same field of business (the Court did not refer to 'trade marks' generally). In later cases, such as *Nichols* and *SAT.2* the CJEU clarified that it is enough that the trade mark enables consumers to identify the origin of the product. The same applies to colour combinations, such as the combination of fuchsia and gold; however, applicants should be familiar with the requirements established in *Heidelberger Bauchemie GmbH v Deutsches Patent- und Markenamt* [2004] ECR I-6129, which we examined in chapter 10, where the CJEU said that the representation must include a systematic arrangement associating the colours in a predetermined and uniform way. JollyBrush should be advised about the changes to UK trade mark law by reference to the graphic representation requirement.

By reference to the shape of the brush, three-dimensional objects are expressly mentioned in s. 1 as examples of trade marks and they are in principle protected. However, a separate set of absolute grounds apply to shape marks in s. 3(2). On the basis of the CJEU ruling in *Linde*, s. 3(2) is an independent ground of objection and should be applied first, *before* s. 3(1), meaning that when an application is rejected under s. 3(2), evidence of acquired distinctiveness will be of no assistance (*Philips v Remington*). The shape of Jolly-Brush's brush cannot be registered as a UK trade mark as it falls under the exclusion of s. 3(2). On the basis of the facts given, the shape is necessary in order to achieve a technical result and, secondarily, it gives substantial value to the product as such. The underlying rationale for this exclusion is the public interest. The CJEU elaborated on this matter in *Philips v Remington*, holding that shapes falling within the wording of the provision had to be left free for all other traders to use. In that case, the word 'necessary' featuring in s. 3(2)(b) was interpreted to mean 'attributable' and it seems that the half-moon shape of the JollyBrush product relies on that shape in order to achieve its intended objective.

JollyBrush should be advised that s. 3(1)(c) bars registration of geographical names (such as 'Bath, Somerset') the meaning of which has been defined in Cases C-108/97 and 109/97 *Windsurfing Chiemsee Produktions und Vertriebs GmbH v Boots und Segelzubehor Walter Huber* [1999] ECR I-2779. Geographical names can only be registered to the extent that they can function as badges of trade origin, not geographical origin. This can be the case with some 'fanciful' geographical names (such as 'North Pole' for bananas) because consumers are unlikely to believe that those goods originate from that location. It is not likely that 'Bath, Somerset' for beauty products, such as a nourishing hair mask, can serve as an indication of origin, unless JollyBrush is in a position to prove that it has acquired a distinctive character as a result of use. It is more likely that the geographical name will be registered by reference to the hairbrush.

Finally, by reference to the words 'super intensive treatment', they cannot be registered as they are exclusively descriptive, falling under the prohibition of s. 3(1)(c).

End-of-chapter questions

After reading the chapter carefully, try answering the following questions. For answer guidance visit the online resources at **www.oup.com/uk/karapapa-mcdonagh/**

1. Why are geographical names excluded from registration as UK trade marks according to s. 3(1)(c) TMA?

2. Under which conditions are marks considered to be devoid of distinctive character by virtue of s. 3(1)(b) TMA?

3. What is the rationale behind the exclusion of marks that have become customary in the current language, or in the *bona fide* and established practices of the trade by virtue of s. 3(1)(d) TMA?

4. To what extent and under which conditions can absolute grounds be overcome?

5. To what extent, can shapes be registered as UK trade marks?

Further reading

For understanding the protection available to trade marks, the following readings are recommended:

Anemaet, L. 'The Public Domain is Under Pressure—Why We Should not Rely on Empirical Data when Assessing Trade Mark Distinctiveness' [2016] 47(3) *IIC* 303

Argues that the threshold for assuming acquired distinctiveness is not efficient enough and should therefore be applied more restrictively.

Bonadio, E. 'Plain Packaging of Tobacco Products Under EU Intellectual Property Law' [2012] 34(9) *EIPR* 599
Offers an overview of the legal problems surrounding plain packaging for tobacco products.

Calboli, I. 'Chocolate, Fashion, Toys and Cabs: the Misunderstood Distinctiveness of Non-Traditional Trademarks' [2018] 49 *IIC* 1
Argues that the expansion of protection to non-traditional marks can have serious effects on market competition as these signs often protect products or parts of products.

Chronopoulos, A. 'De Jure Functionality of Shapes Driven by Technical Considerations in Manufacturing Methods' [2017] 3 *IPQ* 286
Examines the application of the functionality doctrine to cases where the assertion of trade mark rights in product shapes or features is bound to interfere with the ability of the public to practise unpatented methods of manufacture.

Firth, A. Gredley, E., and Maniatis, S. 'Shapes as Trade Marks: Public Policy, Functional Considerations and Consumer Perception' [2001] 23 *EIPR* 86
Explains the underlying policy issues regarding the registration of shape trade marks and the role of the consumer in deciding registrability.

Geiger, C. and Machado Pontes, L. 'Trade Mark Registration, Public Policy, Morality and Fundamental Rights', Centre for International Intellectual Property Studies (CEIPI) Research Paper, No. 2017-01, 2017, 29
Considers if the practices with regard to the refusal to register immoral trade marks on morality and public policy grounds take sufficiently into account fundamental rights.

Gielen, C. 'Substantial Value Rule: how it Came into Being and why it Should be Abolished' [2014] 36 *EIPR* 164
Argues for the abolition of art.3(1)(e) Trade Marks Directive, according to which shapes that give substantial value to the goods are excluded from protection as trade marks.

Griffiths, A. 'Modernising Trade Mark Law and Promoting Economic Efficiency: an Evaluation of the BABY DRY Judgment and its Aftermath' [2003] 1 *IPQ* 1–37
Considers the impact of BABY DRY in the light of the economic role fulfilled by trade marks.

Griffiths, J. 'Is There a Right to an Immoral Trade Mark?' in P. Torremans, ed., *Intellectual Property and Human Rights* (Kluwer Law International, 2008), 309
Considers the influence of the right to freedom of expression under Article 10 of the European Convention on Human Rights upon United Kingdom and European trade mark law.

Strowel, A. 'Benelux: A Guide to the Validity of Three-dimensional Trade Marks in Europe' [1995] 3 *EIPR* 154
Explains the origins of s. 3(2) of the TMA and argues for a narrow interpretation.

12 Relative grounds for refusal of registration

Problem question

Read this problem question carefully and keep it in mind while you are working through the chapter that follows. At the end of this chapter, you will be able to apply what you have learnt to the problem question and advise the relevant parties.

You receive the following email from a new client, Paul Jonas:

As you know, we have two registered UK trade marks for our products (mostly pens and markers but also stationery in general) since May 2002: the word mark LEO and a figurative mark featuring the word LEO in red fonts and the face of a lion replacing the letter O for Class 16, including stationery and office requisites, such as writing paper, paper-clips, folders for papers, paper sheets, drawing pens, fountain pens, pens, marking pens, balls for ball-point pens, pencils, charcoal pencils, pencil sharpening machines, pencil sharpeners.

On 5 September 2018, we were notified that a company engaging in 3D printing has applied to register the mark LEONE for products falling in Class 6, including metals in foil or powder form for 3D printers, and Class 7, 3D printers and 3D printing pens. They also plan to use the face of a lion instead of the letter O, although it is designed very differently from ours. They've not started selling under the name LEONE yet.

On 21 September 2018, we found out that a newly established Birmingham-based company called Aster Pencils Ltd that is also manufacturing stationery has applied to register the mark LIO for products in Class 16, including stationary and office requisites. Instead of the letter I in LIO they plan to use the image of a pen. Is there anything we can do to stop them from using this mark? We fear that when they put their products in the market our customers will be confused that both LEO and LIO are our products.

Finally, we found out yesterday that a company operating in the production of tissues and toilet paper has applied to register the name NEO for products in class 16, including toilet/hygienic paper, bibs of paper, towels of paper, tissues of paper for removing make-up. They currently trade under the registered UK trade mark NEONEX. NEO is written with very similar fonts as LEO. We are very uncomfortable with this development

→

→ *as we fear the risks to our reputation; we are in the market selling quality writing paper and notepads for over 15 years and we are very uncomfortable with a company using such a similar mark to ours by reference to toilet paper.*

Can you please advise?

London, 15 October 2018

Paul Jonas

12.1 Introduction

Whilst absolute grounds are concerned with an analysis of a proposed mark's innate qualities (e.g. their capacity to be distinctive), covering defects in the mark as such, relative grounds involve a comparison of the mark with prior rights (even unregistered rights), with what is already 'out there'. In particular, relative grounds occur when a mark applied for is already in use or when a similar mark is already in use. The Trade Marks Act ('TMA'), s. 5, recognizes three instances in which relative grounds for refusal will succeed:

a. Where the sign is identical to an earlier sign and the goods and/or services applied for are also identical;

b. Where the sign is identical to an earlier sign and the goods and/or services applied for are similar;

c. Where the sign is similar to an earlier sign and the goods and/or services applied for are identical or similar.

Unlike absolute grounds, where anyone can in principle oppose an application, it is only the proprietor of an earlier trade mark or earlier right that may oppose an application on relative grounds.

If the mark conflicts with an earlier mark (whether registered or unregistered) or an earlier copyright or design, then the application will be rejected. Such an objection can be overcome by obtaining the consent of the owner of the earlier right under s. 5(5) of the TMA.

Note that the principal provisions in the TMA dealing with relative grounds (s. 5(1), s. 5(2) and s. 5(3)) are a mirror image of s. 10(1), s. 10(2), and s. 10(3) setting out the owner's rights in infringement.

12.2 Overview of relative grounds

Relative grounds for refusal of trade mark applications are listed in s. 5. Judge Bornkamm (in 'Harmonising Trade Mark Law in Europe: the Stephen Stewart Memorial Lecture' [1999] 3 *IPQ* 283) calls the two sets of provisions, derived respectively from Arts 4 and 5 of the Directive, the 'triad of protection'. Both s. 5 (and the 'mirror provisions' of s. 10 on infringement) cover three distinct situations, in the case of relative grounds when

DIAGRAM 12.1 *Relative grounds: the 'triad of protection'*

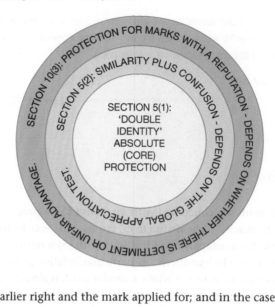

comparing the earlier right and the mark applied for; and in the case of infringement, the registered mark and the infringing sign.

These three situations comprise in essence: double identity between the marks and their respective goods and services; identity and/or similarity between the marks and their goods and services in circumstances where there is a likelihood of confusion; and cases where the senior mark has a reputation which deserves protection against those wishing to take unfair advantage of its distinctive character.

The case law of the Court of Justice of the European Union ('CJEU') on the interpretation of Arts 4 and 5 is completely interchangeable. Just as with the absolute grounds, the average consumer is the person through whose eyes the facts are decided.

The triad of protection can be explained in another way, as set out in Diagram 12.1. There is the absolute 'core' of protection when there is identity between the marks and their products; an outer, more flexible 'core' of protection dependent on similarity and confusion; and an outer rim of protection available only for those marks with a reputation. There is, however, a clear difference between the inner two zones and the outer zone. The former accord with the traditional role of the trade mark in protecting against consumer confusion, the latter is essentially concerned with protecting the owner of the mark against misappropriation. Whichever zone of protection is in issue, however, there must be either identity or similarity of marks. There is no protection against a dissimilar trade mark.

12.3 The list of prior rights

The lengthy list of prior rights comprises earlier registered marks which have effect in the United Kingdom (whether they are on the domestic, EU, or international registers); earlier pending applications for national, EU, or international registrations, provided they mature to registration; subsequent EU registrations claiming seniority from earlier UK or international registrations; well-known trade marks entitled to protection under the Paris Convention; recently lapsed registrations; earlier used but unregistered marks (provided they are capable of protection under passing off); and earlier copyrights, or registered or unregistered designs. Of these, the most important are earlier registered marks.

The list results from a combination of s. 6 and s. 5(4) TMA.

12.4 Applying the provisions

Each of s. 5(1), 5(2), and 5(3) (forming the 'triad of protection') has specific criteria. They must be applied systematically in sequence: *Reed Executive plc v Reed Business Information Ltd* [2004] RPC 767. If the application does not fall within s. 5(1) (because there is absence of identity in either the mark or the goods) you go to s. 5(2). If there is no similarity of goods, or if there is an absence of confusion, you go to s. 5(3).

12.5 Double identity

Section 5(1) provides that a trade mark shall not be registered if it is identical to an earlier mark and is in respect of identical goods and services. There is no need to prove confusion. It is assumed that there will be consumer confusion in cases of total identity: Case C-2/00 *Hölterhoff v Ulrich Freiesleben* [2002] ECR I-4187. The assessment takes place through the eyes of the notional average consumer.

12.5.1 Deciding identity

When deciding whether there is identity for the purposes of s. 5(1), the register entry for the senior mark is crucial. So, the statement of goods on the applicant's Form TM3 is compared with those for which the senior mark is *actually* registered. If the goods are not identical, the case falls under s. 5(2) (*British Sugar*). Likewise, the junior mark as it appears on Form TM3 is compared with how the senior mark is shown on the register: *Philips v Remington* (at p. 312). Where the senior mark is a word, what is registered is the word itself, so the type of lettering is irrelevant: *Bravado Merchandising v Mainstream Publishing* [1996] FSR 205.

12.5.2 The test for identity of marks

Case C-291/00 *LTJ Diffusion SA v Sadas Vertbaudet SA* [2003] ECR I-2799

The test for an identical mark was explained by the CJEU in Case C-291/00 *LTJ Diffusion SA v Sadas Vertbaudet SA* [2003] ECR I-2799 at [50–54]. The Court said that because protection is absolute under s. 5(1) and s. 10(1), 'identity' must be strictly interpreted. The two marks must be the same in all respects. The mark applied for must reproduce, without any modification, all the elements of the senior mark. The Court added that the comparison (an overall one) is made ➡

> → through the eyes of the well-informed, reasonably observant, and circumspect consumer. The consumer will rarely have the opportunity to compare the two marks side by side so that insignificant differences may go unnoticed (this last point is sometimes referred to as the 'doctrine of imperfect recollection'). The consumer's circumstances may mean that the test is not as absolute as might be supposed.

The CJEU did not elaborate on what it meant by 'insignificant differences'. On the facts of the case itself, the addition of a dot over the mark was thought to be insignificant. But what if the mark applied for is ORIGINS when the senior mark is ORIGIN, or HUGGAR when the senior mark is HUGGER? Would the average consumer notice the difference?

12.5.3 Where the senior mark is contained in the junior mark

Where the senior mark is contained within the junior mark (i.e. surrounded by additional words or pictorial matter rather than where the junior mark has more letters), for example, the senior mark is REED and the junior mark is REED ELSEVIER, how is the comparison to be made? In *Reed Executive plc v Reed Business Information Ltd* the Court of Appeal thought it important to decide whether the surrounding matter had trade mark significance (i.e. did it send the consumer a 'trade mark message'?). If it did, then the marks were to be examined to see if they were similar. If it did not, the surrounding non-trade mark matter could be ignored, and the marks would be treated as identical. In the *Reed* case, it was held that ELSEVIER had trade mark significance, so what had to be compared was REED with REED ELSEVIER.

 Pause for reflection

Is the CJEU guidance in *LTJ* as to how identity of marks is to be decided sufficiently clear? How can the test be absolute yet permit insignificant differences to be ignored?

Does the double identity ground apply to any of the cases mentioned in the scenario question? Why not? How is similarity between the junior and senior mark to be assessed?

12.6 Similarity coupled with confusion

Section 5(2) TMA prohibits the registration of a mark which is identical or similar to an earlier registered mark and which is to be for similar or identical goods and services, provided there exists a likelihood of confusion on the part of the public, 'which includes a likelihood of association'.

12.6.1 The scope of s. 5(2)

Section 5(2) offers a figurative outline of a total of 10 permutations, which we set out in Table 12.1:

TABLE 12.1 *Section 5(2) permutations*

A mark applied for in respect of goods will be prevented from achieving registration by the presence on the Register of:	A mark applied for in respect of services will be prevented from achieving registration by the presence on the Register of:
an identical mark in relation to similar goods	an identical mark in relation to similar services
an identical mark in relation to similar services	an identical mark in relation to similar goods
a similar mark in relation to identical goods	a similar mark in relation to identical services
a similar mark in relation to similar goods	a similar mark in relation to similar services
a similar mark in relation to similar services	a similar mark in relation to similar goods

However, whatever the combination is, the overarching requirement is that there must be a likelihood of confusion.

12.6.2 Types of confusion

Section 5(2) demands that there must be a likelihood of confusion 'which includes a likelihood of association'. There is a likelihood of confusion if the association between the marks creates a risk that consumers will wrongly believe that the goods or services come from the same or from economically linked undertakings. Mere association, in that the later mark brings the earlier mark to mind, does not suffice (*Realistic Games Ltd v Goal.com (Holdco) SA* (O/528/17) [2018] ETMR 6).

Case law has identified three types of confusion. First, there may be direct confusion, where the consumer confuses one product with another. Second, there may be indirect confusion, where the consumer thinks that the goods come from an economically linked undertaking or that the trade mark owner has expanded their business. Last, there may be 'mere' association. The consumer 'calls the trade mark to mind' but is not misled about the origin of the goods. This is sometimes referred to as 'non-origin confusion'.

12.6.3 The problem of 'likelihood of association'

The origin of the phrase 'likelihood of association' in the Directive is said to be the Uniform Benelux Trade Marks Act 1971. An example of a case under that legislation is *MONOPOLY v ANTI-MONOPOLY* [1978] BIE 39 and 43. Here it was held that to call a board game 'Anti-Monopoly' would not confuse customers. However, it would make them think of 'Monopoly' and would therefore injure (by dilution) the reputation of the senior mark.

12.6.3.1 The United Kingdom approach

The interpretation of s. 10(2) (and by implication s. 5(2)) was examined by Laddie J in *Wagamama Ltd v City Centre Restaurants* [1995] FSR 713. He applied normal rules of statutory interpretation, and held that 'likelihood of association' was included within the notion of 'likelihood of confusion'. Laddie J rejected all arguments (referring to them as 'Chinese whispers') that the Benelux meaning of association should be incorporated into United Kingdom law. To do so would enhance the trade mark right far too much.

12.6.3.2 The CJEU's approach

> #### Case C-251/95 *Sabel BV v Puma AG* [1997] ECR I-6191
>
> The CJEU first examined the meaning of 'likelihood of confusion' in Case C-251/95 *Sabel BV v Puma AG* [1997] ECR I-6191. Up to a point, the Court agrees with Wagamama (but it should be remembered that the ECJ is not in a hierarchical relationship with national courts). However, the CJEU went much further than Wagamama in its treatment of 'likelihood of association'. It declared that association was not an alternative to confusion but 'serves to define its scope' (at [18]). In other words, although 'calling the trade mark to mind' does not amount to confusion (Case C-425/98 *Marca Mode CV v Adidas AG and Adidas Benelux BV* [2000] ECR I-4861), the thought processes of the average consumer, and the associations which that person makes when seeing the junior mark, play a part in proving confusion. For the purposes of s. 5(2), though, only direct and indirect confusion will suffice.

12.6.3.3 The role of association

Association is not totally irrelevant. It is involved in the way in which direct confusion is assessed, and helps to show indirect confusion. This is attributable to two things, namely Recital 11 to the Directive (as numbered in the consolidated version) and the CJEU's 'global appreciation' test used to determine the likelihood of confusion. Further, 'association' is crucial in the protection for marks with a reputation under s. 5(3).

> **Pause for reflection**
>
> How important is association under s. 5(2)?

12.6.4 The application of s. 5(2)

Recital 11 to the consolidated version of the Directive is the starting point in the application of s. 5(2). It declares that the appreciation of confusion 'depends on numerous elements, in particular, the recognition of the trade mark on the market, of the association which can be made with the used or registered sign, the degree of similarity between the trade mark and the sign and between the goods or services identified'. The Recital mentions two elements of the consumer's comparison of the senior and junior marks, namely 'the recognition of the trade mark' and 'the association which can be made'. Whether or not there is a likelihood of confusion is a question of fact in every case. From *Sabel v Puma*, the issues in s. 5(2) are dealt with in the following order:

12.6.4.1 Similarity of marks

As a precondition to the application of s. 5(2), there must be at least *some* similarity between the senior and junior mark: Case 106/03 P *Vedial SA v OHIM* [2004] ECR I-9573 at [51], [54]. If there is no similarity, the senior mark has no protection.

The first task is to decide whether there is identity or similarity between the two marks, as s. 5(2) covers both. Identity is decided using the test in *LTJ*. If the marks are not identical, are they similar? The CJEU's advice on how to determine similarity of marks was influenced by cases decided under the Benelux Uniform Trade Mark Law 1971, for example, *Union v Union Soleure*, 20 May 1983, Case A 82/5 [1984] BIE 137. In *Sabel v Puma* at [23] the Court said that similarity depends on an aural, visual, and conceptual comparison based on the overall impression given by the marks bearing in mind their distinctive components. To put this another way, how are the words spoken, how do they appear on paper, and what is their underlying idea? The CJEU in *Sabel* added that these issues are decided from the viewpoint of the average consumer, who is assumed to make an overall comparison without going into minute detail.

Case T-112/06 *Inter-Ikea Systems BV v OHIM (IKEA/IDEA)*
[2008] ECR II-212

A good illustration of the aural, visual, and conceptual comparison which must be made and how each of the three elements is to be balanced against the other is Case T-112/06 *Inter-Ikea Systems BV v OHIM (IKEA/IDEA)* [2008] ECR II-212. The Court began by confirming that the average consumer here would be very attentive, as furniture (the goods in question) would only be bought after a period of reflection. When comparing the marks visually, the Court noted that the junior mark had a very dominant figurative element, whilst the senior mark consisted of just a single word. There was only a low degree of aural similarity because even though the sequence of vowel sounds were the same, the consonants 'd' and 'k' were spoken very differently, using different parts of the mouth. Last, there was no conceptual similarity, since the word 'idea' was a word generally understood by the European public whilst 'ikea' was a neologism with no obvious meaning and therefore no associations. There was no similarity.

In *Lloyd* (at [22–23]) the Court expanded on its comment in *Sabel v Puma* about 'the distinctive components' of a mark. The national court had to make an overall assessment of ability of the senior mark to guarantee the origin of goods, including whether it was inherently distinctive and whether it had any descriptive element. In addition, other factors included the market share held by the mark, how intensively and widespread it had been used, how much its owner had spent on advertising, what percentage of consumers recognized it, and how other traders perceived it—in other words, the same list of factors as appears in *Windsurfing Chiemsee* for the purpose of deciding factual distinctiveness under the proviso to s. 3(1).

An example of similar marks can be found in *Neutrogena v Golden Ltd t/a Laboratoires Garnier* [1996] RPC 473 where Jacob J held that NEUTRALIA was similar to

NEUTROGENA. Both marks were for skin care products, and the prefix 'neutra' conveyed the idea to the average shopper that the goods were kind to the skin. The average supermarket shopper would ignore the second part of each word, and would certainly not make a detailed comparison between the two names.

What if the senior mark is included in the junior mark? We have already considered, in the context of s. 5(1) how the Court of Appeal (in *Reed Executive plc v Reed Business Information Ltd*) compared REED with REED ELSEVIER.

Case C-120/04 *Medion AG v Thomson Multimedia Sales* [2005] ECR I-8551

In Case C-120/04 *Medion AG v Thomson Multimedia Sales* [2005] ECR I-8551, the CJEU offered advice on how LIFE (the senior mark) should be compared with THOMSON LIFE when both marks were used on electronic goods. It said that overall assessment of the two marks would make the notional consumer think that the owner of LIFE had expanded its business, leading to indirect confusion. It did not matter that LIFE was not the dominant part of THOMSON LIFE. To require that the senior mark formed the dominant part of the junior mark would in effect deny protection to the senior mark.

Where the only similarity between the marks arose from a common element with low distinctiveness, that tends to weigh against there being a likelihood of confusion (*Whyte & Mackay Ltd v Origin Wine UK Ltd* [2015] EWHC 1271 (Ch)). Such a situation does not preclude a finding of likelihood of confusion but it is a relevant factor and in an appropriate case it may be decisive. Where it is the common concept that is non-distinctive there is no likelihood of confusion (*Nicoventures Holdings Ltd v London Vape Co Ltd* [2017] EWHC 3393 (Ch)).

 Pause for reflection

Is any of the marks applied for that are listed in the scenario question similar to LEO for the purposes of s. 5(2)? Which ones?

12.6.4.2 Similarity of goods

Next, once it is shown that the marks are at least not dissimilar, the goods must be compared.

Case C-39/97 *Canon KK v Metro-Goldwyn-Mayer Inc* [1998] ECR I-5507

The test is that established in Case C-39/97 *Canon KK v Metro-Goldwyn-Mayer Inc* [1998] ECR I-5507. The CJEU explained (at [23]) that all relevant factors must be taken into account, including the nature of the goods, the end users, the method of use, and whether the goods are in competition with each other or are complementary. Whether the goods of both marks

→

> appear in the same class within the Nice Classification of Goods and Services 1957 is of no assistance, as the classification is there for administrative purposes. The *Canon* test depends entirely on the facts of each case.

The test in *Canon* is slightly different from the one adopted in *British Sugar*, where Jacob J reworked the criteria set out in *Jellinek's Application* (1946) 63 RPC 59 (a case decided under the 1938 Act). Though the tests are similar, the one in *British Sugar* is narrower as it asks whether the goods are in competition with each other (i.e. one could be substituted for the other), which is not the same as asking whether the goods are complementary. 'Complementary goods' (for example shoes and shoe polish) are an example of indirect confusion and shows that the CJEU's test is broader. Another issue mentioned in *British Sugar* which is not in the *Canon* test is where the respective goods might be located in a supermarket: given that different supermarkets do not have the same layout and that anyway, the layout is often changed to reflect 'special offers', this is surely not relevant to the issue of similarity.

12.6.4.3 The global appreciation test

According to *Sabel v Puma* and *Canon*, the final aspect of deciding whether there is a likelihood of confusion is to apply the 'global appreciation' test: in other words all the elements are considered together, or, as the CJEU said in *Canon*, there is an interdependence of factors. If the two marks are conceptually similar, and the senior mark has a particularly distinctive character, either inherently, or because of how much it has been used, there will be a greater likelihood of confusion. On the other hand, if (as in *Sabel* itself) the senior mark has hardly been used, and is one of many on the register with the same underlying idea (here, a wild cat) then the chances of confusion are far lower. Further, in *Canon*, the Court said that a lesser degree of similarity between the goods and services could be offset by a greater degree of similarity between the marks and vice versa. In that case, although the goods were not particularly similar (photographic equipment versus video cassettes), because the senior mark was inherently strong, had been extensively used, and heavily promoted, and because the two marks were very close (CANON versus CANNON) there was a likelihood of confusion. As the Court put it in *Lloyd*, the strength of the senior mark may have the effect of making less similar goods similar, or the closeness of the goods may make the junior mark more similar to the senior mark.

The 'global appreciation' test is entirely different from that applied by United Kingdom courts in the early days of the 1994 TMA. In *British Sugar*, it was held that 'likelihood of confusion' was only to be considered *after* it had been established *sequentially* that the goods and the marks were similar. Only notional and fair use of both senior and junior marks was to be assumed; in other words, no account was taken of the circumstances surrounding the senior mark. This 'sterile' test (there was no interdependence of factors) was based on the decision *Smith Hayden & Co Ltd's Application* (1946) 63 RPC 71 under the 1938 Act. Since *Sabel* and *Canon*, the CJEU's more flexible approach has been assimilated into UK case law. An example can be found in *BALMORAL Trade Mark* [1999] RPC 297. In *Reed Executive plc v Reed Business Information Ltd*, the Court of Appeal accepted that in the case of a used trade mark, the circumstances surrounding such use must be taken into account when determining confusion.

 Pause for reflection

Does the global appreciation test provide certainty when dealing with likelihood of confusion? By reference to the scenario question, does s. 5(2) apply to any of the marks applied for? Which ones?

12.7 Marks with a reputation

Section 5(3) contains the final part of Bornkamm's 'triad of protection'. It provides that an earlier registration of the identical or similar mark will prevent the registration of the junior mark where the earlier mark has acquired a reputation and the use of the later mark without due cause would take unfair advantage of or be detrimental to the distinctive character or repute of the earlier mark. The subsection was amended by The Trade Marks (Proof of Use) Regulations 2004 (SI 2004/946), prompted by the CJEU's rulings in Case C-292/00 *Davidoff & Cie SA and Zino Davidoff v Gofkid Ltd* [2003] ECR I-389 and Case C-408/01 *Adidas-Saloman AG and Adidas Benelux BV v Fitnessworld Trading Ltd* [2003] ECR I-12537. Although Art. 4(4)(a) and Art. 5(2) of the Directive (the origins, respectively, of s. 5(3) and s. 10(3)) required the senior mark to be registered for *dissimilar* goods or services, the Court said that there would be a gap in the scheme of protection if the owner of a mark with a reputation could not object to a junior mark where the goods were similar, in circumstances where there was no likelihood of confusion. The 2004 amendment therefore deletes the references in ss. 5(3) and 10(3) to dissimilar goods and services. It may be questioned why the United Kingdom Government saw fit to amend the TMA, as national laws are required to be interpreted in accordance with a parent EU Directive in any event (Case C-106/89 *Marleasing* [1990] ECR I-4135 at [8] and Case C-91/92 *Faccini Dori v Recreb* [1994] ECR I-3325 at [26]). The recast Directive spells out that it matters not whether the goods are identical, similar, or not similar.

12.7.1 The elements of s. 5(3)

The CJEU has stated that s. 5(3) pursues a different objective from s. 5(2) (*Sabel v Puma* at [20]; and Case C-252/07 *Intel Corporation Inc v CPM United Kingdom Ltd* [2008] ECR I-8823 at [50]). For this reason, its criteria are quite specific. The elements of the provision (all of which must be satisfied) are:

- the junior mark must be identical or similar to the senior mark (applying either *LTJ* or *Sabel v Puma* respectively to decide identity and similarity);
- the senior mark must have a reputation;
- the use by the junior mark must be without due cause; and
- the use by the junior mark must take unfair advantage of or be detrimental to the distinctive character or repute of the senior mark.

12.7.2 Similarity

When comparing the senior and junior marks under s. 5(3), the CJEU has said (in Case C-252/07 *Intel Corporation Inc v CPM United Kingdom Ltd* at [41–42] and Case C-487/07 *L'Oréal SA v Bellure NV* [2009] ECR I-5185 at [36–37]) that the similarity must be such that the relevant section of the public makes a connection between the sign and the mark, that is to say, establishes a link between them without confusing them. However, the existence of such a link on its own is not sufficient: there must be injury to the mark. Whether there is a link (i.e. whether the consumer 'calls to mind' the senior mark) is to be assessed globally, taking into account the degree of similarity between the conflicting marks, the nature of the goods or services for which the conflicting marks were registered, including the degree of closeness or dissimilarity between those goods or services, and the relevant section of the public, the strength of the earlier mark's reputation, the degree of the earlier mark's distinctive character, whether inherent or acquired through use, and the existence of the likelihood of confusion on the part of the public.

12.7.3 Reputation

> ### Case C-375/97 *General Motors Corporation v Yplon SA* [1999] ECR I-5421
>
> 'Reputation' was explained by the CJEU in Case C-375/97 *General Motors Corporation v Yplon SA* [1999] ECR I-5421 as requiring the senior mark to be 'known' by a significant number of the relevant public (i.e. the consumers of the product concerned), although it added that it is not necessary to show that a given percentage recognize the mark. 'Known' involves a lower burden of proof than showing that the mark is 'famous' or even 'well-known'. The CJEU in *General Motors* went on to state the factors to be considered when determining reputation. The statement appears to be almost the same as the matters listed in *Windsurfing Chiemsee* when proving factual distinctiveness. These are: the market share held by the trade mark, the intensity, geographical extent and duration of its use, and the size of the investment made by the undertaking in promoting it.

12.7.4 Absence of due cause

The meaning of 'due cause' was considered in *Pfizer Ltd v Eurofood Link (UK) Ltd* [2001] FSR 17 and *Premier Brands UK Ltd v Typhoon Europe Ltd* [2000] FSR 767. Both cases state that it is for the owner of the junior mark to prove 'due cause', rather than for the owner of the senior mark to prove an absence of due cause (proving a negative is impossible). In *Premier Brands*, Neuberger J (as he then was) debated (*obiter*) whether 'absence of due cause' meant 'necessity' or 'bad faith', but on balance inclined to 'necessity'.

12.7.5 Harm to the senior mark

In Case C-252/07 *Intel Corporation Inc v CPM United Kingdom Ltd* at [27] and in Case C 487/07 *L'Oréal SA v Bellure NV* at [38], confirmed in Case C-323/09 *Interflora Inc v Marks & Spencer plc* [2011] ECR I-8625 at [73–74], the CJEU identified three types of harm which can be caused to the senior mark. Any one of these suffices, but in each case the question of harm must be assessed globally:

- detriment to the distinctive character of the mark ('whittling away' or 'blurring'): the mark's ability to identify the goods or services for which it is registered is weakened owing to the 'dispersion of identity';

- detriment to the repute of the mark ('tarnishment' or 'degradation'): the goods or services for which the identical or similar sign is used are perceived by the public in such a way that the trade mark's power of attraction is reduced, particularly where the third party's goods or services possess a characteristic or quality which is liable to have a negative impact on the image of the mark; and

- taking unfair advantage ('parasitism' or 'free-riding'): the third party seeks by their use of the senior mark to ride on its coat-tails in order to benefit from the power of attraction and the reputation and prestige of the mark and to exploit, without paying any financial compensation, the marketing effort expended by the proprietor in order to create and maintain the mark's image.

For the first two categories of harm, the effect must be to make the consumer change their economic behaviour: *Intel* at [77]. However, as Gangjee and Burrell point out (in 'Because You're Worth It: L'Oréal and the Prohibition on Free Riding' (2010) 73 *MLR* 282), the CJEU in *L'Oréal* treats free riding as actionable per se.

12.7.6 Case law on s. 5(3)

A number of UK cases have considered s. 5(3).

Oasis Stores Ltd's Trade Mark Application [1998] RPC 631

The principal decision is that of the Appointed Person in *Oasis Stores Ltd's Trade Mark Application* [1998] RPC 631. An opposition to the registration of EVEREADY for condoms was unsuccessfully opposed by the owner of EVER READY for batteries. It was said that the section is not intended to provide sweeping protection for any mark with a reputation. Whether there is protection is a matter of degree depending on all the circumstances. The gist of the action is 'cross-pollination' between the claimant's and defendant's trade marks. The factors which the court should take into account include the inherent distinctiveness of the earlier trade mark, the extent of its reputation, the range of goods or services for which the reputation is enjoyed, the uniqueness of the senior mark in the market, whether the respective goods or services, even though dissimilar, are in some way related or likely to be sold through the same outlets, and whether the senior mark will be any less distinctive than it was before or whether its reputation is likely to be damaged or tarnished in some material way.

Examples of successful oppositions under s. 5(3) include *C A Sheimer (M) Sdn Bhd's Trade Mark Application (VISA)* [2000] RPC 484 (VISA for credit cards tarnished by the registration of an identical mark for condoms); *Inlima SL's Application for a Three Dimensional Trade Mark* [2000] RPC 661 (the Adidas 'three stripe' mark for sports goods harmed if the applicant was allowed to register a bottle shaped like a football boot, etched with three stripes, for drinks, as sports goods manufacturers would not want to be associated with the evils of drink); and *Quorn Hunt v Marlow Foods Ltd* [2005] ETMR 105 (QUORN for vegetarian meat substitute would be tarnished by being associated with a hunting organization). A key factor in the latter case was that on seeing the defendant's mark, consumers would change their economic behaviour, i.e. they would be put off from buying the opponent's goods.

Pause for reflection

Is there a hidden danger in s. 5(3) in that it offers protection against misappropriation rather than against origin confusion?

In our scenario question, does the mark NEO for goods in Class 16 fall under the relative grounds of s. 5(3)?

12.8 Conflict with an earlier unregistered mark

Section 5(4)(a) implements an optional provision of the Directive. It allows the owner of a prior used but unregistered mark to oppose a later trade mark application. Oppositions under this subsection rarely succeed, because the opponent has to convince the Registry that a passing off action would succeed: *WILD CHILD Trade Mark* [1998] RPC 455. An example of an unsuccessful opposition is *OXFORD BLUE Trade Mark*, Registry, 23 March 2004, where Oxford University failed in its attempt to prevent the registration of OXFORD BLUE for cheese. The name OXFORD BLUE was recognized by the public as a sporting award, but the University had not done business under that name, and so had no goodwill capable of protection.

12.9 Conflict with an earlier copyright or design

The broader definition of trade mark in s. 1 means that a trade mark might conflict with other types of intellectual property right. Section 5(4)(b) gives protection to the owner of an earlier copyright or design. There could be a clash between the trade mark and an earlier two-dimensional artistic work (see *KARO STEP Trade Mark* [1977] RPC 59) or between a shape trade mark and a three-dimensional artistic work, such as a sculpture or registered or unregistered design (*OSCAR Trade Mark* [1979] RPC 173). As music can be a trade mark (*Shield Mark*) there could now be a conflict between the owner of the copyright in the tune and a trade mark applicant.

12.10 Opposition based on a well-known mark

The combination of TMA s. 6(1)(c) and s. 56 means that there is one further form of prior right which is protected in opposition proceedings, and that is a well-known mark. The criteria used to determine a well-known mark were set out in *LE MANS Trade*

Mark Application, Appointed Person, 8 November 2004. A well-known mark can be the basis of a successful opposition under s. 5(1) and 5(2) but cannot be the basis of an opposition under s. 5(3) because of the wording of the Paris Convention: Case T-150/04 *Mühlens GmbH v OHIM*, [2007] ECR II-2353. Individuals or organizations domiciled in the United Kingdom cannot rely on this provision, again because of the wording of the Paris Convention: *Jules Rimet Cup Ltd v The Football Association Ltd* [2008] FSR 254 at [73].

12.11 Conclusion

In this chapter, we have examined the relative grounds for refusal of trade mark registrations as available under s. 5(1)–(3). We have seen that the law recognizes three instances, the so-called 'triad of protection' where rights on earlier marks have prevalence and registrations will be refused or opposed:

a. Where the sign is identical to an earlier sign and the goods and/or services applied for are also identical;

b. Where the sign is identical to an earlier sign and the goods and/or services applied for are similar;

c. Where the sign is similar to an earlier sign and the goods and/or services applied for are identical or similar.

We have explored the scope of each one of these relative grounds, which have to be applied systematically in sequence (*Reed Executive plc v Reed Business Information Ltd* [2004] RPC 767): if the application does not fall within s. 5(1) (because there is absence of identity in either the mark or the goods), we go to s. 5(2). If there is no similarity of goods, or if there is an absence of confusion, we go to s. 5(3).

Going to the scenario question, Paul Jonas should be advised that all three situations he reports on are likely cases of relative grounds for the refusal of the trade mark applications at issue. In order to see how strong are Paul's chances of success we have to apply systematically in sequence the relative grounds listed in s. 5 by reference to each reported case.

- LEONE: With regards to the application to register the mark LEONE (with the face of a lion replacing the letter O) for products falling in Class 6, including metals in foil or powder form for 3D printers, and Class 7, 3D printers and 3D printing pens:

First it is important to assess whether relative grounds under s. 5(1) apply, i.e. whether the mark applied for is identical to an earlier mark and in respect of identical goods and services. There is no need to prove confusion, as confusion is assumed in cases of total identity: Case C-2/00 *Hölterhoff v Ulrich Freiesleben* [2002] ECR I-4187. In order to assess whether the marks are identical for the purposes of s. 5(1), we have to see if the test developed in Case C-291/00 *LTJ Diffusion SA v Sadas Vertbaudet SA* [2003] ECR I-2799 at [50–54] applies, namely to see whether the marks are identical in all respects. In the present case, the mark LEONE does not reproduce, without any modification, all the elements of the senior mark LEO.

In this regard, we have to move on to s. 5(2). In order to assess whether the marks are identical or similar for the purposes of s. 5(2) there has to be at least some similarity between the senior and junior mark (Case 106/03 P *Vedial SA v OHIM* [2004] ECR I-9573 at [51], [54]). Identity is assessed on the basis of the test in *LTJ* and similarity is decided on the basis of cases such as *Union v Union Soleure*, 20 May 1983, Case A 82/5 [1984] BIE 137. *Sabel v Puma* established that the assessment of similarity rests on a comparison of aural, visual, and conceptual elements based on the overall impression given by the marks bearing in mind their distinctive components. In the present case, it can be said that the junior mark LEONE and the senior mark LEO, including the figurative element of the image of a lion replacing the letter O in both marks are similar aurally, visually, and conceptually, by reference to their distinctive components, despite the existence of an extra syllable in the mark LEONE (see e.g. *Neutrogena v Golden Ltd t/a Laboratoires Garnier; Reed Executive plc v Reed Business Information Ltd*).

Since the marks are in principle not dissimilar, the goods have to be compared on the basis of the test established in Case C-39/97 *Canon KK v Metro-Goldwyn-Mayer Inc* [1998] ECR I-5507. All relevant factors must be taken into account, including the nature of the goods, the end users, the method of use, and whether the goods are in competition with each other or are complementary. Whether the goods of both marks appear in the same class within the Nice Classification of Goods and Services 1957 is of no assistance. In the present case, the goods for which the junior and senior mark are applied for do not seem to be in direct competition with each other. The final aspect of deciding whether there is a likelihood of confusion is to apply the 'global appreciation' test (*Sabel v Puma* and *Canon*), in other words all the elements are considered together, or, as the CJEU said in *Canon*, there is an interdependence of factors. If the two marks are conceptually similar, and the senior mark has a particularly distinctive character, either inherently, or because of how much it has been used, there will be a greater likelihood of confusion. There is a likelihood of confusion if the association between the marks creates a risk that consumers will wrongly believe that the goods or services come from the same or from economically linked undertakings. Mere association, in that the later mark brings the earlier mark to mind, does not suffice (*Realistic Games Ltd v Goal.com (Holdco) SA* (O/528/17) [2018] ETMR 6).

- LIO: With regards to the application to register the mark LIO (with the image of a pen replacing the letter I) for products in Class 16, including stationary and office requisites:

As with the mark LEONE, relative grounds under s. 5(1) cannot be established as the marks at issue are not similar in every respect. However, s. 5(2) could apply due to the aural, visual, phonetical, and conceptual similarity between the marks at issue and the fact that the goods on which they plan to attach the mark are identical to the senior mark of Paul Jonas. On the basis of the 'global appreciation test', the marks can be said to be conceptually similar, and it can also be claimed that the senior mark has a particularly distinctive character because it has been used for a considerable amount of time and there will hence be a greater likelihood of confusion. In the present case, confusion is likely to be direct, in that consumers will confuse one product with another, or consider that goods come from economically linked undertakings (indirect confusion).

- NEO: Finally, with regards to the application to register the mark NEO (written in similar fonts as the senior mark) for products in Class 16, including toilet/hygienic paper, bibs of paper, towels of paper, tissues of paper for removing make-up:

As with the other two marks (LEONE and LIO), relative grounds under s. 5(1) cannot be established as the marks at issue are not similar in every respect. Section 5(2) cannot apply as the junior and senior mark may possess some aural and visual similarity as to their distinctive elements even though they are conceptually distinct: NEO connotes something new, whereas LEO is Latin for lion and a zodiac sign. However, the goods for which the marks are sought, although in the same class according to the Nice Classification, are different and it is not likely that any consumer confusion within the purposes of s. 5(2) will occur on a global appreciation of the marks.

It is then necessary to move to s. 5(3). Section 5(3) provides that an earlier registration of the identical or similar mark will prevent the registration of the junior mark where the earlier mark has acquired a reputation and the use of the later mark without due cause would take unfair advantage of, or be detrimental to, the distinctive character or repute of the earlier mark. The elements of the provision (all of which must be satisfied) are:

- the junior mark must be identical or similar to the senior mark (applying either *LTJ* or *Sabel v Puma* respectively to decide identity and similarity);
- the senior mark must have a reputation;
- the use by the junior mark must be without due cause; and
- the use by the junior mark must take unfair advantage of or be detrimental to the distinctive character or repute of the senior mark.

In the comparison of the senior and junior marks under s. 5(3), similarity has to be such that the relevant section of the public makes a connection between the sign and the mark without confusing them (see *Intel Corporation Inc v CPM United Kingdom Ltd* and *L'Oréal SA v Bellure NV*). Similarity of the marks can be established and harm to the senior mark in such a case can take the form detriment to the repute of the mark ('tarnishment' or 'degradation') (*Intel Corporation Inc v CPM United Kingdom Ltd* at [27] and *L'Oréal SA v Bellure NV* at [38]). The difficult aspect would be to prove that the senior mark, i.e. LEO, has acquired reputation by having become known (not famous or well-known) by a significant number of the relevant public (Case C-375/97 *General Motors Corporation v Yplon SA* [1999] ECR I-5421). Factors to be taken into consideration are almost the same with those taken into account to establish factual distinctiveness (e.g. market share, intensity, geographical extent, and duration of its use, investment in promotion of the mark).

End-of-chapter questions

After reading the chapter carefully, try answering the following questions. For answer guidance visit the online resources at **www.oup.com/uk/karapapa-mcdonagh/**

1. How do likelihood of confusion and likelihood of association featuring in s. 5(2) differ?

2. What is the meaning of reputation under s. 5(3) TMA and how is it established?

Further reading

For understanding the protection available to trade marks, the following readings are recommended:

Bornkamm, J. 'Harmonising Trade Mark Law in Europe: the Stephen Stewart Memorial Lecture' [1999] 3 *IPQ* 283
  Explains the scope of protection accorded to the owner of a registered trade mark under Arts 4 and 5 of the Directive.

Davis, J. 'Locating the Average Consumer: His Judicial Origins, Intellectual Influences and Current Role in European Trade Mark Law' [2005] 2 *IPQ* 183
  Examines the way in which the CJEU has developed the average consumer as the arbiter of key issues under the Directive and Regulation.

Gangjee, D. and Burrell, R. 'Because You're Worth It: *L'Oréal* and the Prohibition on Free Riding' (2010) 73 *MLR* 282
  A critique of the CJEU's decision in L'Oréal.

Norman, H. '*Davidoff v Gofkid*: Dealing with the Logical Lapse or Creating European Disharmony' [2003] 3 *IPQ* 342
  Explains how the ECJ broadened the scope of protection under Arts 4 and 5 for trade marks with a reputation.

13 Infringement and loss of registration of trade marks

Problem question

Read this problem question carefully and keep it in mind while you are working through the chapter that follows. At the end of this chapter, you will be able to apply what you have learnt to the problem question and advise the relevant parties.

St James' basketball club is a very popular athletic club in London that owns a registered UK trade mark on the figurative mark featuring the name of the club and its crest, that is based largely on the coat of arms of the Borough of Hillingdon. They have an outlet in the premises of the club and a dedicated website where they sell official merchandise bearing the club's logo, including T-shirts, uniforms, and other memorabilia.

They have recently found out that Mr Alan Green sells memorabilia and uniforms bearing the registered trade mark of St James' club without having requested the club's permission. Mr Green places a tag on each item he sells indicating that this is not official merchandise. He sells his products at considerably lower prices online, along with other items featuring the logos of football and basketball clubs across England, on Etsy and on his own webpage www.funclub.co.uk.

St James' basketball club is not happy with this and would like to bring proceedings against Mr Green and any other responsible party. They come to you for legal advice.

What is more, they want your legal advice regarding the following activities that they have recently found out:

- that a regional competitor, St Regent's basketball club, that owns both a word and a figurative mark 'St Regent's basketball club', has stopped being in the market for the past six years due to financial constraints;

- that AllForTheGame Ltd, has a registered UK trade mark for the words 'Basketball Club' registered in 1962, before basketball took off as a sport and gained popularity in the UK.

13.1 Introduction

The purpose of this chapter is to set out the rights of a trade mark owner (once the mark has been registered) to prevent others from making use of any sign which is the same as, or similar to, the registered mark in the course of trade.

Case law has reinforced the link between the scope of protection accorded to a registered mark and the commercial functions which trade marks perform. As we mentioned in the chapter on relative grounds (chapter 12), there is considerable overlap between the relative grounds for refusal (which enable the registered proprietor to stop another later mark being entered on the Register) and the provisions on infringement (which enable the registered proprietor to stop another later mark being used).

Trade mark infringement is yet another area of trade mark law where European influence is very marked. The wording of the First Trade Marks Directive (Council Directive 89/104/EEC of 21 December 1988 on the approximation of the laws of Member States relating to trade marks [1989] OJ L 40/1, now codified as Directive 2008/95/EC of the European Parliament and of the Council of 22 October 2008 [2008] OJ L 299/25) ('the Directive') and the provisions of the recast Directive (Directive 2015/2436 of the European Parliament and of the Council of 16 December 2015 to approximate the laws of the Member States relating to trade marks, OJ L 336) needs to be compared with that of the Trade Marks Act 1994 ('TMA'). As ever, only the Court of Justice of the European Union ('CJEU') can give a definitive interpretation of the wording of the legislation.

13.2 Infringement: The claimant's arguments

The issues which a trade mark infringement action raises can be conveniently divided into points which the claimant has to prove in order to succeed and those a defendant will wish to raise by way of response (will be discussed in chapter 14).

A claimant who brings a trade mark infringement action will have to show two things: that an act of infringement has been committed, and that such conduct falls within the scope of protection afforded to the registered mark. The two issues can be considered as 'infringement in law' and 'infringement in fact' (the same as in patent law as we will see). Once these two points have been established, the court will normally find in favour of the claimant unless one or more of the counter-arguments raised by the defendant succeeds.

13.3 Categories of infringing acts

Two provisions in the TMA spell out types of infringing conduct. Section 10(4) (based on the wording of Art. 5(3) of the Directive, and partially reflecting the revised approach of Art. 10(3) of the recast Directive) sets out the acts of primary infringement; s. 10(5) (a purely domestic provision) deals with contributory infringement. Section

10(4) and (5) must be read subject to the requirement in s. 9 that infringing conduct must be committed in the United Kingdom and be without the consent of the registered proprietor.

13.3.1 Acts of primary infringement

Under Art. 5(3) of the recast Directive, primary infringement consists of affixing the sign to goods or their packaging; offering or exposing goods for sale, putting them on the market, stocking them for those purposes under the sign, or offering or supplying services under the sign; importing or exporting goods under the sign; using the sign on business papers or advertising. In addition, Art. 10(3) of the recast Directive mentions acts, such as using the sign as a trade or company name or part of a trade or company name and using the sign in comparative advertising in a manner that is contrary to Comparative Advertisement Directive (2006/114/EC). The list covers the act of manufacture (placing the mark on goods) and post-manufacture conduct (distributing goods), and ancillary activities, such as advertising or stocking. Even if the defendant denies having used the claimant's mark when offering goods to the public over the internet, there may still be liability for 'stocking' the goods preparatory to putting them on the market: *Sony Computer Entertainment v Nuplayer Ltd* [2006] FSR 126. The list of conduct which amounts to use of a registered mark should not be regarded as exhaustive, owing to the presence of the phrase 'in particular' in Art. 10(3).

One particular issue is whether the trade mark owner can stop goods which are in transit through the United Kingdom, destined for sale in a third country where there may not be protection for the mark. The CJEU (in Case C-281/05 *Montex Holdings Ltd v Diesel* [2006] ECR I-10881) has stated that the rights of the owner to intervene depend on there having been conduct which results in the goods being 'put on the market'. Consequently, goods have not been imported into the EU (and so have not been 'put on the market') where they have been placed in a transit warehouse for onward transmission to a non-EU state: Case C-405/03 *Class International BV v Colgate Palmolive* [2005] ECR I-8735. These two rulings were applied by the Court of Appeal in *Eli Lilly & Co v 8PM Chemist Ltd* [2008] FSR 313 so that the trade mark owner could not object to goods in transit. It did not matter whether the goods were non-EU goods and on their way to another non-EU state (as in *Class*) or to a Member State where there was no intellectual property (IP) protection (as in *Diesel*), being in transit through the territory of a Member State did not amount to an act of infringement as the goods were not being 'put on the market'. The recast Directive is likely to reverse these cases. Article 10(4) of the recast Directive reads that the proprietor of a registered trade mark shall be entitled to prevent all third parties from bringing goods, in the course of trade, into the Member State where the trade mark is registered, without being released for free circulation there, where such goods, including the packaging thereof, come from third countries and bear without authorization a trade mark which is identical with the trade mark registered in respect of such goods, or which cannot be distinguished in its essential aspects from that trade mark.

Pause for reflection

By reference to the scenario question, which activity/activities are likely to amount to trade mark infringement?

13.3.2 Acts of secondary infringement

Article 11 of the recast Directive (implemented as s. 10(3) TMA) reads that where there is a risk that the packaging, labels, tags, security or authenticity features or devices, or any other means to which the trade mark is affixed, could be used in relation to goods or services and that use would constitute an infringement of the rights of the proprietor of a trade mark under Art. 10(2) and (3) of the recast Directive, the proprietor of that trade mark shall have the right to prohibit the following acts if carried out in the course of trade: affixing a sign identical with, or similar to, the trade mark on packaging, labels, tags, security or authenticity features or devices, or any other means to which the mark may be affixed; offering or placing on the market, or stocking for those purposes, or importing or exporting, packaging, labels, tags, security or authenticity features or devices, or any other means to which the mark is affixed.

13.3.2.1 Blocking injunctions

In certain instances, especially in cases of online trade mark infringements, Courts may find internet service providers liable, unless one of the exemptions available in the e-Commerce Directive 2000/31/EC applies. Once internet service providers become aware that third parties use their services to infringe intellectual property rights, they have the duty to take proportionate measures, upon request, to assist the person wronged to prevent or reduce infringements.

An important case regarding internet service provider liability in light of trade mark infringements is *Cartier International AG v British Sky Broadcasting Ltd* [2016] EWCA Civ 658; [2016] ETMR 43. In this case, the Court of Appeal upheld the High Court's decision to grant Cartier an injunction, effectively requiring major internet service providers to block access to certain websites that were offering for sale counterfeit Cartier products. When considering whether to make a website blocking order, the relief has to be necessary, effective, dissuasive, not unnecessarily complicated or costly; it should avoid barriers to legitimate trade and it should be fair, equitable, and proportionate.

The Supreme Court further clarified certain aspects of website blocking injunctions in *Cartier International AG v British Sky Broadcasting Ltd* [2018] UKSC 28; [2018] ETMR 32. Lord Sumption remarked that:

> In English law, the starting point is the intermediary's legal innocence. An ISP would not incur liability for trade mark infringement under English law, even in the absence of the safe harbour provisions of the E-Commerce Directive. . . . An ISP serving as a 'mere conduit' has no means of knowing what use is being made of his network by third parties to distribute illegal content. Even when it is informed of this, it does not have the limited duty to take proactive steps to stop access to illegal content which is implicit in the conditions governing the immunities for caching and hosting. Its only duty is to comply with an order of the Court (at [33]).

Pause for reflection

Going back to the scenario, could the e-commerce website be found liable for secondary trade mark infringement? Have you seen that various platforms have a 'report abuse' function? What are the responsibilities of such platforms when someone reports abusive behaviour?

13.3.3 Non-graphic use

Whilst the 1938 Act, as amended, contemplated that infringing conduct could only be visual, under the TMA s. 103(2) such conduct can be oral. If this were not the case, then there would be no protection against use of the mark on commercial radio or in sound recordings.

13.3.4 Use within the United Kingdom: websites

The requirement that the infringing conduct must be in the United Kingdom appears at first glance to be straightforward. The claimant needs to show that one of the acts listed in s. 10(4) happened within the territory of the United Kingdom. But what is the position as regards use on a website? When will the inclusion of a UK registered trade mark in a website maintained in another jurisdiction amount to infringement in the United Kingdom? The answer depends on whether the website is 'targeted' at customers in the United Kingdom. If they can order goods on the site for delivery to an address in the United Kingdom and pay in sterling, then that is use 'in the United Kingdom': *Euromarket Designs Inc v Peters and Crate & Barrel Ltd* [2001] FSR 288; *L'Oréal SA v eBay International* [2009] RPC 693 at [402].

By reference to cases of online infringement, it is the seller on an online marketplace who makes use of the signs displayed on a product listing, because the marketplace provided a means for the seller to make its own commercial communications (*Birlea Furniture Limited v Platinum Enterprise (UK) Limited, Mr Mohammed Raheel Baig* [2018] EWHC 26 (IPEC) [37]).

 Pause for reflection

Does the list of infringing conduct cover all ways in which a trade mark could be infringed in the digital era? How could *Birlea Furniture* be relevant by reference to the scenario question?

13.4 The scope of trade mark protection

13.4.1 The impact of the Directive

If there has been infringing conduct within the United Kingdom, it must next be decided whether this falls within the mark's scope of protection. It is here that the Directive has had a significant impact on United Kingdom trade mark law, in two regards.

13.4.1.1 Breadth of protection

Under the 1938 Act, as amended, an infringement action could only be brought where the defendant used the infringing trade mark in relation *to the goods of the registration*. Hence, if the defendant used the claimant's trade mark on goods for which it was not registered, even if such goods were very similar, then the claimant had to seek redress under the law of passing off, something of a lottery. The Directive, by contrast, provides that the registered proprietor can object to use on identical, similar, or even dissimilar goods.

13.4.1.2 Change of language

After the introduction of the TMA there was a debate as to whether, in order to infringe a registered trade mark, the use by the defendant of the alleged infringing sign had to be 'trade mark use'. Such debate was caused in part by the wording of TMA ss. 9 and 10. Rather than copy the exact wording of Art. 5 of the Directive, Parliament split the provision dealing with the rights of the trade mark owner between two separate sections, one (s. 9) declaring the rights which exist in a registered mark, the other (s. 10) providing a definition of when those rights are infringed, that is, setting out the scope of protection. This apparently unnecessary rearrangement of the infringement provision was explained during the passage of the Trade Marks Bill as being simply a matter of drafting technique (*Hansard*, 18 January 1994, col 24). The implications, however, proved to be far more significant.

Analysis of s. 9 shows that it is narrower than Art. 5. Instead of providing that 'the registered trade mark shall confer on the proprietor exclusive rights *therein*. The proprietor shall be entitled to prevent . . . ' (emphasis supplied), the TMA states that 'the proprietor of a registered trade mark has exclusive rights in the trade mark *which are infringed by use of the trade mark* in the United Kingdom without his consent' (again, emphasis supplied). The explanation for the alteration lies in the fact that s. 9 simply copies the language of its predecessor, s. 4 Trade Marks Act 1938, as amended (which had been extensively criticized for being tortuous). This exercise in 'cutting and pasting' led to a debate as to whether, in order to infringe under the TMA, there has to be 'trade mark use'.

 Pause for reflection

Do you find the explanation as to why Art. 5 of the Directive was divided between ss. 9 and 10 TMA convincing? Does the wording of s. 9 TMA correctly implement Art. 5 of the Directive?

13.4.2 **The requirement of trade mark use**

13.4.2.1 The old law

Case law under s. 4 of the 1938 Act had concluded that the section was limited by the definition of 'trade mark' in s. 68 of the same Act, so that if a defendant used the claimant's trade mark for any purpose other than indicating the commercial origin of the goods, this was not trade mark infringement. This point is nicely illustrated by the decision in *Mars (GB) Ltd v Cadbury Ltd* ([1987] RPC 387) where Whitford J held that the registration of TREETS for confectionary was not infringed by the defendants' use of 'treat-size' on packets of miniature WISPA bars.

13.4.2.2 The policy debate

The question under the TMA is whether any use in commerce suffices for infringement or whether the requirement of 'use as a trade mark' is retained. This in turn begs the question of what is meant by 'trade mark use'. Is it use to indicate origin, or is it any use which undermines the wider functions of a trade mark, that is, 'anything which affects the legitimate interests of the trade mark owner or which affects the value of the mark by taking unfair advantage of its distinctive character or repute' (*per* the CJEU in Case C-10/89 *SA CNL-Sucal NV v Hag GF AG* [1990] ECR I-3711 at [14])? In other words, should trade mark law protect the registered proprietor against counterfeiting and confusion only, or should protection extend to any form of 'free-riding', that is, against any form of misappropriation of the value of the trade mark? Such policy debate is linked to the legally recognized functions which trade marks fulfil.

13.4.2.3 A problem of language

The policy choice has to be understood in the light of a difference between the 1938 Act and the TMA. The wording of s. 10(1), s. 10(2), and s. 10(3) refers to the defendant's infringing use of a 'sign'. This is in contrast to the phrase 'trade mark' in s. 9 and its predecessor, s. 4 of the 1938 Act. 'Sign', found in TMA ss. 2, 3, and 10, is a word with a very broad meaning, namely 'anything which conveys information' (*per* Jacob J in *Philips Electronics NV v Remington Consumer Products* [1998] RPC 283 at p. 298) or which sends a 'message' to any of the senses (*per* AG Colomer in Case C-273/00 *Sieckmann v Deutsches Patent- und Markenamt* [2002] ECR I-11737 at [20–21]). What is the effect of the word 'sign' on the requirement of 'trade mark use'?

13.4.2.4 Initial United Kingdom decisions

One possible interpretation of s. 10 is that the word 'sign' merely indicates that use in commerce is all that is required. That was the view of Jacob J in *British Sugar v James Robertson* [1996] RPC 281, who thought that the wording of the section obviated the need to show trade mark use, and that s. 9 was but a 'chatty introduction' to s. 10. Jacob J disagreed with the outcome of an earlier case, *Bravado Merchandising v Mainstream Publishing* [1996] FSR 205, where Lord McClusky had accepted counsel's concession that trade mark use was a necessary component of the infringement action under the TMA. The Court of Appeal subsequently agreed with Jacob J (but only by way of *obiter*), stating that in order to infringe, trade mark use was not necessary (see *Philips Electronics NV v Remington Consumer Products* [1999] RPC 809 and *Marks & Spencer plc and others v One in a Million Ltd* [1998] 4 All ER 476).

The *British Sugar* approach has the advantage of reconciling 'trade mark' in s. 9 with 'sign' in s. 10. However, to state that all that is required is use in commerce ignores the functions performed by trade marks and runs the risk that trade marks are perceived as unfair monopolies.

13.4.2.5 CJEU guidance

> **Case C-206/01 _Arsenal Football Club v Matthew Reed_ [2002] ECR I-10273**
>
> The issue of trade mark use was considered by the CJEU in Case C-206/01 _Arsenal Football Club v Matthew Reed_ [2002] ECR I-10273. The referral for a preliminary ruling under Art. 267 of the Treaty on the Functioning of the European Union ('TFEU') (formerly Art. 234 EC) was made by Laddie J ([2001] RPC 922) who had held that the defendant had not committed trade mark infringement by selling unauthorized merchandise to football fans, as the purchasers would not regard the name 'Arsenal' and the famous 'Gunners' logo as indicating commercial origin. Rather, each sign operated as a 'badge of allegiance' to the club. There was therefore no 'trade mark use'. He also held that the defendant's use of the marks was not passing off, as there was no origin confusion on the part of the public. Laddie J's judgment should therefore be contrasted with that in _British Sugar_: the two cases reach opposite conclusions on the need for trade mark use. Further, Laddie J's thinking has the effect of confining the function of trade marks (whether registered or unregistered) to origin indication only.
>
> The CJEU in its ruling made plain that use in commerce alone does _not_ suffice for infringement. 'Trade mark use' is required. However, 'trade mark use' is given a much wider meaning than before. It means any use which affects the essential function of the trade mark, so that the trade mark owner is entitled to object to anyone who is seeking to take unfair advantage of the status and repute of the trade mark by selling products illegally bearing it. The decision therefore protects the wider function of a trade mark as a vehicle for 'creating and retaining custom'. In its reply, the CJEU made extensive reference to its earlier jurisprudence about the essential function of the trade mark and its role as guarantor of both commercial origin and the quality of the goods, stressing the importance of trade marks in achieving competition within the internal market. The exclusive rights conferred by the Directive (and hence the TMA) are to enable the trade mark proprietor to protect specific interests. These interests will be undermined if a third party's use of the sign is liable to affect the functions of the trade mark, in particular its essential function of guaranteeing to consumers the origin of the goods.

The _Arsenal_ ruling was subsequently accepted as correct by the Court of Appeal despite Laddie J's refusal to apply it on the ground that the CJEU exceeded its jurisdiction ([2003] 1 CMLR 382 (Laddie J), [2003] 2 CMLR 800 (CA)). The Court of Appeal repeated that when considering whether the defendant has trespassed on the scope of the claimant's registration, the question is no longer whether the defendant's use indicates the origin of the goods but whether that use undermines the essential function of the trade mark. In other words, is the use such that it takes unfair advantage of the status and repute of the trade mark? _Arsenal_ appears to suggest that the court should examine the _defendant's_ conduct rather than consider whether the _consumer_ views the trade mark as indicating origin. It therefore introduces notions of unfair competition into the law of registered trade marks.

Since the *Arsenal* case, the CJEU has revisited the requirement of trade mark use and has stepped back from its earlier broad thinking.

Case C-17/06 *Céline SARL v Céline SA* [2007] ECR I-7041

The current view can be found in Case C-17/06 *Céline SARL v Céline SA* [2007] ECR I-7041 where the Court identified four conditions which must be satisfied before the trade mark right is infringed, the second one of which is self-explanatory:

- use must be in the course of trade;
- it must be without the consent of the proprietor of the mark;
- it must be in respect of goods or services; and
- it must affect or be liable to affect the functions of the trade mark, in particular its essential function of guaranteeing to consumers the origin of the goods or services.

 Pause for reflection

Before moving on to explaining each one of these conditions in detail, it is worth going back to the problem scenario. By reference to the use that Mr Green makes of the mark at issue, can it qualify as trade mark use? What does *Arsenal v Reed* instruct and to what extent can this case be applied by analogy to the facts of the present case?

13.4.2.5.1 Use in the course of trade

Any use of a sign in the context of commercial activity with a view to economic advantage (not as a private matter), no matter how modest, would suffice for the requirement for use in the course of trade to be met (*Arsenal Football Club Plc v Reed* (C-206/01) EU:C:2002:651). 'In the course of trade' was considered by the General Court in Case T-195/00 *Travelex Global and Financial Services Ltd v Commission* [2003] ECR II-1677 in which it was held (relying on *Arsenal Football Club v Matthew Reed*) that the Commission had not, when it adopted the official Euro symbol, used a sign which infringed the claimant's trade mark in the course of trade. This was because the adoption of the symbol was not 'use in the course of a commercial activity whereby goods and services are manufactured and supplied in a particular market'. A similar description was given in *RxWorks Ltd v Hunter* [2008] RPC 303 (a case which gives a useful summary of CJEU jurisprudence) as use 'in the course of a commercial activity with a view to gain and not as a private matter'. The same case points out that thanks to *Céline* and *Arsenal*, a trade mark can have significance beyond the point of sale, so it does not need to be visible when the goods are bought, and indeed can be 'embedded' in a product, such as a particular screen display in a computer or on a hidden part in a car engine.

Pause for reflection

In order to reflect on the concept of use in the course of trade consider the following example. Suppose that a famous trade mark is included within a painting, such as Manet's masterpiece *The Bar at the Folies-Bergère* showing a beer bottle with the Bass 'red triangle' mark on the label, or Andy Warhol's picture of a can of Campbell's soup. Depicting the mark in such a manner would not be 'use in the course of trade' as it does not involve 'the manufacture and supply of goods in a particular market' (however, what would be the position if someone started selling postcards of the picture, or making T-shirts with the picture on the front?).

In *Electrocoin Automatics Ltd v Coinworld Ltd* [2005] FSR 79 it was held that the registration for OXO was not infringed by the appearance of the letters O, X, and O on the display of a 'one-armed bandit' gaming machine. Again, although this was a commercial activity, it did not involve making and/or supplying goods.

13.4.2.5.2 Use 'in respect of' goods or services

Use 'in relation to goods' where a third party affixes the sign constituting his company name, trade name, or shop name to the goods which he markets and, even where the sign is not affixed, where the sign is used in such a way that a link is established between the sign which constitutes the company, trade, or shop name of the third party and the goods marketed or the services provided by the third party (*Céline Sarl v Celine SA* (C-17/06) EU:C:2007:497). This suggests that there must be degree of proximity between the mark and the goods. In *RxWorks Ltd v Hunter*, Daniel Alexander QC, sitting as a Deputy High Court Judge, pointed out the inconsistent language found in legislation and case law. Whilst the TMA requires there to be 'use in relation to goods and services' (yet another legacy from the 1938 Act), the Directive simply uses the word 'for' whilst the CJEU has talked about 'use in respect of'. He added that the CJEU appears to assume that 'in respect of' simply refers to the list of infringing conduct set out in Art. 5(3) of the Directive, but that the CJEU has not yet been asked to rule on whether there was 'use in respect of' where the trade mark was 'embedded' in content-carrying media such as CDs or software.

Reference to other cases show that, on the one hand, incidental use of the trade mark will not infringe. In *Trebor Bassett Ltd v The Football Association* [1997] FSR 211, a threats action brought under TMA s. 21 by the alleged infringer, it was held that the appearance of the 'three lions' logo in pictures of English football players appearing on collectable cards inserted in the claimant's sweet packets did not infringe the FA's registration. It was not 'in relation to goods', because the trade mark 'just appeared' (the case may usefully be contrasted with the defence of incidental use in copyright infringement). Equally, use by a *customer* when ordering goods (in contrast to use by the *retailer* when supplying them) will not amount to infringing use (Case C-2/00 *Hölterhoff v Ulrich Freiesleben* [2002] ECR I-4187). By contrast, using the mark on invoices for goods made in the United Kingdom to be shipped abroad is 'use in relation to' the goods (*Beautimatic International Ltd v Mitchell International Pharmaceuticals Ltd* [2000] FSR 267).

Ultimately, whether a mark is used 'in relation to' or 'in respect of' goods depends on the facts. When a customer buys a DUALIT toaster from a John Lewis department store and carries it home in a shopping bag marked 'John Lewis', it cannot be said that the John Lewis mark is used 'in relation to' the toaster (*Daimler AG v Sany Group Co Ltd* [2009] EWHC 2581 (Ch) at [59]). As Jacob J remarked in *Euromarket Designs Inc v Peters and Crate & Barrel Ltd* at [57], only a trade mark lawyer would think that the 'Boots' trade mark had been used 'in relation to' films where a customer who had purchased a KODAK film at Boots took the film home in a Boots bag.

13.4.2.5.3 Consumer perception

The last element in the *Céline* list of requirements for infringement refers to the essential function of the trade mark guaranteeing to consumers the origin of the goods or services. The average consumer plays a key role in deciding issues of registrability, and it now appears that this person is also the arbiter of whether a trade mark has been infringed.

Case C-48/05 *Adam Opel AG v Autec* [2007] ECR I-1017

In Case C-48/05 *Adam Opel AG v Autec* [2007] ECR I-1017, the question which the CJEU had to determine was whether the claimant's mark was infringed when it was used by the defendant on toy cars. The Court's response (at [23–25]) was to say that it all depended on what the consumer thought: did they see the mark as indicating that the toys had been made by the claimant, or did they think that the trade mark was simply part of the authentic appearance of the goods? If the consumer attached great importance to the fidelity of the model car to the original, this would not undermine the function of the trade mark. This is in contrast to the outcome in *Arsenal*, where the end user's perception was that the football club had guaranteed the origin of the merchandise.

In *RxWorks*, it was said that EU law focuses on asking 'what effect is the use likely to have' so that this was a means of controlling the trade mark owner's monopoly. The protection given to the trade mark owner is inversely proportional to the assumed abilities of the notional addressee. The less well informed and observant the average consumer was, the more such a person would assume that a sign intended to perform one function (indicating authenticity) performed another (indicating origin). Consequently, the expectations of the average consumer's ability must not be set too low. In the instant case, the claimant's mark 'vet.local' was buried in the workings of a computer system using the defendant's software, and would only be seen by system administrators. Such a person would not think that it denoted trade origin.

The issue of trade mark use is far from settled. The fourth *Céline* principle appears to mark a retreat from the broad approach of *Arsenal* and its application is always going to be a question of fact. Such questions will often be complex, involving consideration of the nature of the sign, its meaning, the context of use, and the scale of use. One only has to compare the different results in *Arsenal* and *Opel* to see how the context in which the mark is used can affect the outcome. (Were football fans any less perceptive than those who buy authentic model cars?)

Pause for reflection

Is it right that the requirement of trade mark use depends on the view of the notional consumer? Isn't this likely to create uncertainty?

How is the requirement for trade mark use going to apply in the scenario question and the use of the logos on memorabilia by Mr Green?

13.4.2.6 Trade mark use on the internet: adwords and beyond

The digital era means that new ways of infringing are bound to emerge. Reference has already been made to where the mark is 'embedded', whether in computer software or other content-bearing media, where the use of the alleged infringing sign may not send a 'trade mark message'.

There has also been a significant number of CJEU cases involving the use of trade marks as 'adwords' on the internet, whereby a trader purchases a search engine keyword identical or similar to the claimant's mark so that when the user of a website types in the mark, a sponsored link is displayed which has nothing to do with the claimant's business. Is this 'trade mark use'? The various rulings distinguish between service operators (such as Google), marketplace operators (such as eBay), and the trade mark owner's competitors. The CJEU has said that whilst a service operator does not commit trade mark infringement when permitting a competitor to select the proprietor's mark as an adword (Case C-236/08 to C/238/09 *Google France v Louis Vuitton* [2010] ECR I-2417), a marketplace operator who makes use of Google's referencing service to acquire adwords which are then used to advertise its customer-sellers' products does infringe (*L'Oréal SA v eBay International* [2011] ECR I-6011). Competitors who, having purchased adwords, use them to advertise their goods or services also infringe, at least where the reasonably circumspect internet user is unable to ascertain without difficulty whether the goods or services referred to by the advertisement originated from the proprietor of the trade mark or from an undertaking economically linked to it or, on the contrary, originated from a third party (Case C-558/08 *Portakabin Ltd v Primakabin BV* [2010] ECR I-6963). The use by a competitor is likely to affect adversely the origin function of the proprietor's mark, as well as its investment function (Case C-323/09 *Interflora Inc v Marks & Spencer plc* [2011] ECR I-8625).

Pause for reflection

Does the guidance so far given by the CJEU enable us to understand clearly the concept of 'trade mark use'?

13.4.3 The application of the statutory provisions

When considering the scope of protection accorded to the trade mark owner in an infringement action, it will become apparent that s. 10, in its first three subsections, is a

DIAGRAM 13.1 *Trade mark infringement: the 'triad of protection'*

mirror image of the relative grounds for refusal in the first three subsections of s. 5, what Bornkamm (in 'Harmonising Trade Mark Law in Europe: the Stephen Stewart Memorial Lecture' [1999] 3 *IPQ* 283) calls the 'triad of protection'. The two provisions are, however, dissimilar in one respect. The difference is that s. 5 refers to the junior application as a 'trade mark' whilst s. 10 refers to the alleged infringement as a 'sign'. That apart, the case law on the two provisions is interchangeable, and the issues are determined from the viewpoint of the reasonably well-informed and reasonably observant and circumspect consumer (Case C-342/97 *Lloyd Schuhfabrik Meyer & Co KG v Klijsen Handel BV* [1999] ECR I-3819 at [26]).

Bornkamm's 'triad of protection' can be illustrated another way: see Diagram 13.1. By way of reminder, there is the absolute 'core' of protection when there is identity between the marks and their products; an outer, more flexible 'core' of protection dependent on similarity and confusion; and an outer rim of protection available only for those marks with a reputation. There is, however, a difference between the inner two zones and the outer zone: the former accord with the traditional role of the trade mark in protecting against consumer confusion, the latter is concerned with protecting the owner of the mark against misappropriation.

Again, just as with s. 5, s. 10 requires a systematic, indeed sequential, application of the statutory provisions (*Reed Executive plc v Reed Business Information Ltd* [2004] RPC 767).

13.4.3.1 Double identity

Under s. 10(1), use in the course of trade of the identical sign in relation to the identical goods or services will infringe the registered mark. No likelihood of confusion need be proved as it is assumed that there is such confusion where there is absolute identity: *Hölterhoff v Ulrich Freiesleben*.

When applying s. 10(1), the comparison is between the *use* which the defendant has made of the sign and how the claimant's entry on the Register appears. How the claimant has actually used their mark is irrelevant. Hence, 'identical goods' entails a comparison between the defendant's product and the goods for which the claimant's mark is *actually* registered, so that if the goods are not identical, the case falls under s. 10(2): *British Sugar v James Robertson*. Equally, 'identical sign' requires a comparison between the defendant's sign and the entry on the Register in respect of the claimant's mark: *Philips Electronics NV v Remington Consumer Products*.

The test for deciding whether a sign is identical was explained by the CJEU in Case C-291/00 *LTJ Diffusion SA v Sadas Vertbaudet SA* [2003] ECR I-2799. It declared that identity must be strictly interpreted through the eyes of the relevant consumer, who rarely has the chance to make a direct comparison between the products and who may therefore have an imperfect recollection of the claimant's mark. Insignificant differences between the registered mark and the infringing sign may be ignored. An example of an insignificant difference would be a hyphen between two words: *IBM Corporation v Web-Sphere Ltd* [2004] FSR 796.

 Pause for reflection

To what extent can the use that Mr Green amount to infringement on the basis of s. 10(1)?

13.4.3.2 Similarity coupled with confusion

If there is not identity between the infringing sign and the registered mark, or if the goods upon which the infringing sign has been placed are not identical to the goods of the registration, one moves on to consider the next limb of protection, s. 10(2). The provision can be summarized as requiring similarity coupled with a likelihood of confusion. The number of permutations in s. 10(2) can be set out diagrammatically in Table 13.1 as follows:

TABLE 13.1 *The requirement of similarity with likelihood of confusion: Section 10(2) permutations*

A mark registered for goods will be infringed by the use in the course of trade of:	A mark registered for services will be infringed by the use in the course of trade of:
an identical sign in relation to similar goods	an identical sign in relation to similar services
an identical sign in relation to similar services	an identical sign in relation to similar goods
a similar sign in relation to identical goods	a similar sign in relation to identical services
a similar sign in relation to similar goods	a similar sign in relation to similar services
a similar sign in relation to similar services	a similar sign in relation to similar goods

In each case, however, there must be a likelihood of confusion on the part of the public, which includes a likelihood of association. The meaning of 'likelihood of confusion', 'likelihood of association' and the case law of the CJEU which has interpreted Art. 5(1)(b) of the Directive (the parent provision of s. 10(2) TMA) have the same meaning as under the parallel provision in Art. 4(1)(b) (s. 5(2)). In essence:

- three types of confusion have been identified, namely direct confusion (confusing the products); indirect (thinking that the goods come from economically linked undertakings or that the trade mark owner has expanded their product line); and mere association ('calling to mind');

- association' can be traced historically to the Uniform Benelux Trade Marks Act 1971, but in the context of s. 10(2) it must be regarded as a subset of confusion because of the grammatical structure of the provision (*Wagamama Ltd v City Centre Restaurants* [1995] FSR 713; Case C-251/95 *Sabel BV v Puma AG* [1997] ECR I-6191). However, association is not entirely irrelevant, as it 'serves to define [the] scope' of confusion (*Sabel BV v Puma AG* at [18]);

- when applying s. 10(2) (Art. 5(1)(b) of the Directive) the starting point is Recital 11 to the consolidated version of the Directive, which declares that the likelihood of confusion depends on numerous elements;

- when deciding whether the infringing sign is similar to the registered mark, the comparison is to be made aurally, visually, and conceptually (*Sabel BV v Puma AG* at [23]), taking into account the factors listed in *Lloyd Schuhfabrik Meyer & Co GmbH v Klijsen Handel BV*. These include: the greater or lesser capacity of the mark to identify the goods or services, the inherent characteristics of the mark, whether or not it contains a descriptive element, and the market share held by the mark; how intensive, geographically widespread, and long-standing the use of the mark has been; the amount invested by the undertaking in promoting the mark; the proportion of the relevant section of the public which, because of the mark, identifies the goods or services as originating from a particular undertaking; and statements from chambers of commerce and industry or other trade and professional associations;

- when determining whether goods are similar, the test set out by the CJEU in Case C-39/97 *Canon KK v Metro-Goldwyn-Mayer Inc (formerly Pathé Communications Corp)* [1998] ECR I-5507 must be used; that is, all relevant factors must be taken into account, including the nature, the end users, the method of use, and whether they are in competition with each other or are complementary. The fact that the claimant's and defendant's products are in the same class under the Nice Agreement for the International Classification of Goods and Services 1957 is irrelevant;

- assuming that the conditions of similarity of marks and similarity of goods can be satisfied (Case 106/03 P *Vedial SA v OHIM* [2004] ECR I-9573), 'likelihood of confusion' requires a 'global appreciation' of all the issues, there being an 'interdependence of factors' such that a highly distinctive and extensively used mark will be given a wider penumbra of protection, and near-identity of goods may make not-so-similar marks appear similar (*Sabel BV v Puma AG*, *Canon*, and *Lloyd*). In other words, all the surrounding circumstances are to be taken into account (*Reed Executive plc v Reed Business Information Ltd*); and

- likelihood of confusion may also be established where the average consumer might believe that the services come from economically linked undertakings (*Comic Enterprises Ltd v Twentieth Century Fox Film Corp* [2016] EWCA Civ 41; [2016] ETMR 22). This can be the case, for instance, where repair services are offered featuring the mark of the products subject to repair, e.g. a garage using the name BMW by reference to the repair services (*Bayerische Motoren Werke Aktiengesellschaft v Technosport London Ltd & George Agyeton* [2017] EWCA Civ 779; [2017] ETMR 32). Such uses may either be 'informative', i.e. to convey a true message, and 'misleading', i.e. making a false connotation that the service is commercially connected with uses.

13.4.3.3 Marks with a reputation

When considering the final limb of the 'triad of protection', s. 10(3) was amended by The Trade Marks (Proof of Use) Regulations 2004 (SI 2004/946) which deleted the reference to dissimilar goods in the subsection, just as was the case with s. 5(3). The deletion (which has not been made to the Directive) was made in the United Kingdom to take account of the rulings of the ECJ in Case C-292/00 *Davidoff & Cie SA and Zino Davidoff v Gofkid Ltd* [2003] ECR I-389 and Case C-408/01 *Adidas-Saloman AG and Adidas Benelux BV v Fitnessworld Trading Ltd* [2003] ECR I-12537 which were to the effect that there would be a gap in the scheme of protection if the owner of a mark with a reputation could prevent infringement by a junior sign if the goods were dissimilar but not if they were similar in cases where there was no likelihood of confusion. The recast Directive spells out that it matters not whether the goods are identical, similar, or not similar.

The general principles to consider are: whether a trade mark has a reputation if it is known to a significant part of the relevant public at the relevant date; the relevant public are those concerned by the products or services covered by the trade mark; the relevant date is the date on which the defendant first started to use the accused sign; there is no fixed percentage threshold which could be used to assess what constituted a significant part of the public; reputation constitutes a knowledge threshold, to be assessed according to a combination of geographical and economic criteria; all relevant facts are to be taken into consideration when making the assessment (see in this regard *PAGO International GmbH v Tirolmilch Registrierte Genossenschaft mbH* (C-301/07) EU:C:2009:611; *Ornua Co-operative Ltd v Tindale & Stanton Ltd Espana SL* (C-93/16) EU:C:2017:571; *Burgerista Operations GmbH v Burgista Bros Ltd & Ors* [2018] EWHC 35 (IPEC)).

By reference to the reputation of products sold online (Amazon), 'positive reviews by those who bought the product cannot enhance the trade mark as those sales are the acts which . . . have been detrimental to the reputation of the mark' (*Jadebay Ltd/Noa and Nani Ltd (t/a The Discount Outlet) v Clarke-Coles Ltd (t/a Feel Good UK)* [2017] EWHC 1400 (IPEC); [2017] ETMR 34).

The rationale behind the protection of marks with a reputation (regardless of whether it equates to the doctrine of dilution found in other jurisdictions) can be restated thus, bearing in mind that the requirements of the provision are cumulative:

- the purpose of s. 10(3) is distinct from that in s. 10(2) and liability does not depend on there being a likelihood of confusion (*Sabel BV v Puma AG* at [20]; Case C-252/07 *Intel Corporation Inc v CPM United Kingdom Ltd* [2008] ECR I-8823 at [50]);

- there must be identity between the senior mark and the sign (assessed under the *LTJ* test) or at the least similarity (assessed under the test in *Sabel v Puma*). Where similarity is alleged, this must have the effect of making the consumer make a link to the senior mark, although the presence of such a link on its own is not enough as there must be resultant harm to the senior mark (Case C-252/07 *Intel Corporation Inc v CPM United Kingdom Ltd* at [41–42] and Case C 487/07 *L'Oréal SA v Bellure NV*, CJEU [2009] ECR I-5185 at [36–37]). Whether the consumer makes such a link is to be assessed globally, taking into account all the factors listed by the CJEU in *Intel*;

- the provision only applies to marks with a reputation, the meaning of which was explained by the CJEU in Case C-375/97 *General Motors Corporation v Yplon SA* [1999] ECR I-5421. 'Reputation' requires the mark to be 'known', which appears to be a lower standard than requiring the mark to be 'famous' or even 'well-known';

- use of the infringing sign must be 'without due cause', a phrase which probably means 'necessary' (*Premier Brands UK Ltd v Typhoon Europe Ltd* [2000] FSR 767), the onus being on the defendant to establish positively that they had good reason to use the mark;

- three types of harm can be caused to the senior mark, namely detriment to the distinctive character of the mark ('whittling away' or 'blurring'), detriment to the repute of the mark ('tarnishment' or 'degradation') and taking unfair advantage ('parasitism' or 'free-riding') (Case C-252/07 *Intel Corporation Inc v CPM United Kingdom Ltd* at [27] and Case C–487/07 *L'Oréal SA v Bellure NV* at [38]); and

- the section is not intended to provide sweeping protection for any mark with a reputation.

Whether there is protection is a matter of degree depending on all the circumstances. Proof of dilution requires evidence of a change in economic behaviour of the relevant average consumer consequent on the use of the sign, or a serious likelihood that such a change will take place in the future (Case C-252/07 *Intel Corporation Inc v CPM United Kingdom Ltd* at [77]). There is no need for proof of the defendant's subjective intention to exploit the reputation in the claimant's mark in order to establish unfair advantage (*Jack Wills v House of Fraser (Stores)* [2014] FSR at [75]–[80]). However, establishing that there was an advantage is not sufficient and it is necessary to demonstrate that an added factor making it unfair exists (*Whirlpool Corp v Kenwood Ltd* [2009] EWCA Civ 753 at [136]). The fact that there is no longer any likelihood of confusion does not mean that dilution stops happening.

The gist of the action is 'cross-pollination' between the claimant's and defendant's trade marks: *Electrocoin Automatics Ltd v Coinworld Ltd; Oasis Stores Ltd's Trade Mark Application* [1998] RPC 631.

> ### *Pfizer Ltd v Eurofood Link (UK) Ltd* [2001] FSR 17
>
> A good example of 'cross-pollination' can be found in *Pfizer Ltd v Eurofood Link (UK) Ltd* [2001] FSR 17 where the evidence clearly pointed to the defendant's having attempted to 'free-ride' on the success of the VIAGRA mark, not only by the choice of the name VIAGRENE for a drink which was claimed to have aphrodisiac properties, but by the choice of a blue lozenge-shaped logo for the website advertising the drink (VIAGRA tablets are made in the shape of a blue lozenge). The conduct amounted both to 'taking advantage' of the registered mark, and causing it 'detriment' by creating an association with something unwholesome.

By contrast, in *Premier Brands UK Ltd v Typhoon Europe Ltd* there was neither taking advantage of nor creating an unwelcome association with the mark TY.PHOO (registered for tea) when the defendant used TYPHOON for kitchenware. This was despite the claimant's strenuous assertions that its mark would be harmed because consumers might 'call to mind' a ferocious and damaging tropical storm. Equally, in *Daimler-Chrysler AG v Alavi* [2001] RPC 813 the defendant had operated his Carnaby Street shop under the name MERC for many years and there was no evidence that he had attempted to make use of the reputation of the MERCEDES-BENZ trade mark to sell his goods, nor that the cars' image had been tarnished as a result.

 Pause for reflection

When considering the criteria for infringement found respectively in TMA s. 10(1), s. 10(2) and s. 10(3), has the CJEU always provided clear guidance to enable lawyers to advise their clients as to the issues of identity of signs under s. 10(1), similarity of signs and similarity of goods under s. 10(2), and harm to marks with a reputation under s. 10(3)?

13.4.4 Expanded scope of trade mark protection in light of the recast Directive

In addition to provisions featuring in the Directive, the recast Directive expands the scope of trade mark protection by introducing the right to prohibit preparatory acts in relation to the use of packaging or other means (Art. 11).

Article 12 of the recast Directive (implemented as s. 99A TMA) also offers specific protection to the reproduction of trade marks in dictionaries, stipulating that if the reproduction of a trade mark in a dictionary, encyclopaedia, or similar reference work, in print or electronic form, gives the impression that it constitutes the generic name of the goods or services for which the trade mark is registered, the publisher of the work shall, at the request of the proprietor of the trade mark, ensure that the reproduction of the trade mark is, without delay, and in the case of works in printed form at the latest in the next edition of the publication, accompanied by an indication that it is a registered trade mark.

13.5 Loss of registration

Intellectual property litigation tends to be aggressive. In the case of trade marks, entry of a mark on the Register is only *prima facie* evidence of its validity (TMA s. 72). The wording of s. 72 has two consequences: first, registration can never be totally guaranteed (TMA s. 70); and second, the onus is placed on the defendant to challenge the registration. A defendant who is sued for trade mark infringement, besides denying that infringement has been made out or raising one of the statutory defences, will usually try to counterclaim that the mark should be removed from the Register. The grounds of such a counterclaim will be:

- the registered mark should be revoked under TMA s. 46 because it has been mismanaged by its owner since the date registration was completed. Mismanagement comprises non-use, generic use, or deceptive use; and/or

- the mark should be declared invalid under s. 47, on the ground that it failed to comply with TMA s. 3 or s. 5 at the time it was registered.

 Pause for reflection

By reference to the scenario question, which activities could be subject to revocation or invalidity proceedings?

13.5.1 The difference between revocation and invalidity

In contrast to patents and registered designs where, as we shall see, the two terms are interchangeable, trade mark law draws a very precise distinction between revocation and invalidity. They bear completely different meanings. Revocation relates to the conduct of the proprietor *since* registration, conduct which in some way has 'tainted' a previously valid mark. It is essentially concerned with failure to look after the trade mark, to nurture it, since it was registered. The effect of a successful revocation application is that the mark is removed from the Register for the future (from the date of the application to revoke) unless the tribunal directs otherwise. In the context of an infringement action, revocation of the claimant's mark will not exonerate the defendant from past acts of infringement, although it will enable the defendant to continue using their sign in the future. Invalidity, on the other hand, relates to the fact that the trade mark should never have been registered in the first place because at the time it was registered, it did not comply with the TMA. A declaration of invalidity is backdated to the time the mark was filed, so is a much more effective tactic for a defendant to argue than revocation. Invalidity means that the registration never existed (so the defendant cannot have infringed) whilst revocation removes the mark from the Register only for the future, leaving the defendant still liable for acts of past infringement. The actions for revocation and invalidity are independent: *T-Mobile (UK) Ltd v O2 Holdings Ltd*, Appointed Person, 13 December 2007. The difference between revocation and invalidity of trade marks is illustrated in Diagram 13.2.

DIAGRAM 13.2 *The difference between the revocation and invalidity of trade marks*

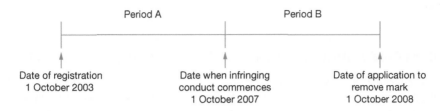

Notes:

1 If the mark is successfully removed under s. 46 TMA (revocation), this will normally operate from 1 October 2008 onwards. Liability for infringement during Period B is *not* affected.

2 If the mark is successfully removed under s. 47 TMA (invalidity), this will operate from 1 October 2003. The mark is treated as if it never existed and so *cannot* be infringed.

13.5.2 Revocation

An application to revoke a registered trade mark can be brought by any person: there is no requirement of *locus standi*. The application can be made directly to the Trade Marks Registry or it can be raised by way of a counterclaim in opposition or infringement proceedings. There are three grounds of revocation listed in TMA s. 46(1).

13.5.2.1 Revocation for non-use

TMA s. 46(1) contains two separate objections to a mark on the basis of non-use. They comprise five years' non-use of the trade mark since it was first entered on the Register (s. 46(1)(a)) and any continuous five-year period of non-use (s. 46(1)(b)); if you don't use it, you lose it! The policy behind revocation for non-use (stated in *Imperial Group v Philip Morris* [1982] FSR 72) is that the Register should be an accurate reflection of marks currently in use. To stockpile marks in case of possible future need or to register a mark as a pre-emptive strike against a competitor is contrary to this policy.

Under s. 46(1)(a), the five-year period runs from the date the registration process is completed, not the date of application (*BON MATIN Trade Mark* [1989] RPC 537), whilst under s. 46(1)(b), any continuous period of non-use counts. An application for revocation can be brought as soon as the five-year period has elapsed. The onus is then on the trade mark owner to show that the mark has been used (TMA s. 100). The only qualification is that no revocation application can be brought where use is recommenced before the application to revoke is made. However, no account is taken of use which is recommenced during the three-month period before the application to revoke if the trade mark proprietor already knew that the application to revoke might be made (s. 46(3)). Granting a licence to use the mark is not evidence of use, simply evidence of preparations to use the mark: *Philosophy Inc v Ferretti Studios SRL* [2003] RPC 287.

The CJEU has confirmed that during the period of five years following registration of an EU trade mark, its proprietor may, if there is a likelihood of confusion, prevent third parties from using an identical or similar sign in the course of trade for goods and services identical or similar to those for which the earlier mark had been registered without having to demonstrate genuine use of that mark in respect of those goods or services (*Länsförsäkringar AB v Matek A/S* (Case C-654/15) [2017] ETMR 10).

Section 46(1)(a) and (b) both require the proprietor to make 'genuine' use of the mark.

Case C-40/01 *Ansul BV v Ajax Brandbeveiliging BV* [2003] ECR I-2439

Use is 'genuine', according to the CJEU in Case C-40/01 *Ansul BV v Ajax Brandbeveiliging BV* [2003] ECR I-2439, where the mark is used in accordance with its essential function. In other words, the mark must guarantee the identity of the origin of the goods or services for which it is registered, in order to create or preserve an outlet for those goods or services. Whereas the test for genuine use is different from that for establishing goodwill in the context of passing off, the central principle is the same (*Johnny Rockets Licensing Corp v Eddie Rockets (Ireland) Ltd* [2016] ETMR 37). Genuine use does not include token use for the sole purpose of preserving the rights conferred by the mark. When assessing whether use of the trade mark is genuine, regard must be had to all the facts and circumstances, particularly whether other traders would regard the use as justified to maintain or create a share in the market for the goods or services protected by the mark. The court should also consider the nature of those goods or services, the characteristics of the market, and the scale and frequency of use of the mark.

The principles for the assessment of whether there has been genuine use of a trade mark were established in *London Taxi Corp v Frazer-Nash Research Ltd* [2016] EWHC 52 (Ch), [2016] ETMR 18 at [219] in a manner which was not criticized on appeal: Genuine use means actual use of the trade mark by the proprietor or by a third party with authority to use the mark. The use must be more than merely token, that is to say, serving solely to preserve the rights conferred by the registration of the mark. The use must be consistent with the essential function of a trade mark, which is to guarantee the identity of the origin of the goods or services to the consumer or end user by enabling him to distinguish the goods or services from others which have another origin. Use of the mark must relate to goods or services which are already marketed or which are about to be marketed and for which preparations to secure customers are under way, particularly in the form of advertising campaigns. The use must be by way of real commercial exploitation of the mark on the market for the relevant goods or services, that is to say, use in accordance with the commercial *raison d'être* of the mark, which is to create or preserve an outlet for the goods or services that bear the mark. It is not the case that every proven commercial use of the mark may automatically be deemed to constitute genuine use. These principles have been repeated in other cases since, such as *W3 Limited v Easygroup Limited v Jean Camille Pons* [2018] EWHC 7 (Ch).

In *Ansul* (which concerned the activities of the trade mark owner supplying parts and chemicals to maintain fire extinguishers it had previously sold), the CJEU added that the fact that a mark is not used for goods newly available on the market but for goods that were sold in the past does not mean that its use is not genuine. It suffices if the proprietor makes actual use of the same mark for component parts that are integral to the make-up or structure of such goods, or for goods or services directly connected with the goods previously sold and intended to meet the needs of customers of those goods. In other words, the nature of the goods and the market for them has to be considered. Also relevant, as in *POLICE Trade Mark* [2004] RPC 693, is the size of the trade mark owner's business. This does not mean that there is one rule for big businesses and one for small firms: rather it is an element in deciding whether the use of the mark has been genuine. In the same way, the quantum of use should be considered, but this does not mean that a small number of sales cannot be genuine use. It all depends on the facts of the case. So, in Case C-442/07 *Verein Radetzky-Orden v Bundesvereinigung Kameradschaft 'Feldmarschall Radetzky'* [2008] ECR I-9223 putting the mark on headed paper sufficed in the case of a voluntary non-profit organization.

The *Ansul* ruling has been applied by the Court of Appeal in *Laboratoires Goëmar SA v La Mer Technology Inc* [2006] FSR 49. In overturning the decision of Blackburne J, it held that although the volume of sales had been small (only £800 worth had been despatched to one intermediary who had then gone into liquidation) and had not been to members of the public, the transactions in question had been at arm's length so that title to the goods had been transferred. That transfer of title had been with a view to creating a retail outlet for the goods. This was not token use for the purpose of protecting the mark from revocation, but genuine use as required by the Directive. It was the quality of the use that mattered, not the quantity.

Under similar provisions under the 1938 Act, the nature of the use made by the proprietor was crucial. Promotional use did not count: see *KODAK Trade Mark* [1990] FSR 49 where it was held that use of KODAK on T-shirts was not enough to maintain the registration for clothing, as the use was advertising KODAK films, not indicating the origin of the T-shirts. Under the current law, the rulings of the CJEU in *Arsenal v Reed*, *Opel* and *Céline* are likely to be relevant. What amounts to 'trade mark use' for the purposes of infringement will be appropriate in deciding what amounts to use for the purpose of maintaining a registration. In Case C-495/07 *Silberquelle GmbH v Maselli-Strickmode GmbH* [2009] ECR I-137 the CJEU ruled that there had not been genuine use of the trade mark (WELLNESS for drinks) where the proprietor had affixed it to bottles of alcohol-free drinks which it then gave away free to customers who bought items of clothing sold under the same mark. The drinks mark (as opposed to the clothing mark) had been correctly revoked for non-use. In this area, just as in other areas of trade mark law, the views of the consumer will be relevant.

ORIENT EXPRESS Trade Mark, Appointed Person, 31 October 2008

In *ORIENT EXPRESS Trade Mark*, Appointed Person, 31 October 2008, the Appointed Person upheld the decision of the Hearing Officer that there should be partial revocation for non-use of the trade mark ORIENT EXPRESS. The trade mark owner had appealed against the decision, arguing that two of the products to be deleted from the specification of goods (whisky and olive oil) were covered by the use of the name 'Orient Express Gift Boutique' on board the trade mark owner's trains, arguing that the Hearing Officer had misapplied the CJEU'S ruling in *Céline*, where it was suggested that use of a name over a shop could be trade mark infringement. The Appointed Person stated that much depended on the perception of the average consumer, and whether they saw the name of the shop as an identifier of the origin of the goods sold there or merely as an identifier of the retail business carried on there. The key issue was whether use of the mark as the name of the on-board shop was use 'in relation to' the goods concerned. Here there was evidence that the shops had sold other companies' goods: it was therefore arguable that the name did not operate as a badge of origin for the goods concerned so that there had not been genuine use.

Under s. 46(1)(a) or (b), the proprietor can prevent revocation by showing that there existed proper reasons for non-use. 'Proper reasons' means obstacles arising independently of the will of the proprietor rather than incompetence or inefficiency on the part of the trade mark owner: *MAGIC BALL Trade Mark* [2000] RPC 439. The CJEU has stated (in Case C-246/05 *Armin Häupl v Lidl Stiftung & Co KG* [2007] ECR I-4673) that obstacles to non-use must have a direct relationship with the trade mark, so that its use is impossible or unreasonable and that these must be independent of the will of the proprietor. This will be a heavy burden to discharge.

Alternatively, the proprietor can show that the mark has been used in a form differing in elements which do not affect the distinctive character of the mark. This alternative argument against revocation is very narrow, so that using NEUTRALIA when what was registered was NUTRALIA did not suffice to avoid revocation for non-use (*Neutrogena v Golden Ltd t/a Laboratoires Garnier*) (the first syllable, though only one letter different, conveyed a totally different meaning to the consumer, suggesting that the product was PH-neutral rather than that it was derived from nuts). Likewise, using similar but different cartoon drawings of penguins from those which were registered did not prevent revocation (*United Biscuits (UK) Ltd v Asda Stores Ltd* [1997] RPC 513), and using VENICE SIMPLON ORIENT EXPRESS differed significantly from the registered mark (ORIENT EXPRESS) so that the owner could not rely on s. 46(2) (*ORIENT EXPRESS Trade Mark*).

 Pause for reflection

Has the CJEU provided sufficiently clear guidance as to what amounts to 'genuine use' in the context of revocation?

To what extent could s. 46(1) apply by reference to St Regent's basketball club?

13.5.2.2 Revocation because the mark has become generic

Under s. 46(1)(c) a registered trade mark will be revoked if, in consequence of the acts or inactivity of the proprietor, the mark has become the common name in the trade for the product or service for which it is registered. In other words the mark has become generic, the name of the product itself. Consider the name ASPIRIN. Originally this was a registered trade mark of Bayer AG but is now the name for a painkiller. Other trade marks which have been lost due to becoming generic include LINOLEUM, CELLOPHANE, and YO-YO.

Section 46(1)(c) will come into play both where the trade mark owner has misused the mark personally, and where they have done nothing to stop others' misuse. Whether the mark has become the common name in the trade for the product is assessed through the eyes of the average consumer: Case C-371/02 *Björnekulla Fruktindustrier AB v Procordia Food AB* [2004] ECR I-5791. This has the effect of reversing the old United Kingdom law in *DAIQUIRI RUM Trade Mark* [1969] RPC 600 (HL) which asked whether other traders used the mark as the common name for the product. The trade mark owner must therefore ensure that the use of the mark, whether by the owner in its advertising or by others, does not lead the public to use it generically.

Pause for reflection

In the light of the CJEU ruling in *Björnekulla Fruktindustrier AB v Procordia Food AB*, consider whether the trade mark HOOVER for vacuum cleaners is liable to be revoked for having become generic in the eyes of the consumer.

What about the trade mark for the words 'Basketball Club' in the scenario question?

13.5.2.3 Revocation because of deceptive use

Under s. 46(1)(d), the last ground of revocation is that in consequence of the use made of it by the proprietor, the mark is liable to mislead the public. The leading decision under the 1938 Act was *GE Trade Mark* [1973] RPC 297 (HL) which emphasized the 'clean hands' doctrine as the basis for this category of revocation. Under the TMA, the deception must arise because of the use of the mark by its owner, which suggests positive misconduct. One suggested example of deceptive use can be found in the somewhat complex facts of *Scandecor Developments AB v Scandecor Marketing AB* [2001] 2 CMLR 645. Here, the House of Lords was prepared (until the case was settled voluntarily) to refer to the CJEU the question of whether the failure to exercise quality control over an exclusive licensee by the trade mark proprietor, so that the public associated the mark with the licensee, amounted to deceptive use under s. 46(1)(d).

On the limited CJEU authority so far available, it seems that this ground of revocation is narrower than the 'clean hands' doctrine in *GE Trade Mark*, and forms a mirror image of one of the Absolute Grounds for refusal where a mark will be rejected under TMA s. 3(3)(b) if it is deceptive.

Case C-259/04 *Elizabeth Emanuel v Continental Shelf* [2006] ECR I-3089

In Case C-259/04 *Elizabeth Emanuel v Continental Shelf* [2006] ECR I-3089, a famous fashion designer had registered her name as a trade mark in 1994. Having subsequently assigned her business to a company, becoming its employee before ultimately resigning, she opposed a number of further applications to register her name made by the eventual successors of her business, arguing that the marks were deceptive under TMA s. 3(3)(b). She also sought revocation of the earlier registration under s. 46(1)(d) on the ground that it had become deceptive as to the origin of the goods. The CJEU ruled that the wording of the Directive required there to be actual deceit or a sufficiently serious risk that the consumer would be deceived. Although a consumer might be influenced by the name 'Elizabeth Emanuel' when buying a garment, the characteristics and qualities of that garment remained guaranteed by the business which owned the mark. Therefore the name itself could not be regarded as being of such a nature as to deceive the public.

The CJEU reached its conclusion in the *Emanuel* case by considering the functions performed by trade marks (set out in its ruling in *Arsenal*), adding that the public interest ground underlying Art. 3(1)(g) (the parent of TMA s. 3(3)(b)) was consumer protection. Its remarks about the interpretation of 'deceive' echo those of AG Colomer, who stated that Art. 3(1)(g) referred to the intrinsic characteristics of the trade mark. The sign must confuse the public by virtue of its inherent qualities, containing incorrect information, which must be deceptive from an objective point of view. The CJEU added that the fact that a mark consisting of the name of an individual had been assigned did not of itself render the mark deceptive (otherwise such marks could never be capable of assignment). There might be circumstances where the assignee of the mark misled consumers into thinking that the named individual was still associated with the business. That might amount to fraudulent conduct, but that would not affect the trade mark itself.

13.5.2.4 Partial revocation

Section 46(5) provides for partial revocation. The objection may be in respect of only some of the goods or services of the registration, so that the effect of partial revocation will be to leave the mark on the Register but with a reduced statement of goods and services. The threat of revocation, particularly for non-use, coupled with the broader protection accorded to registered marks under s. 10, means that there is no need for a trade mark applicant to seek protection for a wide range of goods and services (unless, of course, they do actually trade in such a way).

Several cases have considered how the court ought to approach the task of reducing the scope of the registration in cases of partial revocation, bearing in mind that there is a balance to be struck between the proprietor, other traders, and the public. The problem is that the classification of goods and services set out in Sch. 4 to the Trade Mark (Amendment) Rules 2001 (derived from the Nice Agreement) contains items with a very wide scope. Consider as examples 'computer programs' in Class 9 (*Mercury Communications Ltd v Mercury Interactive (UK) Ltd* [1995] FSR 850) and 'printed matter' in Class 16 (*MINERVA Trade Mark* [2000] FSR 734). 'Beers' was held too wide as a statement of goods when all that the trade mark owner had supplied was 'bitter beer': *David West t/a Eastenders v Fuller Smith & Turner plc* [2003] FSR 816. Even 'household containers' (*Premier Brands UK Ltd v Typhoon Europe Ltd*) is a category covering a wide range of items. The problem therefore, as stated in the last-mentioned case, and over which there has been some debate, is whether it is necessary for the court to 'dig deeper' into how the trade mark owner has actually used the mark. The solution, suggested by the Court of Appeal in *Thomson Holidays Ltd v Norwegian Cruise Lines Ltd* [2003] RPC 586, is to use the viewpoint of the reasonably informed consumer of the product in question. The court should consider the nature of the proprietor's business and then decide how the notional consumer would describe such use. Here the consumer would have described the claimant's business as 'package holidays' and so its registration of FREESTYLE would be cut back accordingly, with other services being deleted from the registration.

In approaching claims for part cancellation of the registration of a trade mark, the important elements to take into consideration are (a) to identify the goods or services in relation to which the mark had been used during the relevant period; (b) to consider the goods or services for which the mark was registered; (c) to take care not to strip the proprietor of protection for goods or services which were not different from them and could not be distinguished from them other than in an arbitrary way; (d) to have regard to the perception of the average consumer and the purpose and intended use of the products or services in issue (*Merck KGaA v Merck Sharp & Dohme Corp* [2017] EWCA Civ 1834; [2018] ETMR 10).

13.5.3 Invalidity

An application to have a trade mark declared invalid can be made directly to the Trade Marks Registry or it can be raised by way of a counterclaim in opposition or infringement proceedings. A declaration of invalidity is based on the simple premise that the trade mark was registered in error. The effect of a successful application for a declaration of invalidity is that the mark is removed from the Register retrospectively, that is from the date of the original registration. In contrast to revocation, this will exonerate the defendant from past acts of infringement, and consequently is a much more effective tactic to pursue. Like revocation, invalidity may be total or partial, so that partial invalidity results in the mark staying on the Register but with a reduced statement of goods and services.

The grounds on which a trade mark can be declared invalid are set out in TMA s. 47(1). The subsection covers two things: first, that the mark was registered in breach of s. 3. However, under the proviso to s. 47(1) (which equates to the proviso to s. 3(1)), where the mark was registered in breach of s. 3(1)(b), (c), or (d), the plea of invalidity may be overcome where the mark has acquired factual distinctiveness since the date of registration. The proviso to s. 47(1) therefore operates in the same way as the proviso to s. 3(1), with one difference. The latter requires that factual distinctiveness be acquired by use *before the date of application* to register the trade mark. The former requires that factual distinctiveness be acquired by use *between the date of registration and the date of the application for the declaration of invalidity*. Apart from this, the effect of the two provisos is the same. The evidence required under s. 47(1) will presumably have to comply with the criteria for acquired distinctiveness set out by the CJEU in Cases C-108/97 and 109/97 *Windsurfing Chiemsee Produktions und Vertriebs GmbH v Boots und Segelzubehor Walter Huber* [1999] ECR I-2779. Article 4(3) of the recast Directive clearly stipulates that a trade mark shall not be declared invalid for the same reasons if, before the date of application for a declaration of invalidity, following the use which has been made of it, it has acquired a distinctive character.

 Pause for reflection

Could St James' basketball club apply for a declaration of invalidity of the trade mark 'Basketball Club' on the basis that it does not meet the conditions of s. 3?

The second ground of invalidity is that the mark was registered in breach of s. 5, unless the owner of the prior right consented. However, and in contrast to challenge under s. 3, the standing to seek a declaration of invalidity under s. 5 is much more constrained. Under the Trade Marks (Relative Grounds) Order 2007 (SI 2007/1976), only the owner of the earlier right can bring an action under s. 5, and the Trade Marks (Proof of Use) Regulations 2004 (SI 2004/946) requires such an action to be brought within five years of the registration of the junior mark. Whilst, therefore, it is not fatal if the owner of the earlier right fails to bring opposition proceedings or is unsuccessful in them, they must nevertheless act within the time limits. No one else can challenge the mark for conflict with earlier rights.

Sub-sections 47(5) and 47(6) allow the Court to make a declaration of partial invalidity in cases where the invalidity grounds affect only some of the goods or services in respect of which the mark is registered (*Caspian Pizza Ltd v Shah* [2017] EWCA Civ 1874; [2018] ETMR 8).

13.5.4 Changes following the implementation of the recast Directive

The recast Directive has introduced changes in invalidity and revocation.

Article 6 establishes invalidity or revocation of a trade mark *a posteriori* in the sense that where the seniority of a national trade mark or of a trade mark registered under international arrangements is claimed for an EU trade mark, the invalidity or revocation of the trade mark providing the basis for the seniority claim may be established a posteriori, provided that the invalidity or revocation could have been declared at the time the mark was surrendered or allowed to lapse. In such a case, the seniority shall cease to produce its effects.

Article 8 stipulates that an application for a declaration of invalidity on the basis of an earlier trade mark shall not succeed at the date of application for invalidation if it would not have been successful at the filing date or the priority date of the later trade mark for any of the following reasons: the earlier trade mark, liable to be declared invalid pursuant to Art. 4(1)(b), (c), or (d), had not yet acquired a distinctive character as referred to in Art. 4(4); the application for a declaration of invalidity is based on Art. 5(1)(b) and the earlier trade mark had not yet become sufficiently distinctive to support a finding of likelihood of confusion within the meaning of Art. 5(1)(b); the application for a declaration of invalidity is based on Art. 5(3)(a) and the earlier trade mark had not yet acquired a reputation within the meaning of Art. 5(3)(a).

Finally, Art. 9 precludes a declaration of invalidity due to acquiescence.

The provisions of the recast Directive were implemented in the United Kingdom on January 2019 through the Trade Marks Regulations 2018.

13.6 Conclusion

In this chapter we have examined the legal framework covering trade mark infringement and we have also discussed the instances where a mark can lose its registration by being revoked or declared invalid. We have seen that the provisions on infringement mirror the provisions on relative grounds for refusal and we have also discussed the concept of trade mark use as a requirement for trade mark infringement and the meaning it has received through judicial interpretation.

By reference to the scenario question, St James' basketball club should be advised that Mr Green uses an identical mark to the one on which they have a registered trade mark by reference to the same goods and services so there is a likely case of trade mark infringement to the extent that the use made takes place in the course of trade. This was highlighted in a very similar case, *Arsenal v Reed*, where the CJEU held that the trade mark owners can rely on the provisions on infringement. In particular, the CJEU held that where a third party uses in the course of trade a sign which is identical to a validly registered trade mark on goods which are identical to those for which it is registered, the trade mark proprietor of the mark is entitled to rely on Art. 5(1)(a) of the directive to prevent that use. Importantly, the CJEU held that it is immaterial that, in the context of that use, the sign is perceived as a badge of support for or loyalty or affiliation to the trade mark proprietor. Although when the case was returned to the High Court, Laddie J applied the principles of law but not conclusions on the facts, as the CJEU was said to exceed its jurisdiction by making findings of fact; the Court of Appeal had a different view. It held that the important question is whether the use is such that takes unfair advantage of the status and repute of the trade mark. Since the *Arsenal* case, the CJEU has revisited the requirement of trade mark use and elaborated on this requirement in C-17/06 *Céline SARL v Céline SA* [2007] ECR I-7041 where it identified four conditions which must be satisfied before the trade mark right is infringed: the use must be in the course of trade; it must be without the consent of the proprietor of the mark; it must be in respect of goods or services; and it must affect or be liable to affect the functions of the trade mark, in particular its essential function of guaranteeing to consumers the origin of the goods or services.

With regards to St Regent's basketball club and their registered trade marks, St James' basketball club can make an application for the revocation of the mark. Section 46(1) contains two separate objections to a mark on the basis of non-use, namely five years' non-use of the trade mark since it was first entered on the Register (s. 46(1)(a)) and any continuous five-year period of non-use (s. 46(1)(b)). As stated in *Imperial Group v Philip Morris* [1982] FSR 72 is the Register should be an accurate reflection of marks currently in use.

With regards to the registered trade mark 'Basketball Club', which belongs to AllForTheGame Ltd, St James's basketball club should be advised that this is a likely case for revocation under TMA s. 46 because the mark has been mismanaged by its owner since the date registration was completed. In particular s. 46(1)(c) states that a registered trade mark will be revoked if, in consequence of the acts or inactivity of the proprietor, the mark has become the common name in the trade for the product or service for which it is registered. In other words the mark has become generic, the name of the product itself. Various trade marks have been lost due to becoming generic, including ASPIRIN, LINOLEUM, CELLOPHANE, and YO-YO. The perspective of the average consumer in assessing whether the mark has become the common name in the trade for the product is paramount: Case C-371/02 *Björnekulla Fruktindustrier AB v Procordia Food AB* [2004] ECR I-5791. By reference to the trade mark 'Basketball Club', St James' basketball club can also make an application to declare that mark invalid. The grounds on which a trade mark can be declared invalid are set out in TMA s. 47(1), including that the mark was registered in breach of s. 3. Here it can be claimed that the mark 'Basketball Club' is descriptive and has not acquired distinctiveness on the basis of the proviso to s. 47(1) (which equates to the proviso to s. 3(1)). The actions for revocation and invalidity are independent (*T-Mobile (UK) Ltd v O2 Holdings Ltd*, Appointed Person, 13 December 2007).

End-of-chapter questions

After reading the chapter carefully, try answering the following questions. For answer guidance visit the online resources at **www.oup.com/uk/karapapa-mcdonagh/**

1. The decision of the European Court of Justice in *Arsenal v Reed* is a disaster for business. Its ruling on what constitutes trade mark use is so wide there is a real danger that powerful brands will become unfair monopolies. Discuss.

2. How is trade mark use established in cases involving 'adwords', i.e. cases where a trader purchases a search engine keyword that is identical or similar to the claimant's mark so that when the user of a website types in the mark, a sponsored link is displayed which has nothing to do with the claimant's business. Does this qualify as 'trade mark use'?

3. What is the difference between revocation and invalidity of trade marks?

Further reading

For understanding the protection available to trade marks, the following readings are recommended:

Bornkamm, Judge J. 'Harmonising Trade Mark Law in Europe: the Stephen Stewart Memorial Lecture' [1999] 3 *IPQ* 283

Explains the relationship between ss. 10(1), 10(2), and 10(3) TMA and how they create a 'triad of protection' for the trade mark owner.

Dawson, N. 'Non-Trade Mark Use' [2012] 4 *IPQ* 204

Considers the role of trade mark functions in the context of infringement.

Dinwoodie, G. B. and Janis, M. D., 'Confusion Over Use: Contextualism in Trademark Law' [2007] *Iowa Law Review* 92(5), 1597

Argues that trademark use theory is flawed and should be rejected, and proposes that trademark law retain its traditional preference for contextual analysis.

Lambert, P. 'More than Meets the Eye: Expert Evidence varies in Intellectual Property Infringement Cases' [2018] 40(3) *EIPR* 178

Argues that industrial and technological advances are likely to increase the need for more specialist experts in intellectual property infringement cases.

Norman, H. 'Davidoff v Gofkid: Dealing with the Logical Lapse or Creating European Disharmony' [2003] 3 *IPQ* 342

Explains how the ECJ set about dealing with the apparently unfair treatment accorded to marks with a reputation when used on similar goods in circumstances where there was no confusion.

Norman, H. 'Time to Blow the Whistle on Trade Mark Use' [2004] 1 *IPQ* 1

The requirement of trade mark use both under the 1938 Trade Marks Act and the 1994 Act. It also analyses the decision in Arsenal v Reed and the consequences of the CJEU's wide view of what constitutes 'taking unfair advantage' of a trade mark.

Simon Fhima, I. *Trade Mark Dilution in Europe and the United States* (Oxford University Press, 2011)
A comprehensive survey and analysis of the protection of trade marks against dilution in two different legal systems.

Simon Fhima, I. 'Dilution by Blurring—A Conceptual Road Map' [2010] 1 *IPQ* 44
Considers the theoretical justifications for dilution.

Simon Fhima, I. 'Exploring the Roots of European Dilution' [2012] 1 *IPQ* 25
Discusses the way in which pre-harmonization national trade mark laws might have influenced the emerging EU jurisprudence.

Simon Fhima, I. and Denvir, C., 'An Empirical Analysis of the Likelihood of Confusion Factors in European Trade Mark Law' (2015) 46 *IIC* 310
An empirical study on how the test for likelihood of confusion is operated by the courts.

Spence, M. 'Section 10 of the Trade Marks Act 1994: Is There Really a Logical Lapse' [2001] 23(9) *EIPR* 423
Explains the potential gap between s. 10(2) (where likelihood of confusion must be proved) and the original wording of s. 10(3) which required a mark with a reputation to be used on dissimilar goods.

14 Defences to trade mark infringement

Problem question

Read this problem question carefully and keep it in mind while you are working through the chapter that follows. At the end of this chapter, you will be able to apply what you have learnt to the problem question and advise the relevant parties.

Since May 2005, Alfred Wolf uses the mark 'Wolf's Deli' written in distinctive blue fonts by reference to corned beef that he sells in supermarkets throughout the United Kingdom. He has not applied to register this mark as a trade mark. He has registered a figurative mark as a UK trade mark for products in Class 29, featuring a minimalist drawing depicting the figure of a wolf. Since March 2008, he is advertising his goods in various local newspapers using the following slogan: 'Hungrier than the . . . Wolf'.

On 6 February 2018, Alfred receives a letter from Adrian Burton, a trade mark attorney based in Reading, Berkshire, that he should stop using the mark Wolf by reference to his products because his clients, The Food Group Ltd, have registered the mark 'Wolf' as a UK trade mark since August 2017 for products in Class 29 of the Nice Classification, which includes 'meat, fish, poultry and game; meat extracts; eggs'. They mostly sell fresh meat and poultry. He stresses in the letter that Alfred has to stop using the slogan as his clients are using a similar advertising slogan by reference to their products ('As hungry as the . . . Wolf'), on which they have registered a UK trade mark since August 2017 for goods in Class 29 and consumers may be misled to think that Alfred's products are better than his client's.

Alfred Wolf asks your legal advice by reference to this letter and also with regards to the following activities:

- he found out that Carnex Ltd exports 'Wolf's Deli' corned beef in Spain, where they sell it at a much lower price. They buy it from one of Alfred Wolf's retailers in the United Kingdom. Alfred would like to know his options against the company that exports the products in Spain without his consent;

- on March 2018 he found out that corned beef of his making is sold in Italy under the name 'Lupo' (i.e. 'wolf' in Italian); an Italian supermarket chain, Marcato, imports corned

→

> beef from one of Alfred's retailers in the United Kingdom; they post a sticker to change
> the mark 'Wolf's Deli' into 'Lupo' and another sticker to add their own name and address
> to the outside of the goods. They do not apply any changes on the figure of the wolf on
> which Alfred has a registered UK trade mark.

14.1 Introduction

A defendant's principal argument will be to deny that there has been any infringing conduct, and/or that what has been done is not within the scope of protection given to the registered mark. There are, however, a number of statutory defences. Some flow from the definition of infringement itself, most are based on the Directive, but some are 'home-grown'. The Court of Justice of the European Union ('CJEU') has repeatedly declared that Arts 5 to 7 of the Directive comprise a complete code of the trade mark owner's rights (Case C-414/99 *Zino Davidoff SA v A&G Imports Ltd,* Cases C-415/99 and C-416/99 *Levi Strauss & Co v Tesco Stores and Costco Wholesale UK Ltd* [2001] ECR I-8691) so it may be questioned whether the 'home-grown' defences are in breach of the Directive.

14.2 The defendant's arguments

The defendant to a trade mark infringement action has several possible counter-arguments:

- first, that there was no infringing conduct and/or that this did not fall within the scope of protection given to the registered mark; in other words, the claimant has failed to establish the key ingredients of the infringement action;

- even if all the ingredients of the infringement action have been proved, one or more of the statutory defences applies to exonerate the defendant. The availability of a particular defence will depend primarily on the facts of the case, as each defence has precise conditions which the defendant must meet in order to succeed; and

- last, that the trade mark should be removed from the Register, either under the revocation provisions (all of which are concerned with post-registration mismanagement of the trade mark by its proprietor) or under the invalidity provisions (which are to the effect that the mark was entered on the Register in error, being in breach of either the absolute or relative grounds). The effects of revocation and a declaration of invalidity are different and from the defendant's point of view, the more effective argument is that the mark should be declared invalid.

Because of the risk of a successful counterclaim for revocation or invalidity, it is standard practice for a trade mark owner to plead passing off as an alternative cause of action. Even if the mark is removed from the Register, its use should confer some degree of protection at common law.

14.3 Consent

Implicit in the definition of infringement of any intellectual property right is that the conduct occurred without the consent of the proprietor. The phrase 'without his consent' occurs in s. 9 and is listed by the CJEU in *Céline* as the second of its requirements for infringement.

Such a defence is most likely to be raised in circumstances where the mark has been licensed. This was the background to the dispute in *Northern & Shell v Condé Nast* [1995] RPC 117, where the trade mark owner, relying on a minimum sales clause in a distribution agreement, appointed another licensee when the initial licensee did not meet its sales target. When sued for infringement by the original licensee, the second licensee successfully argued that it had used the trade mark with the consent of the proprietor.

14.4 Non-trade mark use

The argument that what the defendant has done is not trade mark use and so does not infringe is governed by the CJEU rulings in *Arsenal*, *Opel*, and *Céline*. Not all use in commerce will infringe (*Travelex*). At one time it would have sufficed, in order to raise the defence, to argue that the mark had been used in a manner which did not indicate origin (*Mars v Cadbury*). Today, however, the question is broader, namely whether the defendant's use has affected the essential function of the trade mark, and in turn requires an examination of how the average consumer saw the use of the mark. All the surrounding circumstances will need to be considered.

14.4.1 Decorative use

Under the 1938 Act, decorative use of the mark (for example, putting the mark on a T-shirt) did not infringe because it did not indicate origin (*Unidoor Ltd v Marks & Spencer plc* [1988] RPC 275). Today, at least if the action is brought under s. 10(3) where what matters is the association which the claimant's mark produces in the mind of the customer, even decorative use of a figurative sign may infringe. This was made clear by the CJEU in *Adidas-Saloman AG and Adidas Benelux BV v Fitnessworld Trading Ltd* (where the defendant had used a sign resembling the Adidas 'three stripes' mark to decorate clothing). The CJEU stated that the fact that a sign was viewed as an embellishment by the relevant section of the public was not, of itself, an obstacle to claiming infringement where the degree of similarity was such that the relevant section of the public established a link between the sign and the mark. So, in the case of decorative use of a figurative (i.e. picture) mark, such as the Adidas 'three stripes' mark, it all depends on how the public perceives the decoration: if it creates an association in the minds of the public it may infringe. The Court made the same point in Case C-102/07 *Adidas AG & Adidas Benelux BV v Marca Mode, C&A Nederland, H&M and Vendex* [2008] ECR I-2439, stating that there might be infringement under Art. 5(1)(b) (if the customer was confused) or under Art. 5(2) of the Directive (if unfair advantage was taken of the claimant's mark).

14.5 **Use of another registered mark**

TMA s. 11(1) is one of the provisions with as yet no counterpart in the Directive. It provides that use of another registered mark will not infringe. The section therefore contemplates that there will be two conflicting marks on the Register. This may have come about because the owner of the earlier mark did not file opposition proceedings, or such opposition proceedings failed. It is, of course, open to the owner of the senior mark, having sued for infringement and having been met by this defence, to seek to have the junior mark declared invalid under s. 47, on the grounds that at the time of its registration, it breached the requirements of s. 5. This will be subject to the time limits imposed by s. 48.

The only qualification in s. 11(1) is that the junior mark must have been used in the form in which it is registered. An example of where this was not the case (so that the defence failed) was *Neutrogena v Golden Ltd t/a Laboratoires Garnier* [1996] RPC 473, where the defendant's registered mark was NUTRALIA. However, what it had used was NEUTRALIA, which Jacob J held was not sufficiently similar to the registered mark (because of the different imagery created by the first syllables) for the defence to be available.

The recast Directive makes clear that the right to sue for infringement is subject to prior rights.

14.6 **Protection for other traders**

TMA s. 11(2) (based on Art. 6(1) of the Directive) contains three provisions which are all intended to safeguard the interests of other traders. The three defences are, however, qualified by a proviso which requires the court to consider whether the defendant's conduct, although technically within the wording of the defence, amounted to unfair competition.

14.6.1 **Use of own name**

Paragraph (a) permits the defendant to make use of his own name and address, so that the registration of a surname or geographical name does not amount to a complete monopoly. The subsection contemplates that the defendant's name or address consists of or contains another's registered trade mark (*Céline*). So in *Reed Executive plc v Reed Business Information Ltd*, the claimant's mark REED was included in the defendant company's name REED ELSEVIER, and in *IBM Corporation v Web-Sphere Ltd*, WEBSPHERE (without a hyphen) was a registered trade mark of the claimant. A company can rely on the defence when it was using its trading name rather than its registered name: *Hotel Cipriani Srl v Cipriani (Grosvenor Street) Ltd* [2010] RPC 485.

Note that under UK law, the own name defence applies to both natural persons and corporate entities. This is no longer the case with EU law: Art. 1(13) Regulation 2015/2424 abolished Art.12(a) of Regulation 207/2009 and limited the application of the defence to natural persons only (*Sky Plc v Skykick UK Ltd* [2017] EWHC 1769 (Ch); [2017] ETMR 42); and the recast Directive has limited this defence to use of personal names and addresses, as was originally intended (Art. 14(1)(a)).

The defence is available on condition that such use is in accordance with honest practices in industrial or commercial matters. The defence hence contains a duty to act fairly in relation to the legitimate interests of a trade mark proprietor (*Maier v ASOS* [2015] EWCA Civ 220; [2015] ETMR 26).

 Pause for reflection

To what extent can the 'own name' defence be invoked in the scenario question? Which is the activity it is likely to cover?

14.6.2 Descriptive use

Paragraph (b) permits the use of 'indications concerning the kind, quality, intended purpose . . . or other characteristics of the goods or services', so that one trader can make reasonable descriptive use of another's mark (see *Hölterhoff v Ulrich Freiesleben*). An example would be where a garment manufacturer states on the care label 'Contains LYCRA' (which is a registered trade mark of the Du Pont Corporation). Such use is permissible as long as it does not overstep the limits of the proviso to the subsection. Similarly, a car dealer may advertise that it carries out the servicing of BMW cars (Case C-63/97 *BMW v Deenik* [1999] ECR I-905), or that it is a VOLVO specialist (*AB Volvo v Heritage (Leicester) Ltd* [2000] FSR 253), and a fizzy drinks manufacture can state that its product contains NUTRASWEET.

14.6.3 Use for spare parts and components

Finally, para (c) creates a defence where use of the trade mark is necessary to indicate the intended purpose of a product or service (in particular, as accessories or spare parts). A manufacturer of automotive parts may wish to state that 'these brake pads are suitable for use on the following models of FORD cars'. Whilst para (b) therefore enables the rival manufacturer to indicate the *internal* characteristics of his product ('contains NUTRASWEET'), para (c) is more concerned with its *external* attributes, such as compatibility with the products of others.

The scope of para (c) was considered by the CJEU in Case C-228/03 *The Gillette Company & Gillette Group Finland Oy v LA-Laboratories Oy* [2005] ECR I-2337. It ruled that the phrase 'accessory or spare part' was used in Art. 6 by way of example and should not be given a narrow meaning. Use of a competitor's trade mark was 'necessary' in order to provide the public with comprehensible and complete information about the intended purpose of the product. Such use was necessary if that information could not be provided by a third party without employing the trade mark. That use must, in practice, be the only means of providing such information.

14.6.4 The proviso

Section 11(2) is qualified by the proviso that such use must be in accordance with honest practices in industrial or commercial matters. The proviso seeks to balance the interests of the trade mark owner with those of other traders. Its wording can be traced to Art. 10*bis* of the Paris Convention for the Protection of Industrial Property 1883, where it forms the definition of unfair competition. The proviso to s. 11(2) therefore requires the court to consider the defendant's motives in making use of the registered mark and to examine all the surrounding circumstances.

The CJEU has on several occasions offered guidance as to the meaning of the proviso. In Case C-100/02 *Gerolsteiner Brunnen GmbH v Putsch GmbH* [2004] ECR I-691, relying on its earlier remarks in *BMW v Deenik*, it declared that the phrase 'honest practices' expressed the duty of third parties 'to act fairly in relation to the legitimate interests of the trade mark owner'. Later, in *The Gillette Company & Gillette Group Finland Oy v LA-Laboratories Oy*, the CJEU added that:

> use of the trade mark will not be in accordance with honest practices . . . if it gives the impression that there is a commercial connection between the [defendant] and the trade mark owner; it affects the value of the trade mark by taking unfair advantage of its distinctive character or repute; it entails the discrediting or denigration of the mark; or where the [defendant] presents its product as an imitation or replica of the product bearing the trade mark of which it is not the owner.

It has since explained in Case C-487/07 *L'Oréal v Bellure* at [50] that 'unfair advantage' exists where the third party seeks to ride on the coat-tails of the senior trade mark in order to benefit from its power of attraction, reputation, and prestige, and to exploit the investment made by the owner of the senior mark without paying compensation.

As a result of the CJEU's rulings in *Putsch* (which was applied in *Reed Executive plc v Reed Business Information Ltd*) and *Gillette*, s. 11(2) should *not* be seen as the converse of trade mark use, as previously suggested by the Court of Appeal in *The European Ltd v The Economist Newspaper Ltd* [1998] FSR 283. Instead, in accordance with the policy in *Arsenal v Reed*, it should be asked whether there has been trade mark use by the defendant. If there is not trade mark use, then that is an end of the case. If there has been trade mark use, what then needs to be considered is whether the defendant's conduct has breached the 'duty to act fairly'.

Guidance from the CJEU on the application of the proviso can be found in *BMW v Deenik*. The case also involved a discussion of the Art. 7 exhaustion of rights defence. Mr Deenik ran a garage in the Netherlands, specializing in the sale of second-hand BMW cars, and in the repair and servicing of such cars. He was not part of the dealer network run by BMW. The car manufacturer sued him for trade mark infringement, taking particular objection to the way in which his advertisements described him as a 'BMW specialist'. In reply, Mr Deenik relied on the defences in Art. 6(1)(c) (the origin of s. 11(1)(c)) and Art. 7. The CJEU stated that Art. 7 was the relevant defence to the sale of second-hand cars but that Art. 6(1)(c) was appropriate to the activities of repair and servicing. It then proceeded to apply the same test to each defence, noting that both defences sought to achieve a balance of interests, Art. 7 balancing the rights of the trade mark owner with the interests of the internal market, Art. 6 balancing the rights of the trade mark owner with those of other traders. Whilst use of another's trade mark may be legitimate as a means of informing consumers about the nature of the defendant's business, such use would not be permitted if it was contrary to the duty to act fairly in relation to the legitimate interests of the trade mark owner. Therefore if the advertisements for Mr Deenik's business either misled consumers into thinking that there was a commercial connection with BMW (in particular that the defendant was part of the dealer network) or if they sought to take unfair advantage of the distinctive character or repute of the trade mark, they would lose the benefit of both defences.

It can thus be seen, both from the ruling in *Deenik* and that in the later case of *Gillette*, that there is an element of consumer protection in the defence.

BMW v Deenik was relied on by Rattee J in *AB Volvo v Heritage (Leicester) Ltd* [2000] FSR 253. Here, all the circumstances surrounding the defendant's use of the claimant's trade mark were examined. The defendant, having lost its status as an approved dealer of the claimant car manufacturer, continued to describe itself on headed paper and other advertising materials as an 'independent Volvo specialist', which was true. However, of particular significance was the fact that the words 'independent' and 'specialist', placed adjacent to the registered mark, appeared in much smaller lettering. Rattee J concluded that the effect of the use of the claimant's trade mark would be to mislead the public into thinking that the defendant was still an authorized franchisee. He confirmed that the test under the proviso is objective. No reasonable motor service provider would think that the use complained of was in accordance with honest practices in that line of business.

In *IBM Corporation v Web-Sphere Ltd*, the court had no hesitation in rejecting the defence of use of own name under s. 11(2)(a) because the defendant's conduct clearly took it outside the scope of the proviso. The defendant had changed its corporate name to Web-Sphere shortly after the successful launch of IBM's product of that name. Lewison J held that it was difficult to avoid the inference that the new company name had been chosen to take advantage of IBM's goodwill, as no convincing explanation had been advanced for the change. In *Redd Solicitors LLP v Red Legal Ltd* [2012] EWPCC 54, HHJ Birss decided that had the defendant firm of licensed conveyancers bothered to check before registering their company name, they would have discovered the existence of the claimant, a leading intellectual property law firm.

 Pause for reflection

Do the defences in s. 11(2) TMA provide an effective balance between the interests of the trade mark owner and other traders?

14.7 Prior rights

In common with other intellectual property registration systems, s. 11(3) contains a saving for earlier rights. It is based on Art. 6(2) of the Directive, but unfortunately uses wording which does not match exactly that deployed in the Directive. The main difference is that s. 11(3) requires that the earlier right must have been used continuously, a condition not imposed by the Directive. 'Earlier right' here bears a different meaning from that found in s. 5 when dealing with relative grounds for refusal. Here it means only an unregistered trade mark or sign which has been used continuously in such a manner that it would be protected under the laws of passing off. The prior use must pre-date whichever is the earlier of two events, the use *or* the registration of the claimant's mark. The fact that the defendant must be able to satisfy the court that it would be able to succeed in a passing off action imposes a considerable evidential burden.

In *Caspian Pizza Limited v Shah* [2015] EWHC 3567 (IPEC), HHJ Hacon upheld the s. 11(3) defence despite the fact that the claimant's use of its mark, then unregistered, pre-dated the acquisition by the defendant of its 'earlier right'.

In *Student Union Lettings Ltd v Essex Student Lets Ltd* [2018] EWHC 419 (IPEC), how-ever, the defence could not be upheld. In order for the defence to apply, the defendant has to show that they had an earlier right by the filing date of the mark but also that the right subsisted only in a particular locality (at [44]). In assessing the geographical scope of goodwill it is necessary to consider the facts relating to the specific business in question and to assess the degree to which persons from across England made use of or sought out a party's services. It was not sufficient simply to consider the nature of the services on offer, but to examine how the individual business traded (at [52]).

> **Pause for reflection**
>
> To what extent does the defence on prior rights applies in the scenario question? Can Alfred Wolf invoke this defence regarding the use of 'Wolf's Deli'?

14.8 Statutory acquiescence

Section 48 (based on Art. 9 of the Directive) creates a very limited form of statutory acquiescence. It provides that where the proprietor of an earlier trade mark or other earlier right has acquiesced for a continuous period of five years in the use of a registered mark, they can no longer seek a declaration that the junior mark is invalid, nor can they oppose the use of the later trade mark (i.e. sue for infringement), unless the registration of the latter was obtained in bad faith. The circumstances in which s. 48 will apply are therefore the same as those arising under s. 11(1). *Both* marks must be registered with the later mark being on the Register as a result of failure to oppose or an unsuccessful opposition by the owner of the senior mark. The practical effect of the section is that where there are conflicting registered marks, the proprietor of the first mark has just five years in which to challenge the second mark under s. 47. Once the junior mark is protected against challenge by virtue of s. 48(1), its proprietor is, by virtue of s. 48(2), in exactly the same position as the owner of the senior mark, and so cannot challenge the validity of the senior mark. The section therefore, when it applies, creates a stalemate so that the two marks are forced to coexist for the future.

The scope of Art. 9 was considered by the CJEU in Case C-482/09 *Budejovicky Budvar NP v Anheuser-Busch Inc* [2011] ECR I-8701, yet another episode in the long-running dispute between the two rival producers of BUDWEISER beer. It advised the Court of Appeal that 'acquiescence' in the Directive is a concept of EU law. A proprietor cannot be held to have acquiesced unless it was in a position to prevent the use of the rival mark but chose not to do so intentionally and with full knowledge of the facts. The five-year period only starts to run once the following conditions are satisfied: the later mark has been registered (assuming it was done so in good faith); the later mark has been put to use; and the owner of the earlier mark knows of both the registration and use of the later mark.

 Pause for reflection

The CJEU's criteria should be compared with the general equitable defence of acquiescence, which is available against a claim for the infringement of any intellectual property right. The general defence of acquiescence involves a positive misrepresentation by the claimant, and an intimation to the defendant, on which the defendant relies to their detriment, that the right in question will not be enforced (*Film Investors Overseas Services SA v Home Video Channel Ltd* Times, 2 December 1996). Mere delay in commencing infringement proceedings does not amount to acquiescence (*Farmers Build Ltd v Carier Bulk Handling Materials Ltd* [1999] RPC 461).

Estoppel could not be relied on to provide a defence to trade mark infringement (*Marussia Communications Ireland Ltd v Manor Grand Prix Racing Ltd* [2016] EWHC 809 (Ch); *Coreix Ltd v Coretx Holdings Plc* [2017] EWHC 1695 (IPEC)).

14.9 Comparative advertising

14.9.1 The old law

The law prior to 1994, based on the decision of the Court of Appeal in *Bismag Ltd v Amblins (Chemists) Ltd* (1940) 57 RPC 209, confirmed in the later case of *Chanel Ltd v Triton Packaging Ltd* [1993] RPC 32, was that comparative advertising was trade mark infringement, because, in the words of the 1938 Act, such use by the defendant amounted to 'importing a reference' to the claimant or the claimant's mark. In some extreme instances, comparing the defendant's and claimant's products, their attributes, and prices in an inaccurate manner could also amount to malicious falsehood (*Compaq v Dell* [1992] FSR 93), a form of common law liability which survives the 1994 changes. The pre-TMA UK law (that is, treating comparative advertising as trade mark infringement) was not unlike that found in Germany where, until recently, comparative advertising was regarded as a form of unfair competition.

14.9.2 TMA s. 10(6) (omitted by the Trade Mark Regulations 2018)

There was a change of policy in the United Kingdom in 1994 when it was decided that in the interests of better consumer information, the law on comparative advertising should be de-regulated. In consequence, s. 10(6) was introduced providing (in essence) that a trade mark is not infringed where it is used to identify the goods or services as those of the proprietor of the mark. The wording of the section, which has been omitted from the TMA by virtue of the Trade Mark Regulations 2018, did not actually refer to comparative advertising and potentially covered other situations. Nevertheless, references to *Hansard* indicate that s. 10(6) was intended to reverse the previous law on comparative advertising as a form of trade mark infringement, 'in the best interests of competition and therefore in the interests of the consumer' (*Hansard* (HL) 24 February 1994, col 738). Cases decided under s. 10(6) have all involved comparative advertising.

It is sometimes said that TMA s. 10(6) created a fourth category of trade mark infringement. Such statement must be open to doubt in view of Bornkamm's analysis of the 'triad of protection' and in view of the CJEU's frequent pronouncements that Arts 5 to 7 constitute a complete code of the trade mark owner's right. Further, close examination of its legislative history shows that the provision started out in the family of clauses in the Trade Marks Bill dealing with defences to infringement, but was moved to what ultimately became s. 10 because 'the provision and its relationship with the Directive would be clearer' (*Hansard* (HL) 24 February 1994, col 736). In addition, the opening words of the subsection, 'nothing in the preceding provisions . . . shall be construed as preventing the use of a registered mark' point to the fact that it operates by way of defence, not a cause of action. Indeed, it has been suggested that s. 10(6) was the domestic equivalent of the exhaustion of rights defence (*Scandecor Development AB v Scandecor Marketing AB* [2001] 2 CMLR 645, HL). The conclusion must be, nevertheless, that s. 10(6) was misplaced in the provision dealing with infringement and had to be located with other defences in s. 11.

Two further criticisms have been made. First, as was said at the time of its enactment, the Government should have waited to see what the effect was of the Comparative Advertising Directive (Directive 97/55/EC of the European Parliament and of the Council of 6 October 1997 amending Directive 84/450/EEC concerning misleading advertising so as to include comparative advertising [1997] OJ L 290/18, now consolidated as Directive 2006/114/EC of the European Parliament and of the Council of 12 December 2006 [2006] OJ L 376/21) (hereafter 'the CAD'). It would have been better, it was said, to leave the TMA silent on comparative advertising, to rely instead on the descriptive use defence under s. 11(2)(b) and, if need be, introduce an appropriate amendment once the EU legislative process was complete. In the event, the United Kingdom chose to implement the CAD in such a way that it had no direct impact on the TMA.

A second criticism (one frequently voiced by the judiciary) was that the section is badly drafted. The opening words are qualified by a two-limbed proviso which stated that any such use otherwise than in accordance with honest practices in industrial and commercial matters had to be treated as infringement, if the use without due cause took unfair advantage of, or was detrimental to, the distinctive character or repute of the mark. In effect what the proviso was saying was that comparative advertising would not be permitted where it amounted to unfair competition (the first half of the sentence repeating Art. 10*bis* of the Paris Convention, explained earlier) because the defendant's conduct amounted to unfair competition. The proviso was, to say the least, tautologous.

 Pause for reflection

Given the criticisms of s. 10(6), was the Government wise to 'jump the gun' before the CAD was passed?

14.9.3 **Case law on s. 10(6)**

Several cases have analysed the wording of s. 10(6), the last of which was *British Airways plc v Ryanair Ltd* [2001] FSR 541. The decision in *Ryanair* reinforced the trend evident from the outset, namely the reluctance of the judiciary to find in favour of the trade mark owner under s. 10(6). The case has the added advantage that it involved two advertisments published just before the operative date of the United Kingdom's implementation of the CAD which enabled Jacob J to explore the relationship between s. 10(6) and this Directive. The first advertisement was withdrawn after a number of complaints to the Advertising Standards Authority, the second was the subject of an action for trade mark infringement and malicious falsehood. In regard to the second, Jacob J summarized the law as it then stood on comparative advertising as a defence to trade mark infringement. He stated that the primary objective of s. 10(6) was to permit comparative advertising and as long as the use of the competitor's mark was honest, there was nothing wrong in telling the public of the relative merits of competing goods and services. However, an advertisement which was significantly misleading was not honest. The onus was on the registered proprietor to show that the requirements of the proviso existed. The phrase 'honest practices' was to be interpreted objectively, through the eyes of a reasonable audience: i.e. 'would a reasonable reader be likely to say, upon being given the full facts, that the advertisement is not honest?' Industry-wide codes of practice should be ignored; rather, the advertisement was to be assessed through the eyes of the relevant public. Words were to be given their natural meaning as judged by the general public, who were used to 'hype', and minute textual analysis of the advertisement was to be avoided, as this is something that the reasonable reader would not do. The advertisement was to be considered as a whole. The TMA was not to be used to enforce a more puritanical standard than the general public would expect.

With regard to the impact of the CAD, Jacob J noted that this had amended the earlier Misleading Advertising Directive, but not the Trade Marks Directive so that there was no obligation to interpret the TMA in the light of the CAD. Although the CAD refers to trade marks and although comparative advertisements will usually involve use of other traders' marks, it was as if the Trade Marks Directive and the CAD existed in parallel universes.

 Pause for reflection

Can Alfred Wolf benefit from the comparative advertisement defence by reference to the slogan 'Hungrier than the . . . Wolf'?

14.9.4 **The Comparative Advertising Directive**

The Comparative Advertising Directive ('CAD') starts from a different premise than the former s. 10(6). Whilst the TMA is based on the assumption that comparative advertising is acceptable *unless* it is contrary to honest practices in industrial and commercial matters, the CAD provides that comparative advertising is acceptable *only* if it is *not* misleading.

The CAD, in Art. 4 of its consolidated version, lays down a number of positive criteria to be met:

- the advertisement must compare goods or services meeting the same needs or intended for the same purpose;

- it must objectively compare one or more material, relevant, verifiable, and representative features of goods and services, which may include price;

- it must not discredit or denigrate the trade marks, trade names, other distinguishing marks, goods, services, activities or circumstances of a competitor;

- it does not take unfair advantage of the reputation of a trade mark, trade name or other distinguishing marks of a competitor;

- it does not present goods or services as imitations or replicas of goods or services bearing a protected trade mark; and

- it does not create confusion among traders, between the advertiser and a competitor, or between their trade marks.

14.9.5 Implementation of the CAD in the United Kingdom

Taking advantage of the discretion conferred on it by the CAD, the United Kingdom chose to implement its provisions by means of administrative regulation. Under the Business Protection from Misleading Marketing Regulations 2008 (SI 2008/1276) (replacing the two previous versions of the Control of Misleading Advertisements Regulations), enforcement is by way of complaint to the Advertising Standards Authority which can direct an advertisement to be withdrawn (just as it had done as regards the first advertisement in the *Ryanair* case, on the grounds that it was contrary to good taste). The choices open to the trade mark owner are that if it is felt that a competitor has indulged in unfair comparative advertising, it is better by far (and considerably cheaper) to make a complaint under the Regulations than to bring an action for trade mark infringement.

14.9.6 The CJEU's view

The relationship between comparative advertising and liability for trade mark infringement was considered by the CJEU in Case C-533/06 *O2 Holdings Ltd v Hutchinson 3G Ltd* [2008] ECR I-4231. Here the claimant mobile phone company used bubble images coloured blue to advertise its services and had registered pictures of bubbles (in blue) as trade marks. The defendant's television advertising campaign compared its prices with those of the claimant using black-and-white bubble imagery. It was accepted before the Patents Court that the price comparison was accurate, that the advertisement was not misleading, and that there was no suggestion of any trade connection between the two companies. At first instance it was held that although the use of the bubble imagery fell within s. 10(2), compliance with the CAD provided a defence under s. 11(2)(b). The Court of Appeal sought the CJEU's guidance.

The CJEU began by saying that the use of a competitor's trade mark in a comparative advertisement was use for the advertiser's own goods and services and therefore prima facie infringement. However, the CAD was intended to promote comparative advertising. Further, Recitals 13 to 15 of the consolidated version cross-referred to the Trade Marks Directive and so it was necessary to read the CAD into the limitations on the trade mark owner's rights. The trade mark owner could not object to the use of an identical or similar sign by a third party in a comparative advertisement which complied with the CAD. Compliance with the CAD is therefore a complete defence to trade mark infringement unless the advertisement gives rise to a likelihood of confusion.

This means that most direct comparative advertisements ('our washing powder is cheaper than your washing powder'), where the consumer is alerted to the fact that there are two rival producers, will get the protection of the defence. Only an indirect comparison, where the consumer does not appreciate that there are two different sources of supply and consequently confuses the two, will amount to infringement. The CJEU added that the trade mark owner could not object to the use by a third party of a similar sign if this did not give rise to a likelihood of confusion, regardless of whether the advertisement satisfied all the conditions of the CAD.

By reference to Carrefour's TV advertising campaign that was based on a price comparison rationale, the CJEU held that comparative advertising which omits or hides material information which are necessary for the average consumer in order to make an informed choice or which provides that information in an unclear, unintelligible, ambiguous, or untimely manner, and which may have the effect that the average consumer makes a decision they would not have taken, is considered to be misleading (*Carrefour Hypermarches SAS v ITM Alimentaire International SASU* (C-562/15) EU:C:2017:95; [2017] ETMR 18).

 Pause for reflection

Can the CJEU's interpretation of the CAD in *O2* be reconciled with its statements in *Bellure* that there is liability per se for 'taking unfair advantage' of another's mark?

The recast Directive makes clear that use in a comparative advertisement in a manner contrary to the CAD is trade mark infringement (Art. 10(3)(f), reflected in new s. 10(4)(e)).

The net effect of *O2 Holdings Ltd v Hutchinson 3G Ltd* is that the law of passing off and the law of trade marks now achieve the same outcome. As ever with trade mark infringement issues, everything depends on the consumer's perception. This is entirely in accordance with the Court's earlier statements in *Arsenal*, *Opel*, and *Céline*. How the consumer views the advertisement was to the fore in Case C-159/09 *Lidl SNC v Vierzon Distribution SA* [2010] ECR I-11761. The case concerned a dispute between two rival supermarkets as to the price of the average shopping basket. The CJEU ruled that it was important that the products were interchangeable, so that if the advertiser selected products which had different features which affected the average consumer's choice, the advertisement would be misleading.

Pause for reflection

To what extent does the comparative advertisement defence apply by reference to the scenario question?

14.10 The 'exhaustion of rights'

The term 'exhaustion of rights' denotes that the ability of an intellectual property owner to object to the unauthorized conduct of third parties is spent. The right becomes unenforceable. In consequence, further dealings in trade marked goods cannot be challenged, even though infringing conduct has been committed by a third party. The same applies by reference to patented and copyright protected goods. In common with other statutory defences, exhaustion of rights is not absolute. Much depends on the circumstances of the case. Indeed, the complexity of the case law 'would astonish the average consumer' (*per* Jacob LJ in *Boehringer Ingelheim KG v Dowelhurst Ltd* [2004] ETMR 902 at [79]).

14.10.1 Geographical scope

Like intellectual property rights themselves, exhaustion of rights has a territorial effect. It applies within a geographical area. Exhaustion, therefore, *could* be domestic only, that is, it could operate within a single country, such as the territory of the United Kingdom. The consequence of confining exhaustion to the territory of a particular state would be that once the intellectual property owner has placed trade marked goods in circulation *within* that country, no objection could be made to further dealings in those goods. Importation of goods from elsewhere could be stopped as they would not be 'national' products. An example of exhaustion of trade mark rights being confined nationally (decided by the Court of Appeal under the Trade Marks Act 1938) is *Colgate-Palmolive v Markwell Finance* [1989] RPC 497, where toothpaste imported (somewhat circuitously) into the United Kingdom from Brazil via Nigeria was held to infringe the claimant's registrations, even though the claimant had manufactured the product itself. A significant fact of the case, however, was that the imported product contained different ingredients from the domestic version of the product, which could have caused customer disappointment and harm to the claimant's business.

Alternatively, exhaustion of rights could apply internationally. The right to object to further dealings in the goods would be spent no matter where the goods were first put into circulation by the intellectual property owner. An example of international trade mark exhaustion (decided prior to the 1994 reforms) is *Revlon Inc v Cripps & Lee Ltd* [1980] FSR 87, where a differently constituted Court of Appeal held that the claimant corporate group could not rely on its United Kingdom rights, whether under the law of registered trade marks or passing off, to object to the importation of shampoo from New York. With regard to passing off, there was no misrepresentation as to the commercial source of the goods, as they had originated with the claimant corporate group. Concerning infringement of the REVLON registered trade mark, the whole corporate group was taken to have consented by implication to the use of the mark and to the disposal of the goods. The application of international exhaustion in the *Revlon* case was no doubt helped by the way in which the Revlon corporate group had organized its structure and by the fact that there was no contractual or other stipulation that the goods were not for sale outside the USA. That the grade of shampoo imported from New York had not been previously made available to United Kingdom customers does not seem to have troubled the court.

There is, however, a third possibility. The application of a national approach to exhaustion of rights conflicts with the fundamental principle of the internal market of the EU. The internal market views all 28 Member States as a single territory, within which the four freedoms (free movement of goods, persons, services, and capital) operate. National boundaries are to be disregarded. Further, the effect of the European Economic Area ('EEA') Agreement is that the three European Free Trade Association ('EFTA') countries adhering to the EEA (Norway, Iceland, and Liechtenstein) are treated as part of the EU for the purposes of the four freedoms. Harmonisation Directives enacted in order to give effect to the four freedoms (such as the various intellectual property Directives) also apply throughout the EEA. Free movement of goods within the EEA therefore requires that exhaustion of rights operates on a regional not national basis.

 Pause for reflection

In light of the exit of the United Kingdom from the European Union, what, do you think, will be the most appropriate approach by reference to the exhaustion of trade mark rights? Would UK-wide national exhaustion have benefits for parallel trade?

14.10.2 The role of exhaustion of rights

Exhaustion of rights as a defence to trade mark infringement is found in s. 12 of the Trade Marks Act 1994 ('TMA'), based on Art. 7 of the First Trade Marks Directive (Council Directive 89/104/EEC of 21 December 1988 on the approximation of the laws of Member States relating to trade marks [1989] OJ L 40/1, now codified as Directive 2008/95/EC of the European Parliament and of the Council of 22 October 2008 [2008] OJ L 299/25) ('the Directive'). However, exhaustion of rights is a defence to an action for infringement of *any* intellectual property right. Similar provisions are in various other harmonisation Directives dealing with copyright, designs, and biotechnological patents.

14.10.2.1 Issues to be determined in a case involving exhaustion of rights

As a defence to trade mark infringement, the issues to be determined by a court dealing with the defence will be similar to those raised in any infringement action, namely:

- has there been infringing conduct? Exhaustion is normally pleaded where the defendant has *imported* trade marked goods from another country. Importation is an infringing act under s. 10(4)(c) TMA;

- does the case fall within the 'triad of protection' afforded to the trade mark owner under ss. 10(1), 10(2), or 10(3) TMA? Normally, the applicable provision will be s. 10(1) as the goods will have originated from the claimant or someone acting with the claimant's consent, and will have been marked with the claimant's own trade mark;

- is the defence of exhaustion of rights available on the facts of the case, that is, because the goods were first marketed with the trade mark owner's consent within the EEA? If so:

- does the claimant nevertheless have a valid reason to oppose further commercialization of the goods because the defendant's activities have in some way undermined the trade mark?

 Pause for reflection

Can Alfred Wolf bring infringement proceedings against the exporter of corned beef in Spain successfully? What about the company that exports and repackages beef in Italy under a different mark?

14.10.2.2 Theoretical issues

Exhaustion of rights applies to all forms of intellectual property. It has been argued (see Van der Merwe, 'The Exhaustion of Rights in Patent Law with Specific Emphasis on the Issue of Parallel Importation' [2000] 3 *IPQ* 286) that the defence of exhaustion should apply differently to the various types of intellectual property rights. In Case 40/70 *Sirena v Eda* [1971] ECR 69, the Advocate General suggested that patents merited greater respect and therefore a higher degree of protection than trade marks, so the exhaustion doctrine should be applied less rigorously to patents. The value judgement inherent in this statement raises (again) the justifications for intellectual property rights and the specific economic role which each plays. In relation to trade marks in particular, the debate about the commercial functions which trade marks perform permeates the case law on exhaustion of rights.

 Pause for reflection

Can you think of any arguments which could be made against a rule which states that intellectual property rights are exhausted on first sale of the product?

14.10.3 **The origin of exhaustion of rights**

14.10.3.1 Provisions in the Treaty on the Functioning of the European Union

The origin of the defence of exhaustion of rights is to be found in key provisions in the Treaty on the Functioning of the European Union ('TFEU'), the new name for the Treaty of Rome after the coming into force of the Treaty of Lisbon in December 2009. The case law of the CJEU on these provisions has been crucial to the development of the defence. That case law is now encapsulated in Art. 7 of the Directive, so that the Directive's provisions should always be referred to first (*per* AG Sharpston in Case C-348/04 *Boehringer Ingelheim v Swingward Ltd and Dowelhurst* ('*Boehringer II*') [2007] ECR I-3391 at [15]).

14.10.3.2 Free movement of goods

Part III of the TFEU sets out the policies of the EU, namely the four freedoms mentioned earlier. The fundamental rule in Art. 34 TFEU (formerly Art. 28 EC) is that goods should be able to move freely between Member States. Article 34 is not, however, absolute. Article 36 TFEU (formerly Art. 30 EC) contains a list of exceptions to the principle of free movement, but being a derogation to the basic rule, it should be strictly construed (*per* AG Sharpston in *Boehringer II* at [5]).

Article 34 TFEU declares that 'quantitative restrictions on imports and all measures having equivalent effect shall be prohibited between Member States'. When considering the development of exhaustion of rights, the principle of the supremacy of EU law declared in Case 6/64 *Costa v ENEL* [1964] ECR 585 should be remembered. Free movement of goods as an EU principle prevails over any national rule to the contrary, unless the latter can be justified under Art. 36.

Further, the deceptively simple wording of Art. 34 has been held by the CJEU to have direct horizontal effect, so that it can be relied upon by a defendant to proceedings for the infringement of any intellectual property right.

Case 58/80 *Dansk Supermarked v Imerco* [1981] ECR 181

An example is to be found in Case 58/80 *Dansk Supermarked v Imerco* [1981] ECR 181. Here, to celebrate 50 years in business, the claimant had commissioned commemorative china from an English company. The china was decorated with photographs and engravings of Danish castles, copyright in the pictures belonging to the claimant. The intention was that the claimant would market the china in Denmark, as part of a publicity campaign. The contract allowed the manufacturer to sell any 'seconds' in England, on condition that resale to Scandinavia was prohibited. The defendant supermarket chain nevertheless acquired some 'seconds' which it proposed to sell through its shops in Denmark. The CJEU advised the Danish Supreme Court that neither the law of copyright nor trade marks could be used to stop the sale of goods which had been lawfully marketed in another Member State. However, Danish laws on consumer protection could be relied on to enforce the proper labelling of the china as sub-standard when sold in Danish shops.

The last observation is that Art. 34 has been given a broad interpretation by the CJEU, in line with its judicial activism in developing the internal market. The Court has ruled that the phrase 'quantitative restrictions' means 'measures which amount to a total or partial restraint of . . . imports, exports or goods in transit' (rather than simply 'quotas') in Case 2/73 *Geddo v Ente Nazionale Risi* [1973] ECR 865; and that 'measures of equivalent effect' means 'all trading rules enacted by Member States, which are capable of hindering, directly or indirectly, actually or potentially, intra-Community trade' in Case 8/74 *Procureur du Roi v Dassonville* [1974] ECR 837. Thus Art. 34 covers not just national rules which discriminate against imported goods, but rules which, although applying equally to domestic and imported goods alike, make it more difficult to import products from another Member State: Case 120/78 *Rewe-Zentrale v Bundesmonopolverwaltung für Branntwein* [1979] ECR 649. In other words, it covers both direct and indirect discrimination against imported goods.

14.10.3.3 Free movement of services

A parallel provision to Art. 34 is Art. 56 TFEU, which provides that Member States cannot place restrictions on the freedom to provide services. The Treaty adds (in Art. 57) that goods and services are mutually exclusive. In terms of items covered by intellectual property rights, trade marked (and patented) products will always be regarded as 'goods' and so subject to Art. 34.

 Pause for reflection

In light of the exit of the United Kingdom from the European Union, trade mark exhaustion—as applicable under EU legislation and case law—shall cease to exist in the British territory. Unless the United Kingdom will join the European Economic Area, it will have to decide what is the most appropriate regulatory model, i.e. whether it should introduce regional, national, or international exhaustion.

14.10.3.4 The derogation to Art. 34: Art. 36

Article 36 TFEU contains a list of circumstances which permits Member States to restrict the free movement of goods. The one which concerns us is 'the protection of industrial and commercial property'. For present purposes it can be assumed that the phrase equates to 'intellectual property'. Taken at face value, the first sentence of Art. 36 appears to allow intellectual property rights to take precedence always over the free movement of goods. However, what is equally important is the second sentence of the Article, which provides that 'such prohibitions or restrictions shall not, however, constitute a means of arbitrary discrimination or a disguised restriction on trade between Member States'.

The combined wording of Arts 34 and 36 at first glance creates circularity. Free movement of goods may not be restricted, except to protect intellectual property, but not where such protection restricts trade. The answer to this conundrum lies in the difference between parallel imports and infringing imports. Distinguishing between the two is vital to an understanding of the cases. Mercifully, the distinction is a question of fact, simply requiring the identification of the commercial origin of goods.

In *Schweppes SA v Red Paralela SL & Ors*, ECLI:EU:C:2017:666; [2018] ETMR 13, the General Court held that Art. 7(1) of Directive 2008/95 (now Art. 15(1) of the recast Directive), read in the light of Art. 36 TFEU, must be interpreted as precluding the proprietor of a national trade mark from opposing the import of identical goods bearing the same mark originating in another Member State in which that mark, which initially belonged to that proprietor, is now owned by a third party which has acquired the rights thereto by assignment. This happens when, following that assignment, the proprietor has actively and deliberately continued to promote the appearance or image of a single global trade mark, or there exist economic links between the proprietor and that third party, so that it is possible for them to determine, directly or indirectly, the goods to which the trade mark is affixed and to control the quality of those goods.

14.10.3.5 The difference between parallel and infringing imports

The difference between parallel and infringing imports is determined by answering the following factual question: 'Who first put these goods into circulation?'

14.10.3.5.1 First marketing with the intellectual property owner's consent

Where the first marketing (i.e. in the country of export) was by the intellectual property owner or by another person acting with the owner's express consent (such as a subsidiary or associated company, a licensee, or a distributor) then those goods are treated as parallel imports. In this instance, the second sentence of Art. 36 prevails. For the intellectual property owner to object to further dealings in the goods is 'a disguised restriction on trade' and so free movement of goods takes precedence over intellectual property rights. Intellectual property rights in the Member State of import cannot be used to object to further dealings in those goods unless, in the words of Art. 7(2) of the Directive (now Art. 15(2) of the recast Directive), there exist 'legitimate reasons for the proprietor to oppose further commercialisation of the goods'.

14.10.3.5.2 First marketing by an unconnected third party

Where, however, the goods were first marketed by an unconnected third party (such as a competitor or counterfeiter) then the intellectual property owner can always rely on their rights in the country of import to prevent importation and sale. Such goods are infringing imports, so the first sentence of Art. 36 prevails over the desired goal of the internal market. The conduct of a competitor or counterfeiter, if unchecked, would destroy the right in question (whether patent, design, copyright, or trade mark) which would be contrary to Art. 345 TFEU which declares that 'this Treaty shall in no way prejudice the rules in Member States governing the system of property ownership'. The internal market gives way to the rights of the intellectual property owner, even if this does reinforce national boundaries.

The CJEU was initially somewhat reluctant to accept that the achievement of the internal market had to be tempered in the interests of the intellectual property owner in the case of infringing imports (see Case 119/75 *Terrapin v Terranova* [1976] ECR 1039). It has, however, now recognized that the value of intellectual property rights should be protected in such circumstances.

Deutsche Renault AG v Audi AG [1993] ECR I-6227

In *Deutsche Renault AG v Audi AG* [1993] ECR I-6227, Audi sought to stop Renault using its mark QUADRA in Germany, where Audi had already registered its mark QUATTRO for motor vehicles. Despite the argument that to allow Audi to keep Renault cars out of the

→

→ German market would be contrary to the principle of free movement of goods, the Court accepted that the function of Audi's trade mark (to guarantee the origin of goods) would be seriously undermined if a rival car manufacturer could be allowed to use a confusingly similar name for its products.

The only way that such fragmentation of the internal market could be avoided is by use of the unitary EU trade mark. However, the EU institutions long ago recognized that such a system had to be voluntary and that national trade mark laws had to be allowed to run in parallel to it. Traders have to be free to choose whether to obtain trade mark protection regionally or nationally, depending on the scope of their business activities. The necessary consequence is that national intellectual property rights do create barriers to the free movement of goods.

 Pause for reflection

How easy is it to differentiate between infringing and parallel imports?
By reference to the scenario question, to what extent, do exports in Spain and Italy qualify as infringing or parallel trade?

14.10.3.6 Concepts deployed by the CJEU

The way in which the CJEU has resolved the circularity of wording in Arts 34 and 36 TFEU reveals the nature of the balancing exercise which the Court has to perform. Not only does it have to reconcile the territorial nature of national intellectual property rights with the stated Treaty objective of achieving the internal market, it has to take into account the interests of the rightholder, other traders, and consumers. To this end, the Court has deployed three particular arguments when creating its case law on exhaustion of rights. None of the reasoning used by the CJEU is totally transparent. However, ultimately each concept which the Court has advanced is concerned with whether the intellectual property owner is objecting to parallel or infringing imports.

14.10.3.6.1 Existence and exercise

The first argument utilized by the Court has been to say that there is a difference between the 'existence' and 'exercise' of intellectual property rights. The criteria for deciding whether and how such rights are to be created is left to the laws of the Member States, but the way in which such rights are exploited by their owners is a concern of EU law. Such exploitation (whether this consists of granting licences or suing for infringement) might have the effect of partitioning the internal market along national boundaries. Seeking to rely on national rights to prevent parallel importation from other Member States is a disguised restriction on trade.

The existence-exercise dichotomy has been criticized as being tenuous and difficult to apply. One of the critics is F-K Beier ('Industrial Property and the Free Movement of

Goods in the Internal European Market' (1990) 21 *IIC* 131) who argues that the better approach is to consider the demarcation between legitimate and improper use of intellectual property rights. Indeed, if an intellectual property right exists, then the sole purpose of such existence is for the right to be exercised; conversely, if a right is being exercised, that presupposes its existence.

14.10.3.6.2 Specific subject matter and essential function

The other two concepts used by the Court are based on the notion that each form of intellectual property has a 'specific subject matter' and an 'essential function'. The 'essential function' of a trade mark is 'to guarantee the identity of the origin of the trade-marked product to the consumer or ultimate user, by enabling him, without any possibility of confusion, to distinguish that product from products which have another origin [and to] be certain that a trade-marked product has not been subject at a previous stage of marketing to interference . . . such as to affect the original condition of the product' (Case 102/77 *Hoffmann-La Roche v Centrafarm* [1978] ECR 1139 at [10], repeated in Recital 11 to the consolidated version of the Directive).

 Pause for reflection

Are the arguments advanced by the CJEU to justify the distinction between parallel and infringing imports as clear as they might be?

14.10.4 The case law of the CJEU: parallel imports from within the EEA

14.10.4.1 Early cases: reliance on competition law

The initial jurisprudence of the CJEU on exhaustion of rights arose in the context of competition law. The simple reason for this was that the provisions in the then Treaty of Rome dealing with free movement of goods had a transitional period of 12 years, so that it was 1970 before such provisions could be relied on by litigants before national courts. As a result, early cases show the Court attempting to fit the facts of the cases into Arts 101 and 102 TFEU (formerly Arts 81 and 82 EC). These prohibit, respectively, restrictive agreements which distort intra-EU trade and the abuse of a dominant position. Whilst in some cases, the use of competition law as the vehicle to create the exhaustion of rights defence was non-controversial, in other cases the facts did not really fit the criteria of competition policy, so the CJEU's reasoning appears strained.

Cases 56 & 58/64 *Consten & Grundig v Commission* [1966] ECR 299

The first time the CJEU considered the way in which intellectual property rights could be used to partition what was then called the common market was in Cases 56 & 58/64 *Consten & Grundig v Commission* [1966] ECR 299. Grundig, a German maker of hi-fi equipment,

→

→

appointed Consten to be its exclusive distributor for France. The arrangement gave Consten the right to register Grundig's mark GINT in its own name in France (whether this amounted to a trade mark assignment or licence is irrelevant for present purposes). Consten brought a trade mark infringement action against another trader who had attempted to import Grundig products into France, thereby undercutting Consten (price competition is one of the hallmarks of parallel imports case law). Rather than fight the trade mark infringement action, the other trader complained to the EU Commission that the exclusive distribution agreement breached competition law because it distorted trade between Member States. The CJEU upheld the Commission's decision that intellectual property rights could not be used to partition the common market along national boundaries.

At the time, the decision caused consternation, as it had been assumed that intellectual property agreements fell outside the scope of competition policy. A further assumption had been that what was then Art. 85 of the Treaty of Rome (now Art. 101 TFEU) prohibited only horizontal restrictive agreements rather than vertical restraints. In other words, it was thought that EU competition policy had been intended to operate against cartels of undertakings at the same level in the supply chain (for example, collaboration between rival manufacturers or rival retailers) rather than agreements between manufacturers and distributors.

14.10.4.2 The foundation cases

Once the free movement of goods provisions were fully effective, it did not take long for the CJEU to set out the foundations of the defence of exhaustion of rights.

Case 78/70 *Deutsche Grammophon v Metro-SB-Grossmärkte* [1971] ECR 487

Case 78/70 *Deutsche Grammophon v Metro-SB-Grossmärkte* [1971] ECR 487 concerned sound recordings made by Deutsche Grammophon (DG), a German firm specializing in classical music records. In Germany, at the time, DG was able to require its retailers to sell the recordings at a particular price. It had appointed another company, Polydor, to sell the records in France. Metro, a German supermarket chain, acquired copies of the records in France from Polydor and imported them into Germany where it sold them below list price. The CJEU held that by selling the records in France, DG had exhausted any right it might have to object to their importation and resale in Germany.

Case 15/74 *Centrafarm v Sterling Drug Inc* [1974] ECR 1147 and Case 16/74 *Centrafarm v Winthrop BV* [1974] ECR 1183

The CJEU took matters further in Case 15/74 *Centrafarm v Sterling Drug Inc* [1974] ECR 1147 and Case 16/74 *Centrafarm v Winthrop BV* [1974] ECR 1183. The cases form a classic

→

> →
>
> example of a third-party entrepreneur (Centrafarm) using parallel importation to exploit price differentials, and illustrate the Court's vision of the importance of establishing the internal market. Sterling-Winthrop was a multi-national pharmaceutical group. All patents were held in the name of the USA parent company (Sterling Inc) whilst the relevant trade marks were registered in the name of local subsidiaries. Centrafarm purchased medicines in the United Kingdom (where the prices were low) and transported them to the Netherlands where the prices were higher. It was sued for patent and trade mark infringement. The CJEU ruled that the attempt by the Sterling-Winthrop group to rely on its rights to keep out parallel imports was incompatible with the free movement of goods. Further, the different companies in the corporate group were to be treated as a single undertaking. The consent of one company to the marketing of the goods within the common market bound all.

14.10.4.3 The meaning of 'put on the market'

A key phrase in the *Centrafarm v Winthrop* ruling, repeated in Art. 7(1) of the Directive (now Article 15(1) of the recast Directive), is that the trade mark right doesn't entitle its owner to object to the use of the mark 'in relation to goods which have been put on the market in the Community by the proprietor or with his consent'. What does 'put on the market in the Community' mean? Does it mean that the goods have been driven through a Member State on a lorry or displayed in a shop or kept in a warehouse? Or must there have been a transfer of ownership through an act of sale? The answer was provided by the CJEU in Case C-16/03 *Peak Holding AB v Axolin-Elinor AB* [2004] ECR I-11313. The Court ruled that 'put on the market' requires that goods have been sold, either to members of the public, or to another trader who has the power of disposal over them. Where goods have been kept in a warehouse by the trade mark owner, or displayed in a shop without being sold, then they have not been 'put on the market'. However, once goods have been supplied to another trader, even if there is a clause in the contract prohibiting resale within the EU, the goods are treated as having been 'put on the market', so the defence of exhaustion applies. The trade mark owner cannot use trade mark rights to stop the resale of the goods, even though there might be liability for breach of contract.

The CJEU has since confirmed this in Case C-405/03 *Class International BV v Colgate Palmolive* [2005] ECR I-8735 where a consignment of imported AQUAFRESH toothpaste had been stored in a warehouse before being sent to another non-EEA country. The issue was whether the goods were to be treated as having been 'put on the market' so that the trade mark owner could object to their importation. The Court ruled that mere entry into the EU was not enough. Goods must be introduced into the EU for the purpose of putting them on the market, i.e. for the purpose of resale, so that where goods were merely in transit, no infringing conduct had been committed. Similarly, in Case C-281/05 *Montex Holdings Ltd v Diesel* [2006] ECR I-10881, goods which were in transit to a Member State where there was no trade mark protection could not be treated as infringing goods in an intermediate country where there was such protection. The corollary of these two rulings was that the trade mark owner was unable to ask customs authorities to impound imported goods as counterfeit unless there was clear evidence that they were about to be supplied to EU consumers: Cases C-446/09 and C-495/09 *Philips/Nokia* [2012] ETMR 248. This gap will be closed by Art. 10(5) of the recast Trade Marks Directive.

The CJEU has also stated that where goods such as 'perfume testers' are supplied without transfer of ownership and with a prohibition on their re-sale, they have not been 'put on the market' for the purposes of Art. 7: Case 127/09 *Coty Prestige Lancaster Group GmbH v Simex Trading AG* [2010] ECR I-4965; Case C-324/09 *L'Oréal SA v eBay International* [2011] ECR I-6011. It remains to be seen whether brand owners utilize these two rulings as a means of limiting the effect of the doctrine of exhaustion.

 Pause for reflection

To what extent did Alfred put his goods in the market for the purpose of Art. 15(1) of the recast Directive?

14.10.4.4 The importance of consent to first marketing

The wording of Art. 15(1) of the recast Directive (formerly Art. 7(1) of the Directive) reveals the key element in the defence of exhaustion, namely consent. It took the CJEU quite some time before consent to the first marketing of the goods was clearly spelled out in case law: the Court misled itself for a time in cases where, historically, there had been a change of ownership of the mark even though there was no connection between the trade mark owner and the importer at the time of the case.

14.10.4.4.1 The effect of a change of ownership of the mark

The scenario to be imagined is that Company A owns parallel national trade mark registrations in a number of Member States, for example, France, Germany, and the United Kingdom, but then sells its entire French business to Company B, including the French trade mark registrations. The question to be answered is whether, because of this change of ownership, Company A can now keep trade-marked goods originating from Company B out of Germany and the United Kingdom, and conversely whether Company B can keep the branded goods of Company A out of France.

The difficulty with the cases is that initially, the CJEU treated such goods as if they were parallel imports. It did so as a result of adopting something called the 'common origin' doctrine. The doctrine came about at a time when the Court was obliged to use competition law as the basis of its decisions on exhaustion of rights, and when it was keen to develop the common market. In its enthusiasm to treat all Member States as a single entity, it all but destroyed the value of trade marks. Mercifully (albeit some 20 years later) it set the record straight.

The 'wrong turning' taken by the CJEU occurred in *Sirena v Eda*. Here, there had been parallel trade mark registrations for shaving cream in Germany and Italy. In 1937, ownership of the German mark had been transferred to an unrelated company. Many years later, the Italian trade mark owner sued for infringement when shaving cream bearing the trade mark was imported from Germany. The CJEU treated the 1937 assignment as having continuing effect for the purposes of competition law (a proposition which completely misunderstands the nature of change of ownership) and ruled that the assignment partitioned the market. The Italian trade mark owner could not stop the imports from Germany, even though its links to the German trade mark owner were historical only.

Case 192/73 *Van Zuylen Frères v Hag AG* [1974] ECR 731 *('Hag I')*

The CJEU further developed this 'common origin' doctrine in Case 192/73 *Van Zuylen Frères v Hag AG* [1974] ECR 731 *('Hag I')*. It ruled that even an involuntary change of ownership (by Government expropriation at the end of World War II) did not break the link between the original German owner and the Belgian registration for KAFFEE HAG, so that the current Belgian owner could not object to coffee imported from Germany. The Court's attention was focused on historical origin of the *trade mark* rather than the common origin of the *goods*.

Apart from its failure to appreciate the nature of property transactions, the CJEU's ruling in *Hag I* had the effect of undermining many successful brands, as trade marks often change hands as companies merge, expand, and diversify. In due course the ECJ reconsidered its ruling in *Hag I* in Case C-10/89 *SA CNL-Sucal NV v Hag GF AG* [1990] ECR I-3711 *('Hag II')*. Here, the German trade mark owner objected to imports of KAFFEE HAG coffee coming from Belgium. The Court, no doubt impressed by arguments that consumers would be confused by the availability of two versions of the KAFFEE HAG product, reversed its previous decision, concentrating not on the history of the mark, but whether the owner of the mark in the importing state had consented to the first marketing of the goods. It changed its mind about the effect of voluntary assignments in Case C-9/93 *IHT Internationale Heiztechnik GmbH v Ideal-Standard GmbH* [1994] ECR I-2789, holding that where a German company had sold off its French business, trade-marked sanitary ware imported from France into Germany by the new owners could be stopped. This reversed the decision in *Sirena*, although the Court added, as an afterthought, that it reserved the right to look behind an assignment to see if it was an attempt to partition the market.

14.10.4.4.2 The difference between an assignment and a licence

The effect of the cases discussed in the previous sections can be summarized as follows. The treatment of trade marks which have been assigned and those which have been licensed is different. A change of ownership of the mark means that assignor and assignee can keep each other's products out of their respective territories (in line with the decision in *Audi v Renault*, discussed earlier). However, imports from a licensee, because they have been marketed with the consent of the brand owner, are subject to the full force of the exhaustion defence. In other words, whether exhaustion applies depends entirely on the trade mark owner's consent to the goods being put into circulation in the internal market.

Nevertheless, in some cases the trade mark owner may even be able to object to the circulation of licensed products.

> ### Case C-59/08 *Copad SA v Christian Dior Couture SA* [2009] ECR I-3421
>
> In Case C-59/08 *Copad SA v Christian Dior Couture SA* [2009] ECR I-3421, Dior had concluded a trade mark licence agreement with a company called SIL for the manufacture and distribution of luxury underwear. The contract stipulated that, in order to maintain the repute and prestige of the trade mark, the licensee would not sell to discount stores and the like without the prior written consent of the licensor. Facing economic difficulties, SIL asked Dior permission to market the goods outside of its selective distribution network, but Dior refused. Nevertheless, SIL supplied goods to Copad which ran a discount store. Dior sued both companies for trade mark infringement, arguing both breach of the licence and that lack of consent meant that there was no exhaustion of rights. The CJEU ruled first, that Art. 8(2) of the Directive (which contains an exhaustive list of when conduct by a licensee amounts to trade mark infringement) entitled Dior to sue its licensee for trade mark infringement: it was conceivable that the sale of luxury goods by a licensee to third parties which were not part of a selective distribution network might affect *the quality of the goods themselves*, a factor listed within the Article. Second, although goods marketed by a licensee were put on the market with the consent of the trade mark owner, where, as here, the licence did not amount to absolute and unconditional consent (because of the wording of Art. 8(2)), the contravention of the terms of the licence meant that there was no exhaustion of rights. Finally, where, as here, luxury goods were marketed in contravention of the terms of a licence agreement but this was not sufficient to trigger Art. 8(2), the proprietor could rely on Art. 7(2) of the Directive and could therefore oppose further commercialization of the goods, but only where it could be established that the resale of the goods could damage *the reputation of the trade mark*.

Copad is a significant case for a number of different reasons. It strengthens the argument that the trade mark acts as a guarantee of quality rather than origin. Further, it emphasizes the importance of quality control provisions in a trade mark licence and makes clear that a licensee who breaches these will be liable for trade mark infringement, not just breach of contract. Also, it establishes that where there is breach of quality control provisions in a licence, the goods will have been put on the market *without* consent so that Art. 7(1) does not apply and that even if selling to a prohibited retailer doesn't affect the condition of the goods, it may still give the trade mark owner the right to oppose further commercialization under Art. 7(2) because of damage to the mark.

 Pause for reflection

How important is the role of consent in the defence of exhaustion of rights?
Has Alfred Wolf given consent for the trading of his goods in Spain and Italy? To what extent does exhaustion apply to the export and sale of his goods in these countries?

14.10.5 Exceptions to exhaustion

Over almost four decades, the CJEU has gradually developed exceptions to the defence of exhaustion of rights. In each case, it has said, there are valid reasons why the intellectual property owner can stop the importation of the goods (or, in some cases, object to post-importation conduct). The case law is now expressed in Art. 7(2) of the Directive (now Art. 15(2) of the recast Directive), which provides that the defence of exhaustion shall not apply 'where there exist legitimate reasons . . . to oppose further commercialisation of the goods, especially where the condition of the goods is changed or impaired after they have been put on the market'. Article 7(2) is an exception to the free movement of goods, and should not be generously construed (*per* AG Sharpston in *Boehringer II* at [13]). In applying Art. 7(2), the Court has endeavoured to strike a balance between the interests of a number of key players, namely the intellectual property owner, enterprising importers, and consumers. It may be questioned whether as the law currently stands the CJEU has got the balance right, or whether the scales have been tilted too far towards the rights of the intellectual property owner.

14.10.5.1 Exception 1: alteration of the goods

The first exception to the defence occurs where the parallel importer alters the imported goods. Most (but by no means all) of the cases have concerned pharmaceutical products. As P. Koutrakos explains ('In Search of a Common Vocabulary in Free Movement of Goods: The Example of Repackaging Pharmaceuticals' [2003] 28 *EL Rev* 53), the pharmaceutical market differs considerably from others. The market is dominated by a handful of large, multi-national companies. Size matters because of the research and development costs; further, the time gap between the identification of a new chemical compound and its marketing as an effective pharmaceutical treatment is considerable, so that it takes many years to recoup investment. There are complex EU and national rules for the approval of medicines, and government intervention means that there are significant price differentials between Member States. Nevertheless, medicines are global products. They are needed by patients wherever they live. The products are easy to transport. However, local prescribing and dispensing practices vary enormously. Last, and perhaps most importantly, information about the product needs to be given in the local language. Patients need to know about when and how much of the medicine to take.

These factors provide some of the reasons why importers wish to alter imported pharmaceuticals. It is no good supplying tablets in blister-packs of ten if doctors only prescribe in multiples of seven. Patients used to the United Kingdom trade mark for the product will not recognize the mark used in Italy for the same product. Patients in the United Kingdom will want to read the dosage instructions in English, not Spanish.

The word 'alteration' includes repackaging, rebranding, relabelling, and over-stickering. As these terms are crucial, it will be useful to explain the differences between them. These differences are set out in Table 14.1.

Such alteration of the goods is, according to the CJEU, prima facie infringement of the trade mark right, although there is not an irrebuttable presumption to this effect (*per* Jacob LJ in *Boehringer Ingelheim KG v Dowelhurst Ltd* at [80]). Alteration entitles the trade mark owner to oppose importation and converts the parallel importer into an infringer. At first glance this appears to run contrary to both the origin function of trade marks and the principle of the internal market. What the CJEU has done, as part of its balancing exercise, has been to create *cumulative* guidelines with which the importer must comply in order to render the importation of the altered goods unobjectionable. The guidelines apply equally to repackaging, rebranding, and relabelling: Case C-143/00 *Boehringer Ingelheim v Swingward Ltd and Dowelhurst* ('*Boehringer I*') [2002] ECR I-3759 (*per* AG Jacobs at [86]). The Court disagreed with the advice of AG Sharpston at [42] in *Boehringer II* that over-stickering should not receive the same treatment and instead held that such conduct equally amounted to trade mark infringement (at [29–32]). It has now added that the removal of packaging ('de-branding') has the same effect as re-packaging: Case C-324/09 *L'Oréal SA v eBay International* [2011] ECR I-6011.

TABLE 14.1 *Repackaging, rebranding, relabelling, and over-stickering: definitions and differences*

Term	Meaning
Repackaging	Where the importer leaves the internal packaging intact, but replaces the exterior carton, this being printed in the language of the Member State of import (this should be distinguished from where the internal packaging is altered, for example cutting up blister packs of tablets).
Rebranding	Where the importer removes the trade mark used on the Member State of export and replaces it with that used in the Member State of import (because the trade mark owner uses different marks in different countries).
Relabelling	Where the importer removes existing product labels (including those containing batch codes) and replaces them with its own (possibly inferior) labels.
Over-stickering	Where the importer leaves the original internal and external packaging intact, but then applies an additional label printed in the language of the Member State of import to the outside of the packaging.

 Pause for reflection

Is the identical treatment accorded to repackaging, rebranding, relabelling, over-stickering, and de-branding justified?

To what extent does the exception to the exhaustion rule apply by reference to the use of Alfred's goods in Italy?

14.10.5.1.1 Repackaging the goods

Case 102/77 *Hoffmann-La Roche v Centrafarm* [1978] ECR 1139

The rights of the trade mark owner where the goods have been repackaged were first considered by the CJEU in Case 102/77 *Hoffmann-La Roche v Centrafarm* [1978] ECR 1139. VALIUM tranquilliser tablets sold in the United Kingdom were repackaged by Centrafarm so as to make them acceptable to the prescribing practices of the German market, the importer re-affixing the

→

→

trade mark together with its own name and address to the outside of the repackaged product. Such conduct was held to infringe the trade mark because it undermined its function of guaranteeing the quality of the goods. The Court went on to provide the first repackaging guidelines. The initial four *Hoffmann-La Roche* conditions were that:

- the trade mark owner's conduct must have the effect of partitioning the market. Example of such conduct would be where the goods in question are sold in yellow boxes in Italy but blue boxes in the United Kingdom, or where tablets are supplied in blister packs of seven in the United Kingdom, but packs of ten in Germany;
- the importer must state that the goods have been repackaged;
- notice must be given to the trade mark owner;
- the repackaging must not affect the condition of the goods. This is termed 'physical impairment' and includes the adequacy of any replacement instruction leaflets which the importer adds to the product, *per* AG Jacobs in *Boehringer I*.

The balancing act referred to earlier is evident in the guidelines. The interests of the trade mark owner are met by the requirement that the goods must not be adversely affected by the repackaging, otherwise the essential function of the trade mark is damaged. Equally, the interests of the internal market are met, because the trade mark owner's conduct is examined objectively (i.e. without reference to the owner's intentions) to see whether it has the *effect* of reinforcing national boundaries. The other two guidelines (marking the goods to show that they have been repackaged, and giving notice), whilst underpinning the guarantee function of the mark, appear procedural in nature. The importer in Case 1/81 *Pfizer Inc v Eurim-Pharm* [1981] ECR 2913 successfully complied with these guidelines, thereby escaping liability for infringement.

 Pause for reflection

Does the use of the mark 'Lupo' on Alfred's goods in Italy qualify as repackaging?

14.10.5.1.2 Rebranding the goods

Case 3/78 *Centrafarm v American Home Products* [1978] ECR 1823

In Case 3/78 *Centrafarm v American Home Products* [1978] ECR 1823, the importer not only repackaged the product but changed the trade mark from that used in the United Kingdom (SERENID) to that used in the Netherlands (SERESTA). The importer was held to have infringed the latter registration when it imported the goods into the Netherlands. The CJEU accepted

→

→ that the trade mark owner had good reason (language differences) to have different marks in different Member States, but added the warning that if different marks were chosen simply to partition the internal market, the parallel importer would be at liberty to change the marks without incurring liability.

The difficulty with the ruling is that whereas in *Hoffmann-La Roche* the Court had demanded an *objective* assessment of whether the trade mark owner's conduct divided the internal market, here the Court appears to contemplate a *subjective* test where that conduct consists of having different marks for different Member States. The CJEU has now removed this discrepancy.

 Pause for reflection

Does the use of the mark 'Lupo' on Alfred's goods in Italy qualify as rebranding?

14.10.5.1.3 Relabelling the goods

Relabelling occurred in Case C-349/95 *Frits Loendersloot v George Ballantine & Sons Ltd* [1997] ECR I-6227, which for once did not involve pharmaceutical products. Importers of whisky had removed the labels on the bottles, replacing them with their own. The original labels had included batch numbers, required under EU foodstuffs law to enable the recall of faulty products, but the numbers were also used by the trade mark owner to prevent counterfeiting and to follow dealings in the goods with a view to finding out whether particular traders had breached conditions of sale by supplying known parallel importers. The CJEU held that the removal of labels amounted to trade mark infringement. The use of the labels did not lead to artificial partitioning of the market.

14.10.5.1.4 Over-stickering

In contrast to the facts of *Ballantine*, over-stickering does not involve the removal of any material from the product. Instead, a label is placed onto the exterior packaging, with the objective, at least in the case of pharmaceutical goods, of providing the patient with additional information in their own language. The additions to the *Hoffmann-La Roche* guidelines, discussed next, have added a requirement of proportionality: the importer's over-stickering, where it is the *minimum* that can be done to achieve access to the market, will avoid liability, provided that the labels are of appropriate quality.

14.10.5.1.5 The additions to the *Hoffmann-La Roche* guidelines

In two subsequent rulings, the CJEU added to the *Hoffmann-La Roche* guidelines. In Cases C-427/93 *Bristol-Myers Squibb v Paranova*, C-71/94 *Eurim-Pharm v Beiersdorf*, and C-232/94 *MPA Pharma v Rhône-Poulenc* ('*Paranova I*') [1996] ECR I-3457, the Court said that the power of the trade mark owner to oppose repackaging would be limited where repackaging was necessary to market the product in the importing Member State. It also said that the importer must supply samples of the goods to the trade mark owner if asked to do so, and that the repackaging must not be untidy, of poor quality, or likely to injure the reputation of the mark (referred to as the 'mental impairment' of the mark). In Case C-379/97 *Pharmacia & Upjohn SA v Paranova A/S* *('Paranova II')* [1999] ECR I-6927 it declared that the repackaging must be objectively necessary to enable the importer to have access to the market. *Paranova I* was the first case to be heard by the CJEU under the provisions of the Directive. Its restatement of the rights of the trade mark owner under Art. 7(2) (now Art. 15(2) of the recast Directive) has since been adopted with approval in *Boehringer I* and *Boehringer II*.

Case C-348/04 *Boehringer Ingelheim v Swingward Ltd and Dowelhurst ('Boehringer II')* [2007] ECR I-3391

In Case C-348/04 Boehringer Ingelheim v Swingward Ltd and Dowelhurst ('Boehringer II') [2007] ECR I-3391, the CJEU (at [21], [32]) summarized the restatement Art. 7(2) of the Directive, a trade mark owner may legitimately oppose the further marketing of a pharmaceutical product which has been repackaged, rebranded, relabelled, or over-stickered unless:

- repackaging is necessary for market access;
- the repackaging does not affect the original condition of the product;
- the new packaging clearly states who repackaged the product and the name of the manufacturer;
- the presentation of the repackaged product is not such as to be liable to damage the reputation of the trade mark and of its owner; and
- the importer gives notice to the trade mark owner before the repackaged product is put on sale, and, on demand, supplies a specimen of the repackaged product.

A number of matters in this definitive restatement require further elaboration, namely necessity, 'mental impairment', marking the goods as having been repackaged, the giving of notice, the supply of samples, and the burden of proof.

14.10.5.1.6 Necessity

The requirement that the importer must show the need to repackage has been part of the case law since *Paranova I*. The number of requests for preliminary rulings under what is now Art. 267 TFEU which this has generated shows the inherent difficulty of the concept.

The need to repackage will be a direct result of the conduct of the trade mark owner partitioning the market. Such conduct might consist of choosing different forms of packaging for different Member States, or different trade marks for different Member States (the CJEU in *Paranova I* made clear, in contrast to its earlier ruling in *Centrafarm v American Home Products*, that the choice of different marks for different states was to be determined objectively, not subjectively). It was initially thought the need to repackage had to be in response to restrictions imposed by national legislation (for example, prohibiting the use of particular names as trade marks, as in *Paranova II*) or of local prescribing practices, but the CJEU in *Paranova II* made clear that 'necessity' meant simply whether the importer had to change the goods in order to gain market access. Necessity itself was to be determined objectively. In *Boehringer I*, it said that 'market access' included overcoming consumer resistance to over-stickered boxes (thereby justifying the replacement of the outer packaging) but did not extend to the importer's attempt to secure a commercial advantage (i.e. by free-riding on the success of the claimant's trade mark).

In *Boehringer II*, the CJEU said (at [33–39]) that the requirement of necessity was concerned solely with *whether* the goods had to be reboxed. It did not extend to *how* they were reboxed. To hold otherwise would place an intolerable burden on national courts who would have to take 'numerous decisions on trivial details of pattern and colour', matters not within their judicial remit (*per* AG Sharpston at [54]).

14.10.5.1.7 Mental impairment

The requirement that the importer must not cause harm to the reputation of the trade mark was first established by the CJEU in *Paranova I*. This appears to run contrary to the origin function of trade marks and has not been well received by the United Kingdom judiciary: see *Zino Davidoff SA v A&G Imports Ltd* [1999] 2 CMLR 1056; *Glaxo Group Ltd v Dowelhurst Ltd (No. 2)* [2000] FSR 529. Nevertheless, it does accord with the wider view of trade marks set out by the CJEU in Case C-206/01 *Arsenal Football Club v Matthew Reed* [2002] ECR I-10273. In line with this, the Court stated in *Boehringer I* that the legitimate interests of the trade mark owner must be respected. Further, in *Boehringer II*, the CJEU confirmed (at [43]) that whilst such damage must be serious, it is not limited to defective, poor quality, or untidy packaging. Instead, both the 'inappropriate presentation' of the trade mark and an incorrect suggestion of a commercial link between the trade mark owner and the importer are capable, in principle, of causing damage. Whether 'de-branding', 'co-branding', obscuring the original trade mark, failing to state the ownership of the original mark, or printing the name of the importer in capital letters does damage the reputation of the trade mark is a question of fact for the national court to decide in the light of the circumstances of each case (*Boehringer II* at [47]).

Despite this advice, when *Boehringer II* returned to the national court, the Court of Appeal held that the defendant's conduct in repackaging and over-stickering the claimant's pharmaceutical products had not caused mental impairment: *Boehringer Ingelheim v Swingward* [2008] EWCA Civ 83.

14.10.5.1.8 Marking the goods as repackaged

This is one of the original *Hoffmann-La Roche* guidelines. Surprisingly, the Court seems less concerned that it should be strictly applied, in contrast to some of the other repackaging conditions. In Cases C-400/09 and C-207/10 *Orifarm v Merck, Sharp & Dohme; Paranova v Merck, Sharp & Dohme* [2011] ECR I-7063, it stated that as long as consumers weren't misled, it didn't matter that the name which appeared was not that of the actual repackager but another company in the same corporate group which held the marketing authorization. What was required was to indicate that someone other than the trade mark owner had repackaged the goods.

14.10.5.1.9 Notice

Likewise, the requirement for the importer to given notice to the trade mark owner that the goods have been repackaged originated in *Hoffmann-La Roche*. It has frequently been questioned. One of the key issues in *Boehringer I* was whether the importer had to give notice in person to the trade mark owner. Laddie J, when making the reference, had thought it sufficient if the owner learned of the repackaging from another reliable source. Further, how much notice has to be given? Laddie J thought that 48 hours' notice was enough but the CJEU declared that the trade mark owner had to be given a reasonable time to react and so stipulated that the notice period had to be 15 working days. Notice had to be given by the importer in person.

The matter was revisited in *Boehringer II*, where the Court of Appeal sought further guidance on the penalty to be imposed should the importer comply with all the other guidelines but fail to give the correct notice. AG Sharpston suggested that as notice was a procedural requirement, it ought to attract a less severe remedy than that awarded for breach of the other guidelines. That was not to belittle the importance of giving notice. It was an important safeguard for the trade mark owner and save in the most exceptional cases, failure to give notice would normally be deliberate. The CJEU disagreed on the remedies point: the trade mark owner's right to prevent parallel importation of products marketed in breach of the requirement to give prior notice is no different from the right to object to counterfeit goods. Awarding the same remedy for failure to give notice as for dealing in counterfeit goods is not contrary to the principle of proportionality, although it is for the national court to determine the amount of the financial remedy: *Boehringer II* at [55–64].

14.10.5.1.10 Samples

> **Case C-276/05 *The Wellcome Foundation Ltd v Paranova Pharmazeutika Handels GmbH* [2008] ECR I-10479**
>
> The need to submit samples was the subject matter of the reference in Case C-276/05 *The Wellcome Foundation Ltd v Paranova Pharmazeutika Handels GmbH* [2008] ECR I-10479. Wellcome was the registered proprietor in Austria of the mark ZOVIRAX. Paranova had sold the tablets (bought elsewhere in the EEA) in new packaging, which bore the phrase 'Repackaged and imported by Paranova' in large print, and gave notice to an associated company, enclosing samples of the packaging. The claimant objected that the defendant had not explained the reasons for the repackaging, had not stated where it had bought the tablets (in fact they had been purchased in Greece where the original packs contained different quantities of the tablets), and had not justified using such large print, and asked for samples of all repackaging. The defendant refused. The CJEU stated that the requirement to supply samples was to enable the trade mark owner to check that the condition of the product was
>
> →

> not affected and that the presentation of the product was not likely to damage the reputation of the mark. It was for the national court to decide here whether the packaging did damage the reputation of the mark. It was up to the importer to show necessity to repackage, and to produce sufficient information to enable the proprietor to decide whether repackaging was necessary.

14.10.5.1.11 The burden of proof

In *Boehringer II*, the CJEU saw fit to depart from the Opinion of AG Sharpston. It stated (at [51–53]) that the burden of proof lay on the importer to establish all the conditions set out in para [32] of its ruling. However, with regard to the condition that the repackaging must not affect the original condition of the goods and the condition that the presentation of the product must not affect the trade mark's reputation, it was enough to furnish evidence that led to a reasonable presumption that the condition was fulfilled. As regards mental impairment, the onus then switched to the trade mark proprietor (who was best placed to assess whether the repackaging was liable to damage his reputation and that of the trade mark) to prove that they had been damaged. The Court added that an EU rule regarding the burden of proof was essential to meet the policy set out Recital 10 to the consolidated version of the Directive, namely that trade marks should receive the same level of protection in all Member States.

Pause for reflection

Do the CJEU's guidelines for a parallel importer who wishes to repackage goods give too much power to the trade mark owner?

14.10.5.2 Exception 2: advertising and after-sales service

Two cases illustrate how the exhaustion defence can apply to conduct occurring after goods have been imported. Equally they show how the trade mark owner can object if such conduct affects the essential function of the mark. Both cases make use of the concept of mental impairment first set out in *Paranova I*. In Case C-337/95 *Parfums Christian Dior SA and Parfums Christian Dior BV v Evora BV* [1997] ECR I-6013, the trade mark owner sued for infringement where luxury perfumes were sold in a cut-price chemist's shop, arguing that the positioning of the goods (next to disposable nappies) and the manner of advertising (on cheap leaflets) undermined the 'aura of luxury' associated with the mark. The CJEU ruled that although Art. 7(1) (now Art. 15(1) of the recast Directive) applied to post-importation conduct (such as resale), it was for the national court to decide whether the manner of resale caused harm to the mark. Similarly, in Case C-63/97 *BMW v Deenik* [1999] ECR I-905, the Court said that any sales of second-hand cars by the defendant must not create the mistaken impression on the part of customers that Mr Deenik was part of the authorized BMW dealer network, nor must the manner of sale cause harm to the reputation of the mark.

Pause for reflection

To what extent does exhaustion apply to the export of Alfred's goods in Spain and in Italy? Why does your answer differ by reference to these two instances?

14.10.6 Case law of the CJEU: parallel imports from outside the EEA

It is possible for exhaustion of rights to apply internationally. Marketing of the goods anywhere in the world with the consent of the owner of the intellectual property right would mean that no objection could be made to further dealings in those goods. We consider here the case law of the CJEU on international exhaustion.

Once the EU began enacting harmonization Directives, the question was whether Art. 7 of the Directive removed the discretion left to Member States by *EMI v CBS* to deal with parallel imports from non-EEA Member States in accordance with their own national laws. If (as was logical) Member States no longer had any discretion, but had to apply a single EU rule, should the latter impose a doctrine of international exhaustion or only EU-wide exhaustion of rights?

Case C-355/96 *Silhouette International Schmied GmbH v Hartlauer Handelsgesellschaft mbH* [1998] ECR I-4799

The answer came in Case C-355/96 *Silhouette International Schmied GmbH v Hartlauer Handelsgesellschaft mbH* [1998] ECR I-4799. Silhouette, a manufacturer of spectacle frames at the 'upper end' of the market, sold them under the trade mark SILHOUETTE. In Austria, the frames were supplied to specialist opticians, elsewhere they were supplied through local subsidiaries or distributors. The case came about because Silhouette had 21,000 pairs of spectacles which it no longer required as they were, fashion-wise, out of date. It entered into a contract whereby the goods were sold to an intermediary who was under strict instructions to require the purchaser to resell only in Bulgaria or the states of the former Soviet Union and not to export them to other countries. Predictably, Hartlauer (with whom Silhouette had previously refused to do business because it did not conform to the prestigious image to which Silhouette aspired) acquired the goods and offered them for sale in Austria.

The CJEU ruled that there should be no doctrine of international exhaustion, so that the trade mark owner could object to the importation of the spectacle frames into Austria. EU Member States had to apply intra-EU exhaustion of rights only. The reasoning of the Court is brief. It said that because of what is now Recital 10 to the Directive, trade marks must receive the same level of protection in all Member States, so that in the interests of the internal market, there must be a single rule in order to ensure a 'level playing field'. Articles 5 to 7 of the Directive are a complete code of the trade mark owner's rights. To recognize international exhaustion would reduce the trade mark owner's protection. The key phrase in Art. 7, namely 'put on the market in the Community . . . by the proprietor or with his consent' meant that there should only be intra-EU exhaustion of rights.

The decision in *Silhouette* was extensively criticized because it led to the creation of 'fortress Europe' and because it ignored the origin function of trade marks. Nevertheless, Judge David Edwards has argued that the CJEU had little choice but to adopt a policy of intra-EU exhaustion (see 'Trade Marks: Descriptions of Origin and the Internal Market' [2001] 2 *IPQ* 135). Despite the criticism, the Court confirmed its thinking in *Silhouette* in Case C-173/98 *Sebago Inc & S.A. Ancienne Maison Dubois v S.A. G-B Unic* [1999] ECR I-4103. At the same time, it dealt with a recurring argument as to the meaning of the word 'consent' in Art. 7 (now Art. 15 of the recast Directive). The importer had tried to argue that consent could be implied from a course of dealing, so that once one consignment of goods (here, shoes made in Central America) had been imported into a Member State, all subsequent assignments should be treated as entering the EU with consent. The CJEU dismissed this argument. The wording of its earlier rulings in *Centrafarm v Winthrop*, *Dior*, and *Deenik*, together with the text of Art. 7, made plain that consent had to be given for each individual batch of goods rather than product lines.

 Pause for reflection

Why should a trade mark owner be able to object to goods he has placed in circulation in Singapore or the USA when he cannot object (subject to the repackaging rules) to goods he has placed in circulation somewhere in the EEA?

Predictably, UK judges were not impressed by *Silhouette* and *Sebago*. Indeed, before the rulings were given, Jacob J had hinted (in *Northern & Shell v Condé Nast* [1995] RPC 117) that he favoured a doctrine of international exhaustion. Although Scottish courts had applied *Silhouette* (see *Zino Davidoff SA v M&S Toiletries* [2000] 2 CMLR 735), Laddie J refused to do so in *Zino Davidoff SA v A&G Imports Ltd* [2000] Ch 127. Here, aftershave made in Singapore had, through a chain of dealings, reached the United Kingdom, despite the attempts by the trade mark owner to impose contractual obligations on each purchaser of the goods not to import the goods into the EU. Laddie J, clearly concerned at the enhancement of the trade mark owner's rights, tried to sidestep *Silhouette* by treating consent as a matter of national contract law. Nevertheless, he referred to the CJEU a number of questions on international exhaustion. The CJEU, in a remarkably forthright ruling, insisted that there should be no international exhaustion of rights in EU law.

Case C-414/99 *Zino Davidoff SA v A&G Imports Ltd* [2001] ECR I-8691

The CJEU repeated that Arts 5 to 7 of the Directive were a complete harmonization of the owner's rights. In the interests of the internal market these provisions had to be consistently applied. First marketing outside the EEA did not exhaust the trade mark owner's rights. Further, 'consent' was a concept of EU intellectual property law. Art. 7 was a derogation of the rights

→

> found in Art. 5 of the Directive, and must therefore be narrowly construed, so that consent was the decisive factor. Consequently, the intention of the trade mark owner to renounce the Art. 5 rights must be unequivocally proved. This had to be express, although (exceptionally) consent could be implied. However, said the Court, consent could *not* be implied from failure to communicate an import ban to all subsequent purchasers, from the fact that a warning notice was not placed on the goods, from the absence of any appropriate contractual reservations in any agreement transferring ownership of the goods, nor from the owner's silence. It was also irrelevant that retailers/wholesalers did not pass on the trade mark owner's reservations. Finally, said the Court, the onus of proof was on the importer to show consent, not on the trade mark owner to show lack of consent.

Predictably, the *Silhouette/Davidoff* principle that there should be no international exhaustion of rights continues to attract criticism. One argument is that the *Davidoff* ruling smacks of protectionism. Another which is frequently rehearsed is that consumers are denied the opportunity to buy cheap, non-counterfeit goods made outside the EU. The EU Commission, having initiated research into the effect of the case law, has stated that it does not think consumers are being harmed by the rulings and has indicated that it does not intend to overturn the cases by legislative means. Given the forthright tenor of the *Davidoff* ruling, it looks unlikely that the CJEU can be persuaded to change its mind. The recast Directive will make no change here.

The case law on exhaustion of rights is represented diagrammatically in Diagram 14.1.

14.11 Conclusion

This chapter has explained the various defences against trade mark infringement and the way in which the courts have interpreted them. These span from the use of one's own name to a framework outlining the conditions of comparative advertisement and the role of exhaustion of rights as a defence to an action for trade mark infringement, including the ways in which the intellectual property owner can object to the parallel importation of non-EEA goods.

Going to the scenario question, Alfred Wolf should be advised that a number of defences against trade mark infringement are available to him.

- Regarding the mark 'Wolf' for products in Class 29 of the Nice Classification:

By reference to this case, Alfred Wolf should be advised that s. 11(3) contains a saving for earlier rights, to the extent that they have been used continuously. Earlier rights in this context are either unregistered trade marks or signs which have been used continuously in such a manner that they would be protected under the laws of passing off. The prior use must predate whichever is the earlier of two events: the use *or* the registration of the claimant's mark. In *Caspian Pizza Limited v Shah* [2015] EWHC 3567 (IPEC), HHJ Hacon upheld the s. 11(3) defence despite the fact that the claimant's use of its mark, then unregistered, pre-dated the acquisition by the defendant of its 'earlier right.' In

DIAGRAM 14.1

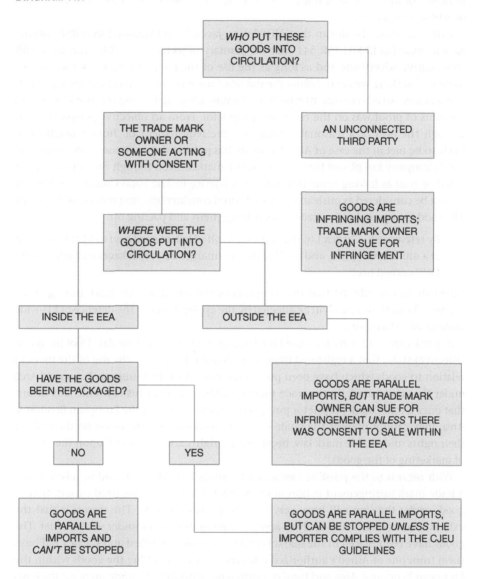

Alfred's case, the mark 'Wolf's Deli' is an earlier mark in this sense and the prior use, on the basis of facts, predates both the use and the registration of the marks belonging to The Food Group Ltd. The same applies to the slogan by which Alfred is advertising his products.

What is more, s. 11(2)(a) permits the defendant to make use of his own name, so that the registration of a surname does not amount to a complete monopoly (see e.g. *Reed Executive plc v Reed Business Information Ltd; IBM Corporation v Web-Sphere Ltd; Hotel Cipriani Srl v Cipriani (Grosvenor Street) Ltd*). A condition for the application of the defence is that it should be in accordance with honest practices in industrial or commercial matters (*Maier v ASOS*). There is nothing in the factual background of Alfred's case to indicate conflict with such honest practices and the use of the mark 'Wolf's Deli' can benefit from s. 11(2)(a).

With regards to the slogan that Alfred uses, Jacob J has explained in *British Airways plc v Ryanair Ltd* [2001] FSR 541 that the primary objective of s. 10(6) was to permit comparative advertising and as long as the use of the competitor's mark was honest, there was nothing wrong in telling the public of the relative merits of competing goods and services. An advertisement which was significantly misleading was not honest and the onus of proof was on the registered proprietor. From an objective perspective and through the eyes of a reasonable audience, the requirement of 'honest practices' is likely to be met in the case of Alfred since he has put the slogan in use years before The Food Company Ltd placed their slogan in the market. Even though the advertisement could be read as having some comparative reference to The Food Company's mark, it cannot be considered as misleading. Alfred could consider bringing proceedings against The Food Company Ltd for trade mark infringement and passing off.

- By reference to Carnex Ltd that exports 'Wolf's Deli' corned beef in Spain, selling it at a much lower price, and the Italian supermarket that repackages and sells 'Wolf's Deli' corned beef:

Alfred should be advised that the prospects of success of a trade mark infringement action in both these cases will be affected by the applicability of the defence of EU-wide trade mark exhaustion.

In particular, s. 12 (which is based on Art. 7 of the Directive, now Art. 15 of the recast Directive) states that a registered trade mark is not infringed by the use of the mark in relation to goods which have been put on the market in the European Economic Area under that trade mark by the trade mark proprietor or with his consent. This means that once a trade mark proprietor puts goods on the market in the European Economic Area, they cannot prevent the resale of those goods within this region on the basis of their rights under trade mark law, because their rights are 'exhausted' upon the first act of marketing of the goods.

With regards to the possible case against Carnex Ltd, Alfred should be advised that a trade mark infringement action under s. 10(4) for the unauthorized exportation of goods under the sign will have very low prospects of success. The reason is that the exhaustion defence is very likely to apply as the conditions set under s. 12 are met. The goods have been placed in the market with the consent of Alfred and Carnex Ltd buys them from one of Alfred's authorized retailers. They are reselling the goods within the European Economic Area and have not interfered with Alfred's trade mark on the basis of the facts given.

By reference to the repackaging and export of Alfred's goods in Italy, this is a prima facie case of infringement under s. 10(4). Section 12(2) stipulates that the exhaustion defence does not apply where the trade mark proprietor has legitimate reasons to oppose further dealings in the goods (in particular where the condition of the goods has been changed or impaired after they have been put on the market). Such legitimate reasons include repackaging, relabelling, and rebranding. In order to avoid liability for trade mark infringer, a repackager has to satisfy five conditions according to *Bristol-Myers Squibb v Paranova*: repackaging the product should have been necessary; there is no effect on the original condition of the product; there is clear identification of the manufacturer and importer; the presentation of the goods does not damage the reputation of the trade mark or its owner; and they ought to give notice to the proprietor. These conditions are also available to cases of relabelling and rebranding of goods (*Pharmacia & Upjohn v Paranova*). It is not likely that the Italian supermarket can successfully invoke the defence as various conditions established in *Bristol-Myers Squibb* are not met, e.g. repackaging does not seem absolutely necessary and there is no clear indication of who the manufacturer and the importer are. This is a likely case of trade mark infringement under s. 10(4) TMA.

End-of-chapter questions

After reading the chapter carefully, try answering the questions which follow. For answer guidance visit the online resources at **www.oup.com/uk/karapapa-mcdonagh/**

1. How does the scope of the 'own name defence' differ under EU and UK trade mark law?

2. In developing its case law on exhaustion of rights under Art. 7 of the Trade Marks Directive, the Court of Justice has all but forgotten the origin function of trade marks. Discuss.

Further reading

For understanding the protection available to trade marks, the following readings are recommended:

Beier, F.-K. 'Industrial Property and the Free Movement of Goods in the Internal European Market' (1990) 21 *IIC* 131

Argues that the concepts deployed by the CJEU in explaining exhaustion of rights are not as clear as they could be.

Burrell, R. and Gangjee, D. S., 'Trade Marks and Freedom of Expression: A Call for Caution' (2010) University of Queensland TC Beirne School of Law Research Paper No. 10-05

Questions the advisability of looking to freedom of expression to address the overreach of trade mark law.

Calboli, I. 'Reviewing the (Shrinking) Principle of Trademark Exhaustion in the European Union (Ten Years Later)' (2012) 16 *Marquette Intellectual Property Law Review* 257

Considers the principle of EU-wide trade mark exhaustion.

Edwards, Judge D. 'Trade Marks: Descriptions of Origin and the Internal Market' [2001] 2 *IPQ* 135

Argues that the CJEU had no choice but to reach the conclusion it did in Silhouette.

Koutrakos, P. 'In Search of a Common Vocabulary in Free Movement of Goods: The Example of Repackaging Pharmaceuticals' [2003] 28 *EL Rev* 53

Explores the problems found in the repackaging cases.

Norman, H. 'Parallel Imports from Non-EEA Member States: the Vision Remains Unclear' [2000] 4 *EIPR* 159

An examination of the Silhouette *decision.*

Simon Fhima, I., 'Nominative Use and Honest Practices in Industrial and Commercial Matters: A Very European History' [2007] 2 *IPQ* 117
Considers what the ECJ's definition of the honest practices proviso means for dilution cases specifically and what lessons can be learned for trade mark law more generally.

Simon Fhima, I., 'Trade Marks and Free Speech' [2013] 44 *IIC* 293
Argues that freedom of speech rhetoric has little impact on EU trade mark law.

Senftleben, M. 'Function Theory and International Exhaustion—Why It Is Wise to Confine the Double Identity Rule to Cases Affecting the Origin Function' [2014] 36 *EIPR* 518

Tritton, G. 'Parallel Imports in the European Community' [1997] 2 *IPQ* 196
Discusses the repackaging cases in detail.

Van der Merwe, A. 'The Exhaustion of Rights in Patent Law with Specific Emphasis on the Issue of Parallel Importation' [2000] 3 *IPQ* 286
Argues that different intellectual property rights should receive different treatment in the exhaustion of rights defence.

Patents

Introduction to patents

Problem question

Read this problem question carefully and keep it in mind while you are working through the chapter that follows. At the end of this chapter, you will be able to apply what you have learnt to the problem question and advise the relevant parties.

John Stevenson is a professional engineer and amateur skateboard enthusiast who recently moved from London to Devon. In advance of competing at the upcoming UK national skateboard championships, John wishes to put in extra practice. Unfortunately, the house he has just moved into is not located close to a suitable concrete practice area. It is, however, very close to a large public park that consists of a wide, grassy field that has several flat areas as well as three hilly points. The grass is cut by the local council every week, so it is always well trimmed. Only for the fact that it is grassy, rather than concrete, it would be an ideal practice area. John realizes that if he could adapt his skateboard wheels so that they could roll easily on fresh cut grass, he would be able to use the nearby field to practice. He puts his engineering knowledge to good use, and after several failed experiments he eventually creates a flexible, tubular-shaped, plastic brace with a click-mechanism that can be attached to each of the wheels of a regular skateboard to improve efficiency. The addition of the braces to each wheel allow the wheels to spin fast on a soft surface such as fresh cut grass. Because of the click-mechanism the braces can be easily removed if the skateboarder wishes to skate on concrete or any other hard service. John attaches the braces and gives the skateboard a quick try in his private garden. It works properly. He is very pleased. He tries out his invention in the local park and a few onlookers cheer him on.

Now that John is satisfied that his invention works, he asks you a question: what is patent law, and is it relevant to what he has created? The top four markets for skateboards are in the US, the UK, France, and Germany. How could he gain protection in all four jurisdictions?

15.1 **Introduction**

In general terms, patents protect inventions—often new medicinal compounds or new aspects of technology—that are novel, inventive, and capable of industrial application. Although the nature of inventions can make them exciting, many students find the law of patents challenging. They find the facts of patent cases, which involve the collision of law and science, difficult to understand, especially when they discover that some patent judgments refer to inventions involving chemical formulae, engineering diagrams or information technologies. Although, at first, patent law may seem impenetrable, it is important not to allow yourself to be mystified. Rather, it is better to accept that the nature of patents means that they are necessarily somewhat 'opaque' and 'uncertain' (S. Thambisetty, 'Patents as Credence Goods' [2007] 27(4) *Oxford Journal of Legal Studies* 707). The skill of the patent lawyer is to define what can be protected, while acknowledging each scientific field on its own terms. Moreover, even if studying patent law is a challenge, it is surely a rewarding one. Many famous figures throughout history have worked as patent examiners, including Thomas Jefferson and Albert Einstein, while many more have created patented inventions, including Alfred Nobel, Thomas Edison, James Dyson, and even entertainers/artists like Harry Houdini, James Cameron, and Prince. (see Appendix 1 for the relevant US patent paperwork for the latter example).

Starting with this chapter, we will go through patent law step-by-step, referring back to John's scenario above in order to bring real world concerns to abstract principles. Furthermore, over the course of this chapter we will also consider patent law's history, nature, and purpose—the historical context in which the law of patents has developed; the origins of current UK legislation; how this type of protection is justified; the key issues likely to be raised in patent litigation; the procedure to be followed when obtaining a patent in the UK and in Europe.

15.1.1 **The origins of patents**

It is worth spending some time considering the history and purpose of patent system. How did it happen that inventors gained the right to a limited monopoly over their inventions? Where did this legal innovation come from?

What is the origin of the patent system?

It is frequently stated that the origins of patents are obscure. The word 'patent' itself derives from the Latin phrase *literae patentes*, meaning 'open letter'. It reflects the practice of the Crown in England from the Middle Ages onwards to grant monopolies to individuals by way of an open letter to which the Great Seal was affixed. The United Kingdom Intellectual Property Office ('UKIPO') itself says that the first recorded patent (for the making of stained-glass windows in Eton College) was granted in 1449; yet, there is extensive academic literature (see Wyndham Hulme, 'The History of the Patent System under the Prerogative and at Common Law' [1896] 12 *LQR* 141) of patents being granted at least a century before.

It has been suggested (see Seaborne Davis, 'Further Light on the Case of Monopolies' [1932] 48 *LQR* 394) that these ancient patents could be subdivided into four categories, namely those involving inventions as we might understand the term today, dispensations from statutory regulation, powers of supervision over particular trades, and personal trading monopolies over everyday items (such as vinegar or playing cards). Even the first category (inventions as such) could be subdivided into those where the patentee had themselves created some sort of technical advance and those where the patentee was merely the first person to introduce into the country technology already in use elsewhere.

During this early period, the principal reason for granting a monopoly over technology already known outside the Kingdom was to encourage the importation of skilled labour and know-how in order to promote local manufacture. The national interest lay at the heart of most of the grants made by the Tudor monarchs: 'new' technology might relate to public works or weapons of war; it might help to make domestic industry more competitive or boost overseas trade; it might reduce unemployment or make a particular commodity cheaper.

The practice of granting patents has existed for many centuries and was by no means exclusive to England. Arguably, the Tudor practice was influenced by legislation elsewhere in Europe, for example, the Statute of Venice (then an independent republic) in 1474.

The Statute of Venice 1474

The Statute of Venice is considered to be one of the earliest to set out patent fundamentals. It reads:

> Be it enacted that, by the authority of this Council, every person who shall build any new and ingenious device in this City, not previously made in our Commonwealth, shall give notice of it to the office of our General Welfare Board when it has been reduced to perfection so that it can be used and operated. It is forbidden to every other person in any of our territories and towns to make any further device conforming with and similar to said one, without the consent and licence of the author, for the term of 10 years. And if anybody builds it in violation hereof, the aforesaid author and inventor shall be entitled to have him summoned before any magistrate of this City, by which magistrate the said infringer shall be constrained to pay him hundred ducats; and the device shall be destroyed at once. It being, however, within the power and discretion of the Government, in its activities, to take and use any such device and instrument, with this condition however that no one but the author shall operate it.

> We have among us men of great genius, apt to invent and discover ingenious devices; and in view of the grandeur and virtue of our City, more such men come to us every day from diverse parts. Now, if provision were made for the works and devices discovered by such persons, so that others who may see them could not build them and take the inventor's honor away, more men would then apply their genius, would discover, and would build devices of great utility and benefit to our commonwealth.

The first paragraph of the above statute contains all the ingredients of a modern patent statute, namely the criteria for protection ('new and ingenious device . . . not previously made . . . when it has been reduced to perfection'), the need to register ('give notice'), the exclusive right conferred on the '**author**', the prohibition on infringement, the penalties for infringing conduct, and power for the Government to make use of the invention. The second paragraph sets out the reasons why patents are desirable.

Not long after patents became widely used in the UK, they began to create controversies (a pattern that has repeated throughout the history of patent law, as we shall see). Criticism of the overuse (and abuse) of patents by Elizabeth I led to legal challenges, such as that in *Darcy v Allin (the Case of Monopolies)* (1602) 11 Co Rep 84b, where (so we are told) the patent for playing cards was held contrary to law. Where, however, the monopoly resulted in the acquisition of new technology, the courts were prepared to uphold the grant as valid (*Clothworkers of Ipswich Case* (1615) Godbolt 252). Later the practice of James I in granting so-called 'odious monopolies' caused even more concern. Resultant disquiet in Parliament led to the enactment of the Statute of Monopolies 1623. Section 1 declared all monopolies to be 'altogether contrary to the laws of this realm, and . . . void'—but s. 6 contained an exception for 'any manner of new manufacture'. This particular provision is not just of historical interest; remarkably, s. 6 was, until 1977, the only substantive provision on patent law in the United Kingdom, and (surprisingly) is still in force today.

Another important aspect to note here is that the law of patents, and indeed intellectual property more generally, is—and has always been—framed around a limited exception to the economic principle that monopolies are bad.

 Pause for reflection

Many economists argue that monopolies have negative effects on the overall economy and lead to restrictions on competition. Why is the law of patents viewed as an exception to the general principle that all monopolies are bad? Perhaps the crucial element of the patent monopoly is that it is strictly *limited*—as we shall see later on in this chapter, the typical patent term is 20 years. Therefore, even if patents remain controversial to some scholars of patents and competition, we must remember that it is not intended to be a permanent monopoly but a temporary one. Duncan Matthews and Olga Gurgula ('Patent strategies and competition law in the pharmaceutical sector: implications for access to medicines' [2016] Queen Mary School of Law Legal Studies Research Paper No. 233/2016) note that achieving a balance between patent rights and competition is conducive to enabling freedom of choice and lower prices for patented drugs, while potentially also serving as an important driver for innovation and access.

15.1.2 **The development of United Kingdom patent law**

Like many areas of commercial law, the law of patents was shaped primarily by 19th-century events, and was a belated response to the Industrial Revolution. Apart from the concerns about the lack of efficiency in the patent system (satirized in Charles Dickens' *Poor Man's Tale of a Patent*), there was vigorous debate about whether there should be patents at all (see F. Machlup and E. Penrose, 'The Patent Controversy in the Nineteenth Century' [1950] 10 *J of Economic History* 1). Some (principally those who favoured untrammelled free trade) called for their abolition, believing that they stifled innovation and production. Such economic objections to patent protection, prompted by but by no means entirely consistent with laissez-faire political philosophy, can be contrasted to the earlier objections to patents in the 16th and 17th centuries, when patents were perceived as an undesirable use of the Crown prerogative. Objections to the patent system as it stood at the start of the 19th century were threefold (see Dutton, *The Patent System and Inventive Activity during the Industrial Revolution 1750–1852* (Manchester University Press, 1984)). First, there was cumbersome administrative machinery; second, patents were expensive to obtain (not least because it was necessary to obtain a separate grant for a patent in England, Scotland, and Ireland); and last, the law was inefficient in protecting the rights of inventors. Ultimately, the anti-patent movement largely failed (despite the contemporary absence of patent laws in several neighbouring European states at the time such as Switzerland) because, as Matthew Fisher has argued (in 'Classical Economics and the Philosophy of the Patent System' [2005] 1 *IPQ* 1) the abolitionists were unable to prove that there was no link between Britain's prosperity and the patent system.

For most of the UK's patent history, legislative reform has tended to be cautious and concerned with procedural improvements to the patent system. At the same time, an important shift occurred in the basis of patent protection from Crown prerogative to Government administration (see Sherman and Bently, *The Making of Modern Intellectual Property Law* (Cambridge University Press, 1999)). Minor changes occurred in 1835 but the real impetus for reform was the Great Exhibition of 1851, which was held in a purpose-built Crystal Palace in Hyde Park. Temporary legislation of that year led in turn to the passing of the Patent Law Amendment Act 1852. This established the UKIPO (under the then name of the Commissioners for Patents). The effect of the Act of 1852, as Dutton explains, was that inventors were to be protected from the date of application rather than the date of grant; there was to be a single patent for the United Kingdom; and an index of patents was to be set up and available for public consultation. The last-mentioned feature marks the start of patents providing an information system for the scientific and engineering communities. Nevertheless, the role of the then Patent Office (the precursor of the modern UKIPO) was limited to receiving and publishing patent applications. Whether or not a patent was granted was the decision of the Law Officers, not the Patent Office itself.

Further significant changes occurred in the Patents, Designs and Marks Act 1883 (which provided for the Patent Office to examine applications and for the Patent Office seal to replace the Great Seal on the formal document of grant); the Patents Act 1902 (which extended the examination system to a limited consideration of whether the invention was new in the light of prior art); and the Patents Act 1949 (which provided an exhaustive list of statutory grounds of invalidity, and also established the posts of specialist patent judges within the Chancery Division of the High Court of England and Wales). All of these innovations—examinations, use of prior art, grounds of invalidity—are important and remain central to UK patenting today. Yet, until the Patents Act 1977, no patent legislation contained any statement of substantive principle: there was no definition of what was a patentable invention, and no statutory explanation of what amounted to infringing conduct. Guidance for examiners and courts was instead found in the wording of s. 6 of the Statute of Monopolies 1623, which we mentioned earlier, and in the formula of the Royal Grant.

Under the Patents Act 1977 s. 1, the patent is said to cover an 'invention' that is new, involves an inventive step and is capable of industrial application. It also must not fall into any of the exclusions. Over this chapter and the chapters that follow we will consider these requirements in detail.

 Pause for reflection

Consider how patent law has evolved over time in the UK. Do you find it surprising that the legislative reforms up to the Patents Act 1977 contained no substantive principle? Which body or institution of the state would therefore have taken the lead, on a case-by-case basis, in defining the precise terms of UK patent law?

15.2 The justifications for patent protection

15.2.1 Academic literature

As noted earlier, the justifications of the patent system can be traced back to 19th-century debates about reform. Scholars such as Machlup and Penrose and Fisher identify four arguments deployed in support of maintaining some form of protection in response to those who wished to abolish the patent system entirely in the interests of free trade. These arguments are as follows: first, a moral justification based on the assertion that there is a natural property right in ideas. Appropriation of ideas is therefore tantamount to stealing. This 'natural law' justification owed much to the writings of John Locke's labour theory, even though it is highly debatable whether Locke contemplated intangible property rights. The second argument is that justice and fairness demand that there should be a reward for services useful to society. Because reward for the inventor cannot be guaranteed if left to market forces, the state should intervene by creating a temporary monopoly for the patentee. The 'reward by monopoly theory' was greatly influenced by the writings of Adam Smith, John Stuart Mill, and Jeremy Bentham. However, as Fisher points out, the theory is not without criticism. Applied logically, the inventor of a groundbreaking patent should receive greater protection than someone who thinks up a minor improvement to existing technology, yet the law draws no distinction between the two. Also, the theory takes no account of how the invention was created, whether by prolonged research, accident, or genius. It is perhaps based on the romantic notion of the inventor as individual hero, imagery which does not accord with the reality of modern research and development carried out by large multi-national corporations.

The third argument is that patents are necessary to secure economic development. In this view, the incentive of patent protection is necessary to ensure that inventions are made. The incentive theory assumes that industrial progress is desirable, that inventions are necessary for such progress, and that granting of patents is the most effective way of providing such incentives. All of these assumptions can, of course, be challenged. Nevertheless, the incentive argument is the one most frequently advanced. Finally, the fourth justification is the 'exchange for secrets' theory. The argument here is that if there were no patents, inventions would be kept secret in perpetuity—e.g. as 'trade secrets' held within companies—and therefore would never be 'open' to allow follow on research by other individuals or businesses. In this view, disclosure by the inventor, via patent publication, is the consideration for the grant of exclusivity. The patent can be viewed, therefore, as a contract between the inventor and the state. In due course, and in particular, after patent term expiry, the information in the patent becomes part of the store of human knowledge to be shared by all. Despite the admitted attractiveness of this argument, it is worth noting that the quality of patent specifications in the Victorian era was poor, and it is only in recent times that the patent information system has lived up to the expectations of the exchange for secrets theory.

 Pause for reflection

The assumption underlying all of these justifications is, of course, that patents are a good thing. This assumption can, and should, be questioned, as we will see later on. Nevertheless, even if they are a good thing, patents still create legal monopolies which prevent competitors from entering the market, something which could cause negative effects on innovation or the overall economy. There are well-documented examples of the holders of key inventions (for example, James Watt's steam engine) using their monopoly power to prevent subsequent developments and thereby hindering or delaying technological change. That being so, how should the law strike a balance between innovation and competition? Is there an economic argument which could be deployed in striking such a balance? Needless to say, there is extensive academic literature on this aspect of patent theory. Of this we mention but one article, simply because it draws together a number of other leading articles and because it has been referred to by the House of Lords in *H Lundbeck A/S v Generics (UK) Ltd* [2009] RPC 407.

Merges and Nelson (in 'On the Complex Economics of Patent Scope' [1990] 90 *Col LR* 839) point out that it is a mistake to assume that technical advance proceeds similarly in all industries, and that it is necessary to separate out discrete inventions (where the patent does not point the way to wide-ranging technical advances); 'cumulative' technologies (such as the aircraft or semi-conductor industries); chemical technologies (which have features of both of the previously mentioned categories); and 'science-based' technologies (for example, biotechnology) where technical advance is driven by developments in science outside the industry. They conclude that public policy ought to encourage inventive rivalry and not hinder it. Although rivalry can be inefficient, it will generate more rapid technical progress, whilst broad patents block progress. The answer lies, they argue, in the way in which courts interpret patent claims in the light of subsequent technological developments. Courts need to be sensitive to the nature of technical advances in particular industries, so that in a handful of cases it may be necessary to curtail broad patent claims, primarily those involving pioneering breakthroughs.

15.2.2 Case law

The justifications for patent protection are from time to time rehearsed in United Kingdom case law, sometimes as part of the conclusions to be reached on the facts of the case. For example, Lord Oliver in *Re Asahi KKK's Patent* [1991] RPC 485 at p. 523 and the Court of Appeal in *Dranez Anstalt v Hayek* [2003] FSR 561 at [25] both refer in general terms to the incentive theory as the reason why patents are granted. Lord Hoffmann in *Biogen Inc v Medeva plc* [1997] RPC 1 at p. 51 appears to pay greater regard to the 'reward by monopoly theory'. He stated that the court should recognize the patentee's technical contribution whilst taking care not to stifle research, an argument which clearly had a bearing on the decision of the House to declare the patent in question invalid. Equally, in *H Lundbeck A/S v Generics (UK) Ltd* at [48], Lord Mance made explicit use of the argument by Merges and Nelson that the scope of patent protection should reflect its inventive contribution (only here the conclusion was that the patent was valid, perhaps because, in contrast to *Biogen*, this was a 'discrete' invention). More recently, Lord Neuberger in *Eli Lilly and Company v Human Genome Sciences Inc* [2012] RPC 102 at [99] overturned the decision of the Court of Appeal that a patent for a protein discovered by 'bioinformatics' should not be granted because it would stultify research by others rather than encourage it. The purpose of the patent system, he said, was to provide a temporary monopoly as an incentive to innovation whilst at the same time facilitating the early dissemination of any such innovation.

 Pause for reflection

The dicta from these cases neatly demonstrate that there is no one settled justification for patents. This leads us back to the point we encountered earlier—the idea that patents are a good thing must not be taken as a token of faith, but rather must be questioned (M. Lemley, 'Faith-Based Intellectual Property' [2015] 62 *UCLA L Rev* 1328, and O. Liivak, 'A Crisis of Faith & the Scientific Future of Patent Theory' [2017] 90 *St. John's Law Review* 639). In fact, some scholars who have conducted empirical research into the effect of patents on the wider economy are highly sceptical of the overall value of the patent system as currently constituted (M. Lemley, 'The Surprising Resilience of the Patent System' [2016] 95 *Texas Law Review* 1). Some academics are worried that an overprotective system may grant numerous broad patents that eventually lead to nuisance patent litigation 'holding up' productive activities (C. Helmers, B. Love & L. McDonagh, 'Is there a Patent Troll Problem in the UK?' [2014] 24 *Fordham IPLJ* 509). Others are concerned that the patent system does not protect inventions strongly enough (K. Madigan and A. Mossoff, 'Turning Gold to Lead: How Patent Eligibility Doctrine Is Undermining U.S. Leadership in Innovation,' George Mason Law & Economics Research Paper No. 17–16). The debate will run.

Linking the theory to the practice, think back to our problem scenario. Do any of the justifications for patent law apply to what John has done? What was his primary motivation for creating the braces? Presuming that his invention meets the criteria of patentability, how could we justify awarding him a patent?

15.3 Understanding the Patents Act 1977

15.3.1 The impact of international conventions

The Patents Act 1977 dealt with the substantive law of UK patents for the first time. The Act's provisions are influenced primarily by the terms of the Patent Co-operation Treaty 1970 ('PCT') and the European Patent Convention 1973 ('EPC'). Also of interest is the Community Patent Convention 1975 and Regulation (EU) No. 1257/2012 of the European Parliament and of the Council of 17 December 2012 implementing enhanced cooperation in the area of the creation of unitary patent protection [2012] OJ L 361/1 (the 'Unitary Patent'), which will be discussed further on.

15.3.1.1 The PCT

The PCT, administered by WIPO, creates a procedural mechanism assisting the intending patentee who wishes to obtain protection in more than one state. At present, PCT membership includes over 125 countries. A single application to a local, national, or regional patent office (the 'receiving office') is subjected to an international search and preliminary examination by one of the International Searching Authorities ('ISAs'). At present these number 14: Australia, Austria, Brazil, Canada, China, Finland, Japan, Korea, the Nordic Patent Institute, the Russian Federation, Spain, Sweden, the USA, and the European Patent Office ('EPO'). The international search report lists references to published patent documents and journal articles which might affect patentability and is accompanied by a written opinion on potential novelty and inventive step. Following the search, WIPO publishes the application. The preliminary examination gives the applicant the opportunity to amend the application in light of the search report and to raise arguments. After this an international preliminary report on patentability is issued. Thereafter, it is up to the applicant, armed with the search report and the preliminary report on patentability, to activate the national phase, in which the patent is examined by designated national or regional patent offices. If successful, a PCT application therefore becomes a series of national patents. Apart from the ability to make multiple filings, the chief advantage of the PCT system is that the applicant can delay the decision whether to proceed with the application in particular countries until armed with the search report, and is not required to file a translation of the patent documents into the local language until 30 months after the priority date of the patent (translation costs are significant in obtaining patent protection). It also means that the designated national or regional patent offices will take as their starting point for substantive examination the report prepared by the International Searching Authority.

15.3.1.2 The EPC

It must be emphasized that the EPC is *not* an EU measure, but an instrument of the Council of Europe. Membership of the Convention is open to any country belonging to the Council of Europe (there are currently 38 members of the EPC), but patent applicants need not be citizens of these states—for instance, a Japanese inventor could apply for a patent under the EPC to obtain patent protection in Europe.

The EPC was revised in 2000, thought the changes did not enter into force until 2007. Changes included amending Art. 52 EPC (dealing with patentability, something we will look at in chapter 17) so that it complies with TRIPs; amending Art. 53 (dealing with exceptions to patentability) so as to comply both with TRIPs and the EU Biotech Directive (Directive 98/44/EC of the European Parliament and of the Council of 6 July 1998 on the legal protection of biotechnological inventions [1998] OJ L 213/13); and amending Art. 54 so as to clarify the practice of allowing 'Swiss form claims' for second medical uses. The other alteration was to Art. 69 and the Protocol thereto to clarify that the scope of patent claims includes equivalent elements. The UK passed the Patents Act 2004 to take account of the EPC 2000 changes by amending ss. 2 and 4 of the 1977 Act.

The key body of the EPC is the European Patent Office ('EPO'), based in Munich, which provides for search, examination, and grant of a European Patent ('EP'). Under the EPC a single application may be made to the EPO. Yet, if granted, the EP is actually a bundle of national patents that must be validated in whichever EPC states protection is sought e.g. UK, Germany, France, the Netherlands, etc. The consequence of this is that, once granted, European patents are treated in law as national patents, which means that infringement actions (claims that a patent has been infringed by e.g. a competitor) and revocation actions (claims that the patent is invalid and should be revoked) are heard by local (national) courts.

Because the EPC does not provide for any supra-national court to rule on European patents once granted (though its Boards of Appeals do oversee post-grant opposition decisions in respect of the validity of the grant of the patent), the various EPC states can, and sometimes do, apply different standards and modes of legal analysis in cases concerned with validity and infringement (L. McDonagh, *European Patent Litigation in the Shadow of the Unified Patent Court* (Edward Elgar, 2016)). In the UK, a classic example of this occurring can be observed from *Improver v Remington* [1990] FSR 181, where the English Patents Court held that the claimant's EPILADY device had not been infringed, whilst sister courts in the Netherlands and Germany came to the opposite conclusion.

15.3.1.3 The Unitary Patent and Unified Patent Court

The lack of uniformity of patent law within the EU, and the difficulties caused by the legal divergences noted above, have long been causes for concern for European jurists. Yet, it was not initially intended for the European patent system to be so fragmented. The EU Patent (as it was called under the Lisbon Treaty) was initially intended to have been implemented via the 1975 Community Patent Convention, which would have worked alongside the EPC as part of a twin-track approach to patents in Europe. However, no real progress was made in its ratification.

In 2000 the EU Commission decided to restart the process by using a different legal instrument, namely a Council Regulation under what is now Art. 352 of the Treaty on the Functioning of the European Union ('TFEU') (the implied powers provision). Crucially, negotiations stalled in 2004—one of the controversies being related to the translation of patent documents. As noted earlier, the current European patent is really a bundle of national patents that must be validated in individual EPC states, which often involves a local translation. The enactment of a unitary patent would largely remove the need to translate patents into local languages in e.g. Italy, Spain, Czechia, etc, and thus would potentially have a negative impact upon the business of local patent translators. This made the unitary patent a hard sell in such countries.

In 2009 another attempt to bring in a unitary system, this time under Art. 118 TFEU—which allows use of the ordinary legislative procedure to enables the creation of unitary European intellectual property rights for the better functioning of the internal market—also failed to progress. The 2009 proposals were declared incompatible with the EU Treaties by the CJEU in Opinion 1/09 of March 2011.

In 2012 the new dawn of European patenting finally seemed on the horizon. The Council of Ministers used 'enhanced cooperation' under Title III TFEU which allows a number of EU Member States to get together to pursue a legislative goal. Twenty-five of the then 27 Member States agreed to proceed with Unitary Patent Protection. The two Member States who decided not to join were Spain and Italy, who refused, once again, due to fears about the impact on their local patent translators. Italy has since opted to join the system, with Poland later deciding to drop out (Croatia joined the EU in 2013 and has not yet opted to join the system). The net result was the creation of two Regulations late in 2012 establishing unitary patent protection and dealing with the thorny issue of translation, together with the International Agreement on the Unified Patent Court in January 2013. Despite these legislative achievements, it remains to be seen whether in practice the Unitary Patent and Unified Patent Court will succeed when all previous attempts have failed. As of 2019, the new system has not yet come into being, with serious doubts about UK participation arising from the 'Brexit' process and whether the system will survive a forthcoming German constitutional challenge (L. McDonagh & M. Mimler, 'Intellectual Property Law and Brexit: A Retreat or a Reaffirmation of Jurisdiction?' in M. Dougan (ed.), *The UK After Brexit: Legal and Policy Challenges* (Intersentia, 2017), 159–179).

 Pause for reflection

Think again about the legal challenges of the current system, which has a single, unified point of application in the European Patent Office, but different, and legally divergent, territories of enforcement (e.g. Germany, UK, France, Italy, etc). What do you think the main benefit of a Unitary Patent and a Unified Patent Court would be for patent holders?

15.3.2 The nature of the 1977 Act

The 1977 Act is a hybrid creature. It introduced substantive provisions on patentability and exclusions therefrom (derived from the EPC) into domestic law, as well as a statutory definition of infringement in s. 60, and new grounds of revocation in s. 72. The Act also introduced, as a purely domestic measure, rules on the ownership of inventions made in the course of employment and a scheme of compensation for employee–inventors (something we will discuss in the next chapter).

15.3.3 The importance of s. 130(7)

The fundamental provision in interpreting the 1977 Act is s. 130(7). It declares that certain key sections (specifically those on patentability, infringement, and revocation) are deemed to have the same effect in the United Kingdom as the corresponding provisions of the conventions discussed earlier have in other states to which those conventions apply. In plain English, United Kingdom courts—which of course, include the separate court systems of England and Wales, Scotland, and Northern Ireland as well as the UK Supreme Court—are to have regard to how courts in other countries interpret the EPC.

The UK courts pay particular regard to the decisions of the EPO Boards of Appeal with regard to patentability (see *Merrell Dow v Norton* [1996] RPC 76 at p. 82 per Lord Hoffmann; and *Bristol-Myers Squibb v Baker Norton Pharmaceuticals Inc* [1999] RPC 253 at pp. 272–3 per Jacob J).

The UK courts also take notice of national court decisions in other EPC member states, especially Germany as it is the most popular venue for patent litigation in Europe (Katrin Cremers, et al, 'Patent Litigation in Europe' 2017 41(1) *European Journal of Law and Economics* 1–44). For instance, courts in the UK have paid attention to how German courts have dealt with the interpretation of patent claims: *Kirin-Amgen Inc v Hoechst Marion Roussel Ltd* [2005] 1 All ER 667 at [72–75] per Lord Hoffmann and *Conor Medsystems v Angiotech Pharmaceuticals Inc* [2008] RPC 716 at [3], again per Lord Hoffmann. German decisions have also been used to interpret s. 60(2) Patents Act, based on what is now Art. 8 of the draft EU Patent, in *Grimme Maschinenfabrik GmBH v Scott* [2010] FSR 193 at [122] per Jacob LJ.

Yet, despite some judicial attempts at keeping UK law in line with EPO decisions, there are several examples where the EPO Boards of Appeal and United Kingdom courts have reached differing conclusions on key questions, e.g. patentability of inventions. As patent law is 'fact-sensitive' such divergences may be attributable to differences in procedure and evidence when evaluating facts (*H Lundbeck A/S v Generics (UK) Ltd* at [35] *per* Lord Walker; *Eli Lilly and Company v Human Genome Sciences Inc* [2010] RPC 429 at [6], [41] *per* Jacob LJ). In this regard, it is notable that the UK system differs from other major patent jurisdictions e.g. Germany, France, Italy, Netherlands, in that the UK courts have a wide-ranging legal requirement that parties must disclose all relevant materials and that lengthy, oral expert testimony can take place at trial.

 Pause for reflection

How have UK courts adapted to the new substantive principles of the 1977 Act (as found in the EPC) in terms of trying to maintain a measure legal unity on patents within Europe? What difficulties could arise for patentees in light of the divergences of legal rulings in different EPC member states? Think back to the proposal for a Unitary Patent and Unified Patent Court: what is the purpose of these reforms?

If, in our problem scenario, John currently seeks protection in Germany, the UK, and France, as well as the US, what advice would you give him about where to file his patent application? Would your advice to John be different if a Unitary Patent were available?

15.4 **UKIPO procedure**

This brief explanation of how to obtain patent protection in the United Kingdom is intended as background information, an aid to understanding the context in which key issues of patent law arise. Procedure before the EPO is broadly similar, except that there is no prescribed time limit for completion of the application, and there is a right of post-grant opposition, whereby a party may 'oppose' the award of a patent to e.g. a competitor based on one or more invalidity grounds.

In essence, there are five key stages in the UK procedure to obtain a domestic patent: application, publication, search, examination, and grant.

15.4.1 **Filing the application**

The documents necessary to support a patent application are set out in the Patents Act s. 14(1) and s. 14(2), namely the request for a grant, the appropriate fee, a specification containing a description of the invention, a claim or claims, and any drawings referred to in the description or claims and an abstract. The last-mentioned document is a key component in the patent information system, and will be entered on the databases maintained by the major patent offices.

 Pause for reflection

Two points are worth noting regarding the patent application filing date:

1   Filing date is the Priority Date for the purposes of validity unless there is an earlier Convention Application. The Priority Date is of great importance for determining whether the patent is valid, as discussed below, and in more detail in chapter 17.

2   Filing Date determines the maximum duration (20 years) and the payment of annual renewal fees (fees to keep the patent in force) from Year 5 onwards.

The term 'specification' is the name for the patent document as a whole; nonetheless, it essentially comprises two parts, the description of the invention and the claims. These require greater elaboration.

15.4.1.1 The description of the invention

The description is deemed to be addressed to the 'skilled addressee' or notional skilled technician or person skilled in the art (the phrase 'skilled addressee' is used throughout this book). The skilled addressee is the hypothetical, objective person through whose eyes the key issues of validity and infringement—which we will consider in chapters 17 and 18—are judged in patent law. This person is the equivalent of the 'reasonable man' in the law of negligence, and their attributes are discussed in greater detail later in the chapter.

In the interpretation of patents, one key principle is sufficiency. Section 14(3) Patents Act 1977 requires the specification to disclose the invention 'in a manner which is clear enough and complete enough for the invention to be performed by a person skilled in the art'. Sufficiency relates to the clarity of the description of the invention, not the claims. It is crucial that a patent description is sufficient as a lack of sufficiency is a ground for revocation under s. 72(1)(c). Examples of lack of sufficiency include *Monsanto Company v Merck & Co Inc* [2000] RPC 709 (there was no guarantee that the skilled addressee, carrying out the instructions in the description, would produce a class of pharmaceutical compounds which had the desired characteristics, namely anti-inflammatory drugs without particular side effects); and *Kimberly-Clark Worldwide Inc v Procter & Gamble Ltd*, unreported, Pumfrey J, 21 July 2000 (a patent for a new type of disposable nappy was insufficient because the skilled addressee, performing the various tests for absorbency set out in the description, would have arrived at contradictory results). Similarly, in *Novartis AG v Johnson & Johnson Medical Ltd* [2010] EWCA Civ 1039, it was held that the skilled addressee would not be able to carry out the invention without prolonged research: the patent claimed extended wear contact lenses by reference both to certain characteristics such as ophthalmic compatibility, corneal health, and wearer comfort, and to physical parameters such as oxygen transmission and ion permeability. Achieving both sets of objectives was too much to expect. However, the House of Lords has stated that the requirement of sufficiency should not be overstated. In *Conor Medsystems v Angiotech Pharmaceuticals Inc* [2008] RPC 716 it said that disclosing that the invention works, and how to perform it, is different from explaining why it works. The latter is not required.

15.4.1.2 The claims

Under s. 14(5), the claim or claims are required to define the matter for which the applicant seeks protection, be clear and concise, be supported by the description, and relate to one invention or a group of inventions so linked as to form a single inventive concept.

As a result of s. 60 Patents Act 1977, claims may relate to a product (a thing) or a process (how to make something or use something or do something). A patent may consist solely of product claims, or solely of process claims, or it may have a mixture of claims: for example a pharmaceutical patent may have claims both for a new compound and how to make it. The infringement provisions in the Patents Act also provide for protection in respect of products which are directly derived from process patents (see s. 60(1) (c), based on Art. 64(2) of the EPC), which removes the need for a separate category of 'product-by-process' patents. As Lord Hoffmann explained (at [90]) in *Kirin-Amgen Inc v Hoechst Marion Roussel Ltd*, this type of claim is relatively rare because the EPO is reluctant to accept it (and indeed has criticized the United Kingdom for being the only Contracting State to permit such a claim). The only time when a 'product-by-process' claim will be allowed is where the patent concerns a new substance whose difference from a known substance cannot be described in chemical or physical terms, in which case the process by which it is obtained is an important element of the invention. As we shall see in chapters 17 and 18, the way in which the claims are described can be crucial when questions of validity and infringement come to court.

15.4.1.3 The significance of the priority date

Under s. 15, the filing date of the patent will be the date on which certain minimum formalities are satisfied. The filing date is to be treated as the 'priority date' unless the application is based on an earlier Convention application. Under s. 5, this will occur where the UK application is based on an earlier filing in respect of the same subject matter in another Contracting State of the Paris Convention. If this is the case, the priority date of the UK application is in effect backdated to the filing in the other Convention country.

Pause for reflection

The priority date of a patent is of crucial importance, as it is the date on which the validity of the patent is assessed. Matter made available to the public before the priority date is known as the 'prior art' and the claims of the patent are compared with the prior art in order to determine whether the invention as set out in the claims meets the requirements of novelty and inventive step. The actual filing date, however, remains relevant in calculating the duration of protection of the patent (Patents Act 1977 s. 25). If it transpires that the patent is not able to claim priority from an earlier Convention application (because, for example, it did not relate to the same subject matter) then the validity of the patent is assessed at the actual filing date, not the earlier priority date (*Biogen Inc v Medeva plc*).

15.4.2 Publication

Eighteen months after filing, the application is automatically published in the *Patents Journal*, early publication being a key feature of the EPC and hence the 1977 Act. If the patent contains information prejudicial to public safety, publication can be prohibited under ss. 22 and 23. A patentee may decide to withdraw the application before it is published (for example, because it has done further tests on the invention and has realised that the initial application was flawed), in which case the information contained therein will remain undisclosed to the public and can be included in a later application (as long as a third party has not lawfully made the same information public in the meantime).

The date of publication is significant in relation to infringement, as once the patent has been granted, the patentee can sue for any acts of infringement committed between the publication date and the date of grant, subject to certain conditions (Patents Act 1977 s. 69). In other words, infringing activities that take place before the patent is granted (but after publication) can lead to an infringement claim.

Unlike EPO procedure, there is no system of opposition at the UKIPO but third parties can make observations to the UKIPO under s. 21. At the EPO patent oppositions are a useful way for competitors to challenge patents that have been granted, and are in force, but which they consider to be overbroad, or invalid. It is comparatively inexpensive to oppose a patent in this way, especially when compared with full blown litigation, and it has the advantage that if a patent is successfully opposed at the EPO, it ceases to be a valid patent in all national jurisdictions of the EPC. However, the EPO oppositions process is a lengthy one, which can mean it takes several years before a final EPO decision is made whether to revoke the patent. In the meantime, UK litigation can take place to revoke a patent or to claim that a patent has been infringed (*Unilin Beheer BV v Berry Floor NV* [2007] EWCA Civ 364). This means that, as happened in *Virgin Atlantic Airways Ltd v Zodiac Seats UK Ltd* [2013] UKSC 46, a court in the UK make a finding of infringement in relation to a European patent, validated in the UK, that is subsequently revoked or amended by the EPO. Where such subsequent EPO revocation/amendment occurs, this can have an impact on whether damages must be paid for the prior UK infringement finding. This type of divergence between national courts and the EPO is another reason the Unified Patent Court was brought forward by EU member states—though it remains to be seen whether it will actually get up and running.

Once a patent has been published, the remaining steps in the procedure must be initiated by the applicant. If they are not, the application is deemed to have been withdrawn. Whilst there is nothing to stop an applicant abandoning its application after publication, the point to remember is that the information contained in the application will have been made public and so cannot form the basis of a fresh application.

15.4.3 Search and preliminary examination

Under s. 17(4), the patent examiner is required to make such investigation as is reasonably practicable and necessary to identify the documents needed for substantive examination to determine whether the invention is new and contains an inventive step. Under s. 15A (inserted into the 1977 Act by the Regulatory Reform (Patents) Order 2004), the examiner shall determine whether the application complies with the formal requirements of the Act.

15.4.4 Substantive examination

Once the search and preliminary examination have been completed, under s. 18 the patent application is examined in detail as to its compliance with the substantive requirements of patentability, including novelty and inventive step, in the light of the search report produced by UKIPO under s. 17. We will discuss these patentability requirements in greater detail in chapter 17. Objections to the application are notified to the patentee by letter, and if these objections cannot be overcome (usually by amendment) then the applicant is entitled to a UKIPO hearing, from which there is a right of appeal to the Patents Court.

15.4.5 Grant

If the application is successful, then upon payment of the correct fee the patent will be granted (s. 18(4)). The grant must be made within a maximum period of four-and-a-half years (54 months) from the priority date. It will last for a maximum of 20 years, calculated from the filing date of the application (s. 25), but from the fifth year onwards, its continued existence is subject to the prompt payment of annual renewal fees, which increase with each year of the life of the patent. The fact of patent grant will be published in the *Patents Journal* (s. 24).

15.4.6 Amendment

A patent applicant can always seek to amend the patent application during the course of its progress through the UKIPO procedure (see ss. 17, 18, and 19), for instance by narrowing the scope of the claims. Similarly, a patent can be amended once it has been granted (see ss. 27, 73, and 75). However, there are restrictions on amendment in s. 76. In essence, the patentee cannot extend the description so as to disclose additional matter—or 'added matter'—and cannot expand the scope of protection in the claims. Any amendment which so broadens the patent can be cited as a ground of revocation under s. 72(1)(d), and (e). Whether an amendment has such a broadening effect is determined through the eyes of the skilled addressee (see *Re Flexible Directional Indicators Application* [1994] RPC 207 as regards pre-grant amendments, and *Bonzel v Intervention (No 3)* [1991] RPC 553 as regards post-grant amendments).

15.4.7 Summary

It is important to note the interaction between the key dates in the timeline of a patent as this is something that will be of importance to prospective patentees such as John in our example above.

 Pause for reflection

Here are the key dates in the patent application timeline:

1. Filing date: duration of term of protection (20 years) calculated from this date; validity of patent to be determined in the light of the prior art at this date (unless Convention priority claimed).
2. Priority date: UK application can be backdated (for purposes of validity only) to first filing date in respect of the same subject matter in another Contracting State of the Paris Convention or WTO (but duration still calculated from actual filing date).
3. Date of publication in the Patents Journal: application may be withdrawn before this date without contents becoming part of the state of the art. If an infringement action is brought (once the patent has been granted), damages may be backdated to this date, in respect of infringing conduct committed between the date of publication and the date of grant, subject to the conditions in s. 69 Patents Act. Publication is followed by the preliminary and substantive examination of the application, but only at the request of the applicant.
4. Date of grant: infringement action may only be brought after this date. Annual renewal fees become payable from the fifth anniversary onwards.

Now that you understand the process for patent applications, how would you advise John regarding the relevance of patent law to what he has created? What first steps could you advise him to take?

15.5 Key issues in patent cases

As we noted at the very beginning of this chapter, many students find the law of patents challenging. As a way of explaining the key patent issues in a practical context, here we look at a well-known and significant case—*Dyson v Hoover* [2001] RPC 473. Having identified the steps taken by the court in resolving the dispute, we then examine some of the factors which affected the outcome. The issues covered in this case do not necessarily occur in every single patent case, but they are sufficiently common to be useful to be used as an aid to our comprehension.

> ### Dyson Appliances Ltd v Hoover Ltd [2001] RPC 473
>
> In this judgment the relevant issues are dealt with in a logical manner, as follows:
>
> - first, the identification of the background of the invention (here it was that the vacuum cleaner industry assumed that vacuum cleaner bags had to be used to collect dirt but that these possessed certain disadvantages, such as loss of efficiency when the bag was full);
> - second, the identification of the inventive concept (or 'epitome') of the invention (here it was the patentee's insight that vacuum cleaners could use a dual cyclone as a means of collecting large and small particles of dirt without the necessity of using a bag);
> - third, the identification of the attributes of the skilled addressee of the patent, namely their qualifications and experience (here it was a graduate engineer with practical experience in the manufacture of vacuum cleaners);
> - fourth, the identification of the common general knowledge which the skilled addressee possessed;
> - fifth, the allocation of meaning to the claims in the light of the description and drawings. The court considered whether the patentee had used everyday English, or whether the patentee provided its own definitions of key words in the specification, or whether the meaning of key words in the specification had to be ascertained from specialist dictionaries. It also analysed each of the claims and identified the integers (or elements) of each one;
> - sixth, the determination of infringement (the court made a comparison of each of the claims with the defendant's product); and
> - seventh, the determination of the validity of the patent (the court made a comparison of each of the claims with the prior art).

We will look at several of these points in much greater detail in chapters 17 and 18. For present purposes, it is merely necessary to outline the basis of each of these issues in patent law.

15.5.1 The inventive concept

One of the tasks a court dealing with a patent infringement action has to undertake is to decide what the patent is all about. This is usually referred to as 'identifying the inventive concept'. Some cases call it the 'epitome' of the invention (*Dyson Appliances Ltd v Hoover Ltd*), others describe the process as identifying the 'core' or 'kernel' or 'essence' of the invention (*H Lundbeck A/S v Generics (UK) Ltd per* Lord Walker at [30]). The inventive concept is not necessarily the same as the invention's technical contribution to the art, which is more concerned with the evaluation of its inventive concept. Thus, in *Biogen Inc v Medeva plc*, the inventive concept was 'the idea of expressing unsequenced eukaryotic DNA in a prokaryotic [non-mammalian] host', described by Lord Hoffmann as a 'brilliant Napoleonic victory' in sequencing the genome for Hepatitis B. However, in terms of its technical contribution to the art it was not of lasting strategic value because within a couple of months the genome had been sequenced by others (*H Lundbeck A/S v Generics (UK) Ltd per* Lord Walker at [32–33], and *per* Lord Neuberger at [101]).

Identifying the inventive concept is done by construing the claims in the light of the description of the invention. When doing so the court should expressly or by implication take into account the problem which the patentee was trying to solve (*Biogen Inc v Medeva plc* at p. 45 *per* Lord Hoffmann). However, using the problem and solution test to identify the inventive concept is not always a straightforward matter.

In *Wheatley (Davina) v Drillsafe Ltd* [2001] RPC 133 there was a division of opinion as to the inventive concept of the patent in suit. The majority (Sedley and Mance LJJ) took a narrow view of the patent's inventive concept, regarding it as the use of a 'centre-less' drill cutter for drilling holes in underground petrol storage tanks without the need for the use of a pilot drill. The minority (Aldous LJ) took a broader view of the inventive concept. To him, what mattered was that the defendant's probe did not enter the tank (thereby avoiding the risk of sparks) which was the problem which the patent had sought to solve. As a consequence, he held that the defendant's device did infringe the patent, whilst the majority had concluded that there was no infringement. Aldous LJ therefore followed the advice of Lord Hoffmann in *Biogen v Medeva* in identifying the problem to be solved as part of the process of ascertaining the inventive concept. The case reveals that it is possible for the underlying inventive concept to be drawn broadly or narrowly by the court.

Another area of uncertainty is in relation to infringement: does the defendant have to take the inventive concept in order to be liable? In *Schütz (UK) Ltd v Werit UK Ltd* [2013] FSR 395, Lord Neuberger disagreed with both Floyd J (who thought that the answer was 'yes') and the Court of Appeal (who thought that the answer was 'no'). Lord Neuberger thought that the matter was more nuanced: whether the defendant had made an infringing product depended on the nature of the invention, the wording of the claims, and what the defendant had actually done. Here, what the defendant had done had been to supply a replacement component which was not the heart of the invention.

15.5.2 The skilled addressee and their common general knowledge

A patent specification is a unilateral statement by the patentee. The specification both describes the invention and demarcates the scope of the monopoly which the patentee wishes to claim as theirs. However, the patent specification does not exist in a vacuum: it is deemed to be addressed to a skilled person.

15.5.2.1 The role of the skilled addressee in patent law

It is important to understand that the skilled addressee is a judicial construct, a legal fiction; she is not a real person, but a hypothetical creature through whose eyes various issues in patent law are determined. The reason for having such a person is to impart objectivity (*Lilly Icos Ltd v Pfizer Ltd* [2001] FSR 201 at [62]). The skilled addressee, armed with common general knowledge, is used in patent law to determine the following issues objectively:

- to construe the claims of the patent in the light of the description of the invention and any drawings contained in the patent specification;

- to determine whether an invention is new under s. 2 Patents Act, i.e. whether the prior art contains enough information by way of enabling disclosure that the skilled addressee could have put the invention into effect before the priority date;

- to determine whether an invention possesses inventive step under s. 3, i.e. it was not obvious to the skilled addressee;

- to determine whether an invention is capable of industrial application under s. 4, or whether the information which it contains is a purely theoretical possibility of exploitation;

- to determine whether the description of the invention is sufficient for the purposes of s. 14(3);

- to determine whether an invention has been the subject of an impermissible amendment contrary to s. 76, so that it is liable to revocation under either s. 72(1)(d) or (e) for having extended the description or claims; and

- to determine whether an invention has been infringed by a product or process which is not literally within the wording of the claims.

It can thus be seen that the skilled addressee plays a crucial role with regard to the validity and infringement of patents, and that the identification of such a person is a task which has to be undertaken by any court dealing with patent litigation. Just like the task of deciding the inventive concept, the choice of the appropriate skilled addressee is a matter susceptible to the vagaries of judicial opinion. In *Dyson v Hoover*, the validity of the patent (which was upheld) was arguably affected by the court's decision that the skilled addressee did not have any practical experience in the use of cyclone technology.

It has been suggested by the Court of Appeal in *Schlumberger Holdings Ltd v Electromagnetic Geoservices AS* [2010] RPC 851 that in rare cases the skilled addressee might not be the same for all purposes: where the invention involves groundbreaking technology (so that the skilled addressee's knowledge is enhanced by reading the patent) a higher standard might be required for sufficiency than for obviousness. This is because the former is assessed post grant, whilst the latter is assessed at the priority date.

15.5.2.2 Characteristics of the skilled addressee

The qualifications and level of experience of the skilled addressee are for the court to determine in each case. These will vary depending on the field of technology with which the patent is concerned and how advanced the invention is. In the case of mechanical patents the skilled addressee is likely to be a graduate engineer in the relevant discipline with practical experience in the field in question (*Dyson Appliances Ltd v Hoover Ltd*). Where the patent involves genetic engineering, as in *Re Genentech's (Human Growth Hormone) Patent* [1989] RPC 613, the skilled addressee will be a team of postdoctoral researchers experienced in recombinant DNA. Where the patent involves hand-held devices for accessing the internet, the skilled addressee will have a Master's degree in computer science: *Research in Motion UK Ltd v Inpro Licensing Sarl* [2006] RPC 517.

In the key case of *Catnic Components v Hill & Smith* [1982] RPC 185, Lord Diplock decided that a patent for a galvanized steel lintel used in cavity-walled buildings was addressed not to a graduate civil engineer, but to a building-site foreman, thereby providing a somewhat surprising addition to the reading matter of those who work in the construction industry. These examples should alert the reader to the fact that the choice of the skilled addressee is capable of being manipulated by the court to produce a desired outcome in a particular case, in the same way that the inventive concept can be viewed in different ways by the court.

Over the last century, the characteristics and abilities of the skilled addressee have been explained in some detail. One description is that in *Lilly Icos Ltd v Pfizer Ltd* [2001] FSR 201 at [62]:

> This is not a real person. He is a legal creation. He is supposed to offer an objective test of whether a particular development can be protected by a patent. He is deemed to have looked at and read publicly available documents and to know of public uses in the prior art. He understands all languages and dialects. He never misses the obvious nor stumbles on the inventive. He has no private idiosyncratic preferences or dislikes. He never thinks laterally. He differs from all real people in one or more of these characteristics.

It has also been suggested that the skilled addressee is 'half way between a mechanical idiot and a mechanical genius' (*Gillette Safety Razor v Anglo-American Trading* (1913) 30 RPC 465 at p. 481 *per* Lord Moulton) or perhaps 'a ventriloquist's dummy' (*Dyson Appliances Ltd v Hoover Ltd* [2002] RPC 465 *per* Sedley LJ at [88]). Such a person does not possess a spark of inventiveness (*per* Lord Reid in *Technograph v Mills & Rockley* [1972] RPC 346 at p. 355) but is sufficiently interested in his or her work to want to improve on the prior art (*per* Oliver LJ in *Windsurfing International v Tabur Marine* [1985] RPC 59 at pp. 69–71). The skilled addressee is expected to try experiments which appear to be technically rather than commercially worthwhile (*Hallen v Brabantia* [1991] RPC 195). Where the technical field is very advanced (such as biotechnology), the addressee is to be credited with sufficient time and the best available equipment to carry out the work (*Genentech Inc's Patent* [1989] RPC 147).

Other cases have described the skilled addressee as 'determined but prosaic' (*Koninklijke Philips Electronics NV v Princo Digital Disc GmbH* [2003] EWHC 1598 at [14]); and a 'nerd', 'if real, would be very boring', but 'not a complete android' (*per* Jacob LJ in *Rockwater Ltd v Technip France SA (formerly Coflexip SA)* [2004] RPC 919, CA at [6–15]). The skilled addressee will possess the prejudices of others working in that field of technology. In *Dyson Appliances Ltd v Hoover Ltd*, the vacuum cleaner industry accepted without question that vacuum cleaners without dust-collecting bags would not work. The court held that the skilled addressee would have such a 'mind set' when reading the claimant's patent.

Last, the skilled reader of the patent may be a team (*Valensi v British Radio Corporation* [1972] RPC 373 at p. 450; *Re Genentech's (Human Growth Hormone) Patent* [1989] RPC 613; *Schlumberger Holdings Ltd v Electromagnetic Geoservices AS*). Even if not in a team, the skilled addressee may well consult another for technical help in understanding the patent. As an example, see *Vericore Ltd v Vetrepharm Ltd*, [2003] EWHC 111 where the patent involved the use of chemicals to treat sea-lice in fish. It was said that the skilled addressee would be either a toxicologist or a fish health expert, and the one would consult the other.

Frequently the courts warn against assuming too high a level of qualifications and ability on the part of the skilled addressee. The skilled addressee is not to be equated with expert witnesses called by the claimant and defendant to assist the court. The former is meant to be the *average* technician in the area to which the patent relates. These latter individuals are usually specialists in their field.

15.5.2.3 Common general knowledge

The skilled addressee is deemed to come equipped with certain background information. This is called 'common general knowledge'. It may be observed that the phrase contains the words 'common' and 'general', words which indicate that such information is known by *all* those working in the particular sector to which the patent relates and is universal not specialist.

Again, there are numerous judicial descriptions of what the phrase 'common general knowledge' means. The leading explanation is by Sachs LJ in *General Tire v Firestone* [1972] RPC 457 at pp. 497, 500, where he described it as 'standard texts or material accepted without question by those in that line of work'. Common general knowledge, however, does not include prior patents.

Other descriptions of common general knowledge include 'a tool-box of knowledge' (*per* Aldous J in *Southco Inc v Dzus Fastener Europe Ltd* [1990] RPC 587 at p. 618); 'the technical background of the notional man skilled in the art' (*Raychem Corporation's Patent* [1998] RPC 31, [1999] RPC 497, CA); 'a good basis for further action' (*Wheatley (Davina) v Drillsafe Ltd* [2001] RPC 133, *per* Aldous LJ); and 'good background technical knowledge' (*Rockwater Ltd v Technip France SA (formerly Coflexip SA)* [2004] RPC 919 *per* Jacob LJ at [16–21]). Where the patent involves sophisticated technology, common general knowledge may be worldwide (*Re Genentech's (Human Growth Hormone) Patent* [1989] RPC 613).

Frequently the courts warn against assuming too high a level of common general knowledge. The fact that something is known to some or indeed recorded doesn't make it common general knowledge and the court should be sensitive to the fact that not all skilled readers will have equal access to information, particularly if the invention is not very complicated (*SEB SA v De'Longhi SpA* [2003] EWCA Civ 952). In *Beloit Technologies v Valmet Paper Machinery* [1997] RPC 489 at pp. 494–5 the Court of Appeal said this:

> It has never been easy to differentiate between common general knowledge and that which is known by some. It has become particularly difficult with the modern ability to circulate and retrieve information. Employees of some companies, with the use of libraries and patent departments, will become aware of information soon after it is published in a whole variety of documents; whereas others, without such advantages, may never do so until that information is accepted generally and put into practice. The notional skilled addressee is the ordinary man who may not have the advantages that some employees of large companies may have.

In other words, the knowledge which the skilled reader possesses should be both common and general to the *average* person in that field of technology.

 Pause for reflection

Think again about the facts of John's scenario. What is the inventive concept? Who do you think would be the skilled addressee in the case of his skateboard braces invention? What characteristics would the court attribute to this person?

15.5.3 **The importance of patent claims**

The claims of a patent fulfil a vital role. They are the patentee's attempt to demarcate the scope of the monopoly. By analogy with land law, a map will show the boundaries of an owner's fee simple estate. In the case of a patent, there is no diagrammatic method of showing the patentee's territory. Instead, this must be done in words.

Claims will usually be drafted by a patent attorney (usually with a scientific or engineering background) on behalf of the patentee (though the patentee may choose to do this themselves, or else the patentee will employ its own in-house patent specialists to do the work for them). The claims will be drafted as a result of the client's instructions to the patent attorney (which presents opportunities for poor communication) and will be written with the objective of obtaining a successful grant from the UKIPO/EPO. One thing which may surprise is that it is entirely down to the skill of the patent attorney how the claims can be drafted to avoid both the prior art *and* the exceptions and exclusions to patentability, in other words, *form* can prevail over *substance*.

The other intriguing aspect of patent claims is that although they may be scrutinized by the UKIPO/EPO (with possible amendment by the patentee in order to meet any objections) when it comes to the scope of the monopoly protection their meaning will be decided in litigation (to determine whether the claims are valid and/or have been infringed).

Thus, patent claims are important in two particular respects. They are compared with the prior art in order to determine whether the patent is valid, and they are compared with the alleged infringement in order to determine whether the defendant's product or process falls within the territory marked out by the patentee's words.

All this flows from two key statutory provisions, namely ss. 125 and 130(1) of the Patents Act 1977. The former incorporates Art. 69 of the EPC together with the Protocol thereto into UK patent law; the latter contains the definition of 'patented invention', namely an invention for which a patent is granted. When combined, the two provisions link the words 'patent', 'invention', and 'patented invention' together to aid in the determination of the scope of the legal protection. Under s. 125 each claim of the patent can be viewed a separate invention for the purposes of the Act.

The claims are to be read purposively through the eyes of the skilled reader. Traditionally, in the UK courts should ask but one question: 'What would a person skilled in the art have understood the patentee to have used the language of the claim to mean?' (*Kirin-Amgen Inc v Hoechst Marion Roussel Ltd* at [34] *per* Lord Hoffmann). However, a recent UK Supreme court case—*Actavis UK Ltd v Eli Lilly & Co* [2017] UKSC 48—suggests that this focuses too much on legal certainty, and not enough on protecting the invention, allowing competitors to 'take the essence of the invention but avoid infringement by reason of a minor variation'. The UK Supreme Court has advocated two questions rather than the single Kirin-Amgen one: first, applying the rules of normal interpretation, does the variant infringe? Second, even if the answer to the first question is no, *should* the variant be held to be infringing because its variance is *immaterial*? We will discuss this change in the law—including the meaning of 'immaterial'—in greater detail in chapter 18.

15.6 **Conclusion**

This chapter has explained the history of UK patents and of patent law to protect inventiveness, the impact on domestic law of the UK's obligations under the EPC and the Patent Cooperation Treaty (PCT), and the key issues in the patent application process.

Looking again at the facts of the problem at the beginning of this chapter it is worth asking: why should inventions like John's be protected? What is the point of giving him a monopoly for something he created initially for purely personal use? Thinking back to the key justificatory theories underpinning patent law, the answer might be a combination of three of the four justifications we examined. First, morally it seems fair to award John protection for what he has done; second, John has created something useful to society at large, and as such, deserves to receive a monopoly on his invention as a form of economic reward; and third, by encouraging him to patent the invention, the invention will be published, and thus will become part of public knowledge (and eventually, upon expiry of patent term, fall into the public domain). The only justification we cannot avail of is the incentive argument—nobody could argue that John's primary motivation was economic development. But the other three justifications appear to favour John.

The question remains, however, what would the process be for John to obtain patent protection? He would need to identify the inventive concept. He would need to engage a patent attorney to write a patent specification, including a description and detailed claims. If he seeks protection in the UK, France, and Germany, he can apply to the EPO and, post-grant, validate the patent in those national jurisdictions. Since he also seeks protection in the US one option would be to file for a patent via the PCT, which would allow simultaneous applications to the EPO and the US Patents & Trademarks Office. The process would be: application, publication, search, examination, and grant. In terms of whether his invention is patentable or not, key would be the skilled addressee's view of his invention in the context of the prior art. Is John really the first person to have invented skateboard braces for using a board on grass? Furthermore, would the skilled addressee think it merely an obvious thing to do? Does the fact that he tests the invention in public have a potential impact on novelty? These are issues we will learn about in much more detail in chapter 17.

End-of-chapter questions

After reading the chapter carefully, try answering the following questions. For answer guidance visit the online resources at **www.oup.com/uk/karapapa-mcdonagh/**

1. Do the various justifications for the patent system seem convincing? How can patent law be reconciled with competition law?

2. Who is the 'person skilled in the art' and why is this person so important to patent law? What defining characteristics does that person have?

Further reading

Cremers, K., M. Ernicke, F. Gaessler, D. Harhoff, C. Helmers, L. McDonagh, P. Schliessler, & N. van Zeebroeck, 'Patent Litigation in Europe' [2017] 41(1) *European Journal of Law and Economics* 1–44

Examines and compares patent litigation in Germany, the UK, France, and the Netherlands using empirical data gathered from courts.

Dutton, H.I. *The Patent System and Inventive Activity during the Industrial Revolution 1750–1852* (Manchester University Press, 1984)

Explores the legal and economic issues leading to the reform of the United Kingdom patent system during the nineteenth century.

Fisher, M. 'Classical Economics and the Philosophy of the Patent System' [2005] 1 *IPQ* 1

Analyses the classical economic theories which are advanced to justify the law of patents and how these were utilized by the nineteenth-century reformers.

Fisher, M. 'The Tyranny of Words' [2007] 36(3) *Common Law World Review* 262

Discusses the nature and importance of patent claims.

Fisher, M. 'The Case That Launched a Thousand Writs, or All That is Dross? Re-conceiving *Darcy v Allen: The Case of Monopolies*' [2010] 4 *IPQ* 356

Argues that our understanding of Darcy v Allen is coloured by Coke CJ's account which was written long after the event and is incorrect.

Helmers, C., Love, B. McDonagh, L. 'Is there a Patent Troll Problem in the UK?' [2014] 24 *Fordham IPLJ* 509)

Examines the issue of 'patent trolls' by reference to empirical case data collected on cases at the Patents Court in London.

Hulme, W. 'The History of the Patent System under the Prerogative and at Common Law' (1896) 12 *LQR* 141

An examination of the practice of granting patents before, during, and after the Tudor monarchs.

Lemley, M. 'Faith-Based Intellectual Property' [2015] 62 *UCLA L Rev* 1328

Takes a critical view of IP discourse, examining whether it has become commonplace to make moral claims for greater IP protection, rather than claims based on empirical evidence.

Lemley, M. 'The Myth of the Sole Inventor' (2011–2012) 110 *Mich LR* 709

Argues that invention is a social not an individual phenomenon and that none of the current theoretical justifications for patent law, including the exchange for secrets theory, adequately explains it.

Lemley, M. 'The Surprising Resilience of the Patent System' [2016] 95 *Texas Law Review* 1

Argues that the patent system has been resilient over the past few decades despite regularly occurring 'crises' that the system is overprotecting or underprotecting patents.

Liivak, O. 'A Crisis of Faith & the Scientific Future of Patent Theory' [2016] 90 *St. John's Law Review* 639

Argues that the 'reward' justification for patent law is a problematic claim because it lacks empirical support.

Machlup, F. and Penrose, E. 'The Patent Controversy in the Nineteenth Century' (1950) 10 *J of Economic History* 1

Explores the debates which took place as a result of the anti-patent movement.

MacLeod, C. and Nuvolari, A. 'Patents and Industrialisation: An Historical Overview of the British Case, 1624–1907', A Report to the Strategic Advisory Board for Intellectual Property Policy 2010 (available from the UKIPO website)

Considers whether the patent system had any effect on industrial development in Britain and the lessons from history for today's 'strong' intellectual property regimes.

McDonagh, L., *European Patent Litigation in the Shadow of the Unified Patent Court* (2016) Edward Elgar

Examines patent litigation in four European jurisdictions in light of the prospective Unified Patent Court and Unitary Patent reforms.

McDonagh, L. & Mimler, M. 'Intellectual Property Law and Brexit: A Retreat or a Reaffirmation of Jurisdiction?' in M. Dougan (ed.), *The UK After Brexit: Legal and Policy Challenges* (Intersentia, 2017), 159–179

Considers whether the patent system will be affected by the UK's exit from the EU.

Madigan, K. & Mossoff, A. 'Turning Gold to Lead: How Patent Eligibility Doctrine Is Undermining U.S. Leadership in Innovation,' [2017] 24 George Mason Law Review 939

Claims that recent US Supreme Court decisions have undermined the eligibility doctrine, leading to the rejection of patent applications that have nonetheless been accepted in other jurisdictions (EPO, China, etc).

Merges, R. and Nelson, R. 'On the Complex Economics of Patent Scope' (1990) 90 *Col L R* 839

Analyses how patent claims can be interpreted both at prosecution and infringement stages and then considers the economics of the patent system.

Seaborne Davis, D. 'Further Light on the Case of Monopolies' (1932) 48 *LQR* 394

A discussion of Darcy v Allin and the Elizabethan practice of granting monopolies to favourite courtiers.

Sherman, B. and Bently, L. *The Making of Modern Intellectual Property Law* Cambridge University Press, 1999)

Explores the historical and economic factors which have influenced present-day intellectual property law.

Thambisetty, S., 'Patents as Credence Goods,' (2007) 27(4) *Oxford Journal of Legal Studies* 707

Examines the obscure nature of patents and the lawyer's role from a critical perspective.

Ownership of patents   16

Problem question

Read this problem question carefully and keep it in mind while you are working through the chapter that follows. At the end of this chapter, you will be able to apply what you have learnt to the problem question and advise the relevant parties.

Felicity Taylor is a biomedical scientist working as researcher for a medium-sized British pharmaceutical company in Cambridge. In her spare time, she enjoys performing her own experiments on DNA sequencing at the work lab, after hours. One evening at 5pm, after her shift ends, she puts away her current work project and takes out her 'pet project'—her investigation into a new method of using crystallized acid to dissolve cancerous cells in dead tissue. To aid her work she 'borrows' old samples of tissue from the lab that would otherwise be thrown away, and uses her employer's lab equipment. She works on her project at the work lab until 9pm, when she discovers a new method of targeting the cancerous cells, which leaving the healthy cells unharmed. She believes that this method would work equally well on live cells. She believes that this piece of research—her pet project—is potentially patentable and could prove to be highly lucrative once commercialized. She wants to know whether she should file for a patent for the invention as its sole owner, or whether her employer has any claims over her invention. Her contract states that she is expected to contribute to patentable research, and that all inventions belong to her employer.

Advise Felicity.

16.1 Introduction

16.1.1 Who is an inventor?

Despite the popular myth of the heroic amateur inventor, most patentable inventions are not devised by sole inventors working at home. Teams of researchers often work together towards a common goal. This means that there are sometimes disputes about who actually invented the product or process covered by a patent. Resolving these disputes is of significance because under patent law the owner possesses the right to grant licences to make use of the patented invention in exchange for a fee or royalties, and the right to sue for infringement.

In terms of law, as we shall see over the course of this chapter, disputes over patent entitlement are more like property disputes than the complex questions of patent validity and infringement we will encounter in the next chapter. Nonetheless, these are important, not least because today many inventions are devised by employees of e.g. multinational companies or universities (J. Pila, 'Professional and Academic Employee Inventions: Looking Beyond the UK Paradigm' in M. Pittard, A. Monitti, and J. Duns (eds.) *Business Innovation: A Legal Balancing Act—Perspectives from Intellectual Property, Labour and Employment, Competition and Corporate Laws* (Edward Elgar, 2013)). One of the important legal questions we will examine is as follows: who is entitled to patent employee inventions, the employee or the employer?

Before deciding who is entitled to the ownership of an invention it is first necessary to examine what is meant in law by the word 'inventor'. This is dealt with in s. 7 of the Patents Act 1977: subsection (1) declares that any person may apply for a patent, but this is qualified by subsection (2) which provides that the patent may only be granted to the inventor or their successor. The word 'inventor' is defined in s. 7(3) as the 'actual deviser' of the invention. The phrase may be compared with that found in earlier legislation, namely 'the first and true inventor'. Cases decided under the old law had concluded that the inventor was the person who was the 'moving spirit' or inventive genius, rather than someone who put the invention into practical effect. Thus, in *Re Smith's Patent* (1905) 22 RPC 57, an application to revoke the patent succeeded, the evidence being that the patentee had not been the inventor but one merely employed to prepare engineering drawings on behalf of the real creator. Similarly, in *Re Homan's Patent* (1889) 6 RPC 104, the challenge by an opponent who alleged that he was the rightful inventor because he had made samples for the patentee was rejected by the court, on the basis that the opponent had not appreciated what it was that the patentee was trying to achieve until it was explained to him.

Cases decided under the Patents Act 1977 have adopted the same thinking as before. The inventor is the *natural* person who thinks up the inventive concept underlying the patent: *Staeng Ltd's Application* [1996] RPC 183, confirmed in *Henry Brothers (Magherafelt) Ltd v Ministry of Defence* [1999] RPC 442.

 Pause for reflection

What happens if there is a dispute between a person who had the original intention to invent and the person who provided the key inventive concept? What happens if both are employees? Establishing ownership can be complex. In the case of *IDA Ltd v Southampton University* [2006]

→

> → RPC 567 a professor from the university published an article in *The Times* setting out his ideas about how to build a better cockroach trap. He was then contacted by one of the claimant's staff who had suggested how to improve the invention via magnetic powder. It was held that the claimant's employee had provided the inventive concept—the 'bright idea' or leap in thinking from what had come before—and thus, the claimant company who was entitled to the patent.
>
> Keep in mind our problem question—think about what the legal situation would be in a case where the IDA employee used his own home phone line to phone up the professor at home. Would their employers still have a claim to the invention? We will consider this later on in the chapter.

Where there is a dispute as to entitlement, the UK Intellectual Property Office ('UKIPO') has jurisdiction to resolve the matter (see ss. 8, 9, 12, and 37 Patents Act 1977). If the matter is a complex one, or raises issues that ought to be considered by a full court hearing, the UKIPO can transfer the dispute to the Patents Court (*Luxim Corporation v Ceravision Ltd* [2007] EWHC 1624). Appeals from a decision of the UKIPO can be heard at the Patents Court, the Court of Appeal, and, potentially, the UK Supreme Court.

At one time, the Court of Appeal took the view that the key word in these provisions was the word 'entitlement', as the sections concern a dispute over property (the patent). Accordingly, someone who sought to challenge entitlement to a patent had to show not only that they had contributed to the inventive concept, but also that that there had been either a breach of confidence or a breach of contract: *Markem v Zipher* [2005] RPC 761 and *IDA Ltd v Southampton University* [2006] RPC 567. Crucially, however, the House of Lords has since overruled both *Markem* and *IDA*. In *Yeda Research & Development Co Ltd v Rhone-Poulenc Rorer* [2008] RPC 1 the House of Lords ruled that the only relevant question is, 'Who came up with the inventive concept?' (either solely or jointly). It is not necessary to show additional factors such as a breach of confidence. Moreover, questions of entitlement, which we are looking at in this chapter, and novelty, which we will look at in chapter 17, ought to be kept separate.

Under s. 72(1)(b) Patents Act 1977, the grant of a patent to the wrong person is also a ground of revocation but the ability to challenge for revocation on this ground is limited to co-inventors and has a strict time limit of two years from grant. The inventor is entitled to be mentioned in the patent even if he or she does not own it: s. 13 Patents Act 1977. Generally, the person entitled to the grant is the inventor—but a non-inventor can become entitled to grant if they have had the rights assigned to them. It is worth noting that a patent application is itself a form of property, and the publication of the application marks the date from which the patentee can claim damages for patent infringement (s. 69 UK Patents Act; EPC Arts 67 and 148).

Finally, it is worth noting that a patent is not the only way that an invention can be 'owned' under intellectual property law—as we shall see in the chapter on breach of confidence, an invention might be protectable as a trade secret. Inventors can, therefore, consider whether they wish to apply for a patent (which can be a long and expensive process) or whether to just keep the invention secret. However, unlike a trade secret, which must be kept secret, and thus cannot be licensed to others for profit, the benefit of a patent is that as the knowledge becomes public with the publication of the application/grant it can be licensed to others during the 20-year period of protection.

16.2 Ownership of employee inventions

Having examined the criteria used by the courts to identify an inventor, we now must consider the special statutory rules concerning employee–inventors. This is a topic where intellectual property law, contract law, and employment law overlap and where each area of law has its different values (J. Pila, '"Sewing the Fly Buttons on the Statute": Employee Inventions and the Employment Context' [2012] 32(2) *Oxford Journal of Legal Studies* 265). Today, the Patents Act 1977 provides that once it has been decided who owns an invention, the employer or employee, there is a scheme of compensation for employee–inventors. The details of the scheme are considered below, as is the question of whether the legislation lives up to aspirations of finding the right balance between the law of patents, employment contracts, and the labour rights of employees.

16.2.1 The pre-1977 law on ownership of employee inventions

Prior to the Patents Act 1977 there were no statutory rules on the ownership of inventions. The matter was governed entirely by a century or more of case law. The court cases placed emphasis on freedom of contract, and the employer's superior economic bargaining power was rarely questioned. In essence, under the law the employer would own an invention made by an employee either by virtue of a provision in the contract of employment, or because the employee was deemed to hold the invention on trust for the employer. Such a trust would arise by virtue of the employee's fiduciary status or by virtue of his or her contractual duties. The Patents Act 1949 conferred (in s. 56) the power to resolve entitlement disputes to courts. However, the restrictive interpretation accorded to the section by the House of Lords in *Sterling Engineering v Patchett* [1955] AC 534 at p. 543 meant that if, either by virtue of contract or via a trust, the employer clearly owned the invention, then there was considered to be no dispute and the section could not be utilized. Employees were in a difficult position, *viz* their employers.

The use of the trust to determine ownership of inventions occurred in one of two situations. In the first scenario, the court could treat a senior employee as having the status of a fiduciary, so that he or she would then be held to be a trustee of the invention (as happened to the managing director in *Worthington Pumping Engine Co v Moore* (1903) 20 RPC 41 and the senior researcher in *British Syphon Co v Homewood* [1956] 1 WLR 119). Alternatively, the court would examine the employment contract and conclude that as the employee was employed to invent, then he or she must be a trustee of the invention as the result of his or her duties: *Triplex Safety Glass Co v Scorah* [1938] Ch 211. It was, of course, open to the employer to draft the employment contract in such a way that the court could easily make such an inference.

With regard to the contractual situation, an employer typically had the economic bargaining power to insert a clause (called a 'pre-assignment clause') into the contract of employment stating that all inventions, whenever and wherever made, belonged to the employer. Employees had little leeway in negotiations and the majority had no choice but to sign.

This practice was widely used but was eventually criticized for being in 'restraint of trade' in *Electrolux v Hudson* [1977] FSR 312. In his ruling, Falconer J declared that a storekeeper who made improvements to a vacuum cleaner was beneficially entitled to the patent. Importantly, it was not the employee's job to invent and the clause in his contract requiring him to hand over all inventions was held unenforceable. By coincidence, this case was decided in the same year as the enactment of the Patents Act 1977, which reformed the law to give employees more rights over their inventions.

 Pause for reflection

Think back to what Felicity has done. How do you think the pre-1977 patent law applies to the facts of our problem question? What might be significant about her employment contract?

16.2.2 The post-1977 law on ownership of employee inventions

As a result of the deliberations of the Banks Committee (*The British Patent System*) (1970) (Cmnd 4407) and the White Paper (*Patent Law Reform*) (1975) (Cmnd 6000), together with lobbying from trade unions, the Patents Act 1977 introduced what was then a new régime for employee inventions. It is worth noting that the European Patent Convention ('EPC') has no influence on this aspect of the 1977 Act, as rules of ownership and property are a matter for domestic law.

The effect of the 1977 Act can be summarized thus:

- it introduced a new (comprehensive) statutory test of ownership which is to the exclusion of anything which applied before;
- it introduced a scheme of compensation for employee inventors; and
- it rendered unenforceable certain terms in contracts of employment.

16.2.2.1 The statutory test of ownership

With regard to ownership of inventions, the key provision is s. 39 Patents Act 1977. The following observations can be made about the wording of the provision:

- it displaces all the previous case law, due to the phrase 'notwithstanding anything in any rule of law';
- the 'default' position is found in s. 39(2): in all cases except those that fall within s. 39(1), the invention belongs to the employee; and
- the circumstances when the invention belongs to the employer under s. 39(1) are precisely set out.

Section 39(1) contains two paragraphs—(a) and (b)—which confer ownership on the employer. In s. 31(1)(a), the section stresses that the invention must be made *in the course of the employee's duties* (either normal duties or those specifically assigned to him); and that the circumstances in either case were such that *an invention* might reasonably be expected to result from the performance of his duties. The section utilizes the phrase 'an invention' not 'the invention'. Consequently, the test is whether, as a result of the employee's duties, he or she is expected to invent—in other words, *is the employee employed to invent?*

Two cases provide apt illustrations of this: *In Re Harris' Patent* [1985] RPC 19 and *Greater Glasgow Health Board's Application* [1996] RPC 207.

In Re Harris' Patent [1985] RPC 19 & *Greater Glasgow Health Board's Application* [1996] RPC 207

In *In Re Harris' Patent* [1985] RPC 19, the court emphasized that the two principal questions to be asked were: what were the employee's normal duties at the material time, and was the invention in suit made by the employee in carrying out those duties? Falconer J held that in the circumstances of the case, the patent belonged to the employee because, employed as a salesman, he was not expected to invent as part of his job.

In *Greater Glasgow Health Board's Application* [1996] RPC 207, a doctor (junior registrar) invented an optical device while he was out of hours and at home. His employer, the Western Infirmary Tennent Institute, claimed ownership under s. 39(1) on the basis of his contractual duties to treat patients and undertake research. On appeal from the UKIPO, Jacob J (as he then was) held that at the time of devising the invention the doctor was clearly 'not acting in the course of his duties' within the meaning of the s. 39(1). Jacob J held that a junior doctor was not expected to invent, even though part of his time was spent teaching and researching in a university, his employer being a 'teaching hospital'. Jacob J stated (at 223):

> Doctors frequently devise new and better treatments. Some of those will involve patentable inventions. Most doctors are employed. If, just because they are employed and because the invention could be used for the purpose of their employment, the invention belongs to the employer then many doctors would be placed in a very difficult position—'Can they publish what they have devised?', 'Do they have to get their employer's permission to publish?' At present they do not. I do not see why they should in the future.

However, whether an employee is employed to invent is not a question to be answered only at the time the person is recruited. A person's job description will necessarily evolve with time, and it is possible that someone not originally employed to invent can be found to be within s. 39(1) as a result of how their job has developed. This requires an examination of all the surrounding circumstances: *LIFFE Administration and Management v Pinkava* [2007] RPC 667.

Under 39(1)(b) (which is wider than para (a), *Staeng Ltd's Application* [1996] RPC 183), the invention will belong to the employer where two cumulative conditions are satisfied. These are that: (i) the inventor made it in the course of his employment duties; and (ii) that when the invention was made, the nature of his responsibilities were such that he was under a special obligation to further the interests of the employer's undertaking. It is not entirely clear whether this provision enacts the thinking, based on trusts and fiduciary duties, discussed above in *Worthington v Moore* and *British Syphon v Homewood*.

The only decision on the provision to date is *Staeng Ltd's Application* [1996] RPC 183. Here, the UKIPO decided that the employee in question fell within s. 39(1)(a), so that his employer was entitled to co-ownership of the invention with another company whose staff had played a part in the creative process. However, in addition, it concluded that the employee whose status was in dispute was also within the terms of s. 39(1)(b) and so had a duty to further the interests of his employer. The UKIPO took into account the wide-ranging nature of the employee's duties found in his job description (these included 'creative thinking') and his remuneration package, under which he received bonuses, and concluded that he was a director of the company in all but name.

16.2.2.2 Pre-assignment clauses

In relation to s. 39, note should be made of the effect of s. 42. The provision renders unenforceable any contractual provision which purports to diminish the employee's rights. The effect of this section means that an employer can no longer attempt to override the rules of ownership set out in s. 39. The section therefore reflects the principle of protecting the employee against the unequal bargaining power of the employer.

Pause for reflection

Think again about how might the post-1977 patent law apply to the facts of our problem question. Did Felicity make her invention in the course of employment? Is she employed to invent? Alternatively, is there any evidence that she has a duty to further the interests of her employer?

16.3 Compensation for employee inventions

The Patents Act 1977 provides for two separate instances when an employee may be awarded compensation in respect of a successful patent of which they are the inventor but not the owner. However, the conditions imposed on the award of compensation are extremely restrictive and employees' claims are rarely successful. Further, the conditions imposed by the Act are cumulative and it takes little imagination, on the part of employers, to work out how to circumvent them.

16.3.1 Compensation where the employer owns the patent

Section 40(1) (as amended by the Patents Act 2004) deals with where the patent is owned by the employer as the result of the operation of s. 39(1).

The cumulative conditions to be satisfied are:

- there must be an invention made by the employee which belongs to the employer;
- a patent for that invention has been granted;
- the patent, the invention, or both must be of outstanding benefit to the employer; and
- it is just that compensation should be awarded.

The second criterion is the most problematic. It requires that a patent must have been granted. This means that if a patent application is unsuccessful (for whatever reason) or if the patent, though successful, is revoked or if the employer decides not to file a patent application, then compensation cannot be claimed.

Moreover, the courts have accorded a restrictive interpretation to the third requirement of 'outstanding benefit' under s. 40(1). What amounts to outstanding benefit is assessed qualitatively. In *British Steel plc's Patent* [1992] RPC 117, it was held that there was no outstanding benefit where the savings in production costs, although totalling several hundred thousand pounds, amounted to 0.01% of turnover. This suggests that the requirement of 'outstanding benefit' is harder to establish in the case of an employer with a large multi-million-pound business than where the employer runs a small or medium-sized enterprise ('SME').

Shanks v Unilever Plc & Others [2014] EWHC 1647 (Pat)

In another case decided under s. 40(1)—*Shanks v Unilever Plc & Others* [2014] EWHC 1647 (Pat)—the dispute was between Professor Shanks and Unilever, concerning a Unilever patent developed pursuant to an invention by Professor Shanks and two others while he worked at Unilever in the 1980s. Arnold J dismissed Professor Shanks' appeal against the decision of the UKIPO Comptroller General of Patents that the patents on his employee invention were not of outstanding benefit to Unilever and thus Professor Shanks was not entitled to an award of employee compensation. This was despite the fact that Unilever had received approximately £24.5m in revenues arising from the patent, because, viewed qualitatively, this was a comparatively small amount for Unilever, whose annual turnover exceeds £40billion. At the same time, Arnold J stated at [69] that 'it would not be correct to construe section 40(1) as meaning that, if the employer's undertaking is large and profitable, no benefit can be outstanding however large it is'. On appeal in *Shanks v Unilever PLC and others* [2017] EWCA Civ 2, the Court of Appeal confirmed the UKIPO and High Court rulings that when considering 'outstanding benefit' the employer group's turnover and profitability are highly relevant factors. Outstanding benefit is therefore a relative concept, which must be measured against the employer's economic and business realities. Notably, Briggs LJ (at [68]) dismissed the appeal 'with some reluctance' because Professor Shanks 'might well have succeeded had his employer been a much smaller undertaking than Unilever'. However, the Court of Appeal felt bound by the wording of s. 41, which specifically refers to the size of the undertaking.

The wording of the section also requires the benefit to the employer to be *the result* of the patent. This can be hard to demonstrate, as there might be many other reasons why the employer's business is successful; for example, the employer might acquire a lucrative contract in which the patent plays only a very small part (*GEC Avionics Ltd's Patent* [1992] RPC 107); or the company's success might be the result of a cordial relationship with a long-term customer (*Memco Med Ltd's Patent* [1992] RPC 403). However, outstanding benefit does not have to be proved over a lengthy period of business dealings: *Entertainment UK Ltd's Patent* [2002] RPC 291.

Despite the stringency of the provision, compensation was awarded in *Kelly & Chiu v GE Healthcare Ltd* [2009] RPC 363 where the claimants were awarded £1 million and £500,000 respectively, representing 2% and 1% of the value of patents worth £50 million for a radioactive imaging agent, the key compound of which had been synthesized by the claimants.

16.3.2 Compensation where the employee owned the patent

The alternative compensation scheme provided by s. 40(2) contemplates that the invention once belonged to the employee (because of the operation of s. 39(2)) but no longer does so because the employee has handed it over to the employer or an associated company. The relevant criteria are:

- a patent must have been granted for an invention made and owned by the employee;
- he has since assigned it or granted an exclusive licence to the employer;
- the benefit from this is inadequate in relation to that derived by the employer; and
- it is just that additional compensation be awarded.

Again, these are cumulative requirements. Their precise nature means that compensation may not always be available, for example, if the invention is not patented or if (as a result of pressure from the employer) the employee grants a non-exclusive licence to the employer rather than assigning the patent or licensing it exclusively. There is no mechanism in the Act for dealing with such an anti-avoidance tactic on the part of the employer, just as there can be no redress if the employer deliberately decides not to seek patent protection. Further, the word 'inadequate' raises similar issues to its counterpart in s. 40(1), 'outstanding benefit'.

16.3.3 Calculating compensation

The factors to be taken into account when calculating compensation under both s. 40(1) and s. 40(2) are in s. 41. This states, in subsection (1), that an employee is to be given a 'fair share of the benefit' and in s. 41(4), lists the factors to be taken into account, including the nature of the employee's duties, his remuneration and other advantages he derives from his employment, the effort and skill devoted to the invention, the efforts of other employees, and the contribution made by the employer. The narrow interpretation accorded under s. 40 to the phrase 'outstanding benefit' suggests that courts are likely to treat the factors relevant to a 'fair share' in a similarly narrow fashion.

In *Kelly & Chiu v GE Healthcare Ltd*, Floyd J took into account the effect which the success of the *patent* had on the claimant's salaries and their subsequent employment and pensions, stating that this exerted 'downward pressure' on the award of compensation. Equally, although their research efforts had been considerable, so had the employer's, in particular further research carried out once the compound was synthesized, in developing the American market for the product, and in bearing the economic risk of the project. He added that an employee's 'fair share of the benefit' of a successful invention might lie anywhere in the range of 0% to 33% but, as already indicated, ultimately awarded a figure at the bottom end of this scale. In fact, the award amounted to 0.1% of the defendant's turnover. In *Shanks v Unilever Plc & Others* [2014] EWHC 1647 (Pat) Arnold J stated that the UKIPO had been correct to state that if Professor Shanks had been entitled to employee compensation, 5% would have been too high as a 'fair share' of the revenues generated and that the share awarded to Professor Shanks would not have been more than the 3% awarded in *Kelly*.

Pause for reflection

Jennifer Pierce (in 'Employee Inventions in the United Kingdom' [2017] LII(3) *Les Nouvelles — Journal of the Licensing Executives Society*) states that historically 'the United Kingdom has been a jurisdiction where, in relative terms, the law is more favourable to employers than to employees'. Do the provisions concerning employee inventions in the Patents Act 1977, including the 2004 amendments, live up to the aspirations of those who lobbied for reform? Why is it so difficult to prove that your employee invention was of 'outstanding benefit' to your employer?

If the patent on Felicity's invention is held to belong to her employer, could an employee invention compensation claim apply in the context of our problem question above? How lucrative do you think the patent would have to be in terms of revenues before Felicity could be awarded compensation? What rate of compensation might she receive?

16.4 Conclusion

This chapter has explained the history of how the UK courts have dealt with the issue of patent ownership. We have examined the definition of 'inventor' under the Patents Act 1977 including the importance of 'inventive concept'. We have looked at the question of employee inventions in detail, including the s. 39 question of when employees, rather than their employers, should be granted ownership of patents on inventions they devise. Finally, we looked at the scheme of employee compensation under ss. 40 and 41.

Looking again at the facts in the problem scenario at the beginning of our chapter, we can advise Felicity. We can inform her that under s. 39 of the Patents Act 1977 the key question is as follows: is she employed to invent? Referring to *In Re Harris' Patent* and *Greater Glasgow Health Board's Application*, we can advise her that given the nature of her job, and the explicit contractual terms, it appears that she is 'employed to invent'. Moreover, she has used her employer's laboratory and leftover samples. These factors indicate that her employer would be entitled to ownership of the patent. However, even if she is held to not be the owner of the patent, she may have a chance to receive employee compensation under s. 40(1). The key issue here would be whether the patent is of 'outstanding benefit' to her employer (*Kelly*). If it turns out to be highly lucrative, the fact that her employer is a medium-sized company means that she is likely to have a strong argument that the benefit accruing to the company from her invention is indeed 'outstanding' (*Shanks*). If she is successful in her compensation claim, the percentage she is likely to receive of the revenues is around 3% (*Kelly, Shanks*).

End-of-chapter questions

After reading the chapter carefully, try answering the following questions. For answer guidance visit the online resources at **www.oup.com/uk/karapapa-mcdonagh/**

1. Is the way the law treats employee inventions, including the rules on compensation, fair to employees?

2. Why is it so difficult for employees to prove that their inventions were of 'outstanding benefit' to their employers?

3. How important are the terms of employment contracts to this area of law?

Further reading

Chandler, P. A., 'Employees' Inventions: Inventorship and Ownership' [1997] 19 *EIPR* 262

Gives a thorough analysis of employee and employer relationship with respect to inventions, including the important issue of compensation.

Lawson, C., 'Academic Inventions Outside the University: Investigating Patent Ownership in the UK' [2013] 20 *Industry and Innovation* 385

This paper investigates the ownership of academic patents for a sample of UK academics and challenges the existing definition of the university invention ownership model. The first descriptive results show that 50% of patents are owned by industry, however, 37% of these firm-assigned patents are in fact owned by university spin-offs.

Pierce, J. 'Employee Inventions in the United Kingdom' [2017] LII(3) *Les Nouvelles—Journal of the Licensing Executives Society*

Considers UK patent law on employee inventions in light of the 2004 amendments to the Patents Act 1977.

Pila, J. 'Professional and Academic Employee Inventions: Looking Beyond the UK Paradigm' in M. Pittard, A. Monitti, and J. Duns (eds.) *Business Innovation: A Legal Balancing Act— Perspectives from Intellectual Property, Labour and Employment, Competition and Corporate Laws* (Edward Elgar, 2013)

Considers academic research in the light of recent UK and Australian decisions on employee inventions and compensation.

Pila, J. '"Sewing the Fly Buttons on the Statute': Employee Inventions and the Employment Context' [2012] 32(2) *Oxford Journal of Legal Studies* 265

Considers UK and Australian case law on employee inventions and calls for further discussion and policy debate.

Stallberg, C.G., 'The Legal Status of Academic Employees' Inventions in Britain and Germany and its Consequences for R&D Agreements' [2007] 4 *IPQ* 489

Takes a comparative perspective of employee inventions in the UK and Germany.

17 Patentability

Problem question

Read this problem question carefully and keep it in mind while you are working through the chapter that follows. At the end of this chapter, you will be able to apply what you have learnt to the problem question and advise the relevant parties.

Siva Patel is a professional engineer, amateur inventor, and keen cyclist who lives in Cardiff. In early May, after spending many weekends toiling away in her home office/work room, she creates a new type of bicycle pump that uses a solar-powered motor to pump air into a bike's wheels. After testing the pump on her bike outside in her garden, she purchases several other pumps on the market in order to compare them. Siva finds that her invention pumps air with 40% more efficiency than any other product on the market, and without requiring any physical exertion from the pump-owner. Moreover, when she searches the market for air pumps online, Siva finds that, as far as she can discern, her pump is unique in that it is the only one that is solar-powered. Having taken a quick look at the academic and journalistic articles on pump technology, as far as Siva is aware nobody has ever suggested that solar energy could ever be used to power an air pump of any kind. Siva is proud of her invention but has yet to show it to anybody. She seeks to understand whether it is patentable in the UK and what she would need to demonstrate to obtain her patent.

Advise Siva.

17.1 **Introduction**

In this chapter we are concerned with the criteria for patentability. In other words, the rules patent examiners and courts use to decide if a patent is valid or not. As we shall see in chapter 18, these criteria are also useful in the context of an infringement action, because a defendant may make a counter-claim to revoke the claimant's patent for invalidity on the basis of one of the criteria.

17.1.1 **The statutory requirements for patentability**

The patentability of an invention is defined by Arts 52 to 57 of the European Patent Convention ('EPC') (translated imperfectly into ss. 1 to 4A Patents Act 1977). The criteria comprise five core elements: three positive and two negative. In terms of the positive requirements, for an invention to be patentable, it must possess novelty (it must be new); inventive step (it must possess something that is not obvious in the field of technology); sufficiency and support (must disclose a claimed invention in sufficient detail for the person skilled in the art to be able to carry out); and industrial applicability (it must have some practical usefulness). Regarding the negative criteria, the invention must not consist of excluded subject matter, and it must not fall afoul of any of the exceptions to patentability.

The factor common to all elements of patentability is the significance of the claims. The combined effect of the Patents Act 1977 ss. 125 and 130(1) means that the scope of a patented invention is determined from the wording of the claims. The claims must be read purposively through the eyes of the skilled addressee. What must be appreciated is that the claims are for the patentee (or rather, a professional advisor, i.e. patent lawyer) to draft. It is up to the patentee to word the claims in such a way that any obstacles posed by the prior art are avoided, and the elements of patentability are met. Successfully granted patents often depend as much on skillful wording and drafting by the patentee (or, invariably, her patent lawyer) as they do on creativity in the invention itself.

 Pause for reflection

Consider what Siva has created in our problem scenario. If you were to define her 'invention' what words would you use? How would you define it?

Performing this task is one of the challenges of patent law and something we will consider in detail later in this chapter with respect to Siva's invention.

17.2 **The meaning of 'an invention'**

As Vaver comments (in 'Invention in Patent Law: a Review and a Modest Proposal' (2003) 11 *International Journal of Law and Information Technology* 286), although one can give a dictionary definition of invention, the parameters of the concept are not so precise. As a legal term of art, its meaning is not immutably fixed and will change over time.

To guide us, we can read the elements of a patentable invention as set out in s. 1(1) Patents Act 1977, with each element in turn being the subject of elaboration in subsequent sections—novelty, inventive step, industrial applicability, etc. It is logical to conclude that if an application meets the criteria of patentability it is an invention. However, before we discuss the criteria in detail, it is worth noting that there is an apparent difference between UK and European Patent Office ('EPO') case law as to whether there is a separate preliminary requirement of 'an invention' which must be satisfied before a patent can be granted.

17.2.1 'An invention': UK cases

There is little discussion in UK case law as to whether there is a separate requirement of 'an invention' per se, probably because of the tacit assumption that if the criteria for patentability were met then, by definition, there must be an invention. The opening words of s. 1(1) ('that is to say') lend support to the conclusion that if all the other criteria for patentability are satisfied there must be an invention.

Three cases have debated whether there is a separate requirement of an invention and all involved biotechnology at a time when the patentability of biotech inventions was a very new and uncertain area of law (Luke McDonagh, 'Biogen v Medeva' in J. Bellido (ed.), *Landmark Cases in Intellectual Property* (Hart, 2017)). There was some judicial disquiet at having to accommodate the law to scientific developments which go beyond the traditional view of patents as involving mechanical or chemical advances.

In *Genentech Inc's Patent* [1989] RPC 147, the principal claims of the patent related to human tissue plasminogen activator ('t-PA'), a protein known to activate an enzyme which dissolved blood clots. Revocation of the patent was sought on various grounds, including lack of inventive step, lack of sufficiency, and that what was claimed was in effect a mere discovery, not an invention. The Court of Appeal upheld the decision of Whitford J that the patent should be revoked. In relation to whether what was claimed was not an invention, Purchas and Mustill LJJ were prepared to state that the requirement of an invention was something which had to be disclosed by the claim *before* the remaining requirements of s. 1(1) became relevant. In other words, the existence of an invention was a prerequisite to patentability.

A differently constituted Court of Appeal in *Chiron Corporation v Organon Teknika Ltd (No. 12)* [1996] FSR 153 took a simpler view of the difference between an invention and a discovery. Morritt LJ pointed out that neither the Act nor the EPC contained a definition of the words 'discovery' or 'invention'. He relied on the words of Nicholls LJ in *Re Gale's Application* [1991] RPC 305 at p. 323:

> I turn now to section 1(2) of the Act. When considering these provisions, it is helpful to have in mind the principles of patent law . . . that an idea or discovery as such is not patentable. It is the practical application of an idea or discovery which leads to patentability. It leads to patentability even if, as frequently happens, the practical application of the discovery is inherent in the discovery itself or is obvious once the discovery has been made and stated.

Pause for reflection

The final case in the trilogy to debate whether 'an invention' is a separate requirement was *Biogen Inc v Medeva plc* [1997] RPC 1, although the views expressed were obiter. Two contrasting opinions were put forward by Lord Mustill and Lord Hoffmann. Taking the latter first (with

➡

→

whom Lords Goff, Browne-Wilkinson, and Slynn agreed), Lord Hoffmann noted that the wording of s. 1 might lead one to conclude that whether what was claimed was an invention should logically be decided as a preliminary issue. This, Lord Hoffmann considered, would be a mistake. The framers of the EPC had been unable to agree a definition of an invention, and were content that one should be omitted because they recognized that 'the question would almost invariably be academic'. The four conditions in s. 1 not only restricted the class of inventions which could be patented, they also contained every element of the concept in ordinary speech. No one had been able to think of an example of something which satisfied all the conditions of s. 1 but was not an invention. Lord Hoffmann considered that if, by working through the four criteria in s. 1, one concluded that they were satisfied, that would be an end to the inquiry. He noted that if one day a case arose where it was necessary to decide whether something which satisfies the conditions should be called an invention 'that question can wait until it arises'. Lord Hoffmann advised that judges should 'put on one side their intuitive sense of what constitutes an invention until they have considered the questions of novelty, inventiveness and so forth'.

Lord Mustill took a different view. Although agreeing with the outcome of the case, he did not concur with Lord Hoffmann that the separate identification of the invention was a waste of time. Although in most cases it would not be necessary to go beyond the four conditions in s. 1, in some instances a close conceptual analysis of the nature of patentability would be appropriate. *Genentech Inc's Patent* had been such a case, where the claim was for a product existing in nature, rather than the mechanical or chemical inventions to which most of patent law relates. There could well be others in the future. Lord Mustill therefore indicated that the criterion of 'an invention' might, in some cases, require separate consideration.

It is a matter of speculation whether biotechnology patents are singled out for special treatment because of their ethical implications or simply because they are based on something found in nature rather than something man-made. Either way, the conclusions of Lord Hoffmann, that the prerequisite of invention will rarely need to be considered by court once the patentability criteria have been met, need to be reconsidered in light of EPO case law.

17.2.2 'An invention': EPO cases

Under the revised Art. 52 EPC (2000), it is stated that 'European patents shall be granted for any inventions, in all fields of technology, *provided* that they are new, involve an inventive step and are susceptible of industrial application'. Subsequent case law of the EPO Boards of Appeal focuses more the question of whether an invention has sufficient technological character (and on patentability with respect to novelty, inventive step, and industrial application) rather than whether it is an invention, per se (*T 258/03 HITACHI/Auction method* [2004] EPOR 548 at [3.1]).

Any variance from the UK position may not make a great deal of difference to most patent decisions, as the EPO's explanation of what is 'technical character' is broad (*T 931/95 PBS PARTNERSHIP/Controlling Pension Benefits System* [2002] EPOR 522). 'Technical character' means that there must be a physical entity or concrete product, man-made for a utilitarian purpose. Thus, the use of pen and paper to write would qualify according to the EPO in *HITACHI* (but that does not mean that such a device would meet the requirements of novelty and inventive step). Anything of an entirely abstract nature, for example theories or mathematical methods or economic calculations, would not be sufficiently technical.

In T 154/04 *DUNS LICENSING ASSOCIATES/Estimating Sales Activity* [2007] EPOR 349 the EPO considered that 'technical character' was a mandatory requirement for any patentable invention, holding an invention must involve 'technical teaching'. Novelty and inventive step were separate, independent, and relative criteria from this analysis. Further, the list of excluded subject matter in Art. 52(2), the common feature of which is the lack of technical character, should not be given too broad an interpretation.

So, how does one decide whether something has 'technical character'? Here we look to the EPO decisions in *PBS PARTNERSHIP* and in *DUNS LICENSING ASSOCIATES*. Once it has been decided that something has technical character because e.g. it is a physical entity, the criterion of technical contribution becomes relevant to the issue of whether the invention possesses an inventive step. This approach was reinforced by *HITACHI*, where the Board held that the first thing to do is to ask if the invention is excluded by Art. 52(2) without any knowledge of the prior art. If the invention possesses any technical means at all (for example, even something as simple as pen and paper), the next stage is to consider whether the invention is new, and if so, whether it has an inventive step, taking account of only those features which contribute to its technical character.

 Pause for reflection

Taking into account the UK and EPO cases, do you think that what Siva has done could be considered as an 'invention' per se under UK law? Looking at the EPO decisions, what 'technical character' does her invention have?

17.2.3 Impact of the EPO case law

It remains to be seen whether UK cases will now follow the EPO in separating out the requirement of an invention. There were indications that this might happen in *H Lundbeck A/S v Generics (UK) Ltd* [2009] RPC 407 where Lord Neuberger (at [70]) appeared to treat an invention as a discrete aspect of patentability. Further, in the same case, the issue of technical character is treated as involving an evaluation of the inventive concept, that is, how far forward the invention has carried the state of the art, rather than part of the definition of 'an invention' (*per* Lord Walker at [30], Lord Neuberger at [101]). For the moment it is necessary to understand both the UK and EPO approaches.

 Pause for reflection

Do you consider that attempting to define an 'invention'—separate from the patentability criteria—is a useful exercise or a waste of time? Is this a case of lawyers and judges perhaps 'overthinking' things?   →

> →
> Keep Siva's invention in mind as we go through the next sections on excluded subject mat-
> ter, novelty, inventive step, and industrial applicability. As we proceed through each category,
> consider whether a separate requirement of 'invention' would help your analysis or hinder it.

17.3 Excluded subject matter

17.3.1 Overview of the exclusions from patentability

The first element of patent law that a patent application must satisfy is that the invention must be of appropriate subject matter (L. Bently, 'Exclusions from Patentability
and Exceptions to Patentees' Rights: Taking Exceptions Seriously' (2011) 64 *Current
Legal Problems* 315). Certain types of intellectual and inventive activity, such as purely
scientific discoveries, e.g. Crick & Watson's 1953 discovery of the double helix structure
of DNA, are prima facie excluded from patentability.

Section 1(2) Patents Act 1977—based on Arts 52(2) and (3) EPC—contains a list of
excluded subject matter. The EPO in *DUNS LICENSING ASSOCIATES* (at [8]), repeating
its earlier views in *T 366/87 STERNHEIMER/Harmonic vibrations* [1989] EPOR 131, stated
that the common feature of the list is 'a substantial lack of technical character', following the classical notion of the difference between intellectual achievements in general
and practical scientific applications. Further, in the same case (at [6]), the EPO appears
to assume that all the items on the list should receive the same treatment and should
be narrowly construed.

UK decisions suggest that the list of excluded items is not a logical class at all and
there are different policy reasons underlying each of the exclusions (*Re CFPH LLC's
Application* [2006] RPC 259 at [21]), so that they should not be accorded the same treatment. In *Aerotel Ltd v Telco Holdings Ltd/Macrossan's Application* it was said that there is
nothing in the EPC itself to indicate whether the list should be read widely or narrowly,
and the list is expressed not as an exception but as positive categories of things not to
be regarded as inventions. By contrast, in *Research in Motion v Inpro* [2006] RPC 517 at
[187], Pumfrey J remarked that the exclusions should not be given too wide a scope.
One must be astute not to defeat patents on the ground that the subject matter is forbidden by Art. 52 EPC unless the invention lies in excluded subject matter as such.

More problematic than such differences of opinion is the interpretation given to
the proviso to s. 1(2). The wording of Art. 52(3) EPC (on which the proviso is based) is
easier to understand, that is, that 'patentability is only excluded *to the extent to which*
the patent relates to such subject matter or activities *as such*' (emphasis supplied). The
qualification 'as such' therefore needs to be read into each paragraph of the list of exclusions, considered in turn in the next section. Indeed, these two words—'as such'—have
led to a great deal of judicial and academic argument.

When applying the proviso, it should be remembered that everything depends on the
wording of the claims. It is the claims which define the subject matter of the invention
(s. 14(5) Patents Act 1977). This means that a patentee can word the specification—a
crucial part of the application—in such a way that it avoids the various exclusions.

There is nothing to stop a patentee from doing this, though it is something that patent examiners will watch out for.

17.3.2 The meaning of 'as such'

The interpretation of the phrase 'as such' was initially explained by the EPO in *VICOM*. It stated that the 'whole contents' approach should be adopted: i.e. the patent should be read as a whole to see if it achieves a technical advance, rather than ignoring those aspects which were excluded from protection and then assessing whether what remained was patentable.

In this view, the emphasis should be on what the invention does, that is, whether it has made a technical contribution. If the invention is merely a quicker way of performing a task which had been done previously by hand, or by the human mind, then even if this resulted in increased efficiency it would not be considered a patentable invention. Following *VICOM*, this was followed by the UKIPO and Court of Appeal in line with s. 1(2) Patents Act 1977: see *Merrill Lynch's Application* [1989] RPC 561, *Re Gale's Application* and *Re Fujitsu's Application* [1997] RPC 608.

Pause for reflection

Think about Siva's invention in light of this. Is there something about Siva's pump that is more than just a 'quicker way of performing a task'?

The EPO has moved on from *VICOM*. The current approach is that of the *PBS PART-NERSHIP* and *HITACHI* decisions, where the Board of Appeal explained that once it has been determined that there is an 'invention', something having technical character, whether that invention falls within the list of exclusions is decided by asking if its novelty or inventive step is in an area of technology. The correct approach therefore is to see if there is an invention featuring technical character and *then* to ask whether it satisfies the requirement of patentability.

In *Re CFPH LLC's Application* [2006] RPC 259 the Patents Court noted that UK case law was out of line with this changed EPO thinking. The difference between the old and new approaches to 'an invention' was helpfully summarized by Peter Prescott QC as follows (at [44–45, 77]):

- the practice of UKIPO was to look at the claim and ask what was its technical contribution. If there was none, the application would be rejected. If there was some technical contribution over the prior art in the form of a new result, it would then be necessary to decide whether the application should be rejected on other grounds;

- the practice of the EPO, on the other hand, was to examine the claim and ask whether, without knowledge of the prior art, it had any technical features. If there were none, then the application would be rejected. If there were any technical features at all, the EPO then asked whether the invention was old or obvious, but in determining whether it is obvious, anything which is not a technical contribution is ignored;

- in summary, the EPO filters out excluded subject matter when considering obviousness, whilst the UKIPO does so when considering novelty.

The lack of accord between the UK and EPO approaches was commented on by the EPO in *DUNS LICENSING ASSOCIATES*. The Board of Appeal went out of its way to criticize the decision of the Court of Appeal in *Aerotel Ltd v Telco Holdings Ltd/Macrossan's Application*. In this case, Jacob LJ had set out a four-step formula for dealing with excluded subject matter: first, one should properly construe the claim; next, one should identify the actual contribution; third, one should ask whether such contribution fell solely within the list of excluded subject matter; and last, one should check whether the actual or alleged contribution was actually technical in nature. There is overlap between these last two requirements.

Since *DUNS LICENSING ASSOCIATES* UK courts have struggled to accommodate the two conflicting approaches because of their obligation under s. 130(7) Patents Act to achieve conformity with EPO case law (though in *Aerotel/Macrossan* Jacob LJ denied that EPO case law was settled). In *Astron Clinica Ltd & others v Comptroller General of Patents* [2008] RPC 339, Kitchen J stated that it was highly undesirable for there to be divergence between the UK and the EPO. It was not open to him to follow the *PBS PARTNERSHIP* and *HITACHI* cases, but it was possible to interpret *Aerotel/Macrossan* in such a way that it was consistent with the *IBM* decisions. He therefore held that claims to computer programs were not necessarily excluded by Art. 52(2) EPC. If claims to a method performed by running a suitably programmed computer or to a computer programmed to carry out the method were allowable (as under *PBS PARTNERSHIP*), then so too 'in principle' was a claim to the program itself. Such a claim, however, had to be drawn to reflect the features of the invention which would ensure the patentability of the method which the program was intended to carry out when it was run. Subsequent to the decision in *Astron*, UKIPO revised its Practice Note on excluded subject matter, in effect restoring its previous practice note issued after the *IBM* decisions.

In *Symbian Ltd v Comptroller-General of Patents* [2009] RPC 1 the Court of Appeal upheld Patten J's decision that the Patents Examiner had misapplied *Aerotel/Macrossan* when holding that a method for accessing data in a dynamic link library was excluded from patentability. The invention was patentable because it resulted in a faster and more reliable computer. Lord Neuberger felt that the court was not able to depart from *Aerotel/Macrossan* but that it was possible to effect a reconciliation between *Aerotel* and *DUNS*. He also warned against blindly following the structured approach in *Aerotel*. Each case needed to be decided on its facts. The court should treat an invention as unpatentable where its technical effect lay solely in excluded matter. Finally, in *AT&T Knowledge Ventures LP v Comptroller-General of Patents* [2009] FSR 743, Lewison J applied the ruling in *Aerotel/Macrossan* when concluding that a computer software invention (used to connect a device such as an MP3 player to a music download site by detecting the characteristics of the storage medium) was devoid of technical effect. It did not make a computer work in a new or different way: all it did was to send particular information to a potential supplier. It did not solve the problem of incompatibility between formats, rather it circumvented the problem by supplying information which minimized the chance of buying something useless, nor did it result in an increase in the speed or reliability of the computer. It was no more than a computerized list of the characteristics of particular devices. Helpfully, Lewison J set out five signposts which would indicate that a program made a technical contribution, including its external effect, whether there was any impact on the architecture of the computer, whether the computer operated in a new way, whether it was more efficient, and whether the perceived problem was overcome rather than just obviated. The 'signposts' have since been considered and applied in other cases.

17.3.3 'As such': conclusions

Vaver states that the practice (as found in Art. 52(2) EPC) of excluding fixed categories of things which cannot be patentable is 'unsound' except for those which, on any view, fall outside the concept of 'an invention'. He further argues that construing the exclusions narrowly, as the EPO does, and allowing the exclusions to be circumvented by clever claim drafting is also unsound. It would be far better, he says, to allow flexibility into the system so that patent offices could deny protection, as under the Statute of Monopolies, to 'generally inconvenient' patents. It is, of course, a matter of debate whether patent applicants would rather face a wide-ranging discretion to refuse protection or have a statutory régime which, although less than transparent, gives the professional advisor/patent attorney the opportunity for creative drafting.

 Pause for reflection

When deciding whether something is excluded from protection 'as such', which approach do you find easier to apply: the EPO's or that of the Court of Appeal?

Would a definition of 'an invention' help to achieve better understanding of when something is not patentable?

What is it about Siva's invention that might make it easier for her to demonstrate a sufficiently technical character?

17.3.4 The list of exclusions

17.3.4.1 Section 1(2)(a): Discoveries, scientific theories, or mathematical methods

This group of exclusions, found in s. 1(2)(a) of the 1977 Act and Art. 52(2) of the EPC, covers 'abstract ideas': i.e. scenarios where there is no applied technology. By analogy, this includes economic calculations (*PBS PARTNERSHIP*). Such abstract ideas can be viewed as non-inventions (*HITACHI*). A common example of an exclusion falling within paragraph (a) is Einstein's theory of relativity ($E = MC^2$), or, as noted above, Crick & Watson's discovery of the DNA double helix.

However, the way in which scientific discoveries are made in university or company laboratories means that there can be a fine dividing line between an unsuccessful patent application which claims a discovery and a successful one which claims its practical application. In *Chiron v Organon (No. 12)*, the Court of Appeal held that although the identification of Hepatitis C amounted to a discovery, the patent was valid because what was claimed were testing kits which enabled doctors to identify whether someone had the disease. Another example can be found in the facts of *Biogen v Medeva* where the identification of the virus which caused Hepatitis B amounted to a discovery, but the process for its artificial replication was an invention, (though the court held that the patent was invalid for other reasons).

In the US the leading case on gene patents as 'discoveries' is *Association for Molecular Pathology v Myriad Genetics, Inc* (2013) 1133 S Ct. 2107. The US Supreme Court held that a naturally occurring DNA segment is a 'product of nature' and it does not become patentable merely because it has been isolated. However, the court held that methods of isolation, as well as synthetic DNA, are patentable. A similar conclusion was reached, over the same patents, in the High Court of Australia in *D'Arcy v Myriad Genetics Inc* [2015] HCA 35. In relation to gene patents, it appears that the EPO is now a more liberal regime for the patenting of genes than the US or Australia (T. Minssen & M. Mimler, Patenting Bioprinting Technologies in the US and Europe–The 5th element in the 3rd dimension' in R.M. Ballardini, M. Norrgård, & J. Partanen (eds), *3D printing, Intellectual Property & Innovation—Insights from Law & Technology* (Wolters Kluwer, 2017).

 Pause for reflection

Consider what Siva has created in our problem scenario. Could Siva's invention be considered a pure discovery, and thus, not patentable?

17.3.4.2 Section 1(2)(b): Aesthetic creations

Aesthetic creations such as the plot of a play, a detective story, or a piece of music cannot be the subject matter of a patent. The policy for this exclusion is that first, such items are best left to the law of copyright; and second, that to permit the patenting of such forms of creativity would confer too great a monopoly, preventing the circulation of cultural ideas (*Re CFPH LLC's Application*). An example of a rejected application falling under this paragraph is *ESP's Application* (1945) 62 RPC 87 which concerned an architect's plans.

17.3.4.3 Section 1(2)(c): a scheme, rule, or method for performing a mental act, playing a game or doing business, or a program for a computer

This group of exclusions covers a wide range of items, which frequently overlap, so that in respect of e.g. an internet gambling system, the objection could be that it is a means of performing a mental act (calculating the odds), doing business (arranging for debiting or crediting money to the gambler), or a specially written computer program to achieve those ends. Nevertheless, for convenience, we divide the list into three separate categories: performing mental acts, computer programs, and means of doing business.

A further complication is that many of the cases involve what might be called 'hybrid' inventions, that is, they are part technical character and part exclusion. In consequence, they raise again the meaning of 'an invention' and the application of the phrase 'as such' when examining the patentee's claims. As if these challenges were not enough, the EPO and the UKIPO have had to decide the relevant cases against the background of demands for the law to be changed. These calls for reform have been prompted partly by the advent of the TRIPs Agreement, Art. 27(1) which declares that 'patents shall be available for any inventions . . . in all fields of technology'. The other major catalyst for change has been the practice of the United States Patent and Trademark Office which in the recent past adopted a far more liberal attitude to the granting of software patents and business methods patents. However, both the EPO and the UKIPO have decided not to drastically redefine these exclusions, so the cases can be viewed as an attempt to hold back the tide. In relation to 'inventions' which involve methods of performing a mental act, two UK cases neatly demonstrate the point made by the EPO in *HITACHI* that merely to computerise something which was previously done in a person's head or on paper is not patentable. In *Raytheon's Application* [1993] RPC 427 patentability for an automated ship identification system was denied as the alleged invention merely mechanized a task previously done by the human eye, and in *Merrill Lynch's Application*, an automated dealing system was held to be no different from the previous manual method of trading in securities.

That this 'mental act' category overlaps with both the computer program exclusion and the business methods exclusion is illustrated by several cases. In *Re Shopalotto.com Ltd's Patent Application* [2006] RPC 293 the decision to deny patent protection for an online lottery was upheld and in *IGT v Comptroller General of Patents* [2007] EWHC 1341 (Ch) a means of controlling gaming machines was equally held to be unpatentable. In *Raytheon v Comptroller General of Patents* [2008] RPC 46 an inventory management system, which was denied patent protection, could be regarded both as a mental act or a way of organizing business regardless of the computer automation involved. Last, in *Oneida Indian Nation v Comptroller General of Patents* [2007] EWHC 954 (Pat), a means of facilitating off-site gaming was held to fall within the Art. 52(2) exclusions.

The mental act exclusion was further reviewed by Birss J in *Halliburton Energy Services Inc's Application* [2012] RPC 297. Birss J stated that the exclusion was to be narrowly interpreted. In the instant case, a simulation process for designing a drill bit in a computer did not fall within any excluded subject matter and made a technical contribution to the art.

Regarding computer programs, there is a widespread misconception that these are not patentable. In fact, you can patent a computer program provided that the subject matter has 'technical character'. Such technical character lies not in the simple operation of computers but in effects which go further than normal computer operations. Also, as indicated earlier, many of the cases involve methods of doing business or the presentation of information and so are liable to be rejected on grounds other than the computer program exclusion. Interestingly, the exclusion for computer programs was based on a different policy consideration—at the time the EPC was being formulated, the assumption was that patent protection would prove too much of a burden for the software industry and would stifle innovation. In consequence, it was thought that protection would be better left to the law of copyright.

Aerotel Ltd v Telco Holdings Ltd [2006] EWCA Civ 1371

In *Aerotel/Macrossan*, the Court of Appeal helpfully set out the various phases in the development of the EPO's case law. Once applications for computer-implemented inventions began to be made ('computer-implemented inventions' is the preferred terminology today), the EPO's

→

→

initial approach was to ask whether the machine as programmed achieved a technical advance: see *VICOM* and *T 26/86 KOCH & STERZEL/X-ray apparatus* [1988] EPOR 72. Both of these cases explained the term 'technical advance' as meaning that some physical change was produced as a result of the operation of the programmed machine.

The 'technical advance' argument was deployed in *Merrill Lynch's Application* where, as previously noted, the Court of Appeal held that an automated dealing system could not be patented as it was simply a way of dealing in stocks and shares. Likewise, in *Re Gale's Patent*, which involved a method of calculating square root stored on ROM, the Court of Appeal held that the instructions contained in the program did not embody a technical process which existed outside the computer, nor did they solve a technical problem lying within the computer. In *Re Fujitsu's Application*, a method of processing crystalline structures by computer was held unpatentable, Aldous LJ making specific reference to the *VICOM* decision whilst stressing the need for a technical contribution. One (rare) successful UK case was *Quantel v Spaceward Microsystems Ltd* [1990] RPC 83, where the patent involved a computerized video graphics system.

The second phase in EPO case law is to be found in *T 1173/97 IBM/Computer program product* [2000] EPOR 219 and *T 935/97 IBM/Computer program product II* [1999] EPOR 301. The Boards of Appeal declared that the purpose of Arts 52(2) and (3) EPC was not to exclude *all* programs from patentability. Instead, the computer programs exclusion was directed only to those programs which amounted to abstract creations lacking in technical character. Those that possessed technical character were patentable.

T 0931/95 (Controlling pension benefits system/PBS PARTNERSHIP) & T 0154/04 (Estimating sales activity/DUNS LICENSING ASSOCIATES)

The third phase of the case law came with the controversial *PBS PARTNERSHIP* 'pensions' decision. This adopted the 'any hardware' approach, so that a method of controlling a pensions benefit program was rejected, but a suitably programmed computer was not excluded (although in fact the patent was eventually refused on the ground that it lacked inventive step).

Last, in *DUNS LICENSING ASSOCIATES*, the EPO refined and to some extent moved away from the 'any hardware' test. If there is something which has technical character because it is a physical entity, then one should treat that as an invention. The prior art is relevant in deciding whether the invention is new and non-obvious, but is not relevant when considering excluded subject matter. Also, as indicated earlier, many of the cases involve methods of doing business or the presentation of information and so are liable to be rejected on grounds other than the computer program exclusion.

The UK courts did not follow *PBS Partnership* on the basis that the EPO decisions were viewed as inconsistent (though there was an attempt by the UK Court of Appeal to reconcile both views in *Symbian Ltd v Comptroller General of Patents* [2008] EWCA Civ 1066). It was hoped that the tensions between the EPO and UK courts about the patentability of computer programs would be resolved by the Enlarged Board of Appeal (EBA) of the EPO in *G 3/08 PRESIDENT's REFERENCE*. The EBA in *G3/08* stated the earlier decisions were in fact consistent. The EBA criticized UK judges for reciting the 'any hardware' approach without also noting that non-technical inventions will be weeded out when it comes to assess them for novelty and obviousness. However, the actual *G 3/08* reference was dismissed, which led UK judges to not follow it (a somewhat controversial decision since even if it was dismissed if there was still a clear statement of EPO doctrine).

In relation to the exclusion relating to business methods, the previously mentioned cases on computer programs remain relevant. However, for business methods there is a difference of approach with respect to these cases, so it will be useful at this point to explore their respective facts and conclusions in more detail.

In T 931/95 *PBS PARTNERSHIP/Controlling Pension Benefits System* [2002] EPOR 52 the application involved two distinct sets of claims. There were those claims which concerned a method of controlling a pensions benefit program by processing data about individual employees, and then working out their contributions, benefits, and associated life insurance. Other claims in the patent related to the apparatus which controlled the system. The EPO treated the two sets of claims separately, holding that the method claims lacked technical effect but the apparatus claims were in principle patentable. Ultimately, however, it held the apparatus claims lacked inventive step because any software developer who knew the structure of the benefit system would have considered the claims obvious.

In case T 258/03 *HITACHI/Auction method* [2004] EPOR 548 the facts concerned a computerized Dutch auction system, which claimed to overcome the technical deficiencies of previous systems by synchronizing key information during the online bidding process. The same Technical Board of Appeal that had decided *PBS PARTNERSHIP* modified its approach. It held that both method claims and apparatus claims in principle were 'inventions' having technical effect. However, applying *PBS PARTNERSHIP* it concluded that both lacked inventive step. The solution to the prior problem which the patent claimed to provide was no more than a modification to the auction method. It was therefore a means of doing business.

A UK decision which makes the same point is *Re Shopalotto.com Ltd's Patent Application*. The patent related to a computer configured to provide a lottery playable via the internet. It had been rejected by the UKIPO as being a scheme, rule, or method for performing a mental act, playing a game or doing business, or a program for a computer, or the presentation of information. On appeal to the Patents Court, the applicant contended that the alleged invention fell within the practice of permitting the patenting of board games as set out in a then UK Patent Office 'Official Ruling' of 1926. Pumfrey J was highly critical of reliance on the Official Ruling, declaring that it could have no application to the 1977 Act. Agreeing with the comments in *CFPH LLC's Application* that the list of exclusions in s. 1(2) was heterogeneous, Pumfrey J concluded that the physical underpinnings of the claims were to a general-purpose computer, connected to the internet, and so squarely within the ambit of excluded subject matter.

 Pause for reflection

Do the criteria established in EPO case law provide clarity on the patentability of computer programs and in particular the criterion of 'technical character'? According to the EPO, just operating a computer is not enough. A program will be patentable, however (subject to

→

> novelty and inventive step), if it produces additional technical effects going beyond the normal physical interaction between hardware and software.
>
> Is it any easier to consider the criteria in the context of business methods?

17.3.4.4 Section 1(2)(d): The presentation of information

Two UK cases neatly illustrate the final exclusion in s. 1(2). *Re Townsend's Application* [2004] EWHC 482 concerned an attempt to patent an advent calendar, which was rejected by Laddie J as it was simply a means of showing dates in December. Similarly, in *Re Crawford's Patent Application* [2006] RPC 345 the patent related to a display system for buses, indicating whether the bus was picking up or dropping off passengers. Kitchin J upheld the rejection of the application by the UKIPO, noting that he alleged invention did not contain any technical contribution but was simply the presentation of information.

17.4 Exceptions to patentability

17.4.1 Overview

The three exceptions in Art. 53 EPC apply when the criteria for patentability—appropriate subject matter, novelty, inventive step, etc—have (in theory) been met—in all three cases the right to obtain a patent will be denied for policy reasons. The three exceptions are (i) morality, (ii) plant/animal varieties and biological processes, and (iii) methods of treatment.

17.4.2 Impact of the Biotech Directive

EU law is highly relevant to two of the exceptions to patentability (patents contrary to morality and patents involving plant and animal varieties). Directive 98/44/EC of 6 July 1998 on the legal protection of biotechnological inventions [1998] OJ L 213/13 ('the Biotech Directive') has had a major impact. The Directive requires EU Member States to protect biotechnological inventions (Art. 1) and declares that inventions which satisfy the criteria for patentability shall be patentable even if they concern a product consisting of biological material (as defined in Art. 2) or a procedure whereby biological material is produced (Art. 3(1)). Further, biological material which is isolated from its natural environment or which is the subject of a technical process is patentable even if it occurs in nature (Art. 3(2)) or in the human body (Art. 5(2)). Nonetheless, there are a number of exclusions in Arts 4–6 of the Directive, reflecting concerns about the ethics of patenting living matter.

The Directive was the subject of an unsuccessful challenge before the Court of Justice of the European Union ('CJEU') in Case C-377/98 *Kingdom of the Netherlands v European Parliament and Council of the European Union* [2001] ECR I-7079. One aspect of the *Netherlands* case is that it explains the relationship between the Directive and the EPC, the former being an EU legislative measure, the latter being a Convention promulgated by the Council of Europe. The Opinion of AG Jacobs and the ruling of the CJEU reveal two things: first, the EPC Implementing Regulations were modified so as to incorporate the wording of Art. 6 of the Directive; and second, when rejecting the challenge to the Directive (on the grounds that the Directive itself was contrary to public policy) the CJEU adopted the case law of the EPO. In effect there has been two-way traffic between the EU and the EPC on the availability of patent protection for living matter. Although each institution operates its own legal system, both systems now contain the same basic principles.

17.4.3 Patents contrary to public policy

One minor complexity of this area is that there are four separate provisions which individually prohibit the granting of patents on public policy grounds. They are: Art. 53(a) EPC, as amended; s. 1(3) Patents Act 1977, as amended; Art. 6(1) of the Biotech Directive; and Art. 27(2) of the TRIPs Agreement. The last-mentioned allows Contracting States, if they wish, to derogate from the principle in Art. 27(1) that patents are to be granted for any inventions in all fields of technology, whilst the other three provisions contain mandatory wording ('patents *shall* not be granted' as opposed to 'members *may* exclude from patentability' (emphasis supplied)). That apart, all four provisions prohibit the granting of patents 'the *commercial* exploitation of which would be contrary to *ordre public* or morality' (emphasis supplied). What is prohibited is not the patent per se, rather it is the *use* to which the invention is put which matters. An example of this might be a patent which explains how to manufacture a new type of letter bomb (applications for inventions involving weapons will generally have their publication in the *Patents Journal* prohibited under s. 22 Patents Act 1977 and may well be the subject of Crown use under s. 55).

Other specific instances of inventions which would be caught by the public policy exception can be found in Arts 5(1) and 6(2) of the Biotech Directive (incorporated into Sch. A2, para 3(a)–(e) Patents Act 1977). These include the human body at the various stages of its formation and development, and the simple discovery of one of its elements, including the sequence or partial sequence of a gene; processes for cloning human beings; processes for modifying the germ line genetic identity of human beings; uses of human embryos for commercial purposes (something that was of controversy in Case C-34/10 *Oliver Brüstle v Greenpeace eV* [2011] ECR I-9821 discussed later on in the chapter); and processes for modifying the genetic identity of animals which are likely to cause them suffering without any substantial medical benefit to man or animal.

17.4.3.1 EPO case law

There has been no UK case law on s. 1(3). In relation to Art. 53(a) EPC, the EPO has adopted a robust attitude to attempts to challenge patents on grounds of morality. Its initial thinking was set out in *T 19/90 HARVARD/Onco Mouse* [1990] EPOR 4, [1990] EPOR 501 and [1991] EPOR 525.

T 19/90 HARVARD/Onco Mouse **[1990] EPOR 4, [1990] EPOR 501 and [1991] EPOR 525**

In this case the patent was for a transgenic mammal modified to grow cancer cells. After the patent's initial rejection (on the ground, subsequently found to be incorrect, that it claimed an animal variety) the Board of Appeal remitted the case to the Examining Division, directing it to reconsider the ethical objections raised against the application. The Examining Division subsequently held

➜

> that the Art. 53(a) objection should be decided in favour of the applicant. Patent law, it was noted, does not give the proprietor a positive right to use the invention but rather a negative right to exclude others from using the invention for a limited period of time. It was up to the legislator to regulate the use of technical knowledge. The risks inherent in new technologies had to be weighed in terms of the harm which might be done to higher life forms. Here the three interests to be reconciled were the need to remedy widespread and dangerous diseases, the need to protect the environment against the uncontrolled dissemination of unwanted genes, and the need to avoid cruelty to animals. The last two considerations might justify treating the invention as immoral, but were outweighed by the significance of improved anti-cancer treatments, the fact that fewer animals would be needed when compared to conventional animal testing, and that no release of the animals into the environment was contemplated.

Article 53(a) was also one of the grounds of the opposition brought by Greenpeace against the grant of the patent in *T 356/93 PLANT GENETIC SYSTEMS/Glutamine synthetase inhibitors* [1995] EPOR 357. The aim of the invention was to develop plants and seeds which were resistant to a particular class of herbicide. This was achieved by integrating into their genome the DNA coding for a protein which neutralized the effect of the weed-killers. The patent contained both process claims (how the plant genome was modified) and product claims to the corresponding plant cells and eventual plants. Greenpeace's opposition was based on three interrelated arguments, namely: that plants were part of the 'common heritage' of mankind and should be available to all without restrictions; that the Opposition Division had failed to carry out the balancing exercise required by *HARVARD*, underestimating the harm to the environment caused by the eventual release of herbicide-resistant plants; and that public opinion (which was against the patenting of genetically engineered plants because it was immoral) had been ignored. Each of these arguments was dismissed. Although the protection of the environment fell within the concept of *ordre public*, plant biotechnology could not be regarded as being any more contrary to morality than traditional selective breeding, and the subject matter of the patent did not concern activities which were wrong as such in the light of conventionally accepted standards of conduct of European culture. Revocation of a patent under Art. 53(a) on the grounds of a serious threat to the environment should only occur if there was sufficient evidence of harm, which here had not been made out. The Board was sceptical of the value of opinion polls, which may not be truly reflective of society, especially if the questions are weighted, and felt that it did not have the authority to carry out those tasks which properly belonged to the regulatory authorities.

> ### T 0272/95 HOWARD FLOREY/Relaxin [2002] EPOR
>
> In *HOWARD FLOREY/Relaxin*, an opposition was brought, inter alia, under Art. 53(a) by the Green Party in the European Parliament against the grant of the patent claiming the relaxin gene. Several arguments were deployed, namely that as the invention depended on the taking of tissue from a pregnant woman, it was contrary to human dignity to make use of the particular

condition (pregnancy) to make a profit; that such conduct amounted to slavery and infringed the right to self-determination; and that the patenting of genes amounted to the patenting of life, which was immoral. Again, the opposition was dismissed. The EPO Opposition Division stated that the function of Art. 53(a) was to ensure that patents would not be granted for inventions which 'would be universally regarded as outrageous' and reiterated that the exception to patentability was to be narrowly construed. It pointed out that many useful products over the years have been produced from human tissue and that the instant case was no different in that consent had been freely given before removing the sample. In any case, once the first sample had been obtained, it could be synthetically reproduced ad infinitum, without the need to obtain further samples. The slavery argument was rebutted by pointing out the negative nature of the patent right, such that it did not confer any right to any particular human individuals, so that the right to self-determination was not affected. Finally, and curtly, the Opposition Division pointed out that the patent did not entail the patenting of life:

> It is worth pointing out that DNA is not 'life', but a chemical substance which carries genetic information and can be used as an intermediate in the production of proteins which may be medically useful. The patenting of a single human gene has nothing to do with the patenting of human life. Even if every gene in the human genome were cloned (and possibly patented), it would be impossible to reconstitute a human being from the sum of its genes.

One important decision which goes against this trend is that of the Enlarged Board of Appeal in *G 2/06 WARF/Stem Cells* [2009] EPOR 129. The patent contained a series of claims involving the use of human embryonic stem cells (hESCs). Combining Art. 53(a) with the text of the Implementing Regulations derived from Art. 6(2) of the Biotech Directive, the Board held that it was not possible to grant a patent for an invention which *necessarily* involved the use and destruction of human embryos from which the stem cells were derived. It was not the fact of the patenting itself which was contrary to *ordre public*, rather it was the *performing* of the invention which included a step which contravened that principle. However, it stressed that the decision did not affect the patentability in general of inventions relating to hESCs, but only those involving the destruction of embryos.

Case C-34/10 *Oliver Brüstle v Greenpeace eV* [2011] ECR I-9821

The use of hESCs has also been considered by the CJEU in Case C-34/10 *Oliver Brüstle v Greenpeace eV* [2011] ECR I-9821. The issue was whether the patent (involving a treatment for Parkinson's disease) was invalid under Art. 6(2). The CJEU ruled that 'human embryo' must be understood in a wide sense, agreeing with the Advocate General that a fertilized egg must be regarded as a human embryo. Likewise, the prohibition in Art. 6(2)(c) on the use of embryos for commercial purposes had to be given a wide meaning, regardless of whether or not the use of the embryo is referred to in the patent and regardless of how long ago the originating embryo was destroyed. The ruling thus goes far beyond that of the EPO in WARF/Stem Cells and has been much criticized, not least because it arguably had the effect of undermining the European biotech industry *viz.* US competitors (E. Bonadio, 'Biotech Patents and Morality after Brüstle' [2012] 34(10) *European Intellectual Property Review* 433–443).

The CJEU made a further ruling in Case C-364/13 *International Stem Cell Corporation v Comptroller General of Patent* (a reference from the Patents Court in *International Stem Cell Corporation v Comptroller General of Patents* [2013] EWHC 807 (Ch)). The CJEU decided that an 'embryo' that includes unfertilized human ova whose division and further development have been stimulated by parthenogenesis, and which, in contrast to fertilized ova, contain only pluripotent cells and are incapable of developing into human beings, is not a 'human embryo' for the purposes of the exception.

17.4.3.2 Conclusions

The inevitable outcome of the EPO decisions is that any challenge to a patent under Art. 53(a) will only succeed in the most extreme case. Examples include where, as the Opposition Division in *HOWARD FLOREY* said, the invention is 'outrageous', or where the claims of the patent fall squarely within the text of the Implementing Regulations as in *WARF*. Further, the previously discussed cases display a subtle shift of emphasis. The initial requirement in *HARVARD* was that the Tribunal carry out a balancing exercise. However, in *PLANT GENETIC SYSTEMS* and *HOWARD FLOREY* the burden of proof was placed on the opponent of the patent to show that the invention is likely to cause serious harm. No regard is to be had to public opinion. That this attitude towards public opinion is now well entrenched is evidenced by the decision of the Opposition Division concerning the patenting of animals, *LELAND STANFORD/Modified Animal* [2002] EPOR 16. The case did not involve a genetically modified animal; instead, the animal had been subjected to xenotransplantation in order to provide a model for HIV infection. The Opposition Division said that so long as a claimed invention has a legitimate use, it is not the role of the EPO to act as a moral censor—simply because technology is perceived as controversial is not a bar to its patentability. Thus, the principle of balancing the benefits to society against harm to the animal was reiterated, but the onus was placed on those challenging the patent to adduce evidence of 'conclusively documented hazards'. Yet, even then it was not for the EPO to monitor such risks: that was for the regulatory authorities charged with overseeing research and medical practice. The current view appears to be that patent law ought not regulate research. The one major exception to this appears to be when the invention concerns a human embryo, within the definition of the Biotech Directive, in accordance with the *Brüstle* case.

 Pause for reflection

How convincing do you find the EPO's statement that patent law does not exist to regulate research? Is it right that there are apparently different standards for human and animal life?

17.4.4 Animal and plant varieties and biological processes

The exclusion in Art. 53(b) EPC (found in Patents Act 1977 Sch. A2, para 3(f)) denies patent protection for any variety of animal or plant or any essentially biological process for the production of animals or plants, not being a microbiological or other technical process or the product of such a process (this wording may be compared with that of the Biotech Directive Art. 4 and with TRIPS Art. 27(3)(b)).

Under this exception, morality aside, the issue is whether it is possible to patent something found in nature. The exception raises yet again the difference between a discovery and its practical application, something we discussed earlier in the chapter with respect to gene patents in Europe, the USA, and Australia. The traditional analysis is that there is a clear distinction, on the one hand, between something found in nature (which is not patentable) and, on the other, two potential innovations: (a) a process for reproducing that substance in the laboratory; and (b) the synthetic equivalent of that substance resulting from the process. The two latter are patentable, subject to novelty and inventive step being satisfied: *per* Lord Wilberforce in *Re American Cyanamid (Dann's) Patent* [1971] RPC 425; and *American Cyanamid v Berk* [1976] RPC 231. This principle is now set out in Arts 3(2) and 5(2) of the Biotech Directive, which draw a contrast between the identification and isolation of living matter.

Article 53(b) contains four separate elements. As with the list of excluded subject matter in Art. 52(2), whether a patent falls within the exception depends on the wording of the claims. The patentee is free to try to word the specification in such a way that the statutory exceptions are avoided.

17.4.4.1 Animal varieties

The first prohibition is against the patenting of animal varieties. The EPO has explained that there is a taxonomy (i.e. system of classification) implicit in the exclusion: animals in general; animal species; varieties within that species. Hence a genetically engineered mouse is not an animal variety, but an animal species (rodents) and so potentially patentable: *HARVARD*. In many respects, it seems counter-intuitive that animal varieties cannot be patented but animals can. Nonetheless, this is the approach taken by the EPO in *HARVARD* and in the case of *LELAND STANFORD*. In *LELAND*, the Opposition Division repeated the point that claims directed to a taxonomic group higher than an animal variety are patentable; and further, that this is in accordance with Art. 4(2) of the Biotech Directive ('inventions which concern plants or animals shall be patentable if the technical feasibility of the invention is *not confined* to a particular plant or animal variety') (emphasis supplied).

17.4.4.2 Plant varieties

The same thinking applies to the second element, plant varieties. However, unlike the animal variety exception, there is a specific reason why plant varieties cannot be patented, and that is because there is an alternative legal mechanism for protecting plant varieties, under the International Convention for the Protection of New Varieties of Plants 1961, as amended in 1991 (the 'UPOV Convention'). There is in place both a regional system of obtaining plant variety protection (Council Regulation (EC) 2100/94 of 27 July 1994 on Community Plant Variety Rights [1994] OJ L 227/1) and a national system (the Plant Varieties Act 1997).

As with animal varieties, the issue is to be decided by interpreting the claims. It must be determined whether the patentee has claimed plants generally or a specific plant variety. Only the latter will fall within the exception. Hence, in *T 320/87 LUBRIZOL/ Hybrid plants* [1990] EPOR 173 it was held that hybrid plants and their seeds were not a 'plant variety' because they did not comply with the definition of a variety. In *PLANT GENETIC SYSTEMS* it was held that genetically modified tobacco plants which were herbicide resistant were not a plant variety. As with the prohibition on patenting animal varieties, the legislative provision contains an implicit taxonomy, whereby a plant variety is the lowest level of the classification system.

The EPO Enlarged Board of Appeal revisited the plant variety exclusion in *G 1/98 NOVARTIS/Transgenic plant* [2000] EPOR 303. One of the questions referred to it was whether a claim which relates to plants, but which does not identify specific varieties, can obviate the prohibition on patenting plant varieties. The Board stated that there was no indication in Art. 53 that patent protection should not be available in respect of matter not covered by the UPOV Convention. The extent of the exclusion from patentability therefore matches the availability of plant variety protection. Whether a claim was in respect of a plant variety depends on its substance. Substance is determined by identifying the underlying invention and the breadth of its application. In the relevant case, the invention could be carried out by modifying plants which might, or might not be, varieties. The genetic modification effected by the claimed process did not necessarily result in a plant variety, and so was not excluded. Further, a claim to a *process* for modifying plants could not be a claim to a plant variety. However, if a claim was in substance for a plant variety (which would be a product claim), it mattered not by what technical means that variety had been produced. Again, it may be noted that Art. 4(2) of the Biotech Directive maintains the distinction between plants in general and plant varieties.

 Pause for reflection

Is the EPO's argument that there is a system of classification which means that only specific varieties of plants and animals cannot be patented logical?

17.4.4.3 Biological processes

The final prohibition is against patenting essentially biological processes. The exception contemplates the difference between technical intervention and traditional cross-breeding methods: the latter are not patentable. According to the EPO in *LUBRIZOL*, whether or not a process is 'essentially biological' has to be judged by the essence of the invention, taking into account the totality of human intervention and its impact on the result achieved. The presence of human intervention is not by itself sufficient to guarantee that the invention falls outside the exception. Human interference may mean that the process is not 'purely biological', but not actually contribute anything of substance to the invention. In *LUBRIZOL*, the human intervention was quite different from that used in classical breeders' processes and so was not essentially biological. Likewise, in *HARVARD*, the EPO felt that the introduction of the oncogene sequence into the mouse cells did not involve an essentially biological process. In *PLANT GENETIC SYSTEMS* it was decided that the process as a whole did not fall within the Art. 53(b) exclusion because the steps taken were 'essentially technical' and could not occur without human intervention.

By contrast, in *PLANT BIOSCIENCE/Broccoli* and *STATE OF ISRAEL/Tomatoes* [2011] EPOR 247, the Enlarged Board of Appeal concluded that a non-microbiological process for the production of plants which consisted of sexually crossing the whole genomes of plants and of subsequently selecting from them was in principle excluded from patentability as being 'essentially biological'. The process did not escape the exclusion of Art. 53(b) EPC merely because it contained a technical step which assisted the performance of crossing and selecting plants.

17.4.4.4 Microbiological processes

The wording of Art. 53(b) creates an exception to the exception, in that microbiological processes are deemed patentable. The only cases which have discussed the meaning of 'microbiological processes' are *PLANT GENETIC SYSTEMS* and *NOVARTIS*. In the former, the Board of Appeal chose to explain that the term microbiological 'qualifies technical activities in which direct use is made of micro-organisms'. In the latter, the EPO agreed that it was tempting to conclude that genetic modification was a microbiological process within the meaning of Art. 53(b), but then added that the two were not identical. 'Microbiological processes', as used in Art. 53(b), was synonymous with processes using micro-organisms which were different from the parts of living beings used for the genetic modification of plants. Genetically modified plants were not to be treated as the product of a microbiological process, because otherwise this would provide a back door means to protecting plant varieties, and give the producers of such plant varieties a privileged position relative to breeders of plant varieties resulting from traditional breeding.

17.4.4.5 Patenting biotechnology: the ethical debate

The role which ethics should play in the decision-making processes of patent offices has provoked considerable debate. Authors such as Crespi ('Biotechnology Patenting: the Wicked Animal Must Defend Itself' [1995] *EIPR* 431 and 'Patenting and Ethics—a Dubious Connection' [2003] 85 *JPTOS* 31) maintain that the patent system is ethically neutral. Further, many of the emotive arguments (Crespi calls them 'blood-curdling') demanding that patent offices take greater account of ethical principles confuse a number of points. Crespi maintains that the issues should be separated as follows:

- objections to patents themselves (reminiscent of the anti-patent debate of the 19th century);
- objections to patents for certain types of inventions, such as gene patents. In particular, the argument goes, 'genes are special' and should be treated differently from other substances because of their inalienable nature, as part of the 'heritage of mankind';
- objections to gene patents because genes are discoveries not inventions; and
- objections to gene patents because genes 'are essentially just information' and hence different from other chemical compounds.

As Crespi points out, all of these arguments can, in principle, be refuted by a proper understanding of the technology and of patent law itself (for example, the difference between a discovery and an invention discussed earlier), as well as of the nature of the patent monopoly as a negative right to stop others.

By contrast, writers such as Drahos ('Biotechnology Patents, Markets and Morality' [1999] 21(9) *EIPR* 441) contend that the creation, operation, and interpretation of the patent system are linked to moral standards. The patent community (i.e. patent attorneys and administrators) take the view that morality has little to do with the grant of patents, inspired no doubt by the decision of the US Supreme Court in *Diamond v Chakrabarty* (1980) 447 US 303 to the effect that it was for Congress not the courts to decide on the ethics of patenting living matter. Nevertheless, the strength of pro-patenting attitudes, the increasing harmonization of global patent law (driven by the demands of technology-exporting countries), and the fear of the major patent offices (the US, Japan, and the EPO) that weakening the patent system will undermine economic growth and prosperity, must be balanced by taking into account the values and attitudes of society.

There is, in fact, a third argument which can be made (see H.E. Norman, 'Patenting Biotechnology: A Case of Legal Abstentionism?' [2002] 14 *ELM* 278). This is to the effect that if the criteria for patentability are strictly applied (particularly inventive step, industrial applicability, and sufficiency) then patent law itself is more than adequate to deal with the perceived threat of biotechnological inventions.

 Pause for reflection

Would it be possible to challenge Siva's invention on the basis of any of the above exclusions?

17.4.5 Methods of treatment

The methods of treatment exception comprises both surgery and therapy (whether on the human or animal body) and methods of diagnosis. The three alternative exclusions are cumulative, so that the claimed method must be neither a therapeutic nor a surgical nor a diagnostic one: *G 1/07 MEDI-PHYSICS/Treatment by surgery* [2010] EPOR 219.

The policy reason why methods of treatment cannot be patented is simply that medical or veterinary practitioners should not be hindered in the conduct of their professional practice by patent protection: *MEDI-PHYSICS*. Other jurisdictions may permit the patenting of methods of treatment, as the TRIPs Agreement allows Contracting States the option of whether or not to allow such patents. As an example, Australia permits the granting of such patents: *Anaesthetic Supplies Pty Ltd v Rescare Ltd* (1994) 122 ALR 141. The need to protect medical or veterinary practitioners from patent litigation can be met (as in the USA) by providing a specific defence to infringement rather than prohibiting the patenting of the particular method, as does the EPC.

17.4.5.1 UK case law

It has been held under the 1977 Act that the phrase 'method of treatment' is to be given a wide interpretation, so that it would include a system of immunization (*Unilever (Davis') Application* [1983] RPC 219). One extreme United Kingdom decision is *Re Stafford-Miller Ltd's Application* [1984] FSR 258, where the judge upheld a method of killing ectoparasites on humans as patentable, a patent application described as being 'on the absolute frontier of the law'.

17.4.5.2 EPO case law

Despite the normal rule of construction that exclusions should be narrowly interpreted, the EPO has interpreted the method of treatment exception broadly, because of its underlying policy: *MEDI-PHYSICS*. In *T 383/03 THE GENERAL HOSPITAL CORP/Hair removal method* [2005] EPOR 357 it was said that 'treatment' could be defined as any non-insignificant physical or psychic intervention performed directly by one human being (who need not be a medical practitioner) on a human being or animal using the means or methods of medical science.

Each of the elements in the exception has been given a wide definition. 'Therapy' was said in *T 58/87 SALMINEN/Pigs III* [1989] EPOR 125 to cover any non-surgical treatment which was designed to cure, alleviate, remove, or lessen the symptoms of, or prevent or reduce the possibility of, contracting any malfunction. In *T 81/84 RORER/Dysmenorrhoea* [1988] EPOR 297 the EPO declared that it was undesirable to distinguish between healing or cure and relief. Further, the treatment does not have to be administered personally by a doctor or vet (*T 116/85 WELLCOME/Pigs I* [1988] EPOR 1; *T 19/86 DUPHAR/Pigs II* [1989] EPOR 10) and indeed can be administered by the patient themselves (*T 964/99 CYGNUS/Device and method for sampling substances* [2002] EPOR 272).

Nevertheless, some early cases (namely *T 144/83 DU PONT/Appetite suppressant* [1987] EPOR 6 and *T 36/83 ROUSSEL-UCLAF/Thenoyl peroxide* [1987] EPOR 1) allowed claims for cosmetic treatment. The correctness of these decisions has been questioned. However, in *T 383/03 THE GENERAL HOSPITAL CORP/Hair removal method*, the EPO allowed a patent for removing hair by optical radiation on the ground that it resulted in an aesthetic improvement of the person even though excess hair can be a symptom of a disease. This case was itself doubted in *MEDI-PHYSICS*.

In relation to 'surgery', the EPO in *T 182/90 SEE-SHELL/Bloodflow* [1994] EPOR 320 pointed out that over the years the term has undergone a change in meaning, so that today surgery can be used for non-curative as well as curative treatment. Nevertheless, a broad meaning should be given, covering both non-invasive and invasive procedures and regardless of the mechanism of the intervention (i.e. whether this was mechanical, electrical, thermal, or chemical). In *MEDI-PHYSICS*, the Enlarged Board of Appeal added that where the invention comprised a number of steps (as here, injecting a special gas into the heart so that a scanner could take clearer pictures of the patient's blood flow), the fact that just one of the steps involved a surgical procedure meant that the whole claim was caught by the Art. 53(c) exclusion. The Board, however, declined to provide a definition of surgery which would once and for all delimit the exact boundaries of the concept.

The term 'diagnosis' was considered by the Enlarged Board of Appeal in *G 1/04 CYGNUS/Diagnostic methods* [2006] EPOR 161. It said that if a claim included features relating to the diagnosis for curative purposes representing deductive decision-making as an intellectual exercise, the preceding steps taken in making such a diagnosis, and the specific interactions with the human or animal body which occur when carrying these out, it would be caught by the wording of Art. 53(c). Further, whether a method was a diagnostic method did not depend on the presence of a medical or veterinary practitioner as long as there was some interaction with a human or animal body.

17.4.5.3 The exceptions to methods of treatment

Section 4A(2) Patents Act 1977 (repeating the wording of Art. 53(c) EPC) provides in effect that any substance used in a method of treatment is patentable. The provision is therefore directed to new and inventive substances. This means that not just pharmaceutical products are patentable but so too is equipment which carries out treatment or diagnosis: *T 426/89 SIEMENS/Pacemaker* [1992] EPOR 149.

But what if there is a *known* substance which can be used in a method of treatment? Section 4A(3), based on Art. 54(4) EPC 2000, provides that where a known substance (for example, egg shells) is used for the first time in a method of treatment (a 'first medical use'), it can be patented for use in that method of treatment even though the substance itself is not new. Novelty is 'borrowed' from its new use, even though the use itself (the method of treatment) cannot be patented. The wording of the claims, however, must be such that the monopoly is limited to the particular use to which the known substance is to be put (i.e. it must be a purpose-limited product claim).

EPO case law extended this to cover *second and subsequent medical uses* (provided such uses were new and inventive): *G5/83 EISAI/Second medical indication*. The case has now been put on a statutory basis by Art. 54(5) EPC 2000, reflected in s. 4A(4) Patents Act 1977. Although UK courts were initially reluctant to recognize the principle (see *Wyeth/ Schering's Applications* [1985] RPC 545), it is now accepted. An example of a successful second medical use patent is that in *American Home Products Corp v Novartis Pharmaceuticals UK Ltd* [2001] RPC 159, where the substance rapamycin, used initially as an anti-fungal agent, was found to be beneficial in transplant surgery. The patent for this unexpected second therapeutic use was upheld. By contrast, where a naturally occurring substance (such as taxol, derived from the yew tree, which is used in treating cancer) had been the subject of a patent, it was not possible to obtain a further patent after research had identified its optimum dosage, as this was simply a clarification of the preferred method of treatment: *Bristol-Myers Squibb Company v Baker Norton Pharmaceuticals Inc* [2001] RPC 1. However, both the Court of Appeal and the Enlarged Board of the EPO have since stated that there is nothing in principle to stop the patenting of a dosage régime where this was new and not directed to a method of treatment: *Actavis UK Ltd v Merck & Co Inc* [2009] 1 WLR 1186; *G 2/08 ABBOTT RESPIRATORY/Dosage régime* [2010] EPOR 262. Thus the new use need not be the treatment of a different disease (*ABBOTT RESPIRATORY* at [5.10.3]).

Where the principle in *EISAI* is to be utilized, it used to be the law that the specification had to contain so-called 'Swiss form' claims, namely 'use of X for the manufacture of a medicament for treatment of Y'. The latest revisions to the EPC remove that requirement, so that it will now be possible to have a claim which reads 'Substance X for use in treatment of disease Y' (see the Explanatory Notes to the Patents Act 2004 and the observations of the Enlarged Board of Appeal in *ABBOTT RESPIRATORY*). Again, this is a purpose-limited product claim.

17.4.6 Conclusions

To summarize this complex area the following propositions can be made:

- methods of treatment are not patentable under EPC Art. 53(c), s. 4A(1) Patents Act 1977, for public policy reasons;

- new substances or equipment used in such treatments are patentable (EPC Art. 53(c), s. 4A(2) Patents Act);
- known substances having a first medical use are patentable under EPC Art. 54(4), s. 4A(3) Patents Act, novelty being found in the new use (this would be have to be in the form of a purpose-limited product claim, e.g. 'substance x for use as a treatment for y'); and
- known substances having a second medical use are patentable under EPC Art. 54(5), s. 4A(4) Patents Act, novelty residing in the subsequent (unexpected) therapeutic use (this would have to be again as a purpose-limited product claim).

 Pause for reflection

Is the availability of patent protection for the first and second medical use of a known substance logical? How can this be related to the justification for the patent monopoly we considered in chapter 15?

17.5 Novelty

17.5.1 Overview of the statutory provisions

Now that we have considered the issue of subject matter, we can move on to the requirement of novelty, as set out in s. 2 Patents Act 1977, based on Art. 54 EPC. Section 2(1) contains the fundamental statement of principle that an invention shall be taken to be new if it does not form part of the state of the art. Section 2(2) explains what is meant by 'state of the art', that is, all matter which has at any time before the priority date of the invention been made available to the public, whether in the UK or elsewhere.

The key word in both subsections is the word 'invention'. An invention is a piece of information (*per* Lord Hoffmann in *Merrell Dow v Norton* [1996] RPC 76 at p. 86), so making matter available to the public under s. 2(2) requires communication or disclosure. The disclosure contemplated by s. 2(2) corresponds with the requirement of disclosure by the patentee for the purposes of sufficiency under s. 14(3) Patents Act 1977. Such disclosures are sometimes referred to in the cases as 'the teaching' of the prior art and 'the teaching' of the patent respectively.

Two other provisions in s. 2 require elaboration. Section 2(3) is intended to deal with the problem of 'double patenting', i.e. where two rival patentees are in a race to the patent office door, as occurred, albeit with differing outcomes, in *Re Asahi KKK's Patent* [1991] RPC 485 and *Synthon BV v Smithkline Beecham plc* [2006] RPC 323. The point to remember when reading s. 2(3) is that the UK and European patent systems are based on the principle of 'first to file', rather than 'first to invent'. This means that the first inventor to file will receive priority, even if the same invention was actually conceived by another inventor who simply did not file the patent in time. The US had a 'first to invent' system until the America Invents Act 2012 facilitated a switch to first to file.

Section 2(3) of the 1977 Act provides that the state of the art includes information contained in an earlier filed, but later published, patent, provided that the relevant information is in both the filed, and the published, version of the first patent, and that the first patent's priority date falls before that of the second patent. In other words, it is the filing date and priority date that are crucial, not the publication date. This can be harsh for an inventor who files a patent application after a rival inventor files for her own patent on the same or similar technology. The earlier filing may destroy the novelty of the later one as it will be included in the state of the art, even though the subsequent inventor was, at time of filing, not aware the earlier filing existed.

 Pause for reflection

In line with Patents Act 1977 s. 2(3), information in Patent A, although unknown when Patent B is filed, becomes part of the prior art when published, as the information is deemed to be available to the public as of the filing date of Patent A.

The net result is that the applicant for the second patent may find that their invention lacks novelty because of the contents of another patent application which was unknown at the time of filing.

Siva, having searched academic journals and journalistic articles, is unaware of anyone else who has created a solar air pump; is this sufficient as a search, or what else would you advise Siva to do when considering prior art?

Next, s. 2(4) (based on EPC Art. 55) contains an exception in respect of two categories of communication, but only if these occurred during the period of six months before the priority date of the patent. These are: information disclosed in breach of confidence; and display of the invention at an international exhibition. Provided the requirements of the section are met, the novelty of the patent is preserved.

17.5.2 Overview of the issues

Anticipation is one of the key technical words of patent law. Put simply, it means that if the prior art matches the claims the invention will have been anticipated—it will not be novel—and thus will not be patentable. For anticipation to be shown the prior art has to fall within the scope of the claim, so contain all the elements, but it doesn't have to cover the whole ground covered by the claim, just overlap with it.

Anticipation occurs where the prior art contains an enabling disclosure. This composite phrase comprises two separate issues which must be dealt with sequentially, namely disclosure and enablement: *Synthon BV v Smithkline Beecham plc, per* Lord Hoffmann at [19–33] and Lord Walker at [58]. Consequently, when considering whether a patent passes the test of novelty, what has to be decided is:

- whether the information was accessible (potentially rather than actually) by any member of the public (even one person) without any fetter of confidentiality; and if so;

- whether that information contained an enabling disclosure such that the skilled addressee, armed with the prior art, could perform the invention without undue burden.

What amounts to the prior art requires an understanding of how information can be made available. Information is usually supplied through documents, but it can be obtained by the supply of goods, the use of an item, or its demonstration. In every case, however, the question to be asked is what would the skilled addressee understand from that information? As with other areas of patent law, novelty is determined objectively from the viewpoint of the skilled addressee, possessed of the appropriate qualifications, practical experience, and common general knowledge. Whether the prior art contains an enabling disclosure depends on a comparison through the eyes of the skilled addressee of each claim of the patent with *each individual* item of prior art. Separate pieces of prior art cannot be taken together for the purpose of anticipation unless they clearly cross-refer to each other. If the item of prior art does not contain *all* the elements (or integers) of a claim, then the claim is valid for novelty (but may still be subject to attack for lack of inventive step as we will discuss below). The importance of the patent's claims should be noted: it is the claims which are individually compared with the prior art. It is possible for one or more claims in a patent to be struck down for lack of novelty, but for other claims to survive (although they may lack validity for other reasons).

17.5.3 Impact of the 1977 Act

In relation to the definition of the 'state of the art' in s. 2(2), the 1977 Act changed the previous law in two respects.

17.5.3.1 Worldwide novelty

Information found anywhere in the world is relevant. Section 2(2) contains the phrase 'in the United Kingdom *or elsewhere*' (emphasis supplied). There is therefore a change from relative to absolute novelty.

17.5.3.2 Prior use

The 1977 Act requires that the information be 'made available to the public'. The result is that under the 1977 Act *all* forms of prior art must contain an enabling disclosure: *Re Asahi KKK's Patent* [1991] RPC 485, confirming a trio of first instance decisions, *Genentech Inc's (Human Growth Hormone) Patent* [1989] RPC 613, *Pall v Bedford Hydraulics* [1990] FSR 329 and *Quantel v Spaceward Microsystems*. However, as we shall see in the next chapter, there is a defence to patent infringement of prior use, found in s. 64 1977 Act.

The thinking on the availability of prior art in *Re Asahi KKK's Patent* is entirely consistent with the case law of the EPO. In *G 1/92 Availability to the Public* [1993] EPOR 241, the Enlarged Board of Appeal noted that Art. 54(2) EPC does not make any distinction between the different means by which information is made available to the public, so that information deriving from use is governed by the same conditions as information disclosed by oral or written **description**. The Board went on to say that an essential purpose of the prior art's teaching is to enable the person skilled in the art to manufacture or use a given product by applying such teaching. Where such teaching results from a product put on the market, if it is possible for that person to discover the composition or the internal structure of the product *and to reproduce it without undue burden* (original emphasis), then both the product and its composition or internal structure become part of the state of the art.

17.5.4 The meaning of 'the public'

The meaning of 'the public' in s. 2 was explained by Aldous J in *PLG Research Ltd v Ardon* at p. 226 as follows:

> Section 2 uses the words 'made available to the public' . . . to form part of the state of the art, the information given by the use must have been made available to at least one member of the public who was free in law and equity to use it. (emphasis supplied)

This statement makes clear two things: 'the public' can consist of just one person; and the key distinguishing characteristic of the recipient of the information is that they must not be bound by confidentiality. Hence, information which is confidential cannot destroy novelty. An example is the EPO case *T 245/88 UNION CARBIDE/Atmospheric Vaporizer* [1991] EPOR 373: novelty was held not to have been destroyed where an invention located on private property (a shipyard) was viewed through a fence. Further, even if the invention had been publicly available, the EPO was not convinced that the skilled addressee would have been able to see all the relevant details, in other words, there had not been an enabling disclosure. Another example of confidentiality protecting novelty is *Re Gallay* [1959] RPC 141, where a duty of secrecy was implied as a contract term in the case of a joint venture. However, in *Re Dalrymple* [1957] RPC 449, the large number of members in a trade association meant that the fact the word 'confidential' was stamped on the front of a document circulated to all had no effect.

 Pause for reflection

In Siva's case, is there any suggestion that someone could have observed what she was doing to the extent that the invention would be 'taught' to the observer? What makes this unlikely?

17.5.5 Anticipation by prior use

Prior use of a later claimed invention may be by a third party of whom the patentee is unaware. This occurred in *Fomento v Mentmore* [1956] RPC 87, where an improved type of ballpoint pen was used by a Canadian visitor to a village shop in England; and, famously, in *Windsurfing International Inc v Tabur Marine* [1985] RPC 59, where a 12-year-old boy built and sailed his home-made sailboard some years before the claimant filed its United Kingdom patent.

Equally, the prior use may be by a competitor, as happened in *Bristol-Myers Co (Johnson's) Application*—the opponents to the patent application had accidentally discovered the same substance, ampicillin, in their laboratories, but being unaware of its properties had put the substance to one side. Finally, of course, the prior use may be by the patentee themselves. This occurred in a pre-1977 Act case, *WL Gore v Kimal* [RPC] 137, where samples were supplied to customers before the patent was filed. Similarly, if the patented device is demonstrated in public—for instance, at a trade show—this will destroy novelty: *Wheatley's Application* [1985] RPC 91. But what if the disclosure occurs not in a public place but on private premises where members of the public (albeit un-skilled people) are present and can examine the device if they wished? In *Folding Attic Stairs Ltd v The Loft Stairs Company Ltd* [2009] FSR 887, Peter Prescott QC thought that it was the *place* of disclosure which mattered, so that there is a significant difference between public and private premises. The visitors to the factory would not have appre-ciated what they had seen, but even if they had, this would not have anticipated claim 1 of the patent which was for the manufacturing process.

17.5.6 Anticipation through documents

Documentary prior art will include earlier patents, such as occurred in two House of Lords decisions we encountered earlier—*Re Asahi KKK's Patent* and *Merrell Dow v Norton*. The only issue in both cases was whether the description of the substance in an earlier patent amounted to an enabling disclosure. In *Asahi*, it was held that the mere identifi-cation of a particular substance (a polypeptide) did not teach the skilled addressee how to replicate it in the laboratory. Thus, there was no enabling disclosure, and novelty was not defeated. By contrast, in *Merrell Dow* the earlier patent gave instructions which, if followed by the skilled addressee, would have led inevitably to the production of the later-claimed substance. This meant that there had indeed been an enabling disclo-sure—novelty had been defeated.

Documentary prior art may also include photographs (*Van der Lely v Bamfords Ltd* [1963] RPC 61); sales leaflets (*Monsanto (Brignac's) Application* [1971] RPC 153); books and magazines as long as they *could* have been read by a member of the public even if no one actually did so (*Lang v Gisbourne* (1862) 31 Beav 133, *Bristol Myers Application* [1969] RPC 146); and information in a library as long as the public have access to it (*Harris v Rothwell* (1887) 35 Ch D 416). A company's private research library may not be accessible by the public, so that documents stored there do not amount to prior art: *Re Tecalemit* [1967] FSR 387, *Re Bakelite* [1967] FSR 582.

17.5.7 The test for enablement

The test for enabling disclosure is to be found in *General Tire v Firestone* [1972] RPC 457 which is generally endorsed by modern cases as being the correct statement on antici-pation, even though in that case the Court of Appeal was only dealing with anticipation through documentary disclosure. Sachs LJ put forward a number of interchangeable tests which can be used in order to decide whether there has been anticipation. First, he suggested, the court should ask the question 'would the prior use infringe if carried out today?' (referred to as 'the infringement test'). The second question to be posed is whether 'the claimed subject matter is derivable directly and unambiguously from the [prior] publication?' The third test is to enquire whether 'the earlier material point[ed] inevitably to the later invention?' Another useful aspect of Sachs LJ's judgment is that he draws a distinction between a 'signpost' and a 'flag-post' contained (metaphorically speaking) in the prior art. A 'signpost' (that is, a general indication which points out one of the possible ways to achieve the later invention) will not suffice to destroy nov-elty; only if the prior art 'plants the flag' at the precise spot claimed by the patentee will there be anticipation.

Interestingly, the House of Lords, although endorsing *General Tire v Firestone* on two separate occasions, has changed its mind about which of the above three tests is to be preferred (without explicitly distinguishing or overruling its own earlier decision). In *Merrell Dow v Norton*, Lord Hoffmann (at p. 86), when discussing anticipation by use, indicated that the infringement test should be avoided:

> The 1977 Act therefore introduced a substantial qualification into the old principle that a patent cannot be used to stop someone doing what he has done before. If the previous use was secret or uninformative, then subject to section 64, it can. Likewise, a gap has opened up between the tests for infringement and anticipation. Acts done secretly or without knowledge of the relevant facts, which would amount to infringement after the grant of the patent, will not count as anticipations before.

The facts of this important case—*Merrell Dow v Norton* [1996] RPC 76—were as follows: the claimant had previously obtained patent protection for terfenadine, a substance used to treat hay fever; but it was later (unexpectedly) discovered that the human body converted terfenadine into an acid metabolite (i.e. the product of a metabolic reaction) and so a second patent was obtained for the acid metabolite. Their Lordships held that the clinical trials conducted by the patentee before the second patent was filed did not anticipate it, because there was no way that patients knew what was going on inside their bodies once the pharmaceutical was swallowed. There was no public information which would enable anyone to work the invention. However, the second patent was anticipated by the information contained in the first patent, because 'the terfenadine specification teaches that the ingestion of terfenadine will produce a chemical reaction in the body and for the purposes of working the invention in this form, this is a sufficient description of the making of the acid metabolite. Under the description the acid metabolite was part of the state of the art' (per Lord Hoffmann at p. 91).

In *Synthon BV v Smithkline Beecham plc*, however, Lord Hoffmann (at [22]) adopted the infringement test from *General Tire*, although he was dealing specifically with documentary disclosure by a prior patent in the context of s. 2(3) Patents Act 1977, rather than anticipation by use (as in *Merrell Dow*). An unusual factor in the case was that the earlier patent contained incorrect information. At first instance Jacob J (with whom the Court of Appeal later disagreed) considered that that the skilled addressee, armed with common general knowledge, would have done further experiments to achieve the correct results and so make the substance claimed in the second patent, despite starting off with the incorrect information. In restoring Jacob J's decision at the House of Lords level, Lord Hoffmann quoted from Lord Westbury in *Hills v Evans* (1862) 31 LJ Ch 457:

> [T]he antecedent statement must be such that a person of ordinary knowledge of the subject would at once perceive, understand and be able practically to apply the discovery without the necessity for making further experiments and gaining further information before the information can be made useful. If something remains to be ascertained which is necessary for the useful application of the discovery, that affords sufficient room for another valid patent.

Lord Hoffmann went on to state that the requirements of disclosure and enablement must be kept distinct (which is incontrovertible). He then declared that the *General Tire* infringement test was the appropriate one to be used to determine whether there had been disclosure (when arguably it, and the other authorities relied on by Lord

Hoffmann, were all concerned with the issue of enablement). Lord Hoffmann did not elaborate on why he had changed his mind since *Merrell Dow* about the suitability of the infringement test. The net result of the two cases, however, is that a gap may have opened up between the treatment of anticipation by use and anticipation by disclosure, even though both statute and EPO case law treat them identically.

 Pause for reflection

Is it possible to reconcile Lord Hoffmann's views in *Merrell Dow v Norton* with his speech in *Synthon*?

Looking again at the facts of Siva's scenario and from the information available, do you consider Siva's invention to be novel? Is it likely there could have been an enabling disclosure to the public that might mean her invention has been anticipated?

Several cases neatly illustrate the need for an enabling disclosure in the case of prior use. All show the key issue is whether the skilled addressee, had they been present when the information was made public, could have implemented the invention.

The clearest illustration of the role of the skilled addressee is found in *Lux Traffic Controls v Pike Signals* [1993] RPC 107. Traffic lights containing a new infrared detector were tested in a public place. It was held that even though there was no evidence that anyone had examined the inside of the device, had the skilled addressee been present at the trial, it would have been possible for such a person to deduce from their observations how the device worked without having to examine the 'black box' containing the electronics.

By contrast, in *Pall v Bedford Hydraulics* samples of microporous filters were supplied for testing which were incapable of analysis so there was no enabling disclosure (the case forms a useful contrast with *Gore v Kimal* as to the differences between the pre- and post-1977 law on prior use). Likewise, in *Quantel v Spaceward Microsystems*, the demonstration of a video graphics system at a trade fair was held not to destroy novelty as those present were not able to get close enough to the device to observe how it worked.

17.5.8 Novelty of purpose

The ability to obtain a patent for the first and second medical use of a pharmaceutical substance was explained earlier. The EPO has further extended this principle to novelty of purpose in non-medical fields in its decision in *G 2/88 MOBIL III/Friction reducing additive* [1990] EPOR 73 which concerned a new use for a substance previously used as a rust inhibitor. The Enlarged Board of Appeal declared that if the new use of the substance had not been made available, then it mattered not that it might have been inherent in its previous use. UK courts have reluctantly accepted the principle (see *Merrell Dow v Norton* and *Bristol-Myers Squibb Company v Baker Norton Pharmaceuticals Inc*), the reluctance stemming from the 'intuitive response' (*per* Lord Hoffmann in *Merrell Dow*) that you cannot patent something which has been done before, even if no one knew that it had been done. To take advantage of the *MOBIL III* principle, the claims have to be worded so as to limit the patentee's monopoly to the particular new use of the known substance.

17.5.9 The link with inventive step

The test of enabling disclosure is very precise, so that if an individual item of prior art does not contain *all* the elements (integers) of the later claimed invention, then the invention is valid for novelty. It is then necessary to consider separately and sequentially whether the invention meets the requirement of inventive step. It is here that Sachs LJ's metaphor in *General Tire* is very handy. If the prior art contains a signpost, pointing in the general direction of the invention, that does not suffice for anticipation. It may well, however, give the skilled addressee sufficient information to make the invention obvious.

17.6 Inventive step

17.6.1 Inventive step: general principles

The next positive element of patentability is that there must be an inventive step, or rather, the invention must not be 'obvious'. It is found in s. 3 Patents Act 1977, derived from Art. 56 EPC. Inventive step should be considered *after* novelty has been decided, and involves different issues. Something may be 'new' but not involve any *contribution to the state of the art*. Whilst novelty is concerned with whether the invention is *quantitatively* different from what has gone before (so that a small difference between the invention and the prior art means that it will still be considered new), inventive step is concerned with whether it is *qualitatively* different. Novelty and inventive step therefore need to be kept distinct.

Inventiveness is a question of fact to be decided objectively and without hindsight. Thus, in *Lilly Icos Ltd v Pfizer Ltd* [2002] EWCA Civ 1, the patent for Viagra was little more than putting into practice the recommendations and suggestions already found in the prior art. At the same time, with an issue such as obviousness, it may be difficult to avoid hindsight where the patent relates to an everyday item and the inventive step is small (see for example *SEB SA v De'Longhi SpA* [2003] EWCA Civ 952, which concerned deep fat fryers). Nevertheless, the court must ensure that hindsight is not used, particularly where the patent is challenged some years after grant.

Many cases assert that the word 'obvious' requires no further explanation, but then proceed to offer synonyms, such as 'very plain' (*General Tire v Firestone*), 'so easy that any fool could do it' (*Edison Bell v Smith* (1894) 11 RPC 389 at p. 398), 'routine development work' (*Lucas v Gaedor* [1978] RPC 297 at p. 377), or 'workshop adjustment' (*Cincinnati Grinders v BSA Tools* (1931) 48 RPC 33 at p. 75). By contrast, it is said, an inventive step involves 'a flash of insight' (*Unilever plc v Chefaro Proprietaries Ltd* [1994] RPC 567 at p. 584), an 'intellectual jump' (*Biogen v Medeva*), or a 'significant advance' (*Schlumberger Holdings Ltd v Electromagnetic Geoservices AS* [2010] RPC 851 at [93]).

17.6.2 Inventive step: the UK test

For many years, the test for inventive step was the one established by Oliver LJ in *Windsurfing International v Tabur Marine* [1985] RPC 59 at p. 73. The test provided a structured approach for determining whether an invention was or was not obvious. Case law was littered with judicial pronouncements on the importance of sticking to such an approach (for example the House of Lords in *Sabaf SpA v MFI Furniture Centres Ltd* [2005] RPC 209).

The Windsurfing test was re-stated and re-ordered by Jacob LJ in the Court of Appeal in *Pozzoli SpA v BDMO SA* [2007] FSR 872. He stated that the court should:

- identify the notional person skilled in the art and their common general knowledge;
- identify the inventive concept of the claim in question, or if that cannot readily be done, construe it. The inventive concept is usually called 'the epitome' or 'essence' of the invention. It is to be extracted from the wording of the claims, bearing in mind the problem which the patent attempted to solve, and hence is subject to the vagaries of judicial opinion (consider the majority and minority views of the inventive concept in *Wheatley (Davina) v Drillsafe Ltd* [2001] RPC 133);
- identify the differences between the matter cited as forming part of the state of the art and the inventive concept; and
- viewed without any knowledge of the alleged invention as claimed, do those differences constitute steps which would have been obvious to the person skilled in the art or do they require any degree of invention?

It is worth noting that some recent UK cases have taken a more flexible approach to the *Pozzoli* criteria. In *Teva UK Ltd & Another v LEO Pharma A/S* [2014] EWHC 3096 (Pat), Birss J complied with the first two steps—identifying the skilled person and the common general knowledge; and identifying the inventive concept—but chose not to identify the differences between cited prior art and the invention as claimed, arguing that it was not useful to his analysis.

 Pause for reflection

Considering the UK case law on obviousness, from the information in our problem scenario, do you think Siva's application would be held to possess an 'inventive step'?

17.6.3 Inventive step: the EPO approach

The test adopted by the EPO in deciding whether an invention possesses inventive step has many similarities with UK law, but there are subtle differences. Both systems deploy the skilled addressee as the person through whose eyes the matter is determined, such person being imbued with the common general knowledge of the relevant technical field and possessing the prejudices of others working in that area. Both systems stress the objective nature of the exercise and the need to avoid using hindsight. The apparent difference between them lies in the EPO's use of what is known as the problem and solution approach:

- the identification of the closest prior art;
- assessing the technical results achieved by the invention when compared with such art;
- defining the technical problem to be solved as the object of the invention; and
- examining whether or not a skilled person, having regard to the state of the art, would have suggested the technical features for obtaining those results.

The fourth stage does not entail asking whether the skilled person *could* have carried out the invention (this involves hindsight), but whether he *would have done so* in the hope of solving the problem or in the expectation of finding a technical improvement.

Despite this linguistic variance with the UK test, in reality there is not a large difference between the two systems. The *Pozzoli* test requires the court to identify the inventive concept of the patent. This should be done, according to Lord Hoffmann in *Biogen v Medeva*, by taking account of the problem which the patentee was attempting to solve. Ultimately, therefore, the differences may be more semantic than real.

 Pause for reflection

Looking at the above EPO problem/solution approach, would your view of the inventiveness of Siva's application change if this test were applied instead of the UK test?

17.6.4 **An objective test**

Inventive step poses a question of fact to be determined by the court objectively, using the standard of the skilled addressee (*Dow Corning's Application* [1969] RPC 544 at pp. 560, 561; *Technograph v Mills & Rockley* [1969] RPC 395 at p. 407 (CA)). This is not subjective—inventive step is determined without reference to the inventor. It doesn't matter how the inventor achieved success, whether by accident, hard work, intuition, or creativity: *Allmanna Svenska Electriska A/B v Burntisland Shipping Co* (1952) 69 RPC 63 at p. 70. What the inventor actually did is therefore irrelevant: *Nichia Corp v Argos Ltd* [2007] FSR 895.

17.6.5 **The meaning of 'prior art' for the purpose of inventive step**

The *Pozzoli* test requires the court to compare the prior art with the invention. A question which remains unresolved is whether the prior art is the same for inventiveness as it is for novelty. The approach of the EPO is to compare the invention with the nearest prior art. UK cases have not been so clear. Initially, it was said that all prior art should be considered (*Woven Plastic Products v British Ropes* [1970] FSR 47). However, the later cases of *Technograph v Mills & Rockley* [1972] RPC 346 (HL) and *General Tire v Firestone* both held that the concept of the 'diligent researcher' should be used, so that the invention was to be compared with items of prior art which such a person would discover. Most recently, it has been said that 'obscure' prior art should be ignored (*Beloit Technologies v Valmet Paper Machinery* [1995] RPC 705, [1997] RPC 489). Nevertheless, in *Windsurfing* itself (which after all is the basis of *Pozzoli*), the Court of Appeal held that all prior art should be considered.

17.6.6 **The prior art: 'mosaicing'**

In contrast to novelty, where each item of prior art has to be considered in isolation, it is possible to combine different items of prior art when arguing that an invention is obvious. This process is called 'mosaicing'. Despite this colourful language, it is unusual for a court to hold that separate, unrelated pieces of prior art can be combined when attacking a patent under s. 3, because it has to be shown that the skilled reader would think it obvious to mosaic, remembering that the skilled addressee has no inventive capacity. One example of where the court decided that the skilled addressee would combine separate items of prior art is *Dow Chemicals (Mildner's) Patent* [1975] RPC 165, where the patent involved a means of covering an electrical cable with a plastic jacket bonded to a metal shield. The Court of Appeal held that it was permissible to combine separate documents about electrical cables and adhesives. A recent case which has also discussed the practice of mosaicing is *SEB SA v De'Longhi SpA* which concerned a patent for deep fat fryers. The Court of Appeal refused to disturb the conclusions of Pumfrey J that the skilled addressee, working in the field of small domestic appliances, would have combined common general knowledge about the use of metals and plastics in the manufacture of such appliances, the use of an air-filled gap as an insulator, and the use of insulating rings in toasters, coffee makers, and irons.

A related issue is where an invention is said to consist of a combination of existing technology. The very act of putting together two or more known features may of itself involve an inventive step especially where the skilled addressee has only basic skills and qualifications in the relevant field and has a technical prejudice against changing accepted technology. However, there will only be a 'collocation' (as it is known) if the invention, considered as a whole, consists of a single inventive concept where the combination of known elements produces a synergy. If each element performs its own function independently of the other, then there is not one invention but two, and each part must be considered on its own in the light of the prior art: *Sabaf SpA v MFI Furniture Centres Ltd*, applying EPO Guidelines and the earlier UK case of *British Celanese Ltd v Courtaulds Ltd* (1935) 52 RPC 171. An example of a combination of known elements which is not inventive (because it does not amount to a collocation) is the putting together of a mincing machine and a filling machine to produce a sausage-making machine.

17.6.7 Inventive step: additional issues

Another subsidiary argument which can be advanced by the patentee to demonstrate inventiveness is that the patent has proved to be highly successful (*Rotocrop v Genbourne* [1982] FSR 241). Commercial success, however, may be attributable to other factors, such as fashion (*Wildey v Freeman* (1931) 48 RPC 405 which involved a patent for an electric comb) or a successful advertising campaign (*Haskell Golf Ball Co v Hutchinson* (1906) 23 RPC 301 which involved a patent for an improved golf ball).

However, if something is inventive, it is not a counter-argument to say that it is simple, as simplicity itself may be evidence of inventiveness. In *Haberman v Jackel International Ltd* [1999] FSR 683 the case concerned the 'any way up' cup—a cup designed for toddlers that had a straightforward mechanism that sealed the cup when it was turned upside down, e.g. by a toddler, thus preventing spillage of liquid. In upholding the patent, despite the (perhaps deceptive) simplicity of the invention, Laddie J put forward a number of factors that ought to be considered by the court when determining inventive step:

- What was the problem which the patented development addressed?
- How long had that problem existed?

- How significant was the problem seen to be?

- How widely known was the problem and how many were likely to be seeking a solution?

- What prior art would have been likely to be known to all or most of those who would have been expected to be involved in finding a solution?

- What other solutions were put forward in the period leading up to the publication of the patentee's development?

- To what extent were there factors which would have held back the exploitation of the solution even if it was technically obvious?

- How well has the patentee's development been received?

- To what extent can it be shown that the whole or much of the commercial success is due to the technical merits of the development, i.e. because it solves the problem?

Significantly, the list takes as its starting point the problem and solution approach. The list was approved by Jacob LJ in *Schlumberger Holdings v Electromagnetic Geoservices* [2010] RPC 33.

Finally, the idea of 'obvious to try' should be considered. Crucial to Birss J in his analysis in *Teva* was an idea that had been emphasised by the House of Lords in *Conor Medsystems Inc v Angiotech Pharmaceuticals Inc* [2008] UKHL 49—the question of whether it was obvious to try a particular solution. In *Teva UK Ltd & Another v LEO Pharma A/S* [2014] EWHC 3096 (Pat), the Court of Appeal actually reversed Birss J's finding on obviousness, saying that the doctrine of 'obvious to try' had been taken too far in this case (*Teva UK Ltd & Another v Leo Pharma A/S* [2015] EWCA Civ 779), noting that the standard of 'obvious to try' requires a higher expectation of success than mere possible inclusion in a research programme. Furthermore, in *Actavis v ICOS* [2017] EWCA Civ 1671 the Court of Appeal stressed that the 'obvious to try' standard should not be take too far, or it would stray into judgements based on hindsight. Thus it is to be remembered that the above criteria should be used to provide balanced guidance for judges, in weighing up obviousness from the perspective of the person skilled in the art, in light of the totality of the circumstances.

17.7 Sufficiency

A patent must have sufficiency and support—essentially it must disclose a claimed invention in sufficient detail for the person skilled in the art to be able to carry it out (Art. 83 and Art. 100(b) EPC and s. 14(3) and s. 72 Patents Act 1977). For example, references to documents or materials provided to support the invention must be sufficiently precise so that the person skilled in the art would not have to make undue efforts to find and gather together the information required to carry out the invention. Thus, the disclosure relates to 'the teaching' of the prior art and 'the teaching' of the patent respectively. The person skilled in the art must be able to perceive the teaching of the claimed invention in order to put it into effect, and this must be the case with respect to the entire scope of the claim (EPO cases).

In T 0409/91 *Fuel oils* the Technical Board of Appeal stated that the 'the extent of the patent monopoly, as defined by the claims, should correspond to the technical contribution to the art in order for it to be supported, or justified'. In G 1/92 *Availability to the Public* [1993] EPOR 241, the Enlarged Board of Appeal stated that an essential purpose of the prior art's teaching is to enable the person skilled in the art to manufacture or use a given product by applying such teaching. Where such teaching results from a product put on the market, if it is possible for that person to discover the composition or the internal structure of the product *and to reproduce it without undue burden* then both the product and its composition or internal structure become part of the state of the art. In T 154/04 *DUNS LICENSING ASSOCIATES/Estimating Sales Activity* [2007] EPOR 349 the EPO considered that in a case involving 'technical character' the invention must involve 'technical teaching' emphasizing that novelty and inventive step were separate, independent, and relative criteria from this analysis.

Turning to UK cases, the classic statement is found in the House of Lords cases of *Biogen v Medeva* [1997] RPC 1 and *Lundbeck v Generics* [2009] UKHL 12. The key principle is that if the invention discloses a principle, the claims must correspond. In *Biogen v Medeva*, Lord Hoffman ruled that it was insufficient for a patentee to merely disclose one way of performing the invention. If other ways of achieving the result were envisaged that made no use of the invention, the patent would be invalid. Therefore, Lord Hoffmann's view was that the patent monopoly must correspond exactly with the claims of the invention. On this point, Lord Hoffmann emphasized the need to allow subsequent research and to ensure competition.

However, in *Generics v Lundbeck* Lord Hoffmann, sitting as a Court of Appeal judge, reduced the scope of 'Biogen insufficiency' due to a belated acceptance that the UK Patents Act s. 60, following the EPC, requires protecting patents for products 'as such'. Thus, the UK Court of Appeal accepted that in the case of a product patent it is inevitable that the monopoly conferred will include all ways of making and using the product—otherwise it would not truly be a product patent; and when preparing, writing, and filing the patent application, the teaching disclosed in the claims of the patent cannot conceivably cover every single way of making/using the product.

In the recent case of *Regeneron v Kymab* [2018] EWCA Civ 671 the Court of Appeal assessed sufficiency of disclosure in a biotechnology case—could the skilled person work the claimed invention without undue burden and was the breadth of the claim in line with the contribution to the art? The Court of Appeal ruled that the patent did disclose the claimed inventions in a sufficiently clear manner that a person skilled in the art could perform the invention.

17.8 The requirement of industrial application

17.8.1 The statutory requirement

According to s. 4(1) Patents Act 1977, derived from Art. 57 EPC, the invention must be capable of industrial application (Art. 57 uses the term 'susceptible' rather than 'capable'). 'Industrial application' means that the invention can be made or used in any kind of industry, including agriculture.

Under the 1977 Act, it has been held that s. 4 requires that the invention must not be something which is useless for any known purpose; in other words, the issue is whether the subject matter of the patent is 'useful': *Chiron v Organon (No. 12)* [1996] FSR 153. Such definition resembles the 'utility' requirement in USA patent law. The EPO has held that cosmetic salons and beauty parlours fall within the meaning of Art. 57 (see *DU PONT/ Appetite suppressant* and *ROUSSEL-UCLAF/Thenoyl peroxide*), stating that 'industry' implies that an activity is carried out continuously, independently, and for financial gain.

17.8.2 Case law

Industrial applicability is not a difficult element of the patentability criteria to demonstrate, so objections to patents under s. 4(1) are rare. Nonetheless, two cases illustrate the role of the provision—it can be useful in the rejection of highly speculative 'inventions'. In *Re Duckett's Patent Application* [2005] EWHC 3140, Kitchin J upheld the decision of the UKIPO to reject a patent application on the basis that it was not capable of industrial application. The application was for, in effect, a 'perpetual motion machine'—a propulsion system (i.e. an engine) involving an electric system and a hydraulic system going against the well-established laws of physics (such machines claim to create energy out of nothing). Similarly, in *Blacklight Power Inc v Comptroller General of Patents* [2009] RPC 173 the UKIPO patent examiner had held that a plasma reactor based on an allegedly new species of hydrogen (christened by the applicant 'the hydrino'), which was supposed to exist in a lower energy state than recognized by the standard laws of physics, was not capable of industrial application because it was inconsistent with generally accepted theories. However, Floyd J allowed the appeal and remitted the case because the examiner had applied too stringent a test: what should have been asked was whether the applicant had a reasonable prospect of showing that his theory was valid, rather than asking whether it was more probable than not that the theory was true.

17.8.3 A particular problem with biotech patents

The requirement of utility may also prove to be a means of challenging biotech patents in the light of the decision of the EPO Opposition Division in *ICOS CORPORATION/ Transmembrane receptor* [2002] OJ EPO 293. Revoking the patent on the grounds of lack of inventiveness, lack of utility, and lack of sufficiency, the EPO seems to have taken the same approach to lack of inventiveness as the Court of Appeal in *Genentech Inc's Patent*, that is, the identification of the relevant genetic sequence was no more than the result of routine procedure which would have been followed by a skilled person in the light of prior art. In relation to utility, the patentee had successfully crossed the boundary between discovery and invention in that they had isolated the particular amino acid sequence. However, the potential uses of the invention were speculative. The patentee had merely 'brainstormed' about how the invention *might* be used. This was not sufficient under Art. 57: the practical applications of the invention had to be clearly spelled out.

The treatment of speculative biotech patents was considered by the Supreme Court in *Eli Lilly and Company v Human Genome Sciences Inc* [2012] RPC 102. Lord Neuberger concluded that Kitchin J and the Court of Appeal had applied EPO case law too strictly. Summarizing that law (at [107]) he stated that the substance in question was part of a wider family of proteins which were known to have certain effects useful in the control of tumours and which were of interest to the pharmaceutical industry. The invention therefore satisfied Art. 57.

 Pause for reflection

Consider the requirement of industrial applicability in light of our problem scenario. Would Siva find it difficult to meet this requirement?

17.9 Conclusion

In this chapter we have examined the concept of 'an invention' and the criteria for patentability. There are five core elements: three positive and two negative. In terms of the positive requirements, for an invention to be patentable, it must possess novelty (it must be new), inventive step (it must possess something that is not obvious in the field of technology), and industrial applicability (it must have some practical usefulness). Regarding the negative criteria, the invention must not consist of excluded subject matter—it must not be a mere discovery; an aesthetic creation; a scheme, rule, or method for performing a mental act, playing a game or doing business, or a program for a computer; or a presentation of information. It also must not fall afoul of any of the exceptions to patentability: (i) morality, (ii) plant/animal varieties and biological processes, and (iii) methods of treatment.

In terms of Siva's invention, we should advise her that to obtain a UK patent she should engage a patent attorney to write a specification and make a patent application as soon as possible. Although she is seeking UK protection, EPO decisions will be of relevance as UK courts take account of them.

We would first need to advise her that there is nothing in the legislative exclusions or exceptions that seems to make her patent application less likely to succeed (Arts 52 –53 EPC, s. 1(2–3) Patents Act 1977). Her invention is not a mere discovery, nor does it fit into any of the other exclusions. Moreover, there are no moral grounds to justify refusal of a patent for her invention; nor is it related to biological life or process, or methods of treatment. Her application would therefore proceed to the positive criteria.

As we have seen, the UK courts, post *Biogen v Medeva*, generally do not spend time considering whether the device is an 'invention' separate from the criteria of novelty, inventive step, and industrial applicability. The EPO does, but Siva's invention would appear to easily satisfy the requirement of 'technical character' (*T 931/95 PBS PARTNER-SHIP/Controlling Pension Benefits System*).

In terms of novelty, Siva has done the right thing in not showing her invention to anybody and keeping it private (EPO case *T 245/88 UNION CARBIDE/Atmospheric Vaporizer*). She must ensure her patent has not been anticipated by an existing piece of knowledge. Anticipation occurs where the prior art contains an enabling disclosure. This comprises two separate issues which must be dealt with sequentially, namely disclosure and enablement: *Synthon BV v Smithkline Beecham plc*; see also *General Tire*. She, with her patent attorney, will need to engage in a prior art search that goes beyond the publications she has searched thus far, including all published patents. The invention will need to be novel in terms of prior use (*Windsurfing International Inc v Tabur Marine*) and prior documentation (*Van der Lely v Bamfords Ltd; Lang v Gisbourne; Bristol Myers Application*). If she is confident there is no prior art that would have taught the 'skilled addressee' (*Lux Traffic Controls v Pike Signals*) the invention, the application would proceed to inventive step.

Inventiveness covers the contribution to the state of the art—whether it is qualitatively different from what has been done before, or merely an obvious step. Inventiveness is a question of fact to be decided objectively and without hindsight (*Lilly Icos Ltd v Pfizer Ltd; SEB SA v De'Longhi SpA*). Following on from *Windsurfing International v Tabur Marine* the traditional test for inventiveness was established in *Pozzoli SpA v BDMO SA*—the court should: (i) identify the notional person skilled in the art and their common general knowledge; (ii) identify the inventive concept of the claim in question, or if that cannot readily be done, construe it; (iii) identify the differences between the matter cited as forming part of the state of the art and the inventive concept; and (iv) consider, when viewed without any knowledge of the alleged invention as claimed, do those differences constitute steps which would have been obvious to the person skilled in the art or do they require any degree of invention? We can note that this was modified somewhat in *Teva*, and also contrast it with the EPO's problem/solution approach, though note that the same result will occur in most cases. At present, we do not have access to all of the prior art, nor are we a skilled addressee, but the indications are that Siva's creation could possess an inventive step. There's nothing in the facts of the problem to indicate that what she has done is obvious. Nor is there any reason to think sufficiency could be a problem for her.

Finally, we can advise Siva that her invention is likely to possess industrial applicability. Her invention is not merely speculative (*Duckworth*) and recent UKSC case law (*Eli Lilly v Human Genome Sciences*) indicates that this criterion should be interpreted broadly.

End-of-chapter questions

After reading the chapter carefully, try answering the following questions. For answer guidance visit the online resources at **www.oup.com/uk/karapapa-mcdonagh/**

1. Think back to the problem in chapter 15 (introduction to patents). Could you give more detailed advice now that you know more about the criteria for patentability?

2. Why is there such an emphasis on an invention being 'new' under patent law?

3. Is it time to move away from the Pozzoli test entirely and embrace the EPO view on inventive step?

Further reading

Bently, L. 'Exclusions from Patentability and Exceptions to Patentees' Rights: Taking Exceptions Seriously' (2011) 64 *Current Legal Problems* 315

Gives a thorough overview of exclusions and exceptions in the context of patents.

Bonadio, E., 'Biotech Patents and Morality after Brüstle' (2012) 34 *EIPR* 433.

Examines the impact of the Brüstle case with reference to prior case law.

Crespi, S. 'Biotechnology Patenting: the Wicked Animal Must Defend Itself' [1995] 17 *EIPR* 431

Explores the arguments concerning whether ethical objections should be taken into account when granting patents.

Crespi, S. 'Patenting and Ethics—a Dubious Connection' (2003) 85 *JPTOS* 31

Revisits the arguments concerning gene patents and ethical concerns.

Drahos, P. 'Biotechnology Patents, Markets and Morality' [1999] 21 *EIPR* 441

Argues that it is vital for patent professionals to take ethical concerns into account.

McDonagh, L. 'Biogen v Medeva' in J. Bellido (ed.), Landmark Cases in Intellectual Property (2017) Hart Publishing.

Examines the Biogen case from the perspectives of law and science and technology studies.

Norman, H.E. 'Patenting Biotechnology: A Case of Legal Abstentionism?' [2002] 14 *ELM* 278

Argues that the concerns about granting biotech patents can be overcome if the patentability criteria are rigorously applied.

O'Sullivan, E. 'Is Article 53(a) EPC Still of Narrow Interpretation?' [2012] 9 *JIPLP* 680

Considers whether the decisions in WARF/Stem Cells and Brüstle v Greenpeace indicate that Art. 53 might be given a broader interpretation in the future.

Parker, S. and England, P. 'Where Now for Stem Cell Patents?' [2012] 7 *JIPLP* 738

Reviews the decisions in WARF/Stem Cells and Brüstle v Greenpeace.

Vaver, D. 'Invention in Patent Law: A Review and a Modest Proposal' (2003) 11 *International Journal of Law and Information Technology* 286

Compares statutory provisions dealing with what are 'patentable inventions' in the light of their historical origins and considers whether it is best to define 'an invention' and to prescribe what cannot be patented.

Warren-Jones, A. 'Morally Regulating Innovation: What is "Commercial Exploitation"?' [2008] 2 *IPQ* 193

Considers the meaning of 'commercial exploitation' in relation to biotech patents, concluding that there is a lack of consensus and that Member States will need further guidance.

Infringement of patents

Problem question

Read this problem question carefully and keep it in mind while you are working through the chapter that follows. At the end of this chapter, you will be able to apply what you have learnt to the problem question and advise the relevant parties.

Siva Patel is a professional engineer, amateur inventor and keen cyclist who lives in Cardiff. Having created a new type of bicycle pump that uses a solar-powered motor to pump air into a bike's wheels, and finding that her invention pumps air with 40% more efficiency than any other product on the market, she successfully files for, and obtains, a patent from the European Patent Office ('EPO'). She validates the patent in the UK, Germany, and France—the three big European markets for bicycle pumps—so that she can bring her product to market before any competitors and take advantage of the patent monopoly.

The primary claim—Claim 1—of the patent reads:

> A bicycle pump with solar power capability, comprising an elongated barrel and a sliding piston-tube, an elastic plug attachment secured in the outer end of said tube, a rubber sleeve surrounding the tube forming a surface which is smooth with the barrel, with a small solar panel on the outer rim and a motor internal to the tube attached to the panel via two wires.

Eighteen months after receiving her granted patent, Siva is about to bring her product onto the market, having partnered with a local business in Cardiff to manufacture and distribute the new pump—the SolaPump. However, as they are on the verge of launching the product Siva notices that a large London-based company—YesTECH—is also bringing out a solar-power bicycle pump—The YesPump. The rival product is broadly the same size and shape as Siva's SolaPump and has a similar solar panel on the exterior, as well as a small motor internal to the pump. The YesPump takes advantage of solar powered technology but only to assist pumping by hand—it is not fully automated, unlike Siva's product. For this reason, YesTECH have rebuffed all of Siva's attempts to seek a negotiated licence for the use of her patented invention. YesTECH recently sent a letter to Siva stating: 'We do not believe we are engaging in infringing activity—and even if we are, the issue is moot as we do not consider Siva's pump patent to be a valid one as we do not believe it to be sufficiently inventive.' Siva seeks your advice about what means of redress she can seek for what she considers to be a clear case of patent infringement; and particularly, what remedies she can seek to prevent her rival's product coming to the market.

Advise Siva.

18.1 Introduction

18.1.1 Patent enforcement via the courts: Taking action for infringement

The central method of the enforcement of patents is undertaking a patent infringement action via the courts. In the UK, s. 60 Patents Act is the key provision on direct patent infringement. Budding patent lawyers must attempt to comprehend the definition of infringing conduct under s. 60, as well as the defences and counterclaims which a defendant to a patent infringement action may raise. It is important to understand the challenge facing the courts in interpreting patent claims when considering if the defendant's conduct falls within the scope of the patentee's monopoly. Moreover, an appreciation of the role of the Protocol to Art. 69 European Patent Convention ('EPC') in determining the scope of the patent monopoly, with respect to the patent's claims, is increasingly important in UK patent law following the UK Supreme Court decision in *Actavis UK Ltd v Eli Lilly & Co* [2017] UKSC 48. During this chapter we will touch upon the remedies a claimant might seek, but reference should be made to the detailed chapter on remedies—chapter 22—for in-depth analysis.

18.1.2 Patent infringement: practical issues

The vast majority of patent litigation in the UK takes places in the courts of England and Wales. Patent actions are assigned by the Senior Courts Act 1981 (previously the Supreme Court Act) to the Patents Court, part of the Chancery Division of the High Court of England and Wales, with an alternative forum for more straightforward and low-value claims being the Intellectual Property Enterprise Court ('IPEC') (also part of the Chancery Division, and which in 2013 replaced the old Patents County Court ('PCC')). Any claimant who considers their patent to have been infringed has to first decide which of these two courts to use. The High Court and IPEC have the same jurisdiction to hear intellectual property ('IP') cases, and both courts can issue injunctions, but the IPEC is restricted in the amount of damages it can award (£500,000) and the amount of costs that can be claimed back from the losing side by the winner (£50,000).

A further issue (depending on the facts) may be choice of defendant. As a matter of common sense, suing the person or undertaking who e.g. made an infringing version of the patented product or used the patented process would seem obvious. However, patent infringement can occur in a number of different ways and may involve multiple defendants. For instance, there can be liability for preparatory acts and for subsequent dealings in infringing products. To come under UK law, infringing conduct must be committed within the territory of the UK. Even if the principal act of infringement (that is, manufacture) occurs in another jurisdiction, it may still be possible to identify other defendants who are within the UK (e.g. importers, distributers).

Pause for reflection

Consider Siva's problem scenario in light of the above. Even at this early stage of our under-standing of patent infringement, several key questions emerge:

In terms of taking a case, should Siva consider taking action at the Patents Court or the IPEC? What are the advantages/disadvantages of either option?

With respect to the facts of her case, is the rival manufacturer based in the UK or elsewhere? Has the product already been manufactured, launched, and distributed to retailers? (Could there be defendants other than YesTECH?)

Have any of the products been exported to other markets where Siva has patent protection? (Might it be necessary to take action in Germany and France?)

These will all be pertinent questions for us to think about when advising Siva over the course of this chapter.

18.1.3 The elements of the case

It is useful at this stage to separate out the issues normally raised in a patent infringe-ment action. The patentee will have to show two things: first, that one or more infring-ing acts have been committed within the UK, and second, that the defendant's conduct falls within the scope of protection afforded to the patent, i.e. within the literal or purposive meaning of the claims. These two issues are sometimes called 'infringement in law' and 'infringement in fact'.

By way of response, the defendant to a patent infringement action can raise a number of different arguments. It can deny that the claimant has established the elements of the infringement action by showing that no infringing conduct has been committed, or even if it has, that the defendant's product or process is not within the meaning of the claims.

Alternatively, or in addition, the defendant may argue that even if the acts are infring-ing within the meaning of the claims, the defendant can counterclaim that the patent is invalid and should be revoked. A defendant may also argue that one or more of the statutory or case law defences to patent infringement apply. Other defensive arguments include: that the patent is no longer in force for a practical reason (e.g. because the an-nual renewal fees have not been paid); or that the claimant has not the standing to sue (because an assignment or an exclusive licence has not been recorded on the register).

Pause for reflection

Consider Siva's situation. What might her opponent do? Attacking the validity of a patent is a standard tactic to adopt when one is accused of infringement (and one which increases the risk and cost of litigation for the patentee). Is it a tactic that YesTECH seem willing to engage in? Is Siva confident that her patent would withstand any challenge to its validity? Think back to our consideration of patentability in the prior chapter.

18.1.4 **Possible outcomes**

It is usually the case that a patent will have more than one claim, though the primary claim (Claim 1) is typically the most important. Forensic analysis of the patent's claims plays a pivotal role in the analysis of whether infringement has occurred in law and in fact.

In the context of patent litigation, the Civil Procedure Rules Part 63 and Practice Direction 63 require a claimant to identify *which* claims have been infringed and how. Likewise, a party seeking a declaration that a patent is invalid must set out clearly the grounds of challenge, which must relate to individual claims.

Consequently, there are several different possible outcomes to a patent infringement action:

- one or more claims are valid and infringed;
- one or more claims are valid but not infringed;
- one or more claims are invalid but had they been valid would have been infringed;
- one or more claims are invalid but had they been valid would not have been infringed.

Further, some of the patent's claims may be accepted by the court as valid, whilst others are invalidated. Similarly, a court may hold that only some claims may have been infringed but not others, so that the above permutations can be multiplied to include partially valid/partially invalid and partially infringed patents. Individual claims in a patent must therefore be treated separately.

 Pause for reflection

Does the fact that the Patents Court can deal with both infringement and validity at the same time, when coupled with the CPR requirement to identify which claims have been infringed and which are invalid, lead to unnecessary complexity in patent litigation? As noted earlier, the Patents Court is highly regarded for the quality of its procedures and judgments, but litigation at the venue can be both lengthy and costly due to the complexity of the above issues. Having said that, if a patentee succeeds in proving infringement of a valid patent at the court, the patentee can be reasonably confident the patent is a strong one which may increase its strategic value in other disputes.

18.2 **Categories of infringing acts**

The Patents Act 1977 defines infringing conduct in s. 60. One critical aspect is that it must involve some sort of commercial activity (*British United Shoe Machinery Co v Simon Collier* (1910) 27 RPC 567 at p. 572). An example of what amounts to taking 'the whole profit and advantage of the invention' is the New Zealand case of *Smith Kline & French Laboratories v Douglas Pharmaceuticals* [1991] FSR 522, where the New Zealand Court of Appeal held there was infringement when the defendant imported a sample of the claimant's patented drug CIMETIDINE into New Zealand for the sole purpose of obtaining a product licence, which would have enabled the defendant to market the drug once the patent had expired (New Zealand law corresponded to the Patents Act 1949). It was use of the invention resulting in a commercial advantage.

18.2.1 Direct infringement

18.2.1.1 The origins of s. 60

As we noted earlier, there is no centralized procedure or law of infringement across the EU. Instead, infringement is dealt with from territory to territory. However, over the past forty years there have been several attempts to create a harmonized European patent law. Examples of European attempts to define infringement include the Community Patent Convention 1975 (Art. 29) (and the EU Patent Regulation 2009 (Art. 7) which did not come into force). The wording of the Patents Act 1977 s. 60(1) was based on Art. 29 of the Community Patent Convention ('CPC') 1975. For this reason, even though the CPC was never implemented, Art. 29 CPC is relevant when attempting to resolve any ambiguity regarding the wording of s. 60 of the Patents Act (*Smith, Kline & French v Harbottle* [1980] RPC 363).

18.2.1.2 The scope of s. 60(1)

Under s. 60(1) (and Art. 29 CPC) there is a clear distinction between patents for products and patents for processes. This distinction ought to be clear from the patent's drafting—whether it relates to a product (a thing) or a process (how to make something or use something or do something) depends entirely on the wording of the claims. A patent may have all product claims, or all process claims, or a mixture of both.

For products, under para (a) infringing conduct consists of making, disposing, offering to dispose of, using or importing the product, or keeping the product for disposal or otherwise.

For processes, both para (b) and (c) are relevant. Under para (b) there are just two infringing acts, using the process or offering it for use. Section 60(1)(b) includes a requirement of knowledge, however such knowledge is only to be proved in respect of the act of 'offering for use', but not 'using' the process. The knowledge required under s. 60(1)(b) is that use of the process which has been offered to another would infringe. This suggests that the defendant must have information about the patent in order to know that use of the process by another will infringe. The test is objective, because of the words 'obvious to a reasonable person in the circumstances'. By analogy to similar wording in s. 22 Copyright, Designs and Patents Act 1988 ('CDPA') 1988, the defendant's conduct is likely to be compared with that of the reasonable trader in that area of commerce: *LA Gear v Hi-Tec Sports plc* [1992] FSR 121. The inference must be that companies which seek patent protection for their own inventions or who exploit patents as part of their business are expected to familiarise themselves with patented inventions in their line of business by conducting regular searches of the UK patent database: *Tamglass Ltd Oy v Luoyang North Glass Technology Co Ltd* [2006] FSR 608. Ignorance of the claimant's patent is unlikely to provide an excuse in such circumstances.

Finally, under s. 60(1)(c), there are further infringing acts in respect of process patents, namely disposing of, offering to dispose of, using or importing any product obtained directly by means of that process, or keeping any such product whether for disposal or otherwise. It has been held by the House of Lords that the infringement provisions in the Patents Act, together with Art. 64(2) EPC, provide for protection in respect of products which are directly derived from process patents, which removes the need for a separate category of 'product-by-process' patents. As Lord Hoffmann explained in *Kirin-Amgen Inc v Hoechst Marion Roussel Ltd* [2005] 1 All ER 667 at [90], this type of claim is relatively rare because the EPO is reluctant to accept it. The only time when a 'product-by-process' claim will be allowed is where the patent concerns a new substance whose difference from a known substance cannot be described in chemical or physical terms, in which case the process by which it is obtained is an important element of the invention.

As a statutory tort, liability under s. 60(1) is strict. This means that, apart from infringement by offering a process for use, the defendant's state of mind is irrelevant as regards liability (*Proctor v Bennis* (1887) 4 RPC 333). Nonetheless, state of mind may have an effect on the award of damages or account of profits. The strict nature of liability for direct patent infringement was stressed by Lord Hoffmann in *Merrell Dow v Norton* [1996] RPC 76 at p. 92. However, one issue which remains to be resolved is whether liability can be strict in relation to inventions which claim a new use of an old product, in accordance with the EPO's decision in *G 2/88 MOBIL III/Friction Reducing Additive* [1990] EPOR 73.

A practical point to remember is that under s. 69 Patents Act 1977 a patent infringement action cannot be brought until the patent has been granted. However, once an action is brought, the claim for damages can, provided certain conditions are met, be backdated to the publication of the patent application, thereby compensating for acts of infringement committed between the date of publication and the date of grant. Publication of a patent application is therefore notice to the world that the invention is the property of the claimant.

Three other observations can be made about the wording of s. 60(1). It requires, first, that the infringing conduct be done without the patentee's consent. Thus, permission to exploit the patent is therefore a complete defence to patent infringement. Second, the section requires that the infringing conduct be committed within the UK (*Menashe Business Mercantile Ltd v William Hill Organisation Ltd* [2003] RPC 575). Conduct occurring in another territory will not infringe a UK-granted patent (by the UK Intellectual Property Office ('UKIPO')) or a European patent (granted by the EPO) validated in the UK. The patentee may well have parallel patent protection in that other jurisdiction, but even so, that will be of no assistance to any UK litigation. Thus, action against an infringer must be brought in the state which granted/validated the patent right (*Coin Controls Ltd v Suzo International (UK) Ltd* [1997] 3 All ER 45). Lastly, the section requires that the infringing conduct be done 'whilst the patent is in force'. This simply means that the annual renewal fees must have been paid and the term must not have expired. Obviously, once patent protection has expired, no infringement claims can be made.

18.2.1.3 Key words and phrases

The first key word we shall look at is 'making'. At first glance, the word 'makes' appears to need no explanation. This is not the case, however, as noted by the UK Supreme Court in *Schütz (UK) Ltd v Werit UK Ltd* [2013] FSR 395.

Schütz (UK) Ltd v Werit UK Ltd [2013] FSR 395

In *Schütz* the defendant supplied replacement plastic bottles to fit the patented cages of the claimant intermediate bulk carriers—it was held to not amount to infringement because the bottles were a subsidiary part of the patented item. What amounts to 'making' does not have a precise meaning—whether an activity amounts to 'making' is a matter of fact and degree.

The word 'disposes' must be understood as involving some sort of commercial dealing. Thus, in *United Telephone Co v Sharples* (1885) 2 RPC 28 the purchase of patented equipment was accompanied by a statement that it was intended for export. This was held to be infringement even though the defendant in fact intended the equipment to be used in experiments by school pupils. Similarly, in *British Motor Syndicate v Taylor* (1900) 17 RPC 723, proof of intention to export was held to amount to a disposal.

'Offer to dispose of' in s. 60(1) should not be interpreted in the sense used by the law of contract. In *Dunlop Tyre Co v British & Colonial Motor Co* (1901) 18 RPC 313, the display of the product at an exhibition was held to be an offer, and in *Gerber Garment Technology v Lectra Systems* [1995] RPC 383 it was held that including pictures of the patented equipment in a catalogue amounted to an offer. In particular, (at pp. 411–12) Jacob J stressed that the words 'offer to dispose of' in s. 60(1)(a) were not intended to reflect the English law of contract but should be construed purposively. Sending details of machinery which infringed a United Kingdom patent by fax to a prospective purchaser has also been held to amount to an offer: *Tamglass Ltd Oy v Luoyang North Glass Technology Co Ltd.*

'Using' was considered in *Merrell Dow v Norton*. Lord Hoffmann indicated that, but for the private use defence (which we look at later on) patients who swallowed terfenadine might have committed such an infringing act (by 'using'). Also bear in mind the discussion in chapter 17 of the *Merrell Dow* case and the distinction between anticipation by use and anticipation by disclosure.

In terms of keeping for disposal, this a new form of liability. In *Hoffmann-La Roche v Harris* [1977] FSR 200 it was held that the word 'keeps' should be treated as requiring some sort of commercial activity which deprives the patentee of the benefit of the invention. However, Oliver J in *Smith, Kline & French v Harbottle* made clear that 'keeps' is not to extend to the activities of a mere warehouse-keeper or carrier.

The word 'directly' appears in s. 60(1)(c)—it creates liability for the infringement of a process patent by dealing in products obtained directly from that process (this is also in Art. 64(2) EPC). The meaning of the word was considered in *Pioneer Electronics Capital Inc v Warner Music Manufacturing Europe GmbH* [1997] RPC 757. The patent was for the processes used to create a master disc as a preliminary to pressing mass-produced compact discs. The defendant denied that its compact discs infringed the patent, as the completed discs were not identical to the master, having undergone three further stages of manufacture and being made of different material. In agreeing with the defendant, the Court of Appeal made extensive reference to German case law, on which Art. 64(2) EPC was said to have been based, observing that the courts of the Netherlands, Switzerland, Denmark, and Austria had also adopted the same approach. The test to be applied was whether the end-product retained the essential characteristics of the patented process, in other words, was there 'a loss of identity' between the process and the end-product?

Pause for reflection

Consider Siva's situation. Is the main claim in her patent a product or a process?

What acts has the rival company actually done (making, using, offering, etc) that could be construed as infringing under s. 60(1)?

18.2.2 Indirect infringement

In addition to direct infringement, the Patents Act 1977 also imposes liability on those who assist the primary infringer. Section 60(2) declares that supplying the means relating to an essential element of the invention in order to put the invention into effect amounts to indirect infringement.

There is an exception in s. 60(3) whereby there is no liability if what has been supplied is a staple commercial product, unless the supply or offer of the staple commercial product is made for the purpose of inducing the person supplied to commit an infringing act falling within s. 60(1).

'Staple commercial product' was explained in *Nestec SA v Dualit Ltd* [2013] EWHC 923 (Pat) at [182] as being something which is supplied commercially for a variety of uses, of the kind which is needed every day and can be generally obtained, such as nails, screws, bolts, and wire. In the instant case, the defendant's coffee capsules had no other use than to fit a limited range of 'portionized' coffee machines.

According to the Court of Appeal in *Grimme Maschinenfabrik GmBH v Scott* [2010] FSR 193, s. 60(2) provides for a novel form of liability within UK law because liability for indirect infringement (or 'contributory infringement' as it is sometimes called) does not depend on the existence of primary, direct infringement being shown.

The following observations can be made about s. 60(2) and (3). First, the conduct in question (the supply of the essential means) must occur within the UK (just like any act of direct infringement). This typically involves providing or offering something tangible ('means') to the primary infringer. Second, the tangible 'means' must be an essential element of the invention. Whether something is an essential element will depend on the court's interpretation of the teaching of the patent (*Nestec v Dualit*), as s. 60 must be read against the background of s. 125, which declares that an invention shall be taken to be as set out in the claims (*Menashe Business Mercantile Ltd v William Hill Organisation Ltd*). Next, the result of the infringing conduct must be that it puts the invention into effect. Quite simply, this means that it makes the invention work. Finally, the provision requires knowledge on the part of the defendant. In contrast to s. 60(1)(b), this is not knowledge of the patent, rather it is knowledge that what has been supplied will make the invention work (implying that the defendant has some sort of appreciation of the technology concerned). However, and just like s. 60(1)(b), such knowledge is to be determined objectively, as the provision contains the phrase 'or it is obvious to a reasonable person in the circumstances that those means are suitable for putting, and are and intended to put, the invention into effect'. Therefore, the defendant's behaviour will be measured against the yardstick of the reasonable trader in that area of commerce.

18.2.2.1 Two examples of indirect (contributory) infringement

One example of where the defendant was alleged to have committed contributory infringement is *Merrell Dow v Norton* [1996] RPC 76. Here the patentee had discovered that the subject matter of its first patent, terfenadine, when swallowed by a patient, was turned into an acid metabolite by the patient's liver. Accordingly, a second patent for the acid metabolite was obtained. The patentee then sued the defendant, another pharmaceutical company, under s. 60(2). The argument was that by supplying terfenadine to patients (the original terfenadine patent had by now expired) the defendant was supplying the means essential for them to make the acid metabolite in their bodies, this being the substance claimed by the second patent. It was held that despite the fact that the patients themselves had not committed infringement (because of the private use defence in s. 60(5)(a)), the defendant would still have been liable for providing something which put the invention, the subject matter of the second patent, into effect. However, the defendant successfully argued that the second patent was invalid on the ground of anticipation. This case therefore demonstrates the value of the revocation counter-claim—even if the defendant loses on the infringing point, by showing the claimant's patent is not valid, the defendant can escape liability.

A second example of contributory infringement can be found in *Menashe Business Mercantile Ltd v William Hill Organisation Ltd* [2003] RPC 575. The patent was for a gaming system, involving a host computer, a terminal computer, a communication means between them, and a program for operating the terminal computer. The defendant bookmaker had supplied its customers with a program on CD-ROM which effectively turned their home computers into the terminal required in the patentee's system and enabled them to participate in online gaming. The defendant denied infringement because its host computer was located outside the UK. The Court of Appeal held that the defendant was liable under s. 60(2). It had supplied the CDs which were suitable for putting the invention, i.e. the gaming apparatus, into effect, because punters could use the gaming system in the UK.

 Pause for reflection

Consider Siva's case. Is there any way a claim of indirect infringement could be made (against e.g. the suppliers of YESTech)?

18.2.3 Europe-wide patent litigation

It is necessary to briefly outline how patent enforcement works in the UK and across territories elsewhere in Europe. As we have already discussed in prior chapters, at present Europe-wide patents can be granted at the EPO (and, post-grant, a European patent's validity can be opposed at the EPO). However, due to the fact that a European patent is, in fact, a bundle of national patents, infringement actions must take place at a territorial level, e.g. at the domestic courts in the UK, in Germany, in France, etc. Thus, it is usually the case that any remedies granted to a patentee are territorial (detailed analysis of specific remedies occurs in chapter 22). This is far from ideal. It means that enforcing a patent throughout the EU and wider Europe (such as in non-EU EPC Member States like Switzerland, Iceland, and Turkey) requires taking multiple cases in several jurisdictions. In light of this, preparations are ongoing to set up a Unified Patent Court ('UPC') for participating EU Member States (25 out of 28 at present, including the UK, Brexit notwithstanding), as well as facilitating the granting of a European Patent with Unitary Effect (Unitary Patent) at the EPO. These measures aim to unify the fragmented European patent litigation system as much as possible. However, as the UPC/UP system is not yet up and running, at time of writing it remains the case that national litigation in one or more of the EPC territories where the patent has been validated is the only way to enforce a patent via the courts. For this reason, it is not necessary to describe the UPC/UP in great detail—instead the key elements of the UPC/UP as pertaining to UK law are explained in the final part of this chapter.

Pause for reflection

What difficulties arise from the fragmented European Patent litigation system? Luke McDonagh argues in *European Patent Litigation in the Shadow of the Unified Patent Court* (Edward Elgar, 2016) that there are, in fact, multiple ways fragmented outcomes on validity and infringement can occur:

> National courts have the ability to issue binding rulings concerning patent infringement within their national territories, and they may also consider questions of patent validity—although the EPO retains the final say on validity via its patent opposition service. Indeed, it is not uncommon for national patent litigation to take place at the same time as parallel EPO opposition proceedings; and the lengthy backlog at the EPO means that national courts sometimes rule on questions of validity and infringement before the EPO Board of Appeals has reached a final decision regarding validity. Moreover, due to the fact that national courts have the ability under the EPC to make decisions based on their own jurisprudence, the courts in one EPC member state (e.g. the UK) may reach different conclusions to the courts of another EPC member state (e.g. Germany) when resolving the central questions of patent litigation: what amounts to infringement of a patent in suit? Is the patent in suit valid or invalid? In what circumstances is it appropriate to grant a preliminary injunction to a patentee? And if EPO proceedings are ongoing, should a stay of national proceedings be granted? (pp. 3–4)

Despite problem of fragmentation, there are some procedural advantages to taking a patent infringement case in a European jurisdiction when compared to e.g. the US.

Pause for reflection

Moreover, in the UK and other European jurisdictions, the 'winner' of the case can generally recover a sizeable portion of its costs from the other side—the 'loser pays' rule (C. Helmers and L. McDonagh, 'Patent litigation in England and Wales and the issue-based approach to costs' [2013] 32(3) *Civil Justice Quarterly* 369).

→

> The 'loser pays' rule may also give the UK and Europe an advantage when compared to the US, where each side bears its own legal costs. One unfortunate aspect of the US costs system is that it is thought to encourage 'nuisance' litigation by so-called 'patent troll' companies. The term 'patent troll' is a derogatory term used to refer to a company that tends not to conduct innovation or manufacture products itself (a non-practising entity), but instead builds up an extensive patent portfolio, often by acquiring patents from other companies, and then aggressively asserts them against companies that are in the process of bringing products to market, threatening litigation—and a potential injunction—unless a fee or settlement is paid to them. In the US, the patent troll can be sure that, even if it loses the case, it only bears its own costs. By keeping its own costs low, the patent troll can limit its risk. In contrast, the UK/European 'loser pays' rule system appears to play a role in limiting 'patent troll' litigation in Europe by increasing the costs risk to troll companies (C. Helmers, B. Love, and L. McDonagh, 'Is there a Patent Troll Problem in the UK?' [2014] 24 *Fordham IPLJ* 509.

18.2.4 Choice of defendant: s. 60 in action

From our discussion of s. 60 Patents Act 1977 it is clear that patent infringement may be committed before, during, and after manufacture. Whilst at first glance the principal defendant ought to be someone who makes an infringing product or uses an infringing process, there may well be liability for others who supply essential ingredients or those who deal in the infringing product subsequently. Choice of defendant ultimately is one for the patentee to make, on the advice of lawyers, but two simple examples will illustrate the breadth of the provisions in the Act. Since we are dealing with an engineering patent in Siva's case, in these examples we will turn our attention to pharmaceutical patents.

18.2.4.1 Example 1: manufacture within the UK

Imagine that a pharmaceutical company, Omnifarm plc, owns a UK product patent for a new antibiotic, Cuprocillin. The product has two key ingredients, copper sulphate (a chemical known for many years and which is readily available) and vandalite, a relatively new compound which is difficult to make. Omnifarm has discovered that Fleming Ltd has made the identical drug without permission and has then supplied the drug to GenPharm Ltd, a wholesaler. GenPharm Ltd has in turn supplied Cuprocillin to Shoes plc, a chain of chemists' shops, and Mercia Hospital. Fleming Ltd obtained its supplies of copper sulphate from Adam and its supplies of vandalite from Julie, who is the only UK manufacturer of the ingredient. The hospital has been administering the drug to its patients.

Potentially, Fleming Ltd, GenPharm Ltd, Shoes plc, the hospital, Adam, and Julie could all be defendants to infringement proceedings. Fleming Ltd is, of course, the prime target, having made the patented product. Regarding those liable for post-manufacture acts of infringement, GenPharm Ltd and Shoes plc have kept the product and have also disposed of it. Further, Shoes plc can be said to have offered to dispose of the product if it is on display in its shops, even if it has not actually sold any. The hospital could be alleged to have infringed by using the product in the treatment of its patients, although the patients themselves (who might equally be said to have infringed by using the product) will have the defence of private use. Adam and Julie may have committed contributory infringement by supplying Fleming Ltd with the essential means of putting the invention into effect. Adam, however, is likely to have the defence of having supplied a staple commercial product. Vandalite, however, would not be a staple commercial product, although Omnifarm plc will have to show that Julie had the requisite knowledge for contributory infringement. As she is the only UK manufacturer of the ingredient, meeting the objective standard of s. 60(2) should not be a problem.

18.2.4.2 Example 2: manufacture outside the UK

An alternative scenario might be that Cuprocillin has been made in France by Curie SA and then imported into the UK by Fleming Ltd for supply to the other parties as in our first example. In this case the act of manufacture will not have been committed within the jurisdiction. Unless Omnifarm plc has a French patent, it can do nothing to stop manufacture in France but will have to be content with suing Fleming Ltd for the act of importation. It would not be possible to allege that Curie SA has 'offered to dispose of goods' in the UK by supplying Fleming Ltd because according to *Kalman v PCL Packaging* [1982] FSR 406 both the offer and the disposal must take place in the UK. However, in the second example, should the claimant wish to pursue Curie SA as the originator of the infringing goods, it may be possible for it to be joined as defendant if it can be proved that Curie SA and Fleming Ltd had acted in concert pursuant to a 'common design' which resulted in infringement. The argument that the primary infringer and a UK importer have been parties to a common design may be useful where a primary infringer is located outside the UK, but a company based within the jurisdiction arranges for them to make the infringing product. However, the mere supply of infringing goods to a UK purchaser is not enough for this type of liability. 'Each person must make the infringing acts his own': *Sabaf SpA v Meneghetti* [2003] RPC 264 at [58].

18.2.4.3 Adding other defendants

The Court of Appeal has held in *Unilever v Gillette* [1989] RPC 583 that it is possible to join a UK company's foreign parent company as a co-defendant if the two have acted in concert, although financial and voting control on their own are not enough (*Unilever v Chefaro Proprietaries Ltd* [1994] FSR 135). The court added (following the House of Lords' decision in relation to copyright infringement in *CBS v Amstrad* [1988] AC 1013) that where someone *procures* the infringement of a patent, this leads to liability as a joint tortfeasor with the *specific* primary infringer of the patent, although there can be no separate liability for *generally* inciting the commission of patent infringement. Finally, *Evans v Spritebrand* [1985] FSR 267, although a copyright infringement case, is generally taken to be authority for the proposition that a director can be personally liable for acts of patent infringement carried out by the company if he (or she) has personally and deliberately participated in the carrying out of the infringing acts. Such personal liability would result in the director becoming a joint tortfeasor with the company.

18.2.4.4 Conclusion

Omnifarm plc will have to decide whether it is worthwhile suing all these parties. Clearly, it will be most efficient to stop the source of manufacture of the infringing product, so where this occurs in the UK, Fleming Ltd is likely to be the first defendant to any infringement action. Where manufacture occurs abroad, then it is the importer who is likely to be sued first, with the manufacturer remaining out of reach unless it is possible to prove a common design. One thing which Omnifarm will need to consider is whether in terms of good public relations it is wise to sue a major wholesaler, a major retailer, and a hospital for patent infringement. It will also need to reflect on whether any potential defendant is worth suing, i.e. do they have the ability to pay damages?

 Pause for reflection

In line with the analysis of Katrin Cremers et al ('Patent Litigation in Europe' [2017] 41(1) *European Journal of Law and Economics* 1–44), if Siva is considering engaging in litigation in Germany and France, as well as in the UK, a number of points need to be made about differences in the procedures. For example, in Germany, patent litigation is conducted before District Courts (*Landgerichte*) but patents can only be annulled by the Federal Patent Court. Thus, separate tribunals deal with infringement and validity separately. This could be advantageous to a patentee like Siva—if she makes a convincing case before the infringement court, she may be able to obtain an injunction quite speedily. By contrast, courts in the UK and France can deal with a claim to infringement and a request to revoke the right in the same action. An advantage of the French system for Siva could be the ability of a patentee to obtain a *saisie* (search and seizure) order to search a potential infringer's premises for evidence of infringement. The UK, meanwhile, provides a very thorough, and highly respected, procedure at the Patents Court, though it is not as quick, nor is it considered to be as 'patentee-friendly' as the German courts due to the Patent Court's willingness to hear wide-ranging evidence on whether the patent is valid or not. Alternatively, a speedy, low-cost procedure at the IPEC is available, though it is not suitable for complex questions of validity which may be raised by YESTech.

18.3 Statutory and case law defences

The most obvious response to an action for patent infringement is for the defendant to say: 'I did not infringe'. Such a denial may entail several quite separate arguments: a plea that no infringing act within the wording of s. 60(1) has been committed; that what has been done is not within the monopoly of the patent's claims (which will require the court to construe the patent); or that the defendant is protected by one or more of the various exceptions and defences provided by case law and statute. It is this final argument—on defences—that we will focus on here. A pure argument of defence should be clearly distinguished from the alternative strategy of counterclaiming that the patent is invalid and liable to be revoked (as we have seen, it is possible for you to accept that your conduct comes within the patent's claims, but to argue those claims are, in fact, invalid). Revocation and construction are considered later in the chapter. The statutory and case law exceptions to infringement will now be considered in turn. The majority of these defences presuppose that infringing conduct has in fact been committed, but that the defendant should be exonerated in the interests of fairness.

18.3.1 Defences derived from EU law

The Patents Act 1977 sets out a number of defences to patent infringement. These are concerned to strike a fair balance between the patentee and third parties, but apply only in specific circumstances.

18.3.1.1 Private not commercial purposes

Section 60(5)(a) provides that an act done for private, not commercial, purposes is not infringement. Aldous J in *Smith, Kline & French v Evans* [1989] FSR 513 suggested that the test is subjective. 'Private' should be contrasted with 'public', meaning something done for one's personal use rather than something done secretly. This is, however, subject to the overriding requirement that the conduct in question must not be done for a commercial purpose. Interestingly, Aldous J added that experiments done in order to conduct legal proceedings (for example, to gather evidence to challenge the validity of a patent) fall within the scope of the defence.

18.3.1.2 Experimental purposes

Section 60(5)(b) provides that an act done for experimental purposes *relating to the subject matter of the invention* is not to be treated as infringement. This is a long-established exception, first recognized in *Frearson v Loe* (1878) 9 Ch D 48 at p. 66 where it was said that 'patent rights were never granted to prevent persons of ingenuity exercising their talents in a fair way'. Hence, the manufacture of patented articles without a licence simply for the purpose of *bona fide* experiments does not give rise to liability. By contrast, in *Monsanto v Stauffer Chemical* [1985] RPC 515, field trials of a herbicide conducted with a view to obtaining safety clearance from two non-statutory, non-regulatory bodies (the Pesticides Safety Precaution Scheme and the Agricultural Chemicals Advisory Scheme) were held outside the exemption, the defendant's case probably not being helped by the fact that it had also proposed trials by a Government Department, the Forestry Commission, and various water authorities.

As Aldous J pointed out in *Smith, Kline & French v Evans*, the wording of s. 60(5)(b) requires the experiments to be done for purposes 'relating to the subject matter of the invention'. Such subject matter must be determined by the claims of the patent. In *Smith, Kline & French v Evans* itself, this meant that experiments carried out on goods which were the subject matter of one patent with a view to challenging a separate but related patent were not protected by this defence. Similarly, in *Corevalve Inc v Edwards Lifesciences AG* [2009] FSR 367, Peter Prescott QC pointed out that s. 60(5)(b) Patents Act does not allow the patented invention to be used for experimental acts relating to a different invention. Here the defendant's device for an artificial heart valve was different. Applying *Monsanto v Stauffer* and the German decision in *Klinische Versuche (Clinical Trials) I* [1997] RPC 623, where, as here, the defendant had mixed purposes (developing confidence in its product by the professionals who would use it, building up technical data through the use of its device in hospitals, and generating revenue) it was necessary to determine what was the preponderant purpose. It could not be said that data gathering was the predominant purpose so, had the defendant's device infringed, the experimental use defence would not have been available.

18.3.1.3 Extemporaneous preparation of prescriptions

Section 60(5)(c) enables the extemporaneous preparation in a pharmacy of a medicine prescribed by a doctor or dentist to be exempt from liability, for the obvious policy reason of protecting healthcare professionals in the conduct of their practice.

18.3.1.4 Vehicles, ships, and aircraft temporarily or accidentally within the territory of the United Kingdom

Sections 60(5)(d), (e), and (f) exempt from liability the use of a patented product or process which forms part of any vehicle, ship, or aircraft temporarily or accidentally within the United Kingdom jurisdiction. The word 'temporarily' was considered by the Court of Appeal in *Stena Rederi Aktiebolag v Irish Ferries Ltd* [2003] RPC 681, a case which concerned a ferry travelling between the Republic of Ireland and the UK. It was said that 'temporarily' meant 'for a limited period of time'. The frequency, persistency, and regularity of the visits were irrelevant.

18.3.1.5 Farmer's privilege

Sections 60(5)(g) and (h) were inserted into the Patents Act 1977 as part of the United Kingdom's implementation of Directive 98/44/EC of the European Parliament and of the Council of 6 July 1998 on the legal protection of biotechnological inventions [1998] OJ L 213/13 (the Biotech Directive). The defences apply where there is use by a farmer of the product of his harvest for propagation or multiplication by him on his own holding of previously purchased plant propagating material, or where there is use by a farmer of an animal or animal reproductive material for agricultural purposes following a sale by the patentee to the farmer of breeding stock or other animal reproductive material. The defence assumes that the farmer has legitimately acquired a patented animal or plant from the patentee. It only operates where the farmer uses the next generation of plants or animals for his own farming activities and not where the farmer undertakes further commercialisation of such items.

18.3.1.6 Prior use

The defence of prior use is set out in s. 64 Patents Act 1977, as amended by the CDPA Sch. 5 para 17. The wording of s. 64 is precise. The use in question must be in the UK and must have been started before the priority date of the patent. Further, the defendant must act in good faith. If these conditions are met, then where the defendant does an act which would infringe the patent were it in force, or makes effective and serious preparation to do such an act, then they have the right to continue to do such an act. Any product which is the subject of the prior use can be disposed of without liability. However, the right is personal to the defendant, who may not license another to perform the act of prior use.

Section 64 was accorded a very narrow interpretation by the Court of Appeal in *Lubrizol Corp v Esso Petroleum Ltd* [1998] RPC 727, building on the earlier decision in *Helitune Ltd v Stewart Hughes Ltd* [1991] FSR 171. The defendant had, before the priority date of the claimant's patent, manufactured a batch of the patented substance in the United States (i.e. outside the UK) and had imported some samples into the UK so that the substance could be tested by potential customers. It was held that the key feature of s.

64 was the word 'act' rather than the prior existence of the infringing product. The act here was one of importation, not manufacture. The defendant could have continued to import the substance, but was not at liberty to commence making the infringing product. Further, although it had held internal discussions about setting up a manufacturing plant in the UK before the priority date, no decision had been taken about the location of the plant, so there had not been 'effective and serious preparations' to make the product.

The role of s. 64 in permitting the defendant to continue what would otherwise be infringing conduct has to be understood in the context of s. 2 and the law on novelty (as considered in the prior chapter). Section 64 contemplates that the prior use in question was not such as to amount to an enabling disclosure, otherwise the patent would be invalidated (*Merrell Dow v Norton*). The section therefore applies only to conduct which is uninformed use.

18.3.2 Case law defences

In addition to the statutory defences outlined in the previous section, there are several other arguments to which a defendant may have recourse.

18.3.2.1 Exhaustion of rights

The defence of exhaustion of rights is relevant to the infringing act of importation and any subsequent dealings in the imported goods. Simply put, this defence states that once the goods have been lawfully placed on the market (with the IP owner's consent) and sold, that first sale terminates, or exhausts, the rights held over the product. Here, EU law is critical—the jurisprudence of the Court of Justice of the European Union ('CJEU') on the meaning of Arts 34 and 36 of the Treaty on the Functioning of the European Union ('TFEU') has established when a patentee can or cannot object to the importation of goods which technically infringe the patent. Because of the supremacy of EU law, the case law of the Court must prevail over any rule, statutory or otherwise, of domestic law (Case 106/77 *Simmenthal v Italian Finance Ministry* [1978] ECR 629, Case C-213/89 *Factortame Ltd v Secretary of State for Transport* [1990] ECR I-2433), so the defence could be available where a patented product has been imported into the UK (at time of writing it is unclear what the situation will be post-Brexit). The defence of exhaustion of rights was examined in detail in the context of trade mark infringement in an earlier chapter, but for the purpose of its role in a patent infringement action, the case law can be summarized as follows.

18.3.2.1.1 The difference between infringing and parallel imports

The crucial question to be determined in any exhaustion case is whether the imports to which the patentee objects are infringing imports or parallel imports. Infringing imports are those which originated from an unconnected third party, such as a competitor or (more usually) someone seeking to make pirated copies of the patentee's goods. Such was the scenario in Case 24/67 *Parke Davis v Probel* [1968] ECR 55, where the claimants were relying on their Dutch pharmaceutical patent to prevent the importation into the Netherlands of goods made in Italy. The case was, however, argued on the basis of the competition law provisions (Arts 101 and 102 TFEU) owing to the lengthy transitional period accorded to Art. 34 TFEU. The ruling of the CJEU was therefore concerned with whether the ownership of a patent placed the patentee in a dominant position which was abused by its seeking to prevent the importation of goods from another Member State (the answer to this was 'no'). Nevertheless, the outcome of *Parke Davis* would be the same today if it were decided under the free movement of goods provision in the TFEU. The derogation in Art. 36 TFEU which permits Member States to restrict the free movement of goods in order to protect 'industrial and commercial property' will always enable a patentee to keep infringing imports out of its territory. This is because the 'specific subject matter' of the patent right is the right to put the goods into circulation for the first time anywhere in the European Economic Area ('EEA') and this subject matter is harmed if the patentee is unable to object to the importation of what are essentially counterfeit goods (see Case C-317/91 *Deutsche Renault AG v Audi AG* [1993] ECR I-6227, a case on the rights of the trade mark owner but equally applicable to patents).

However, where the goods are parallel imports (that is, goods first marketed in another EEA Contracting State which can be traced back to the patentee in some way, whether through a parent/subsidiary relationship, a licence, or a chain of contracts), then Art. 36 TFEU gives way to Art. 34. The principle of the free movement of goods prevails over the interests of the intellectual property owner. Thus, according to Case 15/74 *Centrafarm BV v Sterling Drug* [1974] ECR 1147, the patentee in Member State A (in this case the Netherlands) could not use its patent right to prevent the importation of goods put in circulation in the EU by a subsidiary company in Member State B (the UK), as the sale of the goods in the UK by the subsidiary was deemed to exhaust the patentee's rights. The parallel importer was thus free to exploit price differentials between the two Member States, thereby introducing an element of price competition for the patentee in the latter's own territory.

18.3.2.1.2 The issue of consent to marketing

In determining whether exhaustion has occurred, the key factor is whether the patentee (either personally or through a subsidiary or licensee) consented to the sale of the patented product somewhere in the EEA, not whether the Member State where this first sale occurred granted the patentee protection. In Case 187/80 *Merck v Stephar* [1981] ECR 2063, the CJEU held that the patentee could not use its patent rights in the Netherlands to prevent the importation from Italy of drugs which it had marketed there. The fact that at the time Italy did not grant patent protection for pharmaceuticals was irrelevant, as the patentee had deliberately chosen to market the goods somewhere in the EU and so had to take the consequences. The facts of the case were the opposite of those in *Parke Davis* (the goods in *Merck* had originated with the patentee, rather than having been made by a counterfeiter) and were mirrored in Cases C-267/95 *Merck v Primecrown* and C-268/95 *Beecham v Europharm* [1996] ECR I-6285. Here the patentees were trying to rely on their UK patents to prevent the importation of goods from Spain and Portugal. The CJEU declared that the fact that the Member States of export did not (at the time) grant patent protection for pharmaceuticals was irrelevant. The patentees had chosen to market their products in those countries regardless of any return on their investment. This consent to marketing exhausted any rights they might have had in the UK.

Consent to marketing is assessed on a factual basis, so that where the patentee has been forced to grant a compulsory licence in Member State A, that does *not* exhaust its rights, and the patent can be relied on to prevent importation into Member State B of goods made by another undertaking under the compulsory licence: Case 19/84 *Pharmon v Hoechst* [1985] ECR 2281.

18.3.2.2 Licence to repair

It used to be said that someone who purchased a patented article had the right to repair that article, as long as the repair was not so extensive that it resulted in a new article being made (*Sirdar v Wallington* (1907) 24 RPC 539 and *Solar Thompson v Barton* [1977] RPC 537).

The extent of the so-called 'defence' was considered by the House of Lords in *United Wire Ltd v Screen Repair Services (Scotland) Ltd* [2000] 4 All ER 353. The patents related to mesh screens used in sifting machines deployed in the oil exploration industry. The screens were used to remove solids from drilling fluid and had a relatively short life, the mesh lasting from a few hours to a few days. The frames to which the mesh screens were bonded were often still serviceable. The defendants carried on a screen repair business. They cleaned and recoated the frame made by the claimant, and fitted new meshes. The defendants argued, inter alia, that the repaired screens did not fall within the wording of any of the claims of the patents but, if they did, their acts were merely non-infringing repairs because the patentee had impliedly licensed anyone who acquired a screen assembly to prolong its life by repair. The House of Lords considered that the sale of a patented article could not confer an implied licence to make another. Instead, the repair of a patented product was by definition an act which did not amount to making it. Repair was one of the concepts (like modifying or adapting) which shared a boundary with 'making' but did not trespass on its territory. The notion of an implied licence to repair distracted attention from the question raised by s. 60(1)(a) of the Patents Act 1977, namely whether the defendant had *made* the patented product. The owner's right to repair was not an independent right conferred on him by an express or implied licence, rather it was a residual right, forming part of the right to do whatever did not amount to making the product. *United Wire Screen*, however, was later distinguished by the Supreme Court in *Schütz (UK) Ltd v Werit UK Ltd*: here the defendant's conduct in replacing a part which easily wore out was not 'making'. The implication must be that the implied licence defence can still be raised.

18.3.2.3 That the infringement is 'not novel'

The last case law defence neatly illustrates the intersection of infringement and validity, and the fact that both issues depend on the interpretation of the claims of the patent.

> ### *Gillette Safety Razor Co v Anglo-American Trading Co* (1913)
> ### 30 RPC 465
>
> The defence is called 'Gillette' after the case which first established it. As we shall see, a close examination of the facts of the case shows that this is not so much a defence per se, rather it is a way of pleading which places the patentee (in the words of Lord Mouton) 'on the horns of a dilemma'.

In *Gillette* the patent was for improvements to the safety razor, the main feature being that a thin flexible razor blade was clamped in a curved holder by the handle, the effect of the clamp being to make the blade rigid. The alleged infringement by the defendant consisted of a similar razor, the blade of which was flat. The defendant pointed out the existence of a prior American patent which involved the use of the handle acting as a clamp to hold the razor blade. He then argued that either he had not infringed (because what he had produced, a flat razor blade, was not within the claims which referred only to curved blades) or that what he had done was not novel because the only difference between his razor and the earlier patent was that his razor had a thinner blade, which could still be fitted to the handle of the American razor. Lord Moulton found for the defendant and welcomed the method of arguing the case because it could save time and trouble. The defendant had to succeed either on invalidity or non-infringement. If the claims of the patent were interpreted widely, so as to catch what the defendant had done, the patent would be invalid because it was anticipated by the prior art. On the other hand, if the claimant argued for a narrow construction of the patent so as to avoid the prior art, the defendant's conduct would fall outside the monopoly claimed. The patentee could not have it both ways. The 'heads I win, tails you lose' effect is sometimes known as the 'squeeze' argument.

The *Gillette* defence is a limited one. This was explained by Lord Evershed MR in *Page v Brent Toy Products* (1950) 67 RPC 4 at p. 11. He stated that *Gillette* is not a separate defence. Rather it is a convenient brief form of raising by way of the pleadings the whole of the defendant's case, but only where the defendant is able to raise as alternatives the pleas of non-infringement and invalidity. As noted later on, the applicability of the *Gillette* defence has been thrown into doubt by *Eli Lilly v Actavis* [2017] (and subsequent orbiter comments in the High Court case of *Mylan v Yeda Development* [2017] EWHC 2629 (Pat)).

18.3.3 Restriction on the availability of damages

Section 62 of the Patents Act 1977, rather than providing the alleged infringer with a true defence, restricts the patentee's right to claim damages in three circumstances. Under s. 62(1), damages (or an account of profits) are not available against the innocent defendant, but as pointed out by Lloyd Jacob J in *Wilbec v Dawes* [1966] RPC 513, the onus is on the defendant to prove, objectively, such innocence. The wording of the section includes the phrase 'he was not aware and had no reasonable grounds for supposing that a patent existed' and so the defendant will be judged by the standard of others in that industry (*LA Gear v Hi-Tec Sports plc*). In this case the defence of innocence failed anyway, as the defendant's attention had been drawn to the patent application in earlier correspondence. Section 62(1) goes on to provide, in effect, that in order to ensure knowledge on the part of the defendant, it is not enough merely to mark the goods 'patented': the patent number should also be given.

Section 62(2) confers on the court the discretion to refuse to award damages in respect of any acts of infringement committed during the period when the patentee had failed to pay the annual renewal fees. Finally, there is a discretion in s. 62(3) to refuse the award of damages in respect of infringing acts committed before the patent specification was amended, unless the court is satisfied that the original patent specification was drafted in good faith and with reasonable skill and knowledge. The provision therefore contemplates that the defendant has sought revocation of the patent as a counterclaim to infringement, in response to which the patentee has applied to amend it in order to avoid a conflict with the prior art. It also assumes that the defect in the patent is curable by amendment and that the infringement action succeeded.

 Pause for reflection

Do the various statutory and case law defences strike an adequate balance between the needs of the patentee and those of third parties?

Would any of the above defences be available to YESTech in the dispute with Siva?

18.4 Counterclaiming for revocation of the patent

18.4.1 Overview of revocation

As noted earlier, in addition to raising one or more of the statutory or case law defences, a defendant to a patent infringement action may attempt instead to have the patent declared invalid. Tactically speaking, having the patent revoked is by far the most effective response as its retrospective removal from the register means that there is (literally) nothing to infringe. Nevertheless, the onus is on the defendant to substantiate the counterclaim. The patentee can of course resist the application to revoke by seeking to show the patent is valid, but equally can seek to amend the patent to overcome the objections. The deployment of expert evidence by both parties of necessity increases the length, cost, and complexity of patent litigation at the English Patents Court (the procedures of the IPEC make it unsuitable for complex revocation claims). Revocation may be total or partial (so the court may delete some claims whilst leaving others).

Section 74 Patents Act 1977 sets out when a patent may be challenged. The validity of the patent may be raised as an issue: in infringement proceedings; in a threats action under s. 70; in proceedings for a declaration of non-infringement under s. 71; in revocation proceedings under s. 72; or in any dispute as to Crown use. The Comptroller of Patents (i.e. UKIPO) also has power to revoke of his own initiative under s. 73 where e.g. relevant information has come to the Comptroller's attention. There is no requirement of standing, so that any person can apply: *Cairnstores Ltd v AB Hassle* [2002] FSR 95. The applicant need not have a commercial interest in pursuing such action: *TNS Group Holdings Ltd v Nielsen Media Research Inc* [2009] FSR 873.

18.4.2 Grounds for revocation

The grounds for revocation are to be found in s. 72(1) Patents Act 1977, as amended by the CDPA Sch. 5. The five grounds are:

(a) what has been granted is not a patentable invention under s. 1;

(b) the patent has been granted to the wrong person under s. 7;

(c) the description of the invention is insufficient for the purposes of s. 14;

(d) there has been an impermissible amendment which broadens the description of the invention; and

(e) there has been an impermissible amendment which has extended the scope of the claims.

Section 72 is a self-contained provision which excludes any consideration of the previous law or any other objection to the patent, owing to the presence of the phrase 'but only on' in the opening words of the provision: *Genentech Inc's Patent* [1989] RPC 147; *Mentor v Hollister* [1991] FSR 557.

The grounds of revocation most likely to be encountered are lack of patentability (which raises all the issues we dealt with in the prior chapter, as found in s. 1 Patents Act 1977, particularly novelty and inventive step). As we have covered this in detail in the prior chapter there is no need to revisit it. However, two of the grounds of revocation require further discussion: grant to the wrong person and, more critically, insufficiency.

18.4.2.1 Grant to the wrong person

Despite the apparent breadth of wording of s. 72(1)(b), the ability to revoke a patent on the basis of wrongful entitlement is not wide-ranging. Section 72(2) provides that the application to revoke can only be made by a person who is themselves entitled to be granted the patent (that is, a co-inventor or the inventor's employer); and further, that such an application must be brought within two years of the date of grant of the patent. Therefore, s. 72(1)(b) is concerned with entitlement disputes (often between co-inventors), as in ss. 8 and 37 Patents Act 1977.

In *Yeda Research & Development Co Ltd v Rhone-Poulenc Rorer* [2008] RPC 1 the House of Lords said that the only question under these two provisions is 'who came up with the inventive concept?' (either solely or jointly). Questions of entitlement and novelty ought to be kept separate (the earlier decisions in *Markem v Zipher* [2005] RPC 761 and *IDA Ltd v Southampton University* [2006] RPC 567 which had held that there had to be a breach of confidence or a breach of contract were overruled). The same reasoning must, logically, apply to s. 72.

18.4.2.2 Insufficiency

In terms of the meaning of insufficiency, it was initially uncertain whether s. 72(1)(c) empowered the court to act only where the description of the invention was unclear, or whether the power extended to where the claims of the patent were broader than the description. In other words, can s. 72(1)(c) be used to strike down overly broad claims?

The initial response of the Court of Appeal in *Chiron v Organon (No 12)* [1996] FSR 153 was to say that s. 72(1)(c) was confined to revocation for lack of clarity in the description. If the claims in the patent were too broad, that is, the monopoly contained within them exceeded the description of the invention, that was a matter for the UKIPO to deal with at the application stage; but if the UKIPO did not, then there could not be a subsequent challenge to the breadth of the claims.

However, the House of Lords in *Biogen v Medeva* [1997] RPC 1 took a different approach, saying that if the patentee had claimed protection for matter not set out in the description, then that could be challenged post-grant by third parties under s. 72(1)(c). That led some judges and writers to suggest that there were in fact two types of insufficiency, namely 'classical' insufficiency (failure to explain the invention to the skilled addressee) and *'Biogen'* insufficiency (failure of the claims to match the description). The matter was initially resolved by Aldous LJ in *Kirin-Amgen Inc and others v Hoechst Marion Roussel Ltd and others* [2003] RPC 31, at [71] where he said:

> [The specification must enable the invention to be performed] to the full extent of the monopoly claimed. If the invention discloses a principle capable of general application, the claims may be in correspondingly general terms. The patentee need not show that he has proved its application in every individual instance. On the other hand, if the claims include a number of discrete methods or products, the patentee must enable the invention to be performed in respect of each of them.

Since then, the matter has been revisited by the House of Lords in *H Lundbeck A/S v Generics (UK) Ltd* [2009] RPC 407. Lord Neuberger at [93] (with whom Lord Walker agreed) analysed what Lord Hoffmann had said in *Biogen*. They stated that the issue was not whether the claimed invention could 'deliver the goods', but whether the claims covered other ways in which they might be delivered, ways which owed nothing to the teaching of the patent or any principle it disclosed. In *Biogen*, the disputed claim was very unusual because the molecule was identified partly by the way in which it had been made, and partly by what it did. The patent disclosed one way in which the DNA fragments could produce Hepatitis B antigens, but the claim covered other ways as well. The decision to revoke the patent in *Biogen* for insufficiency was entirely in accord with what the EPO had said in *T 409/91 EXXON/Fuel Oils* [1994] EPOR 149. The case of *Biogen* was distinguished—the patent in *Lundbeck* was entirely different from the 'very unusual' nature of that in *Biogen*, as it was a 'straightforward' claim to a single chemical product.

The key insight of *Lundbeck* is that the ability to revoke a patent for overly broad claims depends on whether the specific claims sufficiently correspond with the description. A general description can have general claims; but detailed claims require a correspondingly detailed (sufficient) description. Much depends, of course, on the identity of the skilled addressee and what is held to be within their common general knowledge.

Where a defendant raises both lack of inventive step and insufficiency as grounds of revocation there is another type of 'squeeze' argument to trap the patentee. If it is alleged that the invention is obvious because the skilled addressee would as a matter of course be able to reach the same point as the invention by relying on the prior art and/or their common general knowledge, then the patentee may respond by saying that the prior art did not contain enough of a signpost (as suggested by Sachs LJ in *General Tire v Firestone* [1972] RPC 457) to guide the reader of the patent. The defendant's rejoinder could then well be that if the prior art did not contain enough information to point the way to the later invention, then the patentee has assumed too much knowledge on the part of the skilled addressee who would be unable to perform the invention from the description found in the specification: *Schering-Plough Ltd v Norbrook Laboratories Ltd* [2006] FSR 302.

 Pause for reflection

Is there really a separate ground of challenge known as *Biogen* insufficiency? If so, how does it fit in with the justifications for patent protection and the requirement that an invention must be capable of industrial application?

→

Biogen v Medeva was the first case involving biotechnology patents that reached the UK's highest court (the House of Lords). As McDonagh notes, the technology was still very new and prior rulings at the High Court and Court of Appeal level had taken divergent views on how patent law should accommodate biotech. In this sense, the House of Lords ruling provided much needed clarity on what the patent law expected from a biotech patent with respect to how the patent described the invention, and whether this was sufficient ('Biogen v Medeva' in J. Bellido (ed.) *Landmark Cases in Intellectual Property* (Hart, 2017)). However, for the same reason, the case can be seen as of its time, and its scope was narrowed in the later case of *Generics v Lundbeck.*

18.5 The scope of the patentee's monopoly

18.5.1 The problem identified: variants

As indicated at the start of this chapter, a key part of the claimant's case is to show that what the defendant has done falls within the wording of the claims of the patent. In other words, the defendant has trespassed on the 'territory' marked out by the claims. However, a defendant will rarely commit what is called 'textual' infringement by producing something that is an 'exact match' of the invention. Rather, there will be differences between the alleged infringing product or process and what is set out in the wording of the claims. These differences are called 'variants'.

When faced with such variants, the task before the court involves two stages: first, it must construe the meaning of the claims; second, it must decide whether the activity of the defendant comes within those claimed invention.

To construe the patent the court will allocate a meaning to the claims. Much will depend on the sort of words used by the claimant (or typically, the patent attorney who drafted the claims) in asserting what was considered to be unique about the invention. Are those words general and descriptive, or specific and technical? In respect of words with specific meanings, has the patentee provided their own definition, or does such definition have to be gleaned from a dictionary? A further factor is that the specification is addressed to the hypothetical skilled addressee, whose identity and attributes will be determined by the court. As noted earlier, the patent specification will probably have been drafted by a patent attorney, someone who is, by training, a scientist or engineer, not a lawyer. Later on, sometimes several years later, it will then be subjected to precise examination by lawyers by each side—primarily solicitors and barristers—in the Patents Court. Opportunities for different interpretations—and even strange results—abound.

Once a meaning has been allocated to the claims, the court will decide whether the alleged infringement falls within the scope of the claimant's invention. The claimant will seek to convince the court that it does; the defendant will, of course, try to argue that it does not. The meaning of the claims, as decided in the first step, will be crucial to this analysis.

18.5.2 The law on patent claim interpretation: from literal to purposive construction

It is often said that the traditional approach to the allocation of meaning to patent claims under United Kingdom law was literal interpretation. Claims (rather like a

map in a conveyance of land) were treated as marking the outer limit of the patentee's protection. They were treated as 'fence-posts' (*EMI v Lissen* (1939) 56 RPC 23;
Henricksen v Tallon [1965] RPC 434.) a term that came to distinguish the UK approach
from the German 'sign posts' approach, which used the claims as guidance rather
than strict limits.

In the UK, whether variants infringed *used* to be determined by the 'pith and marrow
doctrine' (or the doctrine of 'mechanical equivalents') to infringe the defendant must
have taken the 'pith and marrow' of the invention by incorporating all the essential
integers in the alleged infringement (an integer is an element of a claim). If such integers, being the 'substance' of the invention, were present, it did not matter if other,
non-essential, integers had 'mechanical equivalents' substituted for them (Parker J in
Marconi v British Radio Telegraph & Telephone Co (1911) 28 RPC 181 at p. 217 and Lord
Evershed in *Birmingham Sound Reproductions v Collaro* [1956] RPC 232 at p. 245).

Further cases on the literal interpretation such as *Van der Lely v Bamfords* [1963] RPC
61 and *Rodi & Wienenberger v Showell* [1969] RPC 367 exposed the fact that applying the
literal test sometimes resulted in cases that went against justice and perhaps even common sense. In *Rodi*, for instance, the patent described an expandable watch-strap with
'U' shaped links. The defendant's watch-strap had 'C' shaped links. Even though you
can turn a 'U' through 90 degrees to become a 'C' a 3-2 majority of the House of Lords
held that there was no infringement because the defendant's product was not within
the wording of the claims.

In 1982, the House of Lords made a departure from its earlier approach. Lord Diplock
introduced the 'purposive construction' test in the seminal case of *Catnic Components
v Hill & Smith* [1982] RPC 185. The patent related to galvanized steel lintels placed over
doors and windows in buildings with cavity walls. The claim stated that the back-plate
of the lintel had to be 'vertical'. The defendants' lintel (admittedly copied from the
patentees' brochure) had a back-plate which was at a slight angle to the vertical. This
made it less efficient although it still performed the same engineering function (load
bearing). The simple issue for the House of Lords was whether the word 'vertical' was
to be treated as a precise requirement or not. Their Lordships decided that it was not,
instead it meant 'substantially vertical'. Such liberal treatment of a word which to a civil
engineer would have an exact meaning was no doubt helped by the choice of a building
site foreman as the hypothetical skilled addressee of the patent.

Lord Diplock (giving the only speech) stated (without the citation of authority) that
a patent specification should be given a 'purposive' construction, rather than 'a purely
literal one derived from applying to it the kind of meticulous verbal analysis in which
lawyers are too often tempted by their training to indulge'. Lord Diplock then set out
what became known as the '*Catnic* question':

> The question in each case is: whether persons with practical knowledge and experience
> of the kind of work in which the invention was intended to be used, would understand
> that strict compliance with a particular descriptive word or phrase appearing in a claim
> was intended by the patentee to be an essential requirement of the invention so that any
> variant would fall outside the monopoly claimed, even though it could have no material
> effect upon the way the invention worked.
>
> The question, of course, does not arise where the variant would in fact have a mate-
> rial effect upon the way the invention worked. Nor does it arise unless at the date of

publication of the specification it would be obvious to the informed reader that this was so. Where it is not obvious, in the light of the then-existing knowledge, the reader is entitled to assume that the patentee thought at the time of the specification that he had good reason for limiting his monopoly so strictly and had intended to do so, even though subsequent work by him or others in the field of the invention might show the limitation to have been unnecessary. It is to be answered in the negative only when it would be apparent to any reader skilled in the art that a particular descriptive word or phrase used in a claim cannot have been intended by a patentee, who was also skilled in the art, to exclude minor variants which, to the knowledge of both him and the readers to whom the patent was addressed, could have no material effect upon the way in which the invention worked.

 Pause for reflection

How 'revolutionary' was Lord Diplock's speech in *Catnic*? Do you think that moving away from a literal test to a purposive one should allow greater justice to be done, or could it give the courts too much room to interpret claims in ways that were not originally expressed in the literal claims?

Consider Siva's problem. Would YESTech potentially infringe Claim 1 of her patent under the literal or purposive test (or both)?

The Court of Appeal subsequently held in *Codex v Racal-Milgo* [1983] RPC 369 that the *Catnic* 'purposive construction' test had replaced the literal, 'pith and marrow' doctrine.

18.5.3 The impact of the EPC 1973

The *Catnic* decision involved a patent granted under the earlier Patents Act 1949 and so was essentially a product of the 'common law of patents'. Was it relevant to patents granted under the 1977 Act (which followed the EPC)? Two provisions in the current legislation should be noted, both derived from the EPC. First, s. 125(1) (based on EPC Art. 69) declares that an invention is to be as stated in the claims (interpreted in the light of the description which will precede them in the patent specification, together with any drawings) and the extent of the protection conferred by a patent shall be determined accordingly. Second, s. 125(3) replicates the wording of the Protocol to Art. 69 EPC. Because it is so central to the cases which follow, we set out the original wording of the Protocol to Art. 69 EPC 1973, which reads as follows:

> Article 69 should not be interpreted in the sense that the extent of the protection conferred by a European patent is to be understood as that defined by the strict, literal, meaning of the wording used in the claims, the description and drawings being employed only for the purpose of resolving ambiguity found in the claims. Neither should it be interpreted in the sense that the claims serve only as a guideline and that the actual protection conferred may extend to what, from a consideration of the description by a person skilled in the art, the patentee has contemplated. On the contrary, it is to be interpreted as defining a position between these extremes which combines a fair protection for the patentee with a reasonable degree of certainty for third parties.

> ### Pause for reflection
>
> Sherman states that when the EPC was drafted, there was concern that although the process of granting European patents had been centralized at the EPO, once granted such patents would be at the mercy of idiosyncratic interpretations by courts—caricatured as ranging from the UK's (overly) literal approach, to treating the claims merely as guidelines, which was said to be the case in Germany and the Netherlands ('Patent Claim Interpretation: The Impact of the Protocol on Interpretation' [1991] 54 *MLR* 499). It was thought that there would be no point in having a centrally granted patent if its treatment varied wildly from state to state.
>
> Thus, fear of divergency led to the attachment of the Protocol in an attempt to ensure uniformity. However, Sherman questions whether something designed as a compromise at a diplomatic level could achieve internal change in a national legal system. Was the Protocol simply a statement of aspirations? Or was it intended to have significant legal impact on national law? The benefit of hindsight shows us that it is the latter that has occurred. As we shall see, the Protocol has come to play a crucial role in the interpretation of patents before the UK courts.

18.5.4 Catnic reformulated

The first case to consider the impact of the Protocol in United Kingdom law was *Improver v Remington* [1990] FSR 181. The patent involved a hair-removing device in which a coiled helical spring was spun lengthwise by an electric motor, so that as the windings of the spring opened and closed they acted like high-speed tweezers. The defendant's rival device used a bent rubber rod with slits in it instead of the looped spring, but otherwise worked in the same way. As the rod was a variant, the question was deceptively simple. Did it infringe?

The difficulty with the case was that the Court of Appeal, in earlier interlocutory proceedings (*Improver v Remington* [1989] RPC 69) had declared (without explanation) that Lord Diplock's purposive construction test in *Catnic* was the appropriate test for patents granted under the 1977 Act.

In the substantive hearing, *Improver v Remington* [1990] FSR 181, Hoffmann J (as he then was) considered himself bound by that finding. Accordingly, he took Lord Diplock's question from *Catnic* and reworked it into a more complex three-stage test:

> If the issue was whether a feature embodied in an alleged infringement which fell outside the primary, literal or acontextual meaning of a descriptive word or phrase in the claim ('a variant') was nevertheless within its language as properly interpreted, the court should ask itself the following three questions:
>
> (1) Does the variant have a material effect upon the way the invention works? If yes, the variant is outside the claim. If no—
>
> (2) Would this (i.e. that the variant had no material effect) have been obvious at the date of publication of the patent to a reader skilled in the art? If no, the variant is outside the claim. If yes—
>
> (3) Would the reader skilled in the art nevertheless have understood from the language of the claim that the patentee intended that strict compliance with the primary meaning was an essential requirement of the invention? If yes, the variant is outside the claim.

When Hoffmann J's statement is compared with that of Lord Diplock, the *Catnic* question itself becomes the third question, placed after a discussion on the effect of the variant and the skilled addressee's perception of the variant (matters which Lord Diplock treats as subsidiary issues to be looked at later). Hoffmann J's restructuring of *Catnic* into three sequential inquiries has the effect of placing greater emphasis on the wording of the claim, harking back to the days of *EMI v Lissen*. Hoffmann J explained that the first two questions are questions of fact, and are to be used to provide the factual background against which the specification must be construed. He then stated that it is the third question which raises the matter of construction. Lord Diplock's formulation made it clear that the answers to the first two questions are not conclusive. Even though the variant made no material difference and this would have been obvious at the time, the skilled addressee may decide that the patentee for some reason was confining the claim to a specific meaning.

In conclusion, Hoffmann J held that the defendant's device did not infringe, because although the variant did not have a material effect on the way the invention worked, and although it would have been obvious to a skilled addressee that a rubber rod would have the same desired attributes as a looped spring, the wording of the claim was so precise that only the use of a looped spring would infringe.

18.5.5 Application of the *Catnic/Improver* questions

From the time of *Improver* until 2004, UK courts generally applied what became known as the *Catnic/Improver* questions to determine whether a variant infringed. An example is *Daily v Berchet* [1992] FSR 533 where the invention concerned a baby walker. The device had a safety feature, namely an automatic breaking arrangement, so that when downward pressure was exerted on the frame (for example, when the child used the frame to lift itself off the ground) brake pads were applied to the rims of the rear wheels, thus preventing the walker from moving forward. The approach of the Court of Appeal was to take Claim 1 of the patent, and fragment it into its essential integers or features, in many ways not unlike the technique used in the old 'pith and marrow' cases. The resultant emphasis placed on the phrase 'in association with the rear wheels' as a key feature of the invention led inevitably to a finding of non-infringement because the defendant's walking frame (for invalids) had a braking system which applied friction to the ground to stop forward movement, rather than applying pressure to the wheels.

Another example of the use of the *Catnic/Improver* questions include *Electrolux v Black & Decker* [1996] FSR 595 (where the patent for an electric hover mower which used a fan blade to suck up the grass cuttings was not infringed by a rival mower where the fan did not have such an effect).

It is important to consider cases involving 'second medical uses' (Swiss form claims). In *American Home Products Corp v Novartis Pharmaceuticals UK Ltd* [2001] RPC 1 a patent employing 'Swiss form claims' for the second medical use of the substance rapamycin was held not to be infringed by the manufacture of a derivative substance. The wording of the claim was so precise that the skilled addressee would assume that only rapamycin and not any second- or third-generation version of it would be protected.

Warner-Lambert v Generics **[2016] EWCA Civ 1006**

Warner-Lambert is a significant case on the infringement of second-medical use patents. The Court of Appeal upheld the earlier High Court ruling on the patent's invalidity, agreeing that the patent was insufficient. However, the Court of Appeal made *obiter* comments that disagreed with the approach of the High Court to the question of infringement and proposed a new approach, as described below.

In *Warner-Lambert*, in the High Court Arnold J had stated that for a second-medical use claim to be infringed the key elements were (i) that it must have been foreseeable that the manufacturer's product would be used for the claimed indication and (ii) the manufacturer had to actively intend that it be used in this way. The Court of Appeal clarified that Arnold J had not taken the correct approach to intention:

> Intentional use is to be distinguished from use where the drug is prescribed for a different indication and, without it in any sense being the intention of the treatment, a pain condition is in fact treated.

Instead, the Court of Appeal said that for infringement to take place 'it is only essential that the manufacturer is able to foresee that there will be intentional use for the new medical indication'. In the view of the Court of Appeal, this is closer to a pure foreseeability test than one that requires active, subjective intention:

> The intention will be negatived where the manufacturer has taken all reasonable steps within his power to prevent the consequences occurring.

 Pause for reflection

Do you consider that Hoffman J was right to reformulate the *Catnic* question in *Improver v Remington*, or was this a regressive move that laid too much stress on the literal wording of the claims?

18.5.6 Dissent and a re-emphasis of the value of the *Improver* test

In the immediate aftermath of *Improver*, there was only one United Kingdom decision that questioned the correctness of the *Catnic/Improver* questions, namely *PLG Research Ltd v Ardon* [1995] RPC 287. Millett LJ argued that it was preferable to follow the approach at the time of the German courts to claim interpretation (the German approach has since changed). He stated that they used a modified version of the *Improver* questions. The first two questions were identical (namely, as a question of fact, whether the variant worked in the same way as the invention and if so, whether this would have been obvious to the skilled addressee). However, the third question was replaced by an alternative which asked what variants the skilled reader would contemplate as falling within the claims.

PLG v Ardon was immediately criticized (and Millett LJ's remarks were stated to be *obiter*) by Aldous J in *Assidoman Multipack v The Mead Corporation* [1995] RPC 321. It was then repeatedly stated by the Court of Appeal (for example, in *Beloit v Valmet* [1997] RPC 489 and *Kastner v Rizla* [1995] RPC 585) that reliance on the *Improver* questions provided the correct, structured approach to determine patent claim interpretation.

18.5.7 Rebranding *Catnic/Improver* as 'the Protocol questions'

The relationship between the *Catnic/Improver* questions and the Protocol to Art. 69 EPC became clearer when the questions were renamed 'the Protocol questions' in *Wheatley (Davina) v Drillsafe Ltd* [2001] RPC 133. There was a division of opinion in the Court of Appeal as to whether there had been infringement in this case. The differences between the majority and the minority in *Wheatley v Drillsafe* lie in the way in which the court approached the issue of inventive concept.

The majority took a narrower view of the patent's inventive concept, regarding it as the use of a 'centre-less' drill cutter for drilling holes in underground petrol storage tanks without the need for the use of a pilot drill. The minority (Aldous LJ) adopted a broader view of the inventive concept: what mattered was that the defendant's probe did not enter the tank (thereby avoiding the risk of sparks) which was the problem which the patent had sought to solve. Aldous LJ therefore followed the advice of Lord Hoffmann in *Biogen v Medeva* in identifying the problem to be solved as part of the process of identifying the inventive concept. Ultimately, the case reveals that it is possible for the underlying inventive concept to be drawn broadly or narrowly by the court. This means that different answers will be obtained to the Protocol questions in each instance.

With regard to the Protocol questions themselves, *Wheatley v Drillsafe* explained that they were intended simply to assist with purposive construction of the claims. Question 1 envisaged that the claim had an ambit wider than its literal meaning, so as to give fair protection to the patentee, but subject to the safeguard for third parties when taken in conjunction with Question 2. Question 3 also provided a fair result for the patentee, namely the avoidance of an unintended meaning, whilst protecting third parties by emphasizing the purpose of the words.

 Pause for reflection

Does the back and forth over different interpretations and findings—literal, purposive, *Catnic/ Improver*, *Biogen*, and *Wheatley*—illustrate that patent law is a particularly complex, even uncertain, area of law? Or is the nature of technological innovation such that no legal doctrine could ever fully anticipate how and when rival companies trespass onto elements and concepts covered by existing patents?

18.5.8 When *Catnic/Improver* was ignored

Interestingly, not every post-1990 case utilized the three-stage test advocated by Hoffmann J in *Improver v Remington*. For instance, the court dispensed with the questions in *Warheit v Olympia Tools Ltd* [2003] FSR 95, where the invention was very simple and there was literal infringement. Equally, in cases dealing with pharmaceutical patents, it was said that the Protocol questions, though providing a structured approach, were not always appropriate and that the Protocol itself simply required the third question to be put, i.e. what did the skilled addressee think the patentee intended (*Pharmacia Corp v Merck & Co Inc* [2002] RPC 775 (CA) and *Merck & Co Inc v Generics (UK) Ltd* [2004] RPC 607)? As we shall see later on, issues of pharmaceutical patents under the Protocol have recently been re-evaluated by the UKSC.

18.5.9 Kirin-Amgen

In *Kirin-Amgen Inc v Hoechst Marion Roussel Ltd*, the issue of claim interpretation was revisited in the House of Lords by Lord Hoffmann (as he now was). The patent involved the production of erythropoietin ('EPO') by recombinant DNA technology, EPO being a protein which regulates the production of red blood cells. The defendant had developed another way of making EPO which the patentee alleged infringed two claims of the patent. The House of Lords agreed with the Court of Appeal that the patent had not been infringed.

Lord Hoffmann (giving the only speech) made clear that the scope of protection of a patent is determined by the claims. Anything which extends protection outside the claims is expressly prohibited. Crucially, he said that there is therefore nothing in European patent law which equates to the US 'doctrine of equivalents'. When deciding whether a variant infringes, there is only one question to be asked. 'What would a person skilled in the art have understood the patentee to have used the language of the claim to mean?' Everything else, including the Protocol questions themselves, was only guidance to a judge trying to answer that question. Further, the Protocol questions could be unhelpful, because, for example, in an area of rapid change (such as recombinant DNA technology) it cannot be assumed that the skilled addressee would know a variant would work in the same way.

Lord Hoffmann in *Kirin-Amgen* added that the Protocol is concerned with the construction of Art. 69, not the construction of claims. The Protocol says that literalism should be avoided, but otherwise says that one should not go outside the claims. Accordingly, fair protection for the patentee together with certainty for third parties are both catered for by asking 'what is the full extent of the monopoly which the person skilled in the art would think he was intending to claim?' As a result, the original *Catnic* question was in full accord with the Protocol.

Contradicting his own statement in *Improver v Remington*, Lord Hoffmann declared that purposive construction *does* depend on context. Strict compliance is appropriate where 'figures, measurements, angles and the like are given'. The Protocol questions were therefore difficult, if not impossible, to apply where the language used was very exact, and were not a substitute for trying to understand what the person skilled in the art would have understood the patentee to mean by the language of the claims. Lord Hoffmann appears to be saying that where the patent involves sophisticated technology, of necessity the language of the claims will have to be precise (otherwise there might be a risk of '*Biogen* insufficiency'), so that the Protocol questions do not assist the court. The only issue is to ask what the skilled addressee understood the patentee to mean. This appears to mark a complete return to Lord Diplock's question in *Catnic* and an abandonment of the three-stage test in *Improver v Remington*. It also has the effect of conferring narrower protection on what might otherwise be regarded as 'leading edge' inventions.

18.5.10 **Examples of the application of the *Kirin-Amgen* test**

Following the decision of the House of Lords in *Kirin-Amgen*, it became clear that the choice of the skilled addressee, as well as the context of the patent (i.e. how sophisticated it is) and the precision of language used by the patentee, can all have a crucial bearing on how claims are interpreted. A number of cases illustrate the interrelationship of these factors in patent claim interpretation, although ultimately it all comes back to the *Kirin-Amgen* question: what would a person skilled in the art have understood the patentee to have used the language of the claim to mean?

Our starting point is *Corus UK Ltd v Qual-Chem Ltd* [2008] EWCA Civ 1177 where it was held that the use of the word 'tailored' in a patent for an improvement to a process for the manufacture of steel would be understood by the skilled reader to mean 'so chosen to have the desired effect'. It did not mean that there had to be a precise means in the apparatus of adjusting the gas pressure. The context of the patent was significant. The characteristics of the skilled addressee made a difference in *Ancon Ltd v ACS Stainless Steel Fixings Ltd* [2009] EWCA Civ 498, where it was held that the words 'elliptical cone shape' in a patent concerned with bolts used in fixing metal building structures should not be interpreted by a geometer but by a practical designer and manufacturer of fixings for buildings. Lord Diplock's use of a building site foreman as the addressee of the *Catnic* patent might have had something to do with the case.

The unsophisticated nature of the invention played a part in the decision in *Boegli-Gravures SA v Darsail-ASP Ltd* [2009] EWHC 2690 (Pat). The patent involved a system for embossing packaging foils between two rollers with 'pyramidal teeth' to produce an optical effect. Arnold J held the words 'pyramidal teeth' were being used in a figurative sense to denote something roughly shaped like a pyramid rather than a precise geometric shape. By contrast, the invention in *Occlutech GmbH v Aga Medical Corporation* [2010] EWCA Civ 702 was more sophisticated and hence the skilled addressee was more highly qualified. Nevertheless, the case illustrates nicely the difference between the use of words which are precise and those which have a more generalized meaning. The patent involved a device for insertion into a blood vessel or similar, the device being stated to be 'dumbbell-shaped' and with clamps at the ends. It was held not to be infringed by a rival device with a similar shape (having a pinched central section) which had its ends fixed by welding. Although the shape could be described as being like a dumbbell and so was within the wording of the claim, the use of the word 'clamp' in the context of surgical devices indicated a degree of precision.

Last, Lord Hoffmann's remarks in *Kirin-Amgen* about the implication of using 'figures, measurements, angles and the like' are illustrated by *Zeno Corporation v BSM-Bionic Solutions Management* [2009] EWHC 1829 (Pat). Here, the patent was for a hand-held unit 'for' the thermal treatment of insect bites, where the device was to have a maximum temperature in a range from 50 to 65° C, preferably 55 to 60° C, and was to be held in place 'for a time interval ranging from 2 to 12 seconds, preferably 3 to 6 seconds'. Lewison J held that there was no infringement by a device used for the thermal treatment of acne which used a lower temperature and was held in place for a longer period of time. The temperature range and time intervals were held to be precise measurements, and there was no evidence that the defendant's device would have any beneficial effect in the treatment of insect bites.

18.5.11 EPC 2000: revision of the Protocol

The 2000 amendments to the EPC included a revision to the Protocol to Art. 69. The amended Protocol consists of two Articles. Article 1 reproduces the current version of the wording, except that 'patentee' is replaced by 'patent proprietor'. Article 2 is new: it provides that 'For the purpose of determining the scope of protection conferred by a European patent, due account shall be taken of any element which is equivalent to an element specified in the claims'. One may speculate as to whether this will lead, in due course, to a European 'doctrine of equivalents' (which Lord Hoffmann in *Kirin-Amgen* at [44] vehemently denied existed) or whether resort to the skilled addressee and their perception of the wording of the claims will ensure that little change actually occurs.

The idea of a doctrine of equivalents, which exists in Germany, the Netherlands, the USA, and several other states, is that a court may decide that a patent has been infringed even though the infringing acts do not come within the literal scope of the patent's claims—the justification being that the allegedly infringing product could still be considered 'equivalent' to the invention. This doctrine appears to go beyond the purposive interpretation seen in *Kirin-Amgen* and *Improver*.

Fisher (in 'New Protocol, Same Old Story? Patent Claim Construction in 2007; Looking Back with a View to the Future' [2008] 2 *IPQ* 133) notes that German courts have acknowledged that there remains a difference between their style of interpretation of patent claims and that found in the United Kingdom. This difference is due, he says, to the German concern to reward the patentee, whilst United Kingdom courts focus on the patent as incentive rather than reward.

Until very recently, UK courts were adamant that there was now conformity throughout the EPC Contracting States with regard to patent claim interpretation so that nothing further remained to be done (see Lord Hoffmann in *Kirin-Amgen* at [75]). Inevitably, the German and UK views could not both be right—something had to give. As we shall see, in recent years it is the UK courts that have accepted that something close to a 'European doctrine of equivalents' does exist under the Protocol to Art. 69 EPC.

18.5.12 Post-*Kirin*: *Virgin Atlantic*

Following the House of Lords decision in *Kirin-Amgen*, a number of cases attempted to provide a concise summary of the principles of patent claim construction and to deal with the issue of 'equivalents'. A highly significant case is *Virgin Atlantic Airways Ltd v Premium Aircraft Interiors UK Ltd* [2010] FSR 396, where a summary of the effect of *Kirin-Amgen* was given by Jacob LJ at [5]:

- the first overarching principle is that contained in Art. 69 EPC;
- Article 69 says that the extent of protection is determined by the claims. It goes on to say that the description and drawings shall be used to interpret the claims. In short, the claims are to be construed in context;
- it follows that the claims are to be construed purposively—the inventor's purpose being ascertained from the description and drawings;

- it further follows that the claims must not be construed as if they stood alone—the drawings and description only being used to resolve any ambiguity. Purpose is vital to the construction of claims;

- when ascertaining the inventor's purpose, it must be remembered that he may have several purposes depending on the level of generality of his invention. Typically, for instance, an inventor may have one, generally more than one, specific embodiment as well as a generalised concept. But there is no presumption that the patentee necessarily intended the widest possible meaning consistent with his purpose be given to the words that he used: purpose and meaning are different;

- thus purpose is not the be-all and end-all. One is still at the end of the day concerned with the meaning of the language used. Hence the other extreme of the Protocol—a mere guideline—is also ruled out by Art. 69 itself. It is the terms of the claims which delineate the patentee's territory;

- it follows that if the patentee has included what is obviously a deliberate limitation in his claims, it must have a meaning. One cannot disregard obviously intentional elements;

- it also follows that where a patentee has used a word or phrase which, acontextually, might have a particular meaning (narrow or wide) it does not necessarily have that meaning in context;

- it further follows that there is no general 'doctrine of equivalents';

- on the other hand purposive construction can lead to the conclusion that a technically trivial or minor difference between an element of a claim and the corresponding element of the alleged infringement nonetheless falls within the meaning of the element when read purposively. This is not because there is a doctrine of equivalents: it is because that is the fair way to read the claim in context; and

- finally, purposive construction leads one to eschew the kind of meticulous verbal analysis which lawyers are too often tempted by their training to indulge.

One can see from this summary that despite the requirement to strike a middle path between fair protection for the patentee and certainty for third parties, Jacob LJ placed considerable emphasis on the wording of the claim. He also reiterated the view that (despite the EPC 2000 changes) there was no general 'doctrine of equivalents' in European patent law.

18.5.13 *Actavis v Eli Lilly* and the UK's adoption of the 'doctrine of equivalents'

An important ruling that appears to have changed the entire UK approach to purposive construction, at least in the context of equivalents, is the Supreme Court's decision in *Eli Lilly v Actavis UK* [2017] UKSC 48. The case concerned whether drugs manufactured by Actavis infringed a European patent owned by Eli Lilly. The case began when Actavis sought declarations of non-infringement under s. 71 of the Patents Act 1977 that its products did not infringe Eli Lilly's patent. Eli Lilly counter-claimed that Actavis' products infringed their patent, directly and indirectly.

The claims of Eli Lilly's patent describe using the disodium salt of pemetrexed in the manufacture of a cancer drug, for use in combination with vitamin B12 (which mitigates against side-effects). The primary issue before the Supreme Court was the question of whether a drug containing a *different* salt of pemetrexed (used with vitamin B12) would infringe the patent, either directly or indirectly. In the Patents Court, Arnold J. found for Actavis, holding that the Actavis products would not directly, or indirectly, infringe the patent ([2015] RPC 6). The Court of Appeal then held, contra Arnold J, for Eli Lilly in part, stating that Actavis' acts constituted indirect infringement; but the Court of Appeal agreed with the earlier ruling of Arnold J that there was no direct infringement ([2015] EWCA Civ 555 and 556). The UK Supreme Court heard an appeal from Lilly on the issue of direct infringement, and a cross-appeal from Actavis on indirect infringement.

Eli Lilly's central argument was that Actavis' products infringed their patent, reasoning that the Actavis product—*a* pemetrexed salt (or the free acid) with vitamin B12— represented the key essence of the invention within the claims of the patent. Actavis argued that their acts were not infringing because the claims of the patent were limited to a *specific* pemetrexed salt, i.e. the one named in the patent: pemetrexed disodium. (Actavis' drug contained different pemetrexed salts e.g. the dipotassium salt.)

The UK Supreme Court held for Lilly, dismissing Actavis' cross-appeal. The reasoning of the UKSC is worth considering in detail. First, as we outlined above, the SC had to construe the meaning of the patent's claims. The SC stated that 'as a matter of ordinary language' the claims only covered the disodium salt. Nonetheless, the SC stressed the need to take into account the Protocol on the Interpretation of Art. 69 (as amended in EPC 2000). Considering s. 60(1) in light of s. 130(7), the SC felt bound to take account of to the EPC and the Protocol to Art. 69, especially Art. 2 (added by EPC 2000):

> For the purpose of determining the extent of protection conferred by a European patent, due account shall be taken of any element which is equivalent to an element specified in the claims.

In *Kirin-Amgen* Lord Hoffmann had affirmed that the purposive construction approach (Catnic/Improver) had adequately dealt with the requirements of the Protocol—consequently, the Protocol, and the Improver questions, were mere 'guidelines for applying that principle to equivalents . . . more useful in some cases than in others'.

The UKSC was critical of Lord Hoffmann's approach. The UKSC stated that the question of infringement should be answered by addressing the following two issues:

1. Does the variant infringe any of the claims as a matter of normal interpretation? (If not . . .)

2. Does the variant nonetheless infringe because it varies from the invention in a way, or ways, which is, or are, immaterial?

If the court finds that the answer to either 1 or 2 is yes, then infringement is proven. Lord Neuberger stressed that question 1 relies on an issue of interpretation; but question 2 requires an assessment of facts and expert evidence. For the UKSC, the line of authorities from *Catnic* to *Improver* to *Kirin-Amgen* made the error of conflating the two issues as mere interpretation.

Lord Neuberger acknowledged that under the first of these questions Actavis' acts would not infringe the patent as different salts/free acid of pemetrexed did not come within the patent claim as expressed. However, when answering the second question, the issue became more complex. He referred to the view of Sir Hugh Laddie ('Kirin-Amgen—The End of Equivalents in England?' (2009) 40 *IIC* 3, para 68) that the Protocol not only concerns the rules of construction of claims, but also 'determining the scope of protection'.

With this in mind for question 2, the UKSC stated that the *Improver/*Protocol questions needed to be reformulated as follows:

i) Notwithstanding that it is not within the literal meaning of the relevant claim(s) of the patent, does the variant achieve substantially the same result in substantially the same way as the invention, i.e. the inventive concept revealed by the patent?

ii) Would it be obvious to the person skilled in the art, reading the patent at the priority date, but knowing that the variant achieves substantially the same result as the invention, that it does so in substantially the same way as the invention?

iii) Would such a reader of the patent have concluded that the patentee nonetheless intended that strict compliance with the literal meaning of the relevant claim(s) of the patent was an essential requirement of the invention?

Therefore, to demonstrate infringement in a case where, looking at the claims, there's no literal infringement, the patentee must show that the answer to both (i) and (ii) is 'yes' and the answer to (iii) is 'no'. Here, applying these questions, the UKSC was satisfied that the Actavis products did infringe the Eli Lilly patent, holding that Actavis' products achieved: (i) substantially the same result in substantially the same way as the patented invention, and (ii) this would have been obvious to the person skilled in the art at the priority date. Finally, with respect to (iii), the UKSC stated that in light of the Protocol the interpretation of the claims is not the same task as assessing the scope of protection—in the present case, this meant that although the patent's claims were limited to the disodium salt, this did not mean that the patentee did not intend other pemetrexed salts to infringe.

The decision is of great significance. The point made in (iii) above is a definite move away from the *Kirin-Amgen* approach towards a 'doctrine of equivalents' assessment. We do not know as yet the full consequences of the ruling—there appears to be some confusion about the impact of the decision on novelty, as shown by recent orbiter comments in the High Court case of *Mylan v Yeda Development* [2017] EWHC 2629 (Pat)—but on infringement UK patent law is now more in line with the German and wider European-approach described by Fisher, Laddie, and others in academic articles over the past decade.

 Pause for reflection

Do you agree with the UK Supreme Court that it was necessary to move away from Lord Hoffmann's test in *Kirin-Amgen* to fulfil the requirements of the Protocol to Art. 69? Does the current case law on patent claim interpretation provide for certainty and predictability?

18.6 Changes to UK patent law as a result of the UPC/UP system

Since 2012 the EU has been making preparations for the biggest change to the European patent system since the early 1970s. Along with the new European patent with unitary effect ('UP'), the most important reform is the setting up of a new Unified Patent Court ('UPC'), common to participating EU member states. The UPC will have jurisdiction to hear patent disputes and issue remedies to litigants that are binding within an area covering almost the entire EU single market. The UPC will have sole jurisdiction to hear cases involving the new UPs. During a transition period of at least seven years, the UPC will share jurisdiction with national courts for the litigation of European patents (unless the EP owners decide to opt-out of the UPC, in which case the national courts will remain the sole litigation venues). Purely national patents granted at e.g. the UKIPO will remain under the jurisdiction of UK courts.

This represents a huge change from the awkward present system, which requires national litigation involving European patents to take place in each individual member country where the patent is validated. So far, 25 out of the 28 EU Member States have agreed to join the UPC, with Spain, Poland, and Croatia the only ones not participating. The UK has been firmly on board since 2012. The court will include judges from the UK, Germany, France, the Netherlands, and other EU member states.

The EU has passed two Regulations to set up the UP—Regulation (EU) No. 1257/2012 of the European Parliament and of the Council of 17 December 2012 implementing enhanced cooperation in the area of the creation of unitary patent protection (UP Regulation), OJ L 361/1 (2012) and Council Regulation (EU) No. 1260/2012 of 17 December 2012 implementing enhanced cooperation in the area of the creation of unitary patent protection with regard to the applicable translation arrangements (Translation Regulation), OJ L 361/89 (2012). However, the UP will only come into being once the UPC Agreement—the Agreement on a Unified Patent Court (The UPC Agreement), C 175/01 (2013)—has been ratified by the three major patent litigation jurisdictions—UK, Germany, France—and ten other participating Member States.

Until the Brexit referendum, the UK seemed to be well on the way to full ratification of the UPC. Indeed, for the past several years the UK government has been making plans to host one of the new court's central divisions in Aldgate, east London. Although, as of early 2018, the official UK government position is that the UK will ratify the UPC, UK's forthcoming exit from the EU could make this difficult, as the UPC will make references to the CJEU on matters of EU law (such as matters arising under the Biotech Directive). Post-Brexit, UK participation probably requires amendments to be made to the UPC Agreement. Furthermore, German ratification has been held up by a constitutional court challenge, due to be heard in 2018. Until the UK and Germany ratify, the UPC will remain in limbo, and until there is clarity on the post-Brexit UK–EU relationship, we will not know if continued UK participation in the court is legally possible.

18.7 Conclusion

In this chapter we have discussed the fact that parties who consider that their patents have been infringed in the UK should undertake litigation at the Patents Court or the IPEC in London—both courts of England and Wales—choosing between the two venues depending on the value and complexity of the case. We noted that until the UPC is set up, there is no pan-European mechanism for enforcement of patents across EPC and EU Member States so if a patent is infringed in multiple territories, litigation is likely to be required to enforce the patent in each state (UK, Germany, France, etc).

In terms of the specific of the enforcement action, we examined s. 60(1) of the Patents Act in detail, noting that there are a number of possible directly infringing acts, including 'using', 'making', 'offering', or 'keeping' for disposal, and importing the product. For process patents the two acts are 'using' and 'offering'. We looked at s. 60(2) on indirect infringement, which includes supplying the 'means' to infringe.

We looked at the various defence arguments and counter-claims that an accused infringer may make. For defences we paid particular attention to s. 60(5) on the defences of private use, experiments, and prescriptions; and in s. 64 we examined prior use in good faith. As regards counter-claims, we noted that under ss. 70–74, the alleged infringer can counter-claim for revocation of the patent, arguing that it is invalid; and/or that their activities are not infringing. The competitor/alleged infringer can even file for a declaration of non-infringement under s. 71 before a patentee has begun legal proceedings against it.

If a revocation claim is made, the grounds of the legal analysis are found in s. 72(1) of the Patents Act. The most common ones include the elements of patentability we looked at in the prior chapter (novelty, inventive step, etc), as well as 'insufficiency' (*Biogen v Medeva*) and an impermissible (over-broad) amendment of the patent's claims.

Turning to the court's role in assessing the infringement issue, we saw that this primarily consists of the following: first, interpreting and construing the claims; and second, considering the (allegedly) infringing activity in terms of the patent's claims.

Looking at the issues we have considered in this chapter from beginning to end, we can advise Siva to file an action for direct infringement under s. 60(1) at the Patents Court (the likelihood of a revocation counter-claim makes the case unsuitable for the IPEC).

In Siva's case, we can examine Claim 1 of her patent in the context of 'making' under s. 60(1) (direct infringement of a product). In her case we must focus on the *Catnic/ Improver* purposive approach to determine whether the actions of YESTech come within Claim 1 of her patent. The cases of *United Wire* and *Schutz v Werit* would be useful ones to refer to as they refer to 'making' in the context of engineering-style patents, not too dissimilar from Siva's invention. We can note that the specific issue of equivalents and the reformulation of the *Improver*/Protocol questions in *Kirin-Amgen*, and more recently, in *Actavis v Eli Lilly,* is less relevant to Siva's (non-pharmaceutical) patent infringement scenario, as YESTech's acts do seem to come within the scope of the claims, whether considered from a purposive (or even a literal) approach.

In other words, assuming that Claim 1 is a strong one, and capable of withstanding a revocation counter-claim, it is arguable that YESTech's acts clearly come within the terms of Claim 1 of her patent, when considered under the purposive test. Therefore,

Siva would have a good chance of demonstrating infringement. The burden would then shift to the defendant—YESTech—to try to make a defence. It is unlikely, on the facts we possess, that YESTech could avail of any of the defences under s. 60(5) or s. 64.

The primary remedy Siva should seek is an injunction to prevent the rival product coming to market and taking her product's market share; she can also ask for all of the infringing products to be destroyed (here you should refer to the detailed explanation of remedies in chapter 22). If the injunction is granted in time, there may be no need to compensate her for any monetary damage (as none would have been suffered)—but if for any reason her enforcement action takes place after the rival product is already placed on sale, she could claim for damages or an account of profits made from the sales of the infringing product.

End-of-chapter questions

After reading the chapter carefully, try answering the following questions. For answer guidance visit the online resources at **www.oup.com/uk/karapapa-mcdonagh/**

1. Why is the definition of 'making' in patent infringement not as straightforward as it sounds? What guidance have the courts given on interpreting this term?

2. Does the UKSC *Actavis v Eli Lilly* case present a useful clarification of the law on equivalents or a needless complication?

3. What are the positives and negatives of the territorial scope of patent infringement in European jurisdictions such as the UK? Will the proposed Unified Patent Court system provide a better option for patentees?

Further reading

Cremers, K. et al. 'Patent Litigation in Europe' [2017] 41(1) *European Journal of Law and Economics* 1

Empirical analysis of litigation in Germany, the UK, the Netherlands and France.

Fisher, M. 'New Protocol, Same Old Story? Patent Claim Construction in 2007; Looking Back with a View to the Future' [2008] 2 *IPQ* 133

Considers whether the EPC 2000 amendments to Art. 69 will actually have any effect.

Fisher, M. 'A Case-study in Literalism: Dissecting the English Approach to Patent Claim Construction in the Light of *Occlutech v Aga Medical*' [2011] 3 *IPQ* 283

Argues that the current prevailing attitude of the courts favours a literal interpretation of the claims, reinforced by an over-reliance on dictionary definitions.

Helmers, C. & McDonagh, L., 'Patent litigation and the issue-based approach to costs' [2013] 32(3) *Civil Justice Quarterly* 369

Undertakes an empirical assessment of English Patent Court costs rulings.

Helmers, C., Love, B. and McDonagh, L. 'Is there a Patent Troll problem in the UK?' [2014] 24 *Fordham IPLJ* 503

Compares the US 'Patent troll problem' to the UK patent system, and finds that the UK does not encourage nuisance litigation.

McDonagh, L. *European Patent Litigation in the Shadow of the Unified Patent Court* (Edward Elgar, 2016).

Reviews the new Unified Patent Court proposal in light of recent data on patent litigation in European jurisdictions.

Sherman, B. 'Patent Claim Interpretation: The Impact of the Protocol on Interpretation' [1991] 54 *MLR* 499

Explains the origin of the Protocol to Art. 69 EPC and assesses its likely impact in harmonizing national attitudes to patent claim interpretation.

Turner, J. 'Purposive Construction: Seven Reasons Why Catnic is Wrong' [1999] 21 *EIPR* 531

A highly critical analysis of Lord Diplock's speech in Catnic.

Confidential
Information

Part 6

19. Breach of confidence: Trade secrets and private information

Breach of confidence: Trade secrets and private information

19

Problem question

Read this problem question carefully and keep it in mind while you are working through the chapter that follows. At the end of this chapter, you will be able to apply what you have learnt to the problem question and advise the relevant parties.

Thompson Hypermarkets plc is one of the largest supermarket chains in the UK. Its large-scale stores sell not only groceries, but also crockery, bed linen, towels, and clothes. During January and February 2018 they have been making plans to launch a new 'Thompson Summer' range of clothing and housewares (vases, plates, bowls, mugs, etc) in June 2018.

During this period, the marketing team at Thompson entered into a contract with outside consultants New Hygge Trends ('NHT') whereby, in return for a monthly fee of £37,000, NHT will inform them about changing public tastes and opinions. NHT use state-of-the-art data mining software called 'Taste', which they have developed in-house, to trawl the internet, and gather and filter the information. NHT are careful to comply with all applicable intellectual property, privacy and data protection laws when doing so. They do not license 'Taste' to anyone else—it is software deliberately designed for the type of supermarket customers Thompson have.

Having used the software to analyse trends during January and February 2018, on 28 February NHT advised Thompson that that their clothing and houseware should use colours and designs reminiscent of the 1950s and early 1960s as certain key individuals, identified by their research as 'style leaders' within their social groups, are beginning to adopt a mid-century look. Thompson have decided to follow this advice and have ordered a wide range of appropriate goods from their manufactures. NHT have assured Thompson that they will be ahead of their competitors when they launch the new 'Thompson Summer' range in June 2018.

On 1 March 2018, a senior consultant employed by NHT, Saoirse Mullen, announced that she was leaving NHT and to join a competing marketing consultancy: 21st Century Trends →

→

(21CT). Saoirse had been working on the Thompson account as an analyst. Although she is not a programmer, she is aware of how the 'Taste' software works and the underlying technology that results in its unique and ground-breaking nature, as well as the substance of the advice given to Thompson. 21CT recently won a contract to become the new marketing consultants for the Thriftmart chain of UK supermarkets, one of Thompson's main competitors.

The partners in NHT are concerned both at the possibility that Saoirse may (i) tell 21CT how their Taste software works; and (ii) reveal to 21CT details of the advice given to Thompson. If either or both happen, this might put the success of the Thompson campaign in doubt and jeopardize their lucrative deal with Thompson. Advise NHT.

19.1 Introduction

19.1.1 Breach of confidence: the protection of ideas and information

In the UK the area of breach of confidence has traditionally been used to protect ideas and information, including trade secrets. This chapter explains how an action in the area of trade secrets fits within intellectual property law. This area of law concerns a right *in personam* (a trade secret is usually enforceable between a limited set of parties under contract or in contract-like circumstances) as opposed to a strict intellectual property ('IP') right like a copyright, trade mark, patent, or design, which are rights *in rem* (enforceable against anybody who trespasses on the right without permission). As such, one could argue that trade secrets are not IP rights at all; however, although strictly true, to ignore trade secrets would be a grave mistake, as their importance within the world of business is growing. Prominent examples of trade secrets include the Google search algorithm and the recipe for Coca-Cola.

In the UK, the doctrine by which trade secrets are protected (breach of confidence) is judge-made law, rooted in equitable principles (R.G. Hammond, 'The Origins of the Equitable Duty of Confidence' [1979] 8 *Anglo-American Law Review* 71). In consequence, it has developed in a piecemeal, and sometimes contradictory fashion, so that the rationale for the action has not always been clear. Key points remain unresolved. Furthermore, UK courts are typically conservative about broadening the scope of confidence: Lord Walker in *Douglas and Zeta-Jones v Hello! Ltd* [2008] 1 AC 1 (HL) at [292] remarked that 'uncontrolled growth of the law of confidence would . . . tend to bring incoherence into the law of intellectual property' and further added at [300] that relying on the law of confidence to protect 'the exclusivity in a spectacle' would go against the well-established British view (*Victoria Park Racing v Taylor* (1937) 58 CLR 479).

Nevertheless, the law of confidence is broad enough in the UK to encompass: (i) the common definition of a trade secret (commercial, usually technical information); (ii) personal, private information (such as the wedding photos of Michael Douglas and Catherine Zeta-Jones) which may also have a commercial value (including information which may be protected under the right to privacy under Art. 8 of the European Convention on Human Rights ('ECHR')); and (iii) information protected by the state.

We are primarily concerned with (i)—the classic idea of trade secret—but because the law of confidence has developed through all of these avenues, where relevant we will have to look at some cases involving personal info (right to privacy) and some involving state information. Furthermore, as we shall see, because some personal, private information has commercial value—e.g. in the celebrity context—we can link this area of breach of confidence with the idea of a right to control one's image.

In the international realm, meanwhile, the Agreement on Trade-Related Aspects of Intellectual Property Rights ('TRIPs Agreement'), in Art. 39, regards the protection of 'undisclosed information' as an aspect of unfair competition under Art. 10*bis* of the Paris Convention for the Protection of Industrial Property 1883. We have already seen that, unlike e.g. Germany, there is a lack of protection for unfair competition in the UK intellectual property system, though the harmonization of EU trade mark law increasingly fills this gap in the brand context.

Similarly, the EU is moving towards harmonization of trade secrets. In 2016 the EU passed Directive 2016/943 on the protection of undisclosed know-how and business information (trade secrets) against their unlawful acquisition, use, and disclosure. The EU Trade Secrets Directive aims to harmonize this area of law within EU Member States (including, at time of writing, the UK) in mid-2018, when the Directive is due to come into force. Underlying the importance of trade secrets to the EU economy, the European Union Intellectual Property Office ('EUIPO' which, as we have seen, registers EU trademarks and designs, but not patents, which are granted at the European Patent Office ('EPO')) released a report in 2017 which said that use of trade secrets to protect innovative knowledge, products, and algorithms is more common than the use of patents for some types of companies ('Protecting Innovation Through Trade Secrets and Patents: Determinants for European Union Firms' (EUIPO, 2017)). Importantly, the new EU Directive has a focus on trade secrets as business information (not personal or state-protected information) which accords with the focus of this chapter.

In this chapter, and in considering our problem scenario (above), we will first examine the circumstances in which an action for breach of confidence will arise; the defences which may be available; and issues concerning remedies. We will also consider the interaction between confidence and the Human Rights Act 1998 in the context of the 'cult of the celebrity' and 'media intrusion' when considering what information is 'confidential'. Finally, we will examine the effect, if any, the EU Trade Secrets Directive will have in the UK.

19.1.2 Protection for information as such

The action for breach of confidence provides the only legal mechanism in the UK to protect ideas and information *as such*. This marks trade secrets out from the other categories of intellectual property we have looked at in prior chapters typically require ideas and information to be embodied in a tangible form, such as a brand name (trade marks), an invention (patents), a work (copyright), or the appearance of a product (designs).

Nonetheless, even though there is no requirement of creativity or inventiveness in relation to the protected information itself, the right of action only applies in the following circumstances: it requires (i) information which is not in the public domain;

(ii) to be disclosed in circumstances which impose an obligation on the recipient; (iii) that then may be about to be used or further disclosed in a way that requires restraint by injunction (*Boardman v Phipps* [1967] 2 AC 46 at pp.127–8 *per* Lord Upjohn; *Douglas v Hello! Ltd (No. 2)* [2005] 4 All ER 128 (CA) at [119]). Where the defendant has already exploited the information for their own ends, and thus an injunction would serve no purpose, a monetary remedy may also be available.

 Pause for reflection

Consider the above problem scenario. What information might NHT have that could be valuable? Could it have been disclosed in a way that imposed an obligation on Saoirse? What would be the impact of its disclosure to 21CT? These are the issues we will explore in detail in the coming sub-sections.

19.1.3 Types of information: commercial, state, and personal

Information protected by the action for breach of confidence may be commercial, governmental, or personal. The classic idea of a trade secret would be commercial information, e.g. an idea for a new television series; a 'themed' nightclub; a new product (which might or might not be capable of patent protection); steps to be taken in a manufacturing process; the creation of software; test data; or a list of valued customers or suppliers.

Government information, meanwhile, concerns official secrets and other material about the internal workings of the state and its agencies, which the Government would prefer not to be made public. Such information may have been obtained by Crown servants in the course of their duties, or by politicians whilst in Government.

By contrast, personal information will involve facts about an individual which they regard as sensitive, and therefore private. Photographs are included within this category of personal information. Special considerations attach to photographs, because they are not merely an alternative to words, but can be a particularly intrusive way of conveying information. 'A picture is worth a thousand words' (*per* Baroness Hale in *Naomi Campbell v Mirror Group Newspapers* [2004] 2 AC 457 at [155]; *per* Lord Walker in *Douglas and Zeta-Jones v Hello! Ltd* (HL) at [288]).

The leading cases in breach of confidence are drawn from each of these three areas and are often used interchangeably. There are two distinct groups of cases, those dealing with 'traditional' breach of confidence (commercial trade secrets and governmental information) and those dealing with what is now termed 'misuse of personal information'. Generally, these two should be kept separate: *Naomi Campbell v MGN* at [14] *per* Lord Nicholls; *Douglas and Zeta-Jones v Hello! Ltd* (HL) at [255] again, *per* Lord Nicholls. The reason is that the test for what is 'confidential' differs depending on whether the disputed information is commercial or personal. However, there are blurred lines: many cases involving misuse of personal information arise in situations where there is already a contractual obligation in place (for example, an exclusive deal with a magazine to publish photographs of a celebrity wedding) and so could be regarded as commercial rather than personal in nature: see Lord Hoffmann at [124] in *Douglas and Zeta-Jones v Hello! Ltd* (HL).

As stated earlier, our principal focus is on the way in which the action for breach of confidence operates in the commercial world to protect trade secrets, but we will later consider the interaction of the principles of breach of confidence with the Human Rights Act 1998 to create a remedy for the invasion of privacy. Many of the cases in this particular area (usually, but not always, about high-profile celebrities) involve unique facts. The courts have to balance Art. 8 of the ECHR (respect for private and family life) with Art. 10 (freedom of expression). The Court of Appeal in *Douglas v Hello! Ltd (No. 2)* [2005] 4 All ER 128 (CA) at [49] opined that the decision of the European Court of Human Rights ('ECtHR') in *Von Hannover v Germany (No. 1)* (2004) 40 EHHR 1 imposes a positive obligation on Member States to protect an individual against the unjustified invasion of their private life by another individual, and a further obligation on the courts of a Member State to interpret domestic legislation in a way which will achieve that result.

The privacy cases are significant from the intellectual property perspective because they may provide a first step towards the creation of a right of personality; and they enable individuals to exercise a degree of control over the commercial exploitation of their image. As Dinwoodie and Richardson argue, the area of image rights involves not a single right, but messy overlap between privacy, confidence, trade marks, and the law of passing off (as seen in the *Rihanna v Topshop* [2015]) ('Publicity Right, Personality Right, or Just Confusion?' in *Research Handbook on Intellectual Property in Media and Entertainment* (M. Richardson and S. Ricketson (eds) (Elgar Publishing, 2017)).

 Pause for reflection

Is it correct to expand breach of confidence to cover misuse of personal information? Are the rights of businesses to control e.g. their knowledge, software, techniques, etc analogous with celebrity image rights? Does it matter if they are not?

Moreover, the idea of image rights is not limited to celebrities. Could you think of a situation when a regular member of the public might seek to rely on this burgeoning area of law?

19.2 The role of trade secrets in intellectual property law

In relation to trade secrets, breach of confidence has several practical applications, as follows.

19.2.1 An alternative to patents

Keeping information confidential has always been an alternative to patent protection. An inventor may decide not to obtain patent protection for their invention, but instead to rely on trade secrecy (which after all is instant and free). As noted earlier, Coca-Cola to this day relies on secrecy to protect the details of its recipe. Google does the same with its algorithm. The benefit of trade secrets v patent is that it does not require the expensive application and annual renewal fees. A case law example is *Seager v Copydex (No. 1)* [1967] RPC 349 where an inventor had not obtained patent protection for a new type of carpet grip but nevertheless was able to argue successfully that the defendants had misappropriated his ideas.

However, patents are monopoly rights that offer powerful protection against any user. Trade secrets do not give the same level of protection. Relying on secrecy to protect an invention will only be worthwhile if it can truly be kept closed or secret. Although, as Aplin argues, there is no specific 'reverse-engineering' exception, if it is possible for a third party to reverse-engineer the invention—that is, having acquired a legitimate copy of the product, to analyse it to find out how it works before making their own version of the product—then this type of reverse-engineer manufacture would not usually breach any confidential duty under trade secrets (T. Aplin, 'Reverse Engineering Commercial Secrets' [2013] 66 *Current Legal Problems* 341). By contrast, to reverse-engineer a patented item and then manufacture it as your own version/product would be a clear case of patent infringement.

 Pause for reflection

In view of advances in technology, is a company wise to rely on breach of confidence to protect an invention?

Looking at our problem scenario, could NHT have applied for any patents to protect any of the aspects of their business?

19.2.2 An alternative to copyright

Confidentiality can be used to protect ideas which are not yet sufficiently detailed or permanent to fall within the scope of copyright. As an example, in *Fraser v Thames Television* [1983] 2 All ER 101 an experienced television scriptwriter approached the defendants with an idea for a new drama series. His idea was rejected, but some time later the company broadcast a series, *Rock Follies*, based on the claimant's proposal. He was awarded extensive damages.

19.2.3 A supplement to copyright

Confidentiality can offer parallel protection to copyright, so that there can be liability for publication even though there has not been copying. An example of this is *Creation Records v News Group Newspapers* [1997] EMLR 444, which we examined in chapter 2. You will recall that there had been a photo shoot to create the cover for the album *Be Here Now* by the group Oasis, which entailed assembling a number of objects in a swimming pool which were then photographed. Lloyd J declined to hold that the collection of objects in the pool amounted to a collage for the purposes of artistic copyright. Equally, the claimant's photograph had not been copied by the defendant's photograph (a prerequisite for copyright infringement).

However, the conduct of the newspaper in taking its own photograph amounted to breach of confidence as it was clear that their employee knew that the session was secret (notably, however, Lord Walker in *Douglas and Zeta-Jones v Hello! Ltd* (HL) (at [290–291]) regarded the decision as 'scraping the barrel', not least because it involved trivial information).

Trade secrets and copyright were also combined (and both were infringed) in *Shelley Films v Rex Features* [1994] EMLR 134 (an application for interim relief) where a photographer obtained unauthorized photographs of the film set of Kenneth Branagh's *Frankenstein*. Michael Mann QC held that there was both breach of confidence (the photographer knew that the taking of photographs of the film set was forbidden) and breach of copyright (the costumes, masks, and sets were arguably works of artistic craftsmanship so that taking photographs of them infringed).

19.2.4 Ensuring the novelty of a patent or registered design

The use of a confidentiality undertaking can be vital to protect the disclosure of potential patents or designs where it is necessary to have the item evaluated prior to filing the application. The reason for this is that s. 2(4) Patents Act 1977 and s. 1(6) Registered Designs Act 1949, as amended, provide that the **novelty** of a patent or design is not destroyed by a prior disclosure in breach of confidence. Keeping an intended patent or registered design secret is a key aspect to the successful management of intellectual property rights.

19.2.5 Know-how

Imposing confidentiality undertakings is the means (in the context of licensing agreements) to protect non-patentable but commercially valuable information ('know-how') relating to the procedures etc to be used in the manufacture of goods. Such information could relate to a particular sequence to be adopted in a manufacturing process, instruction manuals, systems analysis, software, or other similar technical knowledge. It should be noted that there are competition law implications in the licensing of technology.

 Pause for reflection

Given the EUIPO's 2017 report claiming that in some sectors trade secrets are used more commonly than patents to protect business and technical information, do you think that the government and IP lawyers ought to do more to ensure businesses fully appreciate the importance of breach of confidence as a means of protecting information?

19.3 The historical development of breach of confidence and the basis for its protection

19.3.1 Early cases

It is generally accepted that the first breach of confidence case was *Prince Albert v Strange* (1849) 1 H & Tw 1, where private drawings by Prince Albert had been sent to a printer to be copied professionally. The defendant made unauthorized copies which he had intended to put on public display. An injunction was granted to restrain him. As Lord Cottenham, LC, remarked, 'privacy is the right invaded'.

A more typical trade secret case was *Morison v Moat* (1851) 9 Hare 241, where the son of one of two business partners was restrained by the other partner, after the partnership had been dissolved, from making use of a secret recipe for a medicine.

19.3.2 Basis of protection

The theoretical basis for many of the early decisions on breach of confidence was not entirely clear. Arguments deployed included contract, property rights, and conscience. Because many breach of confidence claims arise when the parties are in a contractual relationship, there were a number of other cases where the courts strove to find some sort of implied contract to justify the outcome, even if the parties were not contractually linked. Such artificiality masked the true nature of the action.

Equally, the proximity of breach of confidence to other intellectual property rights, especially patents and copyright, led to arguments that the basis of the action should be some notion of property.

In the leading case on breach of confidence, *Coco v AN Clark (Engineers) Ltd* [1969] RPC 41 (discussed in detail later), Megarry J remarked that 'whether it is described as originality or novelty or ingenuity or otherwise . . . there must be some *product* of the human brain' (emphasis supplied). This language has property implications.

Yet, the Court of Appeal in *Douglas v Hello! Ltd (No. 2)* at [126] made clear that property law should *not* be used. The court saw fit to distinguish earlier cases which had apparently treated secret information as having the attributes of property, namely *Gilbert v Star Newspaper Co Ltd* (1894) 51 TLR 4 and *Mustad & Sons Ltd v Allcock & Dosen* (1928) [1964] 1 WLR 109, HL. Nevertheless, the Court of Appeal's conclusion that the rights of the claimant's exclusive publishers rested entirely in contract, so that they had no remedy under the law of confidence to restrain a rival magazine from publishing surreptitiously obtained pictures of the claimant's wedding, was overturned by a majority of the House of Lords who held that, as the recipient of commercial confidential information, the defendant's conscience was affected. In order for the recipient's conscience to be affected, they must have agreed, or must know, that the information is confidential (*Vestergaard Frandsen A/S v Bestnet Europe Ltd* [2013] UKSC 31 at [23]; see also *Phillips v Mulcaire* [2013] 1 AC 1).

Even before the pronouncements in *Douglas v Hello! Ltd (No. 2)* (CA), case law had moved away from any theories of implied contract or property law; instead, courts had declared that the action was based on the equitable concept of 'good faith'.

The first statement that breach of confidence is underpinned by a general notion of conscience was in *Saltman Engineering Co Ltd v Campbell Engineering Co Ltd* (1948) 65 RPC 203. Subsequent reiterations include those by Lord Denning in *Fraser v Evans* [1969] 1 QB 349 at 361 ('It is based not so much on property or on contract as on a duty to be of good faith') and Lord Keith in *AG v Guardian Newspapers (No. 2)* [1990] 1 AC 109 (hereafter '*Spycatcher*') ('The obligation may be imposed by an express or implied term in a contract but it may also exist independently of any contract on the basis of an independent equitable principle of confidence').

Pause for reflection

As Bently notes, the overwhelming weight of authority is against using property law as the basis of the action ('Trade secrets: "intellectual property" but not "property"?' in H. Howe and J. Griffiths (eds), *Concepts of Property in Intellectual Property Law* (Cambridge University Press, 2013), pp. 60–93). This leaves trade secrets in an unusual position of being considered by many businesses and lawyers to be akin to intellectual property but not property. Is this sustainable? Or does it, in fact, appropriately reflect the unique place of trade secrets within in the world of business and IP?

19.4 Conditions for protection

Coco v AN Clark (Engineers) Ltd [1969] RPC 41

Coco is the leading case on breach of confidence. Megarry J (at p. 47) set out the requirements: (i) the information must be of a confidential nature; (ii) it must have been communicated in circumstances 'imposing an obligation of confidence'; and (iii) there must be subsequent use or disclosure of that information.

19.4.1 Confidential information

As we have seen several different types of information may be protected. The form which the information takes is irrelevant: it may be in writing, in drawings, in photographs, or oral. It need not be permanent and does not have to be recorded in a document (*Douglas v Hello! Ltd (No. 2)* (CA) at [61]). But according to Lord Goff in *Spycatcher*, it must not be useless, trivial, vague, or immoral. Further, the information must be capable of being identified and certain.

An illustration of this last point is *De Maudsley v Palumbo* [1996] FSR 447 where it was held that vague, preliminary ideas for the Ministry of Sound nightclub were not protectable. The case should be contrasted with *Fraser v Thames Television* (discussed earlier) where the claimant's ideas for a television drama series were much more fully developed. Thus, as with copyright, the law does appear to require a certain amount of detail or development in the ideas for them to be given protection.

Information can be protected even if it discloses conduct that may be viewed by certain members of society as on the boundaries of acceptable behaviour: *Mosley v News Group Newspapers* [2008] EWHC 1777. In *Mosley*, Eady J dismissed the defendant's contention that info about the claimant's sado-masochistic behaviour was not protectable: it was not for the media to expose private, consensual sexual conduct which did not involve any significant breach of the criminal law.

However, whatever the information may be, the one key requirement is that it must not already be in the public domain (*Coco v Clark*). Here, public domain refers to information that is accessible and available in the public sphere (it does not mean the same as when a copyright work has fallen out of copyright into the 'public domain').

In the words of Lord Goff in *Spycatcher*, it must be secret information. Once factual information is in the public domain, then it will no longer be entitled to protection in the law of confidence (*Spycatcher per* Lord Goff at p. 282; *Douglas and Zeta-Jones v Hello! Ltd* (HL) at [122] *per* Lord Hoffmann; *BBC v HarperCollins Publishers Ltd* [2010] EWHC 2424 (Ch)). Thus, in *Woodward v Hutchins* [1977] 1 WLR 760, an injunction preventing disclosure was refused, as gossip about the behaviour of certain pop stars on a transatlantic flight was already known. However, the same is not true of photographs: 'in so far as a photograph does more than convey information and intrudes on privacy by enabling the viewer to focus on intimate personal detail, there will be a fresh intrusion of privacy when each additional viewer sees the photograph' (*Douglas v Hello! Ltd (No. 2)* (CA) at [105]). Republication of a photograph is therefore misuse of personal information.

Unlike the law of patents, the action for breach of confidence is based on the concept of relative, not absolute, secrecy (*Vestergaard Frandsen A/S v BestNet Europe Ltd* [2010] FSR 29 at [77]). Consequently, disclosure to a select few may not destroy confidentiality. But what if the information is a mixture of public and private information? It has been held that protection is still available if the defendant uses the information as a 'springboard' to gain a commercial advantage over competitors.

The 'springboard' doctrine is the product of the judgment of Roxburgh J in *Terrapin v Builders' Supply Co* [1960] RPC 128 where 'mixed' information was protected. Where the 'springboard' test applies, any remedy will be limited to the time it would take a competitor to reverse engineer the claimant's information: *Cadbury Schweppes Inc v FBI Foods Ltd* [2000] FSR 491 (a decision of the Supreme Court of Canada), the information in question here being a secret recipe for a drink, 'Clamato'. It was shown that it would take a competitor 12 months to analyse the composition of the product using laboratory equipment, to test their findings, and bring their own version of the product to market. The injunction against the defendant was accordingly limited to that period of time. The effects of the 'springboard' cannot be indefinite (*Potters Ballotini v Weston Baker* [1977] RPC 202) and will not apply if the information is already in the public domain (*Vestergaard Frandsen A/S v BestNet Europe Ltd* [2010] FSR 29).

 Pause for reflection

How easy is it to apply Lord Goff's *Spycatcher* test of what is protectable information?

How would it apply to our problem scenario? What precise information held by NHT could be subject of a breach of confidence claim? Does that information appear to be private or public?

19.4.2 **An obligation of confidence**

The second requirement from *Coco v Clark* is that the information must have been disclosed by the confider to the confidant in circumstances of confidence. This creates the duty of confidence (or secrecy). It can arise in a number of ways. Commonly, it may arise from a contract between the parties. There may be an express term imposing the duty of secrecy, or the court may impose an implied term in the interests of business efficacy, in accordance with the principles established by the House of Lords in *Liverpool City Council v Irwin* [1977] AC 239 and the speech of Lord Simon in *BP Refinery (Westernport) Pty Ltd v The President, Councillors and Ratepayers of the Shire of Hastings* (1978) 52 ALJR 20. However, it is not necessary to show that there was a contractual relationship, even though evidentially this will help the claimant's case considerably. Instead, the court can infer that there is a duty of confidence either from the parties' relationship or simply from the circumstances of the disclosure, objectively assessed.

Examples of relationships which would give rise to an implied duty of confidentiality include those of employment, banker/customer, professional adviser/client, or a commercial joint venture (*Re Gallay* [1959] RPC 141). The relationship, however, must be of the type which imposes an equitable duty of good faith. An example of where the *circumstances* of the disclosure, as opposed to the parties' relationship, were sufficient to give rise to a duty to keep the information secret is *Stephens v Avery* [1988] Ch 449, discussed further later.

19.4.2.1 An objective test

The weight of authority is in favour of an objective test i.e. the approach of Megarry J in *Coco v Clark*:

> It seems to me that if the circumstances are such that any reasonable man standing in the shoes of the recipient of the information would have realised that upon reasonable grounds the information was being given to him in confidence, then this should suffice to impose upon him the equitable obligation of confidence ([1969] RPC 41 at p. 48).

The objective test was by implication approved in *Spycatcher* by Lords Goff and Keith, and was expressly approved by Lindsay J at first instance in *Douglas and Zeta-Jones v Hello! Ltd* [2003] 3 All ER 996 and by the House of Lords in *Naomi Campbell v MGN*.

An example of an application of the objective test for the existence of the duty of secrecy arising from the circumstances of the disclosure itself is *Stephens v Avery*. Here, one friend disclosed to another that she was in a lesbian relationship. It was held that the confidant should have realized from the circumstances of the disclosure that the information was confidential and not to be disclosed, least of all to a tabloid newspaper.

When dealing with the obligation of confidence employees and third-party recipients deserve particular attention.

19.4.2.2 Employees

An employee owes their employer a duty of fidelity, that is, to further the interests of the employer's business (*Robb v Green* [1895] 2 QB 315). The duty varies depending on the seniority and skill of the employee and not all employees will necessarily receive the same treatment. Very senior employees will be treated as fiduciaries. The duty of good faith can encompass the duty not to compete with or injure the employer's business (*Hivac Ltd v Park Royal Scientific Instruments Ltd* [1964] 1 All ER 350) as well as the obligation to maintain secrecy (*Printers and Finishers Ltd v Holloway* [1965] 1 WLR 1).

19.4.2.3 Ex-employees

> #### *Faccenda v Fowler* [1986] 1 All ER 617
>
> In *Faccenda v Fowler*, it was held that the question of whether a former employee owes an obligation of secrecy to the employer depends on the status, knowledge' and skills of the employee. Moreover, there are three distinct categories of information: (i) trade secrets as such; (ii) commercially sensitive or valuable information; (iii) the employee's general skill and knowledge.

The first *Faccenda* category—trade secrets—is automatically protected during and after the contract of employment. The second—commercially sensitive or valuable information—is automatically protected during the contract of employment because of the employee's general duty of fidelity but will require an express clause to protect it after termination of employment. Such a clause must be limited appropriately in time, geographical area, and as to the relevant activities of the ex-employee, otherwise it may be held void as being in restraint of trade (*Fellowes v Fisher* [1976] QB 122, *Commercial Plastics v Vincent* [1964] 3 All ER 546). The only exception to the requirement to tailor the restriction to the ex-employee's activities would appear to be senior members of the Intelligence Service: *AG v Blake* [2001] AC 268. The final category of information, the employee's general skill and knowledge, is not protectable, on grounds of public policy, so that the employee is free to make use of his or her skills in subsequent employment (*Herbert Morris v Saxelby* [1916] AC 688). 'The law should not discourage former employees from benefiting society and advancing themselves by imposing unfair potential difficulties on their honest attempts to compete with their former employers' (*Vestergaard Frandsen A/S v Bestnet Europe Ltd* [2013] UKSC 31 at [44]). Nevertheless, as the decision in *Faccenda v Fowler* itself shows, the first and second categories are not easy to separate in practice: is a list of customers a trade secret as such, or simply valuable commercial information?

 Pause for reflection

How easy is it in practice to draw the line between the three categories of information mentioned in *Faccenda v Fowler*?

In our problem scenario, would Saoirse possess a 'trade secret' belonging to NHT or merely 'commercial and valuable information'? What about her general skill and knowledge?

19.4.2.4 Involuntary third-party recipients

The starting point here is fairly obvious: unless protection is available against a third-party recipient, the action for breach of confidence would be worthless (*per* Lord Griffiths in *Spycatcher*; and *per* Lords Hoffmann and Brown in *Douglas and Zeta-Jones v Hello! Ltd* at [120–122] and [325] respectively). However, it is in this area that the cases are most contradictory. This stems in part from the difficulty the courts have experienced in deciding the true rationale for breach of confidence: in the absence of a contractual relationship, the justification for the action for breach of confidence is either that information should be treated as a form of property, or that liability rests on whether the defendant's conscience was affected. The courts have been unable to settle on either rationale.

There is a certain attractiveness in adopting the property solution to decide whether an involuntary third-party recipient of secret information is bound by a duty of confidence. Treating information as property would enable the court to adopt concepts such as the *bona fide* purchaser to determine the third party's liability. Nevertheless, there are intrinsic difficulties in applying rules developed in relation to transactions in land in a commercial context (*Bank of Credit & Commerce International (Overseas) Ltd v Akindele* [2001] Ch 437). Alternatively, the third party's conduct could be equated to theft of the information. Here, too, English law has always experienced difficulty in applying the law of theft to intangible property (*Oxford v Moss* (1979) 68 Cr App R 183). There is now extensive authority that the property law approach is not to be adopted: *Boardman v Phipps* at pp. 127–8 *per* Lord Upjohn; *Douglas v Hello! Ltd (No. 2)* (CA) at [119]; *Douglas and Zeta-Jones v Hello! Ltd* (HL) *per* Lord Walker at [282]. Such authority avoids the need to consider whether a third-party recipient can be treated as a *bona fide* purchaser of the information (see *Valeo Vision SA v Flexible Lamps* [1995] RPC 203 for the difficulties which Aldous J encountered in attempting to apply the *bona fide* purchaser rule to trade secrets).

Even if the conscience of the recipient is the key to liability, there is the further difficulty as to what level of knowledge is required. The classic example given by Lord Goff in *Spycatcher*, is of a confidential document left lying on a desk in an office. The document may come into the hands of a third party in a variety of ways, for example by being stolen, acquired by sale or gift from the thief, or blown through an open window onto the street below where it is accidentally found by a passer-by. Consider the implications of these different situations for the recipient's conscience. The third party may acquire the information from the original confidant, either with actual knowledge at the time of the receipt, actual knowledge subsequently acquired, or with some form of constructive knowledge. The recipient may acquire the information from someone who is not themselves bound by secrecy, or the recipient may be a complete stranger. An example of the latter would be the burglar or passer-by.

The variety of circumstances in which a third party may acquire secret information may help to explain the inconsistency in the cases. In some instances, where information has been obtained by unlawful means, the courts have focused on the *conduct* of the third party acquiring the information. There are two decisions which on their facts appear impossible to reconcile. In *Malone v Commissioner of Police* [1979] Ch 344 Megarry J held that there was no duty of secrecy in respect of information obtained when the police intercepted the claimant's telephone calls. By contrast, in *Francome v Mirror Group Newspapers* [1984] 2 All ER 408, the court held that there *was* an obligation of confidence where information was obtained when the claimant's telephone calls were overheard by a private investigator. The Court of Appeal distinguished *Malone* on the basis that the phone tap there was authorized. Because of legislative changes relating to human rights, data protection, and telecommunications laws, these cases today would have different outcomes as regards the legality of the defendants' conduct.

One possible way of reconciling them as regards the law of breach of confidence might be to adopt the approach of Lord Woolf in *A v B (a Company)* [2002] 3 WLR 542, at [11(x)]: that is, that the obtaining of information by unlawful means is an issue which goes to the exercise of the court's discretion as to the award of an injunction.

In most other instances, it is the knowledge of the recipient which determines whether they are bound by confidentiality. Hence, it is necessary to identify whether the subsequent recipient of information steals it, receives it with actual notice, receives it with constructive notice ('turning a blind eye'), or receives it innocently. Ultimately it is a question of conscience. An objective test is applied to determine whether the third party should in conscience be bound. In *Shelley Films v Rex Features* (at p. 146), Michael Mann QC stressed that what mattered was not whether the photographer was a trespasser, but whether the photographer knew that taking photographs was prohibited and therefore confidential. In *Douglas v Hello! Ltd (No. 2)* the Court of Appeal confirmed that Lindsay J had been correct to apply the objective test in deciding whether the defendant magazine was bound by a duty of secrecy in respect of the unauthorized wedding photographs taken by the uninvited paparazzo. In the same case in the House of Lords, Lord Hoffmann (at [121]–[125]) considered that the defendant—*Hello!* magazine—should be liable to the claimants—*OK!* magazine and Michael Douglas and Catherine Zeta-Jones—because the defendant was well aware of the confidential nature of the photographs.

Pause for reflection

Why should the third-party recipient of confidential information not be able to argue that they did not appreciate that the information was secret?

In our problem scenario, could 21CT be viewed as a third-party recipient? What argument might they make? Could NHT take a claim against them?

19.4.3 Wrongful use or disclosure

The final element from the *Coco v Clark* formula which must be proved is that the defendant has gone beyond the purpose of the original disclosure. This may entail using the information for another purpose, or, more usually, passing the information on to somebody else. Even here, there are some unresolved issues in the cases. For example, does there have to be some sort of detriment or harm suffered by the claimant (a useful comparison can be made with the tort of defamation) or is wrongful use *per se* enough? The matter was left open by the House of Lords in *Spycatcher*. Normally in the case of commercial information, the loss of potential sales as a result of the defendant's use of the information to make its own competing product will mean that detriment is not an issue. In the case of personal information, there are cases which hold that the mere fact that there has been disclosure suffices (see *Argyll v Argyll* [1967] Ch 302 and *Michael Barrymore v News Group Newspapers* [1997] FSR 600). By contrast, in the substantive action in *Douglas and Zeta-Jones v Hello! Ltd* (at [199]), Lindsay J suggested that there must be some more tangible detriment to the claimants. The point was not discussed by the Court of Appeal or the House of Lords. The question remains, therefore, whether, for example, in the case of a photograph it is mere publication which suffices, or does the photograph have to show the celebrity in an unfavourable light? If the latter is the case, is it enough that the photograph is of poor quality or shows the 'wrong side' of the celebrity's face, or must there be something more?

These apparent difficulties can be resolved by arguing that the question of detriment is something which goes to the issue of the remedy to be awarded rather than the existence of liability, so that minimal harm will result in the award of nominal rather than substantial damages. However, in *Douglas v Hello! Ltd (No. 2)*, the Court of Appeal did not disturb Lindsay J's 'modest award' for the mental distress caused by the invasion of the claimants' privacy. The low quantum of damages can be contrasted with the force of the court's statement as regards the duty imposed by the ECHR to ensure respect for private life, and its comments about the incorrect discharge of the interim injunction by a differently constituted Court of Appeal.

Pause for reflection

Should the victim of a wrongful breach of confidence have to show detriment or should the mere fact of disclosure suffice? If detriment is required, how is this to be determined? If disclosure alone suffices, is that not tantamount to treating the information as property?

What detriment could NHT show in our problem scenario?

19.5 Privacy and the impact of the Human Rights Act 1998

Prior to the implementation of the Human Rights Act 1998 ('HRA'), UK courts had declared on more than one occasion that there was no right of privacy in UK law (*Kaye v Robertson* [1991] FSR 62). That position changed after the 1998 Act because the HRA incorporated Art. 8 ECHR (right to privacy and family life) into UK law. The free-standing right to privacy is now established. However, subsequent cases have shown that it must be balanced with Art. 10 ECHR (freedom of expression).

The key case was the Court of Appeal decision *Douglas v Hello! Ltd (No. 2)* [2005] 4 All ER 128 (CA) at [251], where the court stated that the extensive imposition of confidentiality undertakings upon guests and staff at the wedding was enough, when coupled with the HRA, to create a right of privacy. Here, the claimants had entered into detailed arrangements to ensure that their wedding was as private as possible, thereby enabling the court to make use of the action for breach of confidence as a means of redress.

Two cases paved the way for the Court of Appeal's declaration in *Douglas v Hello! Ltd (No. 2)* at [53] that United Kingdom courts are required (in fulfilment of their duties under Arts 8 and 10 of the ECHR) to adopt the cause of action formerly described as breach of confidence as the appropriate vehicle for ensuring the protection of private information. Chronologically, the first of these pivotal cases was *Naomi Campbell v Mirror Group Newspapers* [2004] 2 AC 457 where majority of the House of Lords held that the claimant's privacy had been invaded by detailed accounts appearing in the defendant's newspaper of her attendance at a drug rehabilitation clinic in London. The newspaper was entitled to 'set the record straight' after the claimant had denied her drug addiction but had gone too far in disclosing the details of her attendance at the clinic and in publishing pictures, taken surreptitiously, of her leaving a counselling session. According to Lord Hope at [88], at issue were five pieces of information:

- the fact that Naomi Campbell was a drug addict;
- the fact that she was receiving treatment for her addiction;
- the fact that such treatment was provided by Narcotics Anonymous;
- the details of the treatment; and
- photographs of her leaving a treatment session.

The division of opinion in the House of Lords was as to whether the last three items were wrongfully disclosed, not whether there *should* in principle be protection of privacy. On this latter point there was unanimity. Hence, despite being in the minority in his conclusion on the facts, Lord Nicholls accepted that protecting privacy through the action for breach of confidence was a fast-developing area of the law. He suggested that the essence of the action was not so much wrongful disclosure of private information but the *misuse* of private information. The other minority Law Lord, Lord Hoffmann, commented that instead of relying on the duty of good faith, it was better to focus on the protection of human autonomy and dignity, and the right to control the dissemination of information about one's private life. Baroness Hale thought that the cause of action of breach of confidence had within its scope what might be termed 'protection of the individual's informational autonomy'.

The other key case is that of the ECtHR in *Von Hannover v Germany (No. 1)* (2004) 40 EHHR 1, which coincidentally occurred some six weeks after *Naomi Campbell v MGN*. In *Von Hannover v Germany* the applicant, Princess Caroline of Monaco, had applied unsuccessfully on several occasions to the German courts to prevent a number of German magazines from publishing photographs of her and her children. The German Federal Constitutional Court held that as a 'figure of contemporary society' she had to tolerate the publication of the photographs of her in a public place even though she was not engaged in official duties but daily routine, such as shopping and collecting her children from school. The Strasbourg court disagreed, drawing a distinction between facts contributing to a debate about politicians in the exercise of their duties and the reporting of details about the private life of an individual who does not exercise official functions. In the former case, the press had a vital role to play as the 'watchdog' of democracy, but this did not apply where photographs and articles had the sole purpose of satisfying the public's curiosity. In this context, freedom of expression had to be interpreted more narrowly.

The forthright nature of the ECtHR's judgment really left the Court of Appeal in *Douglas v Hello! Ltd (No. 2)* little choice but to develop a right of privacy.

19.5.1 The correct test for liability in privacy cases

One remaining issue was whether the *Coco v Clark* formula for breach of confidence should be applied in cases of misuse of personal information, or whether an alternative test should be developed. What has emerged is that rather than ask whether information is confidential, one should ask whether it is private: *per* Lord Woolf in *A v B (a Company)*. There is a line to be drawn between public and private information, a distinction which is easy to state but less simple to apply. How does one decide whether information is public or private? One test suggested in the context of media intrusion is that of Gleeson CJ in *Australian Broadcasting Corporation v Lenah Game Meats Pty Ltd* (2001) 185 ALR 1:

> There is no bright line which can be drawn between that which is private and what is not. Use of the term 'public' is often a convenient method of contrast, but there is a large area in between what is necessarily public and what is necessarily private . . . The requirement that disclosure or observation of information or conduct would be highly offensive to a reasonable person of ordinary sensibilities is in many circumstances a useful practical test of what is private.

The 'highly offensive' test was cited with approval in *A v B (a Company)*. However, in *Naomi Campbell v MGN*, Lord Nicholls thought the test was more appropriate to the issue of whether it was proportionate to disclose the information, rather than whether that information was protected in the first place. He thought (at [21]) that the correct test was whether there was a reasonable expectation of privacy. Lord Hope (at [99]) put this a slightly different way, namely what would a reasonable person of ordinary sensibilities feel if she were placed in the same position as the claimant and faced with the same publicity?

In *Murray v Express Newspapers* [2009] Ch 48 the Court of Appeal at [35] blends the statements by Lords Nicholls and Hope in *Naomi Campbell v MGN*. The preferred test is whether there is a reasonable expectation of privacy, assessed objectively through the eyes of the reasonable third party. The court provided a list of factors to be considered in deciding whether such an expectation existed. These were:

- the attributes of the claimant;
- the nature of the activity in which the claimant was engaged;
- the place at which it was happening;
- the nature and purpose of the intrusion;
- the absence of consent and whether it was known or could be inferred;
- the effect on the claimant; and
- the circumstances in which and the purposes for which the information came into the hands of the publisher.

Once it is established that there is a reasonable expectation of privacy, the court then has to balance the competing claims of Arts 8 and 10 ECHR.

The same approach was adopted by Eady J in *Mosley v News Group Newspapers* and has also been used in cases where the confider and confidant were in an existing contractual relationship. In *McKennitt v Ash* [2007] 3 WLR 194 the claimant was a successful composer and performer of folk music, whilst the defendant was a former friend who had worked closely with her in connection with merchandising activities, accompanying her on tour as a personal assistant. The defendant wrote a book called *Travels with Loreena McKennitt: My Life as a Friend*. Eady J, confirmed by the Court of Appeal, held that there had been a reasonable expectation of privacy. **Public interest** had to yield to effective protection of private life. The defendant would have been aware that much of the book would cause distress because of its intrusive nature. A number of passages should not have been published.

A similar outcome can be found in *HRH Prince of Wales v Associated Newspapers Ltd* [2007] 3 WLR 222. The claimant had for some 30 years kept personal journals recording his thoughts on various visits he had made to different parts of the world. On his return to the UK, his journals would be photocopied by his staff and selectively distributed to close friends. The copies and any covering letter were marked 'private and confidential'. The originals were kept in a locked safe and it was not anticipated that they would be published during the claimant's lifetime. The defendant had acquired a copy of the claimant's journal (recording his thoughts on the return of Hong Kong to the People's Republic of China) from an undisclosed intermediary who in turn had obtained it from a former secretary. The secretary had tried to retrieve the copy of the journal without success. Blackburne J, having established that there was a reasonable expectation of privacy, carried out the balancing exercise required under the ECHR, holding that as there had been no hypocrisy or wrongdoing on the part of the claimant, the public interest did not favour disclosure. The influence of *Naomi Campbell v MGN* and *Von Hannover v Germany (No. 1)* on both of these cases is very evident.

In *Rocknroll v News Group Newspapers* [2013] EWHC 24 (Ch) the claimant had sought an injunction to restrain the publication on Facebook of a photograph taken at a private party. At [5] Briggs J summarized what he described as the 'well-settled principles' of privacy:

(1) The first stage is to ascertain whether the applicant has a reasonable expectation of privacy so as to engage Art. 8; if not, the claim fails.

(2) The question of whether or not there is a reasonable expectation of privacy in relation to the information 'is a broad one, which takes account of all the circumstances of the case. They include the attributes of the claimant, the nature of the activity in which the claimant was engaged, the place at which it was happening, the nature and purpose of the intrusion, the absence of consent and whether it was known or could be inferred, the effect on the claimant and the circumstances in which and the purposes for which the information came into the hands of the publisher': see *Murray v Express Newspapers* [2009] Ch 481 at [36]. The test established in *Campbell v MGN Ltd* [2004] 2 AC 457 is to ask whether a reasonable person of ordinary sensibilities, if placed in the same situation as the subject of the disclosure, rather than the recipient, would find the disclosure offensive.

(3) The protection may be lost if the information is in the public domain. In this regard there is, per *Browne v Associated Newspapers Ltd* [2008] QB 103 at [61], 'potentially an important distinction between information which is made available to a person's circle of friends or work colleagues and information which is widely published in a newspaper.'

(4) If Art. 8 is engaged then the second stage of the inquiry is to conduct 'the ultimate balancing test' which has the four features identified by Lord Steyn in *In Re S (A Child) (Identification: Restrictions on Publication)* [2005] 1 AC 593 at [17]:

First, neither article [8 or 10] has as such precedence over the other. Secondly, where the values under the two articles are in conflict, an intense focus on the comparative importance of the specific rights being claimed in the individual case is necessary.

Thirdly, the justifications for interfering with or restricting each right must be taken into account. Finally, the proportionality test must be applied to each.

(5) As *Von Hannover v Germany* (2004) 40 EHRR 1 makes clear at [76]:

> the decisive factor in balancing the protection of private life against freedom of expression should lie in the contribution that the published photos and articles make to a debate of general interest.

(6) Pursuant to s. 12(3) of the HRA an interim injunction should not be granted unless a court is satisfied that the applicant is likely—in the sense of more likely than not—to obtain an injunction following a trial.

19.5.2 Loss of privacy

One counter-argument which is often raised in cases involving media intrusion is that those who court publicity have by their own conduct diminished their right of privacy. This was certainly the view of Lord Woolf in *A v B (a Company)* at [11(xii)] where the court refused to restrain the disclosure in the newspapers of the extramarital affairs of a well-known footballer. In *Theakston v MGN* [2002] EWHC 137, Ouseley J likewise refused to restrain the publication of a story concerning the visit to a brothel by a television personality, although he did restrain publication of photographs of the event (again, we may note the more stringent treatment accorded to photographic information).

These two decisions appear to treat the defence of 'in the public interest' as if it meant 'of public interest', thereby lending an aura of respectability to the activities of the media in their attempt to satisfy public curiosity about the rich and famous. This should be contrasted with what was said in *Von Hannover v Germany (No. 1)* about the status of someone who was in the public eye but not holding any office of state, and with the treatment of the public interest argument in *McKennitt v Ash*, the *Prince of Wales* case and *Mosley v News Group Newspapers*. As the Court of Appeal remarked in *Douglas v Hello! Ltd (No. 2)*, English courts for a time appeared to take a less generous view of the protection which a celebrity could expect than the Strasbourg court. There may be a general public interest in maintaining a free press, but in striking a balance between Arts 8 and 10 ECHR, 'one does not start with the balance tilted in favour of Article 10' (*Douglas v Hello! Ltd (No. 2)* at [254], [82]). The comments of the Court of Appeal in *Douglas v Hello! Ltd (No. 2)* (which the court itself stated were *obiter*) must be considered as critical of the treatment of the public interest defence in *A v B (a Company)* and *Theakston*. Nevertheless, the ECtHR itself has recognized that there are circumstances in which the right to privacy may be lost. In *Von Hannover v Germany (No. 2)* [2012] ECHR 228, Princess Caroline sought to restrain the publication of photographs taken of herself and her family on a skiing holiday at a time when her father, Prince Rainier, was gravely ill. The court was of the view that 'not only does the press have the task of imparting information and ideas on all matters of public interest, the public also has a right to receive them'. Here the Prince's illness was an event in contemporary society; in the particular factual context it would be wrong to treat the claimant as an ordinary private individual.

Equally, where the claimant has been untruthful or hypocritical, then the press are entitled to set the record straight (*Woodward v Hutchins per* Bridge LJ). Thus in *Browne v Associated Newspapers* [2007] 3 WLR 289, the Court of Appeal applied the public interest defence by permitting the defendant to publish details of the claimant's homosexual relationship because the claimant had previously committed perjury about it. However, even 'setting the record straight' has its limits. In *Naomi Campbell v MGN* the majority of the House of Lords held that only two out of the five pieces of information (the fact that the claimant was a drug addict and the fact that she was receiving treatment for her addiction) should have been disclosed by the defendant in its attempt to counter the lies which she had told: 'It should [not] necessarily be in the public interest that an individual who has been adopted as a role model . . . should be demonstrated to have feet of clay' (*Naomi Campbell v Mirror Group Newspapers Ltd* [2003] 1 All ER 224 at [41] (CA)).

PJS v News Group Newspapers [2016] UKSC 26

The recent case of *PJS v News Group Newspapers* suggests that privacy is now firmly established as a free-standing right even in cases where the information may be available online. Having initially failed at the High Court level due to the 'public interest' claim of the news organization, a celebrity—PJS—subsequently succeeded at the Court of Appeal level at winning an injunction to prevent publication of a news story about private sexual conduct, which PJS considered to be a private matter which if published could affect the right to privacy and family life. In April 2016, the Court of Appeal decided that the injunction should be lifted, as details of the story had been published widely online. PJS then appealed to the UK Supreme Court which upheld the injunction by a majority of 4-1, emphasizing the right to privacy. Important as well is the fact that the remedy involved a 'super-injunction' which prevented news organizations from reporting not only the details of the specific encounter, but also the identify of the person, a celebrity, who had obtained the injunction.

This case, and the idea of the 'super-injunction' gives rise to the argument previously made by McCamus, that the extension of breach of confidence to protect privacy has primarily boosted the rights of celebrities (J. McCamus, 'Celebrity Newsgathering and Privacy: The Transformation of Breach of Confidence in English Law' [2006] 39 *Akron L. Rev* 1191). In light of *Douglas and Hello! (No. 2)* and *PJS* we can certainly say that the law has empowered celebrities to protect the rights to photographs of their events (birthdays, weddings, etc). Have the UK courts tilted the balance too far in favour of Art. 8 ECHR at the expense of Art. 10?

19.6 Defences

Apart from pleading consent by the claimant or else arguing that the information is already in the public domain, the principal defence to an action for breach of confidence is that disclosure is 'in the public interest'. Some commentators treat disclosure in the public interest as going to the issue of whether the information is protectable. The better view is that public interest is a defence to be raised in order to justify what would otherwise be the wrongful use of secret information which has been imparted in confidence. This is because disclosure in the public interest is also a defence to copyright infringement and there have been several Court of Appeal decisions (notably *Hyde Park v Yelland* [2000]

3 WLR 215 and *Ashdown v Telegraph Group* [2001] 4 All ER 666) involving both breach of confidence and copyright infringement, where disclosure in the public interest was pleaded as a defence to both causes of action, and was dealt with as such by the court. 'In the public interest' is used in a similar way in the privacy cases: once it is established that the claimant had a reasonable expectation of privacy, then the court has to balance Arts 8 and 10 ECHR: i.e. it has to decide whether public interest overrides the claimant's rights.

19.6.1 Disclosure in the public interest: the basis of the defence

Disclosure *in* the public interest (which is not the same as saying that something, such as the latest gossip about celebrities, is 'of public interest') means that the defendant is seeking to justify what has been done by reference to the interests of society as a whole. Disclosure is necessary in order for the rule of law to be upheld. 'There is no confidence in the disclosure of an iniquity' and 'no man can be made the confidant of a crime or fraud' are *dicta* often cited as the reason for the defence (see *Gartside v Outram* (1856) 26 LJ Ch 113 and *Initial Services Ltd v Putterill* [1968] 1 QB 396, CA, respectively). However, even though disclosure to public authorities may be justified (for example where there has been a breach of the law by the claimant) that may not entitle the defendant to tell the world at large. It may be more appropriate to inform the police or regulatory authorities (*Francome v Mirror Group Newspapers* [1984] 2 All ER 408; *Cream Holdings Ltd v Banerjee* [2004] 3 WLR 918).

19.6.2 Public interest: the expansion of the defence

The public interest defence, as originally set out in *Initial Services Ltd v Putterill*, was concerned with where there had been criminal conduct on the part of the claimant, or at least some other serious breach of the law (in *Initial* the employer's breach of competition law justified the 'whistle-blower' employee's conduct in revealing what had gone on). Since that decision, the defence has been raised in many cases, not always successfully.

In *Lion Laboratories v Evans* [1984] 2 All ER 417 publication of the fact that a device (the 'Intoximeter') for breath-testing motorists for drink-driving was unreliable was justified because otherwise there might be wrongful convictions. In *Hellewell v Chief Constable of Derbyshire* [1995] 1 WLR 804, the public interest defence was held to justify the distribution by the police to shopkeepers of photographs of the claimant taken when he was in custody. Although the photographs were confidential, the police could make reasonable use of them for the purposes of crime prevention, detection, and investigation, and they were being distributed to a limited number of shops who had been badly affected by crime.

By contrast, in *Hyde Park Residence v Yelland*, publication in a newspaper of stolen video stills rebutting the claim that Princess Diana was about to marry Dodi Al Fayed was not 'in the public interest' (it might have been 'of public interest') as the information could have been supplied without publishing photographs taken from the CCTV footage (copyright in which was owned by the claimant). In *Ashdown v Telegraph Group*, publication of diaries showing the extent of the Labour/Liberal Democrat negotiations during the 1997 General Election campaign was equally not justified as being 'in the public interest'. Again, the information could have been made available without infringing the claimant's copyright. Further, the fact that key documents had been stolen from the claimant's safe did not lend credence to the defence. Last, of course, there was the division of judicial opinion in *Naomi*

Campbell v MGN as to the extent to which 'in the public interest' allowed disclosure of the five key facts about the claimant's drug addiction, with the majority concluding that only two of the five should be made public in the interest of 'setting the record straight'.

More problematic than these cases is *A v B (a Company)* where Lord Woolf refused to restrain the publication of a footballer's marital infidelities on the basis that this was in the public interest. As a celebrity in the public eye, it was suggested, the claimant had forfeited his right to be let alone. We have already noted the implicit criticism of this thinking (and of Ouseley J's decision in *Theakston v MGN*) by the Court of Appeal in *Douglas v Hello! Ltd (No. 2)*. Subsequent cases, no doubt influenced by the *Von Hannover (No. 1)* ruling with its strict criteria, have been more dismissive of the public interest defence, including *McKennitt v Ash*, *HRH Prince of Wales v Associated Newspapers Ltd* and *Mosley*.

Public interest can be a double-edged sword. In *Volkswagen AG v Garcia and others* [2013] EWHC 1832 (Ch), the defendants wanted to publish an academic paper revealing the weaknesses in a computer chip used by the claimant and other car manufacturers in car immobilizers. One of the arguments they advanced was that there was a strong public interest in exposing the security flaws. Nevertheless, Birss J held that this was outweighed by the greater public interest in not facilitating car crime.

19.6.3 Public interest: government information

In the context of Government information, the public interest defence operates in a slightly different way. In *A-G v Jonathan Cape Ltd* [1976] QB 752, the court refused to restrain the publication of the internal workings of the British Cabinet in a politician's diaries as there was no public interest justification for keeping it secret. Today, where a Crown servant pleads the public interest defence, the Crown must meet the additional burden placed on it by *Spycatcher*, namely that it must be shown not only that the information was confidential but also that it was in the public interest that it should *not* be published.

 Pause for reflection

Do the courts always distinguish clearly between 'in the public interest' and 'of public interest'? Think again about the UKSC case of *PJS v NSN*.

19.7 Remedies

19.7.1 Injunctions

If a claimant is successful in an action for breach of confidence, it will normally want to restrain the defendant from making further use of the secret information. However, case law relating to the award of an injunction for breach of confidence is contradictory. It raises the question of the proper function of an injunction, and in particular whether such relief should be available once the information has become public knowledge. Where publication is the result of the *confider* making the information public, then no injunctive relief is available (*Mustad & Sons Ltd v Allcock & Dosen*). The position is less clear where the information becomes public either through the conduct of the confidant or through the conduct of a third party. Despite the equitable maxim that 'equity does nothing in vain', there are decisions where an injunction has been granted. This raises the question about the purpose of an injunction. Is it to protect the claimant or to punish the defendant?

In *Cranleigh Precision Engineering v Bryant* [1966] RPC 81, post-publication injunctive relief was not granted, the court applying the maxim that equity does nothing in vain. By contrast, in *Schering Chemicals v Falkman* the majority of the Court of Appeal were prepared to grant an injunction, despite the relevant information (about the side effects of the claimant's pharmaceutical) being known. Lord Denning's powerful dissent should be noted. Similarly, injunctive relief was granted in *Speedseal v Paddington* [1986] 1 All ER 91 (probably because of the nature of the defendant's conduct), and in *Spycatcher*. In the latter case, there is a distinct lack of clarity by the House of Lords as to whether Peter Wright, the former civil servant, could be enjoined from publishing his memoirs in the United Kingdom when they were readily available elsewhere. Their Lordships obviously felt some distaste in concluding that there was no point in issuing an injunction once the book had been published, as Peter Wright was profiting from his own wrong.

The role of injunctive relief was revisited by Arnold J in *Vestergaard Frandsen A/S v BestNet Europe Ltd* [2010] FSR 29. He concluded (at [76]) after a detailed review of earlier cases that the so-called 'springboard' doctrine does *not* enable the court to grant an injunction once information has ceased to be confidential and that *Speedseal v Paddington* was wrong. Publication of the confidential information brings the obligation of confidence to an end, regardless of whether this was by the confider, the confidant or a stranger.

19.7.2 Compensation

The case law on compensation for breach of confidence is likewise contradictory. Where the claimant seeks an award of damages, it is necessary to distinguish between those cases where the confidential obligation arises as a result of a contract and those cases where it does not. Where the breach of confidence is also a breach of contract, damages are calculated under the normal contract rules, although in exceptional cases, it is possible to award an account of profits. The ability to award an account is illustrated by *AG v Blake*, where a former security services employee who had defected to the then Soviet Union had published his memoirs, from which he earned considerable royalties. His behaviour was held to be analogous to breach of a fiduciary obligation, for which an account would have been the normal remedy.

Where the parties are not in a contractual relationship, the question is whether damages are awarded under the Senior Courts Act 1981 s. 50 (i.e. in lieu of or in addition to equitable relief) or whether they are awarded independently on a quasi-tortious basis. If the latter is the case, a further question is how are they to be calculated? One answer is in the case of *Seager v Copydex (No. 2)* [1969] RPC 250. Here the Court of Appeal decided that the measure of damages was to be as in the tort of conversion, so that the claimant was to be awarded the retail selling price of each infringing item produced by the defendants. The calculation suggests that damages were awarded independently of the power in s. 50. It might well be, however, that in using such a computation,

Lord Denning was influenced by the fact that at the time conversion damages were available for breach of copyright under the Copyright Act 1956 s. 18. This particular form of monetary relief has since been abolished, which would mean that if *Seager v Copydex (No. 2)* is correct, breach of confidence would be the only area of intellectual property in which such a generous award is allowed. Further, any expansion of the tort of conversion to cover intangible personal property was rejected by a majority of the House of Lords (Lords Hoffmann, Walker, and Brown) in *Douglas and Zeta-Jones v Hello! Ltd*. By contrast, in *Dowson & Mason v Potter* [1986] 2 All ER 418 the court awarded a reasonable licence fee, that is, the sum which the claimant would have charged for permission to use the information commercially, a calculation identical to that used in patent and copyright infringement actions and much more in keeping with the principles enunciated by Lord Wilberforce in *General Tire v Firestone* [1976] RPC 197 concerning damages for infringement of intellectual property rights and with the thinking of the Supreme Court of Canada in *Cadbury Schweppes Inc v FBI Foods Ltd*. That a reasonable licence fee is the correct measure has now been confirmed by the Court of Appeal in *Force India Formula One Team Ltd v Aerolab SRL* [2013] EWCA Civ 780.

A particular problem may present itself in the newly emerging case law on privacy. In *Douglas v Hello! Ltd (No. 2)* the Court of Appeal dismissed the claimant's appeal for damages to be increased from Lindsay J's award of £14,600 so as to accord with what might have been charged as a reasonable licence fee. Apart from the fact that their contract with their authorized publishers prohibited them from agreeing to any further exploitation of their wedding photographs, the difficulty which the court faced was that an interim injunction to prevent the invasion of their privacy should have been maintained but in fact had been wrongly discharged. Damages for this form of harm would have been inadequate. Once privacy is lost, it cannot be recaptured. The question remains, therefore, what form of monetary remedy should the claimants have been awarded for this newly created form of action? We may note that this particular issue was not the subject of appeal to the House of Lords, although Lord Walker (at [295]) expresses doubts about the correctness of awarding 'modest' damages.

The quantum of damages for invasion of privacy was revisited by Eady J in *Mosley v News Group Newspapers*. Noting that an infringement of privacy could never be effectively compensated by money, he decided that £60,000 should be awarded. There should be adequate financial remedy to acknowledge the infringement and to compensate for embarrassment and distress, even though what could be achieved through compensation was limited. However, there should be no award of exemplary or punitive damages (to deter others), but equally, just because some viewed the claimant's conduct with distaste was not a reason to reduce the award.

19.7.3 Proprietary relief

One final question is whether a constructive trust could also be available if the defendant has 'used' the information to make a personal gain. Although this idea was accepted in the Canadian case of *LAC Minerals v International Corona Ltd* (1989) 61 DLR (4th) 14, the Supreme Court of Canada in *Cadbury Schweppes Inc v FBI Foods Ltd* has subsequently declared that a proprietary remedy is not appropriate. Instead, the court should calculate damages on the basis of lost profits during the notional period of one year it would have taken the defendant to 'reverse engineer' the claimant's secret recipe for a drink. Similarly, the House of Lords in *AG v Blake* ruled that a constructive trust should not be imposed on the defendant's gains. There was no proprietary interest to protect. The lack of property right to support a constructive trust was repeated in *Douglas v Hello! Ltd (No. 2)* (CA). However, as noted earlier, their Lordships in *Blake* did suggest that an account of profits should be available instead where the defendant had been in a fiduciary or quasi-fiduciary position. Such reasoning could therefore apply not just to Crown servants (as in *Blake*) but also to high-ranking employees, such as company directors. However, it should be remembered that *Blake* was an exceptional case: *Devenish Nutrition Ltd v Sanofi-Aventis SA* [2009] Ch 390.

19.8 **The EU Trade Secrets Directive**

In 2016 the EU passed Directive 2016/943 on the protection of undisclosed know-how and business information (trade secrets) against their unlawful acquisition, use, and disclosure. The EU Trade Secrets Directive aims to harmonize this area of law within EU Member States (including, at time of writing, the UK) in mid-2018, when the Directive is due to come into force. This means that either via transposition or statutory instrument, the Directive is likely to become part of UK law by the 'Brexit' date in March 2019. Post-Brexit, and pending any UK–EU agreement, the UK courts will determine how to interpret the Directive and can have regard to the decisions of the Court of Justice of the European Union ('CJEU') (though will not be bound by them unless that is part of the UK–EU agreement).

Aplin notes that Recital 1 describes the protection of a trade secret as 'a complement or alternative to intellectual property rights' rather than as an IP right in itself (T. Aplin, 'A Critical Evaluation of the proposed EU Trade Secrets Directive' [2014] 4 *IPQ* 257). This accords with the point made earlier, about the distinction between classic IP rights and trade secrets.

The Directive provides minimum standards of 'trade secret' protection (which means that EU Member States can go beyond the minimum in granting wider protection). Under Art. 2(1) of the Directive a 'trade secret' is information which meets the following requirements:

(a) it is secret in the sense that it is not, as a body or in the precise configuration and assembly of its components, generally known among or readily accessible to persons within the circles that normally deal with the kind of information in question;

(b) it has a commercial value because it is secret;

(c) it has been subject to reasonable steps under the circumstances, by the person lawfully in control of the information, to keep it secret.

Thus, the definition of a trade secret under the Directive appears to be sufficiently broad to cover the protection of 'trade secrets' under UK law of confidence. But is it broad enough to include the kind of confidential information claimed by celebrities under privacy? Aplin argues that although the Directive appears, particular in the Recital 8, to focus on business and technical information, this may not be sufficient to 'exclude commercialised private information because for many celebrities their personal information (and its use and disclosure) is a business' ('A Critical Evaluation'). We will only be able to determine the answer to this once the CJEU gives guidance.

Subtle changes to UK law may arise from the definition of 'unlawful actions' under Art. 4. Article 4(2) makes it unlawful to acquire trade secrets through conduct which is 'contrary to honest commercial practices', a concept which is related to, but which may not be exactly analogous to the case law we looked at above. Article 4(3–5), make clear that third parties can be held liable, including for dealing with 'infringing goods', where they had actual or constructive knowledge that the trade secret had been misappropriated.

Lapousterle et al. state that one gap in the Directive may be that that, looking at Art. 1(3) and Recital 14, post-employment situations do not appear to be harmonized by the Directive, but rather will remain within the purview of Member States (J. Lapousterle, C. Geiger, N. Olszak, and L. Desaunettes, 'What protection for Trade Secrets in the European Union? A comment on the Directive proposal' [2016] 38(5) *EIPR* 255).

19.9 Conclusion

This chapter has explained that in the UK breach of confidence offers protection to trade secrets and other confidential information. As stated in *Coco v Clark*, an action for breach of confidence requires: (i) information which is not in the public domain; (ii) to be disclosed in circumstances which impose an obligation on the recipient; (iii) that then may be about to be used or further disclosed in a way that requires restraint by injunction (*Boardman v Phipps*; *Douglas v Hello! Ltd (No. 2)*).

The information must not already be in the public domain (*Coco v Clark*) and must be kept with relative secrecy (*Spycatcher*; *BBC v HarperCollins*; *Vestergaard Frandsen*). According to Lord Goff in *Spycatcher*, it must not be useless, trivial, vague, or immoral, but rather be identifiable, certain, and detailed—contrast *De Maudsley v Palumbo* with *Fraser v Thames Television*.

Protection may still be available if the defendant uses the information as a 'springboard' to gain a commercial advantage over competitors. The 'springboard' doctrine arose in the case of *Terrapin v Builders' Supply Co* where 'mixed' information was protected. Where the 'springboard' test applies, any remedy will be limited to the time it would take a competitor to reverse engineer the claimant's information (*Cadbury Schweppes Inc*—a decision of the Supreme Court of Canada). The injunction against the defendant was accordingly limited to that period of time.

The second requirement from *Coco v Clark* is that the information must have been disclosed by the confider to the confidant in circumstances of confidence. Commonly, a duty of confidence may arise from a contract between the parties, via an express term it may be a reasonable, implied term in the circumstances of the relationship (*Liverpool City Council v Irwin*; *BP Refinery (Westernport) Pty Ltd*). The weight of authority is in favour of an objective test based on reasonableness (*Coco v Clark*).

An employee owes their employer a duty of fidelity (*Robb v Green*); it varies depending on the seniority and skill of the employee. Very senior employees will be treated as fiduciaries. The duty of good faith can encompass the duty not to compete with or injure the employer's business (*Hivac Ltd v Park Royal Scientific*) as well as the obligation to maintain secrecy (*Printers and Finishers Ltd v Holloway*). Whether a former employee owes an obligation of secrecy to the employer depends again on the status, knowledge, and skills of the employee.

Further, there are three principal categories of information which must be kept distinct: (i) trade secrets as such; (ii) commercially sensitive or valuable information; and (iii) the employee's general skill and knowledge (*Faccenda v Fowler*). The first *Faccenda* category—trade secrets—is automatically protected during and after the contract of employment. The second—commercially sensitive or valuable information—is automatically protected during the contract of employment because of the employee's general duty of fidelity but will require an express clause to protect it after termination of employment. Such a clause must be limited appropriately in time, geographical area, and as to the relevant activities of the ex-employee, otherwise it may be held void as being in restraint of trade (*Fellowes v Fisher; Commercial Plastics v Vincent*). The final category of information, the employee's general skill and knowledge, is not protectable, on grounds of public policy (*Herbert Morris v Saxelby*). Nevertheless, as the decision in *Faccenda v Fowler* itself shows, the first and second categories are not easy to separate in practice: is a list of customers a trade secret as such, or simply valuable commercial information?

What happens to third-party recipients of secret information? Are they bound by a duty of confidence? The conscience of the recipient is the key to liability—but what level of knowledge is required? It is necessary to identify whether the subsequent recipient of information steals it, receives it with actual notice, receives it with constructive notice ('turning a blind eye'), or receives it innocently. Ultimately it is a question of conscience. An objective test is applied to determine whether the third party should in conscience be bound (*Shelley Films v Rex Features; Douglas v Hello! Ltd (No. 2)*).

The final element from the *Coco v Clark* formula which must be proved is that the defendant has gone beyond the purpose of the original disclosure. Normally in the case of commercial information, the loss of potential sales as a result of the defendant's use of the information to make its own competing product will mean that detriment is not an issue.

In our problem, the partners in NHT are concerned both at the possibility that Saoirse may (i) tell 21CT how their Taste software works, and (ii) reveal to 21CT details of the advice given to Thompson. If either, or both, happen, this might put the success of the Thompson campaign in doubt and jeopardize their lucrative deal with Thompson.

To begin your advice to NHT you should tell them that the software and the substance of the Thompson campaign advice could be considered as trade secrets. As we have seen in cases such as *Coco v Clark* and *Spycatcher* it is key that the information is sufficiently detailed and that it is kept private or secret. Here, both the software and the substance of the campaign advice appear to be detailed and private.

In terms of the duty of confidence, Saoirse is an outgoing employee, presumably under contract, who owed her employer a duty of fidelity (*Robb v Green; Hivac*) while employed. Whether she, as a former employee, will still owe an obligation of secrecy to the employer depends on her status, knowledge, and skills. She does seem to be an important part of the team, so we can assume she owes some kind of duty to NHT that is not automatically terminated when she leaves. However, there are three principal categories of information which must be kept distinct: (i) trade secrets as such; (ii) commercially sensitive or valuable information; and (iii) the employee's general skill and knowledge (*Faccenda v Fowler*). The software is likely to be (i) a trade secret—but probably only with respect to its unique functionality, which as a non-programmer, Saoirse probably does not understand. The idea of data-crunching software to enhance marketing advice is probably not protectable in and of itself. The advice to Thompson could be on the border between (i) and (ii) but is likely to be protected. So, we can advise NHT to argue that Saoirse should be considered bound to not reveal either anything she knows about the functionality of the software (which may not be that substantial in any case); and more importantly, the substance of the advice given to Thompson, which could be commercially useful to a competitor. They should seek a court injunction to this effect. If Saoirse has already revealed confidential information to 21CT, they could be viewed as a third-party recipient depending on the knowledge they had or should have had about the information (*Shelley Films; Douglas v Hello! (No. 2)*) and could also be restrained. It is likely, given their client is a direct competitor of Thompson, that a court would seek to prevent 21CT taking advantage of any confidential information Saoirse gave them. Clear detriment would occur to NHT (and Thompson) if the injunction is not granted. NHT could lose their contract and Thompson could lose sales.

But in terms of the length of that injunction, regarding the advice given to Thompson, the 'springboard' doctrine could potentially be relevant (*Terrapin v Builders' Supply*), as any remedy sought by NHT will likely be limited to the time it would take their competitor to create their own mid-century line (Canadian case of *Cadbury Schweppes*) which here seems to be a matter of months up to summer 2018. No public interest defence is available.

End-of-chapter questions

After reading the chapter carefully, try answering the following questions. For answer guidance visit the online resources at www.oup.com/uk/karapapa-mcdonagh/

1. Do you think that it ultimately makes a difference, as an issue of law or as a matter of business practice, whether trade secrets are protected as a right *in personam* rather than as a right *in rem*?

2. Do you think that the area of image rights is sufficiently defined? Do we need a statute to clarify the meaning of this right?

3. Now that privacy is firmly established as an ECHR right independent of the traditional UK case law, do you think the current defences are sufficient, especially in celebrity cases involving 'super-injunctions'?

Further reading

Aplin, T. 'The Development of the Action for Breach of Confidence in the post-HRA Era' [2007] 1 *IPQ* 19

> *Provides a wide-ranging review of the case law.*

Aplin, T. 'A Critical Evaluation of the proposed EU Trade Secrets Directive' [2014] 4 *IPQ* 257

> *Examines the EU Trade Marks Directive and its potential application in UK law.*

Aplin, T. 'Reverse Engineering Commercial Secrets' [2013] 66 *Current Legal Problems* 341

Examines the lack of a specific trade secrets reverse-engineering exception in UK law.

Bently, L. 'Trade secrets: "intellectual property" but not "property"?' in H. Howe and J. Griffiths (eds), *Concepts of Property in Intellectual Property Law* (Cambridge University Press, 2013), pp. 60–93

Explores the paradox that trade secrets are seen as quasi-IP but definitely not property.

Carty, H. 'The Common Law and the Quest for the IP Effect' [2007] 3 *IPQ* 237

Considers in the light of the House of Lords in Douglas v Hello! whether breach of confidence could be expanded to provide wider protection for 'valuable intangibles' against misappropriation.

Carty, H. 'An Analysis of the Modern Action for Breach of Commercial Confidence: When is Protection Merited?' [2008] 4 *IPQ* 416

Argues that the House of Lords in Douglas v Hello! missed the opportunity to state clearly a modern framework for liability.

Dinwoodie, G. and M. Richardson, 'Publicity Right, Personality Right, or Just Confusion?' in M. Richardson and S. Ricketson (eds) *Research Handbook on Intellectual Property in Media and Entertainment* (Edward Elgar, 2017)

Explores the potential of exploitation of a celebrity publicity right.

EUIPO, *Protecting Innovation Through Trade Secrets and Patents: Determinants for European Union Firms* (EUIPO, 2017)

Claims that trade marks are used more commonly than patents in some business sectors and looks ahead to the EU Trade Marks Directive.

Hammond, R.G. 'The Origins of the Equitable Duty of Confidence' [1979] 8 *Anglo-American Law Review* 71

Examines the historical origins of breach of confidence in Equity.

Hunt, C. 'Rethinking Surreptitious Takings in the Law of Confidence' [2011] 1 *IPQ* 66

Criticizes the House of Lords' rulings in Campbell and Douglas for their lack of analysis of how an obligation of confidence can extend to a surreptitious taker.

Lapousterle, J., C. Geiger, N. Olszak, and L. Desaunettes, 'What protection for Trade Secrets in the European Union? A comment on the Directive proposal' 38 [2016] *EIPR* 255

Looks at the issue of harmonization of EU trade secrets via the Directive.

McCamus, J. 'Celebrity Newsgathering and Privacy: The Transformation of Breach of Confidence in English Law' [2006] 39 *Akron L Rev* 1191

Moreham, N.A. 'Privacy in the Common Law' [2005] 121 *LQR* 628

Analyses protection against the invasion of privacy in light of Campbell v MGN, considering in particular the desirable scope of 'private information' and the desirable extension of the action to cover non-information-based intrusions.

Morgan, J. 'Privacy, Confidence and Horizontal Effect: "Hello" Trouble' [2003] 62(2) *CLJ* 443

A critique of the interlocutory decision in Douglas v Hello!

Mulheron, R. 'A Potential Framework for Privacy? A Reply to *Hello!*' [2006] 69 *MLR* 679

Considers the difficulties which arise from any judicial attempt to create a right of privacy and the criteria which ought to be deployed in creating a coherent tort of privacy.

Phillipson, G. 'Transforming Breach of Confidence? Towards a Common Law Right of Privacy under the Human Rights Act' [2003] 66 *MLR* 726

The seminal article on breach of confidence (referred to with approval by Lord Nicholls in Campbell v MGN) which explores the effect of the fusion of the Human Rights Act and breach of confidence.

Schreiber, A. 'Confidence Crisis, Privacy Phobia: Why Invasion of Privacy Should be Independently Recognised in English Law' [2006] 2 *IPQ* 160

Argues that breach of confidence should not be extended to misuse of personal information and that Parliament should legislate to create a separate tort.

Sims, A. '"A Shift in the Centre of Gravity": The Dangers of Protecting Privacy through Breach of Confidence' [2005] 1 *IPQ* 27

Compares the differing approaches of United Kingdom and New Zealand courts in protecting privacy, arguing that it would be better to create a separate stand-alone tort rather than extend the action for breach of confidence.

Designs

PART 7

20. Designs

Designs

Problem question

Read this problem question carefully and keep it in mind while you are working through the chapter that follows. At the end of this chapter, you will be able to apply what you have learnt to the problem question and advise the relevant parties.

Bristol Packaging Technology Ltd (BPT) is a UK-based company that develops and manufactures cardboard packaging systems. It designs, manufactures, and sells bespoke packaging for families moving to a new house and for removal companies who specialise in long-haul moves.

BPT's staff have recently designed a new type of cardboard container aimed at the market for house moves. Unique aspects of the cardboard container are its simplicity and its attractiveness—it consists of a tube of folded cardboard which is cunningly folded at the ends to close the package off, sealing the contents securely inside. The container has eight flat sides. The resulting packaging has an attractive geometrical shape as the folds are visible to customers in one of two different shapes (depending on which version is purchased)—crouching tiger and flying bird. The container packages come in a range of sizes (1kg, 2.5kg, 5kg, 10kg) but are always in the same proportion and shape. BPT's directors hope the package will intrigue the consumer and will prove particularly popular among families with young children, for whom packing up clothes and toys, and moving to a new house can often be a chore, and even something that causes a child to worry.

They wish to test the packaging out on focus groups including consumer families and removal company workers.

Advise about any elements of design protection that might apply and what they need to do to ensure protection.

20.1 Introduction

Design law exists to protect the *appearance* of articles rather than the articles themselves. It is concerned with *how things look*. The underlying idea behind the law on designs is that it involves two distinct elements: an article or product (which under the law as it now stands, need not be mass-produced) and some added ingredient, a design feature, which enhances the appearance of the article. It is the design feature, the added matter, which receives legal protection, not the product itself (unless, of course, the product qualifies in its own right for patent protection). To give a simple example, a bottle would be the article. If the bottle is made in the shape of a human torso (such as the perfume bottles produced by Jean Paul Gaultier), it is the body shape which is protectable under the law of designs (and, incidentally, also under trade mark law).

This chapter deals with the five principal means available to protect the appearance of a product: UK registered design; UK unregistered design right; UK copyright; EU registered design; and EU unregistered design. Thus, a designer who wishes to acquire protection for the appearance of an article under UK and/or EU law has several options. To add to the complexity, various aspects of the design can be protected by registered designs, unregistered designs, and copyright. The upshot is that a designer could end up with several different layers of protection.

20.1.1 Designs: Registered, unregistered, copyright, UK, and EU

The UK registered designs system mirrors the EU system, which like the area of trade marks is harmonized via the EUIPO at Alicante, Spain. The UK also has a doctrine of protection for an unregistered design, as does the EU. As with copyright, for unregistered designs there are questions of subsistence and scope of protection that are relevant to some layers of protection; while patent-style concepts such as novelty are relevant to registered designs. Since our focus is on UK law, in this chapter we will primarily examine the UK registered and unregistered design rights, as well as UK copyright. However, since the UK registered design mirrors the EU Community Registered Design, we will make reference to EU case law. The only element of design law we will not look at in detail is the EU unregistered design right.

The structure of UK design law makes a number of assumptions about what makes a good design and how good designs should best be protected—assumptions that we will aim to investigate over the course of this chapter. The law's view is that an article whose appearance has a greater visual impact on the user is regarded as more deserving of protection than a functional item. The former qualifies for registration (via registered designs), the latter does not; although, as we shall see, there is a second, lower tier of copyright-type protection for designs not having such visual impact.

The duration of protection is longer for registered designs and the owner is given a monopoly-type right so that independent creation is not a defence. Moreover, the counter-arguments available to a defendant in an infringement action are fewer and far narrower. Nevertheless, as with all registrable rights, there is the ever-present risk that the registration may be declared invalid via a challenge by a third-party, thus leaving the designer with nothing. Second-tier protection for non-registered designs—e.g. via copyright—is shorter, narrower, and offers greater scope to the defendant to argue that there has been no infringement. Such protection is, however, automatic and free to the owner, whereas application fees and renewal fees apply to registered designs.

Pause for reflection

The underlying assumptions made by the current UK and EU designs legislation can be challenged in several ways. Separating out the visual impact of a design from its other qualities, such as the usefulness of the product, how sturdy it is, the materials from which it is made, or its price, is not always easy.

In this vein, Suthersanaen states that design law suffers from a lack of consensus as to the nature of protection—some view it as 'industrial property' (like patents) while others see it as 'artistic property' (like copyright works). Courts often struggle to 'draw clear parameters between art (visually relevant designs) and function (technically dictated designs)'. Furthermore, although the EU design regime was set up to attain the best of both worlds, where designs 'would be protected as both industrial property (registration) or as copyright (unregistered rights)' unnecessary complexities and ambiguities plague the system, as national law variances remain under copyright ('Function, Art and Fashion: Do We Need the EU Design Law?' in Christophe Geiger (ed), *Constructing European Intellectual Property* (Edward Elgar, 2013), p. 357).

20.1.2 The justifications for design right protection

Typically, it is said that design law exists either to prevent misappropriation (the stealing of another person's efforts) or to encourage investment in better design for the good of society as a whole (i.e. the utilitarian theory). These arguments (often intertwined) have been advanced by both the UK Government and the EU Commission. The former stated that 'some protection should be available to give the manufacturer who has spent money on the design the opportunity to benefit from his investment, thus providing an incentive to further investment' (White Paper on *Intellectual Property and Innovation* 1986 (Cmnd 9712) para 3.21). The latter has declared (in Recital 7 to the EU Design Regulation (Council Regulation (EC) No. 6/2002 of 12 December 2001 on Community designs [2002] OJ L 3/1), throughout this chapter 'the Regulation') that 'enhanced protection for industrial design not only promotes the contribution of individual designers to the sum of Community excellence in the field, but also encourages innovation and development of new products and investment in their production'.

Pause for reflection

Consider the problem scenario. What is it about what BPT is doing that might justify the award of design protection (either via the registered or unregistered routes)?

20.1.3 Policy

Over the last 50 years, UK Government policy has fluctuated between, on the one hand, insisting that the designer can only obtain protection by registration and, on the other, permitting the designer to choose between registration under the Registered Designs Act 1949, as amended, (throughout this chapter, 'RDA') and reliance on copyright (or an equivalent copyright-type right).

Immediately prior to the introduction of the Copyright, Designs and Patents Act 1988 ('CDPA'), a designer could choose to register the appearance of their design at the Designs Registry (part of the United Kingdom Intellectual Property Office, 'UKIPO'); or, alternatively, argue that the original article was, in itself, an artistic work, such as a sculpture or work of artistic craftsmanship. More problematic, however, was a situation where the design started out as a drawing. The designer in such a case was able, prior to 1989, to rely on the copyright in that drawing to prevent any unauthorized direct or indirect three-dimensional copy of that drawing (*LB (Plastics) v Swish Products* [1979] RPC 551). As a result of the decision of the House of Lords in *British Leyland v Armstrong Patents* [1986] AC 577, which criticized the claimant's reliance on copyright to prevent the manufacture of spare parts for its cars, provisions were introduced in the CDPA which curtail the ability of a designer to rely on the copyright in such 'design documents'. By way of replacement, the CDPA provides a copyright-type right, the unregistered design right, although some residual copyright protection is still available for articles which amount to artistic works in their own right. Interestingly, the UK unregistered design right is unique, having criteria entirely different from those applicable in the UK registered designs and the EU registered and unregistered designs systems.

 Pause for reflection

Given the availability of EU unregistered design right, is there any point any longer in having a separate domestic system of unregistered protection? Is the benefit to the designer of an extra route of protection outweighed by the complexity of the range of (somewhat overlapping) registered and unregistered rights?

20.1.4 Legal choices available to the designer

As we have seen, a designer who wishes to obtain protection for the appearance of an article has a complex and bewildering choice. So, considering our problem scenario, how can we best advise companies like BPT?

The solution best suited to the designer's needs will depend on a number of commercial factors, including the nature of the product, how competitive that sector of the designs industry is, in which countries the product is likely to be marketed, and how long it is expected to be of commercial value (many designs are driven by short-term fashion considerations, as noted by K. Preet, 'Why America needs a European fashion police' [2008] 3(6) *JIPLP* 386).

Legally speaking, the decision on the part of the designer centres on whether the effort of acquiring registered protection (with its consequent monopoly-type right and longer term) outweighs the instant, cost-free, but shorter duration of unregistered, copyright-type protection. It is notable that the former (registered design), as a patent-style monopoly right, will be infringed even if a rival designer independently came up with the same design (there is no need for the claimant to show actual conscious or subconscious copying—*The Procter & Gamble Company v Reckitt Benckiser (UK) Ltd* [2008] FSR 208). By contrast, in the case of the latter (unregistered design), as an exclusive right, the claimant must show copying in order to succeed in an infringement action (genuinely independent creation will always be a defence).

20.1.4.1 Choosing registration

If the designer decides to register the design, they will have to choose between domestic UK registration or registration throughout the EU (or indeed, throughout the world). As regards UK law, the RDA was rewritten in 2001 to take account of the EU Designs Directive (Directive 98/71/EC of the European Parliament and of the Council of 13 October 1998 on the legal protection of designs, [1998] OJ L 289/28, 'the Directive'). The law of registered designs is now harmonized across the EU (including in the UK, Brexit notwithstanding).

At the same time as harmonizing national design laws, the EU, by means of the Regulation, introduced a pan-European system for protecting designs. The EU registered design right provides protection in all Member States by means of a single registration, obtainable from the EU Intellectual Property Office (EUIPO, formerly the Office for Harmonisation in the Internal Market, or OHIM) in Alicante. The criteria for national and EU protection of registered designs, found respectively in the Directive and Regulation, are therefore identical.

 Pause for reflection

Should the designer in our problem scenario (BPT) decide that registration is appropriate, the initial choice is between national (UK) or EU protection. As the criteria for protection are identical in both systems, which one to pursue comes down to the commercial considerations outlined earlier. Does BPT require protection solely in the UK or elsewhere? Where are its biggest markets? Does it compete with companies elsewhere in the EU?

Thinking globally, in September 2007 the EU acceded to the Hague Agreement concerning the international registration of industrial designs. Like the Madrid Agreement for the International Registration of Trade Marks 1891, this operates as a procedural shortcut for the designer so that a single application filed with World Intellectual Property Organization ('WIPO') leads to protection throughout the 60 Contracting States of the Agreement. This allows simultaneous applications to the EU and other contracting states such as the US and South Korea. However, it does have some limitations—some designs submitted to the WIPO register may not qualify for EU protection either because they lack novelty or individual character and WIPO databases for design searches are not as comprehensive as those available at the EUIPO and UKIPO websites.

20.1.4.2 Choosing unregistered protection

For the designer who is unable, or unwilling, to seek registered protection, the choice lies between UK unregistered design right, the EU unregistered design right or, in certain circumstances, UK copyright. Since none of these options requires a registration, any or all of these options might be arguable at trial, depending on what the elements of the design are.

The requirements of the UK unregistered design right, set out in Part III CDPA, are essentially derived from the concept of copyright, and its requirement of originality (s. 213(4) CDPA).

In contrast, the EU unregistered design right (set out in the Regulation) has criteria which mirror those for registered designs (Art. 4). However, here the period of protection is far shorter (three years as opposed to a maximum of 25 years), protection arises immediately the design is published within the EU (Art. 11), and liability for infringement depends on proof of copying (Art. 19). It is possible for a claimant to rely on both UK and EU unregistered design right in the same article even though the criteria for protection differ (*Landor & Hawa International Ltd v Azure Designs Ltd* [2007] FSR 181; *Bailey v Haynes* [2007] FSR 199; *Kohler Mira Ltd v Bristan Group Ltd* [2013] EWPCC 2).

Finally, in limited circumstances (explained later), a designer can rely on artistic copyright under s. 4 CDPA to protect the appearance of an article. Such protection is mutually exclusive with UK unregistered design right (CDPA s. 236).

By way of illustration, the designer's choice can be summarized diagrammatically: see Diagram 20.1.

Our primary goal in this chapter is to consider the principal routes to securing protection for a design under UK law, but it should be remembered that the domestic law on registered designs is a mirror-image of the protection available from EUIPO and as such is relevant to EU protection.

20.2 The UK and EU registration system

Because the criteria for protection and infringement are identical under both the UK RDA and the EU Regulation, we can consider the factors involved in both UK registered designs ('RDs') and EU registered designs (Community Registered Designs—'CRDs') simultaneously. Reference will be made to EU registered and unregistered design cases. These include decisions by the Invalidity Division of the EUIPO, the courts of other EU Member States dealing with the enforcement of the **EU design** right, and UK tribunals.

20.2.1 UK and EU Procedure for registering designs

In line with the Regulatory Reform (Registered Designs) Order 2006 (SI 2006/1974) and the Registered Designs Rules 2006 (SI 2006/1975), the UK registration procedure mirrors the procedure before the EUIPO. It entails just three basic steps:

- filing the application at the UKIPO or the EUIPO, which now can relate to more than one design, rather than one single design, as before. EUIPO statistics show that the majority of EU design applications relate to multiple designs, so designers are clearly taking advantage of the increased flexibility of the new law. As with patents, a design application may claim Convention priority from an earlier national filing.

The validity of the design will be assessed by reference to the available prior art at the filing date, or, if Convention priority is claimed, at the priority date;

- examination for compliance with formalities; and
- grant and publication.

DIAGRAM 20.1 CHOICES OPEN TO A DESIGNER

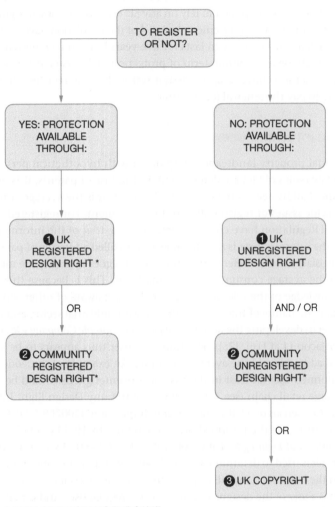

* EACH OF THESE HAS THE SAME
CRITERIA FOR PROTECTION

The application form must show clearly what is the design to be protected (photographs and/or drawings showing the article from various angles are the normal means) and to indicate the products in which the design will be incorporated or to which it will be applied. In both the UK and the EU systems, there is no examination by the Registry at the UKIPO/EUIPO to determine whether the design is new and has individual character (the two positive requirements for a valid design, which we will look at further below). This marks a difference between the process for granting patents (where there is an examination) and registering designs. In the case of designs, it is left to third parties to challenge the design for lack of these requirements in subsequent invalidity or infringement proceedings. It is for this reason that the decisions of courts and the Invalidity Division of EUIPO play a crucial role in the development of case law.

All registered designs are published upon grant, although an applicant has the option to request delayed publication and grant for up to 12 months so that, for example, registration can be timed to coincide with the launch of the new product. During that one-year period, it may be possible for the proprietor to rely on any EU unregistered design right as a further means of protection, provided the criteria in Art. 4 of the Regulation have been met.

Once granted, a registered design lasts for five years but can be renewed on four further occasions, giving a maximum term of protection of 25 years. It is possible for the registered proprietor to have a lapsed design restored to the register where there has been a failure to pay the renewal fees on time.

20.2.2 **The informed user**

The intellectual property landscape is populated with hypothetical persons through whose eyes key issues of fact are determined. In the case of patents, this person is the notional skilled addressee. In the case of trade marks, it is the average consumer who is used to decide issues of registrability and infringement. For registered designs, the Directive and Regulation have created a new persona, that of the informed user.

However, the informed user is *not* the same as the skilled addressee of patent law (otherwise the legislation would refer to the 'informed designer') yet they are more discriminating than the average consumer of trade mark law. This is because they have more extensive knowledge of the relevant design field, being aware of other similar designs, and appreciate the nature of the product, the relevant industrial sector, and the freedom of the designer in developing the design (*The Procter & Gamble Company v Reckitt Benckiser (UK) Ltd, per* Jacob LJ at [16], [25]). The informed user thus appears to be an amalgam of the skilled addressee and the average consumer. An example of someone who might typify an informed user (at least in the case of consumer goods) would be a wholesale buyer for a large retail chain (see T. Headdon, 'Community Design Right Infringement: An Emerging Consensus or a Difference Overall Impression' [2007] 8 *EIPR* 336).

The characteristics of the informed user were set out by HHJ Fysh QC in *Woodhouse UK plc v Architectural Lighting Systems* [2006] RPC 1 at [49–50]. Explaining that this fictional character is used to determine issues of validity and infringement, such decisions are made on the basis of an overall impression, which is, of course, a *visual* impression. Such person is a *user* of the design, and moreover, a regular user, and is neither a manufacturer nor the person in the street. He or she does not possess an 'archival mind' but, having an average memory, is aware of 'what's about in the market' and 'what has been about in the recent past'. He or she has an awareness of product trend and availability, and some knowledge of basic technical considerations. However, as registered design right is concerned with the appearance of articles, the focus is on the appearance of the article, not manufacturing technology.

HHJ Fysh's thinking has since been followed by the Court of Appeal in *The Procter & Gamble Company v Reckitt Benckiser (UK) Ltd* and is in accord with the views of the Court of Justice of the European Union ('CJEU').

> **Case C-281/10P PepsiCo Inc v Grupo Promer Mon Graphic SA and OHIM [2011] ECR I-10153**
>
> PepsiCo appealed against the decision that its design for promotional items for games (known as 'pogs', 'rappers' or 'tazos') was invalid because of Grupo Promer's prior national registration. The CJEU upheld the decision that the designer's freedom of choice was severely constricted, so the small differences between the two designs were insignificant and did not produce a different overall impression on the informed user. As to the identity of the informed user, the CJEU said (at [53]) that the concept lay somewhere between the average consumer in trade marks and the sectoral expert. This person was particularly observant because of their personal experience or extensive knowledge.

In the *PepsiCo* case the informed user would have been a child between the ages of five and ten (someone who played pogs) or a marketing manager in a company that made goods promoted by pogs. The informed user would typically be in a position to compare between two competing products/designs, though at times a direct comparison may not be practical (P.G.F.A. Geerts, 'The Informed User in Design Law: What should he compare and how should he make the comparison?' [2014] 36 *EIPR* 181).

Pause for reflection

Do the characteristics of the 'informed user' provide sufficient certainty and objectivity in deciding registered design cases, or is this another concept which the court can manipulate to achieve a desired outcome?

Who might be the informed user in the case of BPT and its designs? What characteristics might that person have?

20.2.3 Criteria for protection

20.2.3.1 Definition of 'design'

Under the RDA s. 1(2), 'design' means 'the appearance of the whole or a part of a product resulting from the features of, in particular, the lines, contours, colours, shape, texture or materials of the product or its ornamentation'. 'Product' (according to s. 1(3)) means 'any industrial or handicraft item other than a computer program; and, in particular, includes packaging, get-up, graphic symbols, typographic type-faces and parts intended to be assembled into a complex product'. 'Complex product' (also defined in s. 1(3)) means 'a product which is composed of at least two replaceable component parts permitting disassembly and reassembly'.

Particularly notable aspects of the definition include:

- it is possible to obtain protection for part of a product as well as the whole item;
- internal features are capable of registration;
- the design must produce a 'different overall impression' on the informed user;

- handicraft items can be registered (which makes the name accorded by some writers, 'industrial designs', something of a misnomer);

- features of the product other than shape or ornament are included in the definition, so that texture, materials, and colour can be claimed;

- graphic symbols are expressly mentioned as being part of a product, which means that logos are capable of protection both as designs and trade marks. The canny trade mark owner may well consider registering the logo as a design, in part for the simplicity of the procedure, but also for the 25-year period of protection which this would give. J.J.I. Peris suggests (in 'Registered Community Design: The First Two-Year Balance from an Insider's Perspective' [2006] 28 *EIPR* 146) that graphic symbols used as icons in computer menus are registrable.

20.2.3.2 The positive criteria for protection

The amended RDA in s. 1B has two positive criteria which a design must satisfy in order to be registrable, namely novelty and individual character. These requirements are separate and should be applied sequentially, like novelty and inventive step in patents. Both involve comparing the design with the prior art, which, like the prior art in patent law, is potentially worldwide.

Novelty means that a design is new if no identical design or no design whose features differ only in immaterial details has been made available to the public before the relevant date (RDA s. 1B(2)). 'Making available' bears the patent meaning of published (whether following registration or otherwise), exhibited, used in trade, or otherwise disclosed anywhere in the world (RDA s. 1B(5)). However, the requirement of novelty for registered designs is qualified in two respects.

First, and in contrast to patents, such novelty is relative rather than absolute. Section 1B(6) provides that a design is treated as not having been made available if the event in question (publication, exhibition, etc) could not reasonably have become known in the normal course of business to the relevant design circles in the European Economic Area ('EEA'). Unlike a patent, a registered design will not be invalidated by the existence of some obscure prior art (*Green Lane Products Ltd v PMS International Group Ltd* [2008] FSR 1). As Peris explains (in the context of decisions by the EUIPO Invalidity Division) the concept of relative novelty involves a two-stage argument. It is for the party challenging the design to show that there exists prior art which renders the design not new. The burden then shifts to the registered proprietor to show that such prior art could not reasonably have become known to the relevant design circles, and if (for whatever reason) the proprietor fails to do so then the design is invalid for lack of novelty.

So far, the EUIPO Invalidity Division has concluded that publication of an earlier design for an inter-dental brush in the Japanese Patent Office Journal would be known to those in the relevant design circle (*Sunstar Suisse SA v Dentaid SL*, OHIM Ref ICD 000000420, 20 June 2005) and that the inclusion of a design for a convector heater in a commercial catalogue available in Hong Kong would likewise have been known to those concerned in that design field (*Comercial Opera SA v Cata Electrodomesticos SL*, OHIM Ref ICD 000000131, 2 July 2004). Similarly, when considering whether an unregistered EU design was novel, the Landsgericht, Frankfurt, concluded that a design for an abdominal muscle trainer had been invalidated because of distribution of the same device in the United States prior to its launch in Europe: *Thane International Group's Application* [2006] ECDR 71.

However, as Lewison J pointed out in *Green Lane Products Ltd v PMS International Group Ltd*, it is far from clear as to what is meant by the 'sector concerned' in RDA s. 1B(6). Is it the sector in which the registered design falls or is it the sector in which the prior art falls? The problem is neatly illustrated by the facts of *Green Lane* itself, where the claimant's EU registration for spiky laundry balls was challenged by the maker of spiky balls used in body massage. Lewison J concluded (and was upheld on appeal, *Green Lane Products Ltd v PMS International Group Ltd* [2008] FSR 701) that the 'sector concerned' meant the sector relating to the prior art. A design which was old and well known in one sector should not be registrable for a product in any other sector. Such a conclusion was essential in order to achieve consistency with the provisions on the EU unregistered design right, where, provided the design is new, its duration is calculated under Art. 11 of the Regulation from when the design is first launched in Europe. First launch anywhere else destroys novelty. Just as the registered design right gives a monopoly over any kind of goods, 'it makes complete sense that the prior art available for attacking novelty should also extend to all kinds of goods, subject only to the limited exception of prior art obscure even in the sector from which it comes' (*per* Jacob LJ in *Green Lane Products Ltd v PMS International Group Ltd* (CA) at [79]).

The second qualification to the requirement of novelty is that there is no 'making available' where the disclosure was in breach of confidence or if the disclosure was by the designer within the 12 months' 'grace period' calculated from the filing or priority date (RDA s. 1B(5)). The fact that a design will not be treated as having been made available to the public where it was disclosed in breach of confidence emphasizes the practical importance of designs being kept secret prior to the design application being filed. Nevertheless, the presence of a 'grace period' does, according to Recital 20 of the Regulation, give the designer the ability to test the design in the marketplace without endangering the novelty or individual character of the design.

If it is concluded that the design is new, the next issue to consider is whether it has individual character, taking into account the degree of freedom which the designer had. Just as with novelty, 'individual character' involves a comparison between the prior art and the registered design, again through the eyes of the informed user, in order to see whether the design produces a different overall impression. Whilst the comparison for novelty is precise (the prior art must be *identical* to the registered design, or, if it differs, it must do so only in *immaterial detail*), the comparison for individual character is broader and more imprecise, leaving the court 'with a considerable margin for judgment' (*per* Jacob LJ in the Court of Appeal in *The Procter & Gamble Company v Reckitt Benckiser (UK) Ltd* at [34]). The differences in the comparisons to be made are analogous to the differences between novelty and inventive step in the law of patents.

Reference to Recital 13 of the Directive (relevant to Art. 5 of the Directive on which RDA s. 1B(3) and (4) is based) indicates that the registered design is to be compared with the 'existing design corpus' (i.e. 'what's about in the market' and 'what has been about in the recent past' to quote HHJ Fysh in *Woodhouse*), taking into account the nature of the product and the relevant industrial sector.

The Procter & Gamble Company v Reckitt Benckiser (UK) Ltd [2008] FSR 208

The Court of Appeal, in discussing the equivalent provision in the Regulation (Recital 14), observed that these criteria have not been carried over into the text of the actual Articles of the Directive and Regulation but should nevertheless be taken into account when interpreting the substantive provisions. Another phrase not carried over into the Articles from the Recitals is the phrase 'clearly differs'. As Jacob LJ explained (at [18]), only if the 'overall impression' 'clearly differs' from that of the 'existing design corpus' will the design have individual character. In *Procter & Gamble*, there was little doubt that the claimant's design for an air-freshener aerosol had individual character, as it had received a number of industry awards.

LengD'Or SA v Crown Confectionery Co Ltd (OHIM Ref ICD 000000370, 23 February 2005)

An example of the nature of the exercise to be carried out by the tribunal when assessing individual character can be found in the EUIPO (then OHIM) decision in *LengD'Or SA v Crown Confectionery Co Ltd* (OHIM Ref ICD 000000370, 23 February 2005) where the design consisted of a shape for biscuits and was challenged on the grounds that it was the same as a previously registered three-dimensional EU trade mark, also for biscuits. OHIM concluded, first, that the design was novel as there were significant differences between it and the EU trade mark, one having rounded loops, the other having pointed loops; and second, that the impression on the informed user was quite different because one involved six loops and the other eight loops.

The EU General court made an important decision on individual character in joined Cases T-22/13 and T-23/13 *Senz Technologies Bv v OHIM* [2015] ECDR 19. The case concerned an application by Impliva to invalidate two of Senz's Community Registered Designs concerning the appearance of umbrellas. The invalidation challenge rested on the absolute grounds under Art. 52 and Art. 25(1)(b) Regulation 6/2002 on Community designs. Impliva argued that Senz's designs lacked individual character because they produced the 'same overall impression' as a previous registered umbrella in an American registration (design patent) from 1996. At the OHIM (as it then was) both the Cancellation Division and the Board of Appeal held the design invalid. They considered that the informed user in the case of umbrellas would pay attention only to the basic structure, and not the details of the design. With that in mind, they stated that the American registration and the Senz designs produced the same overall impression—a beak-like shape with some asymmetry. The EU General Court annulled the decisions of the EUIPO. The EU General Court stated that in creating umbrellas, the designer would be limited to basic variations on the common design—therefore, minor differences between two designs would be noticed by the informed user. Here, the limited freedom open to the umbrella designer meant that the American registration and the Senz designs would create a different overall impression and did have individual character.

Pause for reflection

In the case of BPT in our problem scenario, if BPT wished to apply for a registered design and it was later challenged, how would you show that the BPT design has novelty and individual character?

20.2.3.3 The negative criteria for protection

The RDA and the corresponding Art. 8 of the Community Design Regulation ('CDR') exclude two types of design features from protection—these are known under the categories of 'technical function' and 'must fit'. The law also provides for certain categories of design to be incapable of registration; and prohibits the registration of designs which conflict with earlier rights.

The exclusions from protection are set out in s. 1C(1) and (2) (Arts 8(1) and (2) of the CDR) and comprise features 'solely dictated by the product's technical function' and 'must fit' features, although this latter exclusion is declared not to prevent the protection of modular systems. The 'solely dictated by the product's technical function' exclusion is justified on the basis that registered designs are intended to protect the aesthetic appeal of a product (rather than the technical benefit, which is potentially protected by patent law). 'Must fit' is a somewhat imprecise summary, and the exact wording of s. 1C(2) should be remembered: 'features of appearance of a product which must necessarily be reproduced in their exact form and dimensions so as to permit the product in which the design is incorporated . . . to be mechanically connected to, or placed in, around or against another so that either product may perform its function'. As yet there is no case law on s. 1C(2), but the interpretation given to the exclusion in s. 1C(1) together with that of the parallel provision in s. 213(3)(b)(i) CDPA suggest that it will have a narrow scope.

Dyson v Vax [2010] EWHC 1923 (upheld on appeal—[2011] EWCA Civ 1206)

In this case Dyson alleged that Vax's Mach Zen Vacuum infringed Dyson's UK Registered Design. Ultimately it was found that there was no infringement. However, what is of importance for our purposes is the analysis of the question of when a design can be said to be dictated solely by technical function and thus ineligible for protection. Arnold J in the High Court held that the configuration of a product is 'solely dictated by technical function' (and thus not protected) if every feature of the design was determined by a technical consideration, and thus the product was created with no consideration of how it appears to the consumer. Thus, Arnold J opted for a 'no aesthetic consideration' test, relying on a UK designs case decided at the House of Lords during the 1970s—*Amp v Utilux* [1972] FSR 572. Arnold J declined to follow a more recent Court of Appeal in *Landor & Hawa International Ltd v Azure Designs Ltd* [2007] FSR 181 that stated that a functional design can be protected if the same technical function could have been achieved via a different configuration, known as the 'multiplicity of forms' approach. Arnold J's decision was upheld on appeal and has been following in subsequent UK case law, including *Samsung v Apple* [2012] EWHC 1882 (Pat). In 2018, the CJEU considered

→

→ a preliminary reference from a German court on the 'solely dictated by its technical function' criterion. Emphasizing the need for a harmonized EU approach, the CJEU stated that 'in order to determine whether the features of appearance of a product are exclusively dictated by its technical function, it must be established that the technical function is the only factor which determined those features, the existence of alternative designs not being decisive in that regard' (Case C-395/16, *DOCERAM GmbH v CeramTec GmbH*; CJEU, 8 March 2018, ECLI:EU:C:2018:172). This assessment should be made from the point of view of the objective observer. This is akin to the 'no aesthetic consideration test' and is broadly in line with the approach of judges in the UK in cases such as *Dyson v Vax* and *Samsung v Apple*.

The RDA in s. 1D prohibits the registration of designs contrary to public policy or morality and Sch. A1 prohibits the registration of designs incorporating specially protected emblems, such as the coat of arms of the Royal family, the flags of other countries, and the Olympic symbol (similar exclusions are found in the Trade Marks Act 1994). Also prohibited from registration by implication are those designs which conflict with earlier EU or UK registered designs or trade marks, or earlier copyrights, as conflict with such an earlier right is a ground of invalidity under ss. 11ZA and 11ZB.

 Pause for reflection

Do the positive and negative criteria for protection effectively balance the interests of the designer with the needs of third parties? Do you agree with the idea that purely technical functions should not be protected by design law, but instead by patents?

In terms of our problem scenario, even if the BPT design has novelty and individual character, does it satisfy the twin negative criteria of 'technical function' and 'must fit'?

20.2.4 Ownership

In summary, s. 2 RDA declares that the design belongs to the designer, except where it was made in the course of employment, in which case it is owned by the designer's employer. All references to commissioned designs have been removed by the Intellectual Property Act 2014 so as to ensure consistency with EU law, which did not recognize the entitlement of a commissioner: Case C-32/08 *Fundación Española para la Innovación de la Artesania (FEAI) v Cul de Sac Espacio Creativo SL and Acierta Product & Position SA*, [2009] ECR I-5611.

Concerning the ability to challenge the validity of the design registration where it has been granted to the wrong person, under the revised RDA only the person properly entitled to the design can challenge its wrongful grant: *Watson v Zap Ltd* [2007] ECDR 209.

20.2.5 Infringement

Section 7(1) RDA declares that registration gives the exclusive right to use the design and any design which does not produce on the informed user a different overall impression.

As with patents, this phrase incorporates two key issues, the nature of infringing conduct and the scope of protection accorded to the registered design.

As regards infringing conduct, 'use' is stated in s. 7(2) to comprise making, offering, putting on the market, importing, exporting, or using a product in which the design is incorporated or to which it is applied, or stocking such a product for those purposes. The list is almost identical to the infringement provisions found in s. 60(1) Patents Act 1977. It may be observed that the scope of protection accorded to the owner is not limited to the articles for which the design was registered but extends to any article to which the design is applied by the infringer because of the use of the indefinite article 'a'. Headdon gives the example of a new design for a saucepan which is then applied to a completely different product such as a hat.

With regard to the scope of protection, this involves a comparison being made between the registered design and the alleged infringement to see if the latter produces a different overall impression. If the impression is the same, then there is infringement, if the impression is different, there is not. The nature of the comparison is similar to that carried out in the context of validity, when the registered design is compared with the prior art to see if it creates a different overall impression. However, according to the Court of Appeal in *The Procter & Gamble Company v Reckitt Benckiser (UK) Ltd*, there is one difference between validity and infringement, because of the wording of the Recitals to the Directive and Regulation. Whilst in relation to validity, there must 'clearly' be a difference between the prior art and the registered design, for infringement the test is simply whether there is a different overall impression.

Pause for reflection

How easy is it to prove that the alleged infringement creates the same overall impression as the protected design?

If a rival to BPT brought out a similar product, what would BPT have to do to show this?

The nature of the exercise means that it is difficult to be precise about the level of generality used in the comparison—after all, what is an 'overall' impression? This is likely to produce a number of apparently conflicting decisions. In *Procter & Gamble* itself, the Court of Appeal disagreed with Lewison J as to whether the defendant's fresh air spray produced a different overall impression on the informed user than the claimant's 'Febreze' spray, ultimately holding that it did, so that there was no infringement. The court was no doubt influenced by the design accolades showered on the claimant's product and the criticisms which had been made of the defendant's. The comparison is likely to be more difficult to make where the infringing product is different from the articles covered by the design registration. To return to Headdon's illustration, how close does the design for the hat have to be before it creates a similar overall impression to the saucepan on the informed user? And who, in this case, is the informed user: a wholesale buyer of saucepans or a wholesale buyer of hats?

The issue of infringement of a Community Registered Design, or CRD, reached the UK Supreme Court in *PMS International Limited v Magmatic Limited* [2016] UKSC 12. The case concerned the popular 'Trunki' suitcase for kids designed and manufactured by Magmatic. Magmatic had registered a CRD for the 'Trunki': a suitcase shaped like a horned animal that allowed children to sit on it and be pulled along by their parents. PMS produced a rival (cheaper) suitcase—Kiddee—available in different shapes, including a case shaped and decorated like an insect, and one shaped and decorated like a tiger.

The Court of Appeal, overruling an earlier infringement decision by the High Court, held that the rival product design by PMS—the Kiddee suitcase—did not infringe the Trunki design. The UKSC agreed with the Court of Appeal. Lord Neuberger remarked that there were three key points that determined the infringement claim.

The first concerned the 'overall impression' of the design—in this case the impression was of a horned animal, and the High Court had erred in not giving this impression its proper weight. The Court of Appeal had rectified this by holding that if a CRD is of a horned animal, any infringing item must make the same impression.

The second concerned the 'absence of decoration' on the CRD. Here, although the UKSC left open the question of whether this minimalist effect was a deliberate part of the CRD, the court considered this absence of decoration reinforced the overall impression of a horned animal. Lord Neuberger stated:

> [I]t seems plain to me that absence of decoration can, as a matter of principle, be a feature of a registered design. Simplicity or minimalism can notoriously be an aspect of a design, and it would be very curious if a design right registration system did not cater for it.

The third element the UKSC highlighted concerned the 'two-tone' colouring of the CRD—grey for the body and horns, and black for the wheels and spokes. The High Court had focused solely on the shape, but the Court of Appeal (and the UKSC in approval) stated that the colour contrasts were potentially significant when considering infringement. The main Trunki features, i.e. the wheels and horns (handles), stood out in the design drawing. By contrast, the Kiddee case had wheels that were almost entirely covered; and, unlike the Trunki, the handles of the Kiddee had the same colour as the body of the case. Lord Neuberger further remarked that the drawings/images filed as part of the registration are not purely descriptive, they are determinative as to what is protected (in the same way that a patent's claims are)—in other words, the drawings/images/representations define the monopoly. Following the EUIPO's own guidance, Lord Neuberger further stated that where a design drawing is filed showing specific colours, those colours are deemed to be claimed; whereas, as a black and white drawing/photo is deemed to cover all colours. In light of this, it was natural to infer that the colour contrasts were a deliberate element of the design—and that the design was limited to contrasting colours. Thus, the CRD was held to claim not merely a shape, but a shape with two contrasting colours (grey/black). The Kiddee suitcase lacked the contrasting colours and this was a factor to take into account when considering infringement.

In agreeing that the Court of Appeal approach, in finding no infringement, was essentially correct, Lord Neuberger remarked (at para. 57):

> It is a conclusion I would have reached with some regret, as the conception of the Trunki, a ride-on wheeled case which looks like an animal, seems to have been both original and clever . . . Furthermore, it appears clear that Mr Beverley of PMS conceived the idea of manufacturing a Kiddee Case as a result of seeing a Trunki, and discovering that a discount model was not available. Unfortunately for Magmatic, however, this appeal is not concerned with an idea or an invention, but with a design.

Pause for reflection

Ashby notes that a key aspect of the *Trunki* decision is the importance it places on getting the design representations right, as any carelessness in the application could lead to a much narrower scope of protection (S. Ashby, 'Magmatic v PMS: UK Supreme Court says no Community registered design infringement by Kiddee cases' [2016] 11 *JIPLP* 490). But do you think the *Trunki* decision limits the scope of design infringement too much?

If BPT fears that a rival company may come out with a similar shaped cardboard container, what steps could they take—in terms of preparing the design representations—to ensure BPT obtain the widest possible protection for their designs?

The defences to infringement (set out in s. 7A RDA) include consent, private and domestic use, experimental use, reproduction for educational purposes, use of equipment on aircraft and ships temporarily within the United Kingdom, the importation of spare parts for the repair of such aircraft and ships, the carrying out of such repairs, exhaustion of rights, and the use of components to repair a complex product. Again, these defences are very similar to those found in s. 60(5) Patents Act 1977. The Intellectual Property Act 2014 adds the further defence of prior use, in wording similar to that found in s. 64 Patents Act 1977.

20.2.6 Invalidity

As a result of the Directive, there are comprehensive provisions as to when a registered design may be declared invalid, which are set out in s. 11ZA RDA. Lack of substantive examination means that revocation actions are likely to be more frequent.

The grounds of invalidity are, first, that the design in question does not satisfy the definition of design in s. 1(2), that it is not new or does not have individual character, that it is dictated by technical function, that it consists of a specially protected emblem, or that it is contrary to public policy. An application to have the design declared invalid on any of these grounds may be brought by *any* person. Other grounds of invalidity are that the registered proprietor is not entitled to the design, or that the design is similar to an earlier registered EU or UK design, or that it infringes an earlier registered trade mark, or that it infringes an earlier copyright. In the case of these further grounds of invalidity, the application may only be brought by the owner of the relevant earlier right (*Watson v Zap Ltd*).

Pause for reflection

To summarize, the Directive and Regulation make clear that a registrable design need not have 'eye appeal' but must create a 'different overall impression' from what was previously available. The product does not need to have been made by an industrial process. The positive criteria of novelty and individual character are to be assessed through the eyes of the 'informed user'. To infringe, a rival design must create the 'same overall impression' as the registered one, with the design representation (drawing/image) a key factor in this assessment.

20.3 United Kingdom copyright as an alternative means of protection

20.3.1 Relevant provisions of Part I CDPA

For many creative industries, particularly those which need to respond quickly to changing fashions (for example, jewellery) the bureaucracy inherent in the registered design system is an anathema. One form of instant protection which might appeal to a designer in such an industry is copyright.

Section 4 CDPA protects two- and three-dimensional artistic works. As regards two-dimensional works, under s. 4(1)(a) there is copyright protection for graphic works, *irrespective of artistic quality*. The phrase 'graphic works' is stated by the section to include drawings. The threshold for protection is low, indeed it has been suggested (in *British Northrop v Texteam Blackburn* [1974] RPC 57, a case in which it was held that drawings for parts of machinery were copyright) that 'anything which goes beyond a single line on a piece of paper is a drawing'. 'Graphic work' also includes engravings and etchings. It should not be assumed that these are necessarily two-dimensional. In *Wham-O Manufacturing Co v Lincoln* [1985] RPC 127, plastic frisbees were treated as engravings, and in *Hi Tech Autoparts v Towergate Two Ltd (No. 1)* [2002] FSR 254, car mats were treated as etchings.

As regards three-dimensional works, s. 4 refers to sculptures and works of artistic craftsmanship. Some cases have given 'sculpture' a wide meaning, but more recently it has been defined (*obiter*) as 'a three-dimensional work made by an artist's hand' (*per* Laddie J in *Metix (UK) Ltd v G.H. Maughan (Plastics) Ltd* [1997] FSR 718). This suggests functional articles should not be treated as sculptures under the CDPA.

The saga of *Lucasfilm Ltd v Ainsworth* [2012] 1 AC 208 is worth considering again in the context of designs.

Lucasfilm Ltd v Ainsworth [2012] 1 AC 208

Laddie J's approach was adopted by Mann J in *Lucasfilm Ltd v Ainsworth* ([2009] FSR 103 at [118]). He reviewed the previous case law on what is a sculpture. Considering the 'normal' (i.e. lay) sense of the word, he stated that not every three-dimensional object should be regarded as a sculpture. To hold otherwise would not be right. Rather, a sculpture should have, as part of its purpose, a visual appeal in the sense that it might be enjoyed for that purpose alone, whether or not it might have another purpose as well. The purpose was that of the creator, the 'artist's hand'. An artist (in the realm of the visual arts) created something because it had visual appeal which was to be enjoyed as such. It had to have the intrinsic quality of being intended to be enjoyed as a visual thing. Items such as model soldiers had correctly been treated as sculptures, but the frisbee in *Wham-O* should not have been, nor should the plates for moulding toasted sandwiches in *Breville Europe plc v Thorn EMI Domestic Appliances Ltd* [1995] FSR 77. What mattered was whether the maker intended the object to have a visual appeal for its own sake. So, for example, a pile of bricks in an art gallery would amount to a sculpture, but a pile of bricks left outside a house by a builder would not. This approach to the meaning of 'sculpture' was subsequently endorsed by the Court of Appeal and the Supreme Court.

More problematic is the composite phrase 'a work of artistic craftsmanship'. Two elements must be present in an object before it will receive protection under s. 4(1)(c): it must possess artistry, which for present purposes can be assumed to equate to 'eye appeal', and it must be made by a craftsman, who is a person who makes something in a skilful way and who takes justified pride in his workmanship (*Vermaat v Boncrest Ltd* [2001] FSR 43). Therefore, if the article is made by machine, it will not count as a work of craftsmanship (*Guild v Eskandar Ltd* [2001] FSR 38). 'Eye appeal' is to be decided by the intention of the maker (*Hensher v Restawile* [1976] AC 64; *Merlet v Mothercare plc* [1986] RPC 115) so that if an article is designed with a particular function in mind it will not qualify for protection under s. 4(1)(c). In *Merlet*, the claimant's baby cape was designed for the purpose of keeping a baby dry, so that this overrode any visual appeal in the garment. In *Lucasfilm*, Mann J (again, confirmed on appeal) decided that the Stormtrooper helmets for the film *Star Wars* were not works of artistic craftsmanship, concluding (at [131]) that 'for a work to be regarded as one of artistic craftsmanship it must be possible fairly to say that the author was both a craftsman and an artist. A craftsman is a person who makes something in a skilful way and takes justified pride in their workmanship. An artist is a person with creative ability who produces something which has aesthetic appeal.'

The significance of relying on copyright protection is that under s. 17(3) CDPA, a two-dimensional artistic work is 'reproduced in any material form' by being converted into a three-dimensional form and vice versa. Consequently, if the design process starts off with the creation of a drawing, such as a fashion sketch (*Bernstein v Sidney Murray* [1981] RPC 303) or diagrams for self-assembly furniture (*LB (Plastics) v Swish Products* [1979] RPC 551), then where the defendant copies the claimant's article, they will infringe the copyright in the drawing even if they never saw the source work. Indirect copying suffices under s. 16 CDPA.

 Pause for reflection

Copyright has the advantage of giving the designer instant protection, but it also has a considerable downside when compared to registered design protection.

In an infringement case the claimant will need to prove that the defendant copied the claimant's work (or at least had the opportunity to do so). The claimant must demonstrate derivation and substantial taking in accordance with Lord Millet's test in *Designers' Guild Ltd v Russell William (Textiles) Ltd* [2000] 1 WLR 2416.

20.3.2 Statutory provisions curtailing copyright

20.3.2.1 The CDPA

The CDPA restricts the rights of the copyright owner when seeking to protect the design of an article. The restriction operates as a defence in a copyright infringement action where the claimant alleges that the defendant has made an article which copies, directly or indirectly, the claimant's artistic work.

20.3.2.1.1 Section 51

The policy iterated in the *British Leyland* case, namely that it is an abuse of copyright protection to rely on an artistic work to prevent others from making articles based on that work, is to be found in s. 51 CDPA. It should not be assumed, however, that the section is a direct enactment of the decision in *British Leyland*: *Mars UK Ltd v Teknowledge Ltd* [2000] FSR 138. Section 51(1) declares that it is not an infringement of any copyright in a design document or model recording a design for anything other than an artistic work to make an article to the design. Section 51(3) defines 'design' as 'the shape or configuration (whether internal or external) of the whole or part of an article, other than surface decoration' and 'design document' as 'any record of a design, whether in the form of a drawing, a written description, a photograph, data stored in a computer or otherwise', wording repeated in Part III CDPA dealing with the unregistered design right. The definition of 'design document' is therefore wide enough to cover any medium in which the designer's efforts are recorded and is not confined to 'drawings' in the conventional sense: *Mackie Designs Inc v Behringer Specialised Studio Equipment (UK) Ltd* [1999] RPC 717 at p. 720 *per* Pumfrey J.

The wording of s. 51(1) is not easy to understand and any commentary on it is best broken down into a series of propositions, as follows.

First, the section does *not* say that copyright does not subsist in a design document for an article. Rather it declares that the copyright existing in a design document *is not infringed* where *an article is made to that design* (it should be remembered that the section is placed in the Chapter of Part I CDPA dealing with defences to copyright infringement). A designer will therefore have copyright in the design document. Such copyright will be infringed if a third party merely copies the document in two-dimensional form, for example, by photocopying it. The designer is prevented from suing for copyright infringement only in one very specific situation, namely where the third party copies the design document directly or indirectly *in order to make articles*. In such a situation, the designer is forced to rely on the protection offered by the unregistered design right in Part III CDPA.

Second, the key word in s. 51(1) is the word 'for'. The question to be asked when applying the provision is whether the claimant is relying on a design document *for* an article. If the document is not *for* an article (for example, if an artist creates a painting of a chair, the painting will not be a design document *for* the chair but *of* the chair), the section does not apply. If a third party then makes a chair based on that shown in the painting, this will fall outside the defence and so will be dealt with under the normal rules on copyright infringement.

Last, it must be determined whether the article to be made from the design document is an artistic work in its own right. If it is (for example, if it is a sculpture, or a work of artistic craftsmanship) then again, s. 51(1) has no application and the full force of copyright law is available to the designer. If, however, the article is not an artistic work in its own right, then the designer cannot bring a copyright infringement action against a third party who has made articles derived from the design document. Instead they must rely on the unregistered design right.

The key to understanding s. 51(1) can be illustrated by the flow chart in Diagram 20.2.

DIAGRAM 20.2 Subsistence and ownership of unregistered design rights

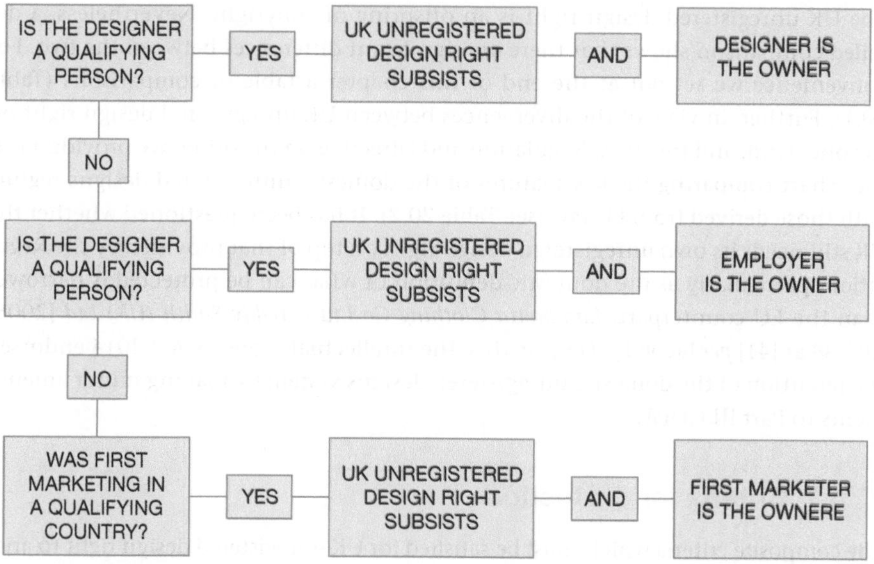

Case law on s. 51

Several cases illustrate the application of s. 51. A case where the s. 51 defence succeeded is *Jo Y Jo Ltd v Matalan Retail Ltd* [2000] ECDR 178 where Rattee J accepted the defendant's argument that the claimant's drawings for ladies' cardigans were design documents for articles and therefore protected only by design right, not copyright. More controversially, Laddie J in *BBC Worldwide Ltd v Pally Screen Printing Ltd* [1998] FSR 665 held that the defendant's use of pictures of the 'Telly Tubbies' on T-shirts fell within s. 51. It could be argued that the designs were being used as two-dimensional decoration *on* articles, but this was an application for summary judgment and the report shows that the judge was clearly irritated by the claimant's handling of its case. By contrast, in *Flashing Badge Co Ltd v Groves* [2007] ECDR 308, Rimer J held that artwork applied to the face of novelty badges was protected by copyright rather than design right and so s. 51 did not apply. Whilst the badges themselves were articles, and so caught by the defence, what the defendant had copied was the artistic work applied to the surface of the badge. The most recent case to apply the s. 51 defence is *Lucasfilm v Ainsworth*: having concluded that the Stormtrooper helmets were neither sculptures nor works of artistic craftsmanship, Mann J (and the appellate courts) had no hesitation in concluding that the action for copyright infringement was barred.

The effect of s. 51 CDPA is to draw a distinction between designs for the shape or configuration of functional articles and designs for articles which are artistic works in their own right, such as sculptures and works of artistic craftsmanship. The latter, to the extent that no protection is sought under the RDA, as amended, obtain full copyright protection for life of the author plus 70 years (the previous limitation of copyright term to 25 years from first marketing where such articles were the subject of mass production no longer applies). The former, although copyright works, cannot be enforced against a defendant who makes articles based on the design and so the designer must rely on the unregistered design right.

20.4 **UK unregistered design right**

The UK unregistered design right is an offspring of copyright. Nevertheless, a detailed comparison shows that there are significant differences between the two. For convenience we set out at the end of this chapter a table of comparisons (Table 20.1). Further, in view of the divergences between UK unregistered design right on the one hand, and the RDA, Regulation and Directive on the other, we provide a further chart comparing the key features of the domestic unregistered designs régime with those derived from EU law (see Table 20.2). It has been questioned whether the UK still needs its own unregistered design right on top of that provided by the Regulation, particularly as the domestic definition of what can be protected is narrower than the EU counterpart: *Lambretta Clothing Co Ltd v Teddy Smith (UK) Ltd* [2005] RPC 88 at [41] *per* Jacob LJ. Despite this, the Intellectual Property Act 2014 endorsed the retention of the domestic unregistered designs system by making minor amendments to Part III CDPA.

20.4.1 **Criteria for protection**

The composite criteria which must be satisfied for UK unregistered design right to arise are set out in s. 213 CDPA. The section begins by declaring that unregistered design right is a property right which subsists in an original design and goes on to provide in s. 213(2) that 'design' means 'the shape or configuration (internal or external) of the whole or part of an article'.

This wording contains the usual dichotomy, namely a three-dimensional object to which design features are applied. In *Farmer Build Ltd v Carier Bulk Handling Materials Ltd* [1999] RPC 461 at p. 483, Mummery LJ observed that the legislation does not confer protection on the article but on the *shape* of the article. An everyday article may have a shape or configuration applied to it which gives it a different appearance. Further, just as with the registered system, design right is concerned with the protection of the design not the article itself, so that if the design is applied to other articles there will be infringement. In *Electronic Techniques (Anglia) Ltd v Critchley Components Ltd* [1997] FSR 401 at p. 418 the example was given of a handle for a spoon which could equally be applied to a fork.

The statutory definition is flexible enough to cover almost any element of an article, so that, as Laddie J observed in *Ocular Sciences Ltd v Aspect Vision Care Ltd* [1997] RPC 289 at p. 422, in the case of a teapot the design could relate to the whole pot, the lid, the spout, the handle, the shape of the interior and so on. There is no need for the design to have artistic merit or eye appeal; it may not be visible during normal use of the article and it may (possibly) even be invisible to the naked eye. There is nothing to stop protection being conferred on simple shapes as long as the design satisfies the other criteria in s. 213. In *Sales v Stromberg* [2006] FSR 89 the claimant, who was a practitioner of complementary medicine, designed two pendants in the shape of a double and triple spiral which were to hold imploded water, said to have a beneficial effect on the wearer. It was held that as a matter of principle, a simple geometric shape was capable of being protected as a design.

20.4.1.1 Positive aspects of the definition

Two elements in ss. 213(1) and (2) require further elaboration, namely 'article' and 'shape or configuration'.

20.4.1.1.1 Article

The starting point is the word 'article'. This, as indicated earlier, means that the section is concerned with something which is three-dimensional, although as Jacob LJ pointed out in *Lambretta Clothing Co Ltd v Teddy Smith (UK) Ltd*, even something which is perceived as being 'flat' or two-dimensional (such as a sheet of paper) can be an article. Examples of 'articles' include cases for mobile phones (*Parker v Tidball* [1997] FSR 680) and contact lenses (*Ocular Sciences Ltd v Aspect Vision Care Ltd*). Even kitchen units can be articles although the whole fitted kitchen will not be: *Mark Wilkinson Furniture v Woodcraft Designs Radcliffe Ltd* [1998] FSR 63.

20.4.1.1.2 Shape or configuration

The word 'shape', it is said, suggests outward appearance or external form. More problematic is the word 'configuration'. In *Mackie Designs Inc v Behringer Specialised Studio Equipment (UK) Ltd* Pumfrey J thought that the word meant 'the relative arrangement of the various parts of an article to each other'. In *Scholes Windows Ltd v Magnet Ltd* [2002] FSR 172 at [37] (a case concerned with replacement windows), Mummery LJ thought that the definition of design did not incorporate the nature or purpose of the article itself, nor its material structure. Hence the fact that the replacement windows were made of u-PVC rather than wood had no bearing on whether they qualified for protection. Nevertheless, it has been suggested that the properties of the material from which the article is made may contribute to its configuration. In *Block v Bath Aqua Glass Ltd* (Decision O/128/06, 22 May 2006), the UKIPO held that the juxtaposition of two or more differently coloured pieces of transparent glass was part of the configuration of some jewellery.

 Pause for reflection

Does the wording of s. 213(2) CDPA assist in deterring what can be the subject matter of unregistered design right under UK law? How could the wording be improved?

20.4.1.1.3 Originality

Just as with copyright, the key element in the definition is the requirement of originality. According to s. 213(4), 'original' means '[not] commonplace in the design field in question at the time of its creation'. Despite this specific wording, the Court of Appeal departed from the language of the CDPA in *Farmer Build Ltd v Carier Bulk Handling Materials Ltd* and declared that 'original' bears the normal copyright meaning of 'not copied', so that the 'not commonplace' requirement is to be considered *separately and subsequently* to proof of originality (see also *Magmatic Ltd v PMS International Ltd* [2013] EWHC 1925). Consequently, even if the design is not copied, it may still lack protection for being 'commonplace'. The court added that given the already restrictive nature of design right, 'commonplace' should be interpreted narrowly. It is for the claimant to prove originality, but it is for the defendant to show that the design is commonplace in the United Kingdom. The phrase 'not commonplace' was suggested by Laddie J in *Ocular Sciences Ltd v Aspect Vision Care Ltd* to mean 'trite, trivial, common-or-garden, hackneyed, or of the type which would excite no peculiar attention in those in the relevant art'.

The nature of the comparative exercise undertaken when deciding whether a design is commonplace was explained by Mummery LJ in *Farmer Build Ltd v Carier Bulk Handling Materials Ltd* The starting point is to identify the design field in question. In *Farmer Build* it was said that this should not be drawn too narrowly, whilst Jacob LJ in *Lambretta Clothing Co Ltd v Teddy Smith (UK) Ltd* (at [45]) stated that a reasonably broad approach was called for. In *Farmer Build* the design field was stated to be slurry separators (the subject matter of the claimant's design) rather than agricultural equipment but in *Scholes Windows*, the design field was declared to be not replacement u-PVC windows, but replacement *Victorian* u-PVC windows. By contrast, in *Rolawn Ltd v Turfmech Machinery Ltd* [2008] RPC 663, a case concerning a design for a wide area mower, Mann J concluded that the relevant design field was not mowers but agricultural machinery in general. It will thus be apparent that the court's choice of design field may well affect the outcome of the case.

Pause for reflection

Is the way in which the courts determine the relevant design field when deciding whether a design is commonplace always consistent?

Thinking about our problem scenario, what advantages, if any, does the UK unregistered design have over a registered design for BPT?

The next step in the *Farmer Build* test is to compare the claimant's design with similar articles in the same field of design made by other unconnected persons (i.e. what is already 'out there'), taking into account (with the help of expert evidence) similarities and differences, but making the comparison objectively. The defendant's design is not considered at this stage of the comparison. Case law has decided that 'commonplace' is limited geographically to what is known to designers in the United Kingdom, but there is no temporal limitation, so that old designs can be taken into account: *Dyson Ltd v Qualtex* [2006] RPC 769. However, the Intellectual Property Act 2014 amends s. 213(4) by specifying that 'commonplace' applies to qualifying countries as defined in s. 217(4). It is possible for design right to exist in a combination of features which individually are commonplace but when amalgamated are significantly different to what is in the design field: *Ultraframe UK Ltd v Clayton and others* [2003] RPC 435 at p. 457. Similarly, the overall design for an article may not be commonplace, even though individual features are: *Rolawn Ltd v Turfmech Machinery Ltd*.

20.4.1.2 Negative aspects of the definition: exclusions

According to *Ultraframe UK Ltd v Clayton and others* [2003] RPC 435 at p. 457 the correct approach is to subtract from the design those features which fall within the exclusions, then apply the 'not commonplace' test to what is left in order to identify the relevant design. For ease of understanding we have already considered the meaning of 'not commonplace' as part of the positive aspect of originality, but the advice of the court in *Ultraframe* should be remembered. Further, as *Copinger & Skone-James on Copyright* (16th edn) points out (at 13.55), these exclusions only operate to exclude design right from the types of features listed in s. 213(3), so that where the design comprises a number of features, some of which fall within these exclusions and some which do not, this does not mean that design right cannot subsist in the design as a whole. It simply means that design right cannot be claimed in those excluded features *on their own*. For that reason, a claimant in an infringement action is required to identify with precision those elements of the design in which protection is sought: *A. Fulton Company Ltd v Grant Barnett & Company Ltd* [2001] RPC 257.

20.4.1.2.1 A method or principle of construction

The purpose of the exclusion in s. 213(3)(a) is to prevent designers from creating an effective monopoly over articles designed and made in a particular way. Despite this, it has been given a narrow interpretation by the Court of Appeal in *Landor & Hawa International Ltd v Azure Designs Ltd*. The exclusion does not apply merely because a design serves a functional purpose, and will only operate where it can be shown that the purpose in question cannot be achieved in any other way. The 'method of construction' exclusion was applied by Mann J in *Rolawn Ltd v Turfmech Machinery Ltd* to deny protection to the folding arms of the mower and to the placing of the fuel tank over the rear wheels of the device. Another example of where the exclusion operated to deny protection was *Bailey v Haynes* [2007] FSR 199 which concerned the design for a micromesh bait bag for carp fishing.

It has been held that s. 213(3)(a) will cover choice of materials. Hence in *Christopher Tasker's Design Right References* [2001] RPC 39 the use of aluminium in sliding wardrobe doors was not protectable, and in *Farmer Build* the choice of laminated rubber to line the roller in the claimant's slurry separator was not protected even though the shape of the roller itself was. The exclusion will also deny protection to how the article is made. So in *Parker v Tidball*, the stitching on the inside of a mobile phone case was treated as a method of construction. However, where the stitching is on the outside of an article and so decorative rather than structural, it may receive protection as part of the 'shape or configuration' of the article: *A. Fulton Company Ltd v Grant Barnett & Company Ltd*.

20.4.1.2.2 'Must fit' and 'must match'

The underlying policy for the two exclusions set out in s. 213(3)(b) is derived from the decision of the House of Lords in *British Leyland v Armstrong* discussed earlier. It has the objective of leaving the manufacturers of spare parts free to compete by making articles which are compatible with the design. The exclusion doesn't apply to other forms of copyright such as software or databases (*Mars UK Ltd v Teknowledge Ltd*). Further, the 'must fit' and 'must match' exclusions are not as broad as the 'spare parts' defence in *British Leyland v Armstrong*, as it was not Parliament's intention to deprive the designer of all protection in relation to spare parts, but only certain aspects of them: *Dyson Ltd v Qualtex*. The same case pointed out that the phrases 'must fit' and 'must match' are a somewhat imprecise shorthand for the wording of s. 213(3)(b). Copinger (at [13.68]) gives an example of a design which might fall within both of these exclusions: the cap of a fountain pen might be caught by both the must fit and must match exclusion but the clip on the cap would not be.

The 'must fit' exclusion ('features of shape or configuration which enable the article to be connected to, or placed in, around or against, another article so that either article may perform its function') is primarily concerned with the 'interface' between two articles or 'things': *Ultraframe UK Ltd v Clayton* and *Dyson Ltd v Qualtex*. Some cases have considered that parts of the human body are an 'article' for this purpose, so that in *Ocular Sciences Ltd v Aspect Vision Care Ltd* the need for a contact lens to fit the eyeball was held to fall within the 'must fit' exclusion and in *Parker v Tidball*, the shape of a mobile phone was dictated by the need to fit comfortably within the user's hand.

But how precise does the 'fit' have to be? In *Amoena (UK) Ltd and Another v Trulife Ltd*, 25 May 1995, unreported, it was held that the shape of a breast prosthesis was influenced but not dictated by the shape of a bra and would have fitted a number of different bras. The exclusion did not therefore apply. The court added that the s. 213(3)(b) exclusion is concerned with 'a much more precise correspondence between two articles'. Likewise, in *A. Fulton Company Ltd v Grant Barnett & Company Ltd* the court considered the need for a case to fit over a folding umbrella. Park J remarked that it would be unacceptable to construe the provision as meaning that any article which is shaped so as to cover or contain another article cannot qualify for design right. He pointed out the very precise language of the provision. It does not provide that design right cannot subsist in *an article* if it can be placed in, around, or against another article, rather it provides that design right cannot subsist in *features of shape or configuration which enable the article to be so placed*.

A further problem of interpretation: has the exclusion concerned with how the component parts of a composite article fit externally to *another* article, as was the case with a child's safety barrier in *Baby Dan AS v Brevi SRL* [1999] FSR 377, or is it concerned with how the components of an article fit together: *Electronic Techniques (Anglia) Ltd v Critchley Components Ltd*? The approach of *Critchley* is to be preferred to that of *Baby Dan*.

The 'must match' exclusion ('features of shape which are dependent upon the appearance of another article of which the article is intended by the designer to form an integral part') was examined in the context of Part III CDPA in *Dyson Ltd v Qualtex*. Both Mann J and the Court of Appeal relied on the registered design case of *Ford Motor Company Ltd's Design Applications* [1995] RPC 167 which concerned the identically worded exclusion found in the pre-2001 version of the RDA. *Ford* had held that in relation to the design for a car, body panels, doors, bonnet, grille, boot, bumper, instrument panel, spoiler, and windscreen were all *dependent* on the appearance of the car as a composite article. However, the steering wheel, wing mirrors, wheels, wheel covers, and seats were not. The key word in s. 213(3)(ii)(b), according to *Dyson* (at [64]), is the word 'dependent'. The question to be asked in each case is whether the overall appearance of the article (a car) would be radically different if the replacement part (for example a door) were not the shape it is. However, the Court of Appeal added that 'design dependency' did not extend to where the replacement part was made to look like the original because of consumer preference. As Amanda Michaels explains (in 'The End of the Road for "Pattern Spare" Parts?' [2006] 28(7) *EIPR* 396) this narrow interpretation enabled the claimant to sue for infringement in respect of vacuum cleaner replacement parts the appearance of which was not totally dependent on that of the original article.

20.4.1.2.3 Surface decoration

The final exclusion in s. 213(3) is 'surface decoration'. In *Mark Wilkinson Furniture v Woodcraft Designs Radcliffe Ltd* it was explained that surface decoration can be two-dimensional (for example a drawing or a painting) or three-dimensional (grooves or beading), though in the case of the latter it is a question of degree when the decoration such as carving becomes 'an aspect' of the shape of the item and hence protectable. An illustration of the last-mentioned point can be found in *Dyson v Qualtex*, where it was held that grooves on the vacuum cleaner's suction wand were not surface decoration but part of the shape of the article as their function was to give a better grip.

Surface decoration may be protected in its own right as an artistic work under s. 4 CDPA, but in some cases may not. The choice of colours for a garment was held not to be an aspect of the shape or configuration of the garment in *Lambretta Clothing Co Ltd v Teddy Smith (UK) Ltd* and being surface decoration, was excluded from protection by s. 213(3). Further, there was nothing in s. 4 CDPA which could afford the designer any protection in the instant case. The court added that 'surface decoration' applied both where the surface was covered by a thin layer and where the decoration ran right through the article (such as the fabric of a garment). The outcome in *Lambretta* was the subject of comment by the Court of Appeal in *Dyson Ltd v Qualtex*, where Jacob LJ explained that normally copyright protection is the converse of design right exclusion in the case of surface decoration, but that *Lambretta* concerned the protection of colour which is not protectable under either United Kingdom copyright or United Kingdom unregistered design right (but is under the EU unregistered design right provisions). Further support for this argument can be found in *Flashing Badge Co Ltd v Groves* where the court distinguished between the shape of novelty badges and the artwork applied to their surface, the latter being protected under copyright.

 Pause for reflection

Do the exclusions from design right protection in s. 213(3) CDPA strike a reasonable balance between protecting the investment of the designer and giving others the freedom to compete?

Recalling our problem scenario, is there any relevant surface decoration in the BPT design?

20.4.2 Subsistence of design right

The rules on when design right protection arises may usefully be compared with those for copyright as there is one similarity but two major differences.

20.4.2.1 Permanent form

The requirement that the design must be in permanent form (CDPA s. 213(6)) is like that for copyright, the Act providing that the recording of the design can either be in a design document or in an article made to that design.

20.4.2.2 Ownership

Our first contrast with the rules on the subsistence of copyright occurs in relation to the ownership of the design. These rules, which are intertwined with those on qualification for protection, must be applied in strict sequence and permit no flexibility. The combined effect of CDPA ss. 214 and 215 is that the designer is treated as the creator (i.e. the author). Further, the designer is also (as under copyright) treated as the first owner *unless* there is:

- a contract of employment, in which case the employer will be first owner; or if not, then,
- the person who first marketed the design in a qualifying country is first owner, provided that person is a qualifying person.

Whilst an employer will own the copyright in the case of works created in the course of employment, there is no equivalent in copyright law of the person who first markets goods becoming the owner of the right.

20.4.2.3 Qualification for protection

The complex rules on ownership of design right have their counterpart in ss. 213 and 218–220 CDPA which set out how a design qualifies for United Kingdom design right protection. The narrow scope of these provisions should be contrasted with the breadth of the copyright rules for qualification for protection.

Under s. 213(5), the designer or his employer must be a qualifying person, or else first marketing must be by a qualifying person within a qualifying country. If one turns to ss. 218–220, it becomes apparent that these sections must be applied in a precise order. If the design was not created in the course of employment, then the designer must be a qualifying person (s. 218). However, if the design was created in the course of employment, the employer must be a qualifying person. Finally, if neither of these applies, then the first marketing must occur in a qualifying country and be by a qualifying person.

The precise order of ss. 218–220 CDPA is exacerbated by the extremely narrow definitions of 'qualifying person' and 'qualifying country', both of which should be contrasted with their equivalent meanings under copyright. A 'qualifying person' must be a citizen of or *habitual* resident in the United Kingdom or an EEA Contracting State or a state listed in the relevant statutory instrument (the Designs (Convention Countries) Order (SI 1994/3219), as amended) or a company incorporated in or having substantial business activity in the United Kingdom or an EEA Contracting State or a state listed in the Order. Because unregistered design right is not covered by the World Trade Organization (WTO) TRIPs Agreement, nor by the Paris Convention, the list of countries in the Designs (Convention Countries) Order is very short and basically confined to those which provide reciprocal protection for United Kingdom nationals. The net effect is that non-European designers are denied protection: *Mackie Designs Inc v Behringer Specialised Studio Equipment (UK) Ltd*.

 Pause for reflection

Given that the unregistered design right is meant to be the 'offspring' of copyright, are the different rules on subsistence justified?

The effect of the provisions on qualification for and ownership of unregistered design right in UK law can be illustrated diagrammatically: see Diagram 20.2.

20.4.3 **Duration of design right protection**

The final contrast to be made between design right and copyright is the length of the term of protection. Section 216 CDPA states that the basic term is 15 years from the end of the year in which the design was first recorded or the end of the year in which the design was first manufactured, whichever is first. However, if marketing occurs anywhere in the world within five years of that date, the duration of protection is reduced to ten years from first marketing. Further, the design right is subject to licences of right in the last five years of protection, which means that any potential infringer is able instead to demand a licence from the owner, the terms of such licence being settled by the UKIPO (CDPA s. 237). In reality, the true term of protection is five years from when articles made to the design were first marketed, a period only marginally longer than the three-year term granted to EU unregistered designs.

20.4.4 **Infringement**

Infringement of UK unregistered design right has much in common with copyright infringement, yet in two key respects is somewhat narrower.

20.4.4.1 Similarities

Just like copyright infringement, the essence of design right infringement is derivation so that independent creation will always be a defence: *Ocular Sciences Ltd v Aspect Vision Care Ltd* Likewise, the rights accorded to the owner are subdivided into primary (CDPA s. 226) and secondary infringement, with the latter (CDPA s. 227) encompassing the usual dealings in infringing copies and requiring the requisite knowledge on the part of the defendant. Broadly speaking, the remedies for design right infringement mirror those for copyright infringement, except that there is no equivalent to the 'self-help' ability to seize infringing copies and there is no criminal liability for design right infringement. The defendant's innocence, whilst not negating liability, can affect the award of damages, so that an innocent primary infringer cannot be made to pay damages, and in the case of innocent secondary infringement, damages are limited to the amount of a reasonable royalty (CDPA s. 233). Where there is an infringement action in the last five years of the right, the infringer can undertake to take a licence of right (CDPA ss. 237–239).

20.4.4.2 Differences

There are, however, three key differences between copyright and design right infringement. First, there is only one restricted act of primary infringement in s. 226, namely reproducing, directly or indirectly, articles to that design for commercial purposes or making a design document for the purpose of enabling such articles to be made. Primary infringement therefore has to involve copying for profit. There is no liability for issuing copies of the design, nor for communicating the design to the public. Second, the test for liability differs from that for copyright.

The reason for this difference was explained by Aldous J in *C & H Engineering v F Klucznik* [1992] FSR 421 at p. 428 where he stated that the wording of s. 226 required the defendant 'to produce articles exactly or substantially to that design'. Therefore, assuming that there has been copying, the comparison to be made is between the design document and the alleged infringement to see whether, viewed through the eyes of the person to whom the design is directed, the infringing article is made exactly or substantially to that design. In contrast, therefore, to the test for copyright infringement set out by Lord Millett in *Designers Guild Ltd v Russell Williams (Textiles) Ltd* at [39–41], what matters is overall similarity rather than substantial taking.

Some decisions did adopt a different approach from that in *Klucznik*, in particular *Mark Wilkinson Furniture v Woodcraft Designs Radcliffe Ltd* and *Mackie Designs Inc v Behringer Specialised Studio Equipment (UK) Ltd*. Both chose to follow the *Designers Guild* test by requiring there to be substantial taking. However, the matter would appear to be beyond doubt now as the Court of Appeal has confirmed that because of the difference in wording between CDPA s. 16 and CDPA s. 226, *Klucznik* is the correct test for design right infringement: *L Woolley Jewellers Ltd v A & A Jewellery Ltd* [2003] FSR 255.

The Intellectual Property Act 2014 has added new defences of private acts, experiments, and teaching, and use on ships and aircraft temporarily within the jurisdiction, so as to reflect certain copyright and RDA exceptions.

The final difference is that unlike copyright, but like other forms of industrial property (patents, trade marks, and designs) there is a remedy for groundless threats to sue for design right infringement (CDPA s. 253), as illustrated by *Quads4Kids v Campbell* [2006] EWHC 2482.

In contrast to the UK unregistered right, the extent of what is protected under the Community unregistered design right is quite different (from the UK equivalent). For instance, the Community unregistered design right covers designs involving texture, colour, and materials—in other words, unlike the UK unregistered right, the Community unregistered design right protects the appearance of a product, including two-dimensional designs which are new and have individual character. The Community unregistered design right provides only three years of protection (the date runs from when it was first made available to the EU public).

20.5 Conclusion

This chapter has explained the five principal means available to protect the appearance of a product: UK registered design; UK unregistered design right; UK copyright; EU Community registered design; and EU Community unregistered design. Thus, a designer who wishes to acquire protection for the appearance of an article under UK and/or EU law has several options. To add to the complexity, various aspects of the design can be protected by registered designs, unregistered designs, and copyright. The upshot is that a designer could end up with several different layers of protection.

In terms of UK and EU registered designs, although there is no examination as part of registration, there are criteria that must be satisfied (but which are only tested post-grant, via an invalidation challenge by a competitor). A registrable design need not have 'eye appeal' but must create a 'different overall impression' from what was previously available. The positive criteria of novelty and individual character are to be assessed through the eyes of the 'informed user'—*Green Lane Products Ltd v PMS International Group Ltd*; *The Procter & Gamble Company v Reckitt Benckiser (UK) Ltd*; *Senz*. The design must also satisfy the negative criteria: exclusions from protection, i.e. features 'solely dictated by the product's technical function' and 'must fit' features, are ineligible: *Dyson v Vax* and the recent CJEU case of *DOCERAM v CeramTec*.

The issue of infringement of a Community Registered Design ('CRD') reached the UK Supreme Court in *PMS International Limited v Magmatic Limited*—any infringing item must make the same impression as the CRD; the representation (drawings/images) are crucial, as are any indicated colour contrasts. The defences to infringement include consent; private and domestic use; experimental use; reproduction for educational purposes; and prior use.

For copyright and unregistered designs (UK and EU) no registration is necessary. Copyright can be used to protect design documents and any artistic work, including a logo or decoration, incorporated within the product. Protection lasts the same as for other copyright works—70 years after the life of the author. UK unregistered design rights are only of limited utility for products where aesthetic quality is a crucial part of the design, because 'ornamentation' and 'surface decoration' are specifically excluded from their scope. Instead, they protect any aspect of the shape/configuration of the whole or part of an article, including internal elements. Protection lasts between 10 and 15 years. The Community unregistered design right protects designs involving texture, colour, and materials, i.e. the appearance of a product, including two-dimensional designs which are new and have individual character. The Community unregistered design right provides only three years of protection.

With respect to our problem scenario, we can advise BPT that registration is appropriate, and in consideration of their specific design/product, likely to prove more advantageous than merely attempting to enforce a copyright or unregistered design (UK). Their initial choice would be whether to register at the national (UK) or EU level. As the criteria for protection are identical in both systems, which one to pursue comes down to the commercial considerations outlined earlier. Does BPT require protection solely in the UK or elsewhere? Where are its biggest markets? Does it compete with companies elsewhere in the EU?

We would advise BPT to consider whether their design has novelty and individual character, from the point of view of the informed user, and whether it would fall afoul of the twin negative criteria of 'technical function' and 'must fit' (*Green Lane Products Ltd v PMS*; *The Procter & Gamble Company v Reckitt Benckiser*; *Senz*; *Landor & Hawa International Ltd v Azure*). These criteria would be vital if a rival company attempted to invalidate their registration.

If a rival attempted to bring a competing product to market, how easy would it be for BPT to prove infringement? In terms of infringement of registered designs an allegedly infringing product must create the same overall impression as the protected design. Taking account of *PMS v Magmatic*, BPT should prepare their design representations (drawings/images) carefully to ensure BPT obtain the widest possible protection for their designs, paying particular attention to shape and colour contrasts. Finally, should BPT not wish to register, they could choose to avail of the EU Community unregistered design right. In an infringement scenario involving this right, BPT would have to demonstrate copying on the part of their rival, something that is not required with a registered design.

End-of-chapter questions

After reading the chapter carefully, try answering the following questions. For answer guidance visit the online resources at **www.oup.com/uk/karapapa-mcdonagh/**

1. The UK unregistered design right has proved to lack clarity, indeed some argue it is unnecessarily complex. By contrast, the Registered designs régime offers far better protection. Would it be best to abolish the former and increase protection of registered designs so that designers can rely on the latter?

2. Having examined the UKSC *Trunki* case in detail, do you think the case offends against common sense? Many members of the public—parents and children—were surprised that such an iconic product was not protected from a 'copycat' product. Should design protection take into account such concerns?

Further reading

Bently, L. and Coulthard, A. 'From the Commonplace to the Interface: Five Cases on Unregistered Design Right' [1997] 19 *EIPR* 401
Reviews some of the early decisions on UK unregistered design right.

Bird, R. 'Registered Community Design: Early Decisions of OHIM Invalidity Division' [2006] 28 *EIPR* 297
Reviews those cases which have so far given guidance as to the likely interpretation of the Regulation.

Geerts, P.G.F.A. 'The Informed User in Design Law: What should he compare and how should he make the comparison?' [2014] 36 *EIPR* 181
Undertakes an in-depth examination of the 'informed user' criterion.

Headdon, T. 'Community Design Right Infringement: an Emerging Consensus or a Difference Overall Impression' [2007] 29 *EIPR* 336
Analyzes some of the early infringement cases decided by national courts under the Regulation.

Michaels, A. 'The End of the Road for "Pattern Spare" Parts?' [2006] 28 *EIPR* 396
Analyzes the Court of Appeal's decision in Dyson v Qualtex.

Peris, J.J.I. 'Registered Community Design: The First Two-Year Balance from an Insider's Perspective' [2006] 28 *EIPR* 146
Analyzes the statistical data for the first two years' operation of OHIM and considers how the Invalidity Division and Board of Appeal have interpreted key words and phrases in the Regulation (the author is a member of OHIM's Invalidity Division and hence is best placed to give an overview of OHIM's case law).

Preet, K. 'Why America needs a European fashion police' [2008] 3(6) *Journal of Intellectual Property Law & Practice* 3(6) 386
Examines US and European design law from a fashion law perspective.

Suthersanen, U. 'Function, Art and Fashion: Do We Need the EU Design Law?' in Christophe Geiger (ed), *Constructing European Intellectual Property* (Edward Elgar, 2013) 357

Examines EU design law from the fashion industry perspective.

TABLE 20.1 *Table of comparisons: copyright and unregistered designs compared*

	Copyright	**Unregistered design right**
Definition	Graphic work, photograph, sculpture, collage, work of architecture, work of artistic craftsmanship (CDPA s. 4)	The shape or configuration (whether internal or external) of the whole or part of an article (CDPA s. 213(2))
Essential requirement	Original (CDPA s. 1(1))	Original and not commonplace (CDPA s. 213(4))
Form	Recorded in permanent form (case law)	Recorded in a design document or an article must have been made to the design (CDPA s. 213(6))
Qualification for protection	The author must be a national of, domiciled in, or resident in the UK, a country to which the Act extends, or a country to which the Act applies (i.e. a Berne, UCC or WTO Contracting State) at the relevant time or else the work must first be published in the UK, a country to which the Act extends, or a country to which the act applies (i.e. a Berne, UCC, or WTO Contracting State) (CDPA ss. 153–159)	The designer or employer must be a national of or habitually resident or incorporated in the UK, the EEA, or a designated country, or first marketing must have been in a qualifying country (CDPA ss. 217–220 plus SI 1994/3219)
Ownership	The author is first owner, unless the work was created in the course of employment, in which case the employer is the owner (CDPA s. 11)	The designer or employer or the first person to market articles in a qualifying country (CDPA s. 215)
Duration	Author's life plus 70 years (CDPA s. 12)	15 years from first recordal in a design document, but if marketed anywhere in the world within the first 5 years, then 10 years from first marketing, with licences of right available during the last 5 years (CDPA s. 216)
Primary infringement	Copying, issuing copies, communicating the work (CDPA ss. 17, 18, and 20)	Reproducing, directly or indirectly, articles to the design for commercial purposes (CDPA s. 226)

Secondary infringement	Importing, possessing, selling, hiring, offering, or exhibiting infringing articles with knowledge in the course of a business (CDPA ss. 22 and 23)	Importing, possessing, selling, hiring, or offering infringing articles with knowledge in the course of a business (CDPA s. 227)

TABLE 20.2 *Table of comparisons: United Kingdom registered and unregistered designs compared*

	UK registered designs	**UK unregistered design right**
Subject matter	A product or part of a product	An article or part of an article
Definition	The appearance of the whole or a part of a product resulting from the features of the lines, contours, colours, shape, texture, or materials of the product or its ornamentation (RDA s. 1(2))	The shape or configuration (whether internal or external) of the whole or part of an article (CDPA s. 213(2))
Essential requirements	Novelty and individual character (RDA s. 1B)	Original and not commonplace (CDPA s. 213(4))
Exclusions	Shapes dictated by technical function and 'must fit' features (RDA s. 1C) Designs contrary to public policy (RDA s. 1D) Designs consisting of specially protected emblems (RDA Sch.A1) Designs conflicting with earlier rights (RDA s. 11ZA)	A method of construction 'Must fit' features 'Must match' features Surface decoration(CDPA s. 213(3))
Qualification for protection	The applicant must be the person claiming to be the owner of the design (RDA s. 2)	The designer or employer must be a national of or habitually resident or incorporated in the UK, the EEA, or a designated country, or first marketing must occur in a qualifying country (CDPA ss. .217–220 plus SI 1994/3219)
Ownership	The designer or the designer's employer (RDA s. 2)	The designer or the designer's employer or the first person to market articles in a qualifying country (CDPA s. 215)
Duration	25 years from the date of filing providing the 5 yearly renewal fees are paid (RDA s. 8)	15 years from first recordal in a design document, but if marketed anywhere in the world within the first 5 years, then 10 years from first marketing, with licences of right available during the last 5 years (CDPA s. 216)

Infringement	The exclusive right to use the design, i.e. making, offering, putting on the market, importing, exporting, or using a product in which the design is incorporated or stocking such a product (RDA s. 7)	Reproducing, directly or indirectly, articles to the design for commercial purposes (CDPA s. 226) (primary infringement) and importing, possessing, selling, hiring, or offering infringing articles with knowledge in the course of a business (CDPA s. 227) (secondary infringement)
Defences to infringement	Private and non-commercial use, experimental use, reproduction for teaching purposes, use on ships or aircraft temporarily within the UK, intra-EU exhaustion of rights, repair of a complex product (RDA s. 7A)	Private and non-commercial use, experimental use, reproduction for teaching purposes, use on ships or aircraft temporarily within the UK (CDPA s. 224A and s. 224B)

Exploitation and enforcement

PART 8

Dealings in intellectual property rights

Problem question

Read this problem question carefully and keep it in mind while you are working through the chapter that follows. At the end of this chapter, you will be able to apply what you have learnt to the problem question and advise the relevant parties.

Sylvia Lyla is the author of a popular book series for young adults called *The Adventures of Sherry Wunderkind*. Since late 2009 she has had a contract with her publisher, Rylance Books, that states:

'The author, Ms S. Lyla, retains the ownership of the literary works, but grants an exclusive licence to Rylance books for a period of 10 years beginning 1 Jan 2009, to publish the books in the UK, EU, USA, Canada and Australia. In return Ms Lyla will receive a fee of £20,000 for every new book delivered to the publisher, as well as a royalty rate of 7% on all net sales of the book in all territories covered by the licence.'

In 2014 Sylvia agreed a contract with Readymade Theatre Company to put on a stage production of the first of the *Sherry Wunderkind* books during the period 1 January 2015 to 31 December 2016. Sherry did not participate in the theatrical transfer of the book to the stage, which was overseen by Readymade's in-house team of staff writers and actors. The production ran from 2015–2016 at the West End in London and was a huge financial success. The play was praised for introducing a new character to the Wunderkind universe—Sam Sunderland. The actors' performances and the innovative set design were also praised. The contract between Sylvia and Readymade stipulates that the copyright in the resulting play is owned by Sylvia, with the exception that the copyright in any new elements, characters, or stage design added to the original text of the book belong to Readymade.

Towards the end of 2017 Sylvia signed a new '360 degree' publishing and rights deal with a multi-media conglomerate—Fashionista Media. The deal, which purportedly takes effect on 1 January 2018, covers the exclusive rights to publish the existing series of *Sherry Wunderkind* books, as well as any new entries to that series; produce theatrical and musical versions of the books; produce a series of feature films based on the books; create a line of merchandise based on the characters; and, finally, publish a new set of books, written by Sylvia, based on the character Sam Sunderland.

→

➡️

In early 2018 Sylvia also registered 'Wunderland' (as a word) and a colourful drawing of Sherry (as a logo) as UK trade marks for a range of goods and services including toys and other merchandise, and a proposed theme park called 'Wunderland Windsor'. However, she does not want to build and operate the theme park herself, but would rather sell the rights to a licensed operator—Funtime Parks plc—who wants to build and run the park. On 1 February 2018 the CEO of Funtime Parks agreed a verbal licence with Sylvia over the phone, covering both the rights to copyright in her characters (for merchandise and the creation of thematic rides) as well the rights to the protected marks (for use in branding) in return for a 10 per cent share of all profits.

Advise Sylvia about how her various dealings with her intellectual property rights are likely to affect the enforcement of the terms of the above licensing agreements.

21.1 **Introduction**

21.1.1 **Dealings in intellectual property rights**

It almost goes without say that intellectual property (IP) rights are a form of property. What is less obvious is that IP rights have some, but not all, of the characteristics of property. Although generally of finite duration—and in the case of registrable rights always at risk of cancellation for invalidity—they can nevertheless be bought and sold, bequeathed and mortgaged. Indeed, under International Financial Reporting Standards, intangible assets *must* be shown on corporate balance sheets. Furthermore, frequent surveys are conducted to establish which is the most successful trade mark—Interbrand is the most prominent ranking of global brands, with Apple, Google, and Coca-Cola usually in the top three spots, while other organizations measure which pharmaceutical company has the most valuable patent portfolio—Pfizer Inc and Novartis are usually viewed as the top IP owners in the pharmaceutical industry.

Given the economic importance of IP rights, it is necessary to understand how IP dealings—or transactions—work. There are two basic forms: (i) assignment, and (ii) licensing. To comprehend these categories, we will explore the UK statutory provisions which govern such dealings, and we will consider the arguments typically used to challenge the validity of certain transactions. It is also crucial to understand how European Union law on free movement of goods affects dealings in intellectual property rights, and how competition law, whether national or EU, may also be of relevance. This is also worth considering in light of the ongoing Brexit process.

The starting point for considering IP transactions is a simple principle—there is a distinction between being the author/creator of the underlying work/invention/mark/design and being the owner of the right. For this reason, being the author/creator does not necessarily mean that you will always have the ability to enter into transactions with others concerning the work, design, invention or mark. Generally, it is owners, or their agents/trustees, who will have the power to engage in IP transactions. Appendix

2, at the end of this book, shows a draft assignment and licensing agreement which you can read through to see the kinds of legal terms that are used when copyright owners (licensors) make agreements with publishers and other commercial users of works (licensees).

21.1.2 Distinction between an assignment and a licence

The two most common forms of IP transactions are (i) assignments, and (ii) licences. It is important to keep the two separate, as different consequences flow depending on which type of dealing occurs.

An assignment involves the outright transfer of ownership from the current owner (the assignor) to the new owner (the assignee). It may be voluntary (i.e. by way of gift), but in most cases will be in exchange for consideration, usually the payment of a lump sum but sometimes for periodic royalties (or a combination of the two). Just as with the conveyance of land or the giving of a present at Christmas, the original owner 'drops out of the picture' and is replaced by the new owner. Nevertheless, in the case of copyright, certain rights, for example an author's moral rights and a performer's right to object to illicit recordings of a performance, cannot be assigned. These rights remain with the author or performer, and despite the transfer of the legal ownership of copyright, provided the conditions of the Copyright, Designs and Patents Act 1988 ('CDPA') are satisfied (e.g. in the case of the moral right of paternity, that this has been asserted).

Lest it be thought that the meaning of 'assignment' is too simple to require explanation, even the Court of Justice of the European Union ('CJEU') has failed to understand the nature of such a transaction and for a time treated it as having continuing effect for the purposes of exhaustion of rights (see Case 40/70 *Sirena v Eda* [1971] ECR 69 and Case 192/73 *Van Zuylen Frères v Hag AG* [1974] ECR 731 ('*Hag I*')).

By contrast, a licence is a mere permission to use the IP right. Like an assignment, this is usually granted by a licensor in exchange for compensation (a licence fee or royalties, or both). The orthodox view in UK law is that this is a personal right and does not give the licensee any proprietary interest: *CBS v Charmdale Records* [1980] 2 All ER 807; *Northern & Shell plc v Condé Nast & National Magazine Distributors Ltd* [1995] RPC 117. Its practical effect is to provide immunity to the licensee from liability for acts covered by the licence that would otherwise be infringing. However, in many instances statute confers certain procedural advantages on licensees so that they can bring infringement proceedings in their own name. These, however, are procedural rights and do not have any proprietary implications.

A licence can take several forms—exclusive, non-exclusive, and sole. An exclusive licence means that the licensee is the only person who can exploit the right in the territory in question (this being to the exclusion even of the owner of the right). A non-exclusive licence means, therefore, that other licensees may be appointed to operate in parallel to the first licensee. A sole licence, by contrast, means that no other licensee can be appointed, but the owner of the right can exploit it at the same time as the licensee. In practice, the term 'sole and exclusive licence' is relatively common, despite the fact that it is a contradiction in terms—in such a case, the courts are likely to look at such a term in light of the entire circumstances and the contractual terms as a whole to determine whether it should be construed as a sole or an exclusive licence.

Pause for reflection

Think back to our problem scenario. What type of licence did Sylvia grant to her publisher from 1 January 2009?

21.1.2 Intangible personal property rights

In England and Wales, property rights are divided into real property and personal property. The latter is subdivided into 'choses in possession' (i.e. assets which can be handed over physically) and 'choses in action' (intangible assets enforced by litigation rather than by taking possession of them). According to Firth and Fitzgerald (in 'Equitable Assignments in Relation to Intellectual Property' [1999] 2 *IPQ* 228) it is arguable that with two exceptions, intellectual property rights are choses in action even though they may appear to share some of the characteristics of real property. The two exceptions are patents which are declared by Patents Act s. 30(1) *not* to be things in action, and confidential information (trade secrets) which has been stated by the courts to be incapable of ownership and to rest on the conscience of the confidant (*Boardman v Phipps* [1967] 2 AC 46 at pp. 127–8 *per* Lord Upjohn and *Douglas v Hello! Ltd (No. 2)* [2005] 4 All ER 128 at [119]).

The general rule for the assignment of choses in action can be found in the Law of Property Act 1925 ('LPA') s. 136, which requires a written document, signed by the assignor and with notice being given to the other party to the chose. All intellectual property statutes follow this basic template, with each requiring a signed assignment in writing, with notice or, in the case of registrable rights, the change of ownership being entered on the relevant register. In such cases notification to the UKIPO can equates to the need in s. 136 LPA to give notice to the other party. The consequences of failing to register the change of ownership can be severe. As a result of the Enforcement Directive (Directive 2004/48/EC of the European Parliament and of the Council of 29 April 2004 on the enforcement of intellectual property rights [2004] OJ L 157/45) the rule is that the new owner is not awarded costs in any subsequent infringement action should there be delay in recording the transaction.

Nonetheless, failure to comply with the requirement of writing does not necessarily mean that the transaction has no effect. The reason is, as Firth and Fitzgerald explain, that principles of equity can step in—even in the absence of writing, equitable (though not legal) title may still pass, so that the assignee, as equitable owner, can demand completion of the appropriate formalities because of the equitable maxim that 'equity looks on that as done which ought to be done'. In such a case, the assignor in effect becomes trustee for the assignee. The right to specific performance can arise, but only where value was given for the assignment. However, being an equitable owner (i.e. a beneficiary under a bare trust) is not something which can be entered on the relevant register, as the Registered Designs Act 1949 ('RDA'), Patents Act 1977 and Trade Marks Act 1994 ('TMA') all declare that no notice of any trust, whether express, implied or constructive, is to be entered on the register. The equitable owner must therefore go to court for the discretionary remedy of specific performance to compel completion of the legal formalities to make them the owner of the right in law.

Whilst s. 136 LPA provides a template for changing the ownership of intellectual property rights, there is no similar provision with regard to giving permission to use such a right. How intellectual property licences are to be effected and recorded at UKIPO therefore depends on the wording of each intellectual property statute. There is no standard pattern, proof again that an overarching code on dealings is overdue.

Pause for reflection

Given the global nature of intellectual property law, does it make sense for someone to be able to claim equitable ownership of a right in England and Wales when statute declares that failure to comply with the appropriate formalities renders an assignment of 'no effect'? Is equity playing a necessary role here or could it be described as interfering with internationally agreed standards?

Are any equitable principles relevant to our problem scenario?

21.2 Assessing dealings involving patents, copyrights, designs, and trade marks in the UK

21.2.1 Patents

In the case of patents, we need to reconsider the popular image of the sole inventor coming up with revolutionary ideas in a home workshop. The reality is that most inventors are employed by large companies—a fact that is crucial to ownership. As we examined in chapter 16 on employee inventions, although the inventor has the right to be named in a patent (Patents Act 1977 s. 13)—and may in certain instances be entitled to compensation where the invention is of outstanding benefit (s. 40)—the patent itself will belong to the employer where the criteria set out in s. 39(1) apply. Thus, the employer will—as owner—have the rights of exploitation set out in the Patents Act s. 60 as well as the rights of property found in s. 30, but equally will have borne the research and development costs and the financial risk of developing the patented product or process. Where an invention has genuinely been created by a sole inventor, the patent will, of course, be owned by that inventor in the first instance.

Pause for reflection

Think back to our consideration of employee inventions in chapter 16. Given that, as we have now learned, only the owner of the patent may engage in lucrative IP dealings, we can now see that the right of companies to own the inventions of their employees is undoubtedly crucial to those companies' continued investment in research and development. This, of course, leaves employees in a weak legal position.

21.2.1.1 Assignment and licensing of patents

Section 30(1) Patents Act 1977 declares that any patent is personal property but without being a 'chose in action'. The section goes on to state that a patent (and indeed, a patent application) can be assigned or mortgaged and can pass by operation of law or on death. Any assignment or mortgage, and any assent (such as by the personal representative of the previous owner), must be in writing and signed, otherwise it will be void. The section also provides for patents to be licensed but is silent as to any formal requirements for such licences. There is a separate provision (s. 31) dealing with property rights under Scottish law.

Section 36 goes on to deal with where a patent is granted to two or more persons, providing that such co-ownership is to be by way of equal undivided shares, in other words creating a tenancy in common. Where there is co-ownership, one co-owner cannot enter into any property transaction (such as an assignment or licence) without the consent of the other.

Section 32 by implication requires all transactions affecting patents to be recorded at UKIPO. The duty to record is emphasized by the *bona fide* purchaser rule set out in s. 33: any person who claims to have acquired property rights in a patent is to be entitled as against someone claiming under an earlier transaction if that earlier transaction had not been registered and there was no knowledge on the part of the person claiming under the later transaction. The need to register is further reinforced by s. 68 (amended as a result of the EU Enforcement Directive). As noted earlier, the penalty is the non-award of costs in any litigation over the patent.

The case of *Thorn Security Ltd v Siemens Schweiz AG* [2008] EWCA Civ 1161 shows that s. 68 can be interpreted in a flexible manner. The question here was whether a company merger under Swiss law (which differed significantly from UK law as to the mechanism for achieving a merger) amounted to an assignment which had not been promptly recorded in the register of patents. It had been held at first instance that an assignment had to involve a consensual document so that a Government order transferring assets on merger did not suffice. The Court of Appeal disagreed. The court stated that a narrow literal approach to s. 68 is to be avoided, and instead a purposive interpretation was adopted. It was wide enough to cover both consensual and administrative transfers of ownership.

The Patents Act provides that voluntary licences can be exclusive or non-exclusive. One important point is that exclusive licensees can be in a stronger position to take infringement actions than the inventor/patent owner. For example, where a small biochemistry research institute with few resources obtained a patent on a compound and licensed it to a multi-national pharma company for drug manufacture, the multi-national licensee could be better placed than the small institute to lead an infringement action against e.g. a competitor who is bringing out a rival drug. As a result, exclusive licensees are often heavily involved in patent litigation. Indeed, under the Patents Act an exclusive licensee has procedural rights to bring an infringement action in their own name under s. 67; but as noted earlier, if the licence has not been recorded on the register, then under s. 68 the licensee will be denied costs in any infringement action. By contrast, no procedural rights are given to a non-exclusive licensee—so such licensees need the co-operation of the patentee to sue infringers. A well-drafted non-exclusive licence will usually contain a provision requiring the patentee to sue infringers if requested by the licensee to do so.

In addition to the voluntary licence regime, a patent may also be the subject of a compulsory licence any time after the third anniversary of its grant if e.g. there is a failure to exploit the patent. The rules on compulsory licences (set out in Patents Act 1977 s. 48, as amended by SI 1999/1899) draw a distinction between where the patentee is a World Trade Organization ('WTO') proprietor and where they are not, with regard to the criteria to be satisfied before the licence can be granted and the steps which the intending licensee must observe. The terms of the licence are determined by UKIPO. Alternatively, the patentee can ask that the entry on the Register be endorsed to the effect that licences of right are available (s. 46 Patents Act, as amended), thus inviting others to request a licence, the terms of which may be decided by the UKIPO. Such an application may be made at any time after grant and has the advantage of halving subsequent renewal fees. Last, under s. 55, the Crown has extensive powers to exploit patents.

Finally, we have to consider FRAND—licensing on fair, reasonable, and non-discriminatory terms. This type of licensing is an obligation in the technology sector where some patented inventions cover 'essential standards' (known as Standard Essential Patents or SEPs). SEPs cover technology that is required in e.g. every new smartphone or tablet computer. In such a case, if the IP owner could refuse to license the essential technology to a competitor, this would create a monopoly in the smartphones market. To allow competition, SEP owners are obliged to license on FRAND terms. This obligation is underpinned by EU competition law (Case C-170/13 *Huawei Technologies Co. Ltd v ZTE Corp., ZTE Deutschland GmbH* [2015]).

The first UK case that dealt with a dispute was *Unwired Planet v Huawei* [2017] EWHC 711 (quickly followed by a decision on the final injunction—*Unwired Planet v Huawei* [2017] EWHC 1304).

Unwired Planet v Huawei [2017] EWHC 711

Unwired Planet offered Huawei a worldwide licence on terms that Unwired Planet considered to be FRAND. Huawei rejected the worldwide licence, arguing that a lower-cost, UK-only licence would be FRAND. Birss J in the High Court assessed whether the licensing offers were FRAND and considered a worldwide FRAND rate.

The main judgment concerned determining FRAND terms. Birss J agreed with United Planet that the FRAND licence should be worldwide, not UK-specific, and evaluated a range of methods for determining the royalty rates of comparable worldwide licences to set what he considered to be FRAND rates in the circumstances of the case.

In the judgment that followed, after Huawei refused the offer of the licence set at these terms, Unwired Planet sought a final injunction. Confirming that United Planet's offer of a worldwide licence was FRAND, Birss J stated:

> Since Unwired Planet have established that Huawei have infringed valid patents EP (UK) 2 229 744 and EP (UK) 1 230 818, and since Huawei have not been prepared to take a licence on the terms I have found to be FRAND, and since Unwired Planet are not in breach of competition law, a final injunction to restrain infringement of these two patents by Huawei should be granted.

Birss J also explained that such a 'FRAND injunction' will be lifted once the defendant has agreed a FRAND licence. The FRAND injunction was suspended pending an appeal.

21.2.2 Copyright

As we saw earlier in this book, copyright amounts to a bundle of rights. Each right listed in s. 16 CDPA—the right to reproduce the work, the right to distribute such copies, the right to perform the work, the right to communicate the work, the right of adaptation, etc—can each be dealt with separately, not just in the UK, but in any state which is a contracting party of the Berne Convention, the Universal Copyright Convention, or the WTO. This means that different people can own—or can be licensed to exploit—different aspects of the same copyright in different countries. The lack of any system of registration makes keeping track of who is entitled to the ownership or exploitation of each right very difficult.

Further to this, the CDPA provides for the author of a work (as defined in s. 9) to be the first owner. However, where a literary, dramatic, musical, or artistic work, or a film (but not any other category of work), is made in the course of employment, the employer is first owner 'subject to any agreement to the contrary' (s. 11(2)). This exception does not apply to Crown copyright or Parliamentary copyright (s. 11(3)).

Thus, being an author does not guarantee that you will own the work—an essential factor if the author wishes to bring an infringement action (*Beloff v Pressdram Ltd* [1973] RPC 765, *Gabrin v Universal Music Operations Ltd* [2004] ECDR 18) or assign or license the work (*R Griggs Group Ltd and others v Evans and others* [2005] FSR 706). Further reference to s. 9, as supplemented by s. 178 CDPA, (the definition section for Part I of the Act) reveals that in respect of entrepreneurial copyrights like films, sound recordings, broadcasts, and computer-generated works, the statutory definition of 'author' does not always reflect creative input. For example, in the case of sound recordings, the producer is first owner, this being defined as the person who made the arrangement for the recording; in the case of a typographical arrangement, it is the publisher.

The common law tradition is to treat copyright as a commodity. In certain industries, such as entertainment and media, there is extensive use of contractual arrangements so that ownership of copyright is far removed from those whose creative efforts are being exploited. In the case of a film, for example, copyright works created by the authors of the story, the screenplay, the dialogue, the costume designers, and the composer of the music (to name but five) will have been assigned in advance to a third party, usually the production company.

 Pause for reflection

Consider our problem scenario. Did Sylvia own the copyright to the works in question when she entered into the first publishing deal beginning 1 January 2009? Is there any doubt over who owns the copyright in the works she negotiates over as part of the 360 degree deal agreed in 2017? How might our consideration of the ownership question affect our advice to Sylvia?

In contrast to employee ownership, s. 11(1) CDPA has an unexpected outcome where a work is commissioned. Contrary to a popular misconception, under the CDPA commissioning a work does not confer any right of ownership. In consequence, someone who pays to have a work created for them must ensure that appropriate contractual provisions are in place with the author which either operate to assign the copyright to the commissioner (under ss. 90 or 91 CDPA) or at the very least give the commissioner a licence to use the work. Should the contract fail to do so, then the court may if it thinks fit imply such a provision in the interests of business efficacy, but the court will only imply the absolute minimum to make the contract work.

Ray v Classic FM plc [1998] FSR 622

The paradigm case dealing with commissioned works is *Ray v Classic FM plc*. Here, the defendant radio station had asked the claimant to create a database of classical music, the contract stating that the claimant was to be treated as a consultant and not an employee. It was held that the defendant did not have any right of ownership. Lightman J restated the principle that in the case of a commissioned work the author was entitled to retain the copyright in the absence of an express or implied term to the contrary effect. The mere fact that an author had been commissioned to produce a work was of itself insufficient to entitle the commissioner to the copyright. In order to imply some rights to fill a hole in the contract, the court should award only the minimum necessary to give the commissioner what the parties to the contract must have intended to confer and in the present case that was the grant of a licence to the defendant to exploit the work. The amount of the purchase price which the commissioner had promised to pay could be relevant. It was only in the rarest cases that an assignment rather than the grant of an exclusive licence would suffice.

Notwithstanding this decision, several cases decided both prior and subsequent to *Ray v Classic FM* provide a contrast to it, showing that the courts are not averse to allocating the ownership of copyright despite the apparent wording of the contract.

For example, in *Ibcos Computers Ltd v Barclays Mercantile Highland Finance Ltd* [1994] FSR 275 the dispute was about ownership of copyright in an agricultural machinery traders' accounting program written at a time when the claimant and defendant were partners. Jacob J (as he then was) decided that both legal and equitable ownership was vested in the partnership because this was necessary to give the partnership 'business efficacy'. Further, copyright in an earlier, general purpose program which had been incorporated into the disputed software also vested in the claimant (as successor in title to the partnership) because of a clause in the defendant's post-employment contract which stated that 'P recognises that all PK software are the sole property of PK', hardly the wording one would expect to see for the assignment of copyright.

In *Hutchison Personal Communications Ltd v Hook Advertising Ltd* [1996] FSR 549 the defendant advertising agency had, through one of its employees, designed a logo for a new mobile phone company. Although clause 8 of the contract stated that copyright in all the artwork should belong to the agency, the court decided that statements made when the agency was bidding for the work resulted in an implied promise that if it was appointed, it would hand over all copyright to the claimant.

Finally, in *R Griggs Group Ltd and others v Evans and others* [2005] FSR 706 a freelance designer had been commissioned by an advertising agency on behalf of its client (the claimant) to combine two existing trade marks for DOC MARTENS footwear so as to produce a new logo. When the claimant subsequently sued a third party for infringement, the latter claimed it was the owner of copyright in the logo as the result of an assignment taken from the freelance designer. The Court of Appeal, confirming the High Court decision, held that the claimant had equitable ownership of the copyright, because in the circumstances this was the minimum necessary to satisfy the 'officious bystander' test for an implied term in the law of contract. The designer had no conceivable further interest in the work being created and was not able to confer property rights on anybody else.

The difference between these three cases and the decision in *Ray v Classic FM* perhaps lies in the fact that the contract in the last-mentioned case had been very carefully drafted and left no room for doubt as to the ownership of the copyright.

Pause for reflection

Does the absence of any statutory rule on commissioned works, when taken in conjunction with the diverging decisions in *Ray v Classic FM* and *Griggs v Evans*, provide sufficient certainty to those entering into IP transactions?

21.2.2.1 Assignment of copyright

Assignment of copyright is dealt with by s. 90 CDPA. The usual declaration is to be found in s. 90(1), namely that copyright is transmissible in the same way as other forms of personal property, i.e. by assignment, by testamentary disposition, or by operation of law. No particular form of wording is required. In the case of testamentary dispositions, there is the practice of appointing literary executors who will deal only with the deceased author's rights, thus separating copyright from the rest of the estate. Further, s. 93 provides that in the case of an *unpublished* work (whether this consists of the original document or some other form of recording of a literary, dramatic, musical, or artistic work, or a 'material thing' embodying a sound recording or film) a bequest of the author's personal estate (whether general or specific) will carry with it the relevant copyright.

As might be expected from the fragmentary nature of copyright, s. 90(2) provides for total or partial assignment, 'partial' referring to rights that are assigned or for a particular period of time. The subsection therefore contemplates copyright reverting to the author (or their estate) after a fixed period. However, in the case of a poorly worded document, the court may find it difficult to decide whether what has been created is an assignment or a licence, in the same way as provisions in contracts of commission may lead to uncertainty as to whether the commissioner is entitled to a licence of the work or to demand that ownership be transferred.

Section 90(3) requires any assignment to be in writing and signed by the assignor if it is to be 'effective'. The ability of a court to treat an imperfect legal transaction as an 'assignment in equity' was discussed earlier. Section 91(1) provides for the automatic assignment of a work to be created at some date in the future where the prospective owner purports to assign such copyright in writing. This can be a useful way of transferring ownership of a commissioned work to the commissioner.

Copyright legislation is always playing 'catch up' with technology. The consequence is to create problems of interpretation of copyright contracts where, subsequent to the drafting of the agreement, there has been either a change in law or a change in technology or both. An example is to be found in *Governors of the Hospital for Sick Children v Walt Disney* [1966] 2 All ER 321.

Governors of the Hospital for Sick Children v Walt Disney [1966] 2 **All ER 321**

J.M. Barrie, the author of *Peter Pan* (a play written in 1904 and adapted into a book in 1911, and consequently governed by the Copyright Act 1842), had, in 1919, granted an exclusive licence to an American film company to produce all his works in cinematograph form. At the time, all films were silent films, and further, under the 1911 Copyright Act there was no protection for films as such. Subsequently, the licence was transferred (with permission) to Walt Disney. In 1939 a further agreement allowed Disney to make a cartoon version of the *Peter Pan* story; but in the meantime, Barrie had assigned his copyright and any residual performing rights to what is now Great Ormond Street Hospital (the hospital has perpetual rights to control the public performance, commercial distribution, communication to the public, and adaptation of the work by virtue of s. 301 CDPA). By the 1960s, the hospital proposed to license another company to make a sound film based on Barrie's book. The majority of the Court of Appeal agreed with the contention that the 1919 agreement was not intended to cover 'talking' films as these were not in the parties' contemplation at the time.

21.2.2.2 Reversionary interests

In a number of cases, copyright ownership can revert—return—to the author or his estate. For example, where a partial assignment under s. 90 CDPA is limited in time, the copyright will revert automatically to the previous owner (who of course might not be the author) when the relevant period has expired. Similarly, where legislation extends the duration of copyright, it has sometimes provided that any additional period of protection should belong to the author. Such reversions can cause problems for users of copyright works because in the absence of any registration system it can be tricky to determine who has the right to authorise a use. From the other perspective, a person claiming to be entitled to a reversionary interest—often, someone who may have inherited it from an ancestor—will have to produce relevant documents that establish a chain of title.

What happens to ownership of rights when they are extended in duration? In 1995 s. 12 CDPA was amended as a result of the Copyright Term Directive (Council Directive 93/98/EC of 29 October 1993 harmonizing the term of copyright protection [1993] OJ L 290/9, now codified as Directive 2006/116/EC of the European Parliament and of the Council of 12 December 2006 [2006] OJ L 372/12) which extended copyright term for authorial works from 50 to 70 years after the life of the author. To deal with this issue, Regulations 16 and 17 of the Duration of Copyright and Rights in Performances Regulations (SI 1995/3297) were brought into law. Regulations 16 and 17 state that any extended or revived copyright belongs to the person who was the owner immediately before the commencement of the Regulations (for extended copyright) or who was the owner immediately before it expired (for revived copyright). In other words, there is no reversion of copyright to the author—the benefit of the extended term goes to the current owner.

21.2.2.3 Copyright licensing

Just like the Patents Act, the CDPA provides for licences of copyright to be granted and for such licences to be binding on the owner's successor in title unless that person is a *bona fide* purchaser for value (s. 90(4)) (although this section is silent as to formalities). Section 92(2) adds that in the case of an exclusive licence (which must be in writing) the licensee is to have the same rights against a successor in title as they have against the person granting the licence. Section 101 confers procedural advantages on an exclusive licensee by stating that they are to have the same rights and remedies (except against the owner) 'as if the licence had been an assignment'. Despite this wording, the nature of an exclusive licence of copyright is to confer a personal right on the licensee so that they are not to be treated as the owner of the right (*CBS Ltd v Charmdale*). Changes made to the CDPA as a result of the Information Society Directive (Directive 2001/29/EC of the European Parliament and of the Council of 22 May 2001 on the harmonization of certain aspects of copyright and related rights in the information society [2001] OJ L 167/10) now give similar rights to a non-exclusive licensee provided the licence is in writing (s. 101A).

As of 2018 there is an EU Draft Directive on Copyright in the Digital Single Market (DSM Directive). One of the concerns of EU legislators is that rights-holders are not sufficiently able to maximize the value of their works (or control their availability) in the digital environment. Article 13 of the proposed Directive would introduce obligations for online content service providers to conclude 'fair and appropriate' licensing agreements with rights-holders for the use of copyright works. This would apply to online content service providers who automatically reproduce or refer to large amounts of copyright works, some of which are uploaded by users. Article 13 would also put online content service providers under a proportionate obligation to prevent infringing content from being made available. The Draft Directive represents a significant attempt by the EU to address the so-called 'value gap' via legislative intervention.

21.2.2.4 Challenging the validity of copyright transactions

Many industries make extensive use of contractual arrangements in order to place the ownership of copyright in the hands of those wanting to exploit works commercially. Creators often have to accept the terms which are offered to them, but in so doing may have no access to independent legal advice. Thus, an aspiring author may have to accept the standard terms offered by a publisher; a musician in the early stages of their career may not appreciate how unfavourable are the terms offered by a record label or a management team.

Brownsword (in 'Copyright Assignment: Fair Dealing and Unconscionable Contracts' [1998] 3 *IPQ* 311) explains that English law has no general doctrine of good faith in contracts but instead has developed piecemeal solutions to deal with unfairness (*Interfoto Picture Library Ltd v Stiletto Visual Programmes Ltd* [1989] QB 433 *per* Bingham LJ at p. 439). Brownsword further suggests that in relation to unfair intellectual property bargains it might be possible to invoke the Unfair Contract Terms Act 1977. Significantly, however, Sch. 1 to that Act specifically excludes intellectual property agreements from its application. We must therefore look to the common law to find a way to protect our aspiring author or budding rock star. Two arguments have been used over the years, namely restraint of trade and inequality of bargaining power.

21.2.2.4.1 Restraint of trade

The argument that a publishing agreement was in restraint of trade was successfully deployed in *Schroeder Music v Macaulay* [1974] 1 WLR 1308, although the terms of the disputed contract were one-sided in the extreme. Here M, a young composer, entered into a standard form agreement with the defendant music publishers in which he handed over the copyright in any songs he might write during the term of the contract. The deal was initially for five years but was extended automatically if royalties exceeded £5,000, an amount described by Lord Reid (at p. 1312) as representing a 'very modest success'. There was no obligation on the defendant to publish the songs, but it could assign the contract at any time whilst the composer could not. Equally, the publisher could end the agreement by giving one month's notice but the composer could not.

The House of Lords had no hesitation in granting the declaration sought by the composer that the agreement was void as being in restraint of trade. In passing, Lord Diplock (at p. 1315) remarked that the public policy which the court was implementing was not some 19th-century theory about freedom to trade, but 'the protection of those whose bargaining power is weak against being forced by those whose bargaining power is stronger to enter into bargains that are unconscionable'. The fact that this was a standard form contract, the terms of which were being offered by a party whose bargaining power enabled it to say 'take it or leave it', did not raise a presumption that the bargain was unconscionable, but did require the court to be vigilant to ensure that it was not.

21.2.2.4.2 Inequality of bargaining power

Lord Diplock's words in the *Macaulay* case were seized upon by Lord Denning in *Lloyds Bank Ltd v Bundy* [1975] QB 326 at p. 339 where he argued that there was a general jurisdiction to set aside contracts where there was inequality of bargaining power:

> By virtue of it, the English law gives relief to one who, without independent advice, enters into a contract upon terms which are very unfair or transfers property for a consideration which is grossly inadequate, when his bargaining power is grievously impaired by reason of his own needs or desires, or by his own ignorance or infirmity, coupled with undue influences or pressures brought to bear on him by or for the benefit of the other.

Lord Denning himself then made use of this principle in *Clifford Davis v WEA Records* [1975] 1 WLR 61. Here, two members of the Fleetwood Mac pop group had signed a management agreement with the claimant under which they assigned the worldwide copyright in any songs they might write over the next ten years, promising to produce one song a month, whilst there was no undertaking from the claimant to publish their work. Having fallen out with the claimant, they composed some new songs which the defendant had recorded and proposed to release. The Court of Appeal held that the terms of the bargain were 'manifestly unfair'. The assignment of copyright had been for consideration which was grossly inadequate, and undue influence had been brought to bear on them. They had not had access to independent legal advice. The assignment of copyright was invalid and would be set aside.

The two lines of thinking, namely restraint of trade and undue influence, were blended together in *O'Sullivan v Management Agency & Music Ltd* [1985] QB 428. The claimant, who became a successful composer and singer, had at the age of 23 entered into a series of agreements with the defendant management company. At the time, he trusted implicitly the defendant's chairman who managed a number of other high-profile pop stars. This enabled the court to conclude that the defendant and its related companies stood in a fiduciary relationship with the claimant, such that undue influence could be presumed, particularly as the claimant had not been offered independent legal advice. Such undue influence rendered the contracts voidable rather than void, but the court nevertheless ordered the contracts to be set aside and required the defendant to account for all the profits made from the arrangement. However, credit was to be given for the skill and labour in promoting the claimant and making a significant contribution to his success, so that the defendant was entitled to a reasonable remuneration including a small profit element albeit one considerably less than would have been received had independent advice been offered.

The willingness of Lord Denning to find that a contract had been vitiated by inequality of bargaining power should be contrasted with the views of the House of Lords in *National Westminster Bank v Morgan* [1985] AC 686. Their Lordships expressly disapproved *Lloyds Bank v Bundy*, stating that a court should not presume undue influence simply from the parties' relationship without more. It had to be shown that the transaction had been wrongful in that it had constituted a manifest and unfair disadvantage to the person seeking to avoid it; in other words, there had to be victimization. They added that it was questionable whether there was any need in the modern law to erect a general principle of relief against inequality of bargaining power, but, conversely, there was no precisely defined law setting limits to the equitable jurisdiction of a court to relieve against undue influence.

Despite the perceived conservatism in *National Westminster Bank v Morgan*, Nicholls J (as he then was) was able to use the case to set aside some of the disputed agreements in *Elton John v James* [1991] FSR 397, a case decided shortly after *Morgan*, but only reported some six years later. The facts of the case follow the familiar pattern, that of a singer-songwriter (and also his lyricist) signing a series of publishing, recording, and management agreements at a time when he was very young (in fact a minor), without receiving independent legal advice, which had it been obtained would have shown the one-sided nature of the deal. Nicholls J stated that the present position (following *Morgan*) is that two ingredients are required before the court will set aside a transaction on the ground of undue influence, namely a relationship in which one person has a dominating influence over another and, second, a manifestly disadvantageous transaction resulting from that influence. Here, to have tied two young men at the beginning of their career to a publishing agreement for six years represented an unacceptably hard bargain. The defendant had assumed a dominating rôle over the claimants so that the original publishing agreement was unfair.

The above cases show a trend of moving away from the now-discredited principle of inequality of bargaining power. What is required is clear evidence from which the court may conclude that there has been undue influence. This will no longer be presumed, but must be shown to have existed as a result of the parties' relationship. In turn, that relationship must have led to the imposition of contractual terms which are manifestly unfair to the creator.

 Pause for reflection

Are the current protections provided by the common law sufficient to protect vulnerable artists, or would the CDPA benefit from having a provision which enabled a copyright assignment to be challenged on the ground that it was unreasonable?

More generally, would IP law benefit by having in place a simple rule that any contract dealing with such rights must be fair and just?

Looking at our problem scenario, is there anything to suggest Sylvia has been in an unduly vulnerable position when concluding any of her contracts?

21.2.3 Designs

21.2.3.1 Registered designs

The RDA (as amended by the Intellectual Property (Enforcement etc) Regulations 2006 (SI 2006/1028)) now contains three new provisions, ss. 15A, 15B, and 15C, which set out the basic rules on property rights. Prior to the 2006 changes, there were no stipulations in the Act as to dealings in registered designs, an omission which the courts refused to rectify: *Oren v Red Box Toy Factory Ltd* [1999] FSR 785 at [42].

Section 15A proffers the standard declaration that registered designs and applications for the same are personal property (or, in Scotland, incorporeal moveable property); whilst s. 15B declares that registered designs may be dealt with in the usual way, that is, by way of assignment, testamentary disposition, by operation of law, or by charge. Assignments must be in writing and signed by the assignor. Any dealing in a registered design is subject to any rights previously entered on the register. Any assignment or transmission of a registered design must be entered on the designs register (RDA s. 19), normally by the person acquiring the right, although s. 19(2) does provide for the original owner to apply for the transaction to be recorded. Further, where an unregistered design right also subsists in a registered design, the change of ownership in the registered design is not to be recorded unless the registrar is satisfied that the new owner is also entitled to a corresponding interest in the unregistered design right (RDA s. 19(3A)).

Section 15B(7) declares that licences may be granted without specifying what formalities may be required, but in the case of exclusive licences, under s. 15C these must be in writing and signed by the proprietor before the exclusive licensee is given the usual procedural right of being able to bring infringement proceedings in their own name. The rights of the exclusive licensee are spelled out in more detail in s. 24F. The licence is to be entered on the register under s. 19(1) RDA. As with patents, there are provisions in the RDA as to Crown use of registered designs, the details of which are to be found in the First Schedule to the Act.

21.2.3.2 Unregistered design right

Section 222 CDPA declares that the UK unregistered design right is to be treated as personal property (or, in Scotland, moveable property) and can be transferred by assignment, testamentary disposition, or by operation of law. Unlike registered designs, there is no provision for an unregistered design to be charged by way of security, yet another instance of the lack of consistency in the rules on the ownership of intellectual property rights. For an assignment to be effective, it must be in writing and signed by the assignor. Section 222(2) (which appears to have been copied in its entirety from s. 90(2)) provides for an assignment to be partial, either with regard to the right transferred or for a fixed period of time. Yet, given the very short duration of unregistered design right (again, in contrast to copyright) the notion of a temporary transfer of ownership followed by a reversionary interest seems odd. The Intellectual Property Act 2014 provides that the default owner of a commissioned design is the author/designer, which means agreements must be in place between the commissioner and the designer to ensure clarity on assignment/licensing.

Section 224 CDPA provides that where a registered design is assigned, such assignment also carries with it any unregistered rights unless there is an intention to the contrary. The parallel provision in RDA s. 19(3B) states that the assignment of the unregistered design right shall be taken to be also an assignment of the right in the registered design unless a contrary intention appears.

Finally, Part III CDPA provides for the granting of a licence to exploit an unregistered design right (s. 222(4)). No formality is prescribed, although for the procedural advantages conferred by s. 225 on an exclusive licensee to apply such an arrangement must be in writing and signed by the design right owner. Licences, whether granted by the design right owner under s. 222, or by a prospective design right owner under s. 223, are stated to be binding on the whole world except a subsequent *bona fide* purchaser for value and without notice (actual or constructive) of the licence. Crown use of unregistered designs is provided for by ss. 240 and 241 CDPA.

 Pause for reflection

Are the differences in detail between the statutory provisions on assignments and licences of patents, copyright, and designs justifiable, or is this just a case of sloppy drafting?

21.2.4 **Trade marks**

TMA 1994 s. 22 declares that a trade mark is personal property. TMA s. 27 states that even a pending application for a trade mark is property. There is a practical reason for such a provision (similar ones appear in the RDA and in the Patents Act) in that a business that is undergoing a sale or merger may want to transfer all of its rights, regardless of whether these have matured to registration. Nonetheless, this conflicts with the spirit and implication of s. 2 TMA which declares that 'a registered trade mark is a property right obtained by the registration of the trade mark under the Act'—which implies that the property right is only created by the act of registration.

The TMA provides for there to be co-ownership of a trade mark. Section 23 of the 1994 Act declares that co-ownership of a trade mark creates a tenancy in common subject to any agreement to the contrary.

21.2.4.1 Assignment of trade marks

Article 22 of the 2015 EU Trade Marks Directive covers assignment of trade marks. In line with this, s. 24(1) TMA states that trade marks are transmissible in the same way as other forms of personal property; and can be assigned with or without the goodwill of the business (acknowledging the fact that TMs are the only IP right that come with some notion of reputation or brand identity). The House of Lords in *CIR v Muller & Co's Margarine Ltd* [1901] AC 217 explained the meaning of 'goodwill' as 'the attractive force which brings in custom' and 'that which distinguishes an old business from a new'. Section 24(2) TMA provides that a partial assignment of a trade mark is possible, either as to some of the goods or services, as to locality or as to manner of use. Unregistered trade marks must still be assigned with the goodwill of the business. This has been confirmed in *Iliffe News & Media Ltd v Commissioners for HM Revenue & Customs* [2012] UKFTT 696 (TC).

There is no mechanism for objecting to deceptive assignments, either by individuals or at the instance of the Registry. Moreover, the CJEU's ruling in Case C-259/04 *Emanuel v Continental Shelf 128 Ltd* [2006] ECR I-3089 indicates that revocations of trade marks are not possible on the ground of deception. The Court said that under EU law 'deceptive' means that the mark must objectively deceive as a result of its inherent qualities. Consequently, where the trade mark was a person's name and had been assigned as part of the business, it did not deceive the public even if it created the mistaken impression that that person took part in the creation of the goods for which the mark was used.

The formalities for the assignment of a trade mark are to be found in s. 24(3). This requires a written document signed by the assignor. More importantly, s. 25 requires the transaction to be recorded on the Register. As with other types of intellectual property, failure to record an assignment exposes the assignee to the risk of a *bona fide* purchaser for value and the inability to claim costs in any post-assignment infringement action.

21.2.4.2 Licensing of trade marks

The current UK provisions on licensing of trade marks must be read in line with Art. 25 of the 2015 EU Trade Marks Directive. The formalities for trade mark licences are to be found in the UK TMA s. 28(2). In contrast to patents and copyright, the TMA requires *all* licences to be in writing. Section 28(3) provides for the licence to bind any successor to the licensor, unless there is an agreement to the contrary. Sub-licences may also be granted 'where the licence so provides' (s. 28(4)). Section 25(2) requires 'all registrable transactions' (which includes licences) to be entered on the register. The sanctions for failing to record are threefold: first, the transaction will be ineffective against a subsequent *bona fide* purchaser; second, the procedural rights given to the licensee by ss. 30 and 31 will not be available; and third, (in accordance with the Enforcement Directive) no costs may be awarded in subsequent litigation for acts of infringement committed between the date of the transaction and the date of registration (s. 25(3) and (4) as amended). Section 25(1) contemplates that it will be the licensee who applies to record the licence (which reflects the sanctions for failing to record) although application may also be made 'by any other person claiming to be affected by such transaction'.

The TMA draws a distinction between exclusive and non-exclusive licensees, 'exclusive licensee' being defined by s. 29 in orthodox language. Section 31 confers procedural rights on the exclusive licensee (in effect to bring infringement proceedings in their own name) whilst other licensees are given lesser rights by s. 30, i.e. to bring proceedings in their own name only after the proprietor has refused a request to sue on behalf of the licensee. Despite both provisions treating the licensee as if they were the owner of the mark, orthodox theory is that trade mark licences do not give any proprietary rights to the licensee but simply confer personal rights which prevent the licensee from being sued for infringement: *Northern & Shell plc v Condé Nast & National Magazine Distributors Ltd* The 2015 EU Trade Marks Directive states that licensees can only bring infringement proceedings where the TM owner consents; although exclusive licensees can bring an action if the owner fails to take a case within an appropriate time frame.

One unresolved question is whether unregistered trade marks can be licensed. There are *obiter* remarks both at first instance and in the Court of Appeal in *GE Trade Mark* [1969] RPC 418 at p. 454 (Graham J) and [1970] RPC 339 at p. 391 (Cross LJ) the consensus being that a licence does not render an unregistered trade mark invalid.

Pause for reflection

Would it be a good idea for all intellectual property legislation to provide (like the TMA) that all licences should be made in writing?

Consider our problem scenario—is there anything in the facts that would affect the validity of the trade mark licence agreed between Sylvia and Funtime Parks?

21.3 Statutory provisions: A lack of consistency

A key inconsistency in this area concerns the statutory provisions on employees which differ from one right to another. In the case of the Community design right, the employer owns the right if the employee did the work 'in the execution of his duties or following the instructions given by his employer'. For copyright, the rule is (as mentioned earlier) framed in much more general language, namely that certain works (but not all works) created 'in the course of employment' belong to the employer 'subject to an agreement to the contrary'. With unregistered design right, s. 215 CDPA uses the same words as s. 11(2) but does not mention the ability to 'contract out' of the basic rule. As the appearance of an article might be protected simultaneously under both copyright and unregistered design right, this lack of consistency could cause practical problems. By contrast, with respect to patents, the provisions in the Patents Act dealing with employee–inventors are stated to be 'notwithstanding anything in any rule of law' which appears to oust any common law rules on ownership. The criteria for when an invention is owned by the employer are set out with far greater precision than in copyright and could well produce a different outcome where creative activity at work leads to both types of right being created.

There are similar discrepancies with regard to co-ownership and even more inconsistencies with regard to how the various intellectual property rights are to be licensed. Moreover, the consequences for failing to comply with the statutory provisions are not what they appear at first glance. The Patents Act s. 30(6) declares that failure to comply with its requirements renders the transaction 'void' and the CDPA s. 90(3) states that non-compliance renders it 'ineffective'; it is unclear whether these two words have identical meaning in law. However, it is still possible that the defective disposal can take effect in equity.

 Pause for reflection

As Vaver notes (in 'Reforming Intellectual Property Law: An Obvious and Not-So-Obvious Agenda: The Stephen Stewart Memorial Lecture for 2008' [2009] 1 *IPQ* 143) the rules on ownership, transfer, and licensing of intellectual property rights require rationalization. They need to be clear and identical wherever possible, and there should be consistency of terminology. With regard to the last point, Vaver says, there is a labelling problem. For example, legislation may refer to either the 'owner', 'proprietor', or 'holder' of the right and it is unclear whether being an owner differs from being a proprietor or a holder. Only an appellate court could provide a definitive answer. As we have encountered, the legislation in this area is riddled with terms that are used interchangeably yet are not of identical legal meaning. This put the courts—as well as those studying IP law—in a difficult position. We must use our legal reasoning to determine what the most probably interpretation will be. Would a new, overarching IP statute help here, or are there simply too many legal factors (UK law, EU law, the European Patent Convention) to achieve consistency across all IP rights?

21.4 Intellectual property transactions and the internal market

One of the challenges facing the CJEU over the last four decades has been to reconcile the territorial nature of intellectual property rights with the concept of the EU internal market in which all 28 Member States—at least until Brexit when the UK will depart from the EU—are treated as a single entity. What emerged as the key to understanding the relationship between Art. 34 of the Treaty on the Functioning of the European Union ('TFEU') (formerly Art. 28 EC) which contains the principle of the free movement of goods and Art. 36 TFEU (formerly Art. 30 EC) which provides for a derogation from this in order to protect intellectual property is the factual distinction between infringing imports and parallel imports. Put simply, the importation of infringing products can always be stopped by the intellectual property owner because such goods undermine the specific subject matter of the right (Case C-317/91 *Deutsche Renault AG v Audi AG* [1993] ECR I-6227); by contrast parallel importation of goods first marketed by the intellectual property owner elsewhere within the EU cannot be prevented (subject to certain specific exceptions), as this amounts to a disguised restriction on trade: Case 15/74 *Centrafarm BV v Sterling Drug* and Case 16/74 *Centrafarm v Winthrop* [1974] ECR 1183.

21.4.1 Assignment and licensing of intellectual property rights and the free movement of goods

As a result of the CJEU's case law, imports originating from an assignee or licensee of the intellectual property right in the exporting Member State now receive different treatment. In light of Brexit, it will be necessary to consider how these rules apply, depending on the final agreement reached between the UK and EU.

21.4.1.1 Article 30 TFEU and intellectual property assignments

Early CJEU case law on IP assignments was not always clear on property issues. The modern approach, which began to correct this, can be traced to Case 19/84 *Pharmon v Hoechst* [1985] ECR 2281, a case concerned with the compulsory licensing of patents. For the first time the CJEU considered the question of whether the intellectual property owner had consented to the marketing of goods, holding that because the goods had been put into circulation in the Member State of export without the agreement of the patentee, the patentee could object to their importation into another Member State.

In Case C-10/89 *SA CNL-Sucal NV v Hag GF AG* [1990] ECR I-3711 ('*Hag II*') the Court accepted that an involuntary assignment broke the connection between the original owner and the intellectual property right in question; and in Case C-9/93 *IHT Internationale Heiztechnik GmbH v Ideal-Standard GmbH* [1994] ECR I-2789 it was held that a voluntary assignment of an intellectual property right has the same effect. The net effect of *Ideal Standard* is therefore that where one of several parallel trade mark registrations is assigned in Member State A to an unrelated company, that will break the connection with the original trade mark owner based in Member State B. Both assignor and assignee can therefore keep the other's branded products out of their respective territories. Because they are independent legal entities with no economic connection to the other, neither has consented to the goods being put into circulation in the Member State of export. However, the Court added (at [59]) that where two businesses enter into a series of trade mark assignments with a view to partitioning the internal market, such an arrangement would breach EU competition law, so that it is necessary to analyse the context, the commitments underlying the assignment, the intention of the parties, and the consideration for the assignment in deciding whether it was a collusive bargain.

21.4.1.2 Article 30 TFEU and intellectual property licences

Licences of intellectual property rights are permission to use the right in question. Consequently, the intellectual property owner has given consent to the use of the right so that the right becomes exhausted on first sale of the goods anywhere in the European Econmic Area ('EEA'). To seek to use a trade mark to prevent the importation of goods marketed under licence elsewhere within the EEA partitions the internal market along national boundaries and so is an abusive exercise of the right: Cases 56 & 58/64 *Consten & Grundig v Commission* [1966] ECR 299. Further, it doesn't matter whether first marketing was carried out by a licensee or an associated company of the intellectual property owner: although the doctrine of corporate personality might suggest that holding and subsidiary companies are to be treated as separate undertakings, for the purposes of the free movement of goods they are to be regarded as a single entity (*Centrafarm v Winthrop*).

The defence of exhaustion of rights applies equally to the sale of patented products (Case 15/74 *Centrafarm BV v Sterling Drug* [1974] ECR 1147) and the sale (but not rental or exhibition) of copyright works (Case 78/70 *Deutsche Grammophon v Metro-SB-Grossmärkte* [1971] ECR 487).

21.4.1.3 Trade mark licences and quality control

In the context of trade mark licences 'quality control' is usually important (it was argued in *Scandecor* that failure to supervise the licensee might affect the ability of the trade mark to remain on the register). However, a recent CJEU case has shown that the presence of quality control provisions in a trade mark licence may give the trade mark owner enhanced powers in the context of the free movement of goods.

Case C-59/08 *Copad SA v Christian Dior Couture SA* [2009] ECR I-3421 shows that breach of the terms of a licence (at least one involving luxury goods) may entitle the proprietor to sue the licensee under EU trade mark law because the quality of the goods might be affected. Further, because of the quality control clause, the licence does not amount to absolute and unconditional consent so that there can be no exhaustion of rights.

Pause for reflection

Does the *Copad* decision undermine the fundamental principle found in *Centrafarm v Winthrop* that marketing by a licensee anywhere in the EEA exhausts the intellectual property right?

21.5 Intellectual property transactions and competition law

21.5.1 General remarks

It is beyond the scope of this book to deal in depth with the application of competition law to intellectual property. What follows, therefore, is no more than a very general overview. A more detailed account can be found in chapter 12 of A. Jones and B.E. Sufrin, *EU Competition Law*.

As Anderman explains (in chapter 1 of *The Interface between Intellectual Property Rights and Competition Policy*), competition policy and intellectual property rights have evolved historically as two separate systems of law, each with its own goals and the means of achieving those goals. Each has the common goal of promoting innovation and economic growth, but intellectual property law seeks to do this by granting exclusive rights, whilst competition law seeks to do this by regulating commercial agreements and monopolies in order to maintain effective competition. He further points out (in chapter 2 of the same) that historically there was a period when a misunderstanding of intellectual property rights led the EU competition authorities to place unduly strict limits on the exercise of such rights. A particular example of this was in the area of patent licensing. More recently, he says, a more realistic approach has been adopted and there is express recognition of the positive contribution which intellectual property rights make to competition.

21.5.2 **EU and national law**

EU competition law is a product of the decisions of the EU Commission under its original task of applying Arts 101 and 102 TFEU (formerly Arts 81 and 82 EC). In turn, judicial review of these decisions, initially by the ECJ, and then by the General Court generated a considerable body of jurisprudence. Such case law has been supplemented by secondary legislation (in the shape of Regulations), in particular those dealing with frequently encountered types of restrictive agreements.

Centralized enforcement of EU competition law proved to be costly and time-consuming, especially once the 2004 enlargement of the EU was contemplated. The Council of Ministers therefore adopted Regulation 1/2003 on the implementation of the rules on competition laid down in Arts 81 and 82 of the Treaty ([2003] OJ L1/1) in order to decentralize the enforcement of competition law. It gives a greater role to national competition authorities and the courts of Member States. As Jones and Sufrin observe, the Regulation entails the voluntary surrender of some of the Commission's powers. The other major impact of the Regulation was to replace the centralized notification and authorization system and to make the whole of Arts 101 and 102 directly applicable.

UK competition law is to be found in the Competition Act 1998 which came into force on 1 March 2000. The Act introduced EU competition law principles into domestic law. It contains provisions parallel to Arts 101 and 102 TFEU, namely Chapter I prohibitions (dealing with restrictive agreements) and Chapter II prohibitions (dealing with the abuse of dominant position).

21.5.3 **Restrictive agreements**

Article 101 TFEU prohibits as incompatible with the internal market all agreements, decisions, and concerted practices between undertakings which may affect trade between Member States and which have as their object or effect the prevention, restriction, or distortion of competition. The Commission (and EU courts) have generally adopted a broad interpretation of the key words in the Article.

21.5.3.1 Vertical and horizontal restraints

One fundamental issue is the difference between vertical and horizontal restraints. This involves an analysis of the position of the parties in the relevant product market. Are they on the same level in the chain of manufacture and supply of goods or services or not? If they are on the same level and so are in effect competitors (for example both are manufacturers) then any agreement between them is a horizontal agreement. The most obvious example of a horizontal agreement would be a cartel under which the parties agree to price fixing or market sharing. If, however, the parties are not on the same level (for example one is a manufacturer and the other is a retailer) then the agreement is a vertical one. The premise of competition law is that agreements between competitors are likely to be more dangerous than agreements between non-competitors. It was assumed in the early days of competition law that intellectual property licences, normally being vertical agreements, would be unobjectionable. It therefore came as a shock when the CJEU held in *Consten & Grundig v Commission* that vertical agreements could be void under Art. 101 TFEU. The Court held that intellectual property licences which use the territorial nature of the right in question (here a trade mark) to partition the internal market by reinforcing national boundaries in order to shield the licensee from price competition from parallel importers was a prohibited restrictive agreement.

21.5.3.2 Patent licences

In the case of patent licences, the policy of the EU Commission has changed significantly over the years. It will be useful first to consider the sorts of clauses which a patentee would wish to insert in a patent licence.

First, and fundamentally, there will be a transfer of technology. The patent may be combined with know-how (i.e. how to exploit the technology more efficiently) or with related software, trade marks, copyrights, and/or designs. Whatever the exact subject matter of the licence, it will grant permission to use the intellectual property rights concerned, although this may be limited to a particular 'field of use' (for example, the use of a patented process to make one particular type of product). In return for this permission, the licensee will undertake to pay royalties, which may be periodic or by way of lump sum. The calculation of such royalties is a matter for negotiation, but, for example, there may be a clause stating that a minimum royalty is payable in any event.

The licensor may want to insert other provisions which are essential to protect their interest in the patent, such as an obligation on the licensee to use their best endeavours to promote the patented product, a duty not to sublicense, and to assist with the pursuit of infringers. In return, the licensee may demand that they be made an exclusive licensee, particularly if the start-up costs of the manufacturing process are considerable. Alongside exclusivity will be the geographic territory of the licence: it may be worldwide, but given the territorial nature of intellectual property rights, is more likely to be confined to a particular country. One particular aspect of territorial protection is that it may be reinforced by a contractual term banning the licensee from exporting from the territory (an active ban) or from responding to potential customers from outside the territory (a passive ban).

Other provisions might oblige the licensee to grant back to the licensor any improvements which are made to the invention: such 'grant-back' obligations could be by way of an assignment, or an exclusive or non-exclusive licence. The licensor may also seek to impose a 'tie-in', that is to require the licensee to purchase particular ingredients from them. Such products may be either essential or non-essential to the exploitation of the patent. There may be a clause prohibiting the licensee from challenging the validity of the patent (an obvious temptation because if the patent is invalid the information it contains is public knowledge and so theoretically free for anyone to use). There may be a desire to prolong the duration of the licence beyond the lifetime of the youngest patent, although this type of clause should be distinguished from a provision which obliges the licensee to keep know-how secret after the licence has ended. Last, the licensor may attempt to impose restrictions on the licensee's freedom to trade by, for example, fixing prices or dictating their choice of retail outlets.

In a series of decisions taken during the 1970s, the EU Commission held that a number of favourite provisions were restrictions on competition, namely: the grant-back of improvements unless by means of non-exclusive licence; 'tie-ins' for non-essential goods; 'no challenge' clauses; prolongation of the licence beyond life of the youngest patent; and restrictions on freedom to trade. It was, however, accepted by the CJEU that exclusivity could be justified under certain circumstances. In Case 258/78 *Nungesser v Commission* [1982] ECR 2015 the Court adopted a far less strict approach than the Commission, taking into account economic considerations and the need to encourage new technology (in this case the development of new varieties of maize).

Since 1984, there have been a number of EU Regulations granting block exemption from Art. 101(3) for patent licences which comply with certain requirements. A Block Exemption does not provide the parties with a standardized agreement; rather it lists those clauses which are acceptable under competition law and those which are not. The latest Technology Transfer Block Exemption Regulation ('TTBER') is Commission Regulation (EU) No 651/2014 of 17 June 2014 declaring certain categories of aid compatible with the internal market in application of Arts 107 and 108 of the Treaty Text with EEA relevance. It includes software and designs as well as patents and know-how. The basic premise of the TTBER (which applies only to bilateral agreements) is to draw a distinction between agreements between competitors and agreements between non-competitors. It will only apply to exempt licences from breach of competition law where certain market thresholds are not exceeded.

21.5.3.3. Trade mark licences

Unlike patent licenses, trade mark licences have not attracted as much attention from the EU Commission, but when considering the competition law aspects, the difference between horizontal and vertical agreements must be kept in mind.

One particular category of horizontal trade mark agreement is a trade mark delimitation agreement. This is an agreement entered into in order to settle litigation, particularly where one party opposes or objects to the use of an allegedly confusingly similar trade mark. A number of Commission decisions on such contracts culminated in the CJEU's ruling in Case 35/83 *BAT Cigaretten-Fabriken GmbH v Commission* [1985] ECR 363. Here the Court stated that an agreement will be outside Art. 101 if there is a genuine risk of confusion and the agreement does not attempt to divide markets within the EU. The subsequent enactment of the Trade Marks Directive means that there is now a harmonized approach to when there is a likelihood of confusion, but nevertheless, the encouragement to settle litigation found in the UK's Civil Procedure Rules has to be balanced against the impact of competition law.

One particular type of trade mark vertical agreement which did attract the Commission's attention is a franchising agreement. Franchise agreements relate to the licence of particular business methods, enabling the franchisor to set up a uniform network for the distribution of goods or services (for example photocopy shops, hairdressers, or pizza shops). The franchisee is enabled to set up business with an established entrepreneur using a tried and tested format. Franchise agreements were considered by the CJEU in Case 161/84 *Pronuptia de Paris GmbH v Schillgallis* [1986] ECR 353 where it was held that two clauses essential to franchise agreements did not amount to a restriction on competition. These were a ban on the franchisee opening a shop of a similar nature for a reasonable period after the end of the contract; and selling the shop without the franchisor's consent. Similarly, other clauses such as laying out the premises in a particular manner, only selling approved products, and getting all advertising approved did not fall within Art. 101.

Although there was subsequently a Block Exemption dealing with franchise agreements, these now fall within the Vertical Restraints Block Exemption, the latest version of which is Commission Regulation 330/2010 of 20 April 2010 [2010] OJ L 102/1, effective 1 June 2010. The Regulation also applies to selective distribution agreements. Like the TTBER, the Vertical Restraints Block Exemption uses a market share test (Arts 3 and 9), below which threshold vertical restraints are presumed to be beneficial to competition (Recital 6), as long as they do not contain certain prohibited clauses (listed in Arts 4 and 5). Agreements not satisfying the Regulation will fall outside its protection. Certain types of provision are considered to render the agreement non-exemptable, including retail price maintenance, cross-supply restrictions, and customer allocation to a given distributor.

Because of the combined effect of the TTBER and the Vertical Restraints Block Exemption, the only trade mark licences not covered by Block Exemptions are those involving merchandising agreements. These presumably would still fall within the scope of Art. 101 TFEU if restrictive of competition.

21.5.3.4 Copyright licences

There have been few decisions on copyright licences, although it is clear that any agreement which partitions the market along territorial boundaries may fall within Art. 101 TFEU: Case 19/77 *Miller International Schallplatten GmbH v Commission* [1978] ECR 131; Case 262/81 *Coditel v Cine Vog (No. 2)* [1982] ECR 3381.

 Pause for reflection

Does the treatment of intellectual property licences under Art. 101 TFEU and the various Block Exemptions recognize, in Anderman's words, the positive contribution which intellectual property rights make to competition?

21.5.4 **Abuse of dominant position**

Article 102 TFEU declares that any abuse by one or more undertakings of a dominant position within the internal market or in a substantial part of it shall be prohibited as incompatible with the internal market in so far as it may affect trade between Member States. It goes on to list particular forms of abuse, such as directly or indirectly imposing unfair purchase or selling prices or other unfair trading conditions; limiting production, markets, or technical development to the prejudice of consumers; applying dissimilar conditions to equivalent transactions with other trading parties, thereby placing them at a competitive disadvantage; and making the conclusion of contracts subject to acceptance by the other parties of supplementary obligations which, by their nature or according to commercial usage, have no connection with the subject of such contracts. The application of Art. 102 to intellectual property rights requires consideration of three separate issues.

21.5.4.1 Ownership of intellectual property rights

It was held by the CJEU at a fairly early stage of the development of competition law that mere ownership of an intellectual property right did not breach Art. 102 because of the negative nature of the right: Case 24/67 *Parke Davis v Probel* [1968] ECR 55. Therefore, although ownership of a patent, copyright, design, or trade mark confers a statutory monopoly, this is not the same as an economic monopoly and does not mean that its owner is in a dominant position. However, how the owner chooses to exploit that right may well have implications under competition law.

21.5.4.2 Refusal to license

More relevant to Art. 102 is if the proprietor declines to deal with potential licensees (the terms of any licence actually granted will fall under Art. 101). The CJEU held in Case 238/87 *Volvo v Veng* [1988] ECR 6211 that a refusal to license copyright in relation to car replacement parts was not automatically a breach of Art. 102 but might be in certain circumstances, depending on the nature of the proprietor's conduct and whether that was abusive; for example, whether it was arbitrary, whether unfair prices were charged, and whether there was a continuation of supply of parts for out-of-date models.

Refusal to license was given a much more detailed examination by the CJEU in Case C-241–242/91P *RTE v Commission (Magill Intervening)* [1995] ECR I-743. The refusal of three broadcasting organizations in the 1980s (the BBC, ITV, and RTE) to license Magill so that he could publish a multi-channel TV guide (common in mainland Europe but at the time unusual in the UK and Ireland) was held to be a breach of EU competition law. The Court did not deny that the organizations had copyright in their respective lists of programmes but did hold, in effect, that such copyright was secondary to the broadcasters' main product, television programmes, and that they were using their market power to stifle the publication of a new product for which there was public demand. One might speculate that the hidden message of the case was that the Court considered the threshold for copyright protection in the UK and Ireland was too low, but did not have the jurisdiction to comment on the point.

The Court revisited the issue of when a refusal to license copyright can amount to an abuse of dominant position in Case C-418/01 *IMS Health GmbH v NDC Health GmbH* [2004] ECR I-5039. The case concerned IMS' alleged copyright in a database of regional sales information about pharmaceutical products and its refusal to license others. The CJEU declared that three conditions had to be satisfied before a refusal to license copyright was a breach of Art. 102 TFEU. First, the undertaking requesting the licence must intend to offer new products not offered by the copyright owner and for which there was a potential consumer demand; second, the refusal could not be justified by objective considerations; last, the refusal had to have the effect of eliminating all the copyright owner's competitors in that market.

21.5.4.3 Collecting societies

Certain copyrights (particularly music) are usually managed on behalf of authors by collecting societies. For a composer to have to obtain royalties from someone who controls premises each time a piece of music is performed on those premises would be manifestly inconvenient. In the UK, wherever you see the sign 'PRS for Music' at a business—e.g. restaurant, bar, gym, venue—you can be certain that business has paid the appropriate licence to PRS for Music, the UK's umbrella body for collecting licences for the Performing Rights Society (PRS) (which collects for composers), and Phonographic Performance Limited (PPL) (which collects on behalf of record companies).

Copyright collecting societies tend to be territorial, and so deal with particular categories of copyright work within a particular country, although there exists a network of reciprocal arrangements between various European societies whereby royalties are collected on behalf of each other's members. Of concern under Art. 102 are the terms on which membership is provided and on which copyright is licensed to potential users. As Rosenblatt explains (in 'Copyright Assignments: Rights and Wrongs—the Collecting Societies' Perspective' [2000] 2 *IPQ* 187) collective administration, in contrast to individual copyright agreements, may not offer the most favourable terms to every right holder in every circumstance, nor to every user. The majority of European collective societies operate on an exclusive basis, usually acquiring the rights they administer by way of assignment.

In *Re GEMA* [1971] CMLR D35, the Commission decided that the German copyright collecting society had infringed competition law because its membership rules tied authors to it for too long a period and in respect of too many rights. Cases decided by the CJEU include Case 127/73 *Belgische Radio en Televisie v SABAM* [1974] ECR 51 where the Court recognized the benefits of collective administration but emphasized the need for collecting societies, when drafting their membership rules, to take account of all interests and to try to balance the needs of authors and composers with effective management of their rights.

The relationship between copyright collecting societies and those wishing to exploit the works has been considered by the CJEU in a number of referrals to it by national courts under Art. 267 TFEU. In Case 22/79 *Greenwich Films v SACEM* [1979] ECR 3275 the Court suggested that the activities of SACEM (the principal French copyright collecting society) should be considered in their totality as their licensing system as a whole might be considered to partition the internal market, even with regard to the granting of extra-territorial licences. SACEM's policy with regard to the licensing of music for use in discothèques has been the subject of extensive litigation in France, culminating with the referral to the CJEU in Cases 395/87 and 241–242/88 *Ministère Public v Tournier; Lucazeau v SACEM* [1989] ECR 2521, 2811. The Court stated that the imposition of significantly higher royalties on specific forms of exploitation might be evidence of the abuse of a dominant position unless the royalty rate could be objectively justified. In Case C-52/07 *Kanal 5 Ltd, TV 4 AB v Föreningen Svenska Tonsättares Internationella Musikbyrå (STIM) upa* [2008] ECR I-9275, it was held that there was no breach of competition law where the remuneration model for commercial TV channels was based partly on the channels' revenue (i.e. it was a flat rate reflecting the commercial success of that channel) unless there was another means of identifying more precisely which musical works had been broadcast, as long as this did not involve disproportionate costs. However, the society might breach Art. 102 if it treated commercial and public sector broadcasters differently where they were in fact offering equivalent services, unless this different treatment could be objectively justified. In all of these cases, it should be remembered that the CJEU was giving advice to the application of EU competition law by national competition authorities, so of necessity the conclusions as to the status of collecting societies under Art. 102 tend to be expressed in general terms. These issues must be considered in light of the 2014 EU Directive on collective management: Commission Regulation (EU) No. 651/2014 of 17 June 2014 declaring certain categories of aid compatible with the internal market in application of Arts 107 and 108 of the Treaty Text with EEA relevance.

21.5.5 **Summary**

EU competition law, by means of Arts 101 and 102 TFEU, controls the ways in which intellectual property rights may be licensed and managed. Of necessity, this law is complex and highly specialized and is driven by the need to achieve the 'level playing field' of the internal market.

21.6 **Alternative licensing models: Free and open-source licensing and creative commons**

Kelty remarks that alternative licensing systems 'rely on the existence of intellectual property (IP) to create and maintain the "commons" . . . even as they occupy a position of challenge or resistance to the dominant forms of intellectual property' (C. Kelty, 'Punt to Culture' [2004] 77 *Anthropological Quarterly* 547). In other words, alternative licensing systems do not follow the standard terms of IP licences—they allow them to be tailored to suit individual creators or communities of creators.

Copyright has been the area most impacted by alternative licensing. The most well-known system of alternative licensing is free and open-source software ('FOSS'). The iconic FOSS licence is the GNU General Public Licence ('GPL'), now in version 3.0, and since the 1990s it has allowed the creators of FOSS to release their Linux software with 'open-source' code. FOSS licences work in the following way: the person who creates the software in the first instance has the right, as the IP-owner, to license the work as that person sees fit. FOSS operates to facilitate linked authorship—at each point, every new creator/collaborator who produces new original modifications to the code must license these new modifications onwards. Therefore, FOSS licences make subversive use of IP law concepts to facilitate a community of shared creativity, rather than a profit-based one.

The most prominent attempt to bring the ethos of FOSS to other cultural fields is the Creative Commons ('CC') licence. CC provides an alternative copyright licence for a wide range of creative works, including music, film, and literature, enabling creators to use licensing to claim 'some rights reserved' rather than 'all rights reserved'. Under a CC licence, copyright in the work typically remains with the author, but the author can choose one of the CC licences in order to regulate further uses of the work by others. The core terms of a CC licence are: attribution, non-commercial reproduction, and derivative use. For instance, it is possible for an author to retain only the attribution right, and to allow (or disallow) commercial uses of the work. By contrast, it is possible to restrict all uses of the work except non-commercial distribution.

 Pause for reflection

In terms of enforceability, several courts, including those in the US and the Netherlands, have accepted alternate licences, such as FOSS and CC, as being legally valid (US case of *Jacobsen v Katser* 535 F. 3d 1373 Fd. Cir. (2008) and the Dutch case of *Curry v Audax* Case no. 334492/KG 06-176 SR (March, 2006)).

→

> Nonetheless, alternative licences still pose some legal difficulties. For example, under FOSS and CC licences works are protected by the underlying copyright law, but are licensed contractually under a set of terms chosen by the licensor. In this context, the question of what each term — e.g. 'commercial use' — means is crucial. To take this one example, CC defines 'commercial use' as use exercised 'in any manner that is primarily intended for, or directed toward, commercial advantage or private monetary compensation'. Yet, different jurisdictions may interpret and define 'commercial use' in their own ways, which means that the line between 'commercial' and 'non-commercial' may not always be clear to users. The same is true of terms used in FOSS licences. Until we get more case law we cannot be certain what legal weight these terms have (L. McDonagh, 'FOSS and Alternative Licensing in the United Kingdom: Assessing the Dual Importance of Contract Law and Copyright Law,' in A. Metzger (ed.), *Free and Open Source Software (FOSS) and other Alternative Licensing Models—A Comparative Analysis of the Main Legal Issues* (Springer, 2016), 461–76).

21.7 Conclusion

In this chapter we have considered two key forms of dealing in IP rights: (i) assignment (usually a permanent transfer of ownership in the IP right), and (ii) licensing (permission to use, can be exclusive or non-exclusive, and is typically time-limited). To comprehend these categories, we have explored the UK statutory provisions which govern such dealings, and we considered the arguments typically used to challenge the validity of certain transactions. We also looked at how European Union law on free movement of goods affects dealings in intellectual property rights, and how competition law, whether national or EU, may also be of relevance.

To begin the analysis of our problem scenario there are three agreements we need to deal with—the contract between Sylvia and her first publisher Rylance Books, beginning 1 January 2009 for a ten-year period thereafter; the agreement between Sylvia and the Readymade Theatre Company beginning 1 January 2015 and ending 31 December 2016; and the '360 degree' contract between Sylvia and her second publisher Fashionista Media, beginning 1 January 2018.

Having studied the requirements of authorship and originality under the CDPA in the prior chapters, we can say with confidence that Sylvia is the author and first owner of her works. As such, she has the right to license or assign the works as she sees fit (ss. 90–95 CDPA). From what we have learned in this chapter, the first agreement she signs, with Rylance Books, seems unproblematic: it clearly states it is an exclusive licence (in line with CDPA s. 92), so we know that she is licensing the works, not assigning; it is clear about the fee and royalty rate levels; and furthermore, it states that the licence agreement is for a limited period of ten years from 1 January 2009 (to 31 December 2018).

The second agreement, between Sylvia and Readymade, is not as straightforward. This involves the adaptation right in the CDPA s. 21 as it involves adapting or transforming Sylvia's book (a literary work) into a stage play (a dramatic work), as well as the right of performance (CDPA s 21). On the plus side, the licence is time-limited, which gives clarity as to how long the stage production can last. However, the provision on the resulting dramatic work—the play—is more complex. It states that the resulting play (dramatic work) will be the property of Sylvia, except for any new original content added by Readymade, such as new characters and set design, which will belong to Readymade. When we consider what we learned about originality (*Infopaq*, *Meltwater*), adaptations/arrangements (*Fisher v Brooker*) and joint authorship of theatrical works (*Brighton v Jones*) in prior chapters, we can see that the important character Sam Sunderland, added to the stage version by Readymade, will not be owned by Sylvia. Crucially, she is not the author of that character, and the agreement she signed appears to give those rights to the creators at Readymade.

This has a knock-on effect on her third agreement, with Fashionista Media. Sylvia cannot license the forthcoming 'Sam Sunderland' books to Fashionista because she does not own the character. For this she will have to obtain a licence from the owners of the character—Readymade—which may mean sharing the royalties with them. By agreeing this licence with Fashionista, Sylvia is breaching copyright law, and she leaves herself open to an accusation of copyright infringement by Readymade. The same goes for any other elements, including stage design, that were created by Readymade—copyright in these vests in Readymade and if any of Sylvia's future stage shows copy their design, she may be liable unless she obtains a licence from them. There is a further problem with the contract with Fashionista—Sylvia has granted Fashionista the right to publish her works from 1 January 2018. But by 1 January 2018 there will still be one year of her original, exclusive publishing licensing agreement with Rylance Books left. This means that the new agreement breaches the earlier one, leaving Sylvia open to court action by Rylance for breaching the terms of the licence.

Finally, the trade mark licence agreed by Sylvia with Funtime Parks plc will be invalid as it is not in writing—as required by TMA s. 28. In addition, with respect to the copyright elements of her agreement with Funtime, prior to this she agreed an exclusive merchandising deal with Fashionista, and thus the copyright elements of the licence she agreed with Funtime are in breach of the earlier agreement with Fashionista, leaving her open to further legal action.

Having unpacked this complex scenario the best advice to give Sylvia is as follows: (i) Sylvia should obtain a licence from Readymade for 'Sam Sunderland' and any other elements she wishes to use in future works/adaptations; (ii) she should delay her new deal with Fashionista until 1 January 2019, when her original publishing licence will expire; (iii) she ought to conclude a written trade mark licence with Funtime Parks plc; (iv) she should agree a deal between Funtime and Fashionista to share revenues generated from merchandise at the theme park so that all three parties are clear about their legal rights and responsibilities.

End-of-chapter questions

After reading the chapter carefully, try answering the questions which follow. If you would like to know what we think visit the online resources at **www.oup.com/uk/karapapa-mcdonagh/**

1. Read through the sample agreement in Appendix II. What are the key terms it uses? Can you think of any ways you could improve it?

2. How could you tell, from reading a legal agreement between two parties, whether it is intended to cover a full assignment of rights, or a mere licence? Look again at the sample agreement in Appendix II.

3. How does open-source licensing provide a challenge to the traditional standard licence agreement?

Further reading

Anderman, S.D. The Interface between Intellectual Property Rights and Competition Policy (Cambridge University Press, 2007)
The book surveys the relationship between competition policy and intellectual property rights in the major trading blocks of the world (the EU, USA, and Japan), in some selected smaller economies and also considers some specific issues, including parallel imports, technology transfers, and economic theory.

Brownsword, R. 'Copyright Assignment: Fair Dealing and Unconscionable Contracts' [1998] 3 *IPQ* 311
Discusses the cases where copyright assignments have been set aside.

Firth, A. and Fitzgerald, J. 'Equitable Assignments in Relation to Intellectual Property' [1999] 2 *IPQ* 228
Puts dealings in intellectual property rights into the broader context of legal and equitable assignment of choses in action.

Jones, A. and Sufrin, B. *EU Competition Law: Text, Cases and Materials* (5th edn) (Oxford University Press, 2014)
A detailed account of all aspects of competition law, with chapter 12 dealing with competition law and intellectual property rights.

Kelty, C. 'Punt to Culture' [2004] 77 *Anthropological Quarterly* 547
Takes a theoretical approach to the phenomenon of FOSS.

McDonagh, L. 'FOSS and Alternative Licensing in the United Kingdom: Assessing the Dual Importance of Contract Law and Copyright Law,' in A. Metzger (ed), *Free and Open Source Software (FOSS) and other Alternative Licensing Models—A Comparative Analysis of the Main Legal Issues* (Springer, 2016), 461–476
Considers the application of contract law and copyright law in the context of FOSS.

Rosenblatt, H. 'Copyright Assignments: Rights and Wrongs—the Collecting Societies' Perspective' [2000] 2 *IPQ* 187
Discusses the role of collecting societies in the administration of copyright with reference to the competition law aspects of the contracts with their members.

Vaver, D. 'Reforming Intellectual Property Law: An Obvious and Not-So-Obvious Agenda: The Stephen Stewart Memorial Lecture for 2008' [2009] 1 *IPQ* 143
Considers ways in which United Kingdom intellectual property law could be reformed, with particular reference to formalities for assignment and licensing.

22 Civil and criminal remedies

Problem question

Read this problem question carefully and keep it in mind while you are working through the chapter that follows. At the end of this chapter, you will be able to apply what you have learnt to the problem question and advise the relevant parties.

Gyo Technology is a start-up company that began trading in 2016. Gyo's main business is in the creation of new video gaming apps for smart phones. During 2016 and 2017 their market share increased rapidly but in early 2018 they noticed a sharp decline in sales that they were unable to explain. Then, during March 2018, the head of the design department at Gyo, Dr Matt Barnstrom, discovered that a new game for the smart phone market—'Go Ryde Along'—was being advertised on the London Underground by a new company—Ryde Games. He noticed that the price of the rival game was only half of what Gyo had been charging. Out of curiosity Matt downloaded the game and found it to be almost identical to his own company's 'Gyo Ride' game. He believes that the rival game make unauthorized use of several of Gyo Technology's intellectual property ('IP') rights, including with respect to the game's graphics, characters, and source code and the branding of the game as 'Go Ryde Along' which he believes is very similar to 'Gyo Ride'. He wishes to take prompt legal action against Ryde Games and wishes to know what the appropriate grounds are for the litigation, what venues would be suitable to make the claim, and what remedies are available to his company for the alleged IP infringements.

Advise Matt about the grounds of the action, where he can take his claim and the legal remedies that might apply.

22.1 Introduction

In this chapter, we consider the means available to the owner of an intellectual property right (whether a patent, trade mark, design, or copyright) to obtain redress for infringement. Having examined assignments and licensing in chapter 21—situations where IP owners voluntarily give permission to others to use their IP, typically in return for payment—here we will focus on another practical reason that businesses obtain IP protection, namely to maintain a competitive edge by excluding rivals from utilizing their IP without permission.

When a dispute occurs, IP holders typically approach their legal advisors for assistance in resolving the situation, i.e. undertaking legal action to stop the competitor and/or counterfeiter from using their IP without permission or license. Unless the dispute is settled between the parties out of court, the court must answer a crucial question—if IP infringement has been proven, what redress should the IP owner receive for the violation of the IP owner's exclusive rights?

22.1.1 Remedies for enforcement of intellectual property rights

The law's exclusionary effect typically occurs by means of the claimant IP owner obtaining one or more remedies from a court against the defendant(s). Common remedies include injunctions and monetary compensation in the form of damages/accounts of profit. It is crucial to comprehend that the court, when granting remedies, attempts to strike a balance between the IP holder's rights (as property rights, benefiting the owner) and the principles of free competition (which tend to benefit competitors and consumers). We therefore return in this chapter to one of our recurring themes, namely how to balance the interests of the intellectual property owner with other operators and users in the wider marketplace.

An injunction is granted to prevent IP infringement taking place, either on an interim (preliminary) basis or as a final measure. Damages or accounts of profit are granted to claimant IP owners who have suffered a financial loss, e.g. where there have been lost sales or lost royalties due to a competitor infringing upon the claimant's IP rights. Depending on the circumstances, the court may grant either, or both, injunctive and monetary relief.

As this chapter will show, most remedies are common to all intellectual property rights. Whether the action concerns the infringement of a patent, design, copyright, or trade mark, the relief a successful claimant can obtain is basically the same. Nevertheless, there are a host of minor differences between the available remedies. Directive 2004/48/EC of the European Parliament and of the Council of 29 April 2004 on the enforcement of intellectual property rights [2004] OJ L 157/45 ('the Enforcement Directive') has produced a degree of standardization previously lacking, but equally has raised questions about some well-established principles of UK law. Occasionally, criminal penalties are of relevance to IP cases, as we will consider these as well.

Thus, in this chapter we will consider the contexts in which intellectual property rights are enforced and what remedies available to a claimant before the full trial occurs, and what remedies are available to a successful claimant after there has been a substantive court ruling on infringement.

Pause for reflection

Day, in 'Competition and Piracy' [2018] 1 *Berkeley Technology Law Journal* 32(2), argues that although all IP infringement tends to be considered as 'akin to theft and trespassing' the imposition of compensatory remedies 'squanders the benefits of piracy'. Rather, he argues that an economic framework should be utilized, with an acknowledgement that while infringement can cause economic harm, certain acts of infringement tend to promote innovation and efficiency within the wider economy. However, this interesting idea has yet to take hold within policy circles—likely because it would face considerable opposition from IP rights-holders.

22.1.2 Forum of litigation

Under the Supreme Court Act 1981 (now renamed the Senior Courts Act by the Constitutional Reform Act 2005) actions for the infringement of patents and registered designs are typically allocated to the specialist Patents Court, part of the Chancery Division of the High Court of England and Wales (see s. 6(1)(a), ss. 61, 62, and Sch. 1). Cases involving copyright, trade marks, and unregistered designs can be heard in the general Chancery Division of the High Court but are typically allocated to judges with IP experience.

In addition, there is the Intellectual Property Enterprise Court ('IPEC') (the successor of the former Patents County Court or PCC) (Copyright, Designs and Patents Act 1988 ('CDPA') s. 287), which provides a less costly and more speedy means of litigation for small businesses and individual IP owners (such as photographers). The IPEC, which has a single specialist judge, is also part of the Chancery Division of the High Court of England and Wales and has the same jurisdiction to hear IP cases as the Patents Court/ High Court and can hand down the same remedies.

The IPEC is subdivided into 'multi-track' and 'small claims track'. The IPEC multi-track features a ceiling on the amount of damages/account of profits that can be awarded (£500,000) to claimants, and there is also a limit on the level of costs (£50,000) which can be recovered from the other side. It covers cases involving copyright, trade marks, passing off, and unregistered designs (not patents or registered designs) where the sum claimed is less than £10,000. The transformation of the IPEC from the old PCC was a response to the concerns of the Hargreaves Report and the Jackson Review, both of which noted the high cost of IP litigation, as well as the realization that there were some procedural problems with the old PCC jurisdiction. The reformed IPEC multi-track and SCT have increased access to justice for small to medium-sized enterprises (SMEs) and small-scale IP owners (Christian Helmers, Yassine Lefouili, and Luke McDonagh, 'Evaluation of the Reforms of the Intellectual Property Enterprise Court 2010–2013' (UK Intellectual Property Office, 2015)) as such IP owners now have greater clarity with respect to the length of the action—IPEC cases hearings typically last no more than a single day—as well as their potential costs burden in the event of a loss.

Cases can be transferred between the High Court/Patents Court and the IPEC depending on factors including the size of the parties, the complexity of the claims, the nature of the evidence, and the value of the action. Appeals lie from the High Court/

Patents Court or IPEC to the Court of Appeal. Further appeal to the UK Supreme Court (formerly the House of Lords) is only possible with leave.

 Pause for reflection

What advice would you give to Matt in our problem scenario about which venue—IPEC or the High Court—might best suit a company of his size?

22.1.3 **Choice of defendant**

The statutory rules on infringement impose liability not only on primary infringers of the right in question, such as those who affix trade marks to goods or who make copies of sound recordings and films, but on contributory infringers (those who assist the primary infringer to commit an infringing act, by the pre-manufacture supply of essential materials, equipment, or packaging) and on secondary infringers (those who post-manufacture sell, distribute, or otherwise deal in infringing products by way of trade). An important question for any claimant will therefore be 'whom should I sue'? Tempting though it may be to sue anyone and everyone, a claimant will need to consider likely expense and complexity if there is a large number of defendants.

22.1.3.1 Conduct outside the jurisdiction

Suing importers, wholesalers, or retailers may, however, be necessary where the primary infringer is an overseas undertaking which has manufactured infringing copies abroad, as all the statutory infringement provisions require acts of infringement to be committed within the UK: see the Patents Act 1977 s. 60; the Trade Marks Act 1994 ('TMA') s. 9; and CDPA s. 16. No such restriction appears in s. 7 Registered Designs Act 1949 ('RDA') but common sense would indicate that a UK registered design can be infringed only by conduct committed within the jurisdiction.

Like its predecessor—Council Regulation (EC) No. 44/2001 of 22 December 2000 on Jurisdiction and the Recognition and Enforcement of Judgments in Civil and Commercial Matters [2001] OJ L 12/1—the recast Brussels Regulation (Council Regulation (EU) No. 1215/2012 of 12 December 2012 on Jurisdiction and the Recognition and Enforcement of Judgments in Civil and Commercial Matters [2012] OJ L 351/1) enables UK courts to accept jurisdiction either on the basis of the domicile of the defendant (Art. 4) (previously Art. 2) or the place where the harm was committed (Art. 7) (currently Art. 5). However, in the case of registered intellectual property rights, the wording of Art. 24(4) (previously Art. 22(4)) confers exclusive jurisdiction on the state granting the right (*Coin Controls Ltd v Suzo International (UK) Ltd* [1997] 3 All ER 45). The ability to sue an enterprise before UK courts for infringing conduct committed abroad is therefore limited to copyright infringement and passing off. Thus, in *Pearce v Ove Arup Partnership Ltd* [1999] 1 All ER 769, jurisdiction for copyright infringement allegedly committed in the Netherlands was accepted on the basis of the defendant's domicile as a UK company, although ultimately the defendant was found not to have infringed. In *Mecklermedia Corp v DC Congress GmbH* [1997] 3 WLR 479, jurisdiction was accepted for passing off, where although the misrepresentation had been made in Germany, the harm to goodwill occurred in the UK.

It may, however, be possible for an intellectual property owner to sue for infringement where a primary infringer is located outside the UK, but an undertaking within the jurisdiction arranges for them to make the infringing product. In such a case, the claimant would be able to argue that the overseas defendant is a joint tortfeasor, either by virtue of having induced the infringing act, or because it was party to a common design. So, for example, in *Puschner v Tom Parker (Scotland)* [1989] RPC 430 there was held to be a common design where as part of a joint marketing agreement, the foreign supplier had provided promotional literature to and trained the sales staff of the UK customer. However, the mere supply of infringing goods to a UK purchaser is not enough for this type of liability: 'Each person must make the infringing acts his own' (*Sabaf SpA v Meneghetti* [2003] RPC 264 at [58] (CA)).

22.1.4 Who can sue

It may seem self-evident that an action in respect of the infringement of an intellectual property right can only be brought by its proprietor. Nevertheless, case law is full of examples of claimants failing because they are not the owners of the IP right. Examples include an employee suing for copyright infringement when the work was owned by the employer by virtue of a contract of employment (*Beloff v Pressdram Ltd* [1973] RPC 765) or a widow suing for infringement of copyright in photographs taken by her late husband where it could not be established that she had letters of administration to his estate (*Gabrin v Universal Music Operations Ltd* [2004] ECDR 18). In the case of registrable rights, the relevant register (of patents, designs, or trade marks) should be checked to see that the claimant is actually entered as the owner of the right alleged to have been infringed before the claim form is issued. Any transactions (such as assignments) affecting entitlement to sue must have been recorded (see Patents Act s. 68, TMA s. 25).

All intellectual property legislation (the Patents Act s. 67, TMA s. 31, CDPA s. 101, RDA s. 24) confers the right to commence proceedings on an exclusive licensee of the right. Such right is procedural only and does not confer any proprietary interest (*Northern & Shell plc v Condé Nast & National Magazine Distributors Ltd* [1995] RPC 117). In the case of registrable rights, the existence of the exclusive licence must be entered on the register. As a result of the Enforcement Directive, the penalty for failing to record a licence is that the successful claimant may not be awarded costs, whereas previously the penalty for failing to record a licence promptly was loss of compensatory relief. In the case of copyright, the exclusive licence must be in writing in order for the procedural rights in s. 101 CDPA to be exercised. Subject to certain conditions, similar rights may also be conferred on a non-exclusive licensee under s. 101A.

22.1.5 Statutory basis of relief

For those intellectual property rights which are statute based (that is, copyright, designs, patents, and trade marks), the remedies are prescribed by the relevant statute. These statutes are largely declaratory of prior case law (*Coflexip SA v Stolt Comex Seaway MS Ltd* [2001] 1 All ER 952). Remedies for passing off and breach of confidence (trade secrets) are the result of case law alone and reflect the historical influence of the Court of Chancery over the development of these causes of action.

Pause for reflection

Are there any doubts about whether Matt is the right person to sue Ryde Games? Should he take a claim in his personal capacity or should the claim be in the name of the company?

22.1.6 The effect of the Civil Procedure Rules

The England and Wales Civil Procedure Rules ('CPR') were introduced in 1999. So far as practicable, in giving effect to the overall objective of dealing with cases justly, courts must seek to:

- ensure that the parties are on an equal footing;
- save expense;
- deal with the case in ways which are proportionate; and
- ensure that the case is dealt with expeditiously and fairly.

CPR Part 63, together with supplementary Practice Direction 63 and the Patents Court Guide, govern intellectual property litigation. CPR Part 63 and its Practice Direction are stated to apply to both the Patents Court/High Court and the IPEC.

22.1.7 Questions to consider before taking action

Litigation can be expensive and time-consuming. For this reason, many businesses view formal legal action as a last resort. Before commencing proceedings for the infringement of an intellectual property right, the potential claimant ought to consider Diagram 22.1 below.

22.2 Pre-trial orders

If an IP owner wishes to sue someone for infringement, a successful action may be of little value to the claimant if, in the meantime, the defendant is allowed to continue trading, thereby increasing their share of the market or doing other harm to the claimant's business. Equally, filing a claim form at the court may have the effect of encouraging a defendant to destroy evidence of their infringing conduct, or to remove assets out of the UK so that no funds exist out of which to pay damages. Finally, an IP owner may decide to sue a retailer who is selling infringing copies, but ideally would like to know who has been making these copies. All these difficulties can be overcome by the award of various pre-trial orders.

22.2.1 Interim injunctions

Interim injunctions are governed by the Senior Courts Act 1981, s. 37 together with CPR Part 25. An interim injunction is a court order directing that certain acts do or do not take place or should continue, pending the final determination of the parties' rights

DIAGRAM 22.1 *Summary of litigation and the IP enforcement process*

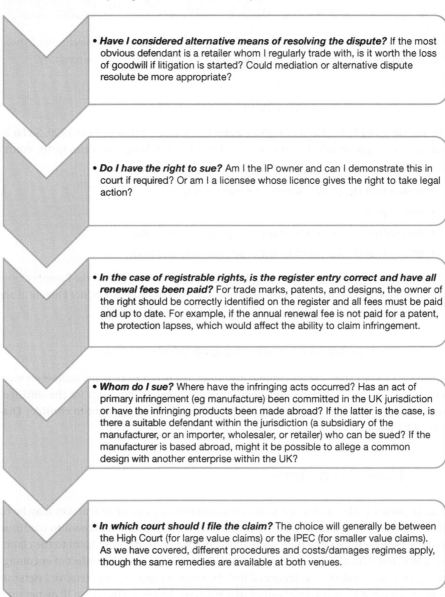

- **Have I considered alternative means of resolving the dispute?** If the most obvious defendant is a retailer whom I regularly trade with, is it worth the loss of goodwill if litigation is started? Could mediation or alternative dispute resolute be more appropriate?

- **Do I have the right to sue?** Am I the IP owner and can I demonstrate this in court if required? Or am I a licensee whose licence gives the right to take legal action?

- **In the case of registrable rights, is the register entry correct and have all renewal fees been paid?** For trade marks, patents, and designs, the owner of the right should be correctly identified on the register and all fees must be paid and up to date. For example, if the annual renewal fee is not paid for a patent, the protection lapses, which would affect the ability to claim infringement.

- **Whom do I sue?** Where have the infringing acts occurred? Has an act of primary infringement (eg manufacture) been committed in the UK jurisdiction or have the infringing products been made abroad? If the latter is the case, is there a suitable defendant within the jurisdiction (a subsidiary of the manufacturer, or an importer, wholesaler, or retailer) who can be sued? If the manufacturer is based abroad, might it be possible to allege a common design with another enterprise within the UK?

- **In which court should I file the claim?** The choice will generally be between the High Court (for large value claims) or the IPEC (for smaller value claims). As we have covered, different procedures and costs/damages regimes apply, though the same remedies are available at both venues.

by the court. An injunction may be ordered in all cases in which it appears to the court to be just and convenient to do so. The objective of an interim injunction is to preserve the status quo in order to prevent irremediable harm. As with other interim remedies, an interim injunction may be sought before, or after, the claim form is issued, although seeking interim relief before proceedings have been started can only be done in cases of urgency. Speed is of the essence in seeking interim relief: whilst not commencing proceedings for several weeks after the claimant becomes aware of the infringement may not be fatal, a delay of several months usually will be. The claimant must offer a cross-undertaking in damages, that is, pay money into court as security in case they lose at the main hearing. If they do not have the means to do so, then interim relief will not be available.

22.2.1.1 Relevant principles

The principles governing the grant of interim injunctions were stated by Lord Diplock in *American Cyanamid v Ethicon* [1975] AC 396, itself a patent infringement case.

American Cyanamid v Ethicon [1975] AC 396

In this case Lord Diplock re-emphasized the basic rule that the award of an interim injunction is essentially a discretionary matter. The need to do this was evident because, as he said, the Court of Appeal in *Cyanamid* had treated the matter as if it were a 'rule of law' by demanding that the claimant establish a prima facie case. The principal issue, according to Lord Diplock, ought to be whether there is *a serious issue to be tried* — arguably a more relaxed test than that of showing a prima facie case.

In line with this Lord Diplock listed the factors to be considered when granting interim relief:

- whether there is a serious issue to be tried;
- whether damages are an adequate remedy. Adequacy has to be considered from the viewpoint of both parties. If the claimant succeeds at trial and obtains a permanent injunction, could they be compensated adequately if the defendant is allowed to continue the harmful conduct between the date of the application for interim relief and the date of the trial? That being so, if the defendant were to succeed at trial, could they be compensated adequately if an injunction were granted between the date of the application and the date of the trial?
- where the balance of convenience lies;
- if factors are evenly balanced, the court should endeavour to preserve the status quo; and
- which party has the stronger case?

The matter of how the court ought to exercise its discretion in the granting of interim injunctions was revisited by Laddie J in *Series 5 Software v Clarke* [1996] FSR 273. Laddie J declared that the most important factor to be taken into account by the court in the exercise of its discretion is the strength of each party's case. The effect of *Series 5*, when combined with the emphasis in the CPR on the expeditious conduct of litigation, means that where a successful claimant's damages would be based on a reasonable licence fee (the normal remedy in many infringement cases) an interim injunction is unlikely to be awarded. Where, however, the right to be protected is incapable of compensation (for example, the right of privacy in photographs) then interim relief ought to be granted (*Douglas v Hello! Ltd (No. 2)* [2005] 4 All ER 128 (CA) at [253–255], relying on *Von Hannover v Germany* (2005) 40 EHRR 1).

At first glance, the views of Laddie J in *Series 5* appear to contradict those of Lord Diplock in *American Cyanamid*. The question is often asked, 'How can that be?' because under the doctrine of precedent, a decision of the House of Lords (now the Supreme Court) is binding on all lower courts. It is, however, instructive to compare in more detail what was said in the two cases.

In *Series 5 Software v Clarke* [1996] FSR 273 Laddie J stated that the issues for the court were:

- interim relief is always a matter of discretion, depending on the facts of the case;
- the rule is that there are no rules—the relief must be kept flexible;
- the court should avoid dealing with complex issues of disputed fact or law at an interim hearing; and
- the major factors to be considered are the adequacy of damages, the balance of convenience, the maintenance of the status quo; and whether there is any clear view of the relative strengths of each of the parties' case.

One obvious difference between the views of Lord Diplock and Laddie J is that the latter places greater stress on the relative strengths of the parties' case. However, looked at more closely, both judgments are saying the same thing. Interim injunctions are always a matter of discretion and flexibility must be maintained. Each case will depend on a number of factors. The conclusion to be drawn from both cases is that periodically the courts need to remind themselves of the discretionary nature of the award. Laddie J was doing no more than Lord Diplock had done 20 years before. More recently, Mei (in 'Interlocutory Injunctions in IP infringement actions in England and Wales and in Ireland—*American Cyanamid* revisited' [2015] 46 *IIC* 175) criticizes the *American Cyanamid* criteria for taking too little account, when assessing the balance of convenience, of the *probability* of damage/injury occurring and placing too much emphasis on the *extent* of the possible damage/injury. Nonetheless, the criteria remain our guide.

22.2.1.2 Effect of the Human Rights Act 1998

Where the action involves a claim for copyright infringement or breach of confidence, and the defendant is a newspaper, magazine, or broadcasting organization, s. 12(3) Human Rights Act 1998 provides that no relief (for example, an interim injunction) which might affect the exercise of the right to freedom of expression is to be granted so as to restrain publication before trial, unless the court is satisfied that the applicant is likely to establish that publication should not be allowed. The relationship between this provision and the *American Cyanamid* test was explored by the House of Lords in *Cream Holdings Ltd v Banerjee* [2004] 3 WLR 918. Lord Nicholls, having declared that the purpose of s. 12(3) was to buttress the protection afforded to freedom of speech at the interlocutory stage (sic), thought that likelihood of success at trial was an essential element in the court's consideration of whether to make an interim order. Flexibility meant that there could be no single, rigid standard. The court should not grant an interim order restraining publication unless satisfied that the applicant's prospects of success were 'sufficiently favourable' in the circumstances. 'Sufficiently favourable' meant that relief should not be granted where the applicant had not satisfied the court that he would probably succeed at trial.

22.2.1.3 The balance of convenience

One of the issues mentioned in Lord Diplock's opinion in *American Cyanamid*, the balance of convenience, needs further elaboration. Much will depend on the circumstances of each individual case, but the court may consider one or more of the following factors, most of which are of a commercial nature:

- the relative size of the parties. They may be equal in size, for example, both being large, multi-nationals. If that is so, both will be able to pay damages if the other succeeds at trial, and both will be able to survive competition in the marketplace in the meantime, as in *Polaroid v Kodak* [1977] FSR 25. In such a case, an interim injunction will *not* be granted. On the other hand, the claimant may be small and the defendant a large enterprise with 'muscle', as in *Corruplast v Harrison* [1978] RPC 761, in which case relief will be granted. Alternatively, relief may be denied where the defendant is relatively new to the market but the claimant is well established and thus able financially to withstand competition until trial, as in *Catnic v Stressline* [1976] FSR 157;

- whether there are public interest grounds for refusing relief. Examples of the public interest prevailing include where an interim injunction would prevent a new life-saving drug from reaching the market (*Roussel-Uclaf v G.D. Searle* [1977] FSR 125) or the need for a 'whistleblower' to disclose the wrongdoing of their former employer even though this involved breach of the employee's duty of confidentiality (*Cream Holdings Ltd v Banerjee*);

- whether there was any delay by the claimant. Interim relief should be sought promptly, i.e. within days or weeks of the infringing conduct, not months;

- whether the parties are in direct competition, and how close their products are in terms of characteristics and quality. Direct competition from a product which is a cheap imitation of the claimant's is more likely to lead to relief being granted, because of the risk of loss of reputation, and hence loss of long-term sales, to the claimant's product;

- whether granting or not granting an injunction might put one of the parties out of business; and

- the risk to either party's investment (as in *Catnic v Stressline* [1976] FSR 157), including the risk of redundancies amongst their employees.

It can therefore be seen that the balance of convenience is far from straightforward. Ultimately, however, the CPR ensure that in many cases, interim relief will be refused and a speedy trial ordered instead.

 Pause for reflection

Is it fair to deny a claimant interim relief where there is clear evidence that there has been infringement? Do the principles set out by Lord Diplock in *American Cyanamid* and Laddie J in *Series 5* ensure that a fair balance is maintained between the interests of the intellectual property owner and those of any competitors?

→

> →
> Could interim relief be of relevance to our problem scenario involving Gyo? Is there any reason why it might not be appropriate?

22.2.2 Search orders

These are now governed by the Civil Procedure Act 1997 s. 7, together with CPR Part 25. The order is addressed to the defendant who, it is thought, might destroy vital evidence of infringing conduct. It requires the defendant to admit the claimant's solicitor to the defendant's premises with a view to copying or removing such evidence. The defendant is not given notice of the request for the order and hence is not in court when it is granted. Surprise is of the essence.

The search order originated in Lord Denning's judgment in *Anton Piller KG v Manufacturing Processes Ltd* [1976] Ch 55, where he laid down the primary criteria:

- the claimant must have an extremely strong prima facie case;
- there must be a serious risk of damage to the claimant's interests;
- there must be compelling evidence that the defendant will dispose of or destroy documents if given warning (for example, on receipt of the claim form); but
- the risk to the defendant's business must not be excessive.

The purpose of the order must be to fulfil a legitimate purpose, such as protecting the claimant's copyright or other intellectual property right (*Columbia Pictures v Robinson* [1986] FSR 367) but the court is required to bear in mind the right to private life enshrined in Art. 8 of the ECHR (*Chappell v UK* [1989] FSR 617).

Search orders have always been of a draconian nature. Indeed, a former Master of the Rolls once described the *Anton Piller* order as 'one of the law's two nuclear weapons', the other 'nuclear weapon' being the *Mareva* order (*per* Donaldson LJ, as he then was, in *Bank Mellat v Nikpour* [1985] FSR 87 at p. 92). At one time, *Anton Piller* orders were granted relatively readily. By the late 1980s, the perception was that they were being misused. Such misuse was that either claimants were using them as a 'fishing expedition' to gain information about a rival's business rather than evidence of infringing conduct, or they were being administered in a very aggressive manner. These concerns led Nicholls VC to state clear guidelines for the grant of an *Anton Piller* order in *Universal Thermosensors v Hibben* [1992] 3 All ER 257. These guidelines have now been incorporated into and updated by the Practice Direction supplementing CPR Part 25.

Universal Thermosensors v Hibben [1992] 3 All ER 257

In *Universal Thermosensors v Hibben* Nicholls VC gave the following guidelines for search orders:

- the order is to be executed during office hours so that the defendant can contact his or her solicitor;

→

- a female solicitor must be present if unaccompanied female family members or office staff will be on the defendant's premises;

- the defendant must be given a list of items which are being removed;

- the injunction restraining the defendant from giving a 'tip off' to third parties is to be limited in time;

- the order must be executed only at company premises before a responsible officer of the defendant's business;

- the claimant is not allowed to make a thorough search of the defendant's premises (that is, the order should not be a 'fishing expedition'); and

- there must be an experienced supervising solicitor who should report back to the court.

As with interim injunctions, the claimant must give a cross-undertaking in damages. The search order must not have the effect of putting the defendant out of business. If documents are copied, these must be returned to the defendant within two days. The CPR contain further detailed guidance where the evidence to be obtained is stored on the defendant's computers.

The guidelines are indicative of the sorts of misuse which occurred before the *Hibben* decision, which may well have justified the description of the order as a 'nuclear weapon'. Because the application for the order is heard in the defendant's absence, the onus is on the claimant to put all material facts before the court. Failure to do so may lead to the order being discharged or the evidence obtained not being admissible (*Naf Naf v Dickens* [1993] FSR 424). The current Practice Direction, when coupled with the requirement to give a cross-undertaking in damages and the risk that evidence incorrectly obtained may be rendered inadmissible, suggests that the opportunity for abuse is much reduced.

Pause for reflection

Do the current rules on the award of a search order meet the concerns expressed by Nicholls VC in *Universal Thermosensors v Hibben*? What type of evidence might Gyo wish to search for at the headquarters of Go Ryde?

22.2.3 Freezing injunctions

These are governed by the Senior Courts Act 1981, s. 37 and CPR Part 25. A freezing injunction (again, obtained without notice, that is, without the defendant being notified or being present in court) is designed to prevent the defendant from moving assets out of the jurisdiction or otherwise dissipating them or concealing them so as to deprive the claimant of any monetary compensation in the event of success at trial. It may relate to assets within the jurisdiction or worldwide. The order origi-nated in *Mareva Compania Naviera SA v International Bulk Carriers SA* [1980] 1 All ER 213.

Mareva Compania Naviera SA v International Bulk Carriers SA [1980] 1 All ER 213

The *Mareva* case established the following requirements:

- a cause of action justiciable within England and Wales;
- a good arguable case on the merits;
- the defendant has assets within the jurisdiction; and
- there is a real risk of removal or disposal.

The safeguards for such a draconian order are that the defendant must be left with enough money to live on and to carry on his day-to-day business. Nevertheless, the order can affect third parties, such as banks.

What type of evidence might Gyo wish to search for at the headquarters of Go Ryde?

22.2.4 Disclosure

The last interim order to consider is that of disclosure. In *Norwich Pharmacal v Commissioners of Customs & Excise* [1974] AC 133 the House of Lords confirmed that an order could be made against the Commissioners of Customs and Excise to reveal the names of a company importing pharmaceutical products which infringed the claimant's patent. In *Ashworth Security Hospital v MGN* [2003] FSR 311, a similar order was granted against a newspaper journalist, requiring him to disclose the name of the person who had supplied the journalist with the medical records of a convicted criminal being held in a secure hospital. The information had been disclosed to the journalist in breach of confidence. The House of Lords stressed, however, that the order in the instant case was issued because of a pressing social need, and that a court issuing such an order should bear in mind the Human Rights Act 1998, in particular s. 10(2) (the freedom of the press). Last, in *The Rugby Football Union v Consolidated Information Services Ltd* [2012] 1 WLR 3333, the Supreme Court rejected the defendant's argument that an order requiring it to reveal the names of those who had supplied it with tickets in breach of the claimant's conditions of sale was unnecessary and disproportionate.

As with other interim relief, the onus is on the claimant to establish that there has been infringement of an intellectual property right. The court will limit the use of the information obtained under the order, so that it can only be used to support further intellectual property litigation.

The order for disclosure of names (as a prelude to further litigation) should not be confused with an order for disclosure of documents. The latter is one of a range of directions which may be made by the court as part of the case management process under the CPR.

Pause for reflection

Do the various forms of interim relief (injunctions, search orders, freezing injunctions, and disclosure) provide effective protection for the IP owner against a serial counterfeiter?

22.3 Post-trial remedies

The successful claimant in an intellectual property infringement action has a range of well-established remedies available to them. These comprise injunctive relief, compensation for financial loss, and a range of court orders intended to ensure that infringing copies do not remain in circulation. Some of these remedies will, however, have to be re-evaluated as the impact of the Enforcement Directive becomes clearer.

22.3.1 Final injunctions

Each of the principal statutes (RDA s. 24A, TMA s. 14, CDPA s. 96, and the Patents Act 1977, s. 61) provides for the award of a final injunction. Once it has been established that there has been infringement of an intellectual property right and the infringement has not completely ceased at the date of trial, an injunction is the normal form of remedy: *Cantor Gaming Ltd v Gameaccount Global Ltd* [2007] EWHC 1914. The injunction protects the claimant from a continuation of the infringements of his rights. The court assumes that the infringement is not a one-off activity and so grants relief to avoid repetition: *Coflexip SA v Stolt Comex Seaway MS Ltd* at [6–7].

Nevertheless, even a final injunction is discretionary in nature. It must be fair to the defendant and will not be awarded where it is unlikely that the defendant will repeat any acts of infringement, because, for example, undertakings have been given: *Landor & Hawa International Ltd v Azure Designs Ltd* [2007] FSR 181 at [46] *per* Neuberger LJ. Equally, a final injunction will not be granted if the interference with the claimant's right is trivial. The injunction will be discharged if the intellectual property right in question is declared invalid in other, parallel proceedings against a different defendant: *Coflexip SA v Stolt Offshore MS Ltd* [2004] FSR 34 at [32]. The same principle also applies to the award of damages: *Virgin Atlantic Airways Ltd v Zodiac Seats UK Ltd* [2013] UKSC 46.

The form of the injunction is governed by the wording of the relevant statutory provision rather than the actual conduct of the defendant: *Coflexip SA v Stolt Comex Seaway MS Ltd per* Aldous LJ at [60]. Thus, even though the defendant may only have infringed the claimant's patent by manufacture, the formula of the injunction will reflect the list of infringing acts set out in the legislation. Normally, the injunction is limited in time to the balance of the term of protection for the intellectual property right in question. However, where the defendant has obtained an unfair competitive advantage from its infringing conduct, so that on the expiry of the claimant's right the defendant could immediately recommence manufacture of a rival product, the duration of the injunction may be extended beyond the expiry date of the right. The defendant will be restrained from competing with the claimant for the length of time it would normally take the defendant, starting afresh and without the knowledge which it has already gained by its infringing conduct, to analyse the claimant's product and set up a manufacturing facility (see *Dyson Appliances Ltd v Hoover Ltd (No. 2)* [2001] RPC 544 for an example of this so-called 'springboard' relief).

The grant of final injunctions is straightforward when an infringer is primarily a manufacturer or a supplier or distributor of the infringing goods to the public. In the age of the internet, however, what should the position be regarding those enterprises whose services are used by a third-party infringer, but who have not themselves committed an infringing act? Specifically, are internet companies, such as Google, eBay, and Yahoo, to be subjected to injunctive relief where their websites are used by others to sell infringing products? The Enforcement Directive provides, in Art. 11, that Member States are required to ensure that owners of intellectual property rights are in a position to apply for an injunction against intermediaries whose services are used by third-party infringers. The UK has not taken any steps to implement Art. 11, it being assumed by the Government that existing law is in compliance with the Directive. However, in *L'Oréal SA v eBay International AG* [2009] EWHC 1094 (Ch) Arnold J pointed out that such an intermediary could not be liable under existing law as a joint infringer under the principle of *CBS Songs Ltd v Amstrad Consumer Electronics plc* [1988] AC 1013 as it had not procured the infringing conduct by inducement, incitement, or persuasion, nor had it participated in a common design. Facilitation was not enough, and eBay was under no legal duty to prevent infringement. Arnold J added that it was unclear whether Art. 11 of the Enforcement Directive had changed these principles so that a domestic court would be obliged to apply s. 37 of the Senior Courts Act to intermediaries. He therefore referred this point to the European Court of Justice for guidance. The reply from the Court (in Case C-324/09 *L'Oréal SA v eBay International AG* [2011] RPC 777) was to the effect that Member States are required to empower their courts to order the operators of online marketplaces to terminate existing infringements and to prevent further ones.

 Pause for reflection

As noted by García Pérez ('Injunctions in Intellectual Property Cases: What is the Power of the Courts?' [2016] 1 *IPQ* 88) despite EU harmonization measures such as the Enforcement Directive, the limited amount of discretion that judges have with regard to the award of injunctions must still be taken into account.

In the context of our problem scenario, provided that infringement of copyright and/or trade marks is proven, what might you argue to convince a judge that a final injunction is an appropriate remedy for Gyo?

22.3.2 Monetary remedies

A successful claimant in an intellectual property infringement action will normally want to be compensated for the trespass to its right. Two forms of monetary remedy are available, common law damages and the equitable action for an account of profits.

22.3.2.1 Damages: general principles

Damages for the infringement of intellectual property rights are tortious in nature, their objective being to restore the claimant to the position he or she would have been in had the defendant not infringed. The principles governing the award of damages for intellectual property rights are set out in detail in *General Tire v Firestone* [1976] RPC 197 by Lord Wilberforce—the key point is to try to put the claimant in the position the claimant would have been in had the infringement not occurred. In the case of patent infringement, where the claimant is in the business of manufacturing goods, and so in competition with the defendant, the measure of damages will be lost profits. In all other cases of patent infringement, the measure of damages will be a reasonable licence fee. 'Lost profits' is also the measure of damages adopted in trade mark infringement actions, and where there has been wrongful use of a competitor's trade secret (*Cadbury Schweppes Inc v FBI Foods Ltd* [2000] FSR 491). In the case of copyright infringement, the normal measure will be a reasonable licence fee. In *Henderson v All Around the World Recordings Ltd* [2014] EWHC 3087 (IPEC) it was held that damages should not be calculated based on both lost profits to the claimant and unfair profits gained by the defendant, as this would be unduly punitive (for more on this and related issues see Scott, 'Damages inquiries and accounts of profits in the IPEC' [2016] 38 *EIPR* 273).

22.3.2.2 'Parasitic' damages

If damages are meant to compensate the claimant for the trespass to the intangible property right, can a patentee recover damages in respect of non-patented items which are normally sold as part of a patented product or process? The original view expressed in *Polaroid v Eastman Kodak* [1977] RPC 379 was that such 'parasitic' damages were not available because the monetary compensation must reflect the precise scope of the patentee's monopoly. Consequently, the patentee could only claim for patented items and not any ancillary equipment. However, a more liberal attitude was shown in *Gerber v Lectra* [1997] RPC 443 where Jacob J held that the loss of sales of ancillary items which were invariably sold with the patented equipment were recoverable as being a direct result of the infringing conduct.

22.3.2.3 Additional damages for copyright infringement

In the case of copyright infringement and unregistered design right infringement (CDPA ss. 97(2) and 229(3)) but not any other form of intellectual property right, the court may award additional damages. A similar provision existed in the Copyright Act 1956 (in relation to copyright only), its purpose being explained in *Williams v Settle* [1960] 1 WLR 1072 to deal with cases of flagrant infringement, where the defendant had exhibited total disregard of the claimant's copyright.

Section 97(2) was considered in *Nottinghamshire Healthcare NHS Trust v News Group Newspapers* [2002] RPC 962 by Pumfrey J. Having reiterated the general principles applicable to damages for the infringement of all intellectual property rights, the judgment reviewed the difference of wording between s. 97(2) and its predecessor. Pumfrey J pointed out that the exact nature of additional damages for copyright infringement under the CDPA had been left undecided by the House of Lords in *Redrow Homes Ltd v Bett Brothers plc* [1998] 2 WLR 198. It had been suggested that the award under s. 97(2) was *sui generis*, but, Pumfrey J explained, a consensus was emerging that such damages were similar to aggravated damages. The reasons for this were, first, the policy restrictions laid down by the House of Lords in *Rookes v Barnard* [1964] AC 1129 on the award of exemplary damages, the latter phrase meaning, according to Pumfrey J at [33], 'an award of damages intended both to compensate the claimant for his loss and to teach the defendant that tort does not pay', this definition reflecting the punitive nature of the award. Second, the possibility of bringing criminal proceedings against the infringer under the CDPA s. 107 pointed to additional damages for copyright infringement being aggravated damages, that is, the award had an element of restitution which took into account the benefit gained by the defendant, and where the normal compensation to the claimant 'left the defendant still enjoying the fruits of his infringement'. These conclusions suggest that there has been a change in the nature of additional damages under the CDPA, as the Court of Appeal in *Williams v Settle* clearly regarded the predecessor to s. 97(2) as giving power to award exemplary damages.

An example of additional damages can be found in *Phonographic Performance Ltd v Reader* [2005] FSR 891, where a disc jockey had failed to obtain a licence for the public performance of sound recordings for at least two years despite previous undertakings. Pumfrey J held, applying his own ruling in *Nottinghamshire Health Care NHS Trust v Newsgroup Newspapers*, that it is permissible for an award of statutory additional damages to include a punitive element provided that the purpose was not simply to punish the defendant. Here, the defendant was well aware of the need for a licence, had previously obtained one only under the threat of legal proceedings, and had no excuse for his failure to seek the appropriate licence. It was therefore a case of deliberate and flagrant infringement.

22.3.2.4 Damages: the effect of the defendant's innocence

The various statutes dealing with the award of damages for intellectual property infringement contain provisions dealing with circumstances where infringement has occurred innocently as this affects the claimant's ability to obtain monetary relief. The defendant's innocence must be as to the *existence* of the right, an objective standard being applied. Innocence prevents the award of damages for copyright, design right, registered design, and patent infringement, by virtue of the CDPA ss. 97(1) and 233(1), RDA as amended, s. 24B, and Patents Act 1977, s. 62(1). There is no such provision in the TMA 1994.

As to why innocence does not affect the award of damages for trade mark infringement (and likewise passing off), the matter was considered in *Gillette UK Ltd v Edenwest Ltd* [1994] RPC 279. Blackburne J pointed out that the trade mark infringement action was derived, historically, from the tort of deceit. What mattered was *the effect* of the defendant's misrepresentation on the claimant's customer, not the defendant's state of mind. If the consumer was misled, it mattered not whether the misrepresentation was innocent.

22.3.2.5 Damages: the effect of the defendant's knowledge

The Enforcement Directive may yet have a further impact on the calculation of damages. Article 13 of the Directive is incorporated in Regulation 3 of the Intellectual Property (Enforcement etc) Regulations 2006 (SI 2006/1028). It provides that where a defendant knew or had reasonable grounds to know that he was engaged in infringing activity, the damages awarded should be 'appropriate to the actual prejudice suffered as a result of the infringement'. The court is required to take into account all appropriate aspects, in particular the negative economic consequences, including any lost profits which the claimant has suffered and any unfair profits made by the defendant and any elements other than economic factors, including moral prejudice caused to the claimant by the infringement. This idea of moral prejudice could be pertinent to claims of infringement of moral rights, particularly the integrity right, where there may be damage to the reputation of the author.

In *Henderson v All Around the World Recordings Ltd* [2014] EWHC 3087 (IPEC), the IPEC had to consider when damages for moral prejudice are justified under Art. 13(1). The claimant's performer's rights in a sound recording had been infringed knowingly by the defendant, and the court had to decide the amount of damages, including whether damages for moral prejudice were appropriate. HH Judge Hacon in the IPEC awarded damages for the infringement, and for unfair profits under Art. 13, but did not consider that any moral prejudice had occurred, and thus no additional damages were awarded. In fact, Judge Hacon remarked that the idea of moral prejudice probably only covered a limited range of circumstances, such as where a claimant had not suffered a direct financial loss, and thus would otherwise have no ground for compensation. However, subsequent to this decision the Court of Justice of the European Union ('CJEU') clarified the issue of when damages for moral prejudice can accrue in *Christian Liffers v Producciones Mandarina SL* C-99/15. Here the CJEU took a purposive approach to Art. 13, deciding that damages based on moral prejudice can be awarded to the IP right-holder in addition to damages based on royalties. This is a broader approach than that of the IPEC in *Henderson*, and it seems to leave open the possibility that wronged parties can make a claim for damages based on moral prejudice even where the circumstances are not as 'limited' as those envisaged by Judge Hacon.

22.3.2.6 Account of profits

Equity provides an alternative form of monetary remedy through the order for an account of profits. The aim here is to transfer to the claimant the profits which the defendant has made from his or her infringing conduct, rather than to compensate the claimant for lost revenue from the intellectual property right. An account of profits can also be the appropriate remedy where there has been either breach of a fiduciary duty or breach of a civil servant's duty to the Crown, as illustrated by *AG v Blake* [2001] AC 268, although the House of Lords was at pains to point out that this was an extreme case.

The remedy of an account of profits can be complex to apply and has the effect of condoning past acts of infringement. Nevertheless, there are instances when it is more advantageous than damages. The decision of *Potton v Yorkclose* [1990] FSR 11 is a good example of when an account is preferable. *Potton* was a case of copyright infringement where the copyright work consisted of an architect's plans for houses. Had the defendant sought a licence before building the houses, the fee would have been governed by the rules of the Royal Institute of British Architects and would have been relatively low. However, by copying without permission and by building houses at a time of a rising housing market, the defendant gained much more from its infringing activities. Despite the complexity of the calculation, an account was a more effective remedy.

Like the award of damages, a plea of innocent infringement by a defendant may have the effect of denying a claimant an account, though the statutory provisions are more inconsistent here. The Patents Act 1977 s. 62(1) and the RDA s. 24B both provide that innocence (again, to be determined objectively) will prevent the award of an account of profits. Innocence does not, however, affect the award of an account for copyright and unregistered design right infringement (see the CDPA ss. 97(1) and 233(1)). Innocence cannot prevent the award of an account of profits for trade mark infringement or passing off for the same reason as innocence does not prevent the award of damages (*Gillette v Edenwest*).

22.3.2.7 Account or damages?

A claimant cannot have both damages and an account—the claimant must elect between them. However, they do not have to do so until after the conclusion of the trial: *Island Records v Tring* [1995] FSR 560. Where, however, a claimant elects for an account, they may not also claim additional damages under s. 97(2) CDPA: *Redrow Homes Ltd v Bett Brothers plc*.

 Pause for reflection

What factors in our problem scenario might influence Gyo's decision to claim damages or an account of profits from Ryde Games?

22.3.2.8 Remedies: discrepancies

As will have become apparent, there are a number of minor discrepancies between the statutory provisions on damages, the most obvious examples being the effect of innocence and the availability of additional damages. Dealing with the latter first, the availability of additional damages for copyright and unregistered design right infringement, but not for the infringement of other forms of IP right, seems at first glance intuitively wrong. Copyright and unregistered design right are not registrable IP rights, so there is no means whereby the defendant can ascertain the existence of the right. By contrast, anyone can check the registers of trade marks, designs, and patents, so why should they not be penalized if they infringe in a flagrant manner? However, additional damages for copyright and unjustified design right infringement can be justified because *copying* the work is the kernel of liability for both types of right. Further, the normal measure of damages will be a reasonable licence fee, which a persistent defendant may regard as an incidental cost. If, therefore, a defendant has deliberately and flagrantly copied a work, or persisted in committing another of the restricted acts, then it seems entirely appropriate that such additional compensation be available to 'top up' the reasonable licence fee normally awarded under the CDPA.

With regard to the effect of innocence on the availability of monetary relief, *Gillette v Edenwest* contains a convincing explanation as to why trade marks and passing off are different from other forms of intellectual property right. What mattered, historically, was the effect of the defendant's conduct on the claimant's customers, not the defendant's state of mind. However, there remain differences between patents, copyright, unregistered design right, and registered design right as regards the effect of innocence on the award of damages and an account of profits. For both patents and registered designs, at present, innocence is a complete bar to any monetary award, whilst with copyright and unregistered design right, innocence prevents the award of damages but not an account. The origin of this may lie in the difference between registered and unregistered rights, or because of the normal measure of damages for copyright and unregistered design right infringement.

Pause for reflection

Would it be better to do away with the remedy of account of profits and repeal all the statutory provisions on the award of damages, replacing the latter with a simple rule which leaves the award of damages at the discretion of the court, guided only by the principles set out in Art. 13 of the Enforcement Directive (or post-Brexit, common law considerations of enforcement)?

22.3.3 Moral rights and rights in performances

Mention has not been made so far of the remedies available for the two rights specifically created by the CDPA 1988, namely moral rights and rights in performances. The CDPA declares (in ss. 103 and 194, respectively) that infringement of such rights is to be actionable as a breach of statutory duty.

22.3.4 Additional statutory remedies

Various ancillary remedies are prescribed by legislation to assist the intellectual property owner in the fight against counterfeiting. These include an order for the erasure of an infringing sign under the TMA s. 15, and an order for the delivery up and destruction of infringing copies of copyright works, performances, designs, patents, and trade marks (see, respectively ss. 99 and 114 of the CDPA in relation to copyright works; ss. 195 and 204 CDPA in relation to illicit copies of performances; ss. 230 and 231 CDPA in relation to designs; s. 61 of the Patents Act 1977; and ss. 16 and 19 of the TMA). The wording of these various provisions means that a court order can be made against an innocent retailer who just happens to have infringing copies in its possession, and not merely the counterfeiter who has made the products in question: *Lagenes Ltd v It's At (UK) Ltd* [1991] FSR 492. Lastly, a copyright owner and a performer have, as a result of the CDPA 1988, ss. 100 and 196 respectively, the 'self-help' remedy whereby infringing copies can be seized. However, there are stringent conditions imposed on this remedy, including the requirement that due notice must be given to the local police. Because the remedy cannot be executed against anyone operating from permanent business premises (which includes market stalls), in effect, it is only available against pavement vendors i.e. those selling counterfeit merchandise outside sports venues and rock concerts. See Diagram 22.2 for an illustration of the process of obtaining a remedy for IP infringement—from case filing to court decision.

DIAGRAM 22.2 *Summary of the process of obtaining a remedy for IP infringement*

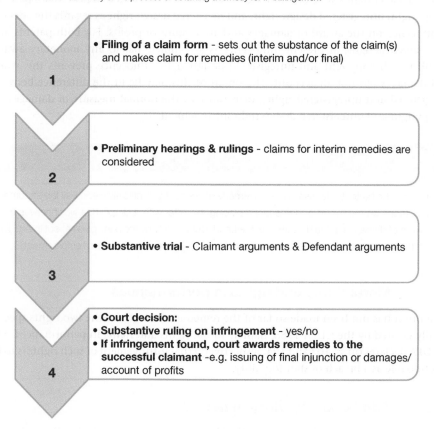

1
- **Filing of a claim form** - sets out the substance of the claim(s) and makes claim for remedies (interim and/or final)

2
- **Preliminary hearings & rulings** - claims for interim remedies are considered

3
- **Substantive trial** - Claimant arguments & Defendant arguments

4
- **Court decision:**
- **Substantive ruling on infringement** - yes/no
- **If infringement found, court awards remedies to the successful claimant** -e.g. issuing of final injunction or damages/account of profits

 Pause for reflection

Why should the self-help remedy in CDPA ss. 100 and 196 not be available for other forms of intellectual property? What is it about the nature of counterfeit merchandise stalls that makes court-approved action difficult?

22.4 Counterfeiting: State assistance for the intellectual property owner

Because of the widespread problem of counterfeiting, UK law provides for the intellectual property owner to invoke the assistance of the state in protecting what is essentially a right of private property. One might question the value judgement inherent in such state support. Why should the infringement of a private property right attract the opprobrium of the criminal law, when the owner of the right in question might be a multi-national corporation, such undertakings being perceived, rightly or wrongly, as being key players in globalization? Why should a company, which has perhaps outsourced the manufacture of branded goods to less-developed countries so as to take advantage of low wage rates, be able to invoke state assistance if imitations of those goods are being supplied to brand-conscious UK consumers? Whatever one's views, the implicit assumption in UK law is that the taking of intangible property should be treated as criminal conduct, a point reinforced by those who contend that counterfeiting forms part of organized crime.

Counterfeiting is facilitated by modern technology. Items which have required the investment of labour and capital to create are easily copied, depriving the creator of their expected return. In particular, films and sound recordings, computer software, fashion garments, shoes, and perfumes are frequently the subject of counterfeiting. More recently (and more worryingly) counterfeiting has extended to pharmaceuticals, with a plethora of illegally manufactured and fake medicines being sold online. The assistance provided by the state is twofold.

22.4.1 Criminal liability

First, to commit copyright and trade mark infringement by way of trade gives rise to criminal liability: see the CDPA 1988 s. 107 (copyright) and s. 198 (performances); and the TMA ss. 92 and 93. There is no such liability in relation to patents, the unregistered design right, nor the theft of trade secrets. The Intellectual Property Act 2014 imposes criminal liability for the deliberate copying of a registered design (whether UK or EU).

Prosecution in cases of criminal enforcement is not confined to those who are counterfeiters, but may be brought against the intellectual property owner's competitors: *Thames & Hudson v Design & Copyright Artists Society* [1995] FSR 153. The enforcement of the criminal provisions relating to IP is delegated to Local Authority Trading Standards Departments. This can include raiding premises where counterfeit goods, often worth thousands of pounds, are being made, or any place where they are sold. Under the Criminal Justice Act 1988 (Confiscation Orders) Order 1995, a magistrates' court can impose a confiscation order in respect of the criminal offences found in the CDPA and the Trade Marks Act 1994. The maximum penalties were increased by the Digital Economy Act 2010.

 Pause for reflection

Is it right that infringement of a private property right should give rise to criminal liability? As noted by Buccafusco & Masur ('Innovation and Incarceration: An Economic Analysis of Criminal Intellectual Property Law' [2013–2014] 87 *S Cal L Rev* 275) there is a legitimate fear that 'using criminal sanctions to protect IP will expand already overgrown rights' and end up having a 'chilling effect' on valuable expressive and inventive behaviour.

Is there any likelihood Ryde Games has committed a criminal offence in our problem scenario?

22.4.2 HM Revenue and Customs

Regulation (EU) No 608/2013 of the European Parliament and of the Council of 12 June 2013 concerning customs enforcement of intellectual property rights, [2013] OJ L 181/15 applies to counterfeit goods and pirated goods. It allows the intellectual property owner to notify the customs authorities, who have power to prevent the importation of suspect goods at the point of entry. The goods in question are liable to forfeiture and destruction.

22.5 Policy restrictions on the intellectual property owner's rights

Civil litigation is the normal means for an intellectual property owner to protect their rights. However, because of the monopolistic nature of intellectual property rights, it would be very easy for a large, multi-national corporation to use the power of litigation to put competitors out of business. UK intellectual property litigation is estimated to be one of the most expensive in the world, and these costs may act as a deterrent to small businesses (on a more positive note, SMEs are able to make use of the low-cost IPEC to enforce their own IP rights). There are therefore various statutory provisions which curtail the litigious intellectual property owner.

22.5.1 Threats actions

UK statutes contain provisions restricting the right of the IP owner to threaten another party with litigation. The presence of the **threats action** in UK legislation can be seen as a safeguard to ensure that the intellectual property owner does not attempt to stifle competition by excessive use of their monopoly power. The underlying assumption is that small competitors may otherwise be intimidated by a 'letter before action', particularly in view of the high costs of litigation. By taking a 'threats action' a claimant can argue that a threat of infringement lacks sufficient grounding in law, and as such an injunction and/or damages should be awarded to prevent such threats or compensate for their effect. Even if most of the threats in a dispute are justified, if one is not, this can result in the award of an injunction in relation to that threat. In *Azumi Ltd v Zuma's Choice Pet Products Ltd* [2017] EWHC 609 the High Court considered that although most threats in the trade mark dispute were justified, one—a requirement that the accused party change the company name—was not. Damages were not a relevant remedy as there was no evidence of loss resulting from this threat—but the High Court awarded a declaration that it was an unjustified threat and an injunction to restrain the making of the threat in future.

The Intellectual Property (Unjustified Threats) Act 2017 provides a harmonized threats regime—a step forward from the previous piecemeal approach. The Act protects against unjustified, or groundless, threats of infringement by a person who owns a patent, trade mark, registered design, or unregistered design right. Not just nationally registered rights are protected, but also EU trade marks and EU designs as well as European and unitary patents. The Act amended: s. 70 of the Patents Act 1977; s. 21 of the Trade Marks Act 1994; s. 26 of the Registered Designs Act 1949; and s. 253 CDPA 1988.

The Act puts forward a new definition of what constitutes an unjustified threat in a communication: whether a reasonable person in the position of the recipient would understand from the communication that (i) an IP right exists; and (ii) that a person intends to bring infringement proceeds in relation to that right. The message is, therefore, that before warning potential defendants of litigation, the IP holder needs to be sure that: (a) there has been an act of infringement; and (b) the right which has been infringed is valid.

At time of writing there is no published case law decided under the new Act, so the prior case law is summarized below—though it must be read in line with the terms of the new Act.

In determining whether a threat has occurred, the court has in the past considered the wording of the communication from the IP owner (it may be written or oral) to see whether viewed through the eyes of a reasonable third party it constitutes a threat to sue. A 'working definition' of an actionable threat was given by Pumfrey J in *Quads 4 Kids v Campbell* at [23] as 'a statement from which a reasonable man in the position of a person to whom the statement is made understands is a statement that might well be the subject of infringement proceedings at some point in the future'. Lightman J in *L'Oréal (UK) Ltd v Johnson & Johnson* [2000] FSR 686 stated that 'the term "threat" covers any intimation that would convey to a reasonable man that some person has . . . rights and intends to enforce them against another. It matters not that the threat may be veiled or covert, conditional or future. Nor does it matter that the threat is made in response to an enquiry from the party threatened.' The words in question do not have to be intimidatory so that even vague language counts, indeed in the *L'Oréal* case the letter in question was described by the judge as 'Delphic' but sufficient to unsettle the alleged infringer. Further, where an IP owner with rights in another country (for example, the owner of a USA trade mark) writes to a UK business intimating that they will take action for trade mark infringement because the UK business operates a website with a domain name identical to the foreign trade mark, then such correspondence is actionable if the threat is received in the UK: *Prince plc v Prince Sports Group Inc* [1998] FSR 21.

A threats action has the effect of shifting the onus to the IP owner to show that there had been infringing conduct and that the right in question is valid. As an example of this shift of onus, we may note *Trebor Bassett Ltd v The Football Association* [1997] FSR 211 where a sweet manufacturer successfully argued that the FA had wrongly threatened litigation for trade mark infringement. No infringing conduct had occurred because the appearance of the 'three lions' logo in collectible pictures of football players found in sweet packets was not trade mark use under ss. 9 and 10 TMA.

 Pause for reflection

There are no such restrictions in relation to copyright infringement, infringement of moral rights, rights in performances, plant breeders' rights, database rights, nor in relation to passing off or breach of confidence (the last two are not statute based anyway). It may be questioned why, if excessive zeal in litigation is regarded as undesirable, the threats action does not apply to all categories of rights.

22.6 **Conclusion**

We have come to the end of this chapter and the textbook as a whole. It should now be clear that the various areas of intellectual property law that we have surveyed—copyright, trade marks, patents, designs, trade secrets—are diverse, yet they contain the same essential building block: exclusivity. By giving exclusive rights to IP owners—whether via e.g. the right to copy in the case of a literary work, or a monopoly right in the case of a patented invention—the law restricts other potential users, such as competitors, from utilizing the protected IP. We have seen how this exclusive legal protection is justified by reference to philosophical ideas such as the personality of the author (copyright), business utility and consumer protection (trade marks), and encouraging the publication of inventions (patents); and we have also explored economic notions of incentive/reward (all forms of IP). Ideally IP law results in a creative environment that is balanced: it must allow creators and businesses to do exciting new things in the confidence they will be able to use exclusive rights to benefit economically from their creations and inventions; yet it must also allow competition within the wider marketplace and fair dealing by consumers and follow-on creators. The cases we have examined in detail over the course of this book illustrate how IP law keeps up with the changing nature of the 21st-century digital economy, where an ever-increasing share of the economy is tied up in intangible assets protected as IP. Indeed, enforcement via litigation is a key element of the IP system—decisions made by courts not only affect the individual parties to the case, but also help to maintain a broader balance within the IP system. Remedies are a crucial element to maintain this balance, and over the course of this chapter we have assessed how the court determines what remedies—injunctions, damages, etc—are appropriate to the facts at hand.

A number of interim remedies are available. Where a claimant is seeking an interim injunction, we have seen how the various factors are weighed up by the court, following the *American Cynamid* and *Series 5* cases. Claimants can also seek search orders under the *Anton Pillar* and *Universal Thermosensors* cases, freezing orders under the *Mareva* case and the Senior Courts Act 1981 s. 37 and CPR Part 25 and claims for disclosure of information under *Norwich Pharmacal*.

Successful claimants are generally entitled to a final injunction—as noted under the *Cantor* and *Coflexip* cases—but where it is unnecessary an injunction will not be granted (*Landor & Hawa International Ltd*).

For damages, the key case is *General Tire v Firestone* which emphasized that the point of monetary compensation is to try to put the key point is to try to put the claimant in the position the claimant would have been in had the infringement not occurred. This could be through a calculation of 'lost profits' (patent cases involving competitors, trade mark cases, and trade secret cases) or through a reasonable licence fee (copyright cases and non-competitive cases of patent infringement). Article 13 of the EU Enforcement Directive is also worth considering, particularly with regard to damages arising from moral prejudice (*Henderson*). Except in the case of trade marks, innocent infringement prevents the award of damages in IP cases. An account of profits can be claimed as an alternative to damages and in some cases may be advantageous to a claimant—in *Potton*, account of profits was a more lucrative remedy than damages based on a copyright royalty.

Criminal liability can arise with respect to copyright, trade mark, and registered design infringement. There is no such liability in relation to patents, the unregistered design right, nor the theft of trade secrets.

Finally, an IP owner must be careful not to make unjustified threats of infringement—the Intellectual Property (Unjustified Threats) Act 2017 protects against unjustified, or groundless, threats of infringement by a person who owns a patent, trade mark, registered design, or unregistered design right.

Turning to our problem scenario, we must first establish what the precise IP rights at stake are and who owns them. This is particularly important given that Gyo could be liable for making 'groundless threats' of IP infringement if it turns out they do not own valid IP rights.

From our understanding of copyright and trade marks undertaken in prior chapters, we can undertake this assessment. Cases such as *Infopaq*, *Meltwater*, *SAS*, and *Nova Productions v Mazooma* indicate that there the graphics and characters created by Gyo are works that are fixed and sufficiently original (as required by the CDPA)—and thus protected by copyright law. It also seems clear that Ryde Games' use of these is unauthorized. Similarly, if Gyo programmers created the original game's source code, and the company owns the copyright to this code, on the facts we can try to argue that this code has been infringed by Ryde Games. However, in the case of the source code we cannot assume infringement from simply looking at how the game 'plays' because the functionality is not what is protected, only the underlying code. Has the underlying code actually been used by Ryde Games, or have they merely emulated its functionality? We must suggest that Gyo investigate further.

For the trade marks element, we need to first establish whether Gyo owns a registered EU or UK trade mark in 'Gyo Ryde' (or, if not, whether we can argue that it should be considered an unregistered trade mark under the tort of passing off). Provided we can establish rights under trade mark law or passing off, the likelihood of a trade mark infringement finding is quite high. The two games will be classed as 'similar goods' and as such we can argue that the similarity of the marks could cause consumer confusion.

We can advise Matt that, given the facts at hand, it is likely that Ryde Games has infringed upon copyrights and trade marks owned by Gyo. The question then turns to the key elements we are interested in: enforcement and remedies.

Regarding the venue of the prospective litigation, given the size of his firm we ought to advise him that the IPEC would best suit, provided that the damages sought fall below the IPEC limit of £500,000. The High Court is also a possible venue but would prove more expensive to litigate at, so the only benefit—given that the same injunctive remedies are available from both venues—is that there is no cap on damages. Has the loss of profits at Gyo in the past months been such that it makes it worthwhile to take a High Court action? If not, the IPEC is the preferable venue.

We must advise Matt that he must ensure that the right person takes action against Ryde Games? In the first instance, it should be the IP owner. Here the owner of the copyrights and trade marks is most likely to be the company—Gyo Technology—and Matt must ensure the litigation is conducted using the company's name; the litigation should not be conducted by him in his personal capacity.

In terms of remedies, Matt could try to claim interim relief in terms of an interim injunction to prevent sales of the Go Ryde game. In such a case, the criteria in *American Cyanamid* remain critical. The court will weigh up the extent of the potential harm and attempt to maintain balance between the interests of the IP owner (Gyo) and those of the competitor (Ryde Games). However, since the game is already on sale, the harm appears to have already occurred, which weakens the case for an interim injunction.

Continuing with interim applications, with respect to the possible infringement of Gyo's source code, Gyo could argue for discovery of documents and computer records to try to establish whether indeed there has been infringement of their code (*Norwich Pharmacal v Commissioners of Customs & Excise* [1974] AC 133; *The Rugby Football Union v Consolidated Information Services Ltd*).

If Gyo have a legitimate concern that Go Ryde might destroy evidence, under the *Universal Thermosensors v Hibben* case Gyo could argue for a search order—but for this they would need to provide appropriate evidence.

As noted earlier, provided that infringement of copyright and/or trade marks is proven at the main hearing, Gyo should argue for a final injunction and monetary relief. A final injunction is an appropriate remedy as it would prevent future infringements occurring, something that is in line with the EU Enforcement Directive (*Cantor Gaming Ltd v Gameaccount Global Ltd* [2007] EWHC 1914; *Coflexip SA v Stolt Comex Seaway MS Ltd* at [6–7]).

In terms of monetary relief, Gyo should weigh up whether it is more advantageous to claim an account of profits, or whether to argue for damages because they will not be entitled to both (*General Tire v Firestone* [1976] RPC 197; *Potton v Yorkclose* [1990] FSR 11; *Henderson v All Around the World Recordings Ltd* [2014] EWHC 3087 (IPEC); *Island Records v Tring* [1995] FSR 560; *Redrow Homes Ltd v Bett Brothers plc*).

Finally, there is no likelihood Ryde Games has committed a criminal offence in our problem scenario, so we do not need to deal with criminal penalties.

End-of-chapter questions

After reading the chapter carefully, try answering the questions which follow. If you would like to know what we think visit the online resources at **www.oup.com/uk/karapapa-mcdonagh/**

1. In what circumstances would an account of profits be more of an advantage than a claim for damages?

2. Why are injunctions—preliminary and final—so important to claimants? What is the potential impact on the defendant?

3. Should the criminal law have a role to play in intellectual property law at all, or is it the case that such remedies are draconian?

Further reading

Buccafusco, C. and Masur, J. 'Innovation and Incarceration: An Economic Analysis of Criminal Intellectual Property Law' [2013-2014] 87 S Cal L Rev 275
Investigates criminal penalties in IP law from an economic perspective.

Day, G. 'Competition and Piracy' [2018] 32 *Berkeley Technology Law Journal* 775
Looks at the balance between IP rights and fair competition from an economic perspective.

Edenborough, M. and Tritton, G. 'American Cyanamid Revisited' [1996] 18 *EIPR* 234

Considers the relationship between American Cyanamid *and* Series 5 *with regard to the grant of interim injunctions.*

García Pérez, R., 'Injunctions in Intellectual Property Cases: What is the Power of the Courts?' [2016] 1 *IPQ* 87, 88–90

Gives an overview of the discretion that judges possess in the light of the Enforcement Directive.

Geiger, C., *Criminal Enforcement of Intellectual Property: A Handbook of Contemporary Research* (Edward Elgar, 2012)

Overview of virtually every aspect of criminal enforcement of IP.

Hall, S. '*Anton Piller* Orders: A Doorstep Too Far' [1995] 17 *EIPR* 50

Explains the background to the guidelines set out by Nicholls LJ in the Hibben *case.*

Helmers, C., Lefouili, Y. and McDonagh, L. 'Evaluation of the Reforms of the Intellectual Property Enterprise Court 2010–2013' (UK Intellectual Property Office, 2015)

Examines the reforms of the IPEC using empirical data gathered at the courts.

Mei, G. 'Interlocutory Injunctions in IP infringement actions in England and Wales and in Ireland— *American Cyanamid* revisited' [2015] 46 *IIC* 175

Argues that the American Cyanamid criteria should take greater account of probability.

Philips, J. 'Interlocutory Injunctions and Intellectual Property: A Review of *American Cyanamid v Ethicon* in the Light of *Series 5 Software*' [1997] *JBL* 486

Considers the relationship between American Cyanamid *and* Series 5 *with regard to the grant of interim injunctions.*

Scott, S. 'Damages inquiries and accounts of profits in the IPEC' [2016] 38 *EIPR* 273

Examines Damages and accounts of profits at the IPEC in terms of judicial decisions.

Seuba, X. 'The Economics of Intellectual Property Enforcement' [2016] 6(2) *WIPO J* 133

Wide-ranging article examines IP enforcement from an economics perspective.

This appendix is an example of the patent paperwork submitted to the United States Patent and Trademark office for a patent to a musical keyboard by the musician Prince.

US00D349127S

United States Patent [19]

Nelson

[11] Patent Number: **Des. 349,127**

[45] Date of Patent: ** **Jul. 26, 1994**

[54] **PORTABLE, ELECTRONIC KEYBOARD MUSICAL INSTRUMENT**

[75] Inventor: **Prince R. Nelson,** Chanhassen, Minn.

[73] Assignee: **Prince Rogers Nelson,** Chanhassen, Minn.

[**] Term: **14 Years**

[21] Appl. No.: **821,470**

[22] Filed: **Jan. 16, 1992**

[52] U.S. Cl. **D17/1**

[58] **Field of Search** .... 84/423 R, 719, 723, 84/743, 744, 670, 718; D17/1, 2, 5, 7, 9

[56] **References Cited**

U.S. PATENT DOCUMENTS

D. 245,197	7/1977	Noury, Jr.	D17/1
D. 254,496	3/1980	Hill	D17/1
D. 278,066	3/1985	Garoogian	D17/1
D. 296,338	6/1988	Sgroi	D17/1
4,314,494	2/1982	de Vries	84/744
4,570,521	2/1986	Fox	84/670

OTHER PUBLICATIONS

The Music Trades, Dec. 1987, p. 122 (Yamaha's SHS–1 Keyboard).
Hong Kong Enterprise Oct. 1989, p. 229.

Primary Examiner—Bernard Ansher
Assistant Examiner—Adir Aronovich
Attorney, Agent, or Firm—Drucker & Sommers

[57] **CLAIM**

The ornamental design for portable electronic keyboard musical instrument, as shown and described.

DESCRIPTION

FIG. **1** is a front elevational view of a portable electronic keyboard musical instrument showing my new design;
FIG. **2** is a top plan view thereof;
FIG. **3** is a bottom plan view thereof;
FIG. **4** is a rear view thereof;
FIG. **5** is a first end view of my new design, which is a left end view of FIG. **1**; and,
FIG. **6** is a second end view of my new design, which is a right end view of FIG. **1**.

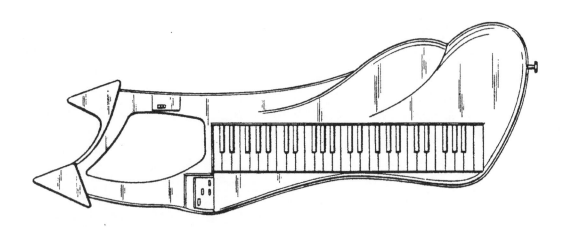

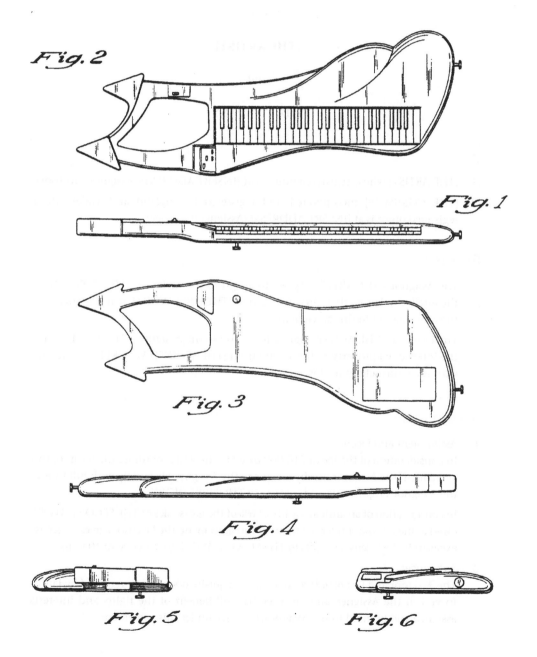

Fig. 2

Fig. 1

Fig. 3

Fig. 4

Fig. 5

Fig. 6

DATED   28-08-2018
DRAFT
ASSIGNMENT AND LICENSING OF INTELLECTUAL PROPERTY RIGHTS

between

[THE ARTIST]

and

[THE COMPANY]

PARTIES

(1) [THE ARTIST] whose registered office is at [INSERT ADDRESS] (Assignor/Licensor).

(2) [THE COMPANY] incorporated and registered in England and Wales whose registered office is at [INSERT ADDRESS] (Assignee/Licensee).

BACKGROUND

The Assignor—THE ARTIST—agrees to assign to the Assignee—THE COMPANY—the intellectual property rights arising from [THE FIRST WORK] in accordance with the terms set out in this agreement.

The Licensor—THE ARTIST—agrees to license to the Assignee—THE COMPANY—the intellectual property rights arising from [THE SECOND WORK] in accordance with the terms set out in this agreement

AGREED TERMS

1. Assignment and Licence
    In consideration of the fee of £10,000 owed to the Assignor under the terms of this agreement, the Assignor hereby assigns to the Assignee absolutely with full title all the Assignor's rights, title and interest in THE FIRST WORK.

    In consideration of an annual royalty of 6% of the gross sales of THE SECOND WORK owed to the Licensor under the terms of this agreement, the Licensor agrees to license exclusively the Licensor's rights to THE SECOND WORK for a period of 10 years.

2. Assurance
    The Assignor and Licensor shall deliver all requisite documents, required by law or to vest in the Assignee and Licensee the full benefit of the rights and interests assigned and licensed to the Assignor/Licensee under this agreement.

3. Governing law and Exclusive jurisdiction
    This agreement and any dispute or claim arising out it shall be governed by and
    construed in accordance with the law of England and Wales. The courts of England
    and Wales shall have exclusive jurisdiction to settle any dispute or claim arising out
    of or in connection with this agreement.

This document takes effect on the date stated at the beginning of it.

SIGNED as a DEED by   )
an authorized signatory of   )

[THE ARTIST]   ) ....
in the presence of:)
W   Signature:
I   Name:
T   Address:
N
E
S
S   Occupation:

SIGNED as a DEED by   )
an authorized signatory of   )

[THE COMPANY]   ) ....
in the presence of:)
W   Signature:
I   Name:
T   Address:
N
E
S
S   Occupation: